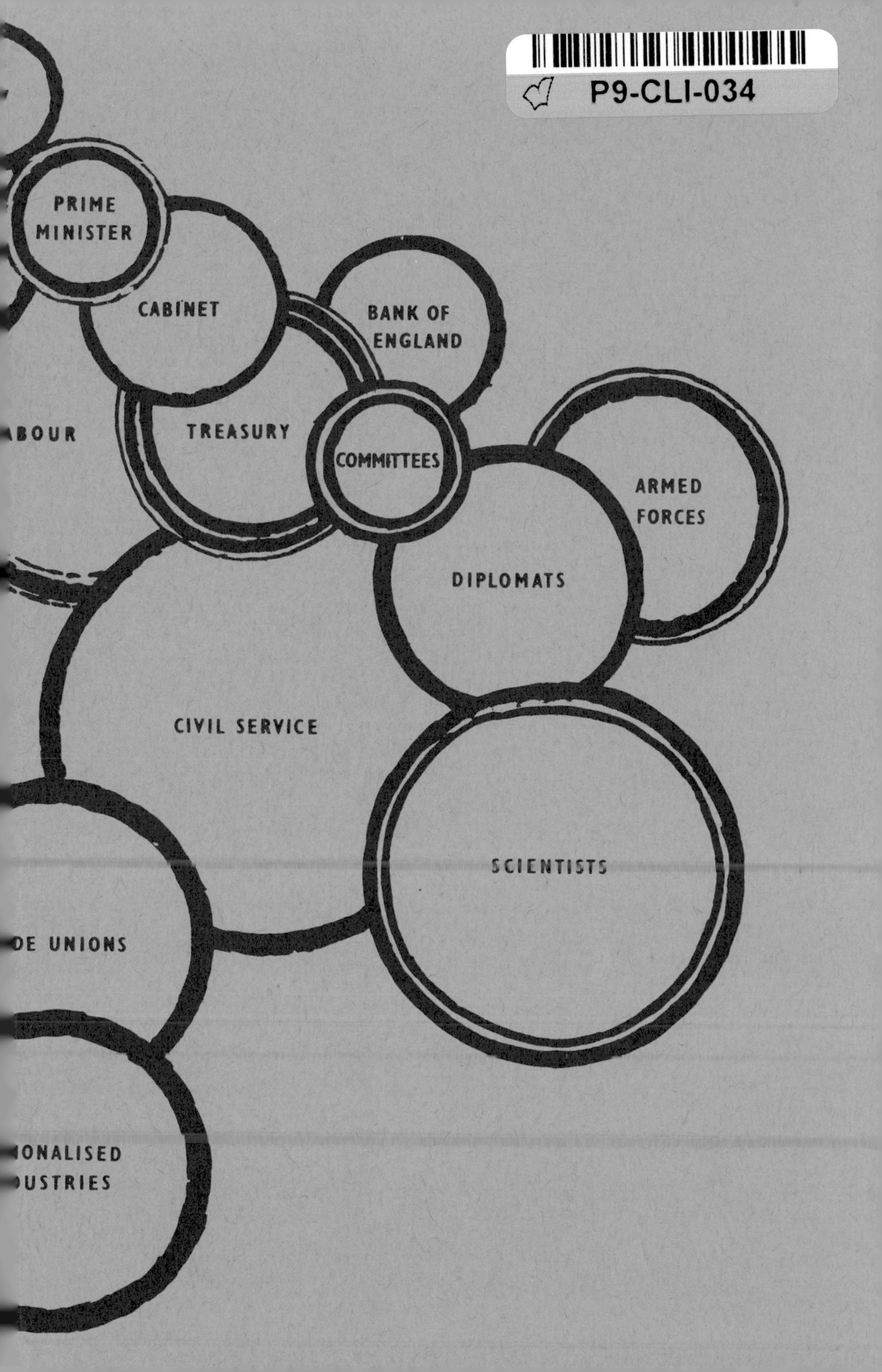

P9-CLI-034
PRIME MINISTER
CABINET
BANK OF ENGLAND
BOUR
TREASURY
COMMITTEES
ARMED FORCES
DIPLOMATS
CIVIL SERVICE
SCIENTISTS
DE UNIONS
ONALISED
USTRIES

ANATOMY OF BRITAIN TODAY

By the same author

DRUM

THE TREASON CAGE

COMMONSENSE ABOUT AFRICA

ANATOMY OF BRITAIN

ANTHONY SAMPSON

ANATOMY OF BRITAIN TODAY

HARPER & ROW, PUBLISHERS, NEW YORK

LIBRARY OF CONGRESS CATALOG CARD NUMBER: *65-21378*

FOR

MY MOTHER

The characteristic danger of great nations, like the Roman, or the English, which have a long history of continuous creation, is that they may at last fail from not comprehending the great institutions they have created.

Walter Bagehot (Essay on Lord Althorp)

Institutions are worth no more than the men who work them.

Amiel

CONTENTS

Contents

INTRODUCTION

It is nearly three years since the original edition of *Anatomy of Britain* came out, and in that time there have been large changes, in structure, in attitude, and in the government. In *Anatomy of Britain Today*, I have tried to present an up-to-date picture of who runs Britain, and how, at the beginning of 1965. I have completely revised the text, and rewritten about a quarter of it. I have found this in many ways a more interesting, and certainly more agreeable task than writing the first book. I have found it easier to pick up information and moods, against the background of the earlier *Anatomy*, and I have been able to look at the shifts and movements within institutions. I have tried, in particular, to convey the process and atmosphere of Harold Wilson's 'hundred days', and the shake-up it induced. Much of the solid substructure of Britain—the aristocracy, the City, the industrial corporations—has hardly changed; but in a large part of Whitehall and politics, in management, education and communications, there have been considerable and exciting upheavals. In the last chapter on 'Britain's Changing Anatomy', I try to sum up the real extent of the changes, to describe the special impact of Harold Wilson, and to pull together the threads that run through the book.

I have retained most of the structure of the original version, but all through the book I have altered emphasis and order, subtracted some sections and added more (this book is considerably longer than the first). Some chapters (like 'The Palace') are now shorter, and others (like 'Scientists') are longer. I begin, in the first five chapters, with the more antique and historical institutions, centring round the aristocracy. I then turn to the sudden and very separate presence of Harold Wilson, and to the Labour party. I then deal, at much greater length than before, with the educational system, which is the main instrument of change: and the charts of schools and universities form a kind of centrepiece to the book. After this, in the chapters on the civil service, I try to trace the effect of the new government on the bureaucracies, and conclude the first part of the book with scientists, in their strengthened position.

In the second part, as before, I turn to the financial institutions of the City of London, culminating with the massive new influence of insurance companies, and their impact on ordinary people. In the third part I look at industrial organisations, the vast, self-contained corporations and the professions that intertwine with them—managers, accountants or advertising men—ending with the upstart and revolutionary world of television.

In each chapter, and particularly in the last, I try to trace not only the changing power, but the changing people. This is primarily a book about personalities, both single and corporate, and I have not hesitated to write about individuals and their idiosyncracies. I have stuck firmly to Britain as it is now, avoiding historical flashbacks whenever possible, but inevitably I have found myself frequently referring to the Victorians, who invented so many of our institutions, and from time to time I have used Walter Bagehot, both as a critic with a very contemporary tang, and as a kind of yardstick for developments since.

I have not tried to approach this task as an historian, or as a student of constitutions, but simply as an enquiring journalist. I first became interested when I returned to England after four years in Africa, and found myself curious about the slowness and complexity of Britain compared to Africa: and later, as a columnist for *The Observer*, writing often about people in prominent positions, my curiosity broadened. So I decided, rashly, to spend eighteen months exploring the ramifications of people and power, and the original edition of this book was the result. Since then, I have got into the habit of watching institutions and top people.

I offer myself as an informal guide to a living museum, describing the rooms and exhibits as I found them, giving basic hard facts and frequent quotations from others, but not hesitating to add my own comments.

I have had to restrict the field. There has been no time or space to cover the broad fields of art, medicine, religion or provincial life and culture which all go to make up the character of Britain; they would need another quarter-million words. I have concentrated on the basic anatomy—the arms and legs and the main blood stream. Nor do I deal with the life of ordinary people. Basically this is a book about the managers—in government, industry, science or communication. But within those spheres I have let my curiosity wander and filled in some flesh and blood. In particular I have tried to give some picture of the metabolism of the anonymous institutions which settle our everyday lives.

Several themes recur in different chapters, and are brought together in the last: the repercussions of a Labour Government; the impact of the new 'meritocracy' on the old aristocracy; the conflict between professionals and amateurs; the gap between prestige and power and (in Bagehot's phrase) between dignified and efficient parts; the proliferation of committees; the obscuring of ends by means; the pressure of conformism; the difficulties of combining democracy with efficiency; the emergence of a more thrusting and self-ambitious young generation of managers, in conflict with the old. Some themes—for instance the dominance of Oxbridge and public schools in some fields--recur regularly, but they have thrown themselves up so repetitively that I do not feel that they can be ignored. Many of the themes are common to America and Europe, and many of the problems are those of all capitalist countries, but in Britain—with her continuous traditions—the contrasts are unusually vivid, in the harsh juxtaposition with the Common Market and America. I have tried to use the quotations at the heads of chapters to illuminate some of the themes.

I have written in a deliberately detached and analytical way, rather as a foreign correspondent reporting territories. I have tried to expose myself to the influences of each of the institutions, and then (the hardest part) to retreat, and consider them dispassionately. I have not thought it necessary to reiterate that I consider Britain the most civilised and humane country, and the happiest to live in, and I have not dwelt on the long traditions of democracy, and the tolerance and humanity of most British institutions, which Englishmen easily forget and which writing this book has brought home to me.

To cover this large canvas before its characters and situations change, to try to catch a moment of contemporary history before it moves on, I have been forced to write this book at high speed—both in the first edition and in this revision. I am well aware that I have often failed to do justice to complex institutions, but writing such a book is like painting the Forth Bridge: if I had spent longer on it, the beginning would have been rusty by the time I had reached the end. But I hope, nevertheless, that this brisk tour through the gallery of power may be of some interest to others, as it has been to me, in understanding the kind of country we live in.

My indebtedness to others is enormous. This has been a brain-picking operation on a large scale, and to all whose brains I have picked I am grateful: there is no space to thank them, and many would prefer not to be mentioned. But the people without whom the book would not have happened are Michael Davie of *The Observer*, who first encouraged me to try it; Robin Denniston of Hodders, whose collaboration and perspective, as with my first book, have been crucial in both editions; and the printers, Tinlings, who have wonderfully faced the difficult task of producing a long book in a short time, and of deciphering untidy handwriting and corrections.

I am greatly indebted to the many people who helped me through the original edition: Professor Asa Briggs, for his advice and encouragement; my colleague Ivan Yates for many patient and perceptive comments; Madeleine Kallay, who had the appalling task of filing, checking, reading my writing and typing 300,000 words twice over; and the research assistants who helped me at various stages—Ann Grant, Corinna Ascherson, Kathleen Halton, Juliet Shubart. I owe a very special gratitude to my friend and colleague Virginia Makins, who saw the first book through the last exhausting stage of rewriting, checking and updating with great perception and who has been of immense help in this revision, particularly in the chapters on schools and universities: and also to her sister Mollie Philipps, who has very efficiently checked proofs and facts. I have also much appreciated the help of T. J. Wardill, who drew the charts, and of my friend Len Deighton for his design of the endpapers. In this revision I have had the help in research and secretarial work of Carol O'Brien, Carol Gaynor and Maureen McConville.

I am also again indebted to R. L. Urwin, for his compilation of a prodigious index in the most difficult and hectic conditions, and for his help with proof-reading and advice.

We have taken great pains to corroborate facts, and the chapters have been read—though not necessarily approved—by people in the institutions concerned. I have taken special pains in this revision to eliminate mistakes, and I have been much helped by the many readers who have taken the trouble to send corrections, and by friends who have made invaluable comments. But I am aware that among over 50,000 facts there will still be errors, and I will remain grateful to anyone who, however angrily, points them out.

Anatomy of Britain Today

PART ONE

I

ARISTOCRACY

The day of the dynasty and the era of nepotism is over.
Harold Wilson, November 1964.

The English aristocracy has been adroit in more than one respect. First of all it has always been involved in public affairs; it has taken the initiative in protecting its rights; it has talked a great deal about liberty. But what distinguished it from all others is the ease with which it has opened its ranks.
de Tocqueville, 1833.

IN the eighteenth century, it was not difficult to answer the question: 'Who rules Britain?' It was ruled by the ruling classes. More specifically, it was governed by the monarch and by two principal families, the descendants of the Churchills, Granvilles and Pelhams on one side, and the Stanhopes, Pitts and Grenvilles on the other. The wealth and dominance of the great British families—only about one hundred and fifty prominent people—reached its climax in the late eighteenth century. They became richer and more separate, competing in domestic splendour: palaces like Chatsworth or Belvoir Castle are their memorials.[1] Then, after the French Revolution, the intrusion of industry and the growth of the towns, the aristocracy began to come to terms with the new world, and to lose its separateness. In five years from 1784, the younger Pitt increased the numbers of peers from 200 to 250.[2] In the famous if exaggerated words of Disraeli: 'He created a plebeian aristocracy and blended it with the patrician oligarchy. He made peers of second-rate squires and fat graziers. He caught them in the alleys of Lombard-street, and clutched them from the counting-houses of Cornhill.'

The end of the old order, or what looked like the end, came with the first Reform Bill in 1832. Lord Bathurst cut off his pigtail—the mark of the superior courtier—and said, 'Ichabod, for the

[1] J. H. Plumb: *Sir Robert Walpole, the Making of a Statesman*, 1956. p. 8–11.
[2] A. R. Wagner: *English Genealogy*, 1960.

glory is departed.' But the glory was a long time departing, and the aristocracy managed to adapt themselves. 'By exercise, temperance and plebeian alliance', wrote G. M. Young of early Victorian England, 'the spindle-shanked lord of Fielding had become the ancestor of an invigorated race. They had shed their brutality and extravagance; their eccentricities were of a harmless sporting kind; they were forward in good works; they habitually had family prayers.' And they succeeded in keeping their wealth. Emerson, visiting Britain in 1856, described how the Marquess of Breadalbane could ride a hundred miles in a straight line, on his own property, and the Duke of Sutherland owned the whole of Sutherland, from sea to sea. He heard how some lords (even then) were forced to earn money showing people round their houses, and how ruined dukes were living in exile for debt: but in general he regarded the British nobles as 'high-spirited, active, educated men born to wealth and power'.[1]

Gradually, with the rise of industry, public schools, the professional civil service, death duties and Lloyd George, the old aristocracy lost its monopoly of power. The growth of the Labour Party and the big business corporations, with their new race of managers and technocrats, had little to do with aristocrats. The first world war was a greater shock to their world than the second. The great London palaces of the Whig oligarchs—Devonshire House, Lansdowne House, Holland House, Grosvenor House—which for so long were the centres of intrigue and influence—gave way to hotels and office blocks. The names remained, but the occupants were quite different. On their country estates they were forced to sell land to pay death duties, and to show the public round their houses to pay for their upkeep.

This is one popular picture of the twentieth-century aristocrat—much promoted by plays, films and aristocrats—a sad, impoverished man, living in a flat in a crumbling Tudor mansion, helping to collect half-crowns and serve the ice-cream, while the public in thousands come out of charabancs, their plastic raincoats squeaking together, to gape at armour, four-posters and tables laid for imaginary banquets.

But it is a misleading picture. In the first place, the aristocracy are, in general, much richer than they seem. With democracy has come discretion. Their London palaces and outward show have disappeared, but the countryside is still full of millionaire peers: many of them, with the boom in property, are richer now than

[1] Emerson: *English Traits*, 1888. p. 178.

they have ever been. Their individual wealth cannot compare with the new corporate wealth of industrial giants or insurance companies, but members of some of the oldest families are still among the richest men in Britain. Death duties, which used to eat into the large fortunes, are now nearly always circumvented by trusts and gifts.

In the second place, the British aristocracy have remained entangled with politics and power to an extent which—one suspects—Lord Bathurst would never have dreamt. Would he have guessed that, more than a century after 1832, an earl would become prime minister?

The British aristocracy has survived partly because it has never been very exclusive, and has always been ready to admit outsider sons-in-law, provided they were rich; this has helped it to keep up with the times. There has never been a nobility as in pre-revolutionary France, where 100,000 aristocrats had a separate, privileged life of their own. By continental standards, the English aristocracy is not very aristocratic, and its history has been mercenary. Only two families, the Ardens and the Berkeleys, can be traced to before the Norman Conquest. There is still a George Arden, a doctor at Windsor, author of *Posterior Dislocation of Both Shoulders*: and there are several Berkeleys, including Baroness Berkeley and Lennox Berkeley, the composer; a Captain Berkeley still lives at Berkeley Castle, where Edward II was murdered. A few aristocratic families, such as the Giffards and Ferrers came over with William the Conqueror: but a large number of titles—including all the dukedoms—were killed off in the Wars of the Roses.

A batch of surviving peers came with the dissolution of the monasteries in 1530, which founded the persistent fortunes of the Dukes of Bedford and Devonshire, and the Marquesses of Bath. But the numbers of the peerage were doubled by James I and Charles I, who made seventy-two peers in twenty-six years: King James charged £10,000 for a barony. Another large increase came with the younger Pitt, and the new aristocrats soon became merged with the old. In the nineteenth century scores of politicians, bankers, and merchants became peers, and a vast increase came with Lloyd George, who raised over three million pounds for the Liberal Party by the sale of peerages. Another boom —without the politics—came after the last war, under Attlee (who made 98 in six years), and continued under Macmillan and Douglas-Home. A new spate of life peers came with the new

Labour Government.[1] There has been a steady inflation in the proportion of peers. In medieval times there were about fourteen peers per million: now there are nineteen—not including life peers. And *over half* the peerages existing today date from 1906 or later.[2]

While new blood was coming into the aristocracy through new titles, peers introduced new blood to their families by marrying heiresses. Long before death duties, gambling, drinking and building had reduced many noble fortunes, which could only be revived by marrying money (it has even been argued that several families brought about their own extinction by marrying single heiresses—the children of less fertile marriages, who were liable themselves to be infertile). And the British aristocracy kept itself rich by the ruthless custom of primogeniture, by which the estate and the title passed only to the eldest son, and other sons had to make their own way in the army, the Church or business, or vanish into obscurity and poverty. It is still possible to find a rich peer living grandly in the family mansion, and his younger brother or his dowager mother living in a three-roomed flat: before the war there was even a second sons' club founded to protest against the custom. The favouritism for the eldest son has kept the old estates intact, for peers could never maintain their pomp if every son of a lord was a lord.

But the greatest strength of the British landed aristocracy is that they are the *only* aristocracy. There is no strong separate mercantile aristocracy as in Holland, nor an intellectual aristocracy as in France, nor an urban aristocracy as in America. The life of the country squire, if not of a peer, remains the ambition of successful Englishmen, whether dons or property developers, and few intellectuals would turn down an invitation from a duke. Before the war, it looked as if intellectuals more successfully rejected aristocratic habits, knighthoods and invitations, but since the war there has been much less revolt, and the aristocrats remain masters of the 'aristocratic embrace', which hugs angry radicals, poets, or working-class novelists into their cosy world. 'Never', said the American sociologist, Edward Shils, writing on post-war Britain, 'has an intellectual class found its society and its culture more to their liking'.[3]

[1] *See* p. 20.

[2] Sir Ivor Jennings: *Parliament*, 1957. p. 384.

[3] *Encounter*, April, 1955.

THE DUKES

'The Parson knows enough who knows a Duke.'
William Cowper, 1783.

Among the peerage, dukes have always been regarded as a class by themselves. Of the twenty-six still surviving—excluding the five royal dukes—the origins are odd. Only two, Norfolk and Somerset, go back before Charles I. Two, Bedford and Devonshire, founded their fortunes on the sacking of the monasteries by Henry VIII. Four were bastard sons of Charles II—St. Albans (by Nell Gwynn), Grafton (by the Duchess of Cleveland), Richmond (by the Duchess of Portsmouth) and Buccleuch (by Lucy Walters). Only two were promoted for obvious merit as opposed to wealth—Marlborough and Wellington.

Up till the first world war, the dukes lived legendary lives—though already diminished. Many were wealthier than the King. To commoners brought up before 1914—men of the generation of Harold Macmillan, Oliver Lyttelton or Duff Cooper (who all married duke's daughters)—ducal families were awesome. They had massive country estates, teams of liveried servants and dominating town houses—Grosvenor House, Norfolk House, Devonshire House: scores of London streets still bear their family names. Grosvenor House was the grandest, with a great grey colonnade along Park Lane and a courtyard behind it: inside was one of the finest picture galleries in Europe, to which the working classes were admitted on Sundays. The house was knocked down in 1930, to build Grosvenor House hotel, which still has a grey colonnade in front of the hotel rooms. The new Norfolk House contains British Aluminium; Devonshire House has motor-car showrooms. Only one of the ducal town houses remains—Apsley House, stranded on an island and surrounded by traffic in the middle of Hyde Park Corner; it has been turned into the Wellington Museum, but it still contains a live Duke of Wellington, devoted to the memory of his forefather, and author of his iconography, living in a large flat on the top.

Most of the dukes lead remarkably similar lives. Nearly all went to Eton (three were there together), and several to Christ Church: half have been Guards officers. All are based in the country, and most have a flat in London. Dukes are apt to be involved in royal occasions, and their daughters often become ladies of the bedchamber. They are referred to by the Queen in official documents as 'right trusty and entirely beloved cousins'; and they are supposed to be addressed as 'your grace'—which makes for conversational embarrassments. Like bishops and other peers, they are referred to by their christian name and their title—Bernard Norfolk, or Walter Buccleuch.

The dukes keep themselves to themselves. The most remarkable case of endogamy is the Duke of Northumberland: his father was the eighth Duke, his brother was the ninth Duke, his mother was the daughter of the Duke of Richmond (who was also related to the Duke of Portland). He married the daughter of the Duke of Buccleuch (who had married the grand-daughter of the Duke of St. Albans). One sister married the Duke of Hamilton, another married the Duke of Sutherland. He and his relations thus account for more than a quarter of the dukedoms. At least half are still millionaires. The Duke of Beaufort—a master of foxhounds whose car-number is MFH1—owns 52,000 acres in Gloucestershire, an area often known as 'Beaufortshire'. The Duke of Buccleuch—the descendant of a medieval Scots chieftain—has three big houses in Scotland and the midlands, all of them full of art treasures and closed to the public, and a flat in Grosvenor Square: he controls businesses, including a harbour, and is chairman of the Royal Bank of Scotland. The Duke of Rutland has 18,000 acres, two big houses in the midlands, and an art gallery. The Dukes of Westminster and Bedford still own areas of London. The Duke who has been closest to having an ordinary job is the new Duke of St. Albans, a large and amiable man who until recently has been head of the films division of the Central Office of Information.

The oldest dukedom is held by Bernard Marmaduke Fitzalan-Howard, sixteenth Duke of Norfolk; his family became earls of Arundel (where they still have 15,000 acres) in 1139, and dukes in 1483. As hereditary Earl Marshal of England, the duke is paid twenty pounds a year—a salary fixed in 1483. He is put in charge of special royal occasions, such as the Coronation and State Funerals, and his teddy-bear features, encased in heraldry, have thus become familiar on television. His stately and Catholic upbringing have given him a natural sense of ritual, and at Sir Winston Churchill's funeral he presided and led the procession with unshakeable dignity.

Into the discreet and sheltered world of the traditional dukes there burst in 1953 a disturbing presence—the new Duke of Bedford, back from South Africa. Faced with the problem of paying £4½ million death duties, he threw open his eighteenth-century mansion in a blaze of publicity, with every kind of ballyhoo and sideshow, including a private zoo, a park with bison and eleven kinds of deer, a playground, two million pounds' worth of pictures, a Chinese dairy, and occasional nudist camps.

The showman-duke was a new phenomenon, and the brashness of his exploits, including special lunch parties for Americans to have lunch with a duke for £10, appalled the more stately dukes, who while using and often enjoying publicity, preferred to maintain a private mystique of dukedom. But Bedford was enjoying himself: 'Being a showman is more fun', he wrote, 'than sitting about in dignity or potting pheasants'; and financially he has been sensationally successful. He moved Woburn Abbey quickly to the top of the 'league table' for stately homes, and although by 1963 he had refused to reveal the number of visitors he had brought in ('There has been a lot of cheating,' he alleged), numbers were said to be up on 1962, when 470,000 people visited Woburn.

The most political, and probably the most interesting of the dukes, is Andrew Cavendish, eleventh Duke of Devonshire. He lies in the centre of the network of interrelated families: his uncles include Harold Macmillan and Lord Salisbury, and he has been related by marriage to President Kennedy and Fred Astaire. Devonshires have been in and out of politics for four hundred years: the first duke, who built the family seat in 1687, was once fined £30,000 for brawling at court; and other Cavendishes discovered the composition of water and founded the Cavendish laboratory at Cambridge.

The present duke was Under-Secretary of State for Commonwealth Relations for four years, in his uncle's and Sir Alec's governments. He is a tall, gay, witty duke who talks fast and irreverently: he is as near as one can get to the debonair young dukes of novelists. He moves between his house in Mayfair, his shooting lodge in Yorkshire, his house in Ireland, and Chatsworth, the colossal palace in Derbyshire with 111 bedrooms, which he moved back into in 1960, where he entertains ducally while the public mill around the lawns: even after £2½ million death duties, much of the family estate is still intact. Devonshire is probably the most active of all the dukes—shooting, racing, politics, City and elaborate social life—but they remain traditional ducal activities, and the earlier Cavendish interest in science and art has subsided.

What will happen to the dukes? The last to be created, apart from royal relatives, was Westminster in 1874, who came from an old Norman family, the Grosvenors, and became one of the richest of all the Victorians, owning a quarter of central London including the whole of Belgravia (named after him), much of which—including Eaton Square—still remains in the family's hands. The present Duke of Westminster's fortune is by far the largest of the dukes' (said to be bigger than Charles Clore's) with big estates in Canada, Australia and South Africa, as well as London. In 1953, when the second duke died, a whole sub-department of the Inland Revenue was engaged in collecting £20 million death duties.

Since 1874 there have been no non-royal dukes: and the fact that Churchill did not accept a dukedom suggests that no more will be made. Churchill, as it happened, very nearly *was* a duke: for the first eighteen years of his life, until his uncle had a son, he was the heir to the dukedom of Marlborough. But Churchill had never taken very kindly to the aristocracy from which he sprang: and even in his old age he preferred the company of self-made men, like Aristotle Onassis, Emery Reeves and Lord Beaverbrook.

Dukes are often spoken of nowadays as if they were men to be pitied, debilitated by their titles, fenced-in like a tribe of aborigines. It is sometimes assumed that to be a duke is itself an all-consuming and productive profession. Thus Lord Kinross, writing in 1943:

'Twenty-six men with few of the average man's opportunities. Men who cannot rise, only descend in the social scale. Men condemned to eternal publicity, whose private lives are seldom their own. Men who may live only where their grandfathers have chosen, and where the public expects. Men hamstrung by an inherited amateur status, to whom barely a profession is open. Men born limited by the responsibilities of too large an income. Men born into a world where there is one law for the duke, and another for the poor, perpetually victims of their own class government.'[1]

But in fact the limitations on dukes' lives are very few. They are not compelled to spend their day in seventeenth-century sports. The management of their estates is nearly always successfully delegated: and in so far that they have publicity—such as attended the wedding of the Duke of Marlborough's heir to Tina Onassis—it is not always unwelcome. There is nothing to stop them taking an interest in new universities, technology, the Commonwealth or contemporary art. Their social prestige gives them, as to Prince Philip, immense opportunities for leadership and enterprise—a duke can make anything fashionable—but most have preferred to live in the world of their ancestors. Their speeches in the House of Lords give some idea of their interests: between 1955 and 1964

[1] Lord Kinross: The Dukes of England. *Life*, November 15, 1943.

only eight spoke at all: Atholl spoke about salmon, game laws, leisure, grey squirrels, birds' eggs and pig meat; Buccleuch spoke about pests, agriculture, deer and trees.

PEERS AND PEERAGE

Altogether in December 1964 there were 931 hereditary peers in Britain, belonging to five different orders:

5 Royal Dukes
26 Dukes
38 Marquesses
204 Earls
133 Viscounts
525 Barons
and 20 Peeresses in their own right

All of them except dukes are called 'Lord': but within the peerage each order has a different aura. The younger sons and the daughters of dukes and marquesses are known as 'Lord John' or 'Lady Ann': but the children of viscounts or barons are merely called 'Honourable'. The hierarchy is rigidly preserved even in divorce rates. The dukes lead with a 30 per cent rate; next marquesses with 26 per cent, then earls 22 per cent, viscounts 21 per cent, and barons 15 per cent.[1]

Marquesses, like dukes, are becoming rarer: none has been created since the Marquess of Willingdon, the Viceroy of India, in 1936. The premier Marquess is Winchester, whose title goes back to 1551, but most of the rest date from the eighteenth and nineteenth centuries. They are noticeably less grand than dukes, though several are very wealthy—like the Marquess of Northampton (known as the 'Boxing Marquess') who moves between the oldest country house, Compton Wynyates, and his Elizabethan mansion, Castle Ashby, and owns 10,000 acres, including a valuable corner of Surrey.

New earls, too, are rare: only thirteen have been created since the war—an odd mixture including a wartime field-marshal (Alexander), an admiral of the fleet (Mountbatten), two ex-prime ministers and two ex-cabinet ministers. Retiring prime ministers are always offered an earldom, though since 1900 five of them

[1] According to Lord Kennet (quoting Ronald Hall), speaking in the House of Lords, June 21, 1963.

(Bonar Law, MacDonald, Chamberlain, Churchill and Macmillan) have turned it down. Douglas-Home, having renounced one earldom, cannot accept another.

Viscounts are scarcer, but more contemporary: they are thought, for some odd reason, to be more in keeping with modern Britain, and forty-seven have been made since the war. Between earls and viscounts are nice distinctions: why, for instance, was Alexander made an earl and Montgomery only a viscount? (Was it anticipated that Montgomery might be more eccentric?) There are two newspaper viscounts (Rothermere and Kemsley), a soap viscount (Leverhulme) and a beer viscount (Younger). It is still thought to be not totally pointless for a man, like Lord Eccles in 1963, to be promoted from a barony to a viscounty.

Last come the barons—much more the commonest of the peers, and the most booming: half were created in this century, and 159 have been made since the war—nearly a third of the total baronage, and a curious reflection on the social revolution. In the past, barons have been something of a joke: G. W. E. Russell, the nineteenth-century diarist, has described how Pitt was once asked by his banker, Smith, for the privilege of driving through the horse-guards: 'No,' said Pitt, 'but I can make you an Irish Peer.' Next day Mr. Smith was Lord Carrington.

A few of the baronies are very old: the premier barony is held by a young baroness who farms in Ireland, whose title goes back to 1264: and the ten oldest baronies, all medieval, still have land and fortunes. But most of them are more modern and mercantile. There are a Unilever baron, a Shell baron, a BP baron, a Rootes baron, a sugar baron (Lyle), tobacco barons (Dulverton, Sinclair), banker barons (Swaythling, Rothschild, Catto, etc.) and several whisky and brewing barons—collectively known as 'The Beerage' (Guinness have an earl, a viscount and a baron). Since Lloyd George's time the new barons have not necessarily been wealthy men, and many of them, like Lord Heyworth of Unilevers, have been managers rather than entrepreneurs.

To the hereditary barons have been added since 1958 the life barons—a device for bringing new peers into the House of Lords without being burdened with their offspring.[1] When life peers were introduced, many people expected that new hereditary peers would no longer be made, but the supply has continued unabated. Sixty-eight life barons had been made by 1965, and thirteen

[1] Life Peers were first proposed in 1856, for distinguished men who were too poor to support the dignity of an hereditary title.

women (whose form of address is still uncertain: they were meant to be called 'Baroness', but the title has not caught on). There is no obvious difference between life peers and ordinary new peers, but the influx of life peers has had a relatively enlivening effect on the House of Lords. 'It's like the BBC and the ITA,' said one peer, 'competition seems to have improved the programmes.'

But the peerage is very far from being synonymous with the aristocracy, and outside the world of Lords and Honourables, there are thousands of families who have continued for centuries, living prosperously in the country—loosely known as 'the gentry': there are 2,400 pages of them in *Burke's Landed Gentry*. There is also the curious title of baronet—a kind of hereditary knight—invented by King James I to pay for the settlement of Ulster, 'so that the King's wants might be relieved out of the vanities and ambitions of the gentry'. There are now about 1,500—nearly twice the peerage, including no less than 34 Tory MPs: but their future seems shaky. The Labour Party, between 1945 and 1951, stopped making them at all—except for one each year to the Lord Mayor of London: but the Conservatives showed a renewed fondness for them, and made 106 between 1952 and 1965. Among the advantages of baronets is the 'Baronetage Standing Council', which gives parties for them occasionally at the House of Lords.

The direct advantages of a peerage are few. A lord finds it easier to get servants, to run up credit, to get the best cuts of beef, to book tables at restaurants and sleepers on trains. He receives parliamentary debates free of charge, and can claim 4½ guineas for every day he sits in the House of Lords. He has the right to wear a hat in Court, to be hanged with a silken halter and (as Lord Mowbray showed in 1962) to claim privilege against a writ of attachment. (The Duke of Atholl even has the special privilege of being allowed to have a private army.) A peer can also, for 150 guineas have a coat of arms designed for him—a process which is supervised by the Garter King of Arms, Sir Anthony Wagner, a scholarly and dedicated herald who has worked his way up from Portcullis Pursuivant. On the other hand any peer receives hundreds of begging letters, is expected to be rich, and to open bazaars, sign letters and 'take things up' with the government.

But if he has social ambitions, the benefits are obvious. Peers are very active in professions where social prestige is important; and for any form of showmanship or salesmanship a title is invaluable. The eighth Marquess of Hertford and the fourth Earl of Kimberley each runs a public relations firm. Lord Montagu of

Beaulieu is a publicist and showman, specialising in vintage cars and jazz. Lord Kilbracken has written *Living like a Lord* and *A Peer behind the Iron Curtain*, and Lord Kinross has written *The Century of the Common Peer*. Lord Vivian has run a Chelsea restaurant with his signature on every menu and a special wine called 'My Claret'. Lord Foley has played jazz in America with a coronet on the piano. The Duke of Argyll has signed Argyll socks, among other well-publicised activities.

The more confused the social structure in Britain becomes, the more attractive, it seems, is the status-symbol of a title. The Englishman's love of a lord remains undiminished. 'Never have class divisions been so acute and anguished', Anthony Crosland has written, 'as since they were, theoretically, abolished.' It is often argued that snobbery—the 'pox Britannica' as it has been called—is most rife when classes are confused. 'Snobbery belongs rather to the situation where one class melts imperceptibly into another', wrote Sir Anthony Wagner, the Garter King of Arms, 'and where fairly free movement from one into another is possible.'

PLUTOCRACY

> Americans relate all effort, all work and all of life to the dollar. Their talk is of nothing but dollars. The English seldom sit happily chatting for hours on end about pounds.
>
> *Nancy Mitford*

Interacting with the traditional Society of old families is the new Society of the self-made rich, the entertainers, the communicators, and the urban hurly-burly sometimes called Café Society. Writing in 1872, Bagehot notices approvingly that there is no country where a 'poor devil of a millionaire is so ill off as in England', and said, in defence of the House of Lords, that 'the order of nobility . . . prevents the rule of wealth—the religion of gold'. 'Money alone—money *pur et simple*', he said, 'will not buy "London Society".' Ninety years later he would be much less certain. The ennobled still have a prestige different from that of the merely rich, but the impact of death duties, America, publicity-machines and gossip columns has helped to confuse the two. Between peers and publicists there is a natural alliance, and in the much-heralded new age of leisure, the aristocrats have a marketable expertise as the most practised leisure-merchants.

Here we might briefly digress to note the numbers of the rich. The British government does not, as the Americans do, publish the *names* of the men with the highest salaries, thus proclaiming its plutocracy; but the Inland Revenue *do* publish the numbers of people in each income bracket. This was the list for 1961–2[1]:

Annual income (before tax)	*Numbers of people*
More than £20,000	4,300
£10,000–£20,000	18,600
£5,000–£10,000	84,000
£3,000–£5,000	193,000
£2,000–£3,000	370,000
£1,500–£2,000	725,000
£1,000–£1,500	3,400,000
£800–£1,000	3,800,000
£700–£800	2,450,000
£600–£700	2,400,000
£500–£600	2,250,000
£400–£500	2,100,000
£300–£400	2,000,000
£250–£300	950,000
£200–£250	900,000
£180–£200	355,000

But these figures are misleading, because they take no account of capital gains. One recent survey has thrown light on capital wealth. Lydall and Tipping, writing in the Bulletin of the Oxford Institute of Statistics in 1961, estimated that the top one per cent of British adults owned 43 per cent of total net capital—whereas in America (in 1954) the top one per cent owned only 24 per cent of personal wealth. The authors estimated that 20,000 people owned more than £100,000, and that their average holding was £250,000. (While at the bottom there are 16 million people with less than £100 each, and an average of £50.)[2] This large number of quarter-millionaires obviously includes only a small proportion of aristocrats in the conventional sense.

A hint of private wealth is provided by servants: the Ministry of Labour in 1963 recorded 22,800 men and 217,400 women in 'private domestic service' (which includes daily helps and gardeners)—though this is a drop of over 7,000 men and 58,000 women on the figures for 1960. It is estimated that there are still about 600 butlers in Britain, many of whom, according to a director of a London employment agency, 'have all the benefits of a £2,000 a year man'.[3] In addition to their pay they have free accommodation, keep and uniform, and tips—which can amount

[1] 106th report of the Commissioners of Inland Revenue.
[2] *The Economist*, April 29, 1961. p. 434.
[3] *The Times*, March 19, 1963.

to £5 from a wealthy weekend guest. This is how *The Times* reckoned the average weekly rates of pay for the following staff:

Male	*Female*
Butler £7–£15	Cook Housekeeper £5 10s.–£7
Footman £5–£8	Cook General £5–£6
Chauffeur:	Nannies £5–£13
Residential £10–12	House Parlour Maid £6–£7
Non-residential £14–£18	Housemaid £5–£6
Chef £15–£20	Mothers' Help £4–£6
	Lady's Maid £6–£8
	Parlour Maid £6–£7

According to agencies, the cost of a big staff—butler, cook, footman, two housemaids, kitchen maid, lady's maid, chauffeur-handyman and dailies—would be about £6,000 a year.

How far, with a large class of new rich, is the old aristocracy losing ground? The 'religion of gold' has probably waned since Victorian times, when Emerson noted: 'There is no country in which so absolute homage is paid to wealth,' and Taine was appalled by the ruthless money-worship. In the gossip columns—a useful if fitful pointer to public interest—the worlds of new millionaires and old aristocrats are often colliding, and it is the aristocrats who usually win.

The two worlds of aristocracy and plutocracy overlap in the 'season'—the succession of private dances and balls given between April and July, which serve as the marriage-market for richer children. The minimum cost for the coming-out of a debutante is a thousand pounds, and a large dance at a hotel costs about £4,000. But nevertheless the season has swelled since the war, with two or three dances a night from May to July, and a new bonus of autumn dances. The season has become an increasingly commercialised affair, with paid hostesses and elaborate publicity arrangements, and since 1959 the Queen has ceased receiving debutantes at the Palace. But the entertainment continues unabated, with a momentum of its own.

HOUSE OF LORDS

Would those who have accepted titles please stop asking us not to call them by the titles they have accepted?

Colin MacInnes (Letter to *The Times*, December 1964).

The centrepiece of the peerage is still the pinnacled building at Westminster, the House of Lords. In the past two years its residual influence has shown signs of faster dwindling; but it still has a charm which few people—least of all radicals—seem able to resist. The more cut-off it becomes from everyday life, the greater its attraction for weary businessmen or politicians. On the road outside, the word 'Peers' is painted across the car-park in large white letters. At the door stands a policeman with a strong sense of occasion; inside a tall liveried ex-guardsman, with the decorum of a Hollywood butler, directs you through the vaulted entrance hall, past a long row of elaborate gothic coat-hooks, each one labelled, beginning with H.R.H. D. Windsor (what would happen, one wonders, if he were to walk in?) progressing through other royal dukes to all the peers from L. Aberconway to M. Zetland—one of the many features of the building reminiscent of a school.

Upstairs you come to a series of high dark rooms, embellished with gothic woodwork and carved ceilings: the powerful architecture gives an atmosphere of peace and timelessness, like an eccentric but well-run country house. A life-size white marble statue of the young Queen Victoria, sitting on the Coronation chair and crowned with laurels, looks down on elderly peers sitting at hexagonal tables, writing letters on gothic writing-paper. Doors lead off to long dining-rooms—one for guests, another for peers only—and to a large bar looking over the river, which serves drinks all day and sells special 'House of Lords' cigarettes. Other closed doors are simply marked 'Peers'—an embarrassing ambiguity for lady peers, for 'peers' can mean the Lords' equivalent of 'gentlemen'. In fact the presence of lady peers in the House is a cause of constant embarrassment—she cannot even get herself a cup of tea unless she is accompanied by a male peer.

In the ante-room and passages, soft-footed attendants take messages, escort visitors, and address all peers as 'My Lord'. But in the dining-rooms a momentary sense of reality breaks in: cosy aproned waitresses are apt to talk about the telly, to call peeresses 'my dear', and to serve a meal of roast beef and two veg.

Ambling between the ante-rooms are elderly men, exchanging reminiscences and comments about debates. There is an aura of contented old age—older than the oldest men's club. The rooms are full of half-remembered faces of famous men, or politicians who had dropped suddenly out of public life twenty years ago, who—how shall one put it—one had forgotten were still around. There is banter between left-wing peers and right-wing peers, and a great deal of talk about operations and ailments and nursing homes. 'You see this is a kind of hospital,' one earl explained to me, after two peers had come up to talk about their recent illnesses: 'you have to be something of an expert on operations.'

Occasionally a young man appears among the old faces—perhaps a young peer well-off enough to be independent, or one of the many young government peers. But, as the number of life peers increases, so the proportion of young faces becomes smaller, and the average age climbs inexorably up. In 1964 there were 10 nonagenarians and 59 octogenarians.

Leading off the main ante-room is the chamber itself—the fine flower of the Victorian romantic style. It is quite small, only eighty feet long—twice the length of a large drawing-room. Stained glass windows shed a dark red light, and rows of statues of the barons of Magna Carta, looking misleadingly like saints, look down from the walls. The hall is extravagantly ornate and reminiscent of a rich private chapel. The difference between it and the House of Commons is (as one observer remarked) rather like the difference between a first-class and second-class railway carriage. On either side of the hall are long red-leather sofas, facing each other across the gangway with dark wood choir-stalls at the back. Between the two sides is something which looks like a huge red pouff, with a back-rest in the middle of it: this is 'the Woolsack', the traditional seat of the Lord Chancellor, stuffed with bits of wool from all over the Commonwealth. Facing the Woolsack are three men in wigs, sitting at a large old desk, full of bits of writing-paper, glue, inkpots, paper clips and an hour-glass.

At the far end, like a reredos, is an immense gilded canopy, stretching half-way up to the roof, with twenty-foot high candlesticks on either side rising from the floor like stalagmites. And in the middle of the canopy, behind bronze rails and a deep red carpet, is the throne.

Sitting on the red-leather sofas, facing each other, leaning back, whispering, putting their feet up, fumbling with papers, making notes, putting a deaf-aid (supplied by the attendants) to their ear, or simply sleeping, are the peers. On a full day— which is rare—you can see them in their groups: a group of bishops or 'Lords Spiritual' (26 of them are allowed to sit in the Lords) in white rochets; a handful of judges (9 sit in the Lords); a cluster of industrial peers—Chandos or Knollys—a row of government peers—Morrison, Longford, Shackleton—and facing them some Conservative peers—Blakenham, Carrington, Dundee. More often there is only a handful of peers in the room and a pleasant somnolence descends while one of them is speaking. The speakers are relaxed, prolix, delighting in the formalities—'My Lords', 'Your Lordships' House', 'The Noble Earl'.

The hours are not strenuous: the peers often sit for only three hours at a time, and never on Fridays. Nor are attendances spectacular: since peers can claim four-and-a-half guineas for attending, young peers have taken to looking in after work, for a sit-down and a drink: the average afternoon attendance has gone up to about 110. Only three peers are needed for a quorum. Lord Chandos did not bother to speak until seven years after becoming a peer, and other recent peers have never spoken. The record number to have attended since the war is 333, for the debate on the death penalty in 1956. 'A policy of militant abstentionism' is how one peer described his absence from a debate. A pleasant tolerance is one main characteristic of the Lords. When Lord Milford, the first Communist peer, made his maiden speech calling for the abolition of the Lords in July 1963, Lord Attlee mildly pointed out: 'there are many anomalies in this country. One curious one is that the voice of the Communist Party can be heard only in this House. That is the advantage of hereditary representation.'

In the imposing surroundings of the Lords, it is sometimes difficult to remember how unimportant they are. (It is odd to recall, too, that the magnificent edifice was built by the Victorians in 1847, after the first Reform Act had been passed which began the eclipse of its power.) The most that the Lords can do now is to delay a bill by one year: and any 'money bill' they can delay only for a month. Their main impact comes from the few inches of space in next morning's papers.

The unimportance of the Lords derives ultimately from the discomforting fact that the prime minister can create as many peers as he wants to, and so flood the chamber with his supporters. Ever since 1712, when the Tories created twelve new peers to pass the Treaty of Utrecht, the threat has been in the background. The threat was used to pass the Reform Bill of 1832 and the Parliament Bill of 1911—when the powers of the Lords were curbed, after they had thrown out Lloyd George's budget of 1909. Actually to *carry out* the threat nowadays would be embarrassing: in 1950, if the Labour Party had wanted a majority in the Lords, it would have had to create about six hundred peers.[1] But the nightmare is real enough to bring the peers to heel.

For years, both political parties have been worried about their

[1] Sir Ivor Jennings: *The British Constitution*, 1946. p. 100.

Lordships' House. As a Second Chamber it is hopelessly unrepresentative—about ninety per cent Conservative, much more conservative than the Conservative Party, and they have not defeated a Conservative motion since 1832. However many Labour peers are made, their sons often turn out to be Conservative. Life peers have hardly redressed the balance, for more than half of *them* are Tories.

In 1963 the Commons and the Lords took quite a bold step. They passed the new Peerage Bill, which allowed peers to disclaim their titles. The Earl of Home has become Sir Alec Douglas-Home, Lord Hailsham has become Mr. Quintin Hogg, Lord Stansgate has become Mr. Anthony Wedgwood Benn, and Lord Altrincham has become Mr. John Grigg. The complexity of the new system was further revealed when it became necessary for Wavell Wakefield, the former Member of Parliament for Marylebone, to be made a peer in order to allow Mr. Hogg to enter the Commons. It is still too early to judge the long-term results of this small and talented exodus; but the implication remains that the political peers who stay in the Lords are those who could not make a career in the House of Commons.

Ironically, the end of a Conservative government and the beginning of a Labour one produced a spate of peerages without precedent in all British history. Between June 1964 and January 1965, no fewer than forty-four peerages were made, increasing the membership of the House of Lords by nearly five per cent in less than six months, and including three viscounts, nine barons and thirty-two life barons and baronesses. Harold Wilson made it clear that he would not create any more hereditary peerages, but he produced a bevy of new life ones—sometimes in return for past services, sometimes to allow ministers to sit in the Lords, sometimes to make way for others to sit in the Commons. They included such varied people as George Cole of Unilever, Fenner Brockway, the left-wing MP, Harold Collison, chairman of the TUC, and Charles Leatherland, an alderman in Essex; and some people suspected that Wilson might be trying to remove the awe of the Lords by flooding it with more ordinary people.

There are aspects of the Lords which are delightful—the kindliness, the clubbiness, the eccentric discussions—about prostitutes, or drunkenness, or forestry, or *Lady Chatterley's Lover*: and some debates are far from fatuous. But this extraordinary assembly of dukes, earls, marquesses, viscounts, barons, bishops and judges remains an apparently insoluble dilemma for both parties in the

Britain of the sixties. Few people are happy about having such an anachronistic assembly in the midst of parliament, but few people can bring themselves to advocate abolishing it. It epitomises the divorce between prestige and power which we shall find elsewhere.

2

PALACE

When there is a select committee on the Queen the charm of royalty will be gone. Its mystery is its life. We must not let in daylight upon magic.

Walter Bagehot.

We live in what virtually amounts to a museum—which does not happen to a lot of people.

Prince Philip, February 25, 1964.

MONARCHS

In Europe in 1900, there were kings or emperors in Germany, Austria, Russia, Italy, Portugal and Spain. Now there are only seven European monarchies left (excluding the Grand Duchess of Luxembourg, the Prince of Monaco and the Prince of Liechtenstein, who has only 14,000 subjects). They are, in order of numbers of subjects:

Queen Elizabeth of the United Kingdom
Queen Juliana of the Netherlands
King Baudouin of Belgium
King Constantine of Greece
King Gustav Adolph of Sweden
King Frederick of Denmark
King Olaf of Norway

They are a select, endogamous profession: five of them are descendants, or married to descendants, of Queen Victoria, 'the matriarch of Europe'. Both the King of Sweden's wives have been descendants of Queen Victoria: and the King of Denmark married the daughter of the King of Sweden. The King of Greece married (in 1964) the daughter of the King of Denmark. The English are German, the Swedes are French, the Norwegians and Greeks are Danes. They might seem an anachronous and dwindling profession; but in fact all the monarchs, with the possible exception of the Greek king, are more secure than they were fifty years ago. All of them have yielded most of their traditional power to prime ministers and cabinets.

But most of the kings and queens have kept the respect of their people by diminishing not only their power, but their style and expense. Outside England, the most formal is King Baudouin, who has a big palace in Brussels and is attended by a large household and heated controversy. The Queen of Holland is probably richer than Queen Elizabeth, with an allowance of £170,000 a year; but she lives a simple life with her husband, Prince Bernhard, who is an active director of the Royal Blast Furnaces and the Netherlands Bank for National Recovery.

The others are aggressively democratic: the King of Denmark —who has a well-tattooed chest—answers his own letters and telephone, bows to his guests, conducts the royal orchestra, and has even made a film of 'a day in the life of a king' to show how ordinary he is. The King of Norway (who is in remote succession to the British Throne) studied political science at Balliol; and his father Haakon began the modernisation of kings by refusing to accept the throne in 1905 unless he was elected. The King of Sweden, an archaeologist and Fellow of the Royal Society, spent years in the civil service as a monarch-trainee.

But the British monarchy is in a class by itself, and in the past fifty years it has become increasingly cut off from the rest. Edward VII, when thrones were shaky, was touchy about monarchic solidarity: 'I cannot be indifferent to the assassination of a member of my profession,' he said when he refused to recognise the Serbian régime after the murder of King Alexander: 'We should be obliged to shut up our businesses if we, the Kings, were to consider the assassination of Kings as of no consequence at all.' But nowadays—though assassinations are of course disapproved of —there is a less close fellow-feeling. British courtiers have been known to talk with contempt about 'those bicycling kings' (it is a measure of the sanctity of the British monarchy that the thought of a sovereign on a bicycle, or even on a bus, is regarded as inherently laughable).

Only in Britain is there still a monarchy on the grand and sanctified scale, supported by religious processions, courtiers, mass adulation and above all by a full-blown titled aristocracy. In its blend of showmanship, religion, diplomacy and occasional public hysteria, the monarchy remains an important part of the national character.

At the head of this unique institution is Her Most Excellent Majesty Elizabeth the Second, by the Grace of God, of the United Kingdom of Great Britain and Northern Ireland and of Her other

Realms and Territories Queen, Head of the Commonwealth, Defender of the Faith, Sovereign of the British Orders of Knighthood. The Queen is the fortieth monarch since the Norman Conquest, descended among others from Charlemagne, Egbert King of Wessex, Rodrigo the Cid and the Emperor Barbarossa.

Behind the official routine, the Queen's own life remains remarkably well concealed. She is known to be shy, conscientious and painstaking: as an employer she is fair, kind, but exacting. Of her homes, her favourite—as was Queen Victoria's—is Balmoral, the grey granite Victorian castle in Scotland, with pepper-pot turrets and a great square keep which has a persistent fascination for British royalty. It is a bizarre place, surrounded by grouse-moors, full of antlers, tartan chairs, and flock wallpaper embossed with 'VR'. It is here, for nine weeks every year, that the Queen retreats from the public—working in the morning, walking, riding or deer-stalking in the afternoon, watching television, playing scrabble or party games in the evenings.

The Queen's circle of personal friends all come from the same landed background. Among them are Lord Rupert Nevill, brother of the Marquess of Abergavenny; the Dukes of Beaufort and Norfolk; Gavin Astor, chairman of *The Times*; Lord Euston, son of the Duke of Grafton; Major-General Sir Harold Wernher, president of Electrolux. Sometimes the Queen and Prince Philip spend weekends with them, but since they must be accompanied by a dresser, a valet, a chauffeur and one or two detectives, the numbers of hosts are limited; entertaining the Queen is not as difficult as in the first Queen Elizabeth's day—when the Queen's visit could almost ruin a nobleman—but it is still a large commitment; and the Queen, realising this, usually prefers to be host rather than guest.

The Queen's life has many ordeals but there is no sign that she has difficulty in the central rôle—being royal. In spite of the intrusion of democracy, the votes of parliament and the pressures of the populace, the world of the palace remains something quite separate from the world of Whitehall, or Westminster, and that world revolves firmly round the personality of the Queen.

However much one discusses the monarchy as an institution, it remains primarily a *person*. 'You can't separate the private and public functions of the Queen,' said one court official, 'that's the main difference between a monarchy and a republic. In a republic you know that the President's life is arranged by the state, and that eventually he'll retire back to his own home. But what most impresses the visitors to Windsor or the royal yacht is the feeling that they're in a private home—that it's part of a family life.'

Dashing in and out of this private and settled world, taking off from the palace garden in a helicopter, is the restless figure of Prince Philip, Duke of Edinburgh, who married Princess Elizabeth in 1947. The Duke, like Prince Albert, has strong ideas about the rôle of a consort. He has been strongly influenced by his formidable uncle, Earl Mountbatten; and he has tried to identify himself with the future rather than the past, and particularly with youth, science, industry and technology. He writes his own speeches, has published two books of them, and appears on television. He has described himself as 'one of the most governed people you could hope to meet', but he has managed to establish a place for himself as a free-booting critic. He has cultivated the art of what he calls 'dontopedalogy'—opening his mouth and putting his foot in it. While narrowly avoiding partisan politics, he has aired views on Anglo-German unity, national service, the VIPs' lounge at London Airport, the rear-lights on lorries, the fitness of Canadians, nature conservation and air safety.

But while the Duke has made forays into the world of science and industry, he has not succeeded in appreciably changing the character of the court itself, and between the Duke's competitive pep-talks and the traditional aura of the palace, there remains a large discrepancy.

THE FADING OF FAIRYLAND

'It is a great mistake to make government too dull.'
Lord Attlee, 1952.

To the unique glory of royalty has been added, since Victorian times, unique wealth, and exemption from death duties has heightened the fairyland. Even after the first world war there were still people, like Lord Derby or the Duke of Devonshire, who were richer than the King. Buckingham Palace, though the biggest, was only one of many great town houses, and the dukes and parvenu millionaires could rival royal entertainment. In two world wars taxation cut down all other palaces, and diminished the great country estates. But the Sovereign's allowance remained exempt from his tax commissioners, and his land and palaces remained the sole relic of the old order, with Buckingham Palace at the centre.

There the Palace stands, between Victoria station and Hyde Park Corner, overlooked by office blocks and surrounded by traffic, a symbol of fantasy in an age of commerce. It has six hundred rooms and half-a-mile of corridors cleaned by a hundred cleaners, forty acres of garden kept up by nine gardeners, and a lake of three-and-a-half acres, big enough to contain the whole of Berkeley Square. There are three hundred clocks, wound under contract by Frodsham's, several TV sets (exempt from licence) maintained by the royal electricians.

The isolation of the palace has transformed the social rôle of the monarch. 'Before it was like a pyramid,' explained one courtier, 'now it is more like a bumpy plain, with an island in the middle.' Sitting on this island, the palace has become much more aware of being watched and judged: royal lunches and garden parties acquire a unique significance and every new guest is interpreted as a national gesture.

Life in Buckingham Palace, it is true, is not as grand as it looks. The front rooms are uninhabited except on a few state occasions: only the first floor of the north wing, looking over Constitution Hill, provides the actual living quarters of the Queen, with the royal nursery above, and the administrative offices below. At the door are not gold-braided flunkeys, but men in a kind of blue battle-dress, with 'E II R' on the front. The offices have dictating machines and intercoms, with a row of names and one in red, saying 'The Queen'. Most of the extraordinary collection of people called the 'Queen's Household'—such as the Master of the Horse, Gold Stick, the High Almoner, or the Mistress of the Robes —are not to be seen wandering through the corridors: they are unpaid, and very part-time, and normally only emerge from mufti for royal processions or coronations. The full-time household—apart from servants and grooms—amount to only sixty people: and in Buckingham Palace, apart from the Queen's own lunch-table, only about fifteen people—private secretaries, privy purse people, equerries or press officers—sit down to lunch.

But still the courtiers are sufficiently formidable to maintain a sense of a court, isolated from the outside world, and to act as cushions between royalty and reality—small change, time-tables or awkward encounters. There is a team of three equerries (to rhyme with ferries) seconded from the services who work in fortnightly shifts, and act as royal ADC's: there are ladies-in-waiting who accompany the Queen everywhere, avoiding difficulties, answering telephones, picking up handkerchiefs, arranging payments in shops (the Queen never carries money). On royal tours a large secretariat prepares every inch of the ground, measures the rooms, works out time-tables—to ensure that the monarchy shall maintain smoothness and dignity. 'It is', as one court observer remarked, 'the Rolls Royce of monarchies.' Courtiers remain a very distinct profession, often handed down from father to son, and with a sense of vocation acquired as a child: even accountants or grooms acquire a special stateliness in the service of royalty.

The most important job in the palace is the Private Secretary to the Queen: for he is the main link between the monarch and the world outside. 'It is he more than anyone else who creates for the Sovereign the background of the régime.'[1] Sir Michael Adeane, the present chief secretary, might seem the quintessence of the professional courtier: his grandfather, Lord Stamfordham, was private secretary to King George V and Adeane himself began his royal service at the age of thirteen, as a page of honour to King George V. He took a first at Cambridge and has been a keen wild-fowler. He is a neat, white-haired man, with old-fashioned courtesy, who arrives at Buckingham Palace every morning from his flat in St. James's Palace. But he is essentially a realist in his approach to the monarchy. He does not, like many courtiers, regard himself as part of the mystery, and he talks shrewdly about his problems. In the changes in the monarch's rôle since the war—particularly in the handling of the Commonwealth—Adeane has played an important part.

But Adeane is on the toughest frontier of the monarchy, and the rest of the Court—particularly the periphery—is very subject to mumbo-jumbo. Even the royal food and equipment acquires its own splendour: the words 'By Appointment', together with the royal arms, adorn over 1,000 firms, all listed in the *London Gazette*: they include the royal dog food (supplied by Clark and Sons), the royal mushrooms (Aylesbury Mushrooms Ltd.), the royal turtle soup (John Lusty Ltd.) and the royal marmalade (Frank Cooper's, now taken over by the US Brown & Polson combine), the royal kippers (John Curtis) and the royal bagpipes (Lawrie Ltd.). In 1964, it turned out, there were still two firms—makers of adjustable chairs and purveyors of confectionery—who were allowed to style themselves 'By Appointment to the late Queen Alexandra' (who died in 1925).

Between this fairyland palace and the practical world there is

[1] Sir John Wheeler-Bennett: *King George VI*. Appendix B.

an effective psychological moat, and a drawbridge which is only let down on special occasions. The palace has succeeded in maintaining not only wealth and dignity but also secrecy. There is not so much secrecy that the public eventually loses interest: the palace is far from unaware of publicity, and the Queen reads nearly all the papers every day. But there is enough hidden to stimulate intense public curiosity, and not only in England but in America or Germany (where a royal picture-cover can still increase a magazine's circulation by 50,000 copies). The palace's chief press officer, Commander Colville, is not a journalist, but an ex-naval officer, a courtier and son of a courtier. He is angrily criticised by the press for withholding information: the Queen has never held a press conference, but on royal tours the Queen and the Duke do meet the correspondents who follow them round. In spite of the hundreds of journalists who have hunted for royal stories, no one yet knows how life is led in the royal palaces, what private views the Queen holds, what she says to her visiting statesmen. Visitors to the palace maintain that embarrassed discretion that is the special mark of the courtier.

The remoteness of the Queen is enhanced by her entourage. Most of her time is spent with people who, from the public's point of view, are in a half-and-half world between royalty and ordinariness. Many of the guests at Windsor or Balmoral have titles, and dukes, particularly racing dukes, make up the foothills to royalty. The monarchy, it is true, is not the undisputed centre of the aristocracy, and since Charles II's time the monarch has ceased to be the acknowledged head of London Society (in so far as that exists). But the monarch and the aristocracy for their prestige are mutually interdependent. The aristocracy would not be the same without a pinnacle and a mystery at the top: and the palace would not have the same mystery if it were surrounded by misters.

Certainly the Queen gives no impression of unhappy isolation. Viewed from the outside, seeing this island of royalty surrounded by ordinariness, preserved as a deliberate symbol, a kind of living flag, by calculating parliaments, one might imagine that to be a British monarch was an unbearably lonely profession—like a caged lion in a field of rabbits. But this is not, apparently, how it strikes the visitor to Buckingham Palace. There it is the visitor who is isolated, coming into a world with apparently limitless ramifications. When, from time to time, the Queen and Prince Philip give informal lunch parties to meet cricketers, balloonists or businessmen, it is not so much they who seem to be glimpsing the world outside as the visitors who are glimpsing the world *inside*.

The problem of how to keep the fairyland under control has caused some worry to the palace. Already before the war, the monarchy had taken over a quasi-religious position. 'In the middle of the last century,' wrote Kingsley Martin in 1937, 'it needed courage to break the religious taboo, to doubt the literal truth of the first chapter of Genesis, or question the scientific basis for belief in the virgin birth. The throne on the other hand was frankly criticised in the newspapers and on the platform. In the twentieth century the situation is exactly reversed.'[1] It is hard now to imagine *The Times* commenting, as they did on the funeral of King George IV, 'there never was an individual less regretted by his fellow-creatures than this deceased King.'

After the war, with the end of secrecy, and with the royal wedding and the royal baby, public excitement began to reach alarming proportions: and with the Coronation in 1953, public adoration seemed to have got out of control—like a captive balloon that had broken loose from its moorings. The public frenzy continued, watched by some palace officials with growing bewilderment, and an uneasy feeling that the balloon might eventually hit something and explode: but in the past few years there have been some signs that the public interest has been moderating, only partly revived by the crop of royal babies in 1964. Malcolm Muggeridge complained to an American television audience in February 1964: 'The story goes on and on. There is a happy family, there was a problem sister, and now all the girls are going to have babies. Here are all the ingredients of a soap opera. The English were getting bored with their monarchy. I think it is coming to an end.'

How to regulate the mystery presents difficult problems: for palace people are aware that once you touch the trappings of monarchy, like opening an Egyptian tomb, the inside is liable to crumble. At the Coronation there were discussions as to whether the procession should be adapted to include Commonwealth leaders: but eventually it was felt that the actual meaning of the procession was anyway so doubtful that to change it could be tricky. Likewise the fact that the Queen is head of the Church of England and yet (when she crosses the border) attends the Church of Scotland does not bear too much theological inspection, and is best left unexplained. The basic dilemma of the

[1] Kingsley Martin: *The Magic of Monarchy*, 1937. p. 9.

palace is that, because of the mystery, the public expects far more to be happening inside the palace than actually does, and the public frenzy brings with it the danger of terrible bathos.

THE COST OF THE QUEEN

The total cost of this apparatus is hotly debated. There are even some—for instance Sir Charles Petrie—who insist that the monarchy makes a profit. This argument assumes that the Queen is the real owner of the Crown Lands of which the revenue, since the time of George III, has been handed over to the state. The Crown is the second biggest landowner in Britain, with 180,000 acres in England, 105,000 in Scotland, and valuable city properties, including Regent's Park, Carlton House Terrace, and chunks of Pall Mall, Piccadilly, Holborn and Kensington. The Crown also has such items as income from wrecks, whales and sturgeons, the excise on beer, cider and wine licences, and treasure troves. All these properties, from whales to terraces, are run by the Crown Estates Commissioner in Whitehall, under the First Commissioner and Chairman, the Earl of Perth, a former minor Tory minister and Hereditary Thane of Lennox. Their surplus profits which after tax and expenses amount to about £2½ million a year, is handed to the Exchequer. This income, it is argued, more than makes up for the Queen's salary. But the Crown Lands should be regarded as belonging to the state, and by any calculation the monarchy is an expensive affair.

The sovereign's salary is fixed by parliament at the beginning of the reign. Queen Elizabeth's allowance amounts to £475,000 a year—which has hardly changed since George V's time, and is worth only a third as much: but when it was increased in 1952, it was described by Emrys Hughes, MP, as 'the largest wage claim of the century'. It is made up by:

	£
Her Majesty's Privy Purse	60,000
Salaries of Household	185,000
Expenses of Household	121,800
Royal Bounty, alms and special services	13,200
Supplementary provision (to allow for inflation, Duchess of Kent, Princess Alexandra, etc.)	95,000
	£475,000

On top of this, separate allowances are voted by parliament for a few other members of the Royal Family:

	£
Queen Elizabeth the Queen Mother	70,000
Duke of Edinburgh	40,000
Duke of Gloucester	35,000
Princess Margaret, Countess of Snowdon	15,000
Princess Royal	6,000
	£166,000

But the actual upkeep of the royal palaces (including Buckingham Palace, at £174,000 in 1963, Windsor Castle and Holyroodhouse) is paid for by that dreary patron, the Ministry of Public Buildings and Works: their total estimated cost in 1963 was £781,000. The cost of the Queen's Flight—four Herons, two helicopters and a Chipmunk, all painted fluorescent red and with eighty people to look after them—is paid for by the RAF. The cost of royal tours is borne by the host governments in the Commonwealth countries. The cost of the royal trains, royal postage, royal telegrams (which have precedence) and telephone calls, all fall on the state. The most obviously extravagant royal perquisite is the yacht *Britannia*, paid for by the Navy: it cost £2 million to build, and its upkeep and crew of 250 cost about £380,000 a year. Altogether the cost to the state of the monarchy is probably not less than two million pounds a year—as much as Omo and Daz spend on advertising.

On top of this, the Queen has her private fortune, a source of interminable speculation. Queen Victoria was said to have left at least £2 million, from savings and gifts (she was given half-a-million by an old miser called John Nield in 1852): and since then the fortune has probably increased. King George V is said to have left a million pounds to each of his four sons: and Queen Mary left £406,000—though to *whom* it was bequeathed is not known. One American magazine reckoned that the Queen is the third richest woman in the world. In addition to her capital, the Queen owns the finest art collection in the world, amassed by Henry VIII, George I, George IV, etc., including more than 5,000 paintings, and an unparalleled collection of French and Italian drawings. The Queen also personally owns Sandringham and Balmoral (when Edward VIII abdicated, George VI had to buy them from him). And there is the fabulous royal jewellery, the royal stamp collection, valued at over a million pounds, the royal racehorses, which yield a profit, the royal pictures, valued at £15 million in 1958, and no less than five tons of gold plate. Kingsley Martin, one of the most thorough critics of the monarchy, reckons that the Queen's private fortune is quite probably between £50 million and £60 million.[1]

But it is doubtful whether the Queen has much scope for saving. There are some very expensive items not allowed for by parliament —including the Duke of Windsor: and other royal relations need financial help. In an age of affluence with full employment, the archaic trappings of royalty have been increasingly expensive to maintain: salaries of grooms and footmen, for instance, have risen steeply: the number of horses in the royal mews dwindled from 86 in 1937 to 30 in 1963: the cost of the fodder went up from two to three thousand pounds. And the Queen has a number of incidental expenses—including such oddments as the salary of the Poet Laureate (£99).

THE POWERS OF THE QUEEN

'A monarch is a kind of referee, although the occasions when he or she has to blow the whistle are nowadays very few.'

Lord Attlee.

The constitutional impotence of the Queen is well enough known. In theory, as Bagehot pointed out, if a bill was passed for the execution of the Queen, the Queen would have to sign it.

The actual political influence of the monarch is difficult to assess. The Queen retains one important attribute of power—information. All cabinet minutes and cabinet papers go in a red box to Buckingham Palace: atomic secrets, correspondence with presidents, budget plans, all make their way to the Queen, whether she is at Balmoral, Windsor, or in Africa. Whitehall goes to tremendous pains to keep the sovereign in the news: the Queen is, on this basis, the second-best informed person in Britain.

And every Tuesday night, when the Queen is in London, the prime minister goes round to Buckingham Palace for a talk with the Queen. The relationship has gradually changed: when Chatham was Prime Minister, according to one witness he bowed so low that you could see his great nose between his knees. When Gladstone went to see Queen Victoria, he remained standing up.

[1] Kingsley Martin: *The Crown and The Establishment. Penguin Books*, 1963. p. 143.

Now the prime minister is allowed to sit down and have a cigarette.

In the past thirty years the meetings between the monarch and the ministers have become much more formalised. The political associations of King George V were often private and personal: he wrote long letters to Haig, supporting him against Lloyd George—an intervention that might not have seemed so odd then as it does now. But now the meetings with ministers are deliberately arranged at fixed and stated times. Lord Attlee has described the kind of conversation he had with George VI:

> It would have been quite natural for George VI to say to me: 'How is Mannie hitting it off with the French generals?' or 'Well, Nye seems to be getting the doctors in line'. I, on the other hand, might have said to the King: 'The Old Man was really rather naughty in the House about India.'[1]

George VI, on his side, was touchy about being kept informed. In America, after long and frank conversations with Roosevelt, he complained: 'Why don't my ministers talk to me as the President did tonight?'[2]

There is nothing to stop a monarch trying to influence his prime minister. According to King George VI, when Attlee came to see him in 1945, after the Labour victory:

> I asked him whom he would make Foreign Secretary, and he suggested Dr. Hugh Dalton. I disagreed with him, and said that Foreign Affairs were the most important subject of the moment, and I hoped he would make Mr. Bevin take it. He said he would . . .'[3]

In theory, the Queen's area of patronage is large: in particular, as Head of the Church of England, she can recommend bishops. The Queen takes an interest in the Church, sees all bishops when they are appointed, and often has them to preach at Windsor. But in fact all episcopal appointments come from the prime minister, after consulting the Archbishop of Canterbury.

The most important residual powers of the sovereign are the

[1] *The Observer*, August 23, 1959.

[2] Sir John Wheeler-Bennett: *King George VI*. p. 389.

[3] Wheeler-Bennett. p. 638. Attlee, on the other hand, denies that he was influenced by the King in choosing Bevin.

right to dissolve parliament, and to choose a prime minister. The first has hardly been exercised in modern times. Attlee has said that the dissolution in 1951 was influenced by the King's anxiety and ill-health, but it was mainly due to the narrow majority and the vulnerability of the Labour cabinet.

Three times in the last twenty-five years has the choice of prime minister been in question. The first was in 1940, when the King made it clear that, if he had been given the choice, he would have chosen Lord Halifax.[1] The second was in 1957, when Sir Anthony Eden resigned. It is still sometimes thought that the Queen's choice depended on three men who she visibly consulted—Eden, Churchill, Salisbury: but in fact her choice of Macmillan depended on the careful sounding-out of the Tory party, the cabinet and the Lords, made by the Chief Whip and the Lord Chancellor.

The third and most controversial occasion was after the announcement of Macmillan's resignation in 1963. It is clear, from the various accounts of this crisis, that Macmillan was anxious that the palace should not be required to settle the choice; Macmillan conducted, from his sickbed, his own elaborate but far from conclusive soundings, and deduced that all sections of the party were in favour of the Earl of Home. And so, on Friday, October 18th, Macmillan's recommendation was taken to the palace by his principal private secretary, Sir Timothy Bligh; and with what appeared to be unseemly haste, Lord Home was summoned to the palace on the same afternoon, invited to try to form a government, and became prime minister next day. The brisk time-table made it seem that the Queen was not intended to have a say in the matter, and although one or two ministers attempted to lobby Sir Michael Adeane, to persuade him to delay the choice, this had no effect. It is clear that if the choice had been delayed, Mr. Butler would have stood a good chance of becoming prime minister; for the original argument in favour of Home—that he was a safe compromise candidate—was losing its weight; it is clear, too, that Macmillan was keen to settle for Home.[2]

Should the Queen, in this instance, have exercised her prerogative, taken her own soundings, and ignored Macmillan's advice? Iain Macleod, the sharpest critic of Macmillan's conduct, maintained that 'there is no criticism whatever that can be made

[1] Wheeler-Bennett. p. 444. But in Iain Macleod's biography of Chamberlain, Lord Halifax is shown as unwilling to accept the premiership, if it was offered him, ostensibly because of the problem of being a prime minister in the House of Lords.

[2] *See* p. 68.

of the part played by the Crown'; but Paul Johnson of the *New Statesman* maintained that the Queen should have made her own enquiries and that 'if there was indeed a conspiracy to foist Lord Home on the nation, it is hard to escape the conclusion that the palace was a party to it'.[1] It is difficult to see how, in this instance, the Queen could have delayed the decision without provoking a further political crisis; but it is clear that the Queen's involvement, such as it was, had the effect of encouraging the obscure and muddled methods of the Conservative electoral process.

THE AURA OF MONARCHY

> I entirely agree that we are old-fashioned: it is an old-fashioned institution.
>
> *Prince Philip, February 25, 1964.*

The main importance of the palace is not its political, but its social influence. It is fashionable to regard the palace as a pleasant irrelevance in British life, a convenient side-show for the masses. But any institution which attracts such vast publicity and bemusement must influence its audience.

There is much to be said for the British device of presenting a façade of a mystic monarchy, surrounded by bearskins, dukes and Gold Sticks, behind which the real machinery of government can function quietly and unnoticed. 'Royalty', said Bagehot, 'is a Government in which the attention of the nation is concentrated on one person doing interesting things. A Republic is a Government in which that attention is divided between many, who are all doing uninteresting things.' During a time of social upheaval, such as the Victorian, an apparently unchanging head can give a sense of stability: and to separate pomp from power makes a safeguard against political megalomania or dictatorship.

But when there is no great social change, and the country is inclined to escape from harsh facts, a mysterious monarchy can easily become a refuge for foggy ideas. Among the more old-fashioned areas of British life, a blurred image of Buckingham Palace often lies in the background. That recurring theme: 'it may seem odd to you, but it *works*', which crops up in British institutions, from Lloyd's to the House of Lords and the election of bishops, has its prototype in the mystery of the monarchy. Businessmen with feudal pretensions; arrogant Guards officers;

[1] *New Statesman*, January 24, 1964.

jingo speakers at Conservative conferences; pompous ambassadors; young blimps (a far less pleasant species than old ones); parliamentarians talking about bogus mystique—all these invoke the palace in support of their mystery. While Britain is having to make the painful transition from imperial splendour to competitive trading, the palace represents in most people's minds a feudal, uncompetitive haven of 'it's not *done*'.

For much of this, it is unfair to blame the palace. Many of the pretensions spring from deeper causes than the monarchy: and Prince Philip himself has said: 'If we are to recover prosperity we shall have to find ways of emancipating energy and enterprise from the frustrating control of timid ignoramuses.' Nor is it fair to expect the royal family to change their private pleasures to suit public education—to abandon the Doncaster races for the Edinburgh Festival, to move from the Beatles to Covent Garden, to spend weekends with industrialists and scientists rather than landed aristocrats.

In one very important respect the monarchy *has* personified change—in the Commonwealth. Ever since Nehru and Cripps invented the ingenious new formula of 'Head of the Commonwealth' for the Queen's role in republican India, the monarchy has kept abreast of a changing situation. The monarchy has ceased to be indivisible—as it was by pre-war doctrines—and has become something divisible and different for each Commonwealth country. Its divisibility can produce embarrassments—as appeared before the visit to Ghana in 1961: but it has impressively typified Britain's new relationships.

Yet inside Britain the changes have been much less spectacular: and the monarchy, like other old institutions, has a heavy drag of tradition and protocol. Bold schemes—like a project that was discussed for rebuilding Sandringham in gay modern style—are defeated by inertia. In spite of Prince Philip's excursions, the palace still gives a powerful impression of being detached from the world of science and trade. The discrepancy between outward show and inner realities reaches its splendid climax in royal processions, where cabinet ministers come well at the back, squeezed between the Vice-Chamberlain of Her Majesty's Household and viscounts' eldest sons. (Only in 1902 was the prime minister promoted to a place after the archbishops: till then he had to follow after the sons of peers he himself had created.)[1] And this outward show has

[1] Any government can change the order of precedence if it wishes to, but this would obviously cause embarrassment and alarm.

curious echoes: even *Whitaker's Almanack*, that important organ of public instruction (although since 1962 it has no longer listed octogenarian peers), still has sixteen pages about the monarchy, and forty pages of peers and orders: but if you look up Unilevers or ICI in the index, you will find nothing.

It is often assumed that the monarchy must stand for non-change —that it is there, like Stonehenge, with the encrustations of centuries. But the monarchy, if it is to be useful, cannot be just a question of Gold Sticks and Black Rods: it must be a living institution, closely related to its country. No doubt there are elements which have long since become fossilised. But in many of the conflicts that appear in this book—between old schools and new, old universities and new, classicists and scientists, public service and trade, old regiments and new corps, the royal magic hangs always over the old. The Victorians were practical and ruthless in their use of the monarchy; they used honours to glorify their new civil service, and made the Queen the focal point of their Empire. But since the nineteenth century the monarchy has become much less associated with the present, and more with the past.

3

PARLIAMENT

You have not a perception of the first elements in this matter till you know that government by a *club* is a standing wonder.

Walter Bagehot, 1872.

Well, it's dead. Nobody attends debates, and this gives a general atmosphere of lifelessness about the whole place . . . power has now by-passed the House of Commons.

Humphry Berkeley, M.P. (Third Programme), July 1963.

SINCE the eighteenth century the heirs to the powers of the monarch and the House of Lords have been the members of the House of Commons. In theory these 630 have sovereignty: they can pass laws, summon anyone to give evidence, cross-examine civil servants and reprimand editors. The judges are waiting to interpret their laws, and the civil servants are waiting to administer them.

And yet the members have been aware of their powers mysteriously oozing away. There is nothing new about this phenomenon. As Enoch Powell wrote in 1964[1]: 'If those who complain that parliament is losing its authority and influence would take the pains to enquire, they would find that at no time for which there are records has that complaint not been heard. If they would immerse themselves in the writing and discussion of 1863—or 1463—they would be startled by the same lamentations over the impending suicide and "the short time left to us".' But with the vast new powers and scope of government and the civil service, this loss of authority is increasingly worrying. The current fashion for belittling parliament does no service to democracy: it is, after all, the only democratic instrument yet devised. But the British parliament has been slow to come to terms with new problems and bureaucracies, and it has long ago acquired a life and momentum of its own.

It is the sense of a club which is the most obvious feature of the Commons. In spite of its range, from earls' sons to engine-drivers

[1] Enoch Powell: Essay in *Rebirth of Britain*, 1964. p. 258.

from all over the country, it retains unity and compactness. The chamber, only sixty-eight feet long, cannot seat all members at once: the public and the press in the steep galleries can sometimes outnumber the members by ten to one. But the parliamentarians continue their ritual—dawdling in from the lobby, bowing to the Speaker, exchanging whispers, and speaking as if they were addressing not a nation, but a room. The members, though mostly very ordinary people, assume the heightened manner of a club—the affectation of an older, more confident generation.

Members love talking about 'The House' as if it were a person—moody, headstrong and feminine. 'The House of Commons', said one Victorian sage, 'has more sense than any one in it.' The building itself has an overpowering atmosphere for any new member, and even when, as in 1945 or 1964, there is a great inrush of tough new members, they are easily intimidated by the traditions and rules. But the traditions are not necessarily very dignified: 'I have noticed that this House has its moods,' said Herbert Bowden, then Labour chief whip, rather curiously arguing against televising parliament, in March 1963; 'It has its hilarious moods, its serious moods, and very often when an important statement is imminent we are often apprehensive and giggle and behave rather like schoolgirls. I think that is right. It is right that Members of Parliament should react in that way.'

The New Palace of Westminster (as it is called) has 100 staircases, 2 miles of corridors, 13 quadrangles, 130 statues, averaging seven feet high, and 1,100 rooms (including one room for the press and one blacksmith's forge). 26 policemen and 31 doorkeepers (who act as chuckers-out) guard the doors: 251 people, including 55 cleaners, look after the upkeep: the maintenance and housekeeping of the Commons costs £333,000 a year, and fuel alone costs £55,000. Three-quarters of a million tourists a year pass through: but most of the palace is closed to the public. No debate has ever been televised: and if a photograph is taken anywhere in the palace, the film is destroyed (only Lord Brabazon has admitted secretly taking a photograph—of Neville Chamberlain's last speech in 1940[1]). 'The building is full of oddities. Not 110 steps from the Bar of this House,' said Tam Dalyell, a Labour Member in a debate in July 1964, 'I can show Hon. Members three completely unused dusty rooms. Why is it that the Parade Room with 390 square feet is unused? I discovered there a man pressing his trousers!' In 1964 there were endless abortive discussions and

[1] *The Times*, October 13, 1961.

debates about rebuilding or extending parliament, but the arguments were so petty and disparate that it seemed that the members collectively could not face abandoning the club atmosphere for the sake of efficiency.

The mystique of the House is deliberately maintained by what Sir Ivor Jennings calls 'The Importance of Being Ancient'. The royal opening of parliament every October, the procession led by Black Rod, the antique methods of beginning and ending the day, all bolster the impression that parliament has a meaning quite apart from its functions; the House is never happier than when debating the exact position of the mace. The day begins with the words 'Speaker in the Chair' being shouted through the lobbies: and the Speaker, who is the centre of the ritual, sits down on an Australian-made throne at one end of the House, wearing a full-bottomed wig.

The present Speaker, Sir Harry Hylton-Foster, began like all Speakers as an ordinary MP. The son of a barrister, he became a barrister and later solicitor-general: he had married the daughter of a previous Speaker, Lord Ruffside (even in the tiny profession of Speakership—there have only been 15 since 1800—a son-in-law tradition has apparently begun). 'All Speakers are highly successful,' wrote Lord Rosebery, 'all Speakers are deeply regretted and are generally announced to be irreplaceable. But a Speaker is soon found, and found, almost invariably, among the mediocrities of the House.' Having been chosen, the Speaker is carefully removed from his fellow-members: he lives in a gothic house with sixty rooms inside the Palace of Westminster, now earns £8,500 a year, gives occasional discreet tea-parties, but remains strictly aloof from politics, and will eventually retire with a viscountcy. He is the 'first Commoner', and the only subject who can hold his own levees, and insist on Court dress. At elections he stands as a non-party member, with no particular policy.

The Speaker maintains the rules. He insists that members call each other 'honourable members', bow to him on entering and leaving, address all their speeches to him. He stops them using 'grossly insulting' language: Speakers in the past have forbidden the words villain, hypocrite, murderer, insulting dog, swine, pecksniffian cant, cheat, stool-pigeon and bastards—but not leper.

Consumption of Alcohol

MEMBERS OF PARLIAMENT

Politics is perhaps the only profession for which no preparation is thought necessary.

Robert Louis Stevenson.

To be a member of parliament is an odd profession, with very odd hours. The House sits for only thirty-six weeks a year, with a break for two-and-a-half months from August till mid-October. It sits from 2.30 p.m. to 10.30 (or later) from Mondays to Thursdays, and from 11 a.m. to 4.30 on Fridays (which can often be cut). When parliament is sitting, an MP is ruled by the clanging sound of the division bell, demanding him to vote. Often at 9.45, a frequent time for divisions, MPs rush from their dinner parties to the House. Wealthier members favour houses in the 'division bell district', just behind parliament—Barton, Cowley or Lord North Streets—within five minutes of the Commons. They have bells fixed in their houses, and you can see them all dashing out into their cars.

Since the war, being an MP has become a much more professional business, which can be seen by the way they use the palace. Far more members, according to the serjeant-at-arms, now use the House as an office in the mornings: usually between two and three hundred, either in committees or dealing with letters. Fewer members use the dining-room, which serves meals at hotel hours, and more take meals when they can in the cafeteria or tea-room, which are always open during debates (if everyone wants tea at once, as in the 1960 filibuster, women members have to help out). Then there is the consumption of alcohol: parliament being a royal palace is exempt from licensing laws, and has bars open all afternoon, with wide scope for drunkenness. Before the war, drunk members laughing or even speaking in the chamber were not unknown. There are still several notoriously bibulous members. In 1963 the seven bars in the Commons consumed 3,124 bottles of whisky, and 1,936 bottles of champagne.

The presence of more members in the House does not necessarily make them more useful. 'A whole day can agreeably disappear', wrote a former MP, Nigel Nicolson, 'in answering a few constituency letters in the morning while attending a standing committee with only a quarter ear open to the debate, listening to Questions and Ministerial Statements from 2.30 to 4 p.m., looking in on two party committees in the evening, entertaining a couple of visiting Americans to drinks on the terrace, and then gossiping in the smoking room until it is time for bed.'[1] But though much time is wasted, it is nowadays harder for Tory members to stay away from the House without comment, and almost impossible for Labour members.

At the same time, members are spending more time in their constituencies: this is the dark side of a member's life—sitting in a dingy local office once a week, seeing constituents about anything from housing to drainage. The average MP receives eighty letters a week from constituents, and spends £100 a year on letters and telegrams. While members have become less grand in Westminster, with less scope for deciding the future of the world, they have become more useful in their constituencies, and closer to their local parties.

MP's have their own lope, their own handshake, their own jokes, their own way of saying to visitors, 'can you find your way out?' They belong to the 'best club in Europe'; they know it and the club dominates their lives, and also those of their wives. 'I hope you're going to write something about the St. Stephen's Widows', said Lord Kilmuir. Few MPs can stop being political, and their wives have to marry both them and their politics. Parliament remains a very nocturnal affair, and this cuts off politicians and their wives still further from ordinary people. 'King Louis Philippe once said to me', said Disraeli, 'that he attributed the great success of the English in political life to their talking politics after dinner.'[2]

Until 1964, the salary of members was in keeping with their part-time status. It was not until 1911, when Lloyd George proposed £400 a year, that members were paid at all: the wage went up to £600 in 1937, to £1,000 in 1945, and to £1,750 in 1957. After much complaint and argument, a committee was appointed in 1963 under Sir Geoffrey Lawrence, chairman of the National Incomes Commission, to recommend changes in the salaries of members and ministers. The Lawrence Committee decided that the salaries were quite inadequate. They reported that members without private incomes or outside earnings 'are forced to endure the discomfort, in spite of tax relief, of cheap and shabby lodgings in London; they cannot afford to use the Members' Dining Room; they have to submit to the humiliation of not being able to return hospitality even at the most modest level of entertainment; they are forced to impose considerable

[1] Nigel Nicolson: *People and Parliament*, 1958. p. 64–65.
[2] Banquet at Glasgow. November 19, 1873.

sacrifices on their families and they find it necessary to cut down the number of days on which they can attend sittings of the House'. The Government accepted their recommendation that the salary of members should be increased to £3,250, of which £1,250 should be allowable as expenses; but halved the rise proposed for Ministers (because of the economic situation) so that the prime minister's salary went up from £10,000 to £14,000; the Lord Chancellor's from £12,000 to £14,500; and other ministers' salaries ranged from £13,000 (for the attorney-general) to £3,750 (for junior ministers). In addition to these stipends, members of parliament are allowed such benefits as free telephone calls from the palace to the rest of London (but no further); free first-class travel to and from their constituency; a car allowance of 4½d. a mile; and a daily ration of 24 large sheets and 24 small sheets of House of Commons writing paper.

These new salaries, for the first time, made it possible for MPs without money of their own to devote their whole time to politics, without financial embarrassment. A large number of members, of course, are quite wealthy men, and two of them actually decline to take their salaries. For the others, the increase made a huge difference, and allowed them to adopt a much more whole-hearted attitude. But in other respects, the Commons continues to assume that its members are no more than periodic visitors. 'It is fantastic of course,' Harold Wilson has said: 'the average MP has a cupboard smaller than an orange-box for keeping all his parliamentary requirements, papers, documents and so on. Lack of secretarial, lack of research facilities—yes, it's a wonder that Parliament works as well as it does.'[1] One newly-elected MP in 1964, Mrs. Anne Kerr, even threatened to bring a caravan into the courtyard, to provide herself with an office.

The range of members might seem impressive—from two dukes' sons to twenty-one miners; from the 'Father of the House', Robin Turton (who first came into the House in 1929) to the 'Baby of the House', Paul Rose, born in December 1935. In theory anyone can become a member of parliament, except for aliens, minors, non-dissenting clergy, lunatics, judges, civil servants, peers, bankrupts, felons and candidates found guilty of corrupt practices at elections: the last time a member went to prison was in 1954. But in fact the range of members is not wide.

These were the leading occupations in November 1964:

[1] Interviewed by Dr Norman Hunt. *The Listener*, November 21, 1963.

Conservative: 83 Company Directors,
64 Barristers,
43 Farmers and Landowners,
31 Journalists, Writers and Broadcasters,
16 Regular Forces,
14 Businessmen.

Labour: 46 Teachers and Lecturers,
43 Trades Union Officials,
40 Journalists, Writers and Broadcasters,
32 Barristers,
29 Businessmen,
24 Industrial workers,
21 Colliery workers.[1]

The figures can be misleading: many barristers have long ceased to practise, and 'farmers' can mean anything from a large landowner to a retired businessman. But they point to the lopsidedness of the House. Nearly a sixth are barristers, and another sixth are company directors. (The record is held by Sir Cyril Black, a former Mayor of Wimbledon, with 61 directorships.) There are a preponderance of journalists and broadcasters, but only nineteen engineers, nine economists and seven accountants.

The education of members, too, is untypical. In 1959 64 Conservative MPs and two Socialists had been to Eton. 93 Conservatives and 43 Socialists were from Oxford: 69 Conservatives and 19 Socialists from Cambridge. Oxford and Cambridge provided just over a third of the House, and other universities only a fifth.[2]

Changes since the war have been slow but significant. Men with private means have decreased, and professional men have gone up from about 45 per cent before the war, to 50 per cent since. The average age of the Conservatives remained at about 48 until 1964, when it rose to 50; but Socialists have become progressively more aged, rising (in average age) from 50 in 1945, to 52 in 1951, to 55 in 1959, until at last in 1964 the average dropped slightly to 54. In 1964 there were 13 septuagenarian Labour members to only three Tories, and although the Conservatives had four members under 30, the Socialists only had one. The number of professional 'communicators' in parliament

[1] *Times Guide to the House of Commons*, 1964.
[2] ibid.

has strikingly increased: to the familiar journalist-politicians have been added a new race of TV-politicians, including such well-known faces as Christopher Chataway, Charles Curran and Christopher Mayhew: and there has been an inrush of public-relations and advertising politicians, who find parliament convenient. Nobody can be very happy about this.

Politics is now more wrapped up in itself, and there is less time for an outside career. It is far harder to combine a first-class bar practice with serious politics, or to be a businessman in the mornings and a politician in the evenings.

With these snags, is parliament still attracting first-class men? At first sight the dedication is impressive: there are many more members who take politics seriously, reading White Papers, attending committees, nursing constituencies, than before the war. The lazy Tory squires and the retired trade unionists are going out fast. Parliament still attracts some of the ablest men in Britain, like Maudling, Wilson or Grimond, who could run almost anything; and in the 1964 election there were many new members, such as Peter Shore or Shirley Williams, who were up to this kind of standard. But the imbalance of parliament, and the new requirements of politics, make it much harder to find all-round cabinets, made up of men who can lead, speak *and* run ministries. There are very few managers, administrators, engineers or scientists in the House: and at a time when the cabinet has to run giant businesses—railways, airways, scientific research or roads—MPs are being selected for totally different qualities. 'They're chosen because they're good at talking, not *doing*', as one cabinet minister put it: 'it's very difficult to find people who can actually *run* things.'

LOBBYING

If we had some way of measuring political power, we could possibly demonstrate that at the present time pressure groups are more powerful in Britain than in the United States.

Professor Samuel Beer.

One sign of the uncertain importance of parliament is in the activities of their 'lobbies'—the unseen pressure groups, pointed at the sources of power. The process of lobbying is a basic part of the mechanism of power, and it might be expected to centre on parliament. At first sight, the attention paid by the lobbies to Westminster has never been greater. Their number and scope have swelled in the past fifty years: 'Their day to day activities', wrote Professor Finer, a prominent lobby-watcher, 'pervade every sphere of domestic policy, every day, every way, at every nook and cranny of government.'[1] 'In no other country', wrote Robert McKenzie, 'are the great sectional interests . . . brought more intimately into consultation in the process of decision-making in government and political parties.'[2] Pressure groups have come to be regarded as a respectable and even necessary instrument of democracy, so that 'if an organised group does not exist, the government helps to invent it.'[3]

The pressure groups range from the hundreds of charitable societies, from the National Society for Promoting the Welfare of the Feeble-minded, to the National Farmers Union, the most pervasive of all, with 200,000 members, representing nine-tenths of all farmers. Several organisations arrange for MPs to represent their views in parliament, and probably half the members—including trade unionists—represent some group. The National Sheep Breeders of Great Britain, the Royal Society for the Protection of Birds, the Association of Drainage Authorities, all have their spokesman. The most visible sign of pressure is the number of MPs from public relations; but usually the PRO's advocacy is less effective than that of the men who are themselves part of the industry they represent.

Every member of parliament is constantly assailed by sectional interests. 'In each day's mail he can safely rely on being pursued by at least 15 different causes, campaigns, companies and cliques. Books, circulars, newsletters, pamphlets and holograph letters all plugging an identical theme pour each morning through his letterbox.'[4]

A vivid example of lobbying in action was the campaign in defence of Resale Price Maintenance, after Edward Heath had announced his intention to abolish it early in 1963. Here, all the interests that might be damaged by the new bill—the brewers, the chemists, the motor trade, and small shopkeepers of all kinds —tried to co-ordinate their protests in the 'Resale Price Maintenance Co-ordinating Committee' in Wimpole Street. They supplied pamphlets and arguments, they lobbied MPs and they organised bombardments of letters from constituents. 'The really

[1] S. E. Finer: *Anonymous Empire*, 1958.
[2] Politics of Pressure. *The Observer*, May 14, 1961.
[3] Allen Potter: *Organised Groups in British National Politics*, 1961. p. 32.
[4] *The Times*, July 17, 1961.

disturbing part of the mail' wrote *The Times* political correspondent in February 1964, 'comes handwritten or unevenly typed bearing his constituency postmark, . . . letters from newsagents, stationers, chemists, garage owners, tobacconists, wine and spirit merchants and all the rest of the small men in the constituencies can chill the backbenchers' blood. . . .' When the first major group of Tory backbenchers rebelled in defence of resale price maintenance in March 1964, they revealed very sectional interests; among the nineteen Tories who voted against their government were the member for Burton-on-Trent (Mr. Jennings), a member of the Institute of Brewing (Colonel Jackson), the President of the International Pharmaceutical Federation (Sir Hugh Linstead), and numbers of directors of anxious industries—particularly textile industries.

But the truth is that the biggest business interests do not bother much about parliament, and few of the big corporations now maintain their own members in the House. They have seen where decisive power lies, and so they now deal directly with cabinet ministers or civil servants: even the trade unions, with their vast representation in the Commons, often prefer to deal direct with Whitehall.[1] Parliamentary lobbying can hinder, not help, this pressure on the government: as Sir Raymond Streat, a lifelong defender of cotton interests, has explained, 'You lose the confidence of Whitehall if you try to use Westminster.'[2] Industrial lobbying may be open—through organised deputations or statements, or covert—through casual social occasions. It is typical of Britain, compared to America, that important lobbying is done over lunches or drinks in clubs or homes. 'It's so much easier here,' a senior manager in one big corporation told me: 'We don't have to organise great formal expeditions, as in Washington. Whitehall is only two tube stations away: we have a permanent secretary to lunch from time to time.'

The chairman of ICI, Paul Chambers, does not need to stir up members of parliament: he is on friendly terms with most of the cabinet and many senior civil servants, and can urge his views there, where they are listened to with respect. The more civil servants who go into industry, the easier such informal pressure becomes. In fact, pressure to make someone do something they don't want to do becomes in the end a sort of like-mindedness in which it may not be clear who is the persuader and who the

[1] J. D. Stewart: *British Pressure Groups*, 1958.
[2] Quoted by Dr. Norman Hunt in 'Power and Parliament', *The Listener*, July 25, 1963.

persuaded. Most important lobbying—on trade agreements, taxes, budgets, or building sites—is done before bills ever reach Westminster. MPs may feel tormented or flattered by the lobbies in parliament: but they are well aware that the most important pressures by-pass them altogether.

PARLIAMENT'S POWER

> What clearly is in train, however, is a rapid trend towards the exaltation of the executive (both cabinet ministers and civil servants) at the expense of the House of Commons.
>
> *The Economist*, August, 1960.

Two main forces have weakened the importance of parliament. First, the leaders of political parties have decided on issues beforehand. 'Parliamentary government has already very largely perished,' wrote one former MP, Christopher Hollis: 'The member is the obedient servant of the party machine. He tramps into the division lobby voting for or against he knows not what upon subjects which as a general rule no opinion save that of the specialist is of the least value.'[1]

'With the single exception of the overthrow of the Chamberlain government in the supreme crisis of 1940,' wrote *The Economist* (which has inherited from Bagehot the rôle of chief critic of the constitution), 'the great deterrent function that once made Parliament an occasional unmaker of ministries has diminished into a small deterrent function of regular parliamentary fuss.'

Members are kept firmly in check by the whips—the party policemen, known for their mixture of jolliness and toughness. The government chief whip is also Patronage Secretary, with the prime minister's ear, and so influential in promotion and honours. The combination is devastating, and often results in the government backbencher having less scope than the opposition for expressing his personality: 'The whips do not want speeches but votes. The ministers regard an oration in their praise or defence as only one degree less tiresome than an attack.'[2]

The Chief Whip lives at No. 12 Downing Street, just round the corner from No. 10, with intercommunicating doors. He sees the prime minister every day, and can slip in at any time unobserved.

[1] Christopher Hollis: *Can Parliament Survive?* 1949. p. 64.

[2] *See* Winston Churchill: *Lord Randolph Churchill*, new ed. 1951. p. 60, quoted in R. Rhodes-James: *An Introduction to the House of Commons*, 1961.

This is how Sir Martin Redmayne, the former Conservative chief whip, described his method of working:

> I have thirteen whips plus my deputy, and each of those has, first of all, what we call an area—a geographical area of the country in which there are thirty or forty Conservative members. His business is to keep contact with them, and not merely to keep contact with them but to know them so well that he may in an emergency be able to give a judgment as to what their opinion will be without even asking them. Then each whip is allocated to one or more party committees; he keeps in touch with the chairman and the officers of those committees, attends their meetings, and reports to me anything of interest—that is anything that is likely to be the subject of adverse comment. And every whip in his ordinary round of the House—and they live in the House most of the time when it is sitting—has his own contacts with those who are his friends or those he may dine with, may meet in the smoking room, and so forth. He is always ready to pick up anything which may be useful to the government—and equally useful to the backbenchers, because no party can succeed unless it works as one in matters of opinion.[1]

The arrival of the new Labour Government in 1964, with a majority of five, brought a special burden to the new Chief Whip, Edward Short (a former headmaster with a passionate interest in military matters—a useful combination for the job). Few, if any, Labour MPs, after thirteen years out of office, would want to actually bring the government down; but a tiny majority could increase the nuisance value of rebels, whether on the left (like Ian Mikardo) or on the right (like Woodrow Wyatt). The danger, in the first few months, was not however as great as it looked; for the Conservatives had no desire to be returned to power in the awkward state of the country, and of their party. So that, if the Labour government *had* been in danger of losing a vote, the Tories would have made sure that some of their MPs were not present.

Opinions vary as to how far a small majority makes backbenchers more important: Sir Martin Redmayne maintains that 'the greater the majority, the greater the power of the opinion of the backbenchers'. 'When you have a government with a small majority you get a much more automatic loyalty . . . in 1951 we had a majority of 18, and even the most junior whip could use the argument: "Well, old boy, you mustn't rock the boat." It isn't much use using that argument when you have a majority of 100 because the boat takes a good deal more rocking.'[2]

[1] Interviewed by Dr. Norman Hunt in 'The Commons in Action', *The Listener*, December 19, 1963.

[2] Interview with Dr. Hunt; *see* above.

The other main force which has defeated parliament has been the sheer size and complexity of government affairs. What is basically a club of talkative amateurs has been faced with discussing a machine which, among other things, controls nearly half Britain's investment. Like indignant shareholders, MPs have tried to supervise the ministries and industries which, in theory, they own. Sometimes their interventions have been successful: but the intricacy of administration has usually defeated them, and most parliamentarians are much more interested in debates than in the less glamorous, but more influential committees, which are the most effective instruments of parliament for inspecting the bureaucracy, as we will note later.[1]

The newspapers have continued to look up to parliament as the maker of policy. The fluctuations of parliamentary reputations, the gossip in the lobbies, the rhetorical performances, are analysed, and the 'feeling of the House' is lovingly recorded. But parliamentary reputations bear little relation to reputations in Whitehall; and while parliament goes on applauding its orators, a new race of manager-politicians, often far from eloquent but very able, looks like emerging. 'Administrator-ministers', wrote *The Economist*, 'are being permitted to treat the House of Commons as little better than a nuisance.'[2]

The rate of diminution of the power of parliament is often exaggerated. Even in the nineteenth century MPs had little influence on policy; they sat for half the year, and debated recondite subjects at length—in 1928 parliament could devote 21 hours to the prayer-book. It is not so much that the influence of MPs has declined, as that the scope of the cabinet and the civil service has grown. The huge industrial and social areas of state control have outgrown parliament: the central power has become fragmented, and the big ministries and corporations, which occupy following chapters, have fitful connections with Westminster.

Perhaps the most drastic threatened by-pass of parliament was one of the most important of all post-war issues—the question of joining the Common Market. When the Treaty of Rome was prepared in 1957, none of the European parliaments were able to discuss it in detail: the Treaty itself had been drafted by delegates from each country, and was put forward to the parliaments virtually as a *fait accompli*, to be either rejected or ratified as a whole. The arrangements were far too technical to be left to ordinary

[1] *See* p. 283.
[2] 'House in Decline': *The Economist*, August 20, 1960.

parliamentarians: faced with a take-it-or-leave-it proposition, they reluctantly took it. With Britain, the same process began in 1961, though parliament did not, as it happened, have the opportunity of voting on the final proposition. But the initial debate, in August 1961, did give members the opportunity of airing their fears about parliamentary power. 'The sovereignty of parliament and the rule of law,' said Sir Derek Walker-Smith, 'are for us the twin pillars of our Constitution and our way of life. For the Six, parliament has its roots less deep; and perhaps the institution is held in less high regard than with us.' Mr. Shinwell, the former Labour cabinet minister, said, 'I wonder what this place will be like during the next ten years. There will not be 630 honourable members. There will be no need for more than 150 or so. It will be like a parish council.'

PARLIAMENT, PRESS AND TELEVISION

As parliament becomes less sure of her importance so, like a waning film star, she becomes more anxious about both her privileges and her publicity. Up till the eighteenth century the press was barred from debates, and to publish them was considered in 1738 'a high indignity and notorious breach of privilege': the *Gentleman's Magazine*—the first to report parliament—employed a memory-man, Guthrie, who memorised speeches and then had them put into classical English by Dr. Samuel Johnson.[1] But today the reporting of parliament has affected parliament itself. Official reports are a major operation: four super-speed shorthand reporters, working in twenty-minute shifts, take down the debates, helped by eight typists (who then allow members to improve their grammar on the typescript). The reports are rushed to the parliamentary presses across the river, where eighty people print 2,300 copies, finishing them by 2.30 in the morning—in time to be delivered to MPs for breakfast. Publicity, once scorned, is now courted: big speeches are made early in the day in order to get into the papers,[2] and many members intervene with a wary eye on the press. Parliamentarians plead for more thorough reporting in newspapers.[3]

Now, television has taken over the rôle of intruder, and the possibility of televising parliament arouses the same kind of

[1] Francis Williams: *Dangerous Estate*, 1957. p. 38.
[2] Sir Ivor Jennings: *Parliament*. p. 165.
[3] For instance, Emanuel Shinwell's letter to *The Times*, August 7, 1963.

arguments as were levelled against the press two hundred years ago. But members of parliament have become uncomfortably aware that television has, through its own debates and question times, taken away a great deal of their thunder. The rôle of the cameras became markedly greater during 1963 when, in the four-and-a-half-month recess, a large part of the Profumo affair and the Conservative leadership crisis was played out on television. After the Denning Report, there was an almost daily TV festival of politics, and in one day Harold Wilson appeared five times. At the Blackpool Conservative Conference the television cameras moved into the heart of the party; every evening, after the day of intrigue, two or three key men would disappear into the basement of the Imperial Hotel, to be questioned by the television inquisitors. The election of Sir Alec Douglas-Home produced a new spate of interviews; Sir Alec announced from the beginning, that he would 'share all the government's thinking' on television, and although he did not keep this promise, both he and Harold Wilson have appeared far more frequently than their predecessors, and their TV statements have commanded publicity that parliament can well envy. Wilson has used the publicity machine more expertly than any previous Prime Minister.

Parliament has become aware of this competition; but it remains very reluctant to take the one step which could bring back its audience. The television cameras have moved closer and closer towards the House, and during the Profumo debate in June 1963 they even came into Parliament Square where, under dripping umbrellas, MPs rushed out of the House to report (like messengers in Shakespeare plays) the latest stage of the battle inside. In November 1964 they were allowed inside the House of Lords (in morning dress) for the opening of parliament, but only as far as the door of the House of Commons. But members are terrified that, if they let the cameras into the chamber, the intimacy and dignity of the debates would be wrecked. In March 1963 the Commons debated the question of parliamentary reform, and many members gave strong views about television: the Labour chief whip, Herbert Bowden, said: 'I do not like the idea . . . I do not want parliament to become an alternative to "That Was The Week That Was", or "Steptoe and Son" or "Coronation Street".' But many other prominent members, including Jo Grimond and James Callaghan, gave their support to televising parliament; Iain Macleod declared that there was a great deal to be said for it, and reminded members about the anxieties that were aroused when it was first proposed to televise the Coronation or the party conferences.

Yet parliament still resists the intrusion of this powerful monster; the conjunction of the brash theatrical empire of television with the enclosed club-like world of parliament is one of the most extraordinary of all clashes between British institutions —a clash between the oldest and the newest. But there cannot be much doubt, in the end, as to which one will win. In the words of Robin Day, the arch-inquisitor of television and a strong propagandist for televising parliament, 'Future generations, accustomed to seeing parliament on their television screens, will wonder what all the fuss was about.'[1]

[1] 'The Case for Televising Parliament'. The Hansard Society, 1963.

4

CLUBS

I'm not going to pay good money to join a club that lets in people like me.

Groucho Marx.

That the Athenaeum should be at its full strength of about 1,700 must augur well for Britain's future.

The Tatler, 1961.

THE club is a pervading image among British institutions. Parliament is a club, and when they discuss the Commonwealth or the Common Market members always like to talk in terms of clubs. The Conservative party has always been bound up with a small group of clubs. The Whitehall bureaucracies all have club-like ideas of corporate solidarity: and the London clubs are themselves an intrinsic part of the life of Whitehall. 'No formal arrangements of committees or staffs', wrote Professor Beer of Harvard, discussing the Treasury, 'could quite free the British Government of its dependence upon the common rooms and lunch tables of the clubs of Pall Mall.' Before we penetrate further into Whitehall or the professions, therefore, we should look, by way of a sidelight, into the insides of London clubs—where I found myself frequently in the course of this enquiry.

Viewed from the outside, the clubs have an air of infinite mystery. Every lunch time, the taxis and government Humbers draw up outside the palazzi of Pall Mall, and bowlers and umbrellas disappear through the great stone doorways, acknowledged by reverent porters. Through the big windows you see men reading *The Times*, hailing each other, exchanging surreptitious conversation with special clubman's gestures—the pat on the shoulder, the grip on the forearm, the steering from the back. When an hour-and-a-half later they all emerge again, they have the look of having changed the world. To Americans, used to snatching a sandwich at their desks, the London clubs seem to suggest a special alchemy.

Clubs are an unchallenged English invention. The Empire was

built round clubs, and they remain one of our most successful exports: the authentic gloom of Pall Mall is almost outdone by the morbid staircase of the Rand Club in Johannesburg, the dim ante-rooms of the Century Club in New York, or even the Hunting Club in Rome. In Karachi, Delhi, Durban or tropical Africa, the grim exclusiveness of the English club successfully defies the gaiety of local life, and they have even penetrated to Scotland. The point of a club is not who it lets in, but who it keeps out; and few things can provoke more anger, from Kitwe to Dar-es-Salaam, than the non-membership of an English club. The club is based on two ancient British ideas—the segregation of classes, and the segregation of sexes: and they remain insistent on keeping people out, long after they have stopped wanting to come in. At their best, clubs are still havens of disinterested friendliness where professions mingle. At their worst, they are havens of humbug.

After the war the London clubs, like so many institutions, seemed on the verge of collapse: the tables were half empty, the entrance fees were high, it was hard to find staffs to maintain the palazzi. Some clubs, like the Marlborough, sold up their sites and shared the (large) profits between members: others amalgamated—like the Bath and the Conservative clubs, now vulgarly known as the Lava-Tory. But as prosperity returned and expense-accounts mounted, so clubland came back into its own: business-men, solicitors, advertising men, salesmen, all found clubs an ideal field for operation, and the buildings, rich with associations of Regency gamblers and Victorian giants, were an invaluable status-symbol. Meanwhile the clubs, like successful flirts, have maintained an aura of exclusiveness while welcoming almost any new member. Very few clubs, in fact, have a waiting-list and only a few have black balls: but all of them convey an atmosphere full of the dread of rejection.

The mystique of clubs was encouraged by Harold Macmillan, who during his premiership belonged to six clubs (the Carlton, Turf, Pratts, the Beefsteak, Bucks and the Athenæum) and frequented all of them. (This is far from the record: Lord Mountbatten belongs to fourteen.) Eden and Churchill were not clubmen —though Churchill did found his own. Attlee in the war used to dine night after night at the Oxford and Cambridge (an extraordinary portrait of him, sitting at one end of a big desk, hangs in the dining-room): but he was not a gregarious clubman. Harold Wilson belongs only to the Athenaeum.

And the clubs have kept their buildings. They occupy some of the finest architecture in the most coveted sites in London, including some of the last surviving town houses: and it is hard to believe that people entering such splendid places are not equally splendid. The Naval and Military—the 'In-and-Out'—occupies Lord Palmerston's old house in Piccadilly. A few clubs have been knocked down: the Royal Thames Yacht Club in Knightsbridge sold its old building, in return for two floors of a new one, but Pall Mall and St. James's Street, the heart of clubland, remain solid with club buildings. And one or two shrewd old clubs, like Brooks's, have been given large compensation for *not* being knocked down.

What does the influence of clubs amount to? Like most things in Britain, they are not what they seem: in the first place, many of them are very unsociable. Clubs can be firmly divided into those where you are expected to talk to your neighbour and those where you are not. The big anonymous clubs favoured by the civil service—the Oxford and Cambridge, United University, or the Union—are places to get away from people, not to meet them. They are deliberate extensions of Oxbridge; the United University Club, for instance, refuses to admit members from London University (United *against* Universities might be a more appropriate name). They have huge libraries with deep and solitary armchairs; and they have book-rests on the lunch-tables where under-secretaries can devour cold pie and *The Times* undisturbed. The most hotel-like club is the Royal Automobile, founded by hearty motoring men in 1897, which has three dining-rooms, twelve thousand members and a swimming pool once much frequented by Bernard Shaw. No one at the RAC appears to know anyone else, except in a small and boisterous bar upstairs, full of seasoned drinkers.

But other big clubs, while leaving scope for solitude, provide a useful venue for intrigue. Two of the most active are the Reform and the Travellers, next to each other in Pall Mall—the haunt of the Treasury and the Foreign Office respectively. Membership qualifications for both are equally stringent. For the Reform you must subscribe to the Reform Bill of 1832: for the Travellers you must have travelled at least *five hundred* miles from London (though the entry marked 'travel' in the candidates book offers scope for showing-off).

The Travellers was founded in 1819 with the support of the Duke of Wellington, whose portraits clutter the walls. It is very conscious of its dignity: it has a special hand-rail on the staircase.

put up to help Talleyrand up the stairs. It has tall West Indian waiters and menus with a silhouette of Ulysses. Diplomats, with their careful arrogance, set the tone, and the lunch-room is known as 'the Foreign Office Canteen'; Sir Alec Douglas-Home was the first Traveller prime minister since Baldwin. A few apparently friendly men are crammed into an underground bar: but the chandeliered dining-room and coffee-room are full of supercilious second secretaries. (The food is said to have improved; the club secretary has written a cookery book.) The contrast in clubs becomes apparent in the summer holidays, when they share each other's premises: the Garrick, where members *are* expected to speak to each other, shares with the Travellers, where conversation with someone you don't know is virtually forbidden. 'I always know when the Garrick's shut,' said one veteran traveller: 'you hear laughter in the bar of the Travellers.'

The Reform next door (from which Phileas Fogg went Around the World in Eighty Days) is architecturally flabbergasting. It has a huge indoor courtyard with orange pillars and economists standing ominously drinking sherry—waiting for the news of a crash—while others look down from tables on the balcony. The Reform was built by Barry, in the Italian style, with a kitchen the size of a ball-room—where the famous chef Soyer, author of a standard work on 'Gastronomic Regeneration', presided over a steam-operated kitchen. Gastronomic reform is still a feature of the club, but other radical instincts have deserted it. The Reform has been the temple of *laissez-faire*, but since October 1964 it has acquired a new significance, as the meeting-place of left-wing economists. It was in a private room at the Reform, too, that a group of shrewd lobbyists—Norman Collins, Robert Renwick, Lord Bessborough—successfully plotted commercial television.

But the most august of the big clubs, of course, is the Athenæum, with its big stucco building, behind the gold goddess Athene, facing the United Service Club (The Senior) in Waterloo Place. It is, in many respects, the most unsociable and uncomfortable of all: 'Where all the arts and sciences are understood', said G. W. E. Russell in 1906, 'except gastronomy': and of its cavernous dining-room the same could still be said. Even outside the Silence Room, which is the real heart of the club, a sense of solitude prevails. Old men wander alone up and down the broad staircase (they always walk up the *right-hand* staircase, one scientific member pointed out: they have to change the carpets round from time to time to wear both down equally).

The Athenæum retains an atmosphere of bleak and uncompromising wisdom: a bust of Charles Darwin broods over the hall, and the Greek letters Alpha Theta Eta evoke intimidating memories. Moreover there is always a cluster of bishops, and the club is never without episcopal activity in the Trollopean tradition. (Trollope himself used to write his novels in the long drawing-room, before breakfast, and it was there that he was persuaded to kill off Mrs. Proudie.)

But the Athenæum, for all its dignity, is not above intrigue. Members have complained that they could hardly hear themselves talk above the noise of lobbying—particularly for university grants: the Athenæum is the favourite meeting place for vice-chancellors. It is also a centre for a very unclubbable breed—the scientists (the Royal Society Dining Club assemble there) who use it as a base for manoeuvre and fund-raising. 'The last war was run by the Athenæum on one side, with the scientists and civil servants, and the Senior on the other, with the admirals and generals': one scientist explained, 'since they all talked very loudly, it wasn't difficult to discover what was going on.'

A more sociable and arrogant group are the eighteenth-century clubs, with their elegant façades down St. James's Street. The most sedate is Boodle's, with its big bow window, from which one eighteenth-century duke used to enjoy watching 'the damn'd people get wet'. Boodle's was originally known as the 'Savoir Vivre', famous for orgiastic feasts; it is now more demure, with a hard core of old country members who can be seen snoozing in the window, but there is a Ladies' Annexe in the adjoining Economist's tower, full of gold lamé, debs, and decor. Brooks's on the other side of the street, founded in 1764, and frequented by Charles James Fox, was the scene of reckless gambling by the Whig aristocrats in Regency times. George Drummond, of Drummonds Bank, only gambled once, when he lost £20,000 to Beau Brummel (and had to resign from the bank). It is now mainly Conservative and much less reckless; but it keeps a certain style, and boasts the best hall-porter in London. The most arrogant club, of course, is White's, the traditional haunt of idle Tories: but that is so much part of the character of the Tory Party that it belongs, together with the Carlton, to that chapter.

In a special class are the cultural clubs, all somewhat confused between a Victorian past and a commercial present. The most ponderous is the Garrick, founded in 1831 in memory of the actor, with a gaudy array of Zoffany portraits up the staircase. Their early members included Trollope, Lord John Russell, Gilbert and Sullivan, Dickens and Thackeray—who quarrelled there, later to be reconciled on the staircase of the Athenæum. Thackeray adored 'the little G' and called it 'the dearest place in the world', but nowadays the Garrick, though it still has actors, is full of lawyers, editors and businessmen.

Less pompous is the Savile, which tries to steer a middle course between gravity and bohemianism. 'There are other places', says the history of the Savile (with a dig at the Savage with which it resents confusion) 'where the self-conscious eccentrics and aggressively Bohemian types can circulate and deviate with more approval.' The Savile is unpretentious and not rich: 'Oh yes, the Savile Club,' said Oscar Wilde, 'a real republic of letters, not a sovereign among 'em.' Their motto is 'sodalitas convivium'—but occasionally the *convivium* gets in the way of the *sodalitas*—as when a few years ago one member lifted up a former Lord Chancellor and dumped him on the mantelpiece. The hard core of the Savile are publishers, authors, actors and broadcasters: Ralph Richardson, Compton Mackenzie and Professor Jimmy Edwards are among its more obvious inmates, and C. P. Snow—an inveterate clubman—an archetypal member. Around the bar there is booksy chat and the atmosphere of a literary salon—of reputations being made and broken, of 'what do you thing of G's new thing?'

The Arts Club in Dover Street has had a sadder transformation. It was founded in 1863, for Art, Literature and Science, and it has a pleasant new building, with flock wallpaper, portraits of artists and a few men with beards: but it is now also concerned with the art of advertising and the science of public relations, and from the bar can be heard the braying sound of admen on the move.

The least reticent of the artistic clubs is the Savage, which occupies a faded Regency house in Carlton House Terrace. It is an extrovert place, full of cartoons of famous men with big heads, and jungle fantasies about 'Brother Savages' wearing straw skirts and shaking spears. There are no bowlers and few umbrellas: instead, lots of friendly comedian artists and actors, dumping large cases in the hall and striding into a small, overcrowded drinking den: the club is noisy with theatrical patter—'yes, he's a sweetie—and quite a good actor too'. The Savage is aggressively sociable, and not to be seen talking to someone provokes comment: its most surprising Brother Savage is the stern octogenarian former Lord Chief Justice, Lord Goddard.

A more likely setting for secret influence might seem to be the smaller clubs, of the kind frequented by Harold Macmillan. The most exotic is Pratt's, in two basement rooms in St. James's; it began its existence in 1841 as the kitchen of the Duke of Beaufort's steward, called Pratt, which became the Duke's dive. It still has a large kitchen dresser, and its small rooms are full of stuffed fishes, birds, bric-a-brac and surprising members—who include Lord Dilhorne, Patrick O'Donovan, Osbert Lancaster and Gavin Young. Another unexpected place is Buck's in a plain Georgian house in Mayfair, founded just after the first world war as a re-union club by Captain Buckmaster, who still owns it. It serves a champagne cocktail called 'Buck's Fizz', oysters and mutton chops, and retains a faint air of rakishness.

Or there is the Beefsteak, at the top of a dingy staircase off Leicester Square, opposite a strip-tease joint: its motto is 'Beef and Liberty'. The Beefsteak is very sociable, and generates remarkable dialogues. Members have to sit wherever the waiters (all called Charles) put them on the single long table, and they like to tell the story of how before the first world war the police, seeing old men emerging happily every evening, assumed it was a brothel and began watching the club: one night they raided it, and found four men sitting round the long table. The conversation went something like this:

'And who might you be?' asked the policeman of one old gentleman.

'I am the Lord Chancellor.'

'Aha! And you, sir?'

'The Archbishop of Canterbury.'

'Oh yes! And the next?'

'I am the Governor of the Bank of England.'

'And I suppose', said the policeman to the fourth, 'that you're the prime minister.'

'As a matter of fact I am,' said Arthur Balfour.

Now only the Governor is a member, together with four dukes, Osbert Lancaster, Sir Malcolm Sargent, Harley Drayton, Edward Crankshaw, Peregrine Worsthorne and three hundred others: but many of the junior members are too frightened to actually go there.

The most select clubs of all have no premises at all. The most famous is 'The Club', the traditional top people's dining-club, which included such men as Balfour, John Buchan, and Geoffrey Dawson, and now includes Basil Spence and J. C. Masterman: and 'The Other Club', which was founded by F. E. Smith and Winston

Churchill in 1911, as a rival body of political bounders. Smith himself wrote the constitution, which states that 'the names of the executive committee shall be wrapped in impenetrable mystery'. Since then the outsiders have become the insiders, and The Other Club is now the more active: it still meets every other Thursday during the parliamentary session, at a private room in the Savoy, and its members include Lord Boothby and Lord Shawcross. Originally there were an equal number of Liberal and Conservative members, who could be paired in parliament: but the rise of socialism has unbalanced it, and there are hardly any Labour members.

But clubland altogether is unrepresentative: a few names recur again and again, while the huge area of socialists, managers, scientists and technologists hardly appear at all. The Labour Party has always been pubbable rather than clubbable: there is no left-wing equivalent to the Carlton or White's, and even a Liberal club like Brooks's has ended up largely Conservative. 'Clubland is as Conservative as the sea is salt,' wrote G. W. E. Russell in 1906: and the ineluctable conservatism—both social and political—continues: English clubs progress in the opposite direction to African night-clubs: they begin by being disreputable, full of wild actors and poets drinking into the night, and end up with cautious lawyers toying with cold beef and *rosé*, reminiscing about the wild old days.

Is the future still being settled among port and cigars in club chairs? Can membership confer a sliver of power? Perhaps there are still a few moments of intrigue when clubs are important. But while the reminiscences ramble on in Pall Mall, the future is being decided in the Cabinet Office canteen, in the directors' dining-room in ICI, or in the pubs round the corner from Transport House.

Two major invasions have troubled clubland since the war. The first has been business, which is anathema to the amateur spirit of clubs: many clubs actually forbid members to produce business documents. But while clubs admitted more and more businessmen, the appearance of amateurism has become hard to keep up: and even in White's—traditionally the enemy of trade—the *Financial Times* and Sir Miles Thomas can be seen.

But a more serious revolution has been the intrusion of women. The most formidable weapon of women has been to found their *own* clubs—the Ladies' Alpine Club, the Women's Press Club, or the Sesame Club, for women explorers and pioneers. One by one the men's clubs have given way, either by inaugurating a ladies' night, or a ladies' annexe (often a converted billiard-room)—but hardly ever by introducing lady *members*. Women are kept carefully segregated. At the Reform, 'LADIES may be entertained for DINNER on FRIDAYS and for LUNCH and DINNER on SATURDAY in the East End of the Coffee Room.' At the Senior the Admirals objected fiercely for years before the billiard-room was finally converted for ladies in 1921. The arrangement of ladies' annexes arouses fundamental controversy, for it raises the problem of the club's *image*, and all clubs are very image-conscious. Should clubs try to adapt their style to welcome women, or should they remain defiantly masculine? The clubs have reacted to the problem in different ways, but the favourite solution is the 'Ladies' Annexe'—a phrase which speaks volumes—where the club can present a different image without interfering with its old one.

A more drastic capitulation has been shown by—of all surprising places—the Army and Navy Club, in the heart of Pall Mall. It decided, under the generalship of Sir Ian Jacob, to pull down its old morgue, sell off half of it to a property company, and rebuild the other half with the profits, in a quite different form; it was opened in 1963, to the astonishment of clubland. It has a dance-floor, a buffet bar, and underground car park, and a big room designed for deb dances and weddings, as well as for regimental dinners. The whole place was designed by a woman interior decorator, Mrs. Eily Donald, and the main drawing-room has soft upholstery and fake coal fires. There are some continuing features, including the head waiter, Fitzgerald, Napoleon's Couch, and some die-hard misogynist members who still have a floor to themselves where women are forbidden. But the whole club displays, quite unashamedly, the central fact that the club has come to terms with women; they are even admitted as members. The new volte-face achieved what the committee had hoped for; the average age quickly came down, and in the evening the club actually has people in it, apparently enjoying themselves. The new Army and Navy has struck a deadly blow at the spirit of clubmanship; for while other clubs are designed as an escape from women, with porters, architecture and members all suitably chosen, this club has welcomed them into its midst.

In all clubs, perhaps, there is an element of imposture. Everyone, as he ushers his guest through those mahogany doors, becomes a slightly less real person, talks a bit louder, shakes hands a bit more heartily. The Arts Club has admen pretending to be artists.

The Garrick has lawyers pretending to be actors, or vice-versa. White's has ordinary men pretending to be eccentric. The Travellers is a Foreign Office canteen pretending to be an amateurs' drawing-room. Only the Athenæum is completely *sui generis*—there the bishops are being bishops, the professors are professors, the eccentrics are eccentric, and the dull, distinguished men sit in their deep leather chairs in the silence room, where no one can disturb them. And they hold to themselves the secret of setting themselves, ostentatiously, at ease, and leaving their interlocutors puzzled, embarrassed, gratified but obscurely discomfited.

Can clubs withstand the pressures of democracy *and* women? At lunch time they seem confident enough, but in the evenings, when the wife and family beckon, the loyalty of clubmen is tested. It is then that the crumbling of clubs is revealed. A few fiercely masculine clubs, like White's, succeed in drinking and gambling till late into the night. But in most clubs, only a handful of bachelors, grass widowers or visitors inhabit the cavernous rooms. No doubt clubs will survive a long time, with their myths, their sites and the convenience, but the old misogynist zeal, which built the Empire and kept wives in their place—that has gone.

5

CONSERVATIVES

'Damn your principles! Stick to your party.'
Disraeli to Bulwer Lytton.

THE world of the preceding four chapters—and above all the world of the aristocracy and the palace—is associated closely with the world of the Conservative party. It has been part of the strength and magic of the Tories that they have been able to appear as *the* ruling party, born and bred to govern, with all the rich panoply of tradition and stability behind them. Although the Palace is meant to be above politics, its surroundings are not: the dukes and the marquesses, the lords lieutenant and high sheriffs, are massively conservative not only in their habits, but in their votes. The ancient social institutions that make up this world, from the Jockey Club and the House of Lords to the clubs of St. James's Street and country-house parties, are likewise entangled with the more conservative section of the Conservative party; so that in a long period of Tory rule, as happened from 1951 to 1964, it is easy for the public to imagine that the older political party is indistinguishable from the old institutions, merging into a solid, irremovable *they*. When that *they* is eventually removed, or at least diminished, the arrival of new faces at the Palace or at Downing Street seems as surprising as the arrival of a jazz band in Westminster Abbey. The mystique of the House of Lords and clubland suddenly appears irrelevant and impotent, its inhabitants seem almost physically smaller, and the Conservative party itself, which in power can rest on tradition as on an old sofa, finds itself suddenly compelled to think out its *raison d'être*, and to set about painfully re-establishing its appeal to the voters. The Conservative party has always been swayed by two contradictory notions—the idea of a ruling class which accepts no other possibility, and the idea of a tough, competitive party luring the floating voters. It is like a stately Bond Street shop trying desperately to attract new customers. When its customers desert it, its stateliness seems much more pointless.

The social contrast between the two main parties is most sharply apparent at the party conferences, held every autumn at seaside resorts, after the summer guests have left. Sometimes both parties choose the same resort, for successive weeks. One week there is the Labour party. The lounge of the main hotel is full of jollity, with large comfortable men sitting in braces; the bar is packed with talkative intellectuals, full of witty disloyalties. Outside the conference hall are salesmen for every kind of cranky organisation. Inside the hall are many of the trade unionists who met a month before at their congress, now diluted with other Labour elements—the middle-class intellectuals, or the intense young radicals, and girls in shiny macs.

The proceedings bear the marks of the origin of the Labour party—non-conformism and Marxism: speeches, addressed to 'Comrade Chairman', are full of time-honoured phrases—'countless millions yet unborn', 'brotherhood of man', or 'commanding heights'. The conference ends with singing the 'Red Flag', sung with visible embarrassment by the intellectuals:

> The people's flag is deepest red
> It's shrouded oft our martyrs dead.
> And ere their limbs grew stiff and cold
> Their heart's blood dyed its every fold . . .

The next week the main hotel is suddenly full of dinner-jackets and large hats. The girls are dressed as if for a weekend in the country. Solid north country businessmen and tireless Tory women talk in the foyer: when one of the great men of the party comes through, the crowd edges respectfully away, murmuring loyal noises.

In the conference hall the bearded cranks have all disappeared: instead there is a Conservative bookstall, full of dark-blue pamphlets. Well-tailored young men and trim, two-piece girls eagerly greet visitors. A huge Union Jack is draped across the dais. The impression that the Queen belongs to the Conservatives is overpowering. Speakers begin 'Mr Chairman, Sir, My Lords, Ladies and Gentlemen', and have their own private idioms: 'worthy of our calling', 'I count myself fortunate', 'you all know what *that* means'. The whole conference has a background of ritual and organ music. At many constituency meetings the Conservatives still sing the now meaningless imperial hymn:

Land of hope and glory
 Mother of the Free.
How can we extol thee
 Who are born of thee?
Wider still and wider
 Shall they bounds be set.
God who made thee mighty
 Make thee mightier yet.

Passing from one conference to the other, one might well imagine that Britain was still unmendably split into two nations. But the contrast can be misleading. Both conferences have inherited archaic trappings from the pre-war world. In both parties delegates are more extreme than MPs, and the MPs more extreme than the leaders—so that the two sides sometimes nearly meet at the top. For both sides, however committed their supporters, are concerned with survival: the Tories, because they feel it is part of their vocation to govern; the Socialists, because only through power can they achieve their ends. To gain votes, they both have to appeal to the mass of middling people who roam in the no-man's land and would not be seen dead in a conference.

POST-WAR CONSERVATIVES

'It was the biggest change in a hundred years,' said Lord Poole, who was one of the architects of the Conservative rebuilding after the war, 'between those who were anxious to put the clock back as far as possible to the pre-war world and those who preferred the post-war. Intellectually, we captured the party.' The actual change in leaders was not as abrupt as some have made out. Tory leaders have always been a mixture of landed grandees and middle-class men. But behind the privilege, the actual power structure of the party did undergo a basic change. Most importantly the influence of wealthy families and business interests gave way to the professional politicians, and the party machine. The Maxwell Fyfe Report of 1948 forbade Conservative candidates to contribute more than £100 to election expenses—making it harder for rich families to dominate constituencies, and increasing the power of the central office. There are still many places, like Southend, where voters remain loyal to old dynasties, and peers' sons still abound in the House. But the war swept away shoals of squires, and brought a new catch of middle-class politicians with political expertise but without landed connections.

The most gruesome assembly of old Tories remains White's Club in St. James's street, with its proud tradition of philistinism, gambling and drinking. Before the Reform Bill of 1832 (according to Lord Russell's *Recollections*) one peer at White's, who owned several pocket boroughs, nominated one of the waiters, called Robert Mackreth, for a seat in the Commons, which he duly occupied. And the club still likes to defy democracy—as when, in 1950, Aneurin Bevan was kicked down the steps. In Regency times White's boasted two-thirds of the 'upper ten thousand'; it would not admit anyone who had made his money through trade. It still maintains the atmosphere of ungainful employment. On a hot summer afternoon loud men can be seen warming themselves in front of a roaring fire, or watching the racing results on the ticker-tape. It keeps its own schoolboy language—about hols, prep, brekker or 'being on our side'. The arrogance still fascinates the Tory party, and the prospect of White's back-benchers howling for blood can still intimidate a cabinet minister. But the political importance of White's nowadays is slight, and many senior Tories, including three of the last four prime ministers, have remained aloof from it. The most serious meeting-place is the Carlton Club, which provides full-length portraits of Tory prime ministers but a less terrifying atmosphere.

The old Tory tradition had grandeur as well as arrogance. At their best, the landed aristocrats were independent, courageous and outspoken: the three great pre-war opponents of appeasement—Churchill, Eden and Salisbury—all came from such backgrounds, and were able to defy their constituents and their party. It is easy and dangerous to over-simplify the division between Old Tories and New Tories, putting all Old Etonians neatly on the first list. There are many cross-currents and confusions, rebellious Etonians and backward-looking grammar-school men. But in times of crisis, as in the leadership crisis of 1963, unless there is some over-riding political issue at stake, the class division comes up to the surface; and if you were to guess that the self-made businessmen and the professional men were in favour of reform, and the aristocrats in favour of the *status quo*, you would not be more than 25 per cent wrong.

WHO RUNS THE TORIES?

'The Tory party is run by five people,' one of the Conservative managers said to me in 1961: 'and they all treat their followers with disdain: They're mostly Etonians, and Eton is good for disdain.' The actual centre of power in the Conservative party has always been a source of mystery; for it does not, like the Labour party, rely on a system of definite ballots and votes to elect its leaders, and the mystery is enhanced by the tradition that, when the Conservatives are in office, it is the Queen who chooses the prime minister. The power lies somewhere in the triangle between the prime minister, the Central Office and the 1922 Committee of the parliamentary backbenchers.

Who, in a time of crisis, actually takes the decisions? The mystery was suddenly illuminated in the biggest crisis in the party since the war—the search for a leader to succeed Harold Macmillan, when he resigned from ill-health in October 1963. The ten-days-wonder of political confusion and intrigue which followed showed not only how obscure the party structure can be, but how valuable that obscurity can be for those who wish to make use of it.

The crisis first came into the open in the bizarre Imperial Hotel at Blackpool, where the party had assembled for its annual autumn conference. Macmillan, already politically weakened by the aftermath of the Common Market negotiations and the Profumo affair, had been afflicted two days before with a prostate gland, and gone into hospital. The pressure for his resignation was growing. To the discontent of his colleagues and backbenchers was added, on the Thursday morning of October 10th, the criticism of *The Times*, which had long before decided that Macmillan should go. 'The prime minister is a realist,' wrote *The Times*; 'he knows that politics is a harsh master. It is necessary for the nation's future political health that the coming election finds both parties at their best and the battle be closely fought.' *The Times* for once was decisive. Macmillan, reading the editorial in bed, and thinking he was iller than he was, decided that he must announce his resignation; he sent a letter up to Blackpool which Lord Home, as President of the Conference, read out that afternoon; 'It will not be possible for me to carry the physical burden of leading the party at the next General Election . . . In these circumstances I hope that it will soon be possible for the customary processes of consultation to be carried on within the party about its future leadership.' A fortnight later, he had regretted his decision.

But what exactly *were* the customary processes? It was known that 'soundings' would be taken in the different sectors of the party. But the question was immediately complicated by the doubt as to who was, and who wasn't, a candidate; and by the fact that two possible candidates, Lord Hailsham and Lord Home, were both in the House of Lords. Although Lord Halifax nearly became prime minister in 1940, it was assumed that the prime minister could not now be a peer; but it was now possible (ironically enough through the Bill induced by a Labour MP, Anthony Wedgwood Benn), for a peer to renounce his title.

Lord Hailsham quickly announced on the same Thursday that he would disclaim his peerage, thus throwing his hat into the ring. His chances for the premiership seemed excellent. It was made known that he had the blessing of Harold Macmillan, through two members of his family, his son Maurice and his son-in-law Julian Amery; and to many Conservatives he seemed to have the right kind of Churchillian qualities—including the doubtful advantage of the support of Randolph Churchill who (arriving back later from America) spent much time in the lobbies of the hotel distributing badges labelled Q, for Quintin. But Hailsham had misjudged his tactics; in the next twenty-four hours, thrilled and released by the prospect of power, he showed such a passionate interest in publicity, television and popular appeal that he had already alienated an important sector of the party (including Harold Macmillan)—so much so that by Friday a 'Stop Hailsham' movement had set in.

The evident candidates at this stage were R. A. Butler, the acting prime minister, who was the candidate of many of the younger, middle-class, reforming members of the party; Reginald Maudling, who was favoured by MP's from the same group; and Hailsham, who attracted many of the more romantic, and more right-wing members, and others who believed that he alone had the vigour and brilliance to lead his party to an electoral victory. But there was great uncertainty as to how far the fourth man, Lord Home, was actually in the running. He had not renounced his peerage; he refused, when asked on television, to say whether he would stand; and he seemed altogether aloof from the struggle around him. This ambiguous aloofness, it turned out, was an immense benefit to him, for it kept him clear of the candidates' fray, and made it hard to mount a 'Stop Home' movement until it was too late.

By the time the Blackpool conference ended on Saturday the party seemed to be in total confusion, split between Hailsham and Butler; the 'Stop Butler' group, who thought that Butler was too timid, too intellectual, too un-military or too dull, were almost as determined as the 'Stop Hailsham' group. After the weekend therefore, Harold Macmillan, who was now recuperating from his operation, decided that he must arrange exhaustive soundings.[1] He recommended to Butler, his deputy, that the Lord Chancellor, Lord Dilhorne, should poll the cabinet; the Chief Whip, Martin Redmayne, assisted by Major John Morrison, chairman of the 1922 Committee, should poll the MPs; the Chief Whip in the Lords, Lord St. Aldwyn, should sound Tories in the House of Lords; and that Lord Poole, Mrs. Shepherd and Lord Chelmer should sound the constituency parties, the women's organisations and the candidates. The proposal was put to the cabinet, who (including Iain Macleod) agreed; and the soundings were duly taken, and were reported to Macmillan on Thursday morning, October 17th.

All four pollsters reported in favour of Home, with varying degrees of enthusiasm; and after lunch Macmillan gathered the four men together, to repeat to each other their findings. 'Never in the history of the Tory party, or indeed of any other British political party,' wrote Randolph Churchill in his ecstatic account of the soundings, 'have such full and diligent enquiries been made in the selection of a new leader. This was no decision made in a "smoke-filled room". Everyone in the party had had an opportunity to make his or her views felt, and the result of the canvass had been decisive. There was no election, no precise counting of noses. It was Tory Democracy in action.'

But others were much less impressed by the diligent enquiries, and as soon as the news filtered out on the Thursday evening that Home would be chosen, an important section of the cabinet, horrified by the news, went to an emergency meeting at the house of Enoch Powell. Heath was not present. The objections of the rebel ministers—particularly of Macleod, Maudling and Powell—were later summed up by Iain Macleod in *The Spectator*.[2] He maintained that, at lunchtime that day, neither he nor Maudling thought that Lord Home was a contender: 'It is some measure of the tightness of the magic circle on this occasion that neither the Chancellor of the Exchequer nor the Leader of the House of Commons had any inkling of what was happening.' Macleod

[1] For the account of Macmillan's involvement, I am indebted to Randolph Churchill's *The Fight for the Tory Leadership* (1964), the information in which clearly comes from Macmillan himself.

[2] 'What Happened': *The Spectator*, January 17, 1964.

complained, perhaps disingenuously, that the impression given by Lord Dilhorne, that in the cabinet 'the overwhelming concensus now pointed to Home' was due to misunderstandings as to whether Home really was a contender; and that 'the expressions of genuine regard for him somehow became translated into second or even first preferences'.

At the midnight meeting (to quote Macleod) 'it was established that Maudling and Hailsham were not only opposed to Lord Home but believed Butler to be the right and obvious successor'. The rebel ministers telephoned the Chief Whip, Martin Redmayne, and asked him to convey their views to Macmillan. Learning the news early the next morning, Macmillan was unshaken, and determined to push through with Home's appointment: he spoke to Home on the telephone and rallied him with the words 'look, we can't change our view now. All the troops are on the starting line. Everything is arranged. It will just cause ghastly confusion if we delay.' Butler asked Lord Dilhorne to chair a meeting of the rebel ministers, in order to give them official recognition; but Lord Dilhorne—presumably on the advice of Macmillan—refused. At 9.15 in the morning Timothy Bligh, Macmillan's intrepid and resourceful private secretary, set out for Buckingham Palace to convey Macmillan's final resignation to the Queen. The Queen said that she wished to consult Macmillan in person, and arrived at the hospital at 11.15. Macmillan read to her a memorandum he had prepared, giving the results of the findings of the pollsters, and the conclusion in favour of Home. The Queen then returned to the palace, summoned Lord Home, and announced at 12.56 that same day that she had invited him to try to form an administration.

Lord Home, immediately after lunch, established his office at 10 Downing Street, and interviewed the other ministers; Butler asked to come together with the other rebel leaders, but Home insisted on seeing them separately. By the following morning Butler had agreed to serve as Foreign Secretary, and all the other leading ministers, with the important exceptions of Macleod and Powell, had joined Home's government. 'The Tory Party,' argued Macleod afterwards, 'for the first time since Bonar Law, is now being led from the right of centre.'

The recriminations about the election continued, and behind them lay the murky question of who was really running the party. It was the key to Macleod's objection that the election had been arranged by the Etonian 'magic circle', and in Macleod's account can be seen the bitter disappointment of a man who, after nearly twenty years of making his way up a party which was to the right of him, feels himself finally defeated by reactionary forces. In reviewing Randolph Churchill's account of the proceedings, he wrote: 'The only interesting part of Churchill's book is the account of the advice Macmillan tendered; of how having first supported Hailsham in the decisive days, he switched to Home; of how he organised the collection of opinions by Lord Dilhorne, Lord St. Aldwyn, Lord Poole, Mr. John Morrison and Mr. Martin Redmayne. Eight of the nine men mentioned in the last sentence went to Eton.'

Who, then, was the most powerful kingmaker in this group? It was not Lord Poole at the Central Office, who had been most billed for the role beforehand; for he had been a keen Hailshamite, and had overplayed his hand. It was not Dilhorne who, although he may have misrepresented the cabinet's enthusiasm for Home, did so in good faith; nor was it Redmayne, who was also primarily a teller. No, the kingmaker, insofar that there was one, was a Tory eminence in the oldest tradition—a big, rich, dull major with an island in Scotland and estates in Wiltshire. Major John Morrison, then chairman of the 1922 Committee, had been an old friend and admirer of Home. He was convinced at Blackpool, after Hailsham's over-excitement, that neither Hailsham nor Butler should be leader; and from the time that Morrison was known to support Home—however improbable it may have seemed to the Chancellor of the Exchequer and the Leader of the House of Commons—the notion of Home for prime minister gathered weight. However much the Conservative party appeared as a modern, mechanised democratic machine, it reverted in this time of crisis to its older, more secretive roots.

SIR ALEC DOUGLAS-HOME

There are two problems in my life. The political ones are insoluble and the economic ones are incomprehensible.

Sir Alec Douglas-Home, 1964.

The most striking testimony to the strength and resilience of the Tory aristocrats is, of course, the career of the leader of the party, Sir Alec Douglas-Home, formerly the Earl of Home; for he was chosen in 1963 at a time when most of the cabinet and the parliamentary party seemed urgently in need of a vigorous modern leader, who could present an image of a thrusting, competitive party. Sir Alec was not quite as unqualified for the job as he seemed to his more extreme Tory critics: he was more adaptable and energetic, and more brisk in debate, than he had seemed beforehand, and he understood the importance of promoting and encouraging the men, like Heath, Maudling or Joseph, who *did* look modern. But by the end of the election, when the leaders stood out above all as the symbols of their parties, the old-fashionedness and irrelevance of Sir Alec's personality had become much more evident, and in the aftermath the ancient division between old and new Tories became wider.

In its outward appearance, Sir Alec's career seemed almost a caricature of the easy advancement of the gifted amateur. His family, from the feudal borders of Scotland, is wealthy, eccentric, ancient. At Eton, Lord Dunglass (as he then was called) was described by his headmaster—whose daughter he later married—as one of the most unambitious boys he had known, and by his contemporary Cyril Connolly, in a much-quoted passage:

> He was a votary of the esoteric Eton religion, the kind of graceful, tolerant, sleepy boy who is showered with favours and crowned with all the laurels, who is liked by the masters and admired by the boys without any apparent exertion on his part, without experiencing the ill-effects of success himself or arousing the pangs of envy in others. In the eighteenth century he would have become prime minister before he was thirty: as it was he appeared honourably ineligible for the struggle for life.

But the eighteenth-century tradition, it turned out, is still strong, and Dunglass was far more ambitious than he appeared. He went to Christ Church, played cricket well, took a third-class degree in history, went into parliament. He became Chamberlain's private secretary, followed him to Downing Street and thus (unlike Churchill, Eden and Salisbury, all aristocrats who stood against appeasement) became implicated in Munich. During the war, he spent two years in bed with TB on the spine and during this time made an exhaustive study of Communism, which showed a much tougher interest in politics than his friends suspected. In 1951, when he moved to the Lords, he was a junior minister under Churchill and then in 1955 was promoted by Eden to the Commonwealth Relations Office. He stayed there for five years. He was charming, popular, conscientious, right-wing and undistinguished: he was apt to come out with embarrassing clichés about Africans never having discovered the wheel, etc.

In 1960 came the bombshell: Macmillan insisted on appointing him Foreign Secretary. The *Daily Mirror* described it as 'the most reckless political appointment since the Roman Emperor Caligula made his favourite horse a Consul'. His opinions and even his name were hardly known, and the papers had to explain that it rhymed with fume and not with foam. Most newspapers assumed that he would be conveniently subservient. But there were soon strong indications that the Foreign Office, for the first time for six years, was being run by the Foreign Secretary. In his social ease, his integrity, his lack of middle-class inhibitions, the Earl was compared to Ernest Bevin.

In 1963 came the second bombshell when, after a week of hectic intrigue and bewilderment, Lord Home emerged as the new prime minister to succeed Macmillan, and relinquished his peerage to become Sir Alec Douglas-Home. The shock to many of his colleagues was great: 'It will put back the Tory party by twenty years,' one cabinet minister said to me at the time, 'his views on Africa are semi-Portuguese'; and the fact that the leader came from the Lords came as a blow to the pride of the Commons. But in the following months many of the objections were forgotten in the general relief that under Sir Alec the party had achieved unity and a new calm and confidence. To many Conservative ladies, his consenting to run the country was a final proof of his true nobility.

Harold Macmillan had always been an intricate and devious leader; he had been half an intellectual, half a would-be aristocrat, and beneath his tired Edwardian façade he nurtured strong radical instincts and a fascination with ideas. This combination proved invaluable in Macmillan's awkward task of persuading his party to retreat from Suez, to come to terms with the wind of change in Africa, and to move towards Europe; the more old-fashioned he looked, the more he was able to move with the times. But when things began to go wrong after Britain's exclusion from Europe, Macmillan's two-sidedness was much less popular: the right-wing realised that he was betraying their principles, while the left-wing grew exasperated by his antique manner.

After six years of this ambiguity, the party turned with relief to a prime minister who was clearly all of a piece. Sir Alec was not a man who nursed doubts or theories about either his own or his party's right to rule. His own political inspiration, as he described it, came primarily from his own ancestors, the Earls of Home and Durham, and he was able to discuss politics with the same cold detachment that he brought to the question of grouse. While Macmillan cultivated with some difficulty his 'unflappability', which often concealed considerable emotion and worry, Sir Alec was genuinely unflappable, and at Downing Street, in the midst of some frightful crisis, he was able to switch off completely to arrange the flowers.

Sir Alec's decisiveness, even if the decisions were wrong, soothed many of his party's troubles. By the summer of 1964 the public opinion polls, which had previously reported widespread discontent, began to show a swing back towards the Tories. Sir Alec's public manner became more assured, and his ignorance of economic and industrial matters was partly covered up by the prominence of his two lieutenants, Maudling and Heath. In the election campaign he showed unexpected stamina and zest, and he gave a public impression of niceness, unstuffiness and thorough integrity. But he did not and could not emerge as a dynamic contemporary leader, with the same kind of thrust and urgency as Harold Wilson. When the party finally sank, after thirteen years afloat, it seemed more like a battered and patched-up dreadnought than an up-to-date warship. Inevitably, as the process of re-thinking and replanning began, Sir Alec began to appear as a liability.

FOUR CONTENDERS

Pressing round Sir Alec were four rivals, all contemporaries, all middle-class intellectuals from Oxford and Cambridge. They all came into parliament after the war, became associated with the revival of the Tory party, and achieved high office during the thirteen years. But they are very divergent personalities, and each of them represents a different facet of the 'New Conservatism'. They are Reginald Maudling, Ted Heath, Enoch Powell and Iain Macleod.

The youngest and (some say) the ablest of them is Reginald Maudling, the big and amiable former Chancellor of the Exchequer. With an agile mind and a powerful frame, he moved up to that height with extraordinary ease. He was the son of an actuary—that austere and demanding profession. At Oxford he was gay and gregarious, but he took a first in Greats; he married an actress, was called to the Bar, and spent the war in the air force. He did not enter parliament until 1950, when he was thirty-three, and he never became a good speaker; but three years later he was already Economic Secretary to the Treasury. He had a superbly efficient brain, and a natural political sense; and although ambitious and quite self-centred, he had the gift, very useful in Conservative circles, of being able to walk backwards into power, and of preserving an amateur façade in front of his tough, professional mind. The price of this façade—as with Macmillan—was an inability to exhort or inspire, and a refusal to rise to great occasions. He was not much involved in political alignments; at the Board of Trade he was known to be lukewarm about the Common Market, and at Colonies he was clearly sympathetic to African advancement, without having the emotional involvement of his predecessor, Macleod. He was humane, compassionate, and decent, and occasionally he spoke out on behalf of the New Toryism. In June 1962, when Macmillan's popularity was beginning to wane, he delivered a well-timed and unusually eloquent message to his constituents which concluded:

> The Conservative party will regain its supremacy if, and only if, it can find the answer to the real needs of the 1960s. They are not the needs of a country haunted by Jarrow and the Rhondda, nor any longer the needs solely of a country breaking away from the austerity of war and the meshes of socialism. They are the needs of a people conscious of the greatness of their past, enjoying the affluence and freedom of the present but feeling in their hearts the lack of a sense of the purpose of this freedom and affluence.[1]

The next month, in Macmillan's drastic reshuffle, he became Chancellor of the Exchequer, and therefore a serious candidate for the future leadership. He was an important asset to his party, and as Chancellor he brought reassurance and calm. He claimed to prepare his budget to the sound of Mozart, and he was endlessly photographed with his good-looking family—his ex-actress wife, his actress daughter and his three sons—as if he were a kind of walking advertisement for Tory prosperity. But the sense of purpose which he spoke about was never very apparent in this genial, contented man, and there was still some relevance in the rhyme

> Reg
> Has no edge
> And Maudling
> Is dawdling.

[1] *Daily Mail*, June 21, 1962.

When his great challenge came at Blackpool in 1963, he seemed more than usually languid. He deplored the excitement and emotion of the occasion. Although he clearly *was* a contender, he made very little effort, and his speech to the conference on economic policy was exceptionally flat and uninspired. When Lord Home was eventually chosen as prime minister, he appeared —while serving him as Chancellor—to be in a sulk, and even to be waiting impatiently for the Tories to go into opposition. Before the election campaign there was bitter rivalry between Maudling and Heath as to who should be front man. Home supported Heath, but Maudling was chosen to take the press conferences, which he did with mastery and warmth, and by the time the Conservatives did go into opposition, Maudling had regained his prestige in the party, and seemed well-placed for the leadership.

Maudling's main rival is a man of quite different temperament and background, Ted Heath. He is a much tenser, more dedicated and emotional man, a bachelor whose over-riding interest is politics. Heath has a blank, boyish face, smooth grey hair, an intense manner which gives way suddenly and disconcertingly to a bright smile and shaking laughter, like a clockwork toy. He comes from a less affluent background than Maudling's, is the son of a master-builder, and that rare thing, a grammar-school Tory leader. He went to Oxford as an organ scholar, then to the army and then to politics. He is, unlike Maudling, a keen churchman— he was once news editor of the *Church Times*, and he still likes to play the organ and conduct a choir at Broadstairs. He went into politics in 1950, the same year as Maudling, and also rose quickly, but by a more energetic and difficult route. He became a Whip, and by 1955 was Chief Whip, renowned for his necessary mixture of charm and bullying. He became Macmillan's loyal confidant, and in 1961 was rewarded with the exacting and exciting job of leading Britain's negotiations to join the Common Market—a job which seemed first to make him, and then very nearly to break him. He threw himself into the job with immense energy and skill, tirelessly touring the capitals of Europe, memorising the intricate statistics of tariffs, and flying to and from Brussels as casually as a commuter. He responded to the challenge as vigorously as a soldier in battle.

And then, in January 1963, the collapse came, and the whole new European world that Heath had built for himself crumbled overnight. For some time afterwards he seemed aimless and lost, but a year later he had recovered his resilience. But Macmillan, who had done much for him, clearly did not favour him for the leadership, and at the Blackpool intrigues, Heath was not a contender. Yet he had quietly established a stronger position. Alone of the new Tories, he supported Home and helped to put him into the job, while at the same time he was not identified with Home's old-fashionedness. In Sir Alec's government, at the Board of Trade, he was depicted as the chief moderniser of Britain, with new responsibilities including regional development, and he was well cast for the rôle, with his obvious enthusiasm and drive.

But his drive was not associated with any obvious policy or vision; he had always seemed more a chief-of-staff than a general. In his short parliamentary career he had been much more involved in handling people and situations than in putting forward policies. In the contest for the leadership he had the advantage of typifying a thriving, ambitious New Britain, without snobbery or amateurism. But in the Tory party he was still apt to be regarded as a creepy technocrat with too much zeal and not enough ballast. And he was still identified with the humiliation of Brussels, which his party were trying hard to forget.

The third rival, Iain Macleod, is the most obviously left-wing and independent of them, and firmly identified with political attitudes. He has represented the sector of young Tories who have liberal views on Africa and race, who resent the dominance of Tory aristocrats, and who look for a more idealistic and romantic leadership. He does not himself look romantic. He is shortish, rather bald, with dark, impersonal eyes: he is unobtrusively dressed, though he blossoms out into double-breasted waistcoats. He watches television, spends weekends in London, and works a lot in bed. He has no large hinterland of learning and culture. He enjoys celebrating and pulling out corks, but he never seems to let himself go. He sometimes inhabits White's Club, but looks separate, surrounded by taller, louder men. He appears a rather solitary person, but he is self-contained and at peace with himself; he likes going for long walks to 'renew himself to himself', and he has a strange layer of romanticism, half real, half assumed. His Conservative career has been full of difficult manoeuvres and compromises, and the real value of his ideals will probably only emerge if he ever becomes prime minister.

He comes from tough Scots stock: his father, a doctor who emigrated from the Western Isles to Yorkshire, sent his son to an exacting Scots public school, Fettes (where Selwyn Lloyd also went). Macleod went on to Cambridge where bridge became his passion, and afterwards had a brief and desultory career in business—appropriately in the playing-card firm of De La Rue. After the war, when he rose to be major, he went into Tory politics, and joined R. A. Butler's research staff. In 1950 he was elected to parliament and helped to found the 'One Nation' group of new Conservatives. In 1952 he had his crucial stroke of luck, when Aneurin Bevan intervened in a debate on the health service, and gave Macleod the chance to show his form. Soon after that, Churchill made him Minister of Health—a sudden promotion—and he rose to be Minister of Labour and then to the hottest seat of all—Colonies, which he occupied perilously but without disaster for two years.

Macleod has an agile mind, and a memory which almost equals Harold Wilson's or Macaulay's (he is distantly related to Macaulay): he can recite lists of thirty-year old Olympic results and Derby winners without any strain. He is a master of any kind of political manoeuvre. He is cool, calculating but also emotional. In his two years dealing with Africans he was genuinely sympathetic: 'I believe in the brotherhood of man,' he said quite simply at the 1961 party conference. The disabilities of his wife, who had polio, and his own pain with fibrositis, have given him experience of suffering, which Africans such as Kaunda and Banda appreciated.

Macleod has always showed signs of being restive with Conservatives. He talks with witty dislike of the 'Deep South'—the right-wing strongholds along the south coast—and he likes to depict himself not as a Conservative but as a romantic Tory, of the Disraelian kind. He is very aware of his Highland blood, and has even written a romantic play about the Hebrides.

His difficulties grew after 1961, when he occupied an awkward combination of jobs—Leader of the House of Commons and Chairman of the Conservative Party. Without a ministry, he was less able to show his abilities, and by 1963 his prospects for the eventual leadership were much more slender, and he seemed physically less strong. Then came the leadership crisis at Blackpool, Macleod's resignation, and his new career as editor of *The Spectator*. He still kept his Scots caution. He made no statement when he refused to serve under Home, and even soon afterwards affirmed his respect for the prime minister; but he was inwardly disgusted with the choice, and after three months came out with his outspoken attack in *The Spectator*. It seemed then that Macleod had finally, even deliberately, burnt his boats, and committed the unforgiveable sin of washing dirty Tory linen in public. But his free-booting courage and independence still compelled the admiration of many young Tories and when—as he had anticipated—his party was defeated at the election, many of his colleagues wanted him back, to bring his militant, missionary energy to the new opposition. He joined the Shadow Cabinet, with the special brief of Steel, to lead the Tory counter-attack against the expected re-nationalisation. He had successfully weathered his rebellion, but it was doubtful whether he could make up the ground that Maudling had gained.

The most courageous and maverick of the four is Enoch Powell, the pale, ascetic ex-professor of Greek, who once shared a flat with Iain Macleod, and who more than Macleod embodies a kind of conscience of the Tory party. Powell is unmistakable: he has piercing, icy, eyes and a discomforting gaze, which breaks through suddenly into alarming laughter. He is one of those straightforward people who go round parties saying 'and what do you do?' He respects bold, plain-speaking people, and has romantic ideas about strength, which emerge in his early poems:

> I only love the strong and bold
> The flashing eye, the reddening cheek.

His background is exotic—Birmingham nonconformist, grammar school and Cambridge, with a brilliant academic career: he taught Greek in Cambridge and Australia, became a Brigadier in the war, joined 'Rabs' boys', and went into parliament. The arrival of his sharp and uncompromising mind fluttered the party, for Powell, for all his hexameters, is a fierce believer in old-fashioned free enterprise: he admires Clore as well as Herodotus, and looks back with nostalgia to the old days before monopolies and nationalisation. His determination to take 'free enterprise' literally embarrassed many protective Tories, who looked with distress at take-overs.

The key to Powell's special hold on his party is his integrity, both intellectual and political, and his austere romanticism, a tougher brand than Macleod's. His reasoning leads him to odd corners, and in economic matters he often sounds wildly reactionary; but he has a respect for truth and principle which makes his resignations particularly impressive. He resigned first with Peter

Thorneycroft from the Treasury, in 1958, in protest against Macmillan's spending; and then resigned again, with Macleod, after Home became prime minister. It seemed that he, too, had burnt a lot of boats. But the Conservatives always feel a little insecure without the presence of Powell, who serves as a kind of confessor to the cabinet. And in October 1964 he, too, came back into the fold of the Shadow Cabinet.

SHADOW MINISTERS

These four outstandingly able and ambitious men all hope to inherit a revivified and up-to-date Conservative party. But they are all in rivalry, and although they have had temporary political alliances—Macleod and Maudling during Blackpool, Macleod and Powell in their rebellion—they are usually in conflict. It is part of the traditional wisdom of the Conservative party that the 'clever young men' should be kept in check by playing off one against another, and both their power and their self-confidence can easily be undermined by cultivating their rivalries. It might seem that the new middle-class, professional Toryism will now finally dawn; but the situation at Blackpool, when the bitter rivalries made way for an aloof compromise candidate, could well be maintained or even repeated. However much the Conservative Shadow Cabinet may want to throw up a bold contemporary leader, they are tempted to fall back on less talented but more rooted men, who have the special Tory ingredients of 'soundness'—particularly Christopher Soames, the big amiable son-in-law of Winston Churchill, with a casualness and courage which inspires trust and affection; or even Lord Blakenham, the rich brother-in-law of Lord Cowdray, who used to be called John Hare, and who suddenly cropped up in 1963 as Sir Alec's friend and Chairman of the Party, which he remained until 1965.

The Conservative leadership remains an odd mixture: apart from the four obvious contenders, there are other quite powerful personalities who represent distinct strands of Conservatism. This was the Shadow Cabinet or, more properly, the 'consultative committee' appointed by Sir Alec after the election in October 1964, with their ages and education:

HOME AFFAIRS

	Responsibility	*Education*
Reginald Maudling (47)	Treasury	Merchant Taylors', Oxford
Edward Heath (48)	Economic affairs, policy	Chatham House (Ramsgate), Oxford

Sir Edward Boyle (41)	Home Office	Eton, Oxford
Quintin Hogg (57)	Education and Science	Eton, Oxford
Christopher Soames (44)	Agriculture	Eton, R.M.C. Sandhurst
Sir Keith Joseph (46)	Social Services, Wales	Harrow, Oxford
Joseph Godber (50)	Labour	Bedford
Ernest Marples (56)	Technology	Stretford Grammar School
Iain Macleod (50)	Steel	Fettes, Cambridge
John Boyd-Carpenter (56)	Housing, Land	Stowe, Oxford
Enoch Powell (52)	Transport	King Edwards (Birmingham), Cambridge
Michael Noble (51)	Scotland	Eton, Oxford
	FOREIGN AFFAIRS	
R. A. Butler (61)	Foreign Office	Marlborough, Cambridge
Duncan Sandys (56)	Commonwealth and Colonies	Eton, Oxford
Peter Thorneycroft (55)	Defence	Eton, R.M.A. Woolwich
	OTHER RESPONSIBILITIES	
Selwyn Lloyd (60)	Opposition, Commons	Fettes, Oxford
Lord Blakenham (53)	Party Chairman	Eton
Lord Carrington (45)	Opposition, Lords	Eton, R.M.C. Sandhurst
Lord Dilhorne (61)	Deputy Opposition, Lords	Eton, Oxford

The two other contenders for the leadership in 1963, Hogg and Butler, are now out of the running, but both are significant in the party's corporate character. Quintin Hogg, the former Lord Hailsham, purveys a militant, sub-Churchillian Toryism which is most vocal in moments of national crisis or folly—as during Suez, or the Profumo affair. Brilliant, charming, theatrical and quixotic, he is capable of a moral fervour and eloquence which outshines all his rivals; but he is capable too of frenzied over-excitement and absurdity, as happened during the Blackpool crisis which seemed finally to dish his chances of the leadership. 'Hogg's worst fault,' said one Tory, 'is his indecisiveness. Behind a fustian manner, he dithers.'

Until his retirement to Trinity College Cambridge, with a peerage, in 1965, Richard Austen Butler represented the most ambiguous streak of the Conservative party: for thirty years he had been defending all sorts of different Tory policies. He is not a typical Tory—he is essentially an intellectual—but he accurately represented that broad slice of his party which, without being excited by social change, knew when to give in to it. He has been an appeaser both in the good and the bad sense. He has appeased Hitler and Franco, but also Gandhi: and there have been moments—in education during the war, or in his stand against flogging—when he has been ahead of his party. But cautious ambiguity has been his consistent feature: and this stood in his road to the top job.

In his background he rested between the landed and the academic strands of his party. He was brought up in a Governor's mansion, but his father later became Master of Pembroke, Cambridge, and other Butlers—a large clan—have been scattered through the universities. He moved in stately circles: but he loved to encourage young men to attack 'the Establishment'.

He has been in all the major ministries in Whitehall. He came into the Government as long ago as 1932, as a brilliant young don. His greatest achievement was probably in the years out of office, when he took over with Lord Woolton the reconstruction of the Tory party; he built up his team of 'Rab's boys'—including Macleod, Maudling, Powell, Maude and Alport, who helped to present an up-to-date party, with slogans like 'property-owning democracy'. But back in office, under Churchill and Eden, he failed to inspire his backbenchers with thoughts of firm leadership. When Eden resigned in 1956, he was defeated by Macmillan, and when Macmillan resigned in 1963 he was defeated by Lord Home. His most attractive weaknesses—his indiscretion and his anxiety to please—seemed to grow during the election campaign, and reached their climax in a disastrous railway-carriage interview with the *Daily Express*, in which he explained that Sir Alec was bored with Heath.

OPPOSITION

Outside the more hectic atmosphere of the contenders are the men who have made their reputation not primarily as politicians but as managers or 'technocrats', and who are usually better at running government departments than as parliamentarians. The most senior are Peter Thorneycroft, the former Minister of Defence, and Duncan Sandys, the unblunted hatchet-man of Tory administrations. Below them are the bevy of tycoonish ex-ministers, such as Ernest Marples, Joseph Godber or Geoffrey Rippon, who appear more as super-civil servants than as political operators. They are sometimes referred to by older Conservatives as 'eager beavers' or 'busy bees', with the usual disdain accorded to serious professionalism, but the party is dependent on them for its policies of 'modernisation'. And also among the 'technocrats' are the two surprising baronets, Sir Keith Joseph and Sir Edward Boyle. Sir Keith is a wealthy businessman, son of a Lord Mayor and with his own suave aldermanic manner, who is also a Fellow of All Souls. At the Ministry of Housing he emerged as a central figure in 'modernisation'. Sir Edward, the former Minister of Education, has a nineteenth-century look to him: he is a huge, rubicund egghead, who talks with unconcealed learning, assuming others to be equally learned. He walks like a bear, with a formidable shuffle, and he has the broad interests and leisureliness of a cultivated squire. But, behind this Victorian appearance, he is one of the most radically-minded men: he was one of only two members of the government to resign (very temporarily) over Suez, and he has an interest in social change and education, a dislike of Conservative snobbery, and a belief in the purposive rôle of government, which is rare in his party.

Once in opposition, the Conservative party inevitably becomes, for a time at least, less tribal and feudal, and turns towards the professionals, the intellectuals and the younger men to provide the ammunition for counter-attack. The Conservative Central Office, with its brisk researchers and publicity experts, comes into the front line, and the Conservative Research Department (under Brendon Sewill) acquires new importance. The more independent young conservatives are represented by the Bow Group, which is a think box for the party, like the Fabians on the left. Its views range from die-hard to radical: but it has an ambience of its own. The Bow Groupers are nearly all young professional men—barristers, executives, journalists or advertising men, with an earnest, professional attitude to politics. There is a story of a girl who joined them thinking they were the 'Beau Group', and was disappointed to find them dull and not very sexy. They are studious and carefully pedestrian—compared to the more equestrian postures of pre-war young Tories. They write long, well-printed pamphlets full of accurate figures and cautious suggestions, and they give sober parties in Kensington and Chelsea. They have an active social conscience, shown in their campaigns for the World Refugee Year and Old-people-for-Christmas. Occasionally they have shown signs of tentative rebellion, and their first chairman, James Lemkin (who later turned out to be Liberal), had an important influence in stirring up interest in Central Africa, but they have since been more firmly hugged by the Conservative party machine, and with age they have become less interesting.

Among the younger Conservatives, the different types from different backgrounds jostle together; rich and reverent scions co-exist with quite cheeky and buccaneering upstarts from advertising, the law, television or public relations. The cry for modernisation and for equality of opportunity has become more insistent since the emergence of Sir Alec as leader, and the opposition to the Etonian 'Old Boy Net' spreads from Sir Gerald Nabarro on the right to Iain Macleod to the left. But somehow or other the Etonians, with their confidence, their disdain and their passion for politics, are still constantly popping up in different disguises; when Sir Alec appointed two young men to party appointments after the general election—the director of publicity, and the director of the Conservative Political Centre—they both turned out to be Old Etonians. The first, Roger Pemberton, is a smooth, sceptical advertising man from Colman, Prentis and Varley; the second, David Howell, is a lanky, frail-looking intellectual from the *Daily Telegraph*, who looks like a stage lordling, but has one of the most open and original minds in the party. The Chairmanship of the party, however, went to a man more obviously in a different mould—Edward du Cann, a very successful young city investment expert, aged only forty. Du Cann was not quite the 'grammar school' man that the party liked to make out. He comes from a Tory family, his father was quite a successful barrister, and he went to Woodbridge, a minor public school, and to St. John's, Oxford. He lives in a fashionable Westminster street, and is imperturbably debonair. But he is a man of driving ability and ambition, thoroughly aware of the new techniques of publicity and persuasion: and it seems likely that he and his deputy Sir Michael Fraser (who built up the Conservative Research Department) will be able to refurbish the Tory shop with the same firm eye on the customers that Lord Woolton showed in the 'forties. 'If Sir Alec had fed all the data relating to the very model of a modern party chairman into a computer', wrote Iain Macleod in *The Spectator*, 'the machine would surely have chattered out the name of Edward du Cann'.

6

PRIME MINISTER

As a man, he might briefly be described as a viable island.
Hugh Massingham.

Yes—I have climbed to the top of the greasy pole.
Disraeli.

WITH the character of James Harold Wilson, forty-fifth prime minister of Britain, we reach an apparently clean break with earlier traditions, and the backgrounds of the preceding chapters. For he is, to a rare extent even for prime ministers, an isolated man. The fact might be guessed by his appearance, the more defiantly grey against the quiet splendour of 10 Downing Street. His face is round and unobtrusive, with still a hint of the chubby look of his youth, but now looking older than his forty-nine years (he is the youngest prime minister since Lord Rosebery, and the third youngest member of his cabinet, but that would not be guessed from his looks). His hair greyed before he was forty, and his shape in the last few years has become more paunchy and hunched. His pale eyes have always looked distant, giving no clue to what he is thinking. His mouth has looked sceptical since he was a baby, now emphasised by his perpetual pipe which, with all the lighting, relighting, scraping, cleaning and tapping, provides an additional smokescreen. His clothes add to the greyness—grey suits bought from Burtons, and dark patterned ties. And the picture is corroborated by the voice—clipped, dry, matter-of-fact, and still with a definite though modified Yorkshire accent.

His Yorkshire background has remained all-important, and serves to explain his strength in isolation. He is the first Englishman outside the traditional middle or upper class ever to have become prime minister; of the two other premiers from humble beginnings, Lloyd George, the son of a schoolmaster, was emphatically Welsh, and Ramsay MacDonald, the son of a miner, was very Scots, and their rural Celtic background gave them both freedom and vagueness. But Harold Wilson was the son of a works chemist in

Huddersfield, the heart of the industrial revolution. His father regarded himself as lower-middle class, but called himself 'working class' to his Tory friends.

From his father, now a sturdy old man of eighty-two who has stayed close to his son all his life, Harold inherited toughness, a superb mind and memory, and a powerful sense of social justice. From his mother Ethel he inherited a calm temperament and low blood pressure. The family was very political—either Labour or Liberal—and by the age of seven Harold was taking a keen interest in the 1923 election. He was brought up in a self-contained family atmosphere, underpinned by a Congregationalist faith; and this sense of the privacy of the family unit, stronger in the north than the south, has remained always with Wilson. He has never, like other ambitious provincials, been lured into the elaborate social rituals of London; and this family containment was dramatically underlined on October 16, 1964, when he was called to the palace and took his family along with him—as no prime minister had ever done—his father, his wife Mary, his sons Robin and Giles, and his sister Marjorie.

His upbringing was puritan but contented. The family lived in a stone, terraced house in Milnsbridge, just outside Huddersfield, and travelled about on a motor-bike and side-car. Harold was sent to Milnsbridge primary school, became a keen Scout, went to church and Sunday school every Sunday. The account of his childhood, as presented in his authorised biography,[1] sounds like a Victorian moral tale of self-improvement in the tradition of Samuel Smiles. By the age of twelve he was already imagining himself in a school essay as Chancellor of the Exchequer: his ambition had been set by his father (who has said 'blame me for his politics'), and kept going by Harold's own single-mindedness. His ambition was never blunted by doubts or conflicts; like his electoral rival Sir Alec, but in the opposite mould, he was a monolithic man, all of a piece.

His ambition continued self-enclosed to an extraordinary extent, through his three years at Oxford. He went up with a scholarship to Jesus College—known for its preponderance of Welshmen and poorer undergraduates—in October 1934, and shared rooms with the son of a Welsh plumber. (Only about 10 per cent of the Jesus men at that time came from public schools.) Oxford was then bustling with socio-political activity: two

[1] Leslie Smith: *Harold Wilson, the authentic portrait*. Hodder & Stoughton, 1964. I am indebted to this important book for several details in this chapter.

members of his present cabinet (Crossman and Longford) were then young Oxford dons, deep in politics. The Oxford Union was constantly debating about Nazi Germany, Spain and unemployment.

Wilson was not much concerned with Spain or Germany but he was very personally involved with unemployment. In his third year his father lost his job for the second time (the first time, when he stayed out of work for sixteen months, was when Harold was fifteen). This kind of shock emphasised the rift between Wilson's experience and that of the fashionable Marxists. 'I reacted against Marxism at Oxford,' he has said: 'I was never a Marxist . . . I've always been a pragmatic socialist.'[1] He maintains that he never got farther than page two of Karl Marx's *Das Kapital*. But he had acquired, as early as the General Strike (when he was ten), an ability to see individual emotional problems in rational economic terms, which gave him his intense personal interest in (for instance) the dry subject of economic organisation.

Wilson joined the Union and was keen on debates, but he only spoke there once—carefully choosing a time at the end of term, when the *Isis*, the undergraduate magazine, could not mock his speech the next week. He was shy and nervous at social occasions, and this shyness remained with him. 'I was very sensitive to the fear of derision at Oxford—what to do at sherry parties and that sort of thing.'[2] He joined the Labour Club, but was appalled by the wealthy, public school Marxists who belonged to it, who could drink away in one night as much as a working-class family would earn in a week, and was not at all impressed by the fashionable Socialists who went to the Union wearing hunting pink as a protest against the Tories. This was one reason, he says, why after a year he switched to the Liberal Club, of which he later became Treasurer, when Frank Byers was President. He was considered by his Liberal colleagues as a painstaking organiser, who yet seemed not much moved by the great issues.

His Oxford life, in spite of the prevailing excitements, remained austere and tautly self-disciplined. He resented the cost of Oxford living, and even had a weekly joint, and his laundry, sent from home by his mother. He worked prodigiously, and the intimidating story is told of how he and another northern boy, Eric Sharpe, who later became a baptist minister, competed in industry. They recorded in a big Boots diary how they each had spent every hour

[1] Interview with Brian Blake. *The Listener*, October 29, 1964.
[2] Smith, p. 206.

of the day, and kept a red-and-blue pencil to record the total. The hardest worker kept the pencil; it was nearly always Wilson.[1] After his first term, Wilson changed his subject from History to the new school of Politics, Philosophy and Economics. He specialised and excelled in Economic Organisation—a choice which was to have great advantages. He won a prize for a long essay on 'The State and the Railways, 1823–63' and then a scholarship for economics. He had few diversions: he went to Chapel every Sunday, he ran for the university, and he read very solemn papers to various clubs, including one on 'The Last Depression—and the Next', and one on 'Two Nations' (the north and the south). In 1937 he took his finals, and was awarded the top first-class degree of the year. He had seventeen alphas out of eighteen.

Wilson had applied for a fellowship at Christ Church, where Longford (then Mr. Pakenham) and Gordon Walker were already dons. He was turned down. Instead he became a fellow of New College, where for the first time he came into contact with the old boy net of public schools, and particularly Winchester, which provided so many Labour politicians. He always felt apart from this network and, as a shy young don tutoring confident young Wykehamists, he became aware of the advantages of public schoolboys. 'They had much more self-confidence, I think, because of their kind of upbringing, than I had. I have always felt that these (problems of economics) were very difficult problems, and, to use the old phrase, I used to wish that I was as certain of anything as they were of everything. I have felt that many times since, with the products of a similar upbringing in different walks of life.'[2]

As a don, first at New College and then at University College, Wilson worked for two years with William Beveridge, the Master of Univ, on research into problems of unemployment. He was stimulated by Beveridge's rigorous methods, but baffled by his limitations. 'I learnt something about the weakness of a dedicated scholar and administrator,' he said later.[3] 'I'd realised for some time that Beveridge hadn't grasped the fact that unemployment on the scale and of the kind he was dealing with was a built-in factor of the pre-Keynesian economy—not an unfortunate accident, frictional, or anything like that, but positively built-in . . . My father was out of work at the time.'

[1] *See* Smith, p. 70.
[2] *The Listener*, October 29, 1964.
[3] Conversation with Kenneth Harris. *The Observer*, June 9, 1963.

Soon after war had broken out, when Wilson was twenty-three, he married Mary Baldwin, the girl he had met six years before at a tennis club in Cheshire. Mary, when they first met, was a secretary at Port Sunlight, the soap works, from the same kind of background—lower-middle class, Congregationalist, temperance; they had been going steady, in the strict north country tradition, all the time Wilson was at Oxford. They were married at Mansfield College (Congregationalist) Chapel, with fifty wedding-guests, and honeymooned in the Cotswolds. Soon afterwards, Wilson was interviewed for a wartime job in the civil service and so, as with hundreds of other dons, began his first involvement with government, and his second career.

Wilson is the first prime minister ever to have been a civil servant. His four years in the civil service were all important to his future, for they enabled him to master the inner workings of Whitehall as few politicians can, and to add practical experience to his knowledge of organisational problems. 'I learned that for about three months the civil servants study a new minister to see where he is vulnerable, so that they shall be able to play on it whenever they want to break him down.'[1] He worked his way quickly up through Whitehall—from the Ministry of Supply to Manpower Statistics to Labour to Fuel and Power—and by 1943, at the age of twenty-seven, he was Director of Economics with a staff of 350. He came in touch with many Labour politicians including Dalton, Bevin and Gaitskell (also then a civil servant). He had already before the war abandoned his Liberal connections and (partly under the influence of G. D. H. Cole) became involved with the Fabian Society. In 1943 he was asked to join the committee of the Fabians, and thus came closer to Labour politics. Towards the end of the war he was invited to be nominated as a Labour candidate for Ormskirk. He won the seat in the general election of 1945 with a majority of 7,000. And so began his third and final profession, at the age of twenty-nine.

Attlee, who had heard about Wilson from Dalton, gave him a junior job immediately, as parliamentary secretary to George Tomlinson, the Minister of Works. Wilson's stint in the civil service had given him a high reputation as a planner, and he was confident enough to over-ride senior civil servants twice his age. Soon after he took office he had a row about building materials with the permanent secretary at the ministry, which he has often described since, and which shows his characteristic mixture of

[1] Interview with Kenneth Harris, *The Observer*, June 9, 1964.

toughness and caution. The permanent secretary complained that Wilson had been consulting junior civil servants without reference to him, and Wilson became convinced that the permanent secretary must go. But he did not ask for him to be moved; he arranged with Tomlinson for a new director general of building materials to be appointed, which further infuriated the permanent secretary. Eventually the public outcry over the shortage of bricks forced Attlee to intervene, and only after Attlee had cross-questioned first Tomlinson, then Wilson, did Wilson agree that the permanent secretary should go.

Wilson moved from Works to the Board of Trade, under Cripps. He negotiated for wheat with Mikoyan in Moscow, which was his first taste of big-time diplomacy—and he still loves talking about his tough tactics with 'Mik'. With this and other successes behind him, he was appointed, at the age of thirty-one, to be President of the Board of Trade, with a seat in the cabinet—the youngest cabinet minister since Pitt. He was established as a technocrat of phenomenal efficiency, but with no strong political line.

Four years later came his clear identification with the left of his party, and with Aneurin Bevan. The economic situation had worsened. The government was pressed by the Americans to a vast increase in defence spending, and decided to recoup some of the cost by introducing charges for part of the health service. Wilson was angry with his colleagues—particularly with Gaitskell, now Chancellor of the Exchequer—for giving in to American pressure, and for betraying the ideals of the health service. When Bevan resigned in April, 1951, Wilson, together with John Freeman (later editor of the *New Statesman*) insisted on resigning too. But he maintains that his reasons for resigning were broader than Bevan's original 'teeth and spectacles' row, and that it was not so much Wilson who was a Bevanite as Bevan who became a Wilsonite.

For the next twelve years—while the Labour party were in opposition—Wilson shifted his position inside the party in a way which baffled many of his colleagues. He remained on the left, frequently critical of American foreign policy and committed to further nationalisation, but never became identified with a single group. When Bevan resigned from the Shadow Cabinet in 1954, Wilson took his place, and when Hugh Gaitskell became Leader in 1955, Wilson served as his Shadow Chancellor of the Exchequer. But after 1959, when the Labour party had lost their third election in succession, he again rebelled against his leader, while remaining aloof from the actual argument.

Wilson and Gaitskell, both first-class Oxford economists and dons, were politically and personally irreconcilable. Gaitskell was to the right of his party, not a radical by temperament, pro-American and not much interested in nationalisation. He was a courageous and precise leader, who retained a don's dislike for the often blurred and irrational arguments that swayed the Labour party. After the disastrous Labour defeat of 1959, he was determined to moderate and clarify the Labour policy; he tried without success to root out the famous 'Clause Four' which prescribed mass nationalisation ('It was like telling the Salvation Army there was no Salvation,' said Wilson), and insisted on bringing to a head the issue of unilateral disarmament. At the famous Scarborough conference of October 1960, when the unilateralists were temporarily victorious, Gaitskell, in a speech of passionate eloquence, said: 'There are some of us who will fight and fight and fight again to bring back sanity and honesty and dignity, so that our party—with its great past—may retain its glory and its greatness.'

Wilson during that speech was conspicuously absent from the conference hall. He was not a unilateralist, but he thought that Gaitskell had unnecessarily split the party, and as leader should have accepted the conference's majority. Wilson's attitude here, as in previous disputes, was regarded by Gaitskellites and others as being slippery and evasive: 'If the Labour party ends this week facing two directions,' commented the *New Left Review*, 'it is certain that the figure of Mr. Wilson will be there, at the end of both of them.' But Wilson maintained that his concern was with party unity and that the unilateralists, though illogical, must be taken note of. After the conference Wilson decided to take the step, unprecedented in the history of the party, of standing against the leader in the annual election by Labour MPs; it was, he said later, the only time he could not sleep at night. He received 81 votes to Gaitskell's 166.

The conflict between Wilson and Gaitskell derived not so much from principles, as from two approaches to politics. Wilson was determined, as one commentator put it, to 'find the point of balance of his party, and then perch on it'. He was constantly veering and backing but never became involved too deeply with principles. He was never a Bevanite, or a unilateralist, but he took advantage of their support. Gaitskellites regarded Wilson as 'Nixonish'; Wilson regarded Gaitskell as dogmatic and prejudiced.

Wilson, in his subtlety and calculation, was more of a politician in the American tradition. But there were nevertheless consistent attitudes and beliefs, which Wilson never forgot. He was always concerned with abolishing charges for the health service, with the 'war on want', with restricting speculation. 'The trouble with Britain is that those who make money are more valued than those who earn it,' has been a consistent theme-song.

Wilson and Gaitskell were divided, too, by temperament. Though they lived only a mile apart, they inhabited quite different worlds. Gaitskell, in his spacious house in Hampstead, was gregarious, gay and fond of sophisticated parties; he was for a time the centre of a 'Frognal Set' of middle-class Labour intellectuals, and he liked to mix politics with friendship. Wilson intensely disapproved of his leader's exclusive social activity: as he put it when *he* became leader, 'It doesn't make sense for me and my wife to go spending three or four hours at the dinner table of one member of the party so that he and his friends can tell me what they think and what they would like, while some other member of the party, who can only afford to live three days a week in a cheap hotel, has to rely on fifteen minutes with me in my private office.'[1] Wilson's own home life remained private and enclosed; he has always lived simply and has (he explains) a puritan inability to relax. Very few political colleagues have ever been inside his house, a modest cottagey semi-detached in the Hampstead Garden Suburb (a favourite area for left-wing economists). The antipathy between Wilson and Gaitskell was not just about tastes; it reflected the divide between north and south, between two classes and two nations.

Wilson kept up his rebellion, and seemed a long way from the leadership. After Gaitskell had successfully fought back at the unilateralists in 1961, Wilson stood for election—again unsuccessfully—as the deputy leader, against George Brown, judging (with some justification) that the Gaitskell-Brown combination was too right-wing to represent the party. He appeared less hostile to Gaitskell, and at the 1962 conference, when Gaitskell came out against joining the Common Market, there was less to divide them. Wilson as a rebel had lost some of his force, and Gaitskell, through his political courage and patience, had achieved a large measure of unity. And then, in January 1963, Gaitskell died. Wilson's prospects were instantly transformed.

It is hard now to recall the agony that confronted the party that

[1] Interview with Kenneth Harris. *The Observer*, June 16, 1964.

icy February. The Gaitskellites were convinced that Wilson was far too slippery, too isolationist or too left-wing, to lead the party; but many of them were very sceptical whether George Brown, the right-wing candidate, was sufficiently steady or reliable. Faced with two evils, this group, who included Denis Healey, Douglas Jay and Michael Stewart (all now in the cabinet), nominated without enthusiasm a third candidate, James Callaghan. In the first ballot of Labour MPs, there were 115 votes for Wilson, 88 for Brown and 41 for Callaghan. In the second ballot Callaghan stood down, and Wilson emerged as the clear leader, with 144 votes to Brown's 103. He took over a party bitterly divided, and it seemed almost absurd to imagine him, eighteen months later, leading his party to victory.

Wilson set about establishing his leadership with speed and subtlety, and three months later his leadership already seemed inevitable. He kept his distance from the Gaitskellites, and did not pay more than lip-service to the dead leader; he saw Gaitskell's widow only once, when he offered her a life peerage. He placated the rebels on the left wing of the party, led by Michael Foot, and brought them back into the whip, and he gained strength from the fact that he appeared to be leading his party from left of centre—as Attlee and others had said it should be led. But as power loomed closer he was in fact moving steadily towards the centre. He saw much less of his old left-wing colleagues. There was no hint of anti-Americanism in his speeches. He vied with the Tories, and outdid them, in claiming close links with Washington, and presented himself more and more in the image of Kennedy.

By the time of the next party conference, in October 1963, Wilson's process of unification was complete, symbolised by the triumphant moment when he and George Brown held up their hands together. Wilson shrewdly chose the theme of 'Labour and the Scientific Revolution' for his main speech, and eloquently identified himself with the technicians and white-coat workers:

> In cabinet room and boardroom alike, those with responsibility must be able to speak with the language of the technical age. For the commanding heights of industry to be controlled by men whose only claim is aristocratic connection, or the power of wealth, or speculative finance, is as irrelevant to the twentieth century as would be the continued purchase of commissions in the armed forces by lordly amateurs. At the very time when even the MCC has abolished the distinction

between amateur and professional, we are content to remain, in science and industry, a nation of gentlemen in a world of players.

In his speeches in and out of parliament, Wilson concentrated on the theme of Tory incompetence more than Tory injustice ('We are living in the jet age but we are governed by an Edwardian establishment mentality'). He had a tougher, cheekier style of debating than Gaitskell, which made for sharper exchanges with the Tory leaders. When Wilson sarcastically asked Macmillan whether, after the Profumo scandal, he would appoint an enquiry into the Philby affair, 'assuming you have enough judges to go round', Macmillan replied in his most arrogant manner: 'You really must learn to distinguish between invective and insolence.' Sarcasm remained a favourite, two-edged weapon, which seemed to express Wilson's defensive anger in the face of Tory complacency. Another tricky weapon was his cleverness: he always loved to demonstrate his brains, his memory, and his nimble 'footwork' on every possible occasion. His memory was certainly astounding (in parliament it was second only, he told me, to Walter Padley's), and it could be devastatingly effective in reminding Tory ministers what they had said years ago. But his quick mind, his international name-dropping, his show-off wit, still had a suggestion of the schoolboy swot or the quiz kid, which seemed de-humanised and mechanical, and was without political sex-appeal. 'Very often in Wilson's witticisms,' complained Iain Macleod, 'the midnight oil reeks through.'[1] As he became more involved in electioneering, he became less deliberate and more obviously emotional; but he still could not quite get rid of the tight cleverness of a man who has outshone all his schoolfellows.

He was an unashamed professional, which was rare in either party. He was fascinated by the plumbing of politics, and it was not for nothing that he devoured Theodore White's *The Making of the President*. He did not, like most politicians, regard the political apparatus as a car, in which the driving was all-important. He loved to look under the bonnet and fiddle with the engine. Above all, he was a master of publicity and the press. His eyes lit up at the mention of details of timing, press releases, TV scripts. He knew how to flatter, cajole or bully journalists, and he never gave the impression, as Tory politicians do, of letting in the press by

[1] *The Spectator*, March 16, 1964.

the tradesmen's entrance; in Wilson's political house there was no front door, and journalists were among the most important tradesmen.

He was a tough and ruthless publicist in politics, but his home life remained remarkably insulated. He drove his son Giles to school every morning, left for Westminster at ten o'clock, and spent evenings working quietly at home. He has no social ambition or competitiveness: 'The old story about keeping up with the Joneses and so on does seem to imply a state of continuing unhappiness.' He was and is still bored by cocktail parties and glitter and, in a famous incident, denounced as repugnant the *Daily Express* view of the London Season: 'The last champagne glass has been smashed, the last gate-crasher has been repelled, the last escort has roared away in his sports car down the empty, dawn streets.' He plays occasional golf (often by himself), and spends family holidays in his bungalow, Lowenva ('the house of happiness'), in the Scilly Isles. He drinks very little alcohol, and at parties prefers to have ginger ale. He enjoys films and light music, but has no interest in art, and no visual memory. He enjoys ballet, and claims to have seen *Swan Lake* seventeen times in Moscow. He has the same fondness for the familiar—surprising in a man with so good a memory—in his reading. Oddly, he enjoys Dorothy Sayers's detective stories, with their mixture of romanticism and Oxford snobbery; he has read *The Nine Tailors* fifteen times.

Many of his patrician political colleagues mocked his philistinism and middle-brow tastes, and complained that Harold was impossibly dull: the *salon* approach to politics was a long time dying, even in the Labour party. But what was chiefly surprising about Wilson's simple life was that it should cause so much surprise; for it represented the way of life of the vast majority of the British population. What was unusual about him as a politician was that he had not changed his way of life on the way up. He was that rare combination, an intellectual who yet had roots. He had the qualities that Bagehot required of a constitutional statesman, which he found in Sir Robert Peel (a Lancashire man whom Wilson admires); that he should be 'a man of common opinions and uncommon abilities'.

His ordinariness and his plain northern roots showed at their strongest in his personal election campaign, canvassing in his constituency of Huyton, full of miners, dockers and glassworkers, near Liverpool. He was at ease and happy in those cosy surroundings. He sounded more sincerely emotional and less cerebral, and when he finally heard the news at Huyton town hall of his own vastly increased majority, a few hours before taking office, he reacted with a slow little speech, as relaxed and parochial as a town councillor's thanking all his helpers and officials, while the nation waited for him to become prime minister.

THE PRIME MINISTER'S POWERS

> One suspects, indeed, that ever since the emergence of Lloyd George as the national leader in the first world war the prevailing tendency has been towards the exaltation of the Prime Minister at the expense both of his colleagues and of the House of Commons.
>
> *Professor Max Beloff (August 1960).*

Is the prime minister's power increasing? Is he becoming less the chairman of a cabinet committee, ***primus inter pares***, and more of a president, with powers quite distinct from his colleagues?

Provided a premier can keep his party, his colleagues and parliament reasonably happy, there are no rules for the job. Churchill established a private court of overlords and personal advisers: he had little cause to worry about his party or parliament, since he was virtually irremovable, but he left great areas of government to departmental ministers. Whatever Churchill was, Attlee wasn't: 'he was much more like a chairman,' as one of his successors put it: 'mediating between his directors—Bevin and Cripps.' Or as Attlee described it: 'The job of a prime minister is to lead and co-ordinate a team, not to seek to be an omnipotent minister.'[1] Sir Anthony Eden bombarded nearly every department with minutes, phone calls and questions. He did not in the long run carry his party with him, though in the short run he revealed dramatically the powers of a prime minister. Macmillan established his own court, less powerful than Churchill's in wartime, but with very personal advisors, who stayed with him for four or five years, and who he rewarded with knighthoods and baronetcies. Sir Alec Douglas-Home had less personal relationships, and became more like Attlee in his delegation and aloofness.

Developments in the last century have altered the prime minister's rôle. The most obvious is universal suffrage. Since the vote was extended to everyone, the prime minister has become more a personification of his party, and general elections have

[1] *See Daily Telegraph*, August 9, 1960.

become, in the public's eyes, a contest between two men—with all others subordinate. There are apparent exceptions to this: for instance in 1945 Bevin with his trade union and war-time career was in many respects a more popular and familiar figure than Attlee. But the pressure of publicity tends to concentrate increasingly on one man: in the 1964 election the Tories were embarrassed by the failure of Sir Alec to become 'Mr Tory', while Wilson was undeniably 'Mr Labour'. Once in office, the press are apt to ascribe all government policies to the boss. The prime minister's special relationship with the electors can short-circuit the powers of the cabinet, and television has given him a powerful new medium for direct access: it is one of which he has to be careful—for it infuriates parliament to be by-passed—but which can be invaluable in a cabinet issue such as Suez, or the Common Market.

Secondly, the government machine has expanded. The growth of the Cabinet Office, the spread of cabinet committees, and the wider scope of the civil service, have all brought a larger concentration of information to 10 Downing Street. The more complicated government becomes, the greater the need for co-ordination, and in the nervous system of Whitehall, the prime minister's office must be the ganglion. Much of the influence of a premier depends on sheer information, and the messages that go to and from the limbs of government. A cabinet minister may know less about the current of Whitehall than the civil servants at 10 Downing Street.

The prime minister is not perhaps as central as he might appear from outside: one might suppose that it would be like being in the middle of the piazza of St. Peter's in Rome, where the pillars, which from the edges seem confused and patternless, suddenly come into line, all pointing to the centre. But that is not, it seems, an accurate analogy: for the area of muddle and fog, so noticeable in government departments, is equally apparent here, and the prime minister, like the cabinet, is constantly having things done *to* him—by America, Russia, the TUC, the Opposition, and even his colleagues, which spoil any pattern he may be devising, and provide further muddle. The more puzzling of the prime minister's actions, like those of the Chancellor or the Foreign Secretary, become less astonishing if one takes into account the vital significance of muddle. But nevertheless, 10 Downing Street is much better informed than other departments, which sets the prime minister apart from his colleagues.

Thirdly, summits, jet planes and international telephones have made foreign affairs much more a matter of exchange between chief executives, rather than foreign ministers or ambassadors. And the heads of smaller countries are at least as sensitive about dealing with the chief executive: to the world at large, Wilson *is* Britain. In theory the Monarch is supposed to take over much of the ceremonial representative rôle: in practice, every visitor knows where the power lies, and wants to be there.

The prime minister's powers and patronage show every sign of increasing under Harold Wilson. For when he took office he not only had a very strong hold on his party: he also enjoyed a unique personal knowledge of Whitehall and how to manipulate it. And he had a team of ministers who were deficient in experience of government, after thirteen years' opposition. Whether he liked it or not—and there is little sign that he disliked it—Wilson had to establish firm control in order to get the machinery moving; and he made no secret of the fact that, for the first months at least, he would adopt a more Presidential system of working, with a strengthened Cabinet Office as the central power-house.

MEN AROUND WILSON

> All men must count with you, but none too much.
>
> *Kipling, quoted by Wilson.*[1]

> Most men can be understood by their friends, but Wilson makes a virtue out of his social seclusion.
>
> *Iain Macleod, 1964.*

In October 1964, backed by a tiny parliamentary majority of five seats, Wilson moved into 10 Downing Street. In spite of the recent storms his position of leadership was now stronger than that of any prime minister since Churchill's. The Conservatives accused the Socialists of being a 'one man band', and it was true that Wilson dominated his party. Yet he seemed surprisingly unsure of his position, and after years in various wildernesses, he seemed still apt to imagine people to be against him. He was scrupulously careful to satisfy all party pressures, and to pay off all obligations—Left, Right, North, South, Welsh, Scottish, Miners, Dockers, Old Guard, New Guard. He appointed a few surprising outsiders, including Sir Charles Snow, the novelist-scientist, and Alun Gwynne Jones, the defence journalist. But his big govern-

[1] To Godfrey Smith, in 'Notes for a Profile of a Politician', *Sunday Times*, February 1964.

ment of 107 seemed much less like a 'New Frontier' than a careful balance of old party people. He did not seem exactly vengeful against his old critics, the able young Gaitskellites and Brownites who had fought his election eighteen months ago. But he was determined to offset them with plenty of trade-union ballast and left-wing counterweight. This preoccupation with balance was in keeping with his political career, but there were some who suggested that now, at last, Wilson could afford to be bolder.

Wilson was determined to maintain his isolation. Characteristically, he did not move in to live in Downing Street until three weeks after the election—after his son's half-term holiday. He intended, clearly, to run his government much more personally, and to make it much easier for him to intervene and 'cut corners' (a favourite phrase), but he did not set about establishing a visible private court or a 'garden suburb' (as Lloyd George's advisors, in the garden of Number Ten, were called). His government was so constructed and balanced that he himself would often hold the balance, and could if he wished 'divide and rule'. In particular, he had split the Treasury between Brown and Callaghan; and this ensured that Wilson could have a decisive say on economic affairs.

Wilson was able to make full use of the existing machinery of 10 Downing Street, and the small groups of civil servants who act as the prime minister's advisors. American observers have been astonished by the compactness of the staff at Number Ten—only a handful of private secretaries compared to the massive White House secretariat. The building itself has the easy, informal atmosphere of a well-run country house, with secretaries strolling about like permanent guests and friendly butlers hovering by the door. But it is an undeniably efficient organisation—one of the few which have not succumbed to Parkinson's Law. It is quick, adaptable, capable suddenly of working through the night: everyone from the typists to the switchboard operators is handpicked. The telephone is always answered immediately—it never rings twice (at the Foreign Office, on the other hand, even the telephones seem afflicted with absence of zeal: they often ring for two minutes). The Number Ten switchboard can get Tokyo in ten minutes, and keeps track of anyone who might be needed, so that the prime minister has only to mutter a name into the telephone for the man to be found. No one who has worked at Number Ten ever seems quite satisfied with the organisation anywhere else.

The most effective mechanism for 'cutting corners' is the 'Number Ten Network'—the web of ministers' private secretaries, each exceptionally well-informed, each keeping in close touch with the prime minister's private secretaries. They work the bush-telegraph of Whitehall, and it is they who actually transact much of the day-to-day business, lubricating the wheels between ministers, and adding their own advice on the way. 'Master's in a bit of a worry over that second bit of the Bill,' one of them might say: 'do you think your master might get it changed?' And the other private secretary will consult *his* master, carefully taking the political temperature, and reporting back the result.

At the heart of this network are the four private secretaries to the prime minister, who sit in offices round the cabinet room, and observe all the comings and goings, the ups and downs, and the ins and outs. The private secretaries are the pick of the younger civil servants. Usually in their late thirties, and destined for high promotion, their task is an odd combination of the menial and the crucial; on a prime minister's tour they can be seen trooping out of the aeroplane at the tail end of the party, carrying the red or black boxes which contain state papers, and standing in a huddle together with the typists. But they also draft telegrams, keep contact with ministers, collect and assess the news and reactions, and frequently give advice. 'The private secretaries function in a very heady atmosphere,' said Richard Neustadt, the White House advisor.[1]

The prime minister's principal private secretary occupies a very special position, for he becomes the main link with the politicians and the civil servants outside, and the guard at the door, who can grant or deny access to the great man. His influence varies with personalities, but the more the prime minister tends towards presidential powers, the more important this proximity becomes. In Macmillan's court, Sir Timothy Bligh, a tall, bold ex-naval officer and Wykehamist, had the job of PPS for over five years; and with his political sense he had an influence greater probably than that of many ministers. His position was thus inevitably resented by older civil servants, and when he was appointed to a new job in the Ministry of Defence he instead left the civil service altogether, to become a director of the Thomson Organisation. He was succeeded in the meantime by a smaller and more unobtrusive PPS, Derek Mitchell, from St. Paul's School and Christ Church, with a quick sceptical mind, a subtle humour

[1] *Sunday Times*, November 8, 1964.

and the shrewd observation of people which marks the best civil servants. Mitchell, at this pivot of government, served under Sir Alec Douglas-Home and then under Wilson, and represented as much as anyone the continuity of administration under very different policies.

To add to this traditional retinue, Wilson imported some of his own personal staff from Transport House, the Labour headquarters—led by Mrs. Marcia Williams, his loyal and able secretary, who was installed with the new post of 'political and personal secretary'. The awkward meeting of the two retinues represented in the most dramatic form the conjunction of the two sides of a prime minister's job—the committed party politician on the one hand, and the chief civil servant on the other. And the fierce loyalty and dedication of the party followers contrasted all the more strongly with the smoothness and sophistication of Downing Street, with its huge drawing-rooms, butlers, banquets and chandeliers.

Outside the actual building of Number Ten, Wilson had his own special advisors in key points in Whitehall, and the 'battle for Wilson's ear' became a large source of speculation. Most evident was the irrepressible Hungarian economist, Dr. Thomas Balogh, installed at the Cabinet Office, with direct access to Number Ten. Equally visible was George Wigg, with the non-commital job of 'paymaster general' and a room in Number Ten. Wigg had been a loyal Wilsonite, and led the lobbying for him in the election of the leader. He is a big man who looks like a well-fed but angry turkeycock, and who addresses people, like Dr. Johnson, as 'Sir', or 'Ma'am'. He was a regular soldier for twenty-five years, and has a passion for details of costings and organisations—particularly the army—and a capacity to turn almost anything into a political issue, which had its triumph in the Profumo Affair which he first brought to light.

Other surprising and picturesque figures, from outside Whitehall, are consulted by Wilson from time to time. They include Arnold Goodman, the huge and shrewd lawyer, expert on television syndicates, who is a master of politico-legal problems; Lord Boothby, the gravel-voiced ex-Tory MP and television personality, who seems to act as a kind of worldly advisor; Professor Kenneth Wheare, the Australian expert on government at Oxford; and Siegmund Warburg, the banker, who provides an important link with the city. Apart from these, there are scores of economists, businessmen, journalists and quasi-political people outside the confines of Whitehall with whom Wilson talks and listens. He likes, too, to have go-betweens to help him make easy contact with new men, for he is not a good ice-breaker. Many claim to have his ear, and there is no doubt that Wilson, like Kennedy, is a great listener. He absorbs everything, remembers everything, and brings up tiny titbits of talk years afterwards. But there is not much sign of any paramount influence on Wilson, except perhaps his father. Nearly every prime minister before him has felt the need for a close confidant—as Sir Alec had Lord Oakshott, Macmillan had Lord Egremont—but Wilson seems to have kept his solitary strength even in the strain of the top job.

For Wilson, a special importance rests with his press secretary, for no prime minister in this century has paid so much careful attention to newspapers and television. Characteristically he picked a loyal old friend from Liverpool, Trevor Lloyd Hughes, who had for fifteen years been political correspondent of the *Liverpool Daily Post*, and had thus frequently reported Wilson's doings and speeches at Huyton. He is a straightforward and conscientious journalist, not obviously radical or left-wing in his opinions, while enjoying Wilson's particular trust. But most of Wilson's public relations are conducted by himself and, again like Kennedy, he has established very close relationships with political correspondents. He calls them by their Christian names, remembers articles they wrote years ago, frequently gives informal off-the-record briefings, and invites them to parties in Downing Street. (It is characteristic of Wilson's determined homeliness that he has sent out ordinary small invitation cards, with 'Mr. and Mrs. Harold Wilson' written in.) This cosy closeness has its dangers for journalism, for it can effectively tame or silence correspondents who are dependent on the intimate briefings: and Wilson has been charged with managing news to suit his political interests.

In his speech-making, too, Wilson is insistent on doing it himself, and he has made frequent cracks against Sir Alec's team of speech-writers. In Downing Street, he has had to make use of the private secretaries and his own assistants for drafts and ideas, but he likes to write out the beginnings and ends of speeches himself, and to dictate the rest, in his own dry style, to his secretary. The 'midnight oil' is much less apparent in his speeches, and he has learnt to bring out prefabricated phrases with a sound of spontaneity. When in his provocative opening speech to parliament he used the word 'leper', it sounded like a burst of uncontrollable anger; but the phrase had been rehearsed and discussed for days before.

With an ease which astonished his staff, Wilson fitted into the clothes of the premiership, and acquired the boldly personal behaviour which the job requires. He seemed to have picked up hints from several prime ministers and presidents—a touch of Attlee in his handling of cabinet and his laconic conversations with colleagues; a strong sense of Kennedy in his way of thinking aloud and scattering ideas; a suggestion of Roosevelt in his 'fireside' TV personality; an element of Lloyd George—but a more cautious Lloyd George—in his hold on his party and his colleagues. Few politicians have moved so quickly and so easily—in a bare eighteen months—from a situation of unknown, ineffectual opposition to one of apparently confident premiership. And in spite of his tiny majority, and his uncertain term of office, and the setbacks of the first months, the influence of Wilson's austere and lonely dynamic is visible already in the bureaucracies which occupy the following chapters.

7

LABOUR

This party is a bit like an old stage coach. If you drive it along at a rapid rate, everyone aboard is either so exhilarated or so seasick that you don't have a lot of difficulty.

Harold Wilson (frequently).

The risk is that one will tend to get caught up in the sheer exhilaration of making decisions and in the desire to make them fast, forgetting the point about getting them right.

George Brown, 1964.

There is nothing socialists nationalise so well as socialism.

Ignazio Silone.

OVER the past hundred years, the majority of British governments have been predominantly Conservative, as the chart on page 109 suggests. After 1959, when the Labour party lost for the third time in succession, the left had nightmares of permanent eclipse—as in France, Italy or Canada—and it was hard to foresee how the Conservatives could ever be defeated. During the 133 years since the Reform Bill there has been a fairly equal swing between left and right: but in the years since 1884—which marked the beginning of universal household suffrage—the right has predominated. 'In the course of the 75 years up to 1959', wrote Richard Crossman soon after that defeat, 'there have been only two left-wing governments with outright majorities, the Liberal government elected after the Boer War and the Labour government elected after World War II. Moreover, within five years each of these left-wing governments had lost most of its popular support'[1]

After 1951, the most obvious factor helping the Conservatives was the increasing prosperity, allowing people to move up in the world. 'Broadly what happened over the decades', wrote Dr. Mark Abrams after the 1959 election, 'was that the already slight middle-class vote for Labour fell still further; and, secondly, and

[1] *Labour in the Affluent Society*, Fabian Society, 1960.

more importantly, the considerable minority of manual workers not voting Labour expanded a little more.'[1]

In 1962, with the collapse of the Common Market talks, the diminishing national morale, and the dwindling prestige of Conservative ministers, public opinion once again began to set against the Tories. The morale of the re-united Labour opposition increased, and it seemed that the British public was expressing once again a surge of radical feeling and impatience. It was not the same kind of radicalism that occurred in 1906 or 1945; there was less sense of injustice or wickedness, less demand for any kind of social revolution. The public were much more concerned with efficiency and 'modernisation'—the catchword which both parties began to use. The dislike of Conservatives—as the 1964 election showed—was not matched by a corresponding enthusiasm for the Labour Party. The pendulum, had nevertheless, begun to swing again.

But both parties seemed uneasily caught between two conceptions of the fight. In the first place, there was the old antithesis between two British parties—the 'ruling class' on the one side, claiming all the weight of tradition, experience and inherited skill, and the revolutionary party on the other, supporting the underdogs and committed to drastic social reform. In the second place there was the newer battle between two parties, each representing a broad mixture of voters, competing in terms of efficiency and competence, as the most effective national administrators—a pattern more like American elections before the Goldwater debacle. In this context the Labour Party was awkwardly placed, for while it had abandoned, or outgrown, much of its revolutionary appeal, it had not very visibly acquired the qualifications of an alternative administration. And this uncertain position was reflected in the mixed character of its leadership. As the Tories were roughly divided between their new 'technocratic' leaders and their old aristocracy, so the Labour party had a mixture of their technocrats and their working-class leaders.

The Labour party, like all European socialist groups, has experienced the painful change from being a passionate 'movement', united against a straightforward enemy, to becoming a major political party, involved in divisions and compromises. It has watched the old bogy America become the crucial ally. Nationalisation, which was once a shining Utopia, has become

[1] *From* 'Class Distinction in Britain', *The Future of the Welfare State*, Conservative Political Centre, 1958.

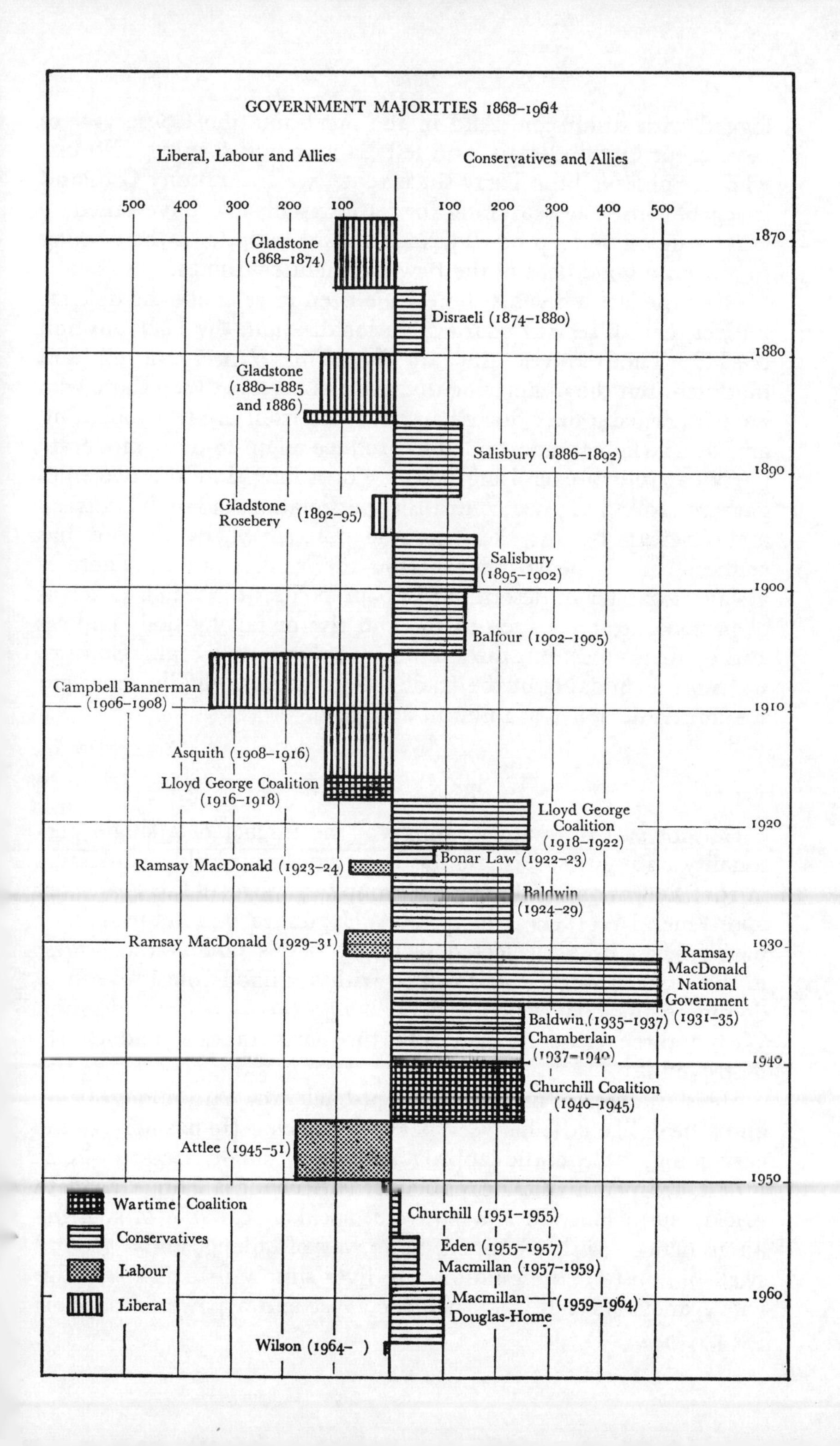
GOVERNMENT MAJORITIES 1868–1964
Liberal, Labour and Allies
Conservatives and Allies
500
400
300
200
100
100
200
300
400
500
1870
1880
1890
1900
1910
1920
1930
1940
1950
1960
Gladstone (1868–1874)
Disraeli (1874–1880)
Gladstone (1880–1885 and 1886)
Salisbury (1886–1892)
Gladstone Rosebery (1892–95)
Salisbury (1895–1902)
Balfour (1902–1905)
Campbell Bannerman (1906–1908)
Asquith (1908–1916)
Lloyd George Coalition (1916–1918)
Lloyd George Coalition (1918–1922)
Bonar Law (1922–23)
Ramsay MacDonald (1923–24)
Baldwin (1924–29)
Ramsay MacDonald (1929–31)
Ramsay MacDonald National Government (1931–35)
Baldwin (1935–1937)
Chamberlain (1937–1940)
Churchill Coalition (1940–1945)
Attlee (1945–51)
Churchill (1951–1955)
Eden (1955–1957)
Macmillan (1957–1959)
Macmillan Douglas-Home (1959–1964)
Wilson (1964–)
Wartime Coalition
Conservatives
Labour
Liberal

fogged with disillusion. And in the meantime the Conservatives have crept up windward, and left Labour sails sagging. 'No one who has observed the Party since 1951', wrote Anthony Crosland in 1956, 'furiously searching for its lost soul, can have failed to sense a mood of deep bewilderment.' And in spite of the coming to power, a good deal of the bewilderment continues.

Over the last ten years there have been rows about the defence budget, health service charges, nationalisation, the H-bomb and NATO. The motives and arguments have been varied and muddled. But the underlying division has been between those who have inherited a fiery doctrinaire attitude from pre-war socialism, and those who are determined to produce an up-to-date, moderate party capable of exercising power. For a long time the two sides gathered round the two contrasting personalities of Hugh Gaitskell and Aneurin Bevan: then, for the past six years, the left has centred round the strident person of Frank Cousins. There is always a danger of describing Labour politics too much in terms of personalities: the men in the end rise or fall by their policies and by their votes. But the character and career of Frank Cousins, the most formidable of the trade union leaders, vividly represent the authentic spirit of militant socialism.

FRANK COUSINS

Cousins is a dramatic example of the impact of a single personality on politics. His rise has been extraordinarily swift. Early in 1956 he was one of the sixteen group secretaries of the Transport and General Workers' Union (TGWU), unheard of in the Labour party. Then he was elected secretary of his union—the largest in the western world—and armed with a million votes[1] set out to dominate the conference and challenge the Labour leadership. Within three years he had split the party in two, and nearly destroyed it.

He is a tall, erect man, with swept-back grey hair, a long stride, and a beak-like nose between heavy spectacles. He has none of the easy-going, phlegmatic approach of most union leaders: he is proud, temperamental, capable of swift changes from charm to prickly suspicion. He is a powerful speaker, capable of swaying an audience—with a clipped, tense way of talking, and a ground swell of constant indignation. He lives simply in a flat with his wife Nancy—herself a left-wing socialist and a powerful support

[1] *See* p. 122.

to her husband—and at all his big speeches she can be seen watching him intently from the gallery.

Cousins comes from the hard old school of union leaders. He was brought up in Doncaster, one of ten children of a miner, went into the coal-pit at fourteen, and later became a driver: 'I was one of the new young men who drove motor vehicles.' He argued in the transport cafés and saw at close quarters the hunger and unemployment of the depression. He has described in a television interview with John Freeman the incident that most stood out in his mind:

> I happened to be in a transport café on the Great North Road, when a young couple came in, with a child in a nearly broken down pram. They were walking from Shields—Shields was one of the places that was hit in the slump, Mr Freeman, as you will remember. They were walking from there to London, because the man understood he could get a job in London. They came into the café and sat down, and they fetched a baby's feeding bottle out, and it had water in it. They fed the baby with water, and then lifted the kiddy's dress up—it was a small baby—and it had a newspaper nappy on. They took this off, and wiped the baby's bottom with it and then they picked up another newspaper and put that on for a fresh nappy. I think if ever I felt a resentment against the system it was on that occasion. I thought somebody ought to do something about it.[1]

He began reading socialist writers, and his young wife encouraged him to militancy: 'We did a lot of our early hand-holding in front of political meetings.' Before the war he became a full-time organiser for the lorry-drivers—still one of the most militant groups in Britain. After the war he moved to the headquarters of the Transport and General Workers, and came sharply up against Arthur Deakin, who infuriated him with his right-wing anti-Communist views (though Cousins himself has never been a Communist). Many trade unionists were softened by the post-war Labour Government, but Cousins kept his militancy, with new outlets. And so, when he strode on to the General Council of the TUC in 1956, with his million votes, he changed electrically the atmosphere of the council-hall. A swing was in fact already occurring in several unions towards the rejection of Britain's H-bomb and more wholesale policies of nationalisation; and the TGWU

[1] *The Listener*, October 26, 1961.

was already hostile to the policy of wage restraint which Deakin and Tiffin had maintained. But Cousins gave the impression of having provoked a crisis single-handed. In his attitude to the bomb and to NATO, Cousins often appeared to be muddled and equivocal: but in this he echoed many of his followers. His indignant oratory appealed to that large slice of the party who felt that they had been cheated of their Utopia by the post-war compromisers, and that Britain's peacemaking rôle had been sacrificed to the Atlantic alliance.

Cousins thus came into immediate conflict with the leader, Hugh Gaitskell, who was trying to steer his party to a more moderate policy of public ownership, and urged the retention of American bases.

The conflict reached its climax at the Labour party's conference at Scarborough in October 1960. Cousins, with large union support, renewed his attack on Gaitskell's defence policy: 'If the two mad groups want to have a go at each other', he said: 'we want no part of them.'

Cousins' motion, rejecting any defence policy based on nuclear weapons, won by 3,282,000 votes to 3,239,000. But Gaitskell stood firm, and by the 1961 conference the mood had changed: when Cousins got up to propose once more, the rejection of nuclear weapons, he was met with jeers and shouts, and his motion was defeated by 4,309,000 to 1,891,000—a fair comment on the fickleness of block votes.

Cousin's militancy was tempered with time, and his rift with Gaitskell was bridged in 1962, when he enthusiastically applauded Gaitskell's anti-Common Market speech. He became more involved in committees, and sat on the council of the Department of Scientific and Industrial Research (DSIR). But he still maintained his political fire and his position on the left, and his perpetual suspicion of the Tories.

When Wilson became leader, it was clear that he enjoyed Cousins' approval, as a man with whom the unions could do business. Wilson, no doubt mindful of the electorate's fears, was discreet about the connection beforehand, but brought Cousins into his cabinet as Minister of Technology. The appointment itself was a shrewd one, for it involved Cousins, as the chief spokesman for the unions, in some of the most crucial and awkward of the unions' problems—particularly automation, his special interest. But the important fact was Cousins's presence in the cabinet, together with that of two other leaders from the left,

Anthony Greenwood and Barbara Castle. For it brought the militant trade union attitudes into the heart of government, and the closeness of Cousins to Wilson offered the prospect of solidarity and trust between the unions and the party.

RUNNERS-UP

Emotion in a politician has become a dirty word.
George Brown to Quentin Crewe, December, 1963.

In the tense struggle for the leadership, in February 1963, between Wilson, Brown and Callaghan, none of the candidates represented the patrician or public-school element that had previously been so evident. All three came from very modest beginnings and, in different ways, represented the rank-and-file of the party.

George Alfred Brown, now deputy prime minister and Minister of Economic Affairs, represents the most crucial ingredient. He comes from the solid working-class core: his father was a lorry-driver, he was born in Peabody Buildings in Southwark, and he had the self-made beginnings which are at a premium in Labour politics. He became an organiser for the Transport and General Workers Union (in left-wing politics, unions often take the place families take in Conservative circles in providing a political stable). He was on the right of the left, and first made his name, just before the war, by attacking Sir Stafford Cripps at a Labour conference. After the war he joined the rush into parliament when he was only thirty-one, became known as the 'boy orator' and was soon noticed: by 1951 he was Minister of Works. Since then, in voluble opposition, he has never ceased to be noticed. In 1960 he succeeded Bevan as deputy-leader, and continued as second-in-command under Wilson.

Brown's relationship with Wilson has, not surprisingly, been tense, since Wilson stood against Brown for the position of deputy in 1962, and for leader in 1963; but Brown has a vigour, a warmth and a political fire which, though frequently embarrassing, gives him a special importance, and makes him hard to exclude or ignore. He is the kind of full-blooded, temperamental politician who in the eighteenth century would have been loved for his faults; but coming into an age of conformity, caution and television, he is much more vulnerable. He is an extrovert, jolly man, different in almost every way from Wilson. He has a round, owlish face, large eyes behind big spectacles, and a full rich voice which emits cosy and expressive remarks, frequently introduced by 'Brother!' which has come to be his political catch-phrase. He has a reputation for plain speech and political courage: he is in the blunt, bull-necked mould of his early hero, Ernest Bevin.

'I react emotionally and not intellectually,' Brown has said. He has an impressive mind, which has constantly surprised his more academic colleagues, and he is well able to keep track of (for instance) the more abstruse areas of nuclear strategy. But his emotional attitudes, his instinctive loves and hates, are constantly bubbling up. He is a man of immense enthusiasm and unlike Wilson, whose drive is very intellectualised and subtle, Brown conveys a sense of physical stimulus and excitement, which infects his co-workers with love or alarm. He is a sociable, convivial man, and in company he is easily over-excited, to the embarrassment of his colleagues, and particularly Wilson. A climax occurred on the night of the death of Kennedy, when Brown was called away from a party to pay tribute to the dead president on television. At the studio he was aggressive and argumentative, and on television he spoke warmly but sincerely about his friendship with 'Jack' and 'Jackie' in a way that offended his more reverent colleagues. Wilson insisted that he should make a private apology to his fellow MP's, which did not improve relations between the two leaders. 'In humiliating his lieutenant', commented Iain Macleod in *The Spectator*, 'Mr Wilson acted shabbily and with incredible clumsiness.'

Once in office, with the challenge of building up the new Department of Economic Affairs, Brown—while remaining quite unpredictable—was able to show the extent of his drive. His first large achievement was the signing of the 'Statement of Intent' towards an incomes policy, by the government, the employers and the trades unions. It was here that Brown's mixture of emotion and intellect was most useful; for he could both work out the tricky negotiations, and also give them a sense of Churchillian urgency and drama which made both sides responsive. He could convince the employers that he was not at all opposed to growing profits, and that he understood their problems (he is, after all, a governor of Repton, an expensive public school). And he could also, with more difficulty, speak to the trades unionists (Lord Collison and George Woodcock) as one worker to another.

James Callaghan, the Chancellor of the Exchequer, the third

in the troika, has less brilliance and more steadiness than George Brown, and stands in the firm centre of his party. He is a big, relaxed, handsome man with, like Brown, an enthusiastic manner, and boyish expressions like 'Oh boy!' and 'My goodness!' which sound strange and refreshing in the Treasury building. His background is very naval, and he still has the swinging stride of a man on a quarterdeck. He was brought up in Portsmouth, his grandfather was a ship's carpenter, his father went to sea at fifteen and became a chief petty officer, and he himself rose in the war to be a lieutenant on the battleship *Queen Elizabeth*. It is his niceness, uprightness and open-ness, rather than his intellect, that has made him so respected by Labour MPs. He began his career as a tax officer when he was seventeen, serving in the Inland Revenue of which he is now the boss. He became Assistant Secretary to the Inland Revenue Staff Federation, under Douglas Houghton, now his cabinet colleague (no cabinet has ever had such personal knowledge of the interior of the bureaucracy). After his war service, Callaghan went into parliament, and held for three years the modest job of parliamentary secretary to Transport, where he left his mark by introducing the zebra crossing, and for a few months was parliamentary secretary to Lord Longford (then Lord Pakenham) at the Admiralty. In opposition he was an effective attacker, with an old-fashioned finger-wagging style of debating, and a confident aggressiveness which sometimes degenerated into swashbuckling; he rose to be Shadow Colonial Secretary—where he made a large mark—and eventually to be Shadow Chancellor. His knowledge of economics sometimes seemed hazy, though augmented by Oxford dons. As the elders of the party retired or died, so Callaghan emerged as an essential element; when Gaitskell died in 1963 Callaghan was persuaded that it was his duty to stand against both Wilson and Brown. It was an embarrassing decision, and Callaghan polled only a sixth of the votes. But Wilson kept him as Shadow Chancellor, while carving off some of his economic territory for George Brown—thus producing a delicate balance of powers. Callaghan, with his simple, breezy approach to politics, often seems at a disadvantage against the bulldozing drive of Brown, or the subtlety of the Oxford intellectuals. But he has large political support, and an earthy sense which give him a fairly safe place in the party.

This was Harold Wilson's cabinet in February 1965, with their ages, education and jobs:

Minister	*Office*	*Education*
Harold Wilson (48)	Prime Minister	Wirral Grammar; Jesus, Oxford
George Brown (50)	Economic Affairs	Secondary school
Michael Stewart (58)	Foreign Office	Christ's Hospital; St. John's, Oxford
James Callaghan (52)	Treasury	Portsmouth Northern Secondary
Herbert Bowden (60)	Leader, Commons	Secondary school
Lord Gardiner (64)	Lord Chancellor	Harrow; Magdalen, Oxford
Denis Healey (47)	Defence	Bradford Grammar; Balliol, Oxford
Sir Frank Soskice (62)	Home Office	St. Paul's; Balliol, Oxford
Arthur Bottomley (57)	Commonwealth Relations	Council school; Toynbee Hall
Anthony Greenwood (53)	Colonial Relations	Merchant Taylor's; Balliol, Oxford
William Ross (53)	Scottish Office	Ayr Academy; Glasgow University
James Griffiths (74)	Welsh affairs	Bettws Council School; Labour College, London
Lord Longford (59)	Lord Privy Seal	Eton; New College, Oxford
Douglas Jay (57)	Board of Trade	Winchester; New College, Oxford
Fred Peart (50)	Agriculture	Wolsingham Grammar; Durham University
Richard Crossman (57)	Housing	Winchester; New College, Oxford
Douglas Houghton (66)	Duchy of Lancaster	County secondary school
Ray Gunter (55)	Labour	Elementary school
Fred Lee (58)	Power	Elementary, Nat. Council Labour Colleges
Tom Fraser (53)	Transport	Lesmahagow Higher Grade School
Frank Cousins (60)	Technology	King Edward School, Doncaster
Barbara Castle (53)	Overseas Development	Bradford Grammar; St. Hugh's, Oxford
Anthony Crosland (46)	Education	Highgate; Trinity, Oxford

LABOUR LEADERSHIP

Behind the three contenders, the Labour party still has a large admixture of middle-class public-school intellectuals, who occupy key jobs in the government and who provide much of the administrative expertise. Many of them are on the right of the party, old allies of Gaitskell, and suspected by the left of betraying socialist ideals; but in power, the doctrinaire divisions become more blurred, and issues become submerged in practical problems. The Labour intellectuals are linked with Oxford, as firmly as Kennedy's were linked to Harvard, and Oxford high tables provide the same kind of common background to these new

Socialists as White's Club and country houses provide for Old Tories. The don-politician has emerged as a recognised type, and the new importance accorded to economics has brought more and more dons into government. At the heart of this world are the group of ex-Oxford politicians who now occupy top positions in the government. Harold Wilson (economics), Lord Longford (politics), Douglas Jay (economics), Richard Crossman (philosophy), Anthony Crosland (economics) were all Oxford dons; and Roy Jenkins (economics), Denis Healey (greats), Lord Gardiner, Sir Dingle Foot and Sir Frank Soskice (law) and Anthony Greenwood all have the equipment and background of Oxford. This enormous infusion from Oxford (and particularly from Balliol, which provided nearly a quarter of the cabinet), stemmed from the Oxford Union debates and the political fervour of the twenties and thirties. It has brought to the Labour party a sophisticated and cultivated element, more urban and entertaining than their Tory equivalents. During Gaitskell's lifetime many of them used to congregate in the 'Frognal Set', but since Wilson's leadership, and the strains of office, they are a less obviously coherent group. The common high-table language nevertheless remains, almost as distinctive, and as maddening to outsiders, as the Tory schoolboys' slang: Six Labour ministers were Presidents of the Oxford Union, and two of the Cambridge Union. Seven out of the eleven cabinet ministers who went to Oxford took first-class degrees. The politics of the dons varies widely, and some men like Harold Wilson and Denis Healey are lone wolves. But most of them are 'revisionists', bored by old party dogma, rather ill-at-ease in trade union gatherings, and looking towards the kind of classless, half-American society outlined in Anthony Crosland's books, particularly *The Future of Socialism.* 'We must learn to be gay', he wrote in that book, 'to appreciate the arts, to burn down the Victorian prejudices.'

Among the younger Oxford men, the two most evident and interesting are Anthony Crosland and Roy Jenkins, both very sophisticated all-rounders with tough political ambition. Jenkins is a subtle and witty intellectual, the son of a Welsh miner, who seems more like a writer than an engaged politician; he is in fact an enterprising journalist and a biographer of Asquith, whom in some ways he resembles. But he has a hidden spring of aggressive energy, which emerges in his tennis, his driving and his political involvement: in Wilson's government, despite earlier rifts, he became Minister of Aviation, faced with the problem of the Concord.

Crosland appears likewise extended between two worlds, of detachment and involvement. He is a tall, handsome man with a boyish face and a brusque, rather petulant attitude. He has expensive tastes, a beautiful wife, and a sharp, vivid style of writing, which shows itself in his important studies of socialism. But he is also capable of immense industry and political dedication. He helped Gaitskell produce a critical report on the Co-op movement, and was the cutting edge of the championship of Gaitskell against the Left. He became, in January 1965, the Minister of Education.

Oxford does not only produce right-wing Socialists, and four Oxford members of the cabinet are more associated with the Left—Richard Crossman, Barbara Castle, Anthony Greenwood and Anthony Wedgwood Benn. The most intricate of them is Richard Crossman, the philosopher and theorist who has been one of Wilson's chief lieutenants. He has been an explosive controversialist, throwing out ideas in the *Daily Mirror*, *The Guardian* or *Encounter* on everything from the cold war to mass media, and his earlier views on education brought terror to Oxford high tables, until to their relief he turned up in the less controversial areas of housing. Wedgwood Benn and Greenwood, both sons of MPs and both obsessively political, enjoy the acclaim of the rank-and-file of the party. Barbara Castle, the red-haired crusader from Bradford, has always enjoyed a special popularity, with her own mixture of passion and brains, and she will appear later as the Minister for Overseas Development.

But these more showy and sophisticated socialists are a misleading guide to the character of the Labour Government, for much of the influence and power rests with men who left school early and climbed up doggedly and steadily through the party, who will crop up in later sections of this book. Most of them are less evident in debates, at elections, or on television, but they are as important to the Labour Party as the squires and majors to the Tories; for they enjoy the trust and loyalty of the party workers and rank-and-file. This core of the party is perhaps most ably represented by Herbert Bowden, who for nine years was Labour Chief Whip in the Commons, until in 1964 he became Leader of the House of Commons and Lord President of the Council (who is neither Lord, nor President, and has no Council). He joined the Labour Party, at the age of eighteen, in Leicester, and became MP for Leicester twenty-two years later, in 1945. In the opposition years he worked unceasingly and sternly to keep the party together first under

Gaitskell and then (perhaps more gladly) under Wilson. He is an austere man, with a dispassionate moustache; he lives in Streatham and, like Wilson, has not been attracted by the more glamorous aspects of politics. He remains close to Wilson and, like many ex-Chief Whips, he is regarded with awe by his colleagues.

Another central influence is Douglas Houghton, a small bespectacled man of sixty-six, whom Wilson put into another nebulous position, Chancellor of the Duchy of Lancaster, and in effect general trouble-shooter. Houghton, like other successful men first cut his teeth as an income-tax inspector, a job which (as for Paul Chambers of ICI) gave him an intimate knowledge of financial operations. He knows the workings of Whitehall almost as thoroughly as George Wigg knows the army, and he first became known to the public in the wartime broadcasts about taxation called 'Can I help you?'; his knowledge was broadened when he became Chairman of the Public Accounts Committee in 1963, in succession to Wilson, where he could cross-question civil servants and probe into their doings. Houghton is not an exciting man, but he has a cosy reliability, and an exhaustive knowledge, which is invaluable to a party with long inexperience of government.

There are many varied backgrounds in the Cabinet, and just outside it, which represent almost every strand of British socialism, from all over the country. There are two Scotsmen: Tom Fraser, Minister of Transport, who left school at fourteen to go down the mines, worked his way up through the miners' union and came into parliament during the war; and William Ross, Secretary for Scotland, a former schoolmaster, in the centre of his party, who was born in Ayr, married a girl from Ayr, lives in Ayr and represents Ayr in parliament. There are two Welshmen, both almost stage Welshmen, full of hwl and talk. James Griffiths, now 74, a venerable ex-miner, seems to belong to an earlier age of Labour politics, with his rich pulpit voice. Ray Gunter, Minister of Labour, is often depicted as a kind of new Aneurin Bevan—he comes from the next-door village to Bevan's, in Monmouthshire, and occasionally, as at Scarborough in 1961, he can bowl over the party with his oratory. He does not have Bevan's intellect, but he has some of his presence, and he is adept at negotiating in a big-minded, no-nonsense way.

Many members of the Labour government, after the long opposition years, have had little opportunity to test their talents, and many present a confused and faint image in the public mind. Such, for instance, are 'the Freds'—Lee, Peart, Willey and Mulley.

Fred Lee, from Lancashire, worked as an engineer at Metro-Vickers, and became involved in politics through the Amalgamated Engineering Union: his appointment was one of the more surprising of Wilson's choices, but he has been one of Wilson's loyallest allies. Fred Peart, as Minister of Agriculture, was more expected: he was PPS at the Ministry twenty years before, and his joint interests have been agriculture and science (he is one of the few Labour MPs who have a science degree). He is an ex-schoolmaster, who first became active in politics at Durham University: he has been a close supporter of Wilson, and like him opposed the Common Market. The other Freds are both Oxford barristers —a commoner breed in parliament. Fred Willey, as Minister of Land and Natural Resources, is a very able lawyer, who gained a first and a Soccer Blue at Oxford, and came into parliament in 1950, when he was forty. Fred Mulley, deputy secretary of Defence, has had a rarer kind of career: he is the son of a labourer, and took his first degree, in economics, while a Lance-Sergeant and prisoner of war. He took another (a first) as an adult scholar at Christ Church, and then became a barrister and MP, specialising in European defence. His earthy background and his spectacular career provide an important link between the dons and the demagogues, or between (for instance) Denis Healey and George Wigg.

NEW SOCIALISTS

The two main streams of Labour—university men and trade unionists—still flow: but the division is less clear-cut than before the war. There are fewer young intellectuals, and some trade unionists win university scholarships, and go into parliament younger, like Reginald Prentice from the TGWU, who went to the London School of Economics and became Minister of State for Education.

Much of the young leadership is made up by the middle-way, middle-class socialists from Oxford and Cambridge. They came into the party with less fire, less sense of outrage, than the pre-war converts: many took to the left after 1945, when the Labour party was already established. Many of them are highly efficient and formidable. It is not always easy to differentiate the Oxbridge Socialists, sipping whisky in Kensington, from the Bow Groupers, or to detect what mysterious force, if any, has pulled one group to the left, the other to the right. There are radicals and reactionaries on both sides, and the words left and right often seem to lose their meaning. But under their moderation, the socialists still have a rooted dislike for upper-class attitudes, and even though they arrange to send their sons to public schools, they have a more fervent belief in the need for social change.

After sixty years the Labour party is beginning to evolve its own dynasties and traditions and among the very young socialists, family groups seem to be taking shape. The son of one ex-Labour MP, Hilary Marquand, has married the daughter of another, Elwyn Jones: the son of Douglas Jay has married the daughter of James Callaghan. Young Gaitskells and young Pakenhams remain in a socialist set, and some schools (most notably the North London Collegiate girls' school at Edgware) seem to acquire a socialist tradition. But there is little sign of the Labour party acquiring the dynastic continuity of the Conservatives or Liberals, and the bulk of the leadership comes from new blood, impelled into socialism by idealism or some personal experience.

Round the outer fringes of the Labour party is the jumble of personalities, pressure-groups, factions, and magazines which make up the left wing of the party. They include such exotic figures as Ian Mikardo, the loud, square leader of the former 'Victory for Socialism' group; Konni Zilliacus, the Finnish-Swedish pamphleteer; Sydney Silverman, the small, bearded lawyer from Liverpool; or the group of fiery young radicals centring on the *New Left Review*, an intellectual quarterly. The most vocal of the radicals is Michael Foot, the political heir to Aneurin Bevan and the third Foot brother in the Labour party—a stooping, haggard-looking man, with swept-back hair who on the platform always manages to appear in the last paroxysms of rage—though off-stage he is charming and kindly.

LABOUR AND LIBERALS

Why are you so obsessed by Mr Grimond?

George Brown to Robin Day, October 16, 1964.

The difficulties of the Labour party, caught between the left and the right, the past and the future, are not helped by the stubborn survival of the Liberal party, which keeps on bobbing up between the two big parties, offering a more daring and forward-looking vision, with special attention to Europe. Since 1922, when the coalition headed by Lloyd George broke up, the

the Liberals have dwindled, eclipsed by the new massed forces of Labour backed by trade unions. But since the early fifties they have shown fitful signs of revival, cropping up in odd corners of the country, particularly in the 'Celtic Fringe' of Wales, Devon and Cornwall. Liberal supporters range from old Whigs who detest all Tories but cannot accept the rough trade-union tactics of Labour, to young technicians who feel that the Liberal party offers an exciting and classless future. In 1964 the Liberals surprised most forecasters by collecting three million votes, though only nine members of parliament.

A large part of the Liberal revival is the achievement of one engaging and inexhaustible man, Jo Grimond. He is a convincing leader for a revivified party. He is tall and handsome, with a shock of grey hair which falls over his face as he becomes excited: he addresses mass meetings with a boyish, school-prefect manner, full of enthusiasm for the future and get-up-and-go. His career has been impeccably Liberal: the son of a Fifeshire laird, he went to Eton and Balliol, and married the daughter of Baroness Asquith, now the formidable high-priestess of Liberalism. Grimond thus came into the midst of the Liberal establishment, which includes Lady Violet's son Mark, the most intellectual of the Liberals, and Lord Byers, a business-man and former chief whip of the party. Grimond's gay oratory and easy exuberance have a suggestion of too-good-to-be-true, and he can sometimes reduce complicated problems to absurd oversimplifications. But he is the most exciting mass speaker, in the flesh or on television, in British politics; and he has precisely the kind of drive and enthusiasm that the other parties most need.

The tiny band of Liberal MPs have been made more significant by the smallness of the Labour majority, but they remain without much impact on parliament. The greater source of influence of the Liberals is their effect on the two big parties, both worried by the encroachments of Liberal voters. For where both parties are old-fashioned and overburdened with pre-war attitudes, with manifestos which do not necessarily reflect live issues, the Liberals have shown the impatience of three million electors. While the big parties are still cluttered with class totems, the Liberals are not associated either with grouse moors or the Red Flag, and they conjure up the new classless, Americanised world of Wimpy bars, coffee-bars, Marks and Spencer, Vespas, minimotors, television and airport lounges.

For Labour voters who are bored with old issues like steel

nationalisation, the Liberals are constantly beckoning, and among Labour MPs there are a cluster who, either secretly or publicly, have Liberal sympathies. The most vocal are the journalist-conspirators, Desmond Donnelly and Woodrow Wyatt, who keep pressing for a new Lib.-Lab. alliance, and enjoy the position of being able, if they wish, to topple their party. The Labour leaders always deny that they will take any notice of the Liberals, but the popularity of this bright little party, like a boutique between two department stores, is a constant reminder of the dangers of old-fashioned political salesmanship.

WHO RUNS LABOUR?

The Labour party does not have the same careful façade of loyalty and leader-worship as the Conservatives: the frictions between its components are more obvious, and paraded in broad daylight every autumn. But a certain discreet confusion nevertheless surrounds the eventual decisions. The Labour party like the Conservatives is not quite what it seems, and its outward decisions do not altogether correspond to results.

First comes the Trade Union Congress, early in September (as we will see in Chapter 33) which propounds its own resolutions. Next, a month later, comes the Labour Party Conference, where trade unionists are joined by delegates from constituencies, which elects the National Executive of twenty-eight—twelve from trade unions, seven from the constituency parties, one from the professional organisations, five women and the three officers. The constituency votes act as a kind of popularity poll, led by well-known and left-wing figures. At the top of the hit parade in December 1964 were:

1. Anthony Greenwood
2. Anthony Wedgwood Benn
3. Barbara Castle
4. Richard Crossman
5. James Callaghan
6. Tom Driberg
7. Ian Mikardo

A month later the Parliamentary Labour Party—consisting entirely of Labour MPs—meets. In opposition, they elect twelve members of their 'Shadow Cabinet', which reveals a very different order of popularity, with moderate men near the top. But when the party is in office, they elect only a Chairman and Vice-Chairman of the parliamentary party. In 1964 the Chairman was Emanuel Shinwell, the veteran ex-cabinet minister who is still, at eighty, a spry and influential figure.

The national executive and the shadow cabinet coexist painfully in opposition. Their conflict arises from the origins of the party, for when it was founded in 1900, the Labour party was little more than the 'political arm' of the Trade Union Congress, with small prospect of power. But as the movement swelled, grew into a parliamentary party and eventually gained office, so inevitably the actual legislators became the centre of power. The frictions were in 1961 exacerbated by Cousins' attacks and at one time threatened to sever the link between the TUC and the Labour party.[1] In theory the parliamentary party is supposed to be responsible to the annual conference and its executive: but in practice the shadow cabinet successfully remained independent. 'By a continuous process of flattery', wrote one Labour critic,[2] 'delegates to Conference are persuaded that they are the ultimate wielders of sovereignty; while simultaneously the leadership is working to ensure that they are never in a position to wield it.'

The chairmanship of the Labour Party Executive rotates every year, and is thus much less influential than the Tory chairmanship. This gives more importance to the general secretary at Transport House, the drab and austere party headquarters in Smith Square, a stone's throw from the Conservative Central Office. For eighteen years the secretary was Morgan Phillips, the shrewd, Welsh organiser who was constantly depicted by Tories as the eminence grise of the Labour party. In 1962 Phillips was succeeded by another Welshman, Len Williams—a big, heavy man with a benign face and silvery hair, whose rock-like presence is reassuring rather than exciting. He worked his way up as agent in the provinces and unlike Phillips, who was always passionately political, he is much more an administrator than a politician. His organisation at Transport House is far less professional and smooth than the Tory headquarters. Its devoted party workers in their bare offices seem to belong to an earlier age of politics, and the party still has a suspicion of modern devices, including advertising and public relations. Impatient reformers have often despaired of Transport House being able to organise a successful

[1] *See* p. 108.

[2] Ivan Yates: Power in the Labour Party, *Political Quarterly*, July, 1960. p. 308.

electoral campaign, and after the Leyton by-election was carelessly lost in January 1965 there were new demands for reorganisation.

A LABOUR ESTABLISHMENT?

> The accursed power which stands on Privilege
> (And goes with Women and Champagne and Bridge)
> Broke—and Democracy resumed her reign:
> (Which goes with Bridge and Women and Champagne).
> *Hilaire Belloc (after the 1906 general election).*

After thirteen years in opposition, it is never easy to visualise a party in power, for the whole apparatus of government, publicity and fame conspires to present one party as masterful, important and dignified, and the other as petty and grasping. The government men make quiet understatements, while the opposition make loud, wild accusations based on inadequate information. But once the last, crucial votes have swung the balance, the whole machinery turns from right to left. The civil servants, the toastmasters, the photographers, the headline-writers, all suddenly switch their devotion, enthusiasm and curiosity, and a chauffeur with a government car is always waiting outside ('I think the one concrete reward of power', said C. P. Snow in September 1964,[1] 'is always having transport laid on)'. The same man who, the day before, seemed ineffectual and even rather silly, now appears, with the magic touch of power, to be vibrating with inner authority. A kind of charisma descends, a mysterious assumption of importance, so that even silliness becomes significant. And the people who before might have appeared quite unqualified or unprepared to govern, now seem natural rulers.

When the Labour party took office in October 1964, the trappings of the Tory 'Establishment' suddenly became unimportant, and diplomats and lobbyists who were used to hanging on the coat-tails of power faced a new and unfamiliar territory. The traditional settings, romanticised and dramatised by novelists from Trollope to Snow, the country-houses, St. James's clubs, Belgravia drawing-rooms, were essentially part of the Tory world, and now their inhabitants were powerless. The Labour party had no such obvious social centres or networks; only a few of the new ministers —such as Lord Longford, Lord Snow, Roy Jenkins or Sir Dingle Foot—were clubmen or country-house-goers. Where was the

[1] *The Sun*, September 21, 1964.

new Labour 'Establishment' to be found? Most Labour MPs had only one club—the House of Commons.

The Labour ministers, in general, are more domestic and home-bound than their Tory equivalents—partly because they are less wealthy, partly, it seems, because they are more content with home life, and particularly with their wives. In the Labour government intellectual women at last came into their own. There were not only a record number (seven) of women in the government, including a woman whip, but there were also more intellectual wives, including Lady Longford, the biographer of Queen Victoria; Lady Taylor, an ex-governor of Holloway Jail; Caroline Wedgwood Benn, a novelist; Susan Crosland, a journalist; Jennie Short, a headmistress; and Peggy Jay, an expert on London government. There are no left-wing streets near Westminster, as Lord North Street, Smith Square, or Eaton Square are Tory streets. Most of the Labour politicians' houses are scattered in the suburbs; but a favoured area is Hampstead Garden suburb, the trim model village, with cottagey houses and neat hedges, between Hampstead and Golders Green in North London. Among its inhabitants are Emanuel Shinwell, Fred Willey, Sir Eric Roll, Patrick Gordon Walker and (until recently) Harold Wilson; and close to it is the Manor House Hospital, a favourite left-wing institution, founded for industrial workers on early socialist principles, with patients helping in the work of the hospital. The Hampstead Garden suburb has no pubs, or restaurants.

But there is in some respects a stronger, more identifiable Labour 'Establishment' than the Conservative one—based on a common Oxford background, a common intellectual confidence, and a sense of camaraderie which comes from long opposition and past defeats. The resemblances can be misleading, and the shared Oxford experience—as with Gaitskell and Wilson—does not necessarily make friendship easier: the complaints of Labour politicians about each other are at least as damaging as those of the Tories. But among many of the Labour intellectuals there is the easy assumption of the in-group, and a telephone network of acquaintances who feel they have been through a struggle together, and that they are 'one of *us*'.

With this compact circle of Oxford intellectuals, the smooth parties and the sophisticated language, it might seem that the election had only replaced one tight group by another. But underneath this more visible 'Establishment' there is another more austere and critical network which is much more concerned with votes, decisions, policies and the bare bones of power. It is a network of civil servants, party workers, trade unionists, who never see each other except at work or at business lunches, and whose talk is too dull to be in a novel. Between the traditional social world and this grey subterranean world there is always mutual suspicion and worry—each feeling that the other holds the real power. And at the centre of the austere non-social world is the remote presence of Harold Wilson.

8

CABINET

The most curious point about the cabinet is that so little is known about it.

Walter Bagehot.

There can be no friendship between the five top men in a cabinet.

Lloyd George.

THE most important job of the political parties is to provide cabinet ministers. For whatever parliament may do, it is on this room-full of men that the week-to-week running of the country depends, and as the state becomes increasingly involved in industry, planning and monetary control, so the area of cabinet decisions becomes larger. The cabinet has no legal existence, beyond the powers of the ministers of the crown. It is merely a committee, whose very existence was originally secret, formed from the majority party in the House, to carry out the business of government. Yet it is in theory the crucial joint on which power ultimately rests. In Bagehot's words: 'A cabinet is a combining committee—a hyphen which joins, a buckle which fastens, the legislative part of the State to the Executive part of the State.' But in the following century the buckle has had to join a far greater area of execution.

When an MP is appointed to the government, the post office engineers arrive at his home to install a green 'scrambler' telephone, which can only be unscrambled by other ministers and senior civil servants. He is provided, too, with a big red leather-covered box with a royal crest and 'ER' on top, (which no spy, incidentally, could fail to notice) to carry state papers. The red boxes and green telephones mark the secret, self-contained world of government to which nearly every member of parliament aspires.

A government consists altogether of about a hundred politicians—about a sixth of the members of parliament—including such unlikely people as the Solicitor-General for Scotland and the Captain of the Yeomen of the Guard; and on top of these hundred there are about fifty 'parliamentary private secretaries' who are unpaid, but who are expected to be loyal to their ministers. The ministers themselves cover a large range. In 1964 there were thirteen 'Ministers of State' (a title created by Churchill during the war) each under a major cabinet minister, who earn from £7,625 to £5,625 a year. There are also ministers who, although heads of important departments, including Pensions and Aviation, are not in the cabinet: they earn £8,500 a year. But it is the cabinet which forms the heart of decisions, and between the cabinet and the rest lies a great divide. Non-cabinet ministers are occasionally invited to the cabinet room to discuss their own topics, but the ordeal is alarming.

It is in the cabinet that the strands of democracy, in theory, meet. Ministers have to run their ministries, attend cabinet and cabinet committees, report to parliament when necessary, and answer privately the complaints of MPs and of their own individual electors. They are company chairmen, barristers and public relations officers all rolled into one, and if not many of them are good at all three, that is not altogether surprising. For this they earn £8,500 a year, together with an official car, parties and travel.

The cabinet meets in a long white room at the back of 10, Downing Street, with awkward pillars in the middle, looking out on to a garden. Ministers leave their hats and coats on a rack outside, labelled 'Lord Chancellor', 'Paymaster-General', etc., and sit down in front of green baize, pens and paper, on a long curved table, the shape of an aeroplane wing, designed so that the prime minister can see everyone. The prime minister—who also often uses the room as his office—sits in the middle, facing the Horse Guards. The prime minister opens the meeting, and ministers address their remarks to him, referring with careful impersonality to their colleagues: 'I can't quite agree with the Lord Privy Seal . . .'

The agenda for the cabinet is short and brisk—the final result of a long process of distillation by the reports of the civil service. It contains usually only about seven or eight points. Once a week is the Foreign Secretary's report, and a report on government business in parliament. The remaining matters are usually brought up either by the prime minister, or by two ministers who have failed to agree. Discussion in cabinet is brief, and speech-making strongly discouraged. 'Democracy means government by discussion but it is only effective if you can stop people talking,' said Lord Attlee. The performance of ministers in cabinet is often quite different to their performance in parliament, or in public.

There are no rules about how to run a cabinet, and each prime minister has his own method. It is the prime minister's main job to sum up discussions at the end, moulding the cabinet's view into one. Discussions hardly ever come to a vote: if there is disagreement, they return to the subject, giving and taking until either a majority view takes shape, or—in extremity—a minister resigns.

'The job of a prime minister,' Lord Attlee has said, 'is to get the general feeling—collect the voices. And then, when everything reasonable has been said, to get on with the job and say, "Well, I think the decision of the cabinet is this, that or the other. Any objections?" Usually there aren't.'[1]

Cabinet ministers used to be overworked, underpaid, and deprived of most of the ordinary pleasures of life. Since the Lawrence Committee's recommendations have been partly adopted, this is no longer so. But even before the increase, very few willingly give up their burden. What keeps them there (I felt more strongly after talking to them) is not so much the love of power—many of them seem to have no clear idea what they want with it—but simply the love of being at the heart of information and events. As Iain Macleod has put it:

> I think the main attraction for me at least, and I believe this would be true of most politicians, is of being at the centre of the web, not just of having power, although I think that is part of the make-up of most politicians, but in the end, in every decision of importance that affects this country, the threads of those decisions run into the cabinet room.[2]

Probably only four or five of them have serious ambitions to be prime minister—in many respects a more agreeable and manageable job than running a department. With many of the others, the fear of losing power is probably as great a motive force as the desire to gain it, and it is this which helps to make resigning so difficult, and so rare. Inside the cabinet room, a minister is caught up in the stream of events, sure of his importance as part of a team, and linked to the network of reassuring officials. Outside, he is alone: and the loneliness of a would-be resigner is terrible. To quote Macleod again:

> Sometimes it's on something that events can't necessarily prove whether you're right or wrong: it's a matter of judgment

[1] Francis Williams: *A Prime Minister Remembers*. 1961. p. 81.

[2] Interview with Malcolm Muggeridge. Granada TV, October 16, 1961.

. . . you come more and more into yourself. You withdraw more and more really from your friends, and then you think it out yourself in the watches of the night, and then you come to whatever conclusion you may have to.

However exhausting or compromising the job, having it is less agonising than losing it. Patrick Gordon Walker has described the experience of *not* being a cabinet minister:

From being at the very heart of affairs and among the few dozen best-informed men in the world, faithfully served day and night, he suddenly reverts to obscurity. The invitations which a short time before had seemed to flow in embarrassing numbers, thin to a trickle. Workmen arrive to remove the direct line which linked him to his Private Office and by which he could control a great Department of State.[1]

And this is how another Labour minister, Lord Longford, described his losing office in 1951, thirteen years before he regained it in 1964:

. . . One had to get used to being out of things, to not being run after. For years one had been leaving word with head porters of clubs, head waiters at restaurants, stewards at golf clubs, that 'there may be a call for me from the ministry'. One was never exactly sorry if by some odd chance there was, although naturally one was profuse in apologies to one's friends, and modest protestations that 'I'm quite sure it's not of the slightest importance'. One's own telephone number was ex-directory, of course. Now the whole world could know one's number without taking advantage of the priceless secret; and porters, waiters and stewards had to be very old friends or new chums to join in the make-believe of an emergency call.[2]

CABINET-MAKING

Duchess of Omnium: 'You ministers go on shuffling the old cards till they are so worn out that one can hardly tell the pips on them.'
The Prime Minister: 'I am one of the dirty old cards myself.'

Trollope: The Prime Minister.

The prime minister in cabinet is officially no more than 'primus

[1] *Encounter*, April, 1956.
[2] Lord Longford: *Five Lives*, 1964. p. 10.

inter pares'—just one member of a committee. But in fact, apart from his political advantage, he has a strong hand. He is chairman of the committee: he appoints it, summons it, guides it, and can eventually dissolve it. Cabinet-making is probably the most important part of a prime minister's job, but the scope is not perhaps as great as might appear from outside. Political rivals cannot easily be demoted, discontented followers must be pacified: left and right must be balanced: the heads of the most important departments cannot be constantly changed: and the number of first-class men in parliament does not give unlimited choice. Cabinet reshuffles are apt to be acclaimed by the press either for their cunning or their aptness: if a man is put into a job which is manifestly unsuitable it is acclaimed as a shrewd political manoeuvre. In fact, the press seems inclined to overestimate the government's cunning; cabinet reshuffling, like so much else, is often more a question of expediency than planning, and prime ministers, like the Duke of Omnium, are well aware of being themselves part of the pack. But a cabinet remains very much the expression of a prime minister's personality. He can introduce peers, and if necessary make peers: he can bring in ballast and he can—up to a point—demote his rivals.

Most prime ministers like to have a kind of ballast in their cabinet: this is how Attlee described it:

> 'You've got to have a certain number of solid people whom no one would think particularly brilliant, but who between conflicting opinions can act as middlemen, give you the ordinary man's point of view . . . You remember little George Tomlinson. I can remember a thing coming up which looked like a good scheme, all worked out by the civil service. But I wasn't quite sure how it would go down with the ordinary people so I said "Minister of Education, what do you know of this." "Well", says George, "it sounds all right, but I've been trying to persuade my wife of it for the last three weeks and I can't persuade her".'[1]

Most people, including Harold Wilson, agree that a cabinet of twenty-three is too big.[2] It has fluctuated over twenty years between fifteen and twenty-three: but since the eighteenth century—as Professor Parkinson has duly noted—it has steadily

[1] *A Prime Minister Remembers*. p. 81.
[2] For the details of Wilson's 1964 Cabinet, *see* Chapter 7.

got bigger. It is much bigger than the American cabinet of ten, though about the same size as the French, German or Italian. Several pressures have blown it up; one has been the need to satisfy groups, by embracing symbolic ministers—such as the Secretary of State for Scotland, the Minister of Labour (to placate the trade unions) or the Minister of Agriculture (to pacify farmers). Another difficulty is that parliament refuses to take non-cabinet ministers seriously, so that departments with heavy pressure of work, the Foreign Office and the Treasury, have to have two in the cabinet. But also there are personal and political pressures: once a man reaches the cabinet, it is painful and dangerous to demote him. (It is a situation echoed in business, where the size of boards has likewise swelled. ICI has twenty-two directors, and Unilever has eighteen. Both are inclined to use their boardrooms as partly honorific affairs, leaving the real planning to a triumvirate.) Big cabinets lead inevitably to formality, and any meeting of twenty has severe limitations. 'The cabinet's a very good jury,' one minister said: 'but it's no good at drafting, which is half the battle: that all has to be done beforehand.'

Inside a big cabinet there nearly always develops an 'inner cabinet'—the small group of ministers who are consulted by the prime minister beforehand and who prepare and guide the decisions. Most prime ministers have had one: Churchill's was open and obvious like a court; Attlee operated in a more impersonal, green-telephone way; Macmillan's was not very finite, but roughly embraced four or five. Harold Wilson has a fairly obvious inner cabinet, centring on the Treasury building—George Brown, James Callaghan, Michael Stewart and Denis Healey—but with his strong personal method of government, the influence of men outside the cabinet, including George Wigg, Thomas Balogh and Sir Solly Zuckerman, may often be greater.

A large cabinet inevitably gives more scope to unofficial groupings. The most potent and celebrated of all recent 'inner cabinets' was Sir Anthony Eden's in the months before Suez: and the power of this cabal has since raised serious doubts as to the effectiveness of the full cabinet. Eden's group consisted of Macmillan, Lloyd, Hailsham and Anthony Head: it was among these that the preparations for the Suez invasion were made, while others like Butler were kept ignorant. Another forty-two years must elapse before the full story emerges: but it is clear that the inner cabinet was able virtually to present cabinet with a *fait accompli*, before they had time to object. 'It seemed to make nonsense of the cabinet,' said one former permanent secretary: 'I still don't understand how it could have happened.'

CABINET NETWORK

Behind the full meetings of cabinet, which only occupy about four hours a week, lies the mechanism known as 'the cabinet network', centring on the cabinet office—an office which has become more important under the premiership of Harold Wilson. The office was established by Lloyd George in 1916, to provide a secretariat for cabinet meetings: before then no record was kept, and two ministers would often embarrassingly interpret the same decision in opposite ways. 'The cabinet,' wrote Lord Hankey, 'often had the haziest notions of what its decisions were.' Lord Hartington's private secretary wrote to Gladstone's PS in 1882: 'My chief has told me to ask you what the devil was decided, for he be damned if he knows.'[1] After the war the cabinet office became permanent, under Sir Maurice Hankey (later Lord Hankey), who was its secretary for nineteen years—under Lloyd George, Bonar Law, MacDonald, Baldwin and Chamberlain.

There have only been four Secretaries of the cabinet—Hankey, Bridges, Brook and Trend. Sir Norman Brook (now Lord Normanbrook), who retired in 1963, combined the positions of Head of the Home Civil Service with Secretary to the Cabinet; but after his retirement the jobs were separated, with Sir Burke Trend as Secretary to the Cabinet, and Sir Laurence Helsby as Head of the Civil Service. The separation made a bigger gap between decision and execution, and cut the Head of the Civil Service further off from the prime minister. But it diminished the pressure on a single man. 'The problem is how to maintain the focus,' as one man in the cabinet office said, 'without overloading the system . . . the greatest threat to orderly government is the sheer pressure of business.'

The Secretary to the Cabinet is at the centre of the focus, and he is responsible for the organisational nexus behind cabinet decisions. 'Cabinet papers' are kept circulating by messengers with red boxes, giving details of matters which one minister wants to bring up, and providing a secret newspaper for Whitehall: a box goes each day to the Queen. From the cabinet papers the prime minister, with the help of Trend compiles the cabinet agenda,

[1] Lord Hankey: *Diplomacy by Conference*. 1946. pp. 53–67.

which is itself an important instrument of policy, playing up some issues and ignoring others.

Sir Burke Trend—as his name suggests—is perfectly qualified for this delicate position in the middle of the web. He has the reputation in Whitehall for having one of the smoothest of all the smooth 'Rolls Royce minds' in the civil service, and he is one of the Treasury mandarins who, as we shall see later, discreetly occupy key points in the administration. He came from a minor public school, Whitgift, took a scholarship to Oxford, and a double first in Mods and Greats. From there he moved up through the civil service, and after the war reached the influential job of Principal Private Secretary to the Chancellor of the Exchequer—first Dalton, then Cripps. By 1956 he was Deputy-Secretary to the Cabinet, under Brook, and since then has been continuously at the hub.

In the cabinet network, too, is the ring of 'cabinet committees', which are offshoots of the full meetings. They are in theory so secret that no one outside the office is supposed to know which are sitting, when and about what. They are appointed by the prime minister (though they do not necessarily include him) for getting particular things done; they include the Defence and Overseas Policy Committee, the Home Affairs Committee, and a Future Legislation Committee. They have the same powers as the cabinet itself, provided they are unanimous, but crucial questions are always passed to the full cabinet. But the more unmanageable the full cabinet, the more important the committees, and gradually they have taken over a large part of the business of government. Small committees inevitably supersede large ones.

The summoning and briefing of all these committees falls on the cabinet secretariat. It is a machine of legendary speed, and its elegant offices in the Old Treasury Building, leading through to 10 Downing Street, constitute a kind of flywheel of government. Some people feel that the cabinet office has become too much the centre of all information, and that its influence gives too much power to civil servants. The civil servants insist that they do no more than co-ordinate the departments: 'All we do,' said one man in the cabinet office, 'is to try to collect together people to get things *done*. Somebody's got to do it.' But (as we have already observed, and as we shall see again) in the modern pattern of government co-ordination is a large part of power, and the gap between policy and execution is a large one.

The most crucial job of the secretariat is the translation of cabinet decisions into action. Trend or his deputy sit at every cabinet meeting, and it is their cabinet minutes which are the frail but effective paperchain between the green table and the departments of state. 'I used to check up to make sure that cabinet decisions were carried out,' said Rab Butler: 'but I soon realised it wasn't necessary. The civil servants come out of their caves like hungry animals and gobble them up.' (What happens inside the caves we will see in subsequent chapters.)

The cabinet secretary miraculously transmutes the rambling arguments into a neat summary of conclusions, with all the art of the de-personalised civil servant. First-person speeches are changed into *oratio obliqua*, angry arguments are transformed into mild disagreements, doubt and muddle become dignified imponderables: and two hours of disjointed discussion is boiled down to a few coherent paragraphs. 'It takes a bit of the personality out of politics,' said one cabinet minister in 1961, 'when Quintin loses his temper, it appears in the minutes as "Lord Hailsham voiced dissent".' The cabinet minutes are the process by which the arguments of twenty men with twenty views are distilled into a collective government, with an apparently solid front of policy. The cabinet office see themselves, above all, as the guardians of the principle of collective authority. If, as can happen, the prime minister tries to push through a personal decision, it is their job to say 'but shouldn't you consult your colleagues?'

THE BUCKLE

It is easy to explain how the cabinet, in theory, is the buckle which joins the two parts of the State, and the core of collective responsibility. Many people might imagine that the cabinet sat down twice a week and said to each other 'What shall we do next?' But one has the disturbing impression that the cabinet are so busy having things done *to* them that they are more often saying, 'How do we get out of this one?' And between the cabinet's policies and its actual execution intervenes the huge area of national and international pressures, conflicting forces, and the nebulous influence which will appear elsewhere in this book, which can only be described as Muddle.

In Victorian times, when parliament sat for half a year, and the government had no hand in industry, the cabinet could have collective discussions about prisons, post offices and foreign policies. But since the first world war the area has spectacularly increased to the point that public investment is over 42% of the whole, and the government has a finger in nearly every industry. As a result of the pressure, as early as 1931 Sir Maurice Hankey drafted a memorandum, saying that ministers should only bring points out to the cabinet after they had been thrashed out with the departments concerned: and since then the cabinet has become more involved in particular disputes and less in general problems. In 1961 for instance the cabinet was repeatedly concerned with Northern Rhodesia, not so much because of a passionate collective interest in African welfare, but because Iain Macleod and Duncan Sandys could not agree.

The sheer pressure of work on a minister, rushing between parliament, his department and cabinet, has strained the buckle apart. There has always been a prejudice against having a 'Minister of Thought', who could sit back and survey long-term problems, and a cabinet minister usually lacks influence if he is detached from a department. But the resulting pressure on individuals has worried most prime ministers since the war. The solution of 'double-banking' in the heaviest ministries—the Foreign Office or the Treasury—helps to relieve the burden, but increases the scope for friction and muddle. When a problem falls between two or three departments—as most serious problems do—their discussion often goes by default: and some of the most disastrous cabinet decisions seem to have arisen as much from lack of discussion as from positive folly. The slowness to come to terms with the problems of the Concord and overseas bases has been not least because few ministers had time to think about them.

The underlying principle of the cabinet, as of all the committees which spread out from it, is that of collective authority or collective responsibility: and this apparent solidarity distinguishes the British government, for instance, from the American—in spite of the fact that American ministers are not elected representatives. 'While in Britain cabinet ministers must support a common policy.', wrote Lord Attlee, 'in America these subordinates of the chief executive are apt to speak with a diversity of voices.' From the outside, the appearance of unanimity, with the help of the cabinet office and its rigid secrecy, is fairly well kept up. But how collective the responsibility really is, is very doubtful. As ministers become more absorbed in their departments, fighting each other for money, the dividing line between their individual departmental responsibility and their collective governmental responsibility becomes very blurred. Sir Ivor Jennings, the constitutional authority, believes that, as departments become more complex and cabinets busier, so the scope for individual ministers within their departments inevitably becomes greater; and a new minister can impose a new policy without much cabinet consultation: he has observed how they nowadays refer less to 'Her Majesty's Government' in their speeches, and more to 'I'. The pressure of time in the cabinet makes it easier for ministers to run their departments without interference: 'It's probably true that as the civil service becomes more complex,' said one Tory minister, 'so ministers become more independent: on the whole the cabinet's prejudice is to let the minister do what he wants with his department.' Many of the ministers are running departments with investments much bigger and more complex than any private company: and for most of their time they are managing directors absorbed in their separate business, which we will see in later chapters.

But while ministers are left more to themselves, their areas of business have overlapped more and more: and the government has become increasingly involved in investment and planning on a national scale. It is difficult, whatever your political doctrine, to think about railways without also thinking about roads, fuel and industrial growth: and the government finds itself no longer running a group of separate businesses, but one large investment company in which one business affects all the others. With the current new wave of planning and attempts at wage restraints, this necessity becomes more apparent, and government requires not a group of separate managing directors, meeting to discuss disagreements, but a single board of directors, with time to make plans for the future. But the ministers are so pressed with work and absorbed in departments, that the opportunities for correlation are few. Gordon Walker remarked in 1956 how, in the Labour government, the pressure of meetings set 'a strict upper limit upon the extent of democratic planning'. As Lord Plowden tactfully put it, in his report on government expenditure: 'There should be an improvement in arrangements to enable ministers to discharge their collective responsibility for the oversight of public expenditure as a whole.'[1] In other words, the cabinet must try to work together.

At a time when Britain needs more than ever before a governing committee with time to plan and look ahead, the cabinet is

[1] Cmd. 1432 of 1961. p. 12.

caught between the exacting treadmills of parliament and departments. Most ministers agree that the system is strained, and that the jobs of managing director, parliamentarian and cabinet minister are becoming more incompatible: but what the outcome will be in this fluctuating political scene is very uncertain. There may be more 'manager-ministers', who run their departments without much care for parliament, or more 'ministers of thought'. There may even be businessmen brought straight into the government on the American pattern, and made life peers to give them a seat in the Lords. But whatever happens, it seems that the buckle is being pulled apart, and that the traditional system of combining parliamentary accountability with collective responsibility is splitting at the centre.

9

PRESS

> Burke said there were Three Estates in Parliament; but in the Reporters' Gallery yonder, there sat a *Fourth Estate* more important far than they all.
>
> *Carlyle.*

> Were it left to me to decide whether we should have a government without newspapers or newspapers without a government, I should not hesitate for a moment to prefer the latter.
>
> *Thomas Jefferson, 1787.*[1]

> Doctors bury their mistakes. Lawyers hang them. But journalists put theirs on the front page.
>
> *Anon.*

SINCE the long fight for the freedom of the press in the eighteenth century, the importance of newspapers as the Fourth Estate, informing and reflecting public opinion, has become unquestioned. The need for independent journalists, free comment and access to information, are agreed by all politicians and administrators. But during the twentieth century several new forces have threatened this independence. Of these, the most spectacular and dangerous is the commercialisation and concentration of newspapers, which reaches probably its most extreme form in Britain.

The British press has the biggest circulations in the Western world. The nearly five million copies of the *Daily Mirror* has no equal in America or Europe, and Britain is so compact and homogeneous that the same newspapers can arrive on the same morning from Land's End to John O' Groats. The British still read more newspapers per head than any other people: they read nearly twice as many newspapers as the Americans (though American papers are fatter), and only the Swedes approach the British consumption.

Four vast newspaper groups now share most of the British popular press between them. These are the four groups of morning

[1] Quoted by Sir William Haley: *The Formation of Public Opinion.* Haldane Memorial Lecture, 1958.

newspapers with their chairmen or owners, and average circulations in the first half of 1964:

Daily		*Sunday*	
International Publishing Corporation (Cecil King)			
Mirror	4,951,488	*Sunday Mirror*	5,052,906
Sun	1,472,279[1]	*People*	5,578,963
Associated Newspapers (Lord Rothermere)			
Mail	2,423,424		
Sketch	923,130		
Beaverbrook Newspapers (Sir Max Aitken)			
Express	4,275,643	*Sunday Express*	4,307,856
Telegraph Newspapers (Michael Berry)			
Telegraph	1,312,582	*Sunday Telegraph*	660,635

Other dailies:	
The Times (Gavin Astor)	242,234
The Guardian (Laurence Scott)	271,739
Financial Times (Lord Robbins)	149,689
Other Sundays:	
News of the World (Sir W. Emsley Carr)	6,224,174
Sunday Times (Lord Thomson)	1,240,239
The Observer (The Observer Trust)	714,424
Sunday Citizen (Co-operative Press)	283,370

This concentration has caused both the opportunity and the crisis of British journalism: for it has put newspapers into the class of heavy industry, on the scale of steelworks and shipyards, and it has led to intense and still growing commercialisation, which has reached a new climax in the past four years. Up till January, 1957, for eighteen years, a truce existed: newsprint was rationed by the Government, and papers agreed not to compete in size, but only in circulation. The smaller papers survived on the advertisements which the bigger ones had to reject. Then newsprint became free, just at the time when commercial television was becoming successful. The top papers in each field—the *Express*, *Mirror*, *Times* and *Telegraph*—became fatter with advertising, while the bottom papers, like the *Herald* and *Chronicle*, became thinner. In 1960 and 1961 one of the nine national dailies and three of the national Sundays collapsed: and two more dailies and one more Sunday lost money heavily. The harsh competition induced a wave of mergers and take-overs, and the concentration of papers—many of them linked with television companies—settled round the four big groups. Since then, the financial

[1] For October, 1964.

position of newspapers has somewhat improved, but the concentration remains.

The impact of the brute strength of big business on the old organs of free speech presents capitalism with an awkward dilemma. Many Western countries face a newspaper crisis: in America dependence on advertising is still greater; in Italy most newspapers are subsidised by political parties or industrialists. In Australia or South Africa a weak and commercialised press (with the exception of the *Rand Daily Mail*) is unable to stand up to a strong government.

While free enterprise may have produced good cars, refrigerators and aircraft, it is much more doubtful whether it has produced good newspapers: yet government involvement strikes (in theory) at the heart of free expression. In Britain this dilemma has come abruptly to the forefront, and the mergers and take-overs of the past six years have produced an unparalleled situation, precipitated by two competitive tycoons, Cecil King and Lord Thomson of Fleet. The events which produced it were so bizarre and illuminating that they must be briefly recorded.

CECIL KING

> The only job I ever wanted was chairman of the *Daily Mirror*. And here I am. *Cecil King to Jocelyn Stevens, 1961.*

The most spectacular result of the mergers was the supremacy of Cecil Harmsworth King, Chairman of the International Publishing Corporation. He controls only four national newspapers—the *Daily Mirror*, the *Sunday Mirror*, the *Sun* and the *People*: but between them they have about 40 per cent of the national circulation. His group also owns the six leading women's magazines, two hundred other magazines, a nine per cent holding in Associated-Television, a controlling interest in the huge Reed Paper Group, and *Debrett's Peerage*. It is the largest publishing house in the free world, and when put together with the Reed Paper Group, it is (by assets) the tenth biggest company in Britain. It was the extent of King's power which precipitated the setting up of a Royal Commission on the Press in 1961.

Cecil King is a large, rumpled man of six foot four with a brusque, dominating manner: he is one of those tycoons who deal with correspondence by returning letters with comments scribbled at the bottom. He lives simply among fine furniture and silver, in a house in Chelsea: he finds people difficult and usually goes to bed at ten. He works on the ninth floor of the red glass *Daily Mirror* cliff in Holborn, looking over St. Paul's in an office with an open-grate fireplace; his status-symbol is the solitary chimney at the top of the building.

The most important fact about Cecil King is his uncle, Alfred Harmsworth, Lord Northcliffe—who invented modern journalism, founded *Answers*, bought *The Times* and *The Observer*, and died of megalomania. Lord Northcliffe's dominating personality still haunts two Fleet Street groups—the *Daily Mail* group of his nephew Lord Rothermere, and the *Daily Mirror* group of Cecil King. King was brought up in the shadow of his uncle, his mother's brother, who was then at the height of his eccentric power; but his father, an Irish Professor of Oriental Languages, was a much milder man. From these two strains, the brash and ruthless Harmsworths and the cultured, public-spirited Kings, came the curious paradox of Cecil King. He is inhibited, cultivated, educated at Winchester and Christ Church: but he is also ruthless, rebellious and fascinated by popular newspapers. He sometimes gives the impression of an intellectual pretending to be Northcliffe: but there is nothing assumed about his ambition. By the time he was twenty-five he was working for the *Daily Mirror*, then owned by Northcliffe's brother, the first Lord Rothermere; he became director three years later. In spite of his fastidious tastes and personal shyness, he loved the rebellious vulgarity of the tabloid, defying everyone—even Churchill in the war. He was one of the team who helped to push the circulation of the *Mirror* in twenty-five years from 800,000 to five million—the largest daily sold outside Russia and Japan. By a mixture of nepotism, ability and drive he increased his power in the *Mirror*: by 1951, after a classic boardroom struggle, he ousted the chairman, Harry Bartholomew, and achieved his life's ambition.

With the *Mirror*'s profits behind him, King looked round for new empires: he acquired a share in television, bought papers in Scotland, and then, unpredictably, bought another part of Lord Northcliffe's old empire, a jumbled group of magazines called Amalgamated Press. This set off a chain reaction. It was a profitable but difficult new empire, and King soon found himself involved in a hectic magazine war. He moved into the musty magazine offices which had been undisturbed for twenty years, sacked editors, shut down magazines, had all the vans painted light blue, renamed the group Fleetway, and advertised massively against his rival magazine group, Odhams, who also owned the *Daily Herald* and the *People.* Then, in January 1961, came the flash-point. Odhams, fearing that King in his difficulties would try to take them over, took fright and tried secretly to merge with Roy Thomson, the other expanding tycoon. King, furious, immediately issued a counter bid, far more attractive than Thomson's proposals, to the Odhams shareholders. A week later, to the astonishment of parliament, the Prime Minister and most of all Odhams, King was in control of the biggest newspaper empire in British history. It had happened, by the irony of big business logic, not because King had been successful with newspapers, but because he had been in difficulties with magazines.

What does King do with his power? He has strong, if not very definable political, views: 'I've never been a Socialist,' he told me before the election in 1964: 'I'm anti-Tory, because I think the Establishment is corrupt and incompetent; in the last thirteen years they've bungled nearly everything. By corruption I don't mean financial bribes; I mean appointing an old school-friend or relation to a public office when you know he's not the best man—which is just as serious in its way. I have a strong feeling of sympathy for underdogs—anyone being trod on by the machine; that's why I am interested in Africans. I identify myself with the underdog—I can't think why.'

In the last few years King has appeared to become much more sensitive to criticism about his newspapers, and a new attitude was apparent when the *Sunday Pictorial* changed its name in 1963 to the *Sunday Mirror*, and took on a more respectable character: during the Profumo scandal in 1963 it decided *not* to print Christine Keeler's memoirs, thus leaving the field open to the *News of the World.* When the *Guardian* in August 1963 attacked the Mirror Group for having 'competed for the privilege of purveying pornography', King protested that 'no newspaper in the *Mirror Group* has glorified these people: the sordid emptiness, anxieties and double-dealing of their lives have been exposed by the courts and the press for all to see'. When in 1964 Lord Boothby sued the *Sunday Mirror* for defamation Cecil King, after settling for £40,000 damages, published a personal apology in his newspapers. 'It is my own view, and the policy of this group, that when a newspaper is wrong it should state so promptly and without equivocation. I am satisfied that any imputation of an improper nature against Lord Boothby is completely unjustified. In these circumstances I feel it my duty to sign this unqualified apology to Lord Boothby and to add the personal regrets of myself and the directors of IPC that the story appeared.'

There were further signs of King's conscience when he announced that, in place of the dying *Herald*, the *Mirror* group would launch a new daily, the *Sun*. ('I admire his courage,' commented Roy Thomson, 'more than I admire his discretion.'). But the *Sun* which rose in September 1964, supervised by King's editorial director, Hugh Cudlipp, revealed the creative weakness of this vast and wealthy corporation; for while nearly £400,000 was spent beforehand on promoting the new product, the newspaper itself revealed a bleak lack of talent, money and new ideas.

King's attitude to newspapers, circulations and political influence emerged very clearly in his provocative chairman's speech in July 1964, which gave a brisk and ruthless round-up of Fleet Street:

As the number of newspapers diminishes, so the political importance of the survivors may increase. Let us take first the *Daily Express*, the only serious rival to our papers, conducted so long by Lord Beaverbrook. Though not as good as it was, the *Daily Express* is a superb journalistic effort in the popular field. As a sort of morning 'pick-me-up' it is evidently what a lot of people want. But here we are talking of politics and this is a field where the *Express* has sought, but failed to find, either power or influence. Its politics, though vaguely Conservative, are so uncertain that no political result could reasonably be expected. Political vendettas have proved ineffective: political campaigns—Empire Free Trade, for instance—have been ignored. It will be interesting to see whether Sir Max Aitken, the new head of the *Express* newspapers, retains the ghost of his father's policies or evolves a policy with more relevance to the times in which we live.

Northcliffe told me, when speaking of the *Daily Mail* many years ago, that an influential paper could amplify a swing of popular opinion but could do nothing to reverse it. Northcliffe, like Beaverbrook, was not one who understood newspaper politics and his efforts to hang the Kaiser and so on after the first war were somewhat embarrassing to Lloyd George, but no more. Of recent years the *Daily Mail* front page comment by George Murray has been one of the best things in the paper, but so dependably Conservative that it can have little influence.

The *Daily Telegraph* shines out with the best news service in Fleet Street, but its political comment is so stodgy as to have little influence on its overwhelmingly Conservative readers. One of the curious aspects of the Macmillan government in its later stages was that it had succeeded in antagonising the whole of the Tory Press. The fact that everyone was out of step except Harold did not seem to bother anyone until the Conservative government found that their critics were right and their majority had gone.

The importance of *The Times*, once so great, has much diminished. It is still a sort of parish magazine for the Establishment, publishing obituaries of people no one else has ever heard of, but its political opinions tend to be so 'balanced' as to be neutral. Every now and then Sir William Haley lashes out, but events like the three articles by 'A Conservative' are too rare to add up to a policy.

Then there are the *Mirror*'s fellow travellers, *The Guardian* and *The Observer*. Though they sometimes appear not to have noticed the fact, we are in fact pursuing similar policies, though with a different technique applied to a different audience. *The Guardian*, which was a great paper under C. P. Scott and a good one under Wadsworth, is now a very pallid version of what it once was. In fact, but for the financial support of the *Manchester Evening News*, the prognosis would be for a future brief as well as undistinguished. *The Observer* was doing very well up to Suez. The Mirror Group, *The Guardian* and *The Observer* were all anti-Suez, and it seems unfair that *The Mirror* and *The Observer* lost sales, while *The Guardian* gained them for pursuing the same fiercely anti-Government policy over the whole crisis. Until Suez *The Observer* and the *Sunday Times* both had increasing sales and *The Observer* was gradually gaining. Since Suez, it has been the other way round and now the *Sunday Times* is more than 500,000 ahead. The experience seems to have shaken *The Observer*, which has been for the last few years less forthright than it used to be.

Of course, the influence of what we call the 'Heavies', and what they call the 'Quality Press', is different in kind from that of the popular Press. The former influence influential people (if at all!); the latter influence the broad masses and, through them, the government of the day. Of the former, since 1945 the most influential paper was the *Economist* under Sir Geoffrey Crowther; of the latter, the *Daily Mirror*. A serious rival to newspaper influence could be that of the BBC or the ITV contractors, but the government has always been careful to sterilise these, beyond allowing them to spread some discreet propaganda for the stodgier parts of the Establishment. This is not really in the interest of the country, but one could quite see that Ministers blench at the thought of handing the television screen over to people who might be no respecters of persons—particularly Governmental persons.

A newspaper that has come up in the world is the *Financial Times*. Instead of being a trade paper for stockbrokers, it is becoming a serious paper in its own right. It is necessarily Conservative in a general way, but it represents Conservatism at its more enlightened. Incidentally, it is curious that Lord Cowdray, who controls the Financial Times and Westminster Press groups, manages to keep almost completely out of the limelight. He is publicised as a polo player, but not as one of the principal newspaper proprietors in the country and, reputedly, as much the largest subscriber to Conservative Party funds.

The latest addition to the ranks of newspaper proprietors has been Lord Thomson, who is frank that his interest in newspapers is purely financial. And we can see in some of his newspapers both here and in Canada what this leads to—high selling prices, stiff advertising rates and poor journalistic contents. The fact that he controls newspapers in Nigeria and the Southern United States shows that his group has no coherent political outlook. But the picture is not all dark. Apart from the coloured supplement, the *Sunday Times*—under the editorship of Denis Hamilton—is a much better paper than it was under Lord Kemsley. Its political viewpoint is indeed Conservative, but an enlightened Conservatism that overlaps with Right Wing Labour.

And now we come to your own papers, which in general support the Labour Party, the only newspapers of any consequence that do. The *Mirror* and *Record* between them cover the same ground as the *Daily* and *Scottish Express* and outsell the latter by a million and a quarter copies per day—a gap which is increasing. The *Mirror* and the *Record* are read by nearly half the adult population of Great Britain every day. Our readers tend to be young with no particular voting loyalties and are more likely to listen to the views of their newspaper than the readers of any other journal. This has been true for a long time and is enhanced by the fact that we have a clearer idea than other newspaper managers and editors of what can, and what cannot, be achieved by newspaper propaganda.

Being read by the masses, our papers can only be expected to be influential in questions which interest the masses—such as General Elections. The *Daily Mirror* was credited with winning the election for Labour in 1945. This is not realistic. The British public was tired of the methods of the Churchill government and pre-war Chamberlain government and wanted a change. The *Daily Mirror* alone voiced that feeling and undoubtedly enhanced that swing. In 1950 Mr. Attlee was in process of throwing away a record majority in record time and it was only thanks to the *Daily Mirror* that he scraped home. In 1951, '55 and '59 the Tories were in whatever any newspaper said or did. Perhaps this time Labour is in on the same terms—perhaps not.

But if our papers have any influence in the matter, it will be because we are in touch with public opinion—real public opinion—not the wishful thinking of which newspaper editors and proprietors are often guilty.

When you know where public opinion is, it is then more possible to guide it into appropriate channels.

LORD THOMSON

> At first he said he wanted to buy 100 newspapers. Now he wants a total of 200. This strikes me as a little odd, a little eccentric.
>
> *Cecil King, February 1964.*

A more sudden intrusion has been that of the small Canadian, Roy Thomson, proprietor, among over a hundred papers, of the *Moose-Jaw Times Herald*, of Saskatchewan, and the *Sunday Times* of London. For Thomson has not only become, in ten years since he first arrived in Scotland, the second biggest newspaper proprietor in the country. He also represents, more forcibly than General Motors or IBM, the impact of traditional North American business attitudes on a sleepy British situation.

The features of 'Uncle Roy', as he is known in Fleet Street, have become very familiar: his benign face beams out, behind pebble glasses, from the reports of the Thomson Organisation. He has a salesman's bonhomie: he is shortish, well-groomed, with a round bland head and a broad mouth which seems fixed in a satisfied smile. He conforms almost exactly to an Englishman's old-fashioned picture of an American. He has a vigorous handshake, calls everyone by his Christian name, mixes easily, jokes, teases and banters, likes to greet recruits with 'you make a dollar for me, I make a dollar for you'. Above all, he talks incessantly, enthusiastically and unashamedly about money; he enjoys being brutally frank about money in the way some people enjoy using four-letter words about sex. He has a paperweight made of imitation sovereigns. It is his commercialism which makes him at the same time so simple, and so baffling.

Thomson's success story is well known. His boyhood as a poor barber's son in Toronto, his peddling of radio sets as a young man in the slump, his beginnings with radio stations in mining camps, his first shaky newspaper in Ontario, all this, so very remote from most British experience, moulded his simple, dynamic philosophy. By 1953, by shrewd costing and mass-produced journalism, he had built up a chain of thirty newspapers, nearly all small ones, from Florida to Ontario.

When he was fifty-nine he took a bold step: he came over to Edinburgh and bought, with the backing of the Royal Bank of Canada, its morning paper *The Scotsman*. He was a widower, and, it seemed, needed something to occupy his mind: and he had a nostalgic affection for Scotland, where his great-grandfather came from. He came to live in Edinburgh, but stayed aloof from its strait-laced social life. Soon afterwards, commercial television was launched, and his ownership of a newspaper gave him the right to apply for the Scottish station. Thomson had a simple rule in assessing business potentials: what works in America will work in Britain. While knowing Scotsmen were shaking their heads over the risks, Thomson, with the help of his paper, bought over 80 per cent of the shares in Scottish Television: it was, as he said later, 'a licence to print your own money'.

Television made him a multi-millionaire, and opened up great new horizons. Only six years after he had bought *The Scotsman*, the ageing Lord Kemsley, proprietor of the *Sunday Times* and twenty-three provincial papers, began to tire of his property. Kemsley, who had worked his way up from poverty like Thomson, had become interested—as the British so often do in late middle age—in prestige and politics more than in profits. He ran his papers with the help of four sons, in a gentlemanly way, with strictly Conservative politics and editorials about the Royal family in italics. He was driven in his Rolls to the office every morning, where he presided over dignified conferences and stately luncheons. At his country house there was a ticker-tape in the hall, and the butler brought in important news on a tray.

Thomson, remembering American precedents, and advised by his very shrewd banker Siegmund Warburg (whose help he freely acknowledges), saw the potential of the Kemsley empire. He bought it quickly for what looked like a very high price, and moved his headquarters to London. Then he found himself for the first time in his life in the big time, at the centre of politics and prestige. Kemsley House, a big half-empty building in the Gray's Inn Road, became Thomson House, and the beaming Canadian strode into the office with zest. He was now running, not a chain of small-town dailies, but a cultural, political weekly which could make authors and flutter cabinets. His arrival in Gray's Inn Road was the most startling event since Northcliffe walked into *The Times*. He walked through the building shaking hands, gave cocktail parties for the staff and told jolly stories to the printers. The exotic literary contributors dreaded the prospect of being costed, but they had no need to worry: Thomson was well aware of the importance, as he put it, of 'salaried eccentrics'.

But he applied to the group the same process of 'consolidation and reorganisation' which he had learnt in the mining camps of Canada. He toured the provinces, fired a few managers and promoted others, increased advertising rates, established strict budgets, and scrutinised everything from wrapping paper to Scotch Tape. He imported a team of aggressive businessmen from Scotland and the provinces, and men who had been leading quiet uncompetitive lives became suddenly activated with profit-mindedness. He bought £2 million worth of printing machinery, and Thomson House rose up to seven storeys. He expanded the *Sunday Times* into a great supermarket paper, added a supplement and hired the Queen's brother-in-law. He even ventured to the perilous field of Africa; he bought half a Nigerian paper; took a small share in the Aga Khan's East African group; and later bought a group of dingy weeklies in Central Africa. He bought a chain of magazines, including the *Illustrated London Magazine* and the *Tatler*, and two publishing houses, Thomas Nelson and Michael Joseph.

As the *Sunday Times* grew, so Thomson enjoyed himself in more spectacular ways; but business remains his obsession. 'It's just a great big hobby,' he said: 'I just can't wait to get to see my mail in the morning.' His office, looking over to St. Pancras Station, is full of striking objects, including a big Nolan painting of an African elephant, but he says he doesn't understand it: 'They tell me it's all right; I take their word for it.'

What in all this frenzied activity had been Thomson's driving motive? He is not, like King, troubled by shareholders: he is in absolute control of his empire, and now personally a very rich man. Yet he has constantly said that he has no political interests. 'Newspaper publication and television,' he said in his 1961 report, 'appeal to me as the most fascinating forms of business enterprise. I do not regard them as instruments for securing or wielding personal power.'

He has a few vaguely political views. He regards himself as an 'independent Tory'; 'I've got money so I'm Conservative; if anyone with much money supports Labour, I suspect it's a gimmick,' he said to me in 1964; 'but I don't always agree with this Conservative Party; I don't like their perpetuation of class rule. The Tories have got to seek membership in the non-ruling classes, much more than they have in the past.'

It seemed extraordinary that given such a powerful political weapon as the *Sunday Times*, he should not wish to wield it. But he has been visibly bored by politics. At one weekly conference, when his editor was explaining a detailed political point, he opened a parcel on his desk, containing a large collection of penknives, and began talking about the pleasures of knife-collecting. Although Thomson had clearly enjoyed mixing with politicians and staying in Tory country-houses, he refuses to commit his papers to any one party. He insists on parading both Socialist and Conservative views in the *Sunday Times*, and has said repeatedly that he would like to own a Labour paper. Many people warned that this was no way to get a barony: but nevertheless in 1964 a barony he got.

Thomson has only one obvious political aim, which is to give the majority of his readers what they want. In America, he has a paper in the South supporting segregation, and others in the North attacking it. He likes to boast of the independence of his editors, but insists that they must be second-in-command to the managers. 'It is not true,' he said at a conference at New Delhi in 1961, 'as some say, that I use editors as mere tools of management —editors should thank their stars I shield them from the worries of business.' But the supremacy of management makes it inevitable that editors with unpopular views will be threatened, and Thomson's speech provoked worried replies. 'Is it a good thing for a man to have the power to sack a hundred editors?' asked Lord Burnham of the *Telegraph*: 'I think not.'

EXPRESS AND MAIL

On Monday, May 25, 1964, six hundred journalists and public men were invited by Lord Thomson to a banquet at the Dorchester Hotel, to celebrate the 85th birthday of Lord Beaverbrook, owner of the *Daily Express*. It was a weird and puzzling evening; a large sector of the British Establishment were assembled to pay tribute to a man whom many of them had hated. Flanking Lord Beaverbrook at the high table were such varied panjandrums as Sir Hugh Greene and Lord Normanbrook of the BBC, Lord Rothermere of the *Daily Mail*, Lord Longford and Iain Macleod. Among the few significant absentees were Cecil King, Sir William Haley of *The Times* and David Astor of *The Observer*; it was one of the very rare occasions when Fleet Street, from the *News of the World* to the *New Statesman* was gathered together. Grace was said by John Gordon, the prickly columnist of the *Sunday Express*, and the banquet was punctuated by processions featuring Lord Beaverbrook, Roast Beef and a sword to cut the birthday cake. Lord Thomson and Lord Rothermere paid fulsome tributes to Lord Beaverbrook, who replied in a self-deprecatory speech. It was the last peak of Lord Beaverbrook's career, at which his opponents and critics had finally capitulated. Three weeks later he died. The obituaries were almost all friendly, and the *New Statesman* commented 'de mortuis nil nisi bunkum'; but in private some journalists were more outspoken. 'I feel the air we breathe this morning is cleaner than it was yesterday,' said one newspaper chairman. 'The only reason I might go to the funeral,' said an eminent editor, 'is to make absolutely sure that he's dead.'

Max Lord Beaverbrook was the Last Tycoon of Fleet Street. Like his friend Churchill, he had the larger-than-life quality of a man who had risen out of the nineteenth century: he seemed to pre-date the world of committees, managers, shareholders and readership surveys. As a young Canadian millionaire, he bought the *Daily Express* for £17,000 in 1916 and moulded its journalism, its politics, and its staff. His biblical Canadian phrases still echo through the editorials—'Be sure', 'Praise this man', 'Not so', 'Let us rejoice'. In its mixture of entertainment, slanted news and violent comment the *Daily Express* proved irresistible to the British public: it has presented a star-spangled fantasy-world to brighten suburban homes. The black glass building of the *Daily Express*, with its hectic, theatrical atmosphere, however much it is hated, has had a dominating influence on the techniques of British journalism.

After Beaverbrook's death the control of his newspapers passed to his son Sir Max Aitken (who renounced his title saying: 'In my lifetime there will be only one Lord Beaverbrook.') Sir Max, a former Battle of Britain pilot, is a tough and formidable tycoon, but without his father's great flair, and it still remains to be seen how the *Daily Express* will fare without a dominating head. For Lord Beaverbrook's bold, decisive leadership, malign though it frequently was, fascinated journalists as much as readers, and gave to the worried and anarchic profession of journalism a sense of direction, bogus but stimulating.

The empire of Lord Rothermere has been far less obviously influenced by its chief proprietor, and its most important paper, the *Daily Mail*, has most of the vigour of the *Express* without its mischief. It retains from its Northcliffe days a refreshing passion for stunts and crusades, ranging from the London-to-Paris air race to banning inflammable nighties or saving a Roman ship from the Thames. Its politics are sometimes confusing; it has a strong liberal element in its staff, including a sympathy for Africans; but it often relapses into antique Tory bombast. Lord Rothermere himself was groomed by his father (who was Northcliffe's brother) for the highest political office; he was Lloyd George's ADC in 1919, and a Tory MP at the age of twenty-one. But since then he has retreated more into the background, and has left his papers to be run by the managers and editors, with only occasional but fundamental control—as in the 1964 election, when the *Daily Mail* unwaveringly supported the Tory Party.

POSH PAPERS

The wheels of big business have involved the highbrow as well as the popular papers. The most striking case has been with the two old Sunday 'posh papers', *The Observer* and the *Sunday Times*. Before the war their combined circulations were less than half-a-million: they had tiny, gentlemanly staffs and a few literary contributors who sent in long articles from the country. St. John Ervine might write 3,000 words about the theatre, and J. L. Garvin would cover a whole page with advice to the government, sent in by Rolls Royce, on the political situation (J. B. Morton talked about 'grazing on the Southern slopes of a Garvin article'): they were both more like estates than competitive business organisations. The war, the rise in the school-leaving age, and the expansion of universities have changed all that: their combined circulations are now over two million, and both have become far fatter, more competitive, and richer, augmented with magazines and supplements. But they have also become much more dependent on advertising, with all its attendant dangers: more than three-quarters of the revenue of the *Sunday Times* now comes from advertisements.

Equally spectacular has been the advance of the *Daily Telegraph*, controlled by a branch of the Berry family—the surviving part of the empire of the Berry Brothers which until 1937 had the biggest concentration in Fleet Street. The *Telegraph* has a simple formula: it looks like *The Times*, but is cheaper and less demanding. It has unwavering Conservative views, letters from angry colonels in Tunbridge Wells, columns of Births, Deaths and Marriages. It reports murder trials in a detailed and stately way, and it has the largest quantity of news of any daily paper. Compared to the *Express*, which is hip and glittering, the *Telegraph* is square and flat. But the *Telegraph* strikes a chord in the growing managerial middle-class, and its rise is an important clue to the social pattern of Britain. The *Telegraph*'s circulation has doubled since 1937, and in 1961 it extended its territory by introducing the *Sunday Telegraph*, which intensified still further the competition among 'posh papers'. When the *Observer* and the *Sunday Times* were both competing with colour magazines, the *Telegraph* entered the fray, not on Sundays, but on Fridays, with a flashy magazine included with their daily edition. The fight between these three magazines, each demanding a large capital investment, is the latest and most perilous phase in the war for the 'quality readers'.

THE TIMES

Even *The Times* has changed. For a hundred and eighty years *The Times* has lived in a sheltered world of its own. Northcliffe, who owned it for fifteen years, could not bend it to his will: he was baffled by the 'black friars'—as he called its stately leader-writers —and talked of writing over its door 'abandon scope all ye who enter here'. After Northcliffe died it was bought for £1½ million by J. J. Astor, now Lord Astor of Hever. Its circulation, which in 1800 was bigger than all other newspapers combined, is now one of the smallest—240,000 a day, or hardly more than a twentieth of the *Daily Mirror*'s. But it gives the impression of being read by everyone that matters. Its editorials suggest an intimate correspondence with the government, its letters constitute a private debating-chamber, and its social columns provide a House Magazine for Society. 'Lady Violet Bonham Carter wishes to express her deep gratitude', said an entry on December 6, 1964, after her Life Peerage was announced, 'for all the generous messages she has received, to which she will reply individually as soon as possible'.

The Times is so sedate that it is often regarded, like Eton or Buckingham Palace, as strictly non-commercial—an impression strengthened by the existence of five impeccable Trustees—the Lord Chief Justice, the Warden of All Souls, the President of the Royal Society, the President of the Institute of Chartered Accountants and the Governor of the Bank of England. But the sole object of the Trustees is to ensure that *The Times* does not fall 'into unworthy hands'[1] a duty which has not so far been onerous. *The Times* has to pay its way like any other newspaper. Even its nineteenth century supremacy was due as much to its steam-printing press as to its journalism, and today, with the *Guardian* overtaking and the *Telegraph* imitating and undercutting, its position is increasingly challenged. But *The Times* still regards itself as the only 'journal of record'—the only paper which puts information, however dull, above everything else.

In 1963 *The Times* commissioned a survey of so-called 'top people' to discover their reading habits. They sent questionnaires to 6,474 people mentioned in *Who's Who*, of whom 63 per cent replied. The results showed that 70 per cent of the total read *The Times*, with the professions broken down thus:[2]

	The Times	*Daily Telegraph*	*Daily Mail*	*Daily Express*	*The Guardian*	*Financial Times*
'Top Dons and Teachers'	70%	23%	11%	7%	32%	5%
'Top Businessmen'	79%	52%	36%	29%	15%	55%
'Top Civil Servants'	85%	41%	18%	18%	22%	24%
'Top Politicians'	71%	54%	35%	43%	39%	27%
'Top Executives' (Administrators in Public Services)	85%	41%	26%	22%	24%	22%
'Top Professional Men' (in Government Service)	83%	43%	24%	16%	17%	9%

[1] *See* History of *The Times*, Vol. IV, Part II, 1952, p. 790.
[2] Survey by Research Services Ltd., 1963.

The Times is now being further threatened by the growth of *The Guardian.* Before the war the *Manchester Guardian*, as it then was, sold only 48,000 copies a day—equivalent to half-a-year's increase for the *Daily Express*: but in the past four years it has dropped its prefix, printed in London as well as Manchester, and increased its circulation to over a quarter of a million, nearly overtopping *The Times*: and under a very independent Glaswegian editor, Alastair Hetherington, it has mixed its own curious whimsy with 'robust North Country commonsense'. But *The Times* insists that no other paper approaches its coverage and reliability, with solid foundation.

However, the most important feature of *The Times* is not its circulation but its political influence: and here the change has been striking. Before the war, Geoffrey Dawson, who edited *The Times* (with a four-year gap) for twenty-nine years, moved in the heart of Conservative politics. Baldwin, Chamberlain and Halifax were his close personal friends, and at All Souls, Cliveden and other country-house weekends he talked incessantly about diplomatic policy, pressing always the importance of appeasing Hitler. That closed, compact circle, revealed in memoirs of pre-war politicians, has done much to cultivate the idea of 'The Establishment' among the next generation—one of the many examples of the history of one generation providing the myths for the next. Dawson appropriated to himself the job of Foreign Editor of *The Times*, cut and trimmed the despatches of his European correspondents, and preferred to take the advice of his Government friends: in one terrible, self-revealing phrase he described his editorial approach to the Germans:

'I did my utmost, night after night, to keep out of the paper anything that might hurt their susceptibilities.'[1]

The pre-war rôle of *The Times*, with its deliberate suppression of news, caused a deep trauma in Printing House Square since the war, and *The Times*' own history—a remarkable piece of corporate psycho-analysis—mercilessly exposes the faults of the paper.

The present editor, Sir William John Haley, shows a total change from the Dawson tradition. He is a self-made, retiring man who regards himself above all as a professional journalist. He is very self-contained, with an impersonal gaze and an intimidating habit of resting his teeth on his fingers. He talks long and precisely about the rôle of journalism, with self-generating enthusiasm.

[1] *See Times History*, Vol. IV, Part II, p. 907.

He has had a romantic success story: the son of a Yorkshire clerk, who died when he was two years old, he was brought up in the Channel Islands and left school—a bookish, introverted boy—at the age of sixteen. He went to sea as a wireless operator, found a job on a Jersey newspaper and then reached *The Times* as telephonist. At the switchboard he thought out a scheme for saving continental calls and was sent to Brussels to work it—in the meantime having married the Foreign Editor's secretary. But *The Times* offered no chance of writing, so Haley moved to the *Manchester Evening News* as a reporter, and then as sub-editor. He had self-discipline and ambition rare in journalists, and eight years later he had become Managing Editor at the age of twenty-nine. He was not much interested in editorial policy: his pre-occupations were accurate news, making the paper pay, and writing book reviews—which he still enjoys more than almost anything.

In journalism he became a figure of legendary and alarming efficiency: he was made joint-managing director of the *Manchester Guardian*, and undertook negotiations for Reuters. He was asked —through Brendan Bracken—to join the BBC, which was in one of its periodic states of muddle, as Editor-in-Chief; six months later he became its Director-General at only forty-three. He ruled the corporation with firmness and austere idealism: he admired Lord Reith, extended popular education, and invented the Third Programme.

After eight years' broadcasting, he was asked to become Editor of *The Times*: the man who had refused to promote him thirty years before was still there. He made gradual, unspectacular changes: he moved out of the Editor's traditional gloomy room into a more cheerful place. He introduced a women's page and wrote his own booksy column under the name 'Oliver Edwards'. He insisted on professional reporters who knew shorthand, rather than the retired diplomats or generals or the old-style amateur 'Men from the Times'. He did not mix much with cabinet ministers, and insisted on supporting the Liberal Party during the 1964 election campaign. He preferred quiet evenings at home to political pow-wows. Of his predecessors—whose miniatures hang above his desk—it is Barnes, who rescued *The Times* from the Government's embrace in the 1820's, and dined off tripe in his office, whom Haley most admires.

JOURNALISTS

Your connection with any newspaper would be a disgrace and a degradation. I would rather sell gin to poor people and poison them that way.

Sir Walter Scott to Lockhart, 1829.

You cannot hope to bribe or twist
Thank God, a British journalist:
But seeing what the man will do
Unbribed, there's no occasion to.

Humbert Wolfe.

In the final analysis, the only people who can preserve the freedom of the press are the journalists themselves.

The Times, March 1963.

Caught unhappily in the commercial cogs are the journalists—over fifteen thousand of them in the National Union of Journalists and thousands more outside it—more journalists in Britain than solicitors. British journalists are aware of being less respected than Americans; there is no British equivalent to the American journalist-pundit—Reston, Lippmann, or the Alsops—and a successful British journalist will usually like to think of himself as something else, a writer, a diplomat or a politician. American newspapers helped to create their democracy, spreading news from coast to coast—in a country without traditional social networks, journalism was crucial. But in Britain, the secretive ruling classes in the eighteenth century had no love of journalism, and it began as an eavesdropping profession, where even parliamentary reports had to be smuggled out. In spite of such eminent journalists as Churchill, Milner or Dickens, journalism has never quite recovered from this backdoor feeling. Cabinet secrecy, which has become almost complete since the first world war, has made it hard for newspapers to drive a wedge into politics: compare the Cuban fiasco in Washington in 1961, when cabinet disagreements were immediately leaked to the press, with the Suez crisis of 1956, whose inner history remains to this day largely a secret.

Part of the difficulty of British journalists comes from its concentration: journalism has lacked the greatest safeguard of professional standards—a multiplicity of clients. The pressure of profits and the shortage of space make press lords unwilling to employ good reporters for the sake of prestige, and the business of reporting—which is often inevitably dull—has become more and more mixed with entertainment and comment. The contrast with America is not as unfavourable as Americans make out: transatlantic reporters, because of cheap newsprint and copious advertisements, have room to be dull, and their turgid prose is often unread and unreadable: like provincial dons, they lose touch with their audience. But journalists in Britain have never had the cosy sense of profession, nor the sense of duty, which Americans enjoy. In America journalism is apt to be regarded as an extension of history: in Britain, as an extension of conversation. As the Alsop brothers (perhaps oversimply) described the difference, in Britain 'the national debate can be and actually is quite largely carried on in the House of Commons itself. The British press therefore has far less national responsibility than the American press.'[1]

On the other hand, British papers can be more vocal, and more varied in their views, than American. At the time of the Vietnam crisis in 1964, or the Castro affair in Cuba in 1961, there was not the same sense of fierce public debate in the American press as arose over Suez in 1956 or even Immigration in 1961. There is no American equivalent to the national controversies in *The Times* letter-columns; and even though the British popular papers may be often opportunist and absurd, they can occasionally produce an uproar which can change the government's mind. Every journalist has his own view of the power of the press: my own impression is that the British government often takes newspapers more seriously than the journalists do.

Broadcasting has added to the problems of journalism. Before the war, radio had already usurped some of the news-providing side of papers, and had pushed them towards magazines: and during the war the prestige of the nine o'clock news, as the voice of the government, put it above all newspapers. Since then television has broken that monopoly, and there are some (including Sir William Haley) who believe that this gives journalism a new opportunity as a serious medium. But television has infected much of journalism with its hectic aggressiveness: jet planes and TV cameras between them have made news seem more like a series of sudden and disconnected crises and shows. Special correspondents rush from Cuba to Berlin to Ghana, discovering crises, plots and disasters, and then moving hurriedly on. Television, too, has broken down some of the old anonymity of journalism, and has tended to drag journalists, not reluctantly, into show business.

[1] Joseph and Stewart Alsop: *The Reporter's Trade*, 1958, p. 11.

Another unpleasant intruder has been the subterranean machinery of public relations, creating its own fake news, organising airlifts of journalists, stimulating bogus controversies and presenting prefabricated images—most extremely in fashion reporting, where news is entirely invented by the publicity machine. But the machinery has also penetrated to industry and politics, where the façade of handouts and pre-arranged news often bears little relation to what actually happened.[1]

THE PRESS AND PROFUMO

The question of the rôle of the press came to an angry climax after November 1962, when William Vassall, a junior official in the Admiralty, had been arrested and sentenced to eighteen years for spying. Soon afterwards several newspapers demanded the resignation of Thomas Galbraith, the Civil Lord of the Admiralty, implying that he was intimate with Vassall. Galbraith offered his resignation. Macmillan reluctantly accepted it, and later appointed a tribunal, under Lord Radcliffe, to investigate the charges. Radcliffe called several journalists to give evidence, many of whom refused to disclose the sources of their sensational accounts. Two of them, Reginald Foster of the *Daily Sketch* and Brendan Mulholland of the *Daily Mail*, were then found guilty of contempt and sentenced by the High Court to periods of imprisonment.

The imprisonment produced an uproar in Fleet Street, particularly (and most unexpectedly) from *The Times*, which thundered against the powers of the Executive. A leading article on March 7, 1963, called 'A Proper Defiance', and believed to have been written by Sir William Haley, said:

> The techniques of power, of political manipulation, of the predatoriness of officialdom, become ever more insidiously efficient. Against these, the community and the individual have all-too-few safeguards. Parliament is not a sure one. The Law is even less so. In spite of all the boasting of politicians that they no longer need to worry as they once did about newspapers, the most effective is still a vigilant press. No one is going to claim that the press is perfect. It has many shortcomings. It can be irresponsible. None the less, it does inform. The basis of political freedom and the essence of democracy is the public's right to know. That right is more constantly being eroded than any other.

This outburst produced a wave of readers' letters, most of them hostile; but Sir William, undeterred, returned to the fray with

[1] *See* Chapter 35.

another celebrated editorial on March 18, called 'It *Is* Happening Here', which was entirely justified in its sentiments, if not in its context.

> What makes the business so grave is the degree of ignorance, complacency and apathy towards the particular dangers perpetually threatening every free society that now stands revealed. There really are people who believe that the encroachments of authority, the corruption of society, and maladministration can safely be left to the powers-that-be to put right . . .
>
> Part of the rot is shown by the accusations of exaggeration and hysteria against anyone who sees the issue in such terms. How ridiculous to imagine that in Britain anything could ever go seriously wrong. The truth is that in a quiet way very much is going seriously wrong. The Executive has taken over power from Parliament. It rules, or fails to rule, by a tacit agreement with outside forces in the community that *their* authority also shall not be challenged. The administrators at all levels decide more and more without the citizen having effective redress. Many ways of thought in the Law are restrictive, secretive, and hamper efforts to preserve the true public interest. And all these hazards are faced by a middle-class that, either through comparative affluence, weariness, or disgust, has thrown in its hand or lost sight of its responsibilities.

But in the meantime the popular press were preparing a counter-attack after the humiliation of the Vassall affair; and here we come into the wake of Christine Keeler who, in the course of a year, seemed to leave her mark on nearly every British institution. Early in 1963 the press had become aware that John Profumo, then the War Minister, had had an affair with Christine Keeler, who was also involved in a West Indian's trial for attempted murder. Without actually stating the scandal, they published several innuendoes until eventually, on March 31, the question was taken up in parliament by George Wigg, the irrepressible Labour defence expert. The next day Profumo denied any impropriety in his friendship with Miss Keeler; and his denial, with varying qualifications, was accepted by the press.

But when, ten weeks later, on June 5 Profumo had to admit his impropriety, the press were cock-a-hoop with excitement; for the following month it seemed to most of the public that not only Profumo, but several other members of the government were implicated in sexual scandals; and the salaciousness of the press seemed triumphantly justified. The *News of the World* published Christine Keeler's own story, and every week the government awaited with dread the next Sunday's revelations. The arrest of

Stephen Ward, the evidence of Christine and Mandy Rice-Davies, and then Ward's suicide, marked the apotheosis of popular journalism; and it seemed as if the press, improbably led by *The Times* and the *News of the World*, was about to bring down the government. But again, there was bathos, and when Lord Denning published his report in September, the whole froth of allegations —about kinky ministers, connivance at the top, the leaking of secrets and suppression of evidence—had subsided into the single known fact of Profumo's brief affair; and the political repercussions, which had seemed so vast, were now scarcely perceptible. The Profumo scandal had apparently disappeared without trace, leaving only a good deal of recrimination about the rôle and ethics of the press. With subsequent decency, the press left Profumo and Christine Keeler alone.

NEWSPAPERS AND WHITEHALL

The financial operations in the press over the past six years have been so bizarre, so like the juggling with other industrial investments, that it is sometimes difficult to remember that these properties are supposed to be the basic instruments of democracy. In spite of all the other elements mixed with them—entertainment, comment and advertising—newspapers remain the principal channels of communication, and if readers do not obtain their facts from them, they are unlikely to find them elsewhere. There are some who believe that the press has already become so mixed with absurdities that its further commercialisation is hardly worth worrying about. But for those who still have hopes for the press as a moulder of public opinion, the position is certainly alarming.

Probably the most serious effect of commercialisation is its swamping of minority views. The fewer and more competitive the papers the less any one paper will be liable to embrace an unpopular view, at the risk of losing readers and advertising: at the present pace no paper, not even *The Times*, can be oblivious to its circulation graph. Every paper must strive after the majority of readers in its own field, and this necessity is enormously enhanced by the demands of advertisers.

Advertising has not influenced journalism in the direct, corrupt way that many people forecast: advertisers have not, except in a few angry moments such as at the time of Suez, tried to bring pressure on to editorial opinion. But it has had more indirect, and equally dangerous effects. It has in the first place compelled journalists, without bribing or twisting, to play in with the uncritical world of advertisements, beginning in the relatively harmless region of fashion and travel but spreading imperceptibly to other areas. When for instance one journalist consistently recommended readers to buy clothes at Marks and Spencer, the more expensive shops quietly withdrew their advertising from that paper. If a journalist adopts a critical attitude to a company, their prestige advertisements will be withdrawn, and no newspaper can survive a cut of 25 per cent in its advertising. But more serious is the effect of advertising in pressing towards mass markets: advertisers are not much interested in the diversities of opinion, they are only interested in the main income groups—A, B, C, D—and the papers which lead in each group are quite adequate. Advertising, which itself exists to build up mass markets, has forced journalism to do the same.

But it is not only commercialism which limits the journalists' scope. It is the increasing difficulty, as the bureaucracies take over from parliament, of finding anything out. While parliament remains a convenient outward show, full of drama, intrigue and gossip, vast areas of government remain quite unpenetrated by journalism. In the civil service and the big corporations, protection from publicity is a sacred principle, and arguments are perpetually put forward to explain why making issues public will make matters worse. 'The mumbo-jumbo words *sub judice*,' wrote Sir William Haley, 'are applied to all kinds of proceedings which are not in the remotest way legal, in order to stifle opinion about them.' Bureaucrats, by their rule, prefer, in Haley's words, to 'cloak their proceedings and present accomplished facts only.'[1] 'The British press is as censored as most censored presses,' said Cecil King in June 1962, 'though in an arbitrary and indeterminate way.'

Over the last forty years the blanket of secrecy round government affairs has become much more impenetrable: the difference is in the immense tightening-up of the government machine. The Whitehall bureaucracies which we encounter later in this book have learnt to suppress all unofficial news, to channel their information through a single well-disciplined official, and specialist journalists are dependent on that official's goodwill for their sources. Every day a Foreign Office spokesman sees the diplomatic correspondents of the daily press—adjusting his information to the

[1] Sir W. J. Haley: *The Formation of Public Opinion.* Haldane Memorial Lecture, 1958.

acceptability of the paper, with plenty of news for *The Times* and very little for the *Worker.* If a paper offends against Foreign Office rules, and publishes embarrassing information, the co-operation of the Foreign Office will be quietly withdrawn: correspondents find it harder to maintain an aggressive fact-finding attitude, and become sucked into the diplomatic machine.

All bureaucracies are secretive, but the British civil service, with its self-contained corporate tradition is more successfully secretive: and in the great contemporary debates within Whitehall—about the deterrent, foreign bases, or economic planning—it is becoming increasingly difficult for journalists to discover the issues before the decisions are actually reached.

10

LAW

Every profession is a conspiracy against the laity.

George Bernard Shaw.

For my part I must own that I wish the country to be governed by law, but not by lawyers.

Edmund Burke.

I think all lawyers are conservative.

Lord Gardiner.[1]

While the Press has no history but considerable political importance, the two older Estates, the Law and the Church, are powerfully interlocked with the History of Britain. Both take a large place in pageantry; judges and bishops sit in the House of Lords, join in processions, are honoured with ancient titles and are received by the Queen. Both reached a climax of fame and splendour in Victorian times. Judges and bishops alike have been intensely conservative and resistant to change—as their votes in the House of Lords, from the Reform Bill onwards, showed. Many have become diverted by the workings of their profession, rather than its ultimate ends, and have found themselves increasingly out of touch with the movements of contemporary Britain. In both professions there is a loving attachment to the phrase, 'It may seem odd to you, but it works.'

The Law is the most striking example of a profession which has become trapped in its conservatism and mystique. Its proud independence and remoteness have given it magnificent strength as a bastion of liberty and justice; but have also made it totally unsusceptible to pressures of change. The Victorian prestige of the law is expressed in the Royal Courts of Justice, built in 1880 by the architect G. E. Street, when the legal profession was at its height. A broad doorway leads into a fake-medieval hall, like a stripped-down cathedral, adorned with big black-letter notices announcing 'Lord Chief Justice's Court', or 'Wash and

[1] *The Economist*, March 28, 1964.

Brush Up'. Ordinary dark-suited men carrying blue or red bags walk into a room by the entrance, and emerge a few minutes later solemnly wearing horse-hair or nylon wigs and flowing gowns.

The 1880s were the heyday of private property: lawyers were the advisers and protectors of the rich men's estates and the law courts were their battleground. And, with the rush of reforming legislation between 1830 and 1880, the great Victorian lawyers had been interlocked with politics: they could argue in court in the morning, and in parliament in the afternoon. But in the past eighty years the pattern of the rest of the country has changed, and left the lawyers behind. Rich individuals have been replaced by the big business corporations, trade unions, insurance companies and civil service departments, and the immense new area of state administration has crept up on the old powers of the law. Eighty per cent of the common law cases fought in the courts are now about compensation for accidents—in factories or motor-cars—often fought by one institution against another, for instance, a trade union against an insurance company. The whole territory of taxation, which has enveloped both corporations and individuals, has been largely neglected by lawyers (who proverbially have never been good at sums) and annexed by the new profession of accountants.[1]

While lawyers have gone on preparing title deeds in Victorian offices, filled with black tin boxes and stiff paper, a whole new world has grown up outside them. And while accountants have multiplied, the proportion of lawyers has fallen in sixty years from about one in 1,400 to one in 2,000. There are now three times as many accountants as lawyers. The change has worried many attorneys. 'We must retain in a world of changing customs and changing values our position as men of affairs,' wrote Sir Leslie Peppiatt, a recent President of the Law Society: 'men (and women, too) to whom our clients will turn for help in their problems. Do not let us force them to seek this help from their accountants or bankers.' Recently the law has become increasingly worried by its image, and has tried to make itself more attractive to the public, on whom ultimately it depends.

British lawyers do not have the same influence as their American counterparts, who play an important rôle in big business decisions. A few eminent British barristers like Lord Shawcross and Lord Monckton have left the bar for business, but practising barristers are not allowed to hold working directorships. The American

[1] *See* Chapter 28.

lawyers, sometimes at the cost of professional standards, have become much more free-ranging, embracing the world of tax and finance, and often taking over the running of companies.

Nor do the British courts have the same obvious impact as in countries with a written constitution, and a court to interpret it (though ironically it is Britain which has *exported* more written constitutions than any country). The Supreme Court of America can visibly affect the lives of ordinary men, and can openly contradict the government: the names of its nine members are constantly in the headlines. But the decisions of British courts, gradually establishing precedents and rights, do not challenge the government, and few ordinary people know the names of the nine Law Lords. Compared to America or the Continent, the Law in Britain is less closely related to society and its problems. At the time of Blackstone's commentaries—in 1787—the Law was regarded as revealing the pattern of society, and lawyers the great interpreters and prophets.[1] Today, it is the economists and the historians who interpret society, while the lawyers—at least in the public's view—are relegated to the position of long-stop rather than wicket-keeper.

The conservatism of English lawyers is reinforced by their strict division into solicitors and barristers—found only in South Africa, New South Wales and Great Britain. Only solicitors are allowed to deal directly with the public. There are 20,683 practising ones and they perform all the routine business: but when they have to take a case to the central courts, they must employ a barrister to plead—much as a GP employs a specialist to operate. The two sides—the wigged and the unwigged—are kept severely apart. Recently some attempts have been made at social liaison, but solicitors still cannot have lunch or dinner in the barristers' Inns of Court.

The system has its advantages. For solicitors it is a special form of subcontracting which often makes for lower total costs. It provides a group of specialists, none tied to a particular firm, all individualists and carrying only minimal overheads, all skilled in pleading and so providing a fairly smooth system of trial. But the division, and the traditions that have grown round it, have produced a web of archaic restrictive practices designed unashamedly to maintain the employment of lawyers. A client, having engaged a barrister, cannot even talk to him except in the presence of his solicitor: in court, he has to employ both solicitor

[1] *See* Asa Briggs: *The Age of Improvement*, 1959, p. 89.

and barrister together. If a client wants to employ a Queen's Counsel or senior barrister, he must also employ—at two-thirds the QC's fee—a junior barrister as well. The bar often seems designed more to maintain full employment for lawyers than to meet the needs of clients. But if it wasn't that the public needed them, there would be no lawyers.

SOLICITORS

The old 'family solicitor' was designed as the adviser to prosperous middle-class clients. He worked in an office which closely resembled a Victorian gentleman's study, and he regarded himself strictly as a legal adviser as a doctor was a medical adviser: he shrunk, like a good professional man, from giving general opinions. But with the complexities of modern business affairs, people—both companies and individuals—look more and more for opinions: they need not merely an occasional adviser, but an agent, to take charge of their affairs, and to advise on policy as well as procedure. 'It is because he is rarely qualified to give such policy advice', wrote Professor L. C. B. Gower of London University, one of the few radical lawyers, 'that the lawyer is losing more and more work to the accountant and the banker.'[1]

A new kind of lawyer's office is emerging. A third of the solicitors are still practising alone: but large partnerships—up to the maximum of twenty partners allowed by law—have grown up to deal with a specialist age. Four large ones dominate the City of London, with stately Dickensian titles which—like the big auditors or bankers—have become stamps of respectability. They are, in order of size:

Linklaters and Paines
Slaughter and May
Freshfields
Allen and Overy

The new kind of lawyer is a more adaptable and positive person: he is staking his claim in the new corporate world, and prepared to deal with any business, including tax, pensions and hire purchase, that his client might have. The new rôle is reflected in the Law Society—the great stone building in Chancery Lane, which serves as a solicitors' lunch-club and their professional headquarters. The Law Society prides itself on go-ahead methods,

[1] Quoted by Michael Birks: *Gentlemen of the Law*, 1960, p. 281.

and gradually it is coaxing its members into more up-to-date habits, with the help of efficiency experts, a cinema room, a photo-copying machine, a large information service, and a committee on Law Reform.

In the new situation, solicitors often have more scope than barristers. They are more adaptable, and they often make more money: and an able barrister may now change over to being a solicitor—instead of the other way round. Solicitors are far better educated than they were: in 1922 17 per cent were graduates; in 1960, 60 per cent.[1] But their education is still very backward: 'as far as I know,' said Lord Gardiner in 1964, 'we are the only Western country in which a law degree isn't an essential qualification for a lawyer to have.'[2] Solicitors remain the 'junior branch of the profession': most of the mystique and prestige of the law settles on barristers, and only a barrister can reach the top of the profession—a judgeship.

BARRISTERS

There are only about 2,100 practising barristers—roughly a tenth of the solicitors: the whole profession could be shipped off on one voyage of the *Queen Mary*. Half the barristers in Britain work in an area of London half-a-mile across, in one of the four Inns of Court. There they enjoy a recondite life of their own. At lunch they sit at long wooden benches in big hammer beam halls, like the halls of a public school or an Oxbridge college. They work in groups in 'chambers', approached by stone steps, with their names proclaimed in elegant eighteenth-century lettering. The Inns have their own elaborate snobberies and peck-order. The oldest and richest is the Inner Temple, alongside a round Saxon church, which has produced the largest number of judges. Next to it, the Middle Temple is less exclusive, though frequently visited by the Queen Mother. Across the road, Lincoln's Inn is almost entirely frequented by Chancery lawyers: while Gray's Inn, the newest of them, is known for its numbers of provincial barristers.

The Inns, like Oxbridge colleges, have very large powers: they are responsible for admissions and discipline, and have refused to delegate real power to the Bar Council. They are a 'survival of medieval republican oligarchy, the last to be found in Europe'.[3]

[1] *The Times*, November 14, 1961.
[2] *The Economist*, March 28, 1964.
[3] Sir Frederick Pollock: *Essays in the Law*, 1922.

They have large endowments in land, but no one knows the extent of their wealth since, unlike most institutions, they are exempted from publishing their accounts. They are ruled by Benchers—a self-perpetuating group of senior lawyers, who sit at a high table at one end of the hall, and run the Inn. To be elected a Bencher brings a barrister into the heart of the small society of the Bar. The Benchers are among the most die-hard and self-centred groups in the country, and the Inns of Court find it difficult to come to terms with each other, let alone with the public. A former Tory Attorney-General, Reginald Manningham-Buller (now Lord Dilhorne), tried to reform legal education to allow interchange between barristers and solicitors, and remarked on 'the archaic and time-wasting procedure' of consulting the Inns: 'there seems in the circumstances little prospect of getting the agreement of all four Inns in the near future to a proposal which the Bar Council on behalf of the Bar has advocated since 1907'.[1] The Inns are among the most absurd anachronisms in Britain, and their selfishness has done real harm: for instance, their reluctance to make decent arrangements for colonial students, who stream into the Bar[2] has contributed to the embittered and anti-British attitudes of many African and Indian barristers.

But the most striking characteristic of barristers is not so much their corporate life, as their loneliness. In an age of organisation men they remain individuals—which gives to the profession both its charm and its hazards. By their own decree, barristers cannot, as doctors or solicitors do, share their risks with anyone else. If they make money, they make it only for themselves, and if they fall ill they have no one to take their place. Barristers have the self-indulgent and idiosyncratic appearance of men who work by themselves, with none of the sameness of bureaucrats. They include a high proportion of bachelors or half-bachelors, and a surprising proportion of private incomes: barristers are apt to be shambling, bulging figures, looking rather obsolete in their penguin outfits, and (as one of them put it) the wrong shape for the twentieth century. They love discussing their profession and its faults, provided they don't have to change it. When one QC, R. E. Megarry, delivered the Hamlyn Lectures in 1963 on the state of the legal profession, Professor Gower commented: 'Most lawyers will love it, since it panders to the narcissism which goes with our complacency and self-deception.'

[1] *The Times*, July 11, 1961.
[2] *See* Lord Denning's Report of January, 1961.

Living, as some of them do, a quarter of their life in the courtroom, they have an odd mixture of scholarship and showmanship. There is an old fellow-feeling between the Bar and the stage, and at the Garrick Club, which they share, it is hard to tell them apart. Sir Patrick Hastings had only two interests—the Law and acting—and the Lord Chancellor, as we shall see, was surprisingly close to being an actor instead. But in the past thirty years the barristers have had to come to terms with a more humdrum age, and histrionics have been at a discount. They are more likely to be recounting the details of a factory accident to a sceptical judge, than passionately urging the virtues of a client to a weeping jury; and even to juries their style is now cosy and confidential. The decline of juries has discouraged acting, and full-throated advocates have found themselves without their audience. In 1933 36 per cent of common law cases were tried by jury: today less than 3 per cent have juries.

Like the army or the air force, the Bar has had much of the glamour taken out of it—and some of its profits too. Today there are perhaps ten barristers earning over £20,000. Recently the increase of legal aid has revived the profession, and helped to make it more secure; but taxation has made the Bar less popular, and judgeships more desirable. Today, a judge's salary of £8,000 with pension is worth more than most successful barristers' practices, and ambitious young barristers are more inclined to look to the bench as their ultimate aim.

JUDGES

There is a certain discrepancy between the public picture of judges, influenced by their wigs and majesty, as men of acknowledged wisdom, picked from a very competitive profession—and the actual situation. In fact the judges as a whole are not a spectacular élite. Out of fewer than 2,000 barristers, less than 150 judges are appointed (including county court judges)—a ratio of about fifteen barristers to one judge: and barristers themselves are a much less carefully selected profession than, for instance, administrative civil servants. Allowing for the fair proportion of impossible barristers, and a large number who do not want to be judges or who go into parliament or business, it is not too difficult for a hardworking man to be some kind of judge by the age of fifty. Every profession likes to appear more competitive than it is; but judges, who are thicker on the ground than admirals or bishops, have been unusually successful. While the senior judges are mostly men of exceptional intellect, the inflation among junior ones, and the resulting quality, has caused some criticism, even from *The Times*[1]: and the fact that a judge must be chosen from the ranks of barristers, at a time when many solicitors are more able, has been repeatedly criticised. The appointment of judges has never had the same radical reorganisation which the civil service underwent in the 1870's.

Nor do judges necessarily have a wide experience to furnish their wisdom: while they give their views on morals, criminology and politics, their actual experience outside the law is usually small. They rarely visit prisons to which they sentence criminals. Their own lives revolve round medieval institutions. And their preoccupation has been with the interpretation of the law, rather than its making. As Lord Devlin has said:

> The judges of England have rarely been original thinkers or great jurists. Many have been craftsmen rather than creators. They have needed the stuff of morals to be supplied to them so that out of it they could fashion the law.

More than any other group, judges are detached from everyday life. For two hundred and twenty-five days in the year they sit in their wigs from 10.30 to 4.15, listening to barristers arguing abstruse points of law. Their presence is deliberately surrounded with pomp, to emphasise the majesty of the law, and even in their private lives they are expected to remain fairly remote. Judges are not seen in pubs and cafés: their usual habitat is their cavernous office in the Law Courts, the high table of an Inn of Court, the Reform, the Garrick or the Oxford and Cambridge, a house in the country and a London flat. The Assize judges tour round the country with their own cook, their marshal and their clerk, not staying at hotels but at luxurious special houses deceptively called 'lodgings'.

Much more than American or continental judges the British bench has grown up detached from society and social developments. They have regarded the new sciences of psychology and sociology with scepticism, and many judges have prided themselves on their ignorance of everyday life. (Before the war the comedian George Robey was once cross-examined by Sir Patrick Hastings, in front of Mr. Justice Darling: 'Who *is* Mr. Robey?' asked

[1] *The Times*, November 2, 1961.

Darling. Sir Patrick quickly replied: 'The Darling of the Music Halls, My Lord.') But judges, like barristers, have become less eccentric, and since 1959 parliament has fixed an age limit for new judges of 75.

Judges are not as dispassionate as they appear: two have even been divorced, three have sat as members of parliament, and several have strong and known political views. But some young barristers feel that their pomp is excessive—making trials increasingly unrealistic and deferential—and complain that the majesty of the law becomes muddled with the majesty of the judges. I asked Lord Devlin about this: 'I don't think it's very serious,' he said: 'of course judges are bound to be a bit behind the times: you can't expect men with an average age of sixty to be as up-to-date as undergraduates. But I don't think the majesty of the law gets in the way of justice.'

Judges come from a small and conservative section of the community—their section is not growing much larger. In 1963 Dr. Philip Abrams, a Cambridge sociologist, analysed the social backgrounds of a hundred judges—current or recently retired. He found that 18 were sons of, or closely related to, peers or baronets; 17 were 'unequivocally upper-class' (meaning that they had been to major public schools, and their fathers were knights, generals or their equivalent, or in Burke's landed gentry); 39 were of upper-middle-class origin (from good public schools); 24 came from middle-class professional families; and only two came from humbler homes. 81 of the hundred came from Oxford or Cambridge; 39 came from Eton, Winchester, Harrow or Rugby.[1]

The Lord Chief Justice of England, Lord Parker of Waddington, is in keeping with the sequestered tradition of the British Law. He is head of the Queen's Bench Division, which deals with all common law and criminal cases. He can sit in any court, from the Queen's Bench to the House of Lords: he can decide which judge hears which case, he can make bold public statements, and he has the ear of the government. But most days he can be seen in his own large green room in the Law Courts, with brass chandeliers and velvet curtains, sitting with two of his colleagues in red robes and flapping white tabs, in front of a carved lion and unicorn.

Lord Parker is the son of a famous judge (he wears his father's old wig), took a double first in science at Cambridge, and has a nephew who is a QC. He began as a barrister for commercial cases, became a Treasury counsel and was appointed a judge at

[1] *Sunday Times*, August 18, 1963.

the age of fifty: he became Lord Chief Justice in 1958. He belongs to the non-histrionic school of judges, in contrast to his opinionated predecessor, Lord Goddard, Parker is unobtrusive and patient. He has not, as Goddard did, made known his political views, and he belongs to a more single-minded generation. He farms in the country, and is an expert on the genetics of cattle. When he was elevated, it was assumed that he would be much more lenient than his predecessor, and scores of convicted men appealed to his court, hoping for diminished sentences. But Parker soon dashed these hopes. He embarked on a tour of America in which he strongly advocated flogging, and back in London made speeches urging sterner sentences: he astonished the Bar by passing a record sentence of 42 years on George Blake, convicted of spying. And when the flood of appeals came up to him, he and his colleagues later actually increased the sentences.

The progress of a judge is elaborate, and marked by an archaic confusion of titles. Every judge must begin as a barrister: after ten years or more he may become a Queen's Counsel, known as John Smith, QC, with higher fees and the assistance of a junior. From there he may be appointed one of the 79 county court judges, when he will become known as His Honour Judge Smith, with a salary of £5,300 a year. Alternatively, a QC may be chosen for the High Court, where he becomes known as 'The Hon. Mr. Justice Smith', or 'Smith, J.', or 'Sir John Smith' (acquiring a knighthood automatically), earning £8,000 a year. From there he may become one of eleven judges in the Appeal Court, where he will wear black robes, become a privy councillor, and be known (although he is not a Lord) as 'Lord Justice Smith', 'Smith, L. J.', or 'the Right Honourable Sir John Smith'. Finally, he may become one of the nine Law Lords, who are life peers, sitting in the House of Lords, earning £9,000 a year, and known as 'the Right Honourable Lord Smith'.

Each court has a different atmosphere: as Lord Asquith of Bishopstone described it: 'A trial judge should be quick, courteous and wrong. That is not to say that the Court of Appeal should be slow, rude and right, for that would be usurping the function of the house of Lords.'[1]

The Law Lords are the supreme judiciary of Great Britain: (the Scottish courts have a separate hierarchy of judges, but one or two Scots judges sit in the House of Lords.) They are a very homogeneous group, and they can often be seen lunching together

[1] Quoted in *Law as Literature*, edited by Louis Blom Cooper, 1961.

at a special table at the House of Lords. Of the nine English Law Lords, four went to Oxford, four went to Cambridge. One (Lord Reid) is seventy-four, and only one is under sixty. Their sittings are undramatic and impressive; a group of five men, not in wigs and robes but in plain grey suits, sit in a room in the House, listening to the intricate arguments of counsel, which have by now reached a rarefied plane. They have about forty appeals a year, sitting a hundred days.

What are the qualities of a successful judge? 'Ability isn't the most important thing,' Lord Devlin told me: 'In most cases the facts aren't really very difficult to get at: no, the most important thing for a judge is—curiously enough—judgment. It's not so very different from the qualities of a successful businessman or civil servant. I'm always struck by how alike men in high positions seem to be. It's rather like seeing a lot of different parts of the stage, and finding that they're all Gerald du Maurier in the end.'

THE LAW AND POLITICS

The House of Commons doesn't like lawyers.
Hazlitt.

Lord Kilmuir, the former Lord Chancellor, told me how, when he first came to the House of Commons, Sir John Simon said to him: 'Remember that you have just been elected to the one legislative assembly in the world where lawyers as such are not popular. You will be hailed with almost perennial suspicion as the "Honourable and Learned Member".' Lawyers have excelled in politics, but not often reached the peak. The last career barrister to become prime minister was Asquith: the last (and only) solicitor was Lloyd George. The only law officer who ever became prime minister was Spencer Perceval in 1809, and he was shot dead two years later.

But nevertheless lawyers—more than any other profession—have gravitated to politics, and barristers make up a sixth of the House of Commons. For successful barristers politics has been a natural climax, and they have been able to combine a lucrative practice with a successful political career. The careers helped each other, and QCs and judges in the past have been often chosen for partly political reasons.

It is doubtful whether this close connection can continue. Both careers are more specialised and professional: to maintain a successful Bar practice while sitting on the back benches is much more difficult, and first-class barristers are more inclined to keep out of parliament: 'All of us' said one QC, 'are much more in grooves than we were.' This grooviness will make it difficult to find future Lord Chancellors who can be both politicians and judges, and this ancient intertwined job may have to be disentangled.

But while the Law has become a much more self-contained profession, split off from politics, it still likes to cling to its old authority and prestige, rather than to interest itself in the exciting new developments of society. The Law, more than any other profession, is imprisoned in its own myths and shibboleths, and while the benchers preserve their traditions, and the solicitors tie up their thick paper in pink tape, their protected world has become increasingly irrelevant to the great corporate world outside.

THE LORD CHANCELLOR

> I really went to the Bar because I thought it would be easier to go on the stage after failing at the Bar than to to the Bar after failing on the stage.
>
> *Lord Gardiner.*

At the top of the intricate legal pyramid is the ancient and confusing position of Lord High Chancellor. For the Lord Chancellor (as usually abbreviated) combines three quite separate functions: he is the head of the legal profession and senior judge—selecting judges, Queen's Counsel, the 16,000 Justices of the Peace, and 35,000 members of tribunals, and presiding (if he wishes) over the hearings of the Law Lords. He is also Speaker of the House of Lords, sitting on the Woolsack. He is also a member of the cabinet, and the government's chief legal adviser. He is the only man who combines the powers of the cabinet, the judiciary and the executive: he helps to make the laws, to carry them out, and to interpret them.[1] This combination has obvious advantages, and obvious perils; the legal side of the Lord Chancellor is always in danger of being over-influenced by the political side—as was alleged by the opposition to have happened in the Enaharo Case in 1963. The Lord Chancellor's post is the most ancient one in the government, five centuries older than the prime minister's, dating back to the medieval court, when the Chancellor was the

[1] The negation of Montesquieu's theory of the separation of powers.

'Keeper of the King's Conscience': and this seniority is still reflected by his salary of £14,500 a year, the highest in the government and £500 more than the prime minister's: at formal dinners or royal processions he walks in front of the prime minister. He lives in a Victorian house inside the Palace of Westminster, above a special 'Lord Chancellor's Courtyard' adjoining the House of Lords, and he works in a long high room overlooking the Thames, with heavy Gothic lamps hanging from the ceiling, and a tapestry at one end.

Lord Kilmuir has described how he reached the job: 'You remember in musical chairs that two things had to coincide, the stopping of the music and being opposite a chair. For those who want office, the office must be vacated and the candidate must be ripe. For the lucky law officer of the Crown, the chair was the Woolsack which was empty when the political music stopped.'[1] 'The Lord Chancellor's main job,' Kilmuir told me, 'is to be responsible for seeing that the machinery of law and administration is in working order. Because he is well placed to do this, public opinion accepts the anomaly of his three different powers. The rest of the cabinet looks to the Lord Chancellor to see that criticisms of the law are not unheeded: that justice is neither denied nor delayed; and that the law is moulded to the changing needs of society.'

Lord Chancellors, with their pomp, their burden and their odd mixture of duties, are not often bold reformers; but in October 1964 there arrived in this lonely job a very new kind of man, Lord Gardiner, to whom lawyers on both sides of politics looked for radical action. He was sixty-four when he reached the Woolsack, but he still had the outlook and simplicity of a young rebel. He had been tirelessly engaged in left-wing and humanitarian causes. He was chairman of the *New Statesman*, he had been a joint-chairman of the campaign against hanging, which had its triumph late in 1964, and he had defended *Lady Chatterley's Lover* against prosecution. His tall, well-tailored shape, with a bald, handsome head and a look of sea-green incorruptibility, was a portent for great changes.

Gardiner's career was romantic and spectacular, in the older legal tradition. He was the son of a prosperous shipping director, Sir Robert Gardiner, and he went to Harrow and Magdalen, Oxford (with a short interval in the Coldstream Guards, just

[1] *See* The Lawyer-Statesman: speech reprinted in the American Bar Association Journal, November, 1954.

after the first world war). At Oxford he was a gay and elegant rebel, with a reputation for smoothness which led to the formation of the 'SRGGH'—the Society for Ruffling Gerald Gardiner's Hair. He spent much of his time acting, and played in a variety show with Ivor Novello and Mrs. Patrick Campbell. He took part in politics as a Liberal, and became President of the Union. He devoted little time to law, and took a fourth class degree. He was eventually sent down for writing a pink pamphlet in defence of a girl undergraduate (Dilys Powell) who had been sent down for climbing into college.[1]

But as soon as he began practising as a barrister in London, he revealed his phenomenal mind, his energy and dedication. In the thirties he was already a well-known figure in the law courts, and by the fifties he was a Queen's Counsel of legendary skill. His acting ability still showed, in the discreetly histrionic twirls of his gown, and he could both master the intricacies of the common law, and put questions sharply, swiftly and dramatically. He was said to earn £30,000 a year, and his great performances, as in Lady Chatterley or the case against the Communist ballot-riggers in the Electrical Trades Union, were watched and admired as works of art. At the same time he became closely involved in the Labour Party, which he had first joined in the thirties. He stood for West Croydon in 1951, and lost by two thousand votes. He was outspoken in his views against hanging (which prevented him becoming a judge), and took a large part in 'Justice', the lawyers' society for protecting the law: he flew to Johannesburg to watch the Treason Trials, to Bizerta and to Portugal to investigate charges of torture. At the bar, his mixture of brilliance and do-gooding made him a hero to younger left-wing lawyers.

He became particularly interested in law reform, having been chairman of the Bar Council and having served on the Lord Chancellor's Committee. In an interview with *The Economist* six months before he took office, he outlined very plainly his ideas: he was determined to consolidate and simplfy the law ('our statute law consists of 43 volumes of statutes going back to 1235, and 99 volumes of delegated legislation, and on any one point you may have to look at 60 different acts of parliament'). He advocated a more thorough legal education, including knowledge of sociology and criminology. He supported the liberalisation of the laws of homosexuality and abortion, as well as the abolition of hanging.

[1] For this and other details, see Godfrey Smith's 'Gardiner, *QC*', *Sunday Times*, April 5, 1964.

And he intended to appoint (if he came into power) five Law Commissioners in the Lord Chancellor's Office, with responsibility for reforming the law.

And so, when Gardiner did become Lord Chancellor in October, expectations were high. Perhaps inevitably, anticlimax followed. Gardiner seemed too preoccupied with his new duties —particularly with the time-wasting duty of sitting on the Woolsack, presiding over a few sleepy peers—to have time to press quickly ahead. As Gardiner's deputy, Harold Wilson appointed a more conservative MP, Eric Fletcher, an expert on legal procedure who had been one of only six Labour members to vote for the retention of hanging. The appointment of Law Commissioners required legislation and time: and there were some who feared that Gardiner, being himself so high-minded, was too little aware of the limitations of his colleagues: 'One trouble with Gerald,' said one of his legal admirers, 'he's not a good judge of people.' It remains to be seen how far this dedicated and incisive man can cut through the tangles of tradition and confusion that jam up the English Law. Many lawyers are looking towards him with the fear that, if he cannot do it, nobody can.

11

CHURCHES

> What bishops like best in their clergy is a dropping-down-deadness of manner.
>
> *Sydney Smith, 1859.*

> There is in the Church of England a deliberate cult of amateurishness which is responsible for the futility of much that it tries to do.
>
> *Crockford's Preface, 1964.*

LIKE the Law, the Church is part of the ancient fabric of the country. It is not within the scope of this book, which is concerned with temporal power, to examine the character of the Churches, or to discuss the decline of religion. Yet the Churches of England and Scotland, since their establishment, have been too intertwined with the state to be left out, and the minorities have helped to mould the social structure of the country. In the course of its involvement, the Church of England, like the Law, has often been distracted by means rather than ends: its leaders have often become more interested in their archaic trappings than in their contemporary functions, more interested in vestments than in the H-bomb; and the public fame of the Archbishop of Canterbury reaches its climax in the astonishing Tudor ceremony of the Coronation. The more obvious oddities, such as the appointment of bishops, the patronage of livings and the parochial system are justified with the same kind of argument 'it's odd but it works' which might be heard in the Inns of Court. The fact that the system is of no value unless it builds up the religious life of the country may be forgotten, as barristers are apt to forget that their sole justification is to serve the ends of justice. However, the publication of the Paul Report, *The Payment & Deployment of the Clergy*, in January 1964, suggested that the system was certainly odd but that it *didn't* work.

THE PAUL REPORT

Leslie Paul's brief from the Church Assembly seemed fairly

harmless, but in fact the Deployment of the Clergy at once involved the researcher in the parson's freehold (you can't sack parsons except for gross and consistent immorality), and so in the nature of the Establishment and the whole future of the Church of England. Paul advocated not the abolition of the freehold but its transformation into a ten-year leasehold, extendable for a further five years. As it stood this suggestion pleased few sections of the Church—for some parsons fifteen years was too little and for others one year was too much. But the effect of the report was less notable for the 62 principal recommendations that it made, or the statistics it laid out, than for the discussion it initiated into the whole function of the Church in modern society. The Church Assembly, as the commissioning body, 'received' (though did not accept) the report; but there is evidence of considerable resistance to it among the country clergy and the evangelical wing. The evangelicals see in the discussed recommendations the underminging of the link between Church and State which they have always seen as the sheet-anchor against any tide in the direction of Rome.

LAMBETH

Every ten years, three hundred bishops of the Anglican Communion converge on London for the Lambeth Conference, from all over the world. At the opening, they gather at a garden party at Lambeth Palace to meet their spiritual head, the Archbishop of Canterbury. There are bishops from Korea, South Western Brazil, Ceylon, Japan, and even from Wales. There are Oriental bishops with exotic crosses; there is an Arab bishop, from Jordan and Syria; and there are ninety American bishops—outnumbering the English by two to one—looking more like businessmen. They all possess the same bonhomie, rubbing their palms together, reminiscing and stretching out welcoming hands. To the splendour of their appearance is added the splendour of their names, which give a Damon Runyon sound to them—Donald the Arctic, Edward Barbados, Kenneth Matabeleland, Victor Rangoon.

Most of the overseas bishops have only a loose relationship with the English Church: Canterbury is given special spiritual prestige, but exercises no authority. The six bishops in Wales and the seven bishops in Scotland have their own jurisdiction and autonomy. Out of the three hundred bishops, only forty-three are in England, under the jurisdiction of the Archbishops of Canterbury and York; and it is they who form the core of that puzzling institution, the Established Church of England.

The extraordinary origins of the Anglican Church still set its character and determine its relations with the State—ever since the break with Rome in 1534, when Henry VIII assumed the title of 'Supreme Head of the Church of England'. In theory, the Church exchanged its independence for a close moral influence on the sovereign and the government—including twenty-six seats for bishops in the House of Lords and the right of the Archbishop to crown the sovereign. It has never exerted a radical influence. Throughout the eighteenth and nineteenth centuries, it remained closely identified with the aristocracy and conservatism. The Anglican Church supported the persecution of dissenting Churches and Roman Catholics: only since 1829 have Catholic priests been allowed to live within five miles of towns, and only since 1871 have dissenters been allowed to teach at Oxford and Cambridge. The sovereign and the Lord Chancellor must both be Anglicans, but the prime minister can now be of any religion: Lloyd George was a Welsh dissenter, Ramsay MacDonald and Campbell-Bannerman were both Scottish Presbyterians, Neville Chamberlain was a Unitarian, Harold Wilson is a Congregationalist. It is the prime minister, as adviser to the sovereign, who appoints the bishops[1] (with the help of a special patronage secretary at 10 Downing Street, sometimes known as the 'bishop-spotter'). A commission under Lord Howick to survey the appointments system reported in November 1964 that the present method—despite being unique among churches everywhere—required no change.

The Church of England is not actually *owned* or subsidised by the State. Its income comes (apart from the offerings of the faithful) from its own land and capital, and only five of the 97 Church Commissioners who administer it are appointed by the Crown. The Church is one of the biggest proprietors in the country: its total assets are more than £300 million—a third of ICI's—providing an income of over £17 million a year: it owns 223,000 acres of land, third only to the Forestry Commission and the Crown. The money is looked after by a team of three commissioners, headed by Lord Silsoe, the same man who handles the crown lands. Over half its assets (£187 million) are now in stock exchange securities, and since 1948 it has moved most of that out of government stock into industrial shares, to the delight of the

[1] Unless he is a Roman Catholic: but there has not yet been a Catholic premier.

stock exchange. It has also co-operated with Charles Clore and other property financiers to develop their more valuable properties in the centre of cities. The development round St. Paul's Cathedral in London is a particularly celebrated example. But the Commissioners still refuse to invest in drink, gambling or armaments.

BISHOPS

The splendour and wealth of bishops has diminished in the past fifty years. In the nineteenth century the discrepancy between the bench and the clergy was grotesque. In 1906 the average income of a parson was about £150, while the Archbishop of Canterbury had £15,000 a year. The incomes of bishops and deans are among the very few which have *not* gone up over the past century.

Most of the forty-three bishops today earn £2,500 or less—together with a house and garden (the total upkeep of bishops' gardens cost £28,000 p.a.). The Archbishop's salary is £7,500—together with two fine houses in London and Canterbury: the first Archbishop Temple, at the end of the nineteenth century, sold the country estate of the Archbishop of Canterbury, believing it wrong for the primate to be associated with landed wealth.

The bishops in England are much more unobtrusive than they were: they inhabit their antique palaces without pomp or splendour, and often without gaiters. They are still addressed as 'My Lord', and archbishops, like dukes, are called 'Your Grace'. But they come from the same kind of Oxbridge stock as judges or top civil servants, and nowadays a good deal of their time, like permanent secretaries', is spent in committees. In 1961 three-quarters of the bishops had been to public schools, and all but three to Oxford and Cambridge, mostly Cambridge: two of the others were at Trinity College, Dublin. Half the bishops were sons of clergymen, only one was the son of a bishop, and only one was an old Etonian. Eight had been Oxford or Cambridge dons. But there is still a muscular tradition: Lichfield and Chester rowed in their university boat, Exeter played hockey for the West of England, Portsmouth was a Rugger blue, and Norwich was an explorer-geologist in Iceland and the Antarctic.

Among the bishops probably the most eminent theologian is Robert Mortimer, Bishop of Exeter, a handsome grey-haired former Professor at Oxford, who is the Church's main authority on gambling, sex and moral problems. The most prominent administrator is Robert Stopford of London, who organised the 1958 Lambeth Conference. Most bishops keep out of politics, but a few display opinions, including William Manchester, a former civil servant from Northern Ireland, who talks against the H-bomb and capital punishment, and several show a talent for showmanship. The most politically voluble is Mervyn Southwark, an elegant bachelor well-known for his left-wing views, who has written articles in the *Evening Standard* (like Dean Inge, 'from being a pillar of the Church, he became a column in the Standard'). He seems to have made the classic episcopal transformation from poacher to gamekeeper, and in his diocese he has built up a group of dynamic and controversial priests. It was he, together with Dr. Donald Soper and Canon Stanley Evans, who took the Labour Government's service of dedication in November 1964. One minister explained this unprecendented occasion: 'We wanted to show that God wasn't Tory'.

On most contemporary political issues, including capital punishment, the bishops have till recently been divided. At the time of Suez, Bishop Mortimer of Exeter and Bishop Harland of Durham wrote to *The Times* in defence of the government; Bell of Chichester, Greer of Manchester and Martin of Liverpool attacked the invasion; Ramsey said in the Lords that a Christian could equally conscientiously support or reject the Suez policy. But Dr. Fisher, then Archbishop of Canterbury, though he made an ambiguous speech in the Lords, went to Downing Street to express his concern.

One man who combines learning with administration is Donald Coggan, Archbishop of York. He was the son of a businessman, and after leaving Oxford he became a don, a curate, and later Professor of the New Testament in Toronto. He is an evangelical bishop, and is particularly concerned with preaching and the Bible. Known as a friendly, unpompous man, he is also a skilful mimic—mimicry and story-telling are favourite ecclesiastical pastimes—and one of his favourite imitations is of the Archbishop of Canterbury. (Christina Foyle—who runs the Foyle's literary luncheons—is a connoisseur of speeches, and has reported that bishops make the wittiest speeches but lawyers make the best ones.)

Two centres of religious activity are at Coventry, where the new cathedral acts both as a spur and a symbol, and Southwark where the Bishop of Woolwich (whose *Honest to God* has sold over 300,000 copies) and other bright speakers arouse the enthusiasm of their supporters and the suspicion of quite a lot of other people.

But some of the most testing bishoprics are abroad, in the East and Africa—where Christianity is on the way out. One bishop, more than any other, has become associated with politics—though more by accident than design: he is Trevor Huddleston, Bishop of Masasi in Tanganyika. Huddleston's tall and gentle presence has made a unique mark on Africa. Though still regarded as a political priest, he is primarily a pastor, impelled by a warm, simple approach to people, and only reluctantly did he become involved in politics. He came from a distinguished Anglo-Catholic family, and after Oxford entered the monastery at Mirfield—a stark old mill-owner's mansion, with a stone chapel on top of a grey hill in Yorkshire. From there he was sent out to Johannesburg and over twelve years became steadily more deeply involved in African rights, at a time when the Anglican Church was slow to commit itself. 'It has been the teaching of the Church through the centuries,' he said at the time of the Defiance Campaign in 1953, 'that when government degenerates into tyranny, laws cease to be binding on its subjects.' He was recalled from South Africa by his Superior in 1955, spent five years at Mirfield and in London, and then, to his relief and delight, was elected Bishop in Tanganyika. In Africa and London, Huddleston has come to stand for a radicalism and simplicity of religion which becomes lost in the intricacies of the Anglican Church at home.

CLERGY

The contrast between bishops and clergy is less sharp than it was, but still striking. The average salary of a clergyman is still only £850 a year—less than a steelworker's—and his pension after the age of seventy is £300 a year. The poverty of clergymen is proverbial. There are a few wealthy town parishes where priests can live in style, and in some fashionable London churches the Easter offering can amount to £300. But most parsons are poor, and some have to subsist on as little as £600 a year—less than the wage of a bus-driver.

At the end of 1962 there were 20,247 clergymen in the Church of England (an increase of 686 over the previous year), and about 18,000 churches. But the distribution among the population is uneven: 'I'll tell you what's wrong with the Church,' said a man at the Information Office: 'the people are all in the towns, and the clergy are all in the country.' As Leslie Paul says, 'some 4,630 clergy are in charge of parishes of 1,500 population or less, while a roughly equal number, 4,794 ,are concerned with parishes which rise from 5,000 to over 20,000 in population'. The total number of parsons has fallen steadily since 1900, when it reached a peak of 23,670: since then old clergymen have died, fewer young ones have come forward, and the average age has gone up from 49 in 1901 to 54 in 1962. Parishes have doubled-up, and curates have dwindled. Even since 1948 the number of clergymen has fallen by 1,000: but recently there has been an upturn, and in 1962 more clergymen were ordained than in any year since before the first world war. All the same, the average age remains a serious problem. The Bishop of Gloucester estimated for his diocese that whereas in 1960 the average age of incumbents was 51·2, by 1980 it would be 62.5.

The Victorian idea of having 'a gentleman in every parish' is being dropped. In the nineteenth century a large proportion of parsons were parsons' sons, or the younger sons of the gentry: the large country rectories which still remain next to country churches are the reminders of their wealth, and from the parsonages have come an extraordinary high proportion of distinguished people—including Addison, Swift, Goldsmith, Wesley, Coleridge, Sterne, Crabbe, the Brontës, Kingsley, Tennyson, Samuel Butler, Nelson and Rhodes. But the contemporary clergyman is less part of society than his forebears, and less certainly a part of the small-town community—with the solicitor, bank manager, doctor or magistrate. Parsons are more apt to be eccentric, independent men, who find in their parish and church a retreat from the world, and the isolation of the Church increases this tendency.

The placing of clergy remains a curiously feudal affair: over half the 12,000 livings are still in the gift of private patrons—including trusts. Lord Salisbury, for instance, has seven livings in his gift, and the Duke of Norfolk has five—though being a Roman Catholic he is not allowed to exercise his choice. It is still possible to buy an 'advowson'—as the patronage of a living is called—though there are now fewer on the market. Of the remaining 6,000, 800 livings are in the hands of universities and colleges, who give preference to old college men. Another 850 are under the Crown and its officers, and only the remaining 5,000 are directly under the diocesan bishops. Some clergy defend the system of patronage on the grounds that it provides variety of choice, and avoids 'one opinion', but private livings are gradually falling into disuse, and passing to the bishops.

Apart from 20,000 clergymen there are immense numbers of people engaged in Church activities—including (at the end of 1962)

85,254 Sunday school teachers
6,571 Licensed readers
295,000 Members of Church youth clubs
380 Moral Welfare workers

How many Englishmen are active members of the Church of England? More than sixty per cent are baptised, but only thirty per cent are confirmed, and only eight per cent go to Easter Communion. Over half the marriages in England are in Anglican churches: but the proportion of Anglican marriages has fallen steadily since 1840[1]—when it was as high as ninety per cent—while the number of civil marriages and Roman Catholic marriages has gone up. But for Easter Communion the numbers have begun to rise since 1947—when they reached their lowest figure of five per cent. Since the war there has been an increase in the congregations in suburbs and new towns—where churchgoing seems to be becoming part of the social pattern, as in America. But it does not appear that the Church exercises any more power through its parishes than it does through its synods and bishops. It does, however, seem that it is a less discredited institution now than it was before the war.

CANTUAR

At the head of the Church of England is the Most Reverend Michael Ramsey—the hundredth Archbishop of Canterbury and Primate of All England since St. Augustine, the Roman missionary, was appointed in AD 597. Since his appointment in 1961, Ramsey's unmistakable presence has suddenly loomed out from television and newspapers. He is a big man, with a venerable medieval look, tufts of white hair and big eyebrows, which wobble up and down in a friendly way while he listens. To meet, he gives an immediate impression of unworldliness and compassion. He could not, like other bishops, be mistaken for a businessman or a headmaster: he sits back in his chair, encased in purple, listening intently and nodding with frequent mmms, and talking in a simple biblical language—'right glad', 'mark that', 'be sure of that'. He

[1] Though the 1957 figures were the same as in 1952.

is apt to say 'let, however, a caveat be here made', when he means 'but'.[1] He is much less vague than he seems: he takes a close interest in other people's problems, has a good memory for names, and is not unaware of Church politics. But he is, unlike his predecessor Dr. Fisher, primarily a theologian and a pastor; he lives more at Canterbury than Lambeth, is driven in an Austin Princess, and spends his holidays with his wife (they have no children) in a small village pub in Devon, chatting and walking. Under him the Church of England may not obviously become a greater force in the land, but is quite likely to become more religious.

Ramsey's career has been academic and rarefied: his father was a Congregationalist Cambridge don and his brother, who died very young, was a brilliant Cambridge philosopher and mathematician, author of *Foundations of Mathematics.* At Cambridge Ramsey changed from classics to theology, took a first, and became a Liberal President of the Union—just before Selwyn Lloyd. He was ordained, took to teaching at Lincoln Theological College and, after a brief interval in a parish, became professor of divinity, first at Durham, then at Cambridge. Then came the bishopric of Durham and the Archbishopric of York.

When Dr. Fisher was due to retire, there was great uncertainty and much lobbying about his successor: Fisher himself favoured the Bishop of Peterborough, or Dr. Coggan, then Bishop of Bradford. Some people regarded Ramsey as too much a pure theologian, and too High Church, and too ineffectual for the big job, with its heavy administrative burden. But others insisted that he alone had the necessary theological toughness and preoccupation with religion, and after a period of 'consultation' (more probably a rarefied form of horse-trading) Macmillan got his man in—Ramsey. Peterborough got London, Bradford got York. As a sop to the low church (Coggan) faction, a number of new episcopal appointments were from amongst evangelicals—John Taylor at Sheffield, Gordon Savage at Southwell, John Tiarks at Chelmsford.

Ramsey approached his job with caution: 'We are here as a Church to represent Christ crucified and the compassion of Christ crucified before the world,' he said in a television interview, 'and because that is so, it may be the will of God that our Church should have its heart broken, and perhaps the heart of the Archbishop broken with it, just because we are here to represent Christ and Christ's compassion. But if that were to happen it wouldn't mean that we were heading for the world's misery but quite likely

[1] *Sunday Times*, December 20, 1964.

pointing the way to the deepest joy.'[1] It is only fair to add that Dr. Ramsey has not in the last three years made any impact on the world at large either in what he has done or said. Many sections of the Church find him baffling, too.

How great is the influence of the Church on the government? In the past few years, all the most prominent men in the conservative cabinet have been regular church-goers: Harold Macmillan still reads the lesson in his village church; Sir Alec Douglas Home, R. A. Butler, Quintin Hogg, Henry Brooke (who owns the copyright of 'Silent Night') and Ted Heath (an excellent organist) have all been active churchmen. But their contact with the Church is largely at parish level, on Sundays only: and the relationship between Archbishop and Prime Minister has been much less obviously significant than it was in the days of Cosmo Lang and Stanley Baldwin. With the Labour Party, which has many more nonconformists and agnostics at the top, the relationship is even more remote.

CHURCH OF SCOTLAND

In remarkable contrast to the Church of England is its neighbour, the Church of Scotland, and the co-existence of these two disparate bodies is one of the oddest features of the kingdom. When the Queen comes to Edinburgh every year, she becomes suddenly Scottish, and attends a Church which is Calvinist, Presbyterian and hostile to bishops and quite pathological about the Pope (in the Westminster confession).

Every year the Church of Scotland meets for the General Assembly, when about 1,400 commissioners gather to debate Scottish and world affairs. The membership is impressive: 1,281,000 Scotsmen are communicant members, out of 3,500,000 adults—compared to only 2,000,000 communicants in the whole of the Church of England. The Assembly comes near to taking the place of a Scottish parliament, and is often regarded as the 'Voice of Scotland': 'It is (said the *Glasgow Bulletin* in 1948) perhaps the nearest thing to Parliament that we have had since 1707.' The splendour which surrounds Assembly Week, some Scotsmen suggest, is a substitute for the gap left by the departure of a Scots king and a Scots parliament.

The General Assembly is much more politically outspoken than the Convocations or Church Assembly in England, and it does not

[1] 'Three Archbishops', ATV June 4, 1961.

confine itself to Scottish affairs. Their most angry debates in recent years have been over Nyasaland (now Malawi)—which is a kind of African Scotland—and many Presbyterian ministers have emerged to champion Nyasa rights. The most persistent of them has been the Very Reverend George Macleod, a former Moderator who was the founder of the Iona Community (where he lives in the summer).

NONCONFORMISTS

The influence of dissenters, on the other hand, has weakened since the beginning of the century—when the number of nonconformist marriages reached its peak of about fourteen per cent, and nonconformity was optimistic and strong: the Liberal party of 1906 was said to be the first since the time of Charles II with most of its members non-Anglican. Since then, some of the impetus of the Chapel has waned, in striking contrast to America; partly this has come from the general decline of working-class zeal, and partly from the tendency for nonconformist families, once they become prosperous, to turn to Anglicanism: 'The coach and pair,' says the old Victorian saw, 'does not pass the church door for more than two generations.' There are prominent Methodists in business, including Lord Mackintosh, the toffee-maker, and Lord Rank, the film magnate; but there is no real Methodist aristocracy.[1] Harold Wilson and his family have always attended a nonconformist Church, but there is little sign of a Congregationalist 'Establishment' inside the Labour Party.

Some Methodists have been worried about the effects of the official 'conversations' between them and the Anglicans about reunion. 'We have been walking out long enough and it is time we got busy with a marriage ceremony', said Dr. Coggan, Archbishop of York, in October 1964. The narrowing of the old rift between Church and Chapel has obvious benefits, but the dissenting Churches had a radicalism and fervour which did much to break into British complacency, and which is much less apparent today. Now the Free Churches are apt to be as conformist as the Church of England, and have lost much of their hold on significant developments. But the nonconformist conscience remains a powerful force, and has moulded men as different as Lord Franks, Lord Rank, Harold Wilson and Sir Ivan Stedeford.

[1] *See* D. W. Brogan: *The English People*, 1943. p. 122.

These are some of the denominations, with their membership in 1963:

Methodists	4,921 Ministers	918,440 Members
Baptists	2,136 Pastors and and Deaconesses	300,382 Members
Congregationalists	1,724 Ministers	202,275 Members
Presbyterian, Church of Wales	441 Ministers in pastoral charge	210,126 Adherents
Congregational, Union of Scotland	158 Ministers	30,763 Members
Independent Methodists	269 Ministers	7,926 Members
Wesleyan Reform Union	20 Ministers	5,576 Members

ROMAN CATHOLICS

A recurring British topic is the idea that Roman Catholics are taking over key sectors of British life—usually the Foreign Office, the BBC, *The Times*, and the House of Lords.

About one in ten of the population of Britain is Catholic. The great majority are working class, from poor Irish immigrants; many are upper class, but there is no great middle class core of Catholicism. (Upper-class Catholics are said to talk about mass to rhyme with *pass*, middle class rhyme it with *lass*, working class rhyme it with *fuss*.) The social superiority of Catholics has been emphasised by the novels of the two great Catholic novelists, Evelyn Waugh and Graham Greene ('I'm sure between them they're responsible for the idea that Catholicism is a snob religion,' said one Catholic). But the aristocratic Catholic families do have a social exclusiveness of their own, and spend a great deal of time in each other's homes. Some of them, such as the Duke of Norfolk, have remained Catholic ever since the Reformation, under considerable persecution, which has given a tradition of close-knit, protective loyalty: and there are pockets of England, such as the Arundel Estate, North-East Suffolk, Stonor near Henley, or parts of Lancashire, which have a strong Catholic territorial influence. To the old Catholic families have been added the many Victorian converts, and the twentieth-century Catholic intellectual converts, such as Alec Guinness and Lord Longford.

Catholics favour certain professions: the army, for instance—'There's a tradition of fighting in the Church, and it's a way, if you're a minority, of proving your patriotism.'[1] Medicine is becom-

[1] *See* Ampleforth and Downside Schools, p. 260.

ing less popular, partly because of the prohibition of contraceptives, which could make a GP's life difficult. Some good Catholics avoid politics, because they are afraid of a conflict of loyalties, but the Catholics hold their own in parliament, with nineteen Labour MPs and thirteen Tories. Besides Lord Longford in the Cabinet, there are two other Catholics in the Labour Government, Bob Mellish and Maurice Foley—more than for a very long time.

The numbers of Catholics are increasing. The proportion of Catholic marriages has risen steadily since 1910, from 4 per cent to 11 per cent: and all children of Catholic marriages must be brought up in the Catholic faith. The increase has come partly from conversion—about 15,000 people are converted every year with the help, among other things, of an Enquiry Centre, a well-organised advertising campaign, and twenty-one leaflets about the Pope, sin, confession, etc.

The Catholic Enquiry Centre reported in 1964 that since it began in 1954

157,324 people have applied for the course,
100,000 took the course up to 1959
7,300 were received.

The total of converts to Catholicism were

1954	11,920
1955	13,291
1956	14,770
1957	14,581
1958	14,363
1959	15,794[1]

Since 1959 figures have not been given. There has been in fact a sharp decline in the number of converts, and this is causing much concern in the English Catholic hierarchy. Some of the bishops blame the new friendly, ecumenical attitude issuing from Rome. Converts now have not the satisfaction of being seen entering the enemy camp, and they tend to be muddled about what the various Churches do, and do not, stand for.

But the numbers are also increased by the tendency for Catholic families to be larger than Protestant ones. And when Protestants marry Catholics, they have Catholic children: in this way a num-

[1] On the other hand in 1958, 3,771 Roman Catholics were received into the Church of England, according to *Facts and Figures*, 1962.

ber of old aristocratic families—for instance the amilies of the Duke of Rutland and the Earls Ferrers and Dalhousie, who have all married Catholics—will become Catholic in the future. Eleven peerages have become Catholic since 1900 and another twelve are expected to do so in the next generation.

12

SCHOOLS

Look out Gentlemen, the Schoolmaster is abroad!

Lord Brougham.

AFTER the unchanging institutions of the Church and the Law, we come to an area of almost total uncertainty and flux, the schools. Nowhere has the British passion for letting institutions just grow, and the British distaste for centralised control, been more evident than in the educational system. Yet education is the main instrument of change: it is the schools that mould the future attitudes of society, and must lay the foundation of new skills and adaptability. As Britain's overseas problems diminished, in the late fifties, so with remarkable suddenness education came to the forefront as the largest political problem, studied and discussed as never before. Britain's confident assumption of her superiority gave way, in the current malaise, to new doubts as to what kind of country she should be, and what kind of schooling was needed to change her.

When the Labour Government took office in October 1964 they had a clear radical blueprint for education. They were to get rid of segregation at the age of eleven, to reorganise secondary education on comprehensive lines, and to set up an Educational Trust to advise on the best way of integrating the public schools in the state programme. The Minister of Education, Anthony Crosland, who took over from Michael Stewart after his promotion in January 1965, is not (as Stewart was) an obvious reformer. He went to a public school, became an Oxford don, and is not at all averse to enjoying himself. He has a sharp and sceptical mind, more at home with seminars than speeches, and 'does not suffer fools gladly'. He is a 'revisionist' who is not convinced of the necessity for nationalisation, or the villainy of private enterprise. But he also has an underlying layer of puritanism (his parents were Plymouth Brethren), and he believes passionately in the need for genuine equality of opportunity, and the reform of public schools. In particular, Crosland is firm on the most controversial educational reform—the replacement of grammar schools with 'comprehensives', to give children the chance to change educational streams after eleven. The Labour insistence on comprehensives became, quite suddenly, one of the most bitter of all political controversies.

Education in Britain is not solely run by the minister—not yet, anyway. It is run by what ministry men optimistically call the Partners. Education is the last great fief left to local government in Britain: local education authorities spent £1,001 million out of the total public spending on education, £1,277 million, in 1962–3.[1] The ministry decides how much they can spend on new building, and how many teachers they can employ, but it is the authorities who decide the shape of education in their fief. There have been cracks in the rigid tripartite system of the 1944 Act, and experiments have provided reformers with valuable ammunition and shown change was both practical and desirable. These experiments were the work, not of a great reforming minister, but of unsung local education officers like Mason of Leicestershire or Clegg of the West Riding. And unlike the school boards in America the local authorities have little control over what goes on in the schools. That is the jealous province of the third group in the partnership, the teachers.

In January 1965 the view from Curzon Street was bewildering and exciting. Reorganisation had suddenly become fashionable: 65 out of 148 local authorities had already drawn up a detailed plan to go more or less comprehensive, and another 55 were considering some kind of reorganisation. But although the tide was moving towards the Labour blueprint, only a handful of authorities had yet coped with the hard practical problems of putting schemes into operation. In general, the schools system was still the old class-ridden one of 1944. And, as we shall see, the reforming authorities were beginning to hit the submerged rocks in the way of reform.

THE STREAMS OF SCHOOLS

'British sociologists have sometimes been accused of being obsessed with the underprivileged. But I regard the eighty per cent of children in secondary modern schools as underprivileged; and in the circumstances I am prepared to be viewed as obsessed.'

Professor David Glass, 1964.

The education of three-quarters of British children, as every

[1] This includes capital expenditure, in current expenditure alone, the local education authorities spent £858 million out of £1,059 million.

parent knows, begins with one decisive selection at the age of eleven—the sorting machine of Britain's élite. Until recently, this was the standard European pattern: after eleven, the clever boys went off to grammar schools in Britain, to lycées in France and Italy, to gymnasien in Germany and Sweden. Only America could afford to avoid this segregation, and to keep all their children together, without a special élite, until sixteen or eighteen. In 1926 the Hadow Report rationalised the break at eleven:

> 'There is a tide which begins to rise in the veins of youth at the age of eleven or twelve. It is called by the name of adolescence. If that tide can be taken at the flood, and a new voyage begun in the strength and along the flow of its current, we think that it will move on to fortune. We therefore propose that all children should be transferred, at the age of eleven or twelve, from the junior or primary school.'

The present educational structure in Britain was the result, as Harold Dent, the London educationalist has said, of a 'curious amalgam of educational aspiration, administrative expedients and end-products of extraneous pressures'. It began in 1944, when the great Education Act which provided secondary education for all children to the age of fourteen (with specific provision that it should be raised to fifteen, then sixteen, when possible) transformed 3,000 senior elementary schools into secondary schools at the stroke of a pen. These, renamed Secondary Moderns, were to educate the great bulk of English children (the word 'modern', both here and in the French colleges 'modernes', was a curious euphemism for 'less clever'.) They were to provide a 'good all-round secondary education, not focused primarily on the traditional subjects of the school curriculum, but arising out of the interests of the children'. Dent comments: 'No brief could have been more formidably vague.' Clever children, as before, would go to the grammar schools, and children 'good with their hands' should go to technical schools. This was the tripartite system: three kinds of school for three kinds of children. In most areas it was bipartite: the proportion of technical schools remained tiny. The educational philosophy behind it had already been discredited by the Spens Report six years before, in 1938: 'There is in fact no clear line of demarcation, physical, psychological or social, between the pupils who attend grammar schools and those who attend modern schools . . . The line as drawn up at present is always artificial and often mistaken.'

The Education Act was much less rigid than its interpretation by most local education authorities (LEA's). Most of them followed the recommendations of the Butler White Paper that preceded the Act: 'such then will be the three main types of secondary school . . .', and missed the next three sentences: 'It would be wrong to suppose that they will necessarily remain separate and apart. Different types may be combined in one building or on one site. . . . In any case the free interchange of pupils from one type to another must be facilitated.'

The outrageous piece of special pleading behind the Act was the idea that the three kinds of school should have 'parity of esteem'. Instead, at eleven, all British schoolchildren were divided into two classes, 'eggheads and serfs'. How could the old elementary schools compete with grammar schools with their large grants and long tradition of preparing boys for the universities? Virtually no national effort was put into research into what the secondary moderns should be doing. Some did experiment: but the decentralised education structure did not promote controlled experiment or the extension of successful ideas to other schools. Too many just remained what Martin Mayer has called 'custodial institutes'. Teachers referred to the 'submerged three-quarters'. Only gradually did the schools begin to turn to the obvious solution for their brighter children and introduce courses to the General Certificate of Education: the key to further education. In 1962–3 the submerged three-quarters provided 41,056 candidates for O-level compared with 35,076 from the privileged five per cent at independent schools. At A-level, the secondary moderns had 318 candidates, the private schools, 9,838.

In 1963 the Newsom Report, on the education of average and below-average children, presented a bleak picture. It revealed slum schools with fifteen-year-olds cramped into primary school furniture and the teachers changing every term, and made a powerful plea for more grown-up education for the fifteen- and sixteen-year-olds, and for a curriculum that was 'practical, realistic and vocational'. Their main recommendation, as they said, was implicit in the whole report: 'their' children 'should receive a greater share of the national resources devoted to education . . . and by resources we do not mean solely finance.' They asked for a change of attitude: 'This cannot be achieved solely by administrative action. It involves a change of thinking and a change of heart.' And they summed up the theme of the report in its title, 'Half our Future'.

The eleven-plus, the most impartial test that could be devised, was flagrantly unfair. There are wide regional differences in the provision of grammar school places. Wales has the most, the eastern region the least. In 1963 33 per cent of Welsh secondary schoolchildren were in maintained grammar schools; in the east only 22·6 per cent. Far worse than the regional differences are the social ones. Survey after survey showed the idea of equal opportunity was a myth. The fullest, a study of the educational performance of every child born in a week of March 1946, by J. W. B. Douglas, showed the astonishing difference class, parents' attitudes, even physical housing conditions, made to children's progress at school.[1] The survey showed that middle-class children have a far higher chance of getting to grammar school—54 per cent of upper middle-class children got places, compared with 11 per cent of lower manual working-class ones. Douglas gave all the children in the survey standard intelligence tests. They found that middle-class children had an advantage over working-class children *of equal intelligence* in the scramble. Only the cleverest children, the top two per cent of the intelligence range, were sure of a place whatever their background. Douglas compared the results of children who scored 55–57 in his tests, a borderline grammar school score: 51 per cent of the upper middle-class children got grammar school places; 34 per cent of lower middle; 21 per cent of upper manual and 22 per cent of the lower manual working classes. Surveys in other European countries produced the same results: children from what the French sociologists call *les familles educogènes* were getting the grammar school places. Most European countries have now modified their selection procedures: Sweden has 'gone comprehensive' and in the late 1950s the French introduced a scheme delaying selection until 13. The problem is not just one of social justice. It is one of wasting the greatest national resource—able manpower.

The chart overleaf shows the streams of schools, and the progress of children in them. The most striking feature of the flow is the abrupt dam at fifteen—the official school-leaving age. In America, 75 per cent of children are still at school at seventeen: in Britain, only 12·9 per cent are. It is true that more and more children

[1] *See The Home and the School*, J. W. B. Douglas (Macgibbon and Kee, 1964).

THE STREAMS OF SCHOOLS

Children in England and Wales with percentages of total age group (Jan. 1963)

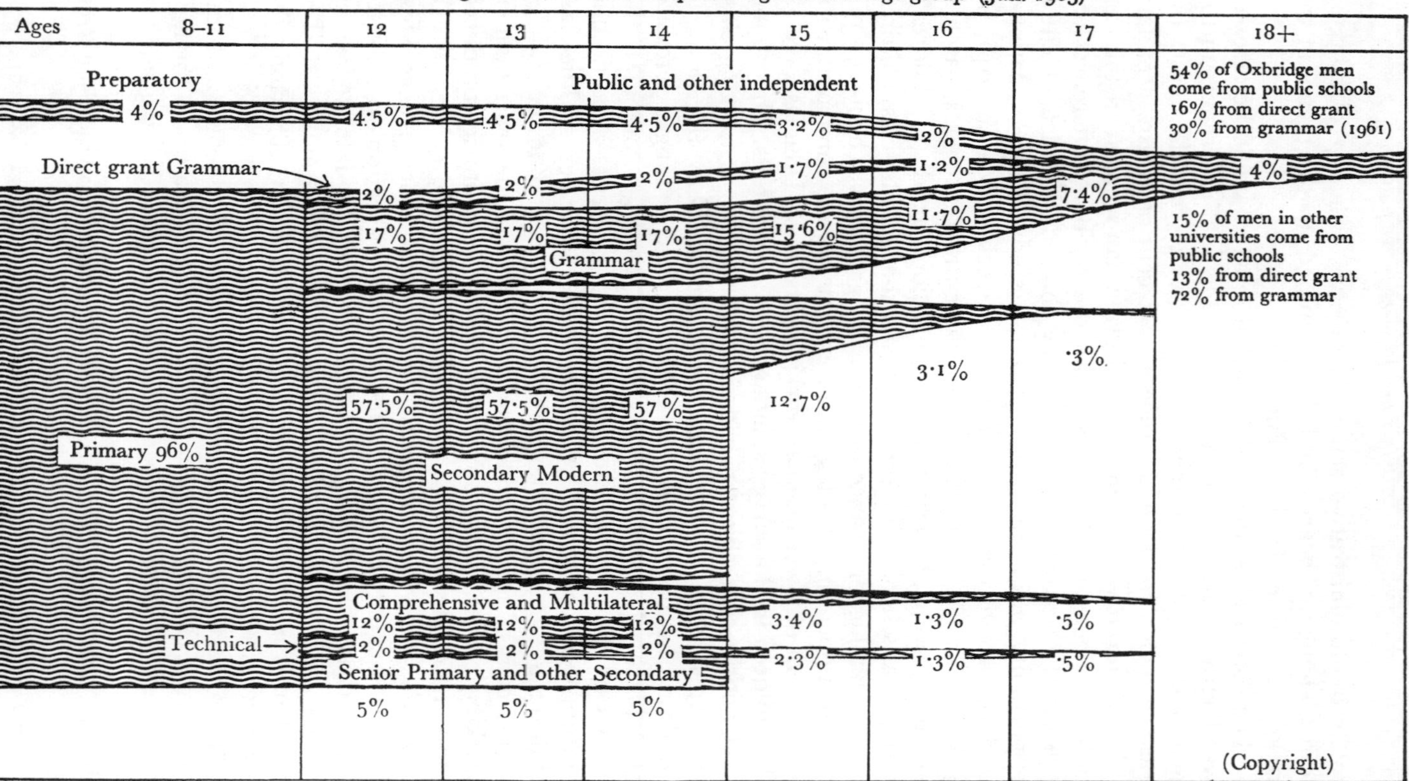

are staying on voluntarily beyond the school-leaving age—the phenomenon known to schoolteachers as 'Trend'. But Trend is again affected by regional variations—in 1963, 28 per cent of London children stayed on at school at 16, in the north only 14·9 per cent did—and by social class.

The great proportion of children still go out to work at 15. The 1944 Education Act provided for an extension of the school-leaving age to 16 as soon as possible, but by 1959 nothing had been done, and Sir Geoffrey Crowther's Report, 'Fifteen to Eighteen', the most important and the most ignored of the post-war education reports, recommended that the leaving age should be raised to sixteen by 1966–9. In 1963 Sir John Newsom's Report repeated the plea. Only then did the Conservative government capitulate, and announced that the age would go up from 1970–1.

For the purposes of this book, the most significant streams remain the two at the top of the chart: the children in the public schools and the grammar schools. For these are the ones who will to on to the universities, and from the university graduates, the future managers of Britain will be chosen.

PUBLIC SCHOOLS

> I should agree with those who hold that moribund class distinctions are being given artificial respiration by our educational system.
>
> *John Dancy, Headmaster of Marlborough, 1963.*

In the midst of the last war most people imagined that the post-war educational system would be turned upside down. The Fleming Committee of 1944, with members of unimpeachable respectability, emphasised how the war, to which 'all classes of society have contributed without distinction of origin' had increased the impatience with the exclusiveness of fee-paying public schools, and remarked that 'it may almost be said that nothing could have been better devised to perpetuate them (social distinctions) than this educational development'. They recommended that a minimum of 25 per cent of public schoolboys, in the first place, should be chosen from primary schools and educated free of charge. With the 1944 Education Act, giving greater opportunities for clever boys to go to grammar school and thence to university, many people assumed that the expensive public schools would wither away from lack of funds from overtaxed parents. But the revolution, of course, never happened: and the changes were blurred and confused. The Fleming proposals were quietly abandoned—partly because responsibility for financing them was shifted from the central government to local councils; partly because public schools took boys at a later age (13), and insisted on Latin or Greek; and partly because of heavy opposition from grammar schools. Middle-class parents, including left-wing ones, saved to send their sons to fee-paying schools, helped by the system of tax-free 'covenants', and industrialists subsidised the public schools with laboratories and scholarships. The most extraordinary result of the war, which no headmaster would have predicted in 1941, was that the public schools—133 of them, many of which before the war had been close to bankruptcy—emerged stronger than ever before, with over 20 per cent more pupils.[1]

ETON

And since the war, the most celebrated of all schools, the College of the Blessed Mary of Eton, has emerged with more stability and prestige than ever. The supremacy of Eton is not old: in the seventeenth century it was Westminster, under Dr Busby, which set the pace, and in the early nineteenth century it was Rugby. Even fifty years ago Harrow was, in social terms, almost co-equal with Eton, acceptable enough to educate Winston Churchill and Jawaharlal Nehru, and to include five members of Baldwin's cabinet ('One of my first thoughts', wrote Baldwin in a famous passage, 'was that it should be a government of which Harrow should not be ashamed.'). But during this century Eton has become established as the unique symbol not so much of expensiveness (in 1964 it cost £535 a year, only £1 more than Harrow, and £59 less than Gordonstoun, Prince Charles's school) but of social exclusiveness. Already the word Eton has cropped up several times in this book and it will crop up again in diplomacy, banking, insurance and industry; it is impossible to avoid it. Eton has educated 64 out of 303 of the Conservative MPs, more than a fifth, and 17 out of the 26 dukes. It has produced Humphrey Lyttelton, Lord Longford, and the chairman of BOAC. It induces in its pupils a relaxed confidence in dealing with the world and the near-certainty of a good job, which scions of other public schools observe with envy.

[1] Estimated by Headmasters' Conference.

Ever since its foundation by King Henry VI in 1440, Eton has been closer to the Crown than other schools, and this has backed up its authority. The Provost, who is a kind of chairman of governors, is still appointed by the Crown, and other governors are elected by Oxford, Cambridge, the Royal Society, and the Lord Chief Justice. Eton is thought to be the richest of the schools,[1] with medieval endowments which pay for the upkeep of the seventy scholars, the choir school and the ancient buildings.

The Eton school buildings are scattered round the gothic pinnacled chapel—an early edition of the King's College Chapel at Cambridge (founded by the same king, for the same kind of boys). Through the courtyards and across the street surge boys of all sizes—the small ones in big white Eton collars and short black Eton jackets, like picture-book scholars, the big ones in morning coats and white ties tucked under the collars—the academic dress of the 19th century. (There are occasional complaints about the dangers of tailcoats in modern laboratories). A few stride like peacocks through the streets, wearing bright damask waistcoats, spongebag trousers and a look of unassailable arrogance. These are the twenty members of 'Pop', the schoolboys' club which provides special monitors for the school, with powers of beating and fining.[2] Pop is the youngest of the many self-perpetuating oligarchies which we will find in this book. It was founded in 1811, has included Sir Alec Douglas-Home, Quintin Hogg, John Grigg and Peter Fleming among its members, but not Harold Macmillan or the Duke of Kent.

The headmastership of Eton is regarded as the peak of the teaching profession, though it combines some of the duties of a bishop, a diplomat and a tycoon. In 1963 a young new headmaster was appointed, at the age of only forty-three. Anthony Chenevix-Trench has nearly all the traditional public-school qualities, and his career has been a schoolmaster's dream. He comes from an old Anglican family, with a tradition of scholarship and service in the Indian Army. His ancestor was the famous Archbishop Trench of Dublin, who invented the Oxford English Dictionary and evening services in Westminster Abbey, and his father, an Indian civil servant, wrote a grammar of the Gondi language. During the war, Chenevix-Trench, in the family tradition, went into the Indian Army, was captured by the

[1] Though its endowments amount to far less than a third of its income, as has been suggested (*see*, *Whose Public School?*, Bow Group, 1957).

[2] *See* 'What Pop means to Eton', by Peter Fleming. *The Times*, October 25, 1961.

Japanese in Singapore, and translated Housman into Latin while working on the Death Railway. He came back to Christ Church after the war, took a classical double first, spent a year as a don, and by the age of thirty-six was headmaster of Bradfield. He is a man of engaging casualness and effortless charm, who seems to have sailed to the top without any obstacle, but he is a more conventional, and sterner person than he appears. At Bradfield he was known by the boys as Whacker Trench, and he has not so far shown signs of being a radical reformer at Eton.

Much of the post-war character of Eton was established by Robert Birley, who was headmaster for fourteen years and was known, because of his mild reforms, as 'Red Robert'. He tried to break down the division between the 'two cultures' of science and the arts, and to make sure that boys do not leave school being 'scientifically illiterate'. 'Our ambition,' he told me in 1961, 'is to have the head of Harwell research station an Old Etonian, who learnt Greek at Eton, and reads the lesson at Harwell parish church.' Etonians, he said, are still going into the Foreign Office, the Civil service, the merchant banks and politics in much the same proportion as before. 'It's a very political school, you know . . . The boys have a sense of service and political responsibility here which is fairly rare—and hardly known in American schools.' After the war Birley had worked devotedly under Ernest Bevin in the Foreign Office, and when he left for Eton, Bevin said: 'Birley, keep on sending us your boys: we can't get along without them.'

Eton is not a very intellectual place: its boys are traditionally chosen in a quaint and personal way by the individual housemasters. But recently, the pressures of competition—particularly for university places—have affected even Eton, which now demands a stiffish standard at Common Entrance, the public schools' joint entrance exam. The teaching is personal but not intensive, and its record (see page 210) is not outstanding. The seventy 'King's Scholars' at Eton, some of whom are entirely supported by scholarships, are kept in a separate hot-house, and the other boys, Oppidans, are apt to regard the 'tugs' as eccentric and rather beyond the pale. The seven hundred or so ex-scholars of Eton show a mixture of ambition and literariness, and although eighteen Old Etonians have been prime ministers, only two—Walpole and Macmillan—have been King's Scholars. Former Eton scholars include

Lord Keynes	John Lehmann
George Orwell	Julian Slade
Cyril Connolly	Sir Henry Willink
Harold Macmillan	Julian Huxley
Sir John Maud	Aldous Huxley
Andrew Sinclair	Quintin Hogg

They are far from typical Etonians, and Eton is proud not so much of its scholastic achievements as of its breadth of interest, and its capacity to produce happy eccentrics of all kinds, giving more emphasis to self-expression than to ambition.

It is important to distinguish between the influence of Eton on careers and the influence of the families that send boys there. The Etonians in the cabinet and in merchant banks are more remarkable for their ancestry than for their Etonianism. Much more than other schools, Eton is full of the sons of prominent men: 60 per cent of Etonians (Birley told me) have Old Etonian fathers: and the proportion is still rising. Eton's contribution to social change is thus strictly limited and even its rôle of turning a plutocracy into an aristocracy is dwindling. As Eton's position grows more unique, so it becomes a more tribal school.

WINCHESTER

Eton and Winchester sometimes seem to be conspiracies rather than educational establishments.

Anthony Hartley.

One public school above others *does* produce an intellectual cream: Winchester. It was founded by William of Wykeham, Bishop of Winchester, in 1394—as 'a perpetual college of poor scholars clerks', with the contentious motto 'Manners Makyth Man'. For the last century Wykehamists have had a unique reputation for cleverness and public service. Winchester's entrance examination is the stiffest, and it produces many more university scholarships, in proportion to its numbers, than any of the other public schools (see page 210). Its headmaster, Sir Desmond Lee, is the son of a clergyman, a rigorous philosopher, and editor of Aristotle and Plato. About 80 per cent of Wykehamists (I was told in 1961) go on to universities, and 70 per cent to Oxford and Cambridge—compared to Eton's 33 per cent. Winchester is a much less dynastic school than Eton, and only about 30 per cent of its boys are sons of Wykehamists. While Eton provides a separate study for each boy (the only school to do so) Winchester has a mass of boys in the same room—which is sometimes thought to explain the eccentricity of Etonians on the one hand and the conformism of Wykehamists on the other. Lack of privacy also makes Wykehamists closed-in, cautious and reticent: 'You never know what a Wykehamist is thinking,' a New College don once said: 'In fact you never know if he's thinking at all.' Incredibly, in the early nineteen-sixties, the school's governors thought it necessary to take positive steps to encourage the boys to be more friendly to each other, so they started up a beer cellar.

Winchester has produced boys ranging from Cecil King to Lord Eccles ('The only Wykehamist,' one of his colleagues said, 'who could possibly be mistaken for a Harrovian'). But Wykehamists have often a common denominator of tough ambition and single-mindedness. In the psychological warfare between public schools, they are depicted as smug and dedicated bores:

> Broad of Church and broad of mind
> Broad before and broad behind
> A keen ecclesiologist
> A rather dirty Wykehamist.[1]

Like Eton, Winchester has its hot-house of scholars, but they are apt to become men of a more single-minded stamp than Old Etonian scholars—including:

Richard Crossman	Prof. Nowell-Smith
John Sparrow	Prof. Andrewes
Lord Simonds	Prof. Driver
Anthony Asquith	Prof. Macartney
William Empson	Prof. Seton Watson
Arnold Toynbee	Prof. Champernowne
Sir William Hayter	Dr. A. L. P. Norrington

HEADMASTERS AND REFORM

Officially, a 'public school' is a school whose headmaster belongs to a group of about two hundred, known as the 'Headmasters Conference', which includes sixty-six 'Direct grant grammar' and fifteen ordinary grammar schools: but usually a public school is taken to mean one which is independently financed—that is, the

[1] John Betjeman: *Mount Zion*, John Murray, 1932.

other 133. They vary from old medieval foundations to a bevy of schools founded in the twenties. Many unknown ones have survived because they gave a grammar school education to middle-class children who failed the eleven-plus. But a small number have had a quite disproportionate influence, and in this book only about twenty schools appear regularly. Below are the nine schools which were singled out by the Clarendon Commission of 1861–4, as 'significant of the position that a few schools had gained in the public eye'.[1] Since then a few old schools have risen in prestige, and a few new ones, like Stowe (1923) and Gordonstoun (1934), have become prominent; and there are famous Roman Catholic schools, notably Ampleforth, which takes more A-levels than any school except Winchester.[2] But the 'Clarendon Schools', a hundred years later, remain among the most important,[3] and in public schools there is no real substitute for antiquity and tradition.

(*December* 1964)	*Fees*	*No. of boys*	*Headmaster*	*Date of foundation*
Charterhouse	£537	650	A. D. Van Oss	1611
Eton	535	1,190	A. Chenevix-Trench	1440
Harrow	534	650	R. L. James	1571
Merchant Taylors	381	600	H. Elder	1561
Rugby	504	730	Walter Hamilton	1567
St. Paul's	395	660	T. E. B. Howarth	1509
Shrewsbury	501	544	A. R. D. Wright	1552
Westminster	528	442	J. D. Carleton	1561
Winchester	537	525	Sir Desmond Lee	1394

The 5 per cent who go to public schools has no real parallel in other countries. In 1942 the Fleming Committee were told that out of 830 bishops, deans, judges, stipendiary magistrates, highly paid home civil servants, Indian civil servants, governors of Dominions and directors of banks and railways companies, 76 per cent came from public schools, and of those, 48 per cent came from twelve major public schools.[4]

Public schools are distinguished from the rest not only by their cost, but by their segregation. Of these nine, only two, St. Paul's

[1] *See* Fleming Report, p. 34.
[2] *See*, *Which?*, Jan. 1964.
[3] R. K. Kelsall: *High Civil Servants in Britain*, 1955. p. 119, etc.
[4] Fleming Report, p. 54.

and Merchant Taylors are mainly for day-boys: most public school boys spend nine months a year, for five years, in the exclusive company of other boys. The drastic weaning and intensely introverted society thus created provide an experience from which many public school boys never recover—as appears for instance in the horrific reminiscences of *John Bull's Schooldays*:[1] and the boarding system has been blamed for most faults of public school boys—their excessive respect for authority, their obsession with tradition, their prolonged adolescence. And the separateness has been prolonged by the 'prep schools' which have grown up to prepare boys for them, often from the ages of 7 to 13—thus deepening the gulf and making it harder for primary schoolboys to change over.

In the Victorian ethos it was by uprooting boys from their parents, and forging them into a tough society, that imperial leaders were created. Many Victorian schools were built round imperial service, or the army: the 'Imperial Service College', now merged with Haileybury, was founded to provide recruits for the East India Company. In Britain itself, the segregated world of public schools crops up in all kinds of institutions: a boy can pass from Eton to the Guards to Oxford to the Middle Temple to parliament, and still remain in the same male world of leather armchairs, teak tables, and nicknames. They need never deal closely with other kinds of people, and some never do, with consequences which are to be found scattered through this book.

Since the war the public schools have becomc slowly aware that there is no longer an empire out to which to send their boys. They have become less philistine and brutal, and art is no longer regarded as pansy: they have become more conscious of industry and trade. They have enormously expanded their science sides—helped by a special investment fund, raised by a group of Britain's leading firms. The industrialists did not extend their cash to the state grammar schools; that, they said, was the province of the Ministry of Education.

But no one visiting a public school can fail to be struck by the continuity of these isolated communities: they roll on with their Latin jokes, their founders' prayers, their fags and private languages, still perpetuating vestigial aspects of a Victorian world. Only half the non-Etonian public schoolboys are sons of public schoolboys: as Chesterton put it, 'The public schools aren't for the sons of gentlemen, they're for the fathers of gentlemen.' But, in the

[1] *John Bull's Schooldays*: edited by Brian Inglis, 1961.

words of *The Times*, 'Once the boys get to the schools the insidious element of accent unifies them all.'[1] The public schools remain, as they were designed by the Victorians, a device by which the new rich can become absorbed with the old rich, and the sons of tradesmen can be removed from the taint of trade. But in contemporary Britain the demand is for the reverse. What is needed is to turn the sons of gentlemen into businessmen: the sons of amateurs into professionals.

The isolation of the public schools is enhanced by their rulers, the headmasters. These are awesome and formidable men, whom no ex-public school boy can recollect in tranquillity; wielding immense power, maintaining exact if sometimes irrelevant standards. They are figures of massive integrity and moral uprightness: a divorced headmaster is unimaginable. Their way of life combines monasticism with worldly ambition. They are insulated against the outside world, living in the midst of the country, surrounded by inferiors, both masters and boys. Most of the major headmasters are sons of schoolmasters, clergymen or civil servants, and several are the sons or brothers of headmasters. Groves of Dulwich is the son-in-law of a former headmaster of Dulwich, An extraordinary number have won the Porson Greek Prize at Cambridge.

The protective attitude of the headmasters does not necessarily set them against change—they have realised that if they are to survive, their isolation from contemporary Britain must end. The Headmasters Conference, in a major public relations effort, have thrown open their annual discussions to the press; they have set up a (secret) enquiry into the public schools; and they have even produced a magazine called *Conference* to counteract, they said, the impressions given in *Anatomy of Britain* and elsewhere. More seriously, in 1961, they made a determined effort to revive the Fleming proposals. The leading reformer, John Dancy of Marlborough, wants the public schools to become direct grant schools, taking up to 50 per cent of their boys from the state system. He has written almost lyrically of the effect of mixing the two systems:[2] 'That passionate concern for justice, that knowledge of the world and the ordinary person in it would complement the detached, objective approach to social and personal matters which characterises the middle classes. The questioning, even suspicious attitude of the newcomers to authority would stimulate the decorous

[1] 'The Public Schools are not Static': *The Times*, September 25, 1951.
[2] John Dancy: *The Public Schools and the Future*, Faber, 1963.

stability and group loyalty which is traditional in middle-class institutions . . . It would all be extremely exciting. . . .' But Dancy specifically says the questioning, suspicious element should never become a majority. His scheme would strengthen the pre-eminence of the top public schools while preserving their essential character—a classic example of the aristocratic embrace at work. The Labour party is more than unlikely to add a group of super-prestigious grammar schools to a state system they are trying to turn comprehensive.

MERITOCRATS AND ARISTOCRATS

The debate about comprehensive schools has had one startling effect: it is eroding the old rivalry between public schools and grammar schools. The great public schools have retained much of their old influence, but a new caste of men from the grammar schools have come up alongside them to share the positions of power. The 'meritocracy' owed nothing to family money or influence; it was sifted out by intelligence tests, and groomed for positions of influence. The impact of the meritocracy of clever boys from grammar schools on the public school aristocracy still produces a sharp juxtaposition, and its repercussions will pop up at various stages of this book. But the public and grammar schools were only ever separated by a thin barrier—although a strong one, with the strength of subtle English class divisions. Both kinds of schools share the same history, the same aims, the same education, the same middle-class manners, with prefects and uniforms. The tiny proportion of boys in the public schools that matter still have advantages—more and better teachers; the old, confident ethos. But in the face of a common threat, the barrier is melting away: they are all grammar schools now.

The brain race is not new: it goes back at least a century, to when the civil service introduced competitive examinations. T. H. S. Escott, writing a book about England in the eighteen-eighties, lamented the shortcomings of the 'competition wallahs' who were replacing young aristocrats in the Indian Civil Service. But the intrusion of those wallahs, disconcerting though it seemed at the time, was limited to university men and therefore, almost necessarily, public school men: only after the first world war was there a large flow of grammar school boys (such as Frank Lee and Norman Brook) to Oxford and Cambridge, and thence to the civil service. The new post-war meritocracy can come from any class of British life, and nearly half of the sixth-form boys in grammar schools are now the sons of manual workers.[1]

The implications of the meritocracy, with its ruthless selectivity, have caused many educationalists to be worried. One nightmare of the future is contained in the brilliant essay by Dr. Michael Young, 'The Rise of the Meritocracy', purporting to have been written in the year 2033, and describing the gradual extension of sifting and segregation, denying all opportunity to the rest—who eventually, goaded by the constant reminders of their inferiority, rise in angry revolt.

The pressure of competition forces nearly all schools to segregate their cleverest children. *The Times* commented in 1961 that:

> 'It is remarkable that the great movement towards educational equality initiated by Locke and Rousseau should at the end, faced with the demands of scientifically based industry, threaten to produce a hierarchical society which, though status in it would depend on educational parchments, would have some resemblance to that of the Middle Ages. There will not even be the satisfaction of being able to claim that a man's place is at least the reward of his own merit, for the experts in examinations agree that proficiency in them is owed partly to inherited intelligence and partly to family environment, and both endowments are as fortuitous as noble birth.'[2]

TWO KINDS OF GRAMMAR SCHOOLS

The production of the meritocracy in Britain is the job of the grammar schools: they prepare boys for the universities, the new sorting-ground for Britain's élite. Most of the oldest, largest, and most famous are not state schools at all, but semi-independent ones. These are the 'direct grant' grammar schools, financed partly by fees and funds, partly by the Department of Education (the direct grant). They earn the grant by taking not less than a quarter and not more than half of their pupils from the state system: the rest are fee paying. They must have local government people on their boards of governors, but unlike ordinary grammar schools, the local authorities can't really interfere. There are 179 direct-grant grammar schools. Some are just small denominational schools (especially Roman Catholic), but the important ones are the great schools—Bradford; Bristol; Manchester; Birkenhead;

[1] Crowther, p. 230.

[2] *The Times*, April 6, 1961.

Dulwich, Haberdashers' Aske and Latymer Upper in London; the Royal Grammar School, Newcastle; King Edward's, Birmingham. These schools make up an important part of the Headmasters Conference. With their traditions and their huge sixth forms, they rival the top public schools in the number of boys they get into Oxford and Cambridge (see table). They benefit too, from their big city 'catchment areas' as their recruiting territory is gruesomely called. The direct-grant schools introduce yet another status distinction into the British educational system. Their existence is a major stumbling block to bringing in a comprehensive system, as we shall see. In comparison with the 1,500 ordinary grammar schools, 'maintained' (and often interfered with) by the local authorities, they are privileged schools. Sixteen per cent of the entrants to Oxford and Cambridge came from direct-grant grammar schools in 1961, compared with thirty per cent from maintained ones. Yet only two per cent of secondary school age group are in the direct-grant schools.

The biggest and most famous of them, with 1,400 boys, is Manchester Grammar School, a low brick building outside the city, surrounded by playing fields. 'MGS' has become a by-word at Oxford and Cambridge for scholarship and success. There is nothing very new about the success of Mancunians: their alumni include Sir Herbert Andrew; the chairman of Marks and Spencer (Israel Sieff); the playwright Robert Bolt; a bishop and an ambassador. But since the war, the success of MGS at the universities has been more widely spread. 75 per cent of their boys go on to university, 25 per cent to Oxbridge. Out of one group of sixty who joined the school in 1946, 30 per cent became scientists, 10 per cent lawyers, 10 per cent teachers, and 8 per cent accountants. Among public schools there is an idea that the clever Old Mancunians 'fizzle out': in fact many of them go into the world of industry and technology, with large and important jobs; and the Robbins Report showed that it was the public schoolboys who did most of the fizzling.

The man most closely associated with MGS has been Lord James of Rusholme, who was High Master for sixteen years, until he became Vice-Chancellor of York University in 1962. Then Peter Mason, a persuasive man who looks like a stage bishop and was educated at another great grammar school (King Edward's, Birmingham), took over the school and the *ex-officio* leadership of the direct-grant lobby. Lord James is still the senior prophet of the 'meritocracy' (though he did not coin the word). He was a scientist from Oxford, who taught at Winchester until he became High Master at only thirty-six. He has insistently championed the grammar schools and attacked the comprehensives. 'This place exists as the spearhead of social mobility', he told me at MGS, 'ten per cent of the boys are sons of manual workers, and we probably have a wider social cross-section than anywhere in the western world. But the change is blurred by the question of families: as you equalise opportunity, family background becomes more important —to take advantage of the opportunity.

'One may be worried by the idea of a "meritocracy"—but what's the alternative? If you want to have equality of opportunity, you inevitably have a meritocracy: but you can mitigate the dangers, by producing essentially *humane* meritocrats. The grammar schools must have their own *noblesse oblige*—but in order to have that, they have to *know* that they are a new kind of aristocracy—as Etonians know it.'

The big grammar schools have caught up with the public schools in the competition for places to Oxford and Cambridge. 'The grammar schools realised quite suddenly', Birley told me back in 1961, 'about three or four years ago that they could get as many boys into Oxford and Cambridge as were clever enough, and that made things far more competitive. Ten years ago half the boys at Eton went to Oxford and Cambridge: now it's only a third.' 'They are giving us a terrific run for our money,' one public school headmaster told me: 'I've been trying to get my head boy a place at Oxford for the last few months.' The public schools, even Eton, have been forced to stiffen their entrance requirements, and they now throw out stupid boys quite ruthlessly. The grammar schools on their side are becoming more confident of their potential. 'I think we've got the Establishment on the run,' said one leading headmaster.

An index of the relative success of the grammar schools is provided by the awards of scholarships to Oxford and Cambridge every July. Because of the intense competitiveness which it encourages, some schoolmasters say the list should never be published: but it does give some indication of a school's intellectual status. The list opposite shows the schools which won most scholarships and exhibitions to Oxford and Cambridge, in proportion to their sixth forms, in the five years covering 1960 to 1964.[1]

[1] Excluding 1963, for which no research is available. These figures are compiled from *The Times Educational Supplement*'s annual compilations, made by G. D. N. Worswick, of Magdalen College, Oxford.

	Total open scholarships	*Average sixth form*	*Percentage of sixth-formers taking scholarships*
Dulwich	110	475	5·9
Winchester	78	345	5·7
Manchester Grammar School	120	540	5·5
King Edward's, Birmingham	59	280	5·3
Christ's Hospital	51	290	5·2
*King Edward VII, Sheffield	54	255	5·2
St. Albans	39	185	5·2
Nottingham High School	37	130	5·1
King's, Canterbury	66	330	5·0
Bradford Grammar School	58	295	5·0
Latymer Upper, Hammersmith	57	310	4·6
City of London	49	265	4·6
KCS, Wimbledon	43	230	4·6
St. Paul's	70	385	4·5
Highgate	37	205	4·5
Downside	43	250	4·3
Bristol Grammar School	49	290	4·2
Birkenhead	34	205	4·2
Rugby	60	395	3·8
Wolverhampton Grammar School	24	290	3·7
Wyggeston	33	225	3·5
Tonbridge	36	230	3·5
*Liverpool Institute High School	30	230	3·3
Westminster	34	260	3·2
Chislehurst and Sidcup Grammar School	26	210	3·1
Bryanston	26	210	3·1
Ampleforth	34	280	3·0

* Not in Headmasters Conference

The most successful scholarship-winners do not necessarily correspond to the most celebrated public schools, and alongside the famous public schools are grammar schools, such as Wyggeston and Chislehurst, which few public schoolboys will have heard of. But all except two of the schools are public or direct-grant, and represented on the Headmasters Conference. (The list omits the 'restricted awards' which are available to only one school: in the case of Winchester and Westminster this adds considerably to the total.)

EGGHEADS V SERFS
(OR THE CASE FOR COMPREHENSIVES)

'Me, I failed the eleven plus and I felt bitter. From then on it was if you can't beat them with your brains, beat them with your fists.'
A Rocker.[1]

The ruthless division of all but a privileged stream of rich children into two castes at the age of eleven has come under heavy attack. The eleven plus was inefficient: Robin Pedley (the pioneer of British comprehensives, who helped to invent the Leicestershire Scheme) has written, "The result of all this immensely honest effort by educational psychologists and administrators is this: that out of every twenty children picked for the grammar school, six or seven turn out to be unsuited . . . and they keep out another six or seven of the remaining eighty, who should have been admitted.'[2] People began to realise that segregation of 'eggheads and serfs' was also dangerous on social and economic grounds.

Abandoning the eleven plus requires an entirely new kind of school organisation. 'Once it is agreed,' wrote Crowther in his report, 'as more and more people are coming to believe, that it is wrong to label children for all time at eleven, the attempt to give mutually exclusive labels to the schools to which they go at that age will have to be abandoned.'[3] It was to avoid these labels, and to mix the streams, that the most spectacular of the post-war experiments were invented—the comprehensive schools. The comprehensives were designed after the war to contain all kinds of children under one roof. But they were *not*, as in America, to be all in one stream: the comprehensives have their own 'grammar school' classes, leading on to university, and their own technical and modern classes. The importance of comprehensives is that they allow children to change streams after eleven, and also to mix out of class with other children cleverer or stupider than themselves.

The comprehensive schools, together with other variations, are growing rapidly. In 1963–4 seven per cent of children were at

[1] Quoted in *Generation X* by Charles Hamblett and Jane Deverson. Tandem Books, 1964.
[2] Robin Pedley: *The Comprehensive School*. Pelican, 1963.
[3] Crowther, p. 23.

some kind of comprehensive school, as opposed to only two per cent in 1956. Two thirds of the local authorities were investigating ways of avoiding the eleven plus in 1964: some had already abandoned it. But there was strong opposition from the middle classes and the grammar schools: comprehensives run against the whole Jamesian grammar school idea of segregating an élite.

The first and one of the most famous of comprehensive schools, founded in 1954, is Kidbrooke, a school for 2,200 girls at Blackheath, which became the subject of renewed controversy in 1965, after complaints by the musical director, Miss Lang. Its architecture expresses both the idealism and the size of the concept, and the atmosphere of a brave new world of schooling. It is a huge triangle of buildings of brick and glass and cedar-wood, with a low copper-covered hall in the middle of it, big enough to hold all two thousand girls at prayers every morning. Inside there are rows of glassy, brightly painted classrooms, including a room of typing girls, a room of dressmakers, a row of model kitchens, a pottery, a model flat, laboratories, libraries and three gymnasia. It certainly has some of the appearance of mass-production: there are long rows of pegs, numbered from 1 to 2,200, two thousand steel chairs in the hall, two thousand girls dressed in identical light grey skirts. The school timetable, showing the criss-crossing of fifty different classes, looks like a Continental railway timetable. But it shows the freedom, as well as the intimidation, of bigness: it is clear at Kidbrooke, as is far from clear at most British schools, that you can do almost anything. and find any kind of girl. And the school is split up into smaller units: there are eight houses (Dolphin, Salamander, Unicorn, etc.), which cut across classes and ages, and a huge range of unacademic activities, like an orchestra, an Old Vic Club, rounders or fashion shows.

Behind a yellow door in the entrance hall is a light office more like a sitting-room—with a loud-speaker, a microphone, and a mass of charts and timetables—inhabited by the headmistress. Mary Green, who was the first headmistress, is now regarded as one of Britain's most important educationalists. She herself went to Wellingborough High School in the midlands, took a first-class degree at Westfield College, London. She has, from the beginning, been heart-and-soul behind the idea of comprehensives. She is a relaxed, undominating administrator, with rimless glasses, greying hair, and a neat grey suit which matches the girls'.

When Kidbrooke started there was an acrimonious quarrel with the local grammar school at Eltham, which Kidbrooke was intended to replace. The Eltham girls, and still more their parents, hated the idea of mixing with the *hoi polloi*: eventually the grammar school was allowed to continue, while Kidbrooke built up its own senior classes. The jealousy of Eltham towards Kidbrooke was symptomatic of the way most grammar schools regarded comprehensives, which challenged the idea of keeping all clever children *socially* separate, and the class-consciousness that often lingers round grammar schools. Although the comprehensives were brought in by a coalition government, they have become firmly associated with Socialism and egalitarianism. In fact, both kinds of school believe in special courses for clever children, and neither is preoccupied with rich men's children. But there remains a strong political prejudice against comprehensive schools. 'I wish', said Miss Green, 'that we could keep politics out of it.'

But while the comprehensives are at odds with the grammar schools, they have much more friendly relations with the public schools—partly because they are not in serious competition; and partly because the public schools are themselves a bit like comprehensives, with both stupid and clever boys. On her side Miss Green is a strong supporter of public schools. 'They set us a standard of teaching, which we wouldn't otherwise have', she said, 'and they set a pattern of eccentricity too, which is useful.'

The comprehensives seem to be achieving their object, although it is still too early to judge their final effects. Only in Sweden has a controlled experiment taken place. The south of Stockholm was reorganised on comprehensive lines in 1954, the north was left with segregation at eleven. The results delighted the comprehensive faction. The oldest criticism of comprehensives is the grammar school one, that clever children are held back. In Stockholm, the grammar streams in the new schools did just as well as the ones in the north, and the lower streams did significantly better. In Britain too, the comprehensives are beginning to show academic results. Pedley has looked at the GCE results of twenty comprehensives all over the country, compared with an average grammar-modern system. The comprehensives got 14 per cent 'good' O-level results, compared with the average of 10 per cent.[1] And it is clear that in their main purpose—allowing children to switch streams after eleven—the schools are succeeding. Miss Green has a chart showing, like a bumps race at Cambridge, the children moving up and down between streams in the years after eleven.

[1] Pedley, *op. cit.*, pp. 95–7.

Like the new universities, the comprehensives have the glamour of youth, and so have attracted good staff, keen on the cultural and social possibilities of the schools. At Eltham Green, another giant London comprehensive, the staff collect paperbacks for the school library, and reminisce with astonishment about English Set $3B_4$'s production of Peter Grimes. But the schools' success is more surprising because they are not in fact comprehensives at all. Only in two small islands, Anglesey and the Isle of Man, is there a fully comprehensive schools system—and they hardly have a middle class. Everywhere else authorities that have tried to go comprehensive have been forced to compromise: they have not been able to destroy the grammar schools. London has the highest number of children in comprehensives—28 per cent, but it still has 150 grammar schools which cream off the cleverest children. Sheffield, Coventry and Wolverhampton are stuck with grammar schools and Manchester, with new plans to go fully comprehensive, is in 1964 faced with the dilemma of what to do about Manchester Grammar school.

Other local authorities have been prevented from going comprehensive because it was physically impossible. The average English school has three to six hundred pupils: a comprehensive needs over 1,250 to support a big enough sixth form. In many districts, 'going comprehensive' would mean pulling down brand new school buildings. A cunning way around the double obstacles of the grammar schools and the limitations of existing plant is the 'two-tier system', started in Leicestershire in 1957. There all children but a very few 'flyers' go to the same high schools until fourteen, then the ones who want to continue their education until at least sixteen transfer to senior highs—the old grammar schools. Other authorities, like Cardiff, have invented their own pet versions of the Leicestershire 'two-tier system'. Others still—the first was Croydon—have plans to turn all their schools comprehensive to 16, and then to have a sixth form college.

Before the Labour government came in, pledged to reorganise education on comprehensive lines, the decisions rested entirely with the local authorities, but even they have sometimes hit trouble, as happened at Bristol. Since the mid nineteen-fifties, Bristol had been gradually going comprehensive; but parents in all districts had still been able to send children to the seven direct grant grammar schools in the centre of the city. In 1964, just before the general election, Bristol announced that the LEA would no longer take up places in the direct grant schools, and that parents must use their neighbourhood schools. The result was a middle-class parents' revolt, protest marches, and a swing against Labour in the general election.

Bristol is a hint of the troubles that may face the Labour government. The fashion for reorganisation among local authoritoes has caught on enormously, but there are still many LEAs with no plans for change—even Labour-controlled ones. Many people still argue, with Lord James, that Britain must have an élite of clever boys trained in hard, tough schools of their own. And many post-war meritocrats, raised to positions of power by a grammar school education, will fight hard, and with missionary zeal, to defend the schools that put them where they are.

TEACHER CRISIS

Unless one stark fact is taken into account, any discussion of reforming British schools is pointless. There is a critical shortage of teachers. Sir Edward Boyle, Conservative Minister for Education, summed it up in 1964: 'We are still 60,000 teachers short of the number needed to get rid of oversize classes. . . . On present plans we expect to recruit a total of about 300,000 during the nineteen-sixties, of whom 200,000 will be women. Of these we shall probably lose about 190,000 . . . By 1970 we shall still be 35,000 teachers short of our target, and the raising of the school-leaving age will add another 20,000 to our total demand'.[1]

The hazards of teacher recruitment are well known. Between 1953 and 1963 the capacity of teacher training colleges went up from 24,000 to 54,000. The standard of the trainees also went up, helped by the shortage of university places: in 1964 40 per cent of the entrants had minimum university qualifications. Sir Edward's estimates are a minimum, worked out for primary classes of 40 children and secondary ones of 30. If primary classes are brought down to 30 too, at least another 60,000 teachers would be needed. But no sooner have girl teachers finished their expensive, three-year training, and gained a little practice on the job, than they get married. In 1962–3 19,000 girls were recruited, and 17,000 women teachers left. By far the worst shortage is in the primary schools, but even in the state secondary schools in 1963, 43·7 per cent of the classes were over the theoretical limit of 30. The teacher shortage in the state schools increases the advantages

[1] Quoted in Tyrrell Burgess' brief and excellent survey: 'Not Enough Teachers', *New Society*, March 19, 1964.

of the independent ones: pupil-teacher ratios in 1963 were 20–1 in maintained grammar schools; 16–1 in direct grant schools, and 13–1 in independent schools.

How is the crisis being met? Training colleges and universities are expanding fast. The Ministry of Education has launched 'Come back and teach' campaigns to lure married women. But there has been no drastic re-thinking. Other countries have met the crisis with crash programmes of research into economical teaching methods, like the French audio-visual centre at Saint-Cloud, or the American team teaching. But in Britain, when the Ministry suggested introducing short-training 'teaching auxiliaries' the teaching profession refused to allow anyone without a three-year training to do anything that could be interpreted as 'teaching.' 'They even solemnly discussed keeping checks on auxiliaries through spy-holes into the next room, and finally decided they could only be used in the corridors, not in the classrooms,' said a senior ministry man.

For years, the government failed to do anything to raise the status of teachers—always lower in England than in America or France, partly because of the murky roots of British state schools, partly perhaps because of the segregation of the training colleges. The golden age of teacher recruitment was in the slump of the thirties, which induced a high proportion of first-class minds to go into teaching. Before the war teaching was also a way up the social ladder for a bright, working-class boy. But since the grammar schools and universities have widened their gates, and the competition for graduates—notably from industry—has been much stronger, teacher recruitment has passed (in Crowther's phrase) into an 'ice age'. They have a basic salary of only £630, rising in 15 years to £1,250, and a maximum chance (with special allowances) of less than £3,000 for the headmaster of a big grammar school.

The Robbins Report recommended another way of raising the status of the profession—integrating the training colleges with the universities. The proposal ran into a tangle of vested interests—the universities, jealous of their scholarship, the local education authorities, jealous of their control. In December 1964 the Labour government bitterly disappointed the training colleges by leaving them under local authorities. The history of the teacher supply question in the last decade is not an extraordinary one in post-war Britain; it is part of the refusal to surrender to facts.

FREEDOM OR PRIVILEGE

Whether the teacher situation improves or not, the large question remains. Should a tiny group of children continue to have privileged education, cut off from their contemporaries from the age of eight? And as the comprehensive movement gains momentum, this problem is enlarging: the cloak of privilege is stretching round the grammar schools.[1] Underlying the whole debate there is a major political dilemma: whether parents should be allowed to choose how their children are educated. And complicating the debate there is the undoubted fact that it is the professional classes, whose children are now in the public schools and dominate the grammar schools, who are most concerned about education. Bringing them into the state system could only benefit the schools. As Robin Pedley has written: 'Without a doubt the most valued and powerful argument for bringing all independent schools into the State system is that it would bring the young Macmillans, Hailshams, Gaitskells and Bonham Carters into the local classrooms. The chance of early vigorous action to wipe out the black spots in national education would be transformed overnight.'[2]

But whatever happens, educational change is the slowest of all to take effect, and its results are not seen for thirty years or more. For the next generation, the men and women who rule Britain, with whom this book is concerned, will more than ever come from the public and grammar schools; the schools which get people in to the universities.

[1] Particularly the direct-grant schools: the state can always cut off their grant, but then the great grammar schools might become entirely independent, and the distinctions inside the Headmasters Conference would be abolished

[2] Pedley, *op. cit.*, p. 170.

13

UNIVERSITIES

In the conditions of modern life the rule is absolute: the race which does not value trained intelligence is doomed. Not all your heroism, not all your social charm, not all your wit, not all your victories on land or at sea, can move back the finger of fate. Tomorrow science will have moved forward yet one more step, and there will be no appeal from the judgment which will then be pronounced on the uneducated.

Alfred North Whitehead, 1916.

For the first time in recorded history the survival of the country depends upon the universities.

Lord Bowden.

WHATEVER happens to the schools, the most important question among ambitious men is no longer, 'What school did you go to?' but 'Which university, or which college? or did you go to university at all?' And the most important function of a successful school is to send a boy on to the right university.

The fewness of Britain's universities has become notorious. In 1901 Ramsay Muir observed that Britain had fewer universities per head than any other civilised country in Europe except Turkey. In 1957 UNESCO showed that this situation had hardly improved: out of twenty-eight countries, Britain was fourth from the bottom—better only than Ireland, Turkey and Norway.

In 1961 the government responded to more than half a century's protest in the usual way: they set up a Committee of Enquiry under Lord Robbins. The Robbins Report showed the international position more clearly than ever before. This table gives the percentage of the age-group entering full-time higher education *of British degree level* in 1958–9;[1] and the projections for 1968–9.

Even if you add in teacher training colleges and technical colleges as equivalent to universities, only 8·5 per cent of the age group entered full-time higher education in Britain in 1962. In fairness, Robbins did also show that a higher proportion of British

[1] This answers the usual defence that Britain has higher standards: at all levels of higher education, Britain came seventh in the Robbins international league for 1958–9.

students finished their courses than in most Western European countries. 'But', they commented, 'the output is, in very important respects, smaller than that of the Soviet Union, or the United States.' In science and technology, for instance, 4 per cent of the Russian age-group finished degree courses in 1961–2, compared with 2·4 per cent in Britain. And Robbins adds: 'Moreover, the total advantage of higher education to a country or to its people cannot be fully described in terms of the numbers who successfully complete it. Those who abandon higher education in other countries may yet be more useful citizens in the community on account of their experience.[1]

Country	*1958–9*	*1968–9*
USA	20	26
Canada	13	18
France	8	12
Sweden	7	13
USSR	6	14
New Zealand	5	7
Switzerland	5	9
Great Britain	4·6	6[2]
Germany	4	6
Australia	4	4
Netherlands	3	5

For a country so rich for so long, this weakness in university education remains astonishing. The Victorians, while they revolutionised schooling, seldom regarded universities as a national necessity. The industrial revolution and the expansion of trade and empire had happened without any help from universities, and the supply of cheap labour and materials kept Britain supreme. While Germany quickly realised that technical education was the key to economic expansion, Britain somehow evaded this truth: the results are apparent elsewhere in this book, and in British plumbing, telephones, or railways. For the whole interwar period the university population hardly increased, and even the post-war expansion, which resulted in one much-heralded but skimped new university at Keele, now seems ridiculously small.

At last, there are signs of unprecedented change. Since 1945, while the Empire was disappearing, universities have gradually loomed larger. The energy and missionary zeal which had been

[1] Robbins, p. 44–5.

[2] Fulfilment of the Robbins demands for expansion would put the British figure up to 6·5 per cent.

devoted to colonies slowly began to turn towards improving Britain itself. 'The New Empires', said Sir Winston Churchill, 'are the Empires of the Mind.' Between 1960 and 1970 there will be eight new universities and the ten colleges of advanced technology will become full-scale universities.

Only a year after they reported, the Robbins Committee's recommendations, backed by the most important set of statistics a government committee ever produced, were generally accepted as *minimum* targets. Robbins said students in full-time higher education (counting ones in teacher training colleges, which would become part of the universities) should go up from 216,000 in 1961–2 to 390,000 in 1973–4 to 560,000 in 1980–1. Spending should go up from £206 million in 1962 (or 0·8 per cent of the GNP) to £742 million in 1980 (1·6 per cent). And to forestall criticism, the report adds in stern economists' terms: 'The country would have to go a good deal beyond what is contemplated in our recommendations before the returns in terms of social net product could be said to suggest general over-investment in this sector.'

This stretching is causing strains and groans. For the old British universities have been preoccupied with their own values, and detest the idea that universities should be an expanding national investment producing practical results. The anti-expansionist attitude has been summed up simply and surprisingly by Kingsley Amis: 'More Means Worse': or by John Wain: 'There's a natural ceiling in the population who are able to profit by academic education, and I think we've reached that ceiling.' But even before the Robbins Committee reported, the climate of opinion was changing. 'It is easily forgotten that the report was written at a time when the expansion of the universities had been slowed down by a government decision', John Vaizey has written, 'and virtually no machinery existed for the co-ordination of the different sectors of higher education with each other, and with the schools. The atmosphere in the last three years or so has changed. We are all expansionists now.'[1] Most expansionists would now go beyond Robbins. The Labour party's Taylor Report wanted 700,000 full-time students by 1983–4, and more new universities built up out of further education colleges.

Sir Geoffrey Crowther insists that 20 per cent of young people should have some form of further education. Visualising Britain's position in the technology of the twenty-first century, he has

[1] 'The Conservative Robbins'. *The Spectator*, August 14, 1964.

asked: 'Can we conceive that it will be adequately run by a generation of whom only one in twenty-five will have reached even a first degree? Is this not, in fact, a formula for national decline?' And his answer to the 'more means worse' school has been: 'If more Minis are admitted to the roads, does that dilute the standards of Rolls Royces?'

Over the last century the idea has slowly grown that Britain's survival depends on higher education. 'University competition between states', said Joseph Chamberlain, 'is as potent as competition in building battleships'; but parliament did not show the same interest in dons as in battleships. The universities, on their side, have resisted this 'menace of the practical', and have always been able, by their powerful alchemy, to make useful subjects rarefied. Noel Annan at Cambridge described to me how after the war the government had been worried by the lack of experts on the Middle and Far East, where Britain had important interests: the Scarborough Report recommended giving the universities money to teach the languages and culture of the countries there. 'What happened? The universities created posts in Egyptology, Sanskrit, Mandarin Chinese and Middle Persian—apart from London they seem to be uninterested in teaching modern languages or culture.'

The demand for degrees has hugely increased since the war, and with the growth of big corporations, the break-up of family firms, and the need for professional managers, 'graduatisation' has spread through industry and even into parts of the City. An Arts degree is no longer regarded as an agreeable cultivation before starting serious work, but more as a vital qualification for the higher rungs of government and industry. In another twenty years, it seems likely that the graduate population in Britain will correspond much more closely to the managerial élite.

OXBRIDGE

> It's terribly difficult for anyone to get out of the Oxford-Cambridge feeling: like class itself in Britain, it's the last thing we let go after our clothes, I think.
>
> *Richard Hoggart, 1960.*

> Oxford and Cambridge are the last medieval islands, all right for first-class people. But their security is harmful to second-class people—it makes them insular and gaga.
>
> *Bertrand Russell.*

For seven hundred years two universities dominated British

education, and today they dominate more than ever, with a fame enhanced by their isolation and their sheer hypnotic beauty. Like dukes, Oxford and Cambridge preserve an antique way of life in the midst of the twentieth century, and the dreaming-spires legend is supported by tourists, the Ford Foundation, conventions of chartered accountants and international fame. Oxford and Cambridge in 1961 provided 87 per cent of permanent secretaries, nearly 40 per cent of members of parliament, and 71 per cent of the vice-chancellors of other universities. Eleven members of Harold Wilson's cabinet were at Oxford. In 1964 Oxford and Cambridge provided 76 successful candidates (by examination and interview) for the senior civil service and foreign service, while other universities provided 17. The 18,000 students of Oxbridge make up, from the outside, at least, one of the most élite élites in the world. Less than one per cent of Britain's population go to Oxbridge but, once there, they are wooed by industry and government. A BA (Oxon) or BA (Cantab.) is quite different from an ordinary BA. Sir Alexander Carr-Saunders told me that when he was invited to sit in on interviews for the civil service, he found 'everyone on the board was prejudiced in favour of the Redbrick candidates: yet they always ended up by choosing Oxbridge men. You see, they speak the *same language*'.

Oxford is different from Cambridge. Oxford is older, more worldly, more philosophical, classical and theological (seven professors of theology to one of engineering in 1965) and with a flair for self-congratulation and public relations. ('It may be, after all', wrote one editor-don, John Hale, 'that Oxford's prominence in the press is due less to the inherent fascination of the place for the public, than to the efficiency of the local news gathering services.'[1]) Cambridge is more isolated, more theatrical, more scientific: five of the heads of Cambridge colleges are scientists; only one in Oxford. Cambridge has a more self-contained intellectual class, with the tradition of intermarried Huxleys, Darwins, Keyneses, Wedgwoods, and is less obsessed with London. But compared to the others, these two stone cities with their quadrangles, cloisters, damp staircases and punts are uncannily alike. Like the monarchy, they are a fairyland in the heart of Britain: but more successfully than the monarchy they have deflected criticism—by casting their spell on the alumni and would-be alumni, particularly in the mass media and politics. (*Whitaker's Almanack*, for instance, lists every Oxbridge professor including

[1] *Oxford Magazine*, March 2, 1961.

the Vigfussan Professor of Icelandic Literature and Antiquities, but no Redbrick ones.)

Oxbridge is only in session for half the year, and the universities adjourn for four months in the summer—a relic from medieval times, when scholars had to bring in the harvest. Lord Bowden has remarked on the appallingly low 'plant utilisation factor', reckoning that their buildings are only used for 125 days a year. 'If education is an industry', he said in November 1964, 'then it is the most extravagant and inefficient I know.' Sir Geoffrey Crowther, in a celebrated attack, has suggested that dons could do twice the work for (if necessary) twice the pay, working a shift system with two universities using each set of buildings.[1]

Slowly the population of Oxford and Cambridge has been changing. In the nineteenth century it was a mixture of some boys who were poor and clever, and others who were rich and idle. The pattern was already changing before the war, when the (Conservative) government gave more grants to poorer boys. But since the war, government grants enormously increased, and now over 80 per cent of university students are paid for by the state. And at the same time, brains have come increasingly into demand. Not surprisingly, therefore, the competition to become part of the Oxbridge stable grew steadily. The Oxford and Cambridge examinations became the great challenge to the schools, distorting their syllabus for three or four years before. The most intense battle was among girls. Only since the 1870s have women been admitted, and the eight women's colleges constitute only 12 per cent of the Oxbridge population, so that competition to reach them was fierce.

Ostensibly, the amenities of Oxbridge are now wide open to the meritocracy, but in fact the proportion of grammar school boys has not spectacularly increased. In 1961, 54 per cent of Oxford men came from independent schools; 16 per cent from the direct-grant grammar schools and only 30 per cent from ordinary maintained grammar schools. At other universities, 72 per cent came from maintained grammar schools.[2] The change since before the war is not very striking: and in fact (because of the expansion of places) *more* public school boys are going to Oxbridge than in the thirties. Comparatively few grammar schools so far are straining to get their boys into Oxbridge. 'I'm surprised how few grammar schools are really trying to get their boys

[1] Schools and Universities: oration for LSE, Dec. 1960.

[2] Robbins, p. 80.

into Cambridge,' said Sir Eric Ashby, the most radical of the Cambridge heads of houses, in 1961: 'It's part of an old tribal pattern: many grammar schools would rather send their boys to a provincial university, which they know, rather than risk being turned down by Oxbridge. We don't get anything like as many grammar school boys applying as we'd like: we only awarded two-thirds of our scholarships in 1960. Cambridge is still regarded as a finishing school for a small set of schools.'

In the early 1960s the Oxbridge reputation for exclusiveness began to harm them, and the numbers of students trying for Oxbridge places dropped alarmingly. Where there had been five applicants for every place, by 1964 there were only two. The standards had not dropped appreciably: headmasters still nursed their cleverest boys for Oxbridge—but the pool of talent Oxbridge used to select from disappeared. Many schools and candidates apparently couldn't be bothered with special Oxbridge exams, (which needed an extra sixth-form year) especially after the newly-created Universities Central Council on Admissions (UCCA)[1] had simplified entrance procedures for all other universities to filling in a single form. Gingerly, the colleges began trying to woo the maintained grammar schools; both Oxford and Cambridge tried to unify the admissions procedures of the different colleges, and finally, in 1963 negotiations were opened with UCCA, and terms were agreed for Oxbridge to join in the national system. Some of the Redbrick universities were sorry to let them in: they were afraid, with some reason, that the trend away from Oxbridge would be immediately reversed.

Gradually the atmosphere of Oxbridge is changing. 'They used to be undergraduates, they're students now,' said one don who returned to Oxford in 1962 from the provinces. The new students are inventing new organisations, with Redbrick names, like the Students Representative Councils: there is even a lobby in Oxford to turn the famous political Union into a Redbrick-style social centre Union for everybody. But one gets the impression the students are still a minority, self-consciously reacting against the old, quasi-aristocratic life that has continued, remarkably unchanged, fostered by draughty college rooms and rheumy college servants.

Much of the attraction of Oxbridge depends on the individual teaching, the range of peculiar lecturers, the sense of being an

[1] *See* p. 244.

international centre, exposed to some of the best minds in the world. But much, too, depends on the social climate—the unchanging calendar of boat-races, college balls and summer frolics. A careful amateurism is still the style (you can still be 'sconced' at some colleges for talking shop at dinner). From outside Oxbridge might appear as a citadel which can only be stormed by the cleverest invaders; but from inside it looks curiously as it always was, with its surface of pageantry, idleness and sport.

COLLEGES

The main resistance to change comes from the fact that admissions to Oxford and Cambridge are still controlled by their forty individual colleges which, like Inns of Court or Eton houses, foster eccentric muddle and fissiparous groups. They retain a jealous autonomy, and they differ as much as Southend differs from Bournemouth. They constitute in themselves a miniature social history of Britain, beginning with University College, Oxford, in 1249 and reaching the new St. Catherine's College, Oxford, in 1964. They range from wealthy old colleges with loud, rich undergraduates to poor new colleges, with no endowments and quiet grammar school boys (like Jesus, Oxford, or Selwyn, Cambridge).

Probably the richest is Christ Church, Oxford, founded in 1532 by King Henry VIII, with endowments which now bring in more than £100,000 a year. It is the largest Oxford college, with 500 undergraduates and a cathedral—the smallest in England—in its garden. It has produced thirteen out of forty-six prime ministers, and the road from Eton to Christ Church to politics has been well travelled for two hundred years. In 1964, it had both one of the largest proportion of public school boys and the largest proportion of failures in the final examinations (5 per cent). 'The House', as it's called, has changed little in thirty years: it now takes one hundred and twenty schoolboys a year, compared to ninety before the war. It is obviously impossible for any Christ Church man to write objectively about his own college, and it generates a love-hate relationship in many of its alumni. It contains all kinds of divisions—between canons and anti-clerical dons, between classicists and scientists, or between the four quadrangles with their social labels. Behind the stone walls lurk all kinds of surprising rebels and nonconformists. I have found (for instance) some of my Christ Church contemporaries some of the most outspoken sources for this book. But the dominant group is still made up of beaglers, sports-car drivers and champagne-party-givers, known to the rest of Oxford as the 'Christ Church bloodies'. From the annual newsletter, which records the KCMGs, the ambassadorships and cabinet changes of alumni, one might suspect that the whole of government provided a kind of after-care treatment for Christ Church men; and the influence of the college has managed to promote the question of whether a road should pass through a neighbouring meadow into an unending national debate. Its surviving extravagance and wealth was shown in 1964 when it succeeded in raising £300,000 for a new quadrangle to house sixty undergraduates—an average of £5,000 per student.

King's College, Cambridge produces a less conventional group. It began as an annexe to Eton, and until 1856 only Etonians went there: but since then, King's has broken loose from their sister-foundation, and although they still include a wodge from Eton, they like to picture themselves as blending Etonian urbanity with a rebellious independence and intellectualism. 'King's doesn't exist', said the Provost, Noël Annan, an urbane and gregarious humanist, 'to discover reasons for agreeing with the pronouncements of the Archbishop of Canterbury and the Lord Chamberlain.' King's has surprisingly transformed itself from a religious foundation—still with the finest chapel and choir in Britain—into a group of agnostic fellows, including E. M. Forster. They have a far higher proportion of fellows to undergraduates—seventy-five to three hundred—than any other college, and thus allow more contact between teachers and taught. Kingsmen specialise in the civil service, teaching, and the 'cultural bureaucracy'. Up till 1961 the college insisted on handpicking their boys *before* examination, and chose a very noticeable type—precocious, fastidious, very arts-conscious.

In terms of sheer wordly success, the most formidable college is Balliol, Oxford. Ever since Benjamin Jowett was Master, from 1870 to 1893, Balliol has been preoccupied not so much with scholarship as with success, producing with considerable effort 'a sense of effortless superiority'. In 1964 they once again had the highest proportion of first-class degrees (18·8 per cent) of any Oxford college: they also, in 1961, startled Oxford by appointing a lecturer in management studies. 'Life is one Balliol man after another,' Lord Samuel said, and it still is. They include:

Balliol Men

Harold Macmillan (plus son and grandson)	King Olaf of Norway
Lord Kilmuir	Sir Denis Brogan
Ted Heath	Arnold Toynbee
Henry Brooke	Ivor Brown
Lord Monckton	Cyril Connolly
Julian Amery	Graham Greene
Sir Dingle Foot	Julian Huxley
Prince Wan of Thailand	Raymond Mortimer
Hugh Fraser	Harold Nicolson
Sir Frank Soskice	Beverley Nichols
Denis Healey	Anthony Greenwood
Mark Bonham Carter	Roy Jenkins
John Fulton	Sir Timothy Bligh

Balliol men are marked not only by their achievements but by their awareness of Balliol, which (like Winchester) gives the impression of being more a cult than a college: they love talking about each other, and in 1957 Balliol men held a special dinner in the City to celebrate the fact that, for the first time since Asquith's government in 1908, the Prime Minister and Lord Chancellor were both Balliol men.[1]

With the growing pressure on Oxbridge from schools on the one side and from industry on the other, the process of 'Ballioliza-tion' is spreading, and colleges are judging themselves increasingly by intellectual and worldly standards, less by the social standards of pre-war Oxbridge. The most obvious criterion is the first-class degree: about 8·5 per cent of Oxford's undergraduates take a first,[2] and 10 per cent of Cambridge's. This 10 per cent does not necessarily correspond to outside success. Eight out of the eleven Oxford graduates in the cabinet took firsts, but one of the cleverest of them, Lord Gardiner, the Lord Chancellor, took a fourth.

DONS

Don different from those regal Dons!
With hearts of gold and lungs of bronze,
Who shout and bang and roar and bawl
The absolute across the hall . . .

Hilaire Belloc.

[1] *See The Observer*, July 7, 1957.

[2] In 1964, 9·1 per cent took firsts, 56·8 per cent took seconds, 27·9 per cent took thirds, 2·8 per cent took fourths, and only 1·7 per cent failed. *See The Oxford Magazine*, October 22, 1964.

Oxbridge not only takes the pick of British undergraduates. It also, still more markedly, takes the best of the university teachers or 'dons'. In purely academic terms, Oxbridge dons are better qualified than those at other universities: 76 per cent of them took first-class degrees, compared to about 55 per cent elsewhere. They are also very inbred, and only 22 per cent graduated from another university, compared to 74 per cent in the other universities.[1] And Oxbridge still sets the pattern—an elaborate one—for dons' behaviour, and clockwise port and high tables have even been exported to Ghana. It was only in 1871 that dons in Oxford and Cambridge were allowed to marry, and Oxbridge still provides a semi-celibate way of life, centring on the senior common room, with special tables for rotating the port and madeira. (Two colleges, Trinity Hall, Cambridge and New College, Oxford, have a special device—a kind of port railway—to solve the appalling problem of how to get the port round without moving it anti-clockwise.) Since 1871 matrimony has gradually crept in, but domesticated dons still lead split lives, spanning two centuries, with white-coated men servants and port in the colleges, and nappies and washing up in North Oxford. This does not apparently lead to broken homes or mental breakdowns, and the two ways of life, like those of diplomats at home and abroad, exist uneasily together.

Most Oxbridge dons maintain a determined detachment from contemporary problems. Some indication can be seen in the postgraduate theses, which show a preference for tiny segments of the distant past, encouraged by their professors to 'crawl along the frontiers of knowledge with a hand-lens'—in Sir Eric Ashby's phrase. These, for instance, were the first four entries in the list of candidates for the degree of Bachelor of Letters in Modern History at Oxford in 1961:

A study of the 'Narratio de Fundatione' of Fountains Abbey.
The rise and influence of the House of Luxemburg-Ligny from 1371 to 1475.
A bibliography of Henry St. John, Viscount Bolingbroke.
The Archiepiscopate of William de Corbeil 1123–36.

Since the war the outside world of industry and mass media has made inroads on the dons' seclusion, and the trains from Oxford and Cambridge to London have been full of dons travelling up to advise on investment or research, or to appear on television. With

[1] Robbins: Appendix III.

the Labour government of 1964, there was a new rush of dons—particularly Oxford economists—into government. Some scientific dons make more money as industrial consultants than from their university work. The worldly involvement of dons is periodically attacked as a selling-out of their values—'*La Trahison des Clercs*'—especially by those who have not been offered jobs. But industrialists who subsidise the universities complain on their side that dons do not contribute enough thought and study to Britain's industrial and economic problems.

Dons, like everyone else, have become much more professional; mad, drunken or absent-minded dons are all rarer. There is a new race of them with both feet in the outside world, like Alan Bullock, of St. Catherine's, Oxford, or Sir John Cockcroft of Churchill, Cambridge, who both preside over brand-new colleges with new ideas. But many Oxbridge ones—particularly Oxford—maintain a profoundly unserious façade: they cultivate frivolous interests and a subtle mortar-board humour, centring on the minutiæ of university rivalries: their outward passions are most deeply aroused on questions such as elections for sinecures or *Lady Chatterley's Lover*, and social snobs encourage them to behave like stage characters. They appear to be delighted, not appalled, by the picture of them painted by Lord Snow.

Outside this small and not very relevant circle, the large new profession of university teaching is facing a crisis. Already not enough young men are prepared to endure the rat-race to publish which is intrinsic in the present academic ethos, while with the present expansion plans, thousands more dons will be needed by the 1970s. At the same time there is growing discontent with the narrow syllabuses of the old universities: there are many reforming parties, but the structure of tutors and professors is so entrenched, like the ramifications of any *ancien régime*, that it is hard to reform one part without upsetting the whole.

Former dons will be scattered all over this book—don-diplomats, don-politicians, don-bishops, even don-bankers and don-chairmen. Scores of them—people like Lord Franks, Lord Radcliffe, Sir Ivor Jennings, Harold Wilson, Barbara Wootton—have had an oustanding influence, moving from the world of books and ideas to politics and committees with astonishing ease: and many towards the end of their career go back to Oxbridge as heads of colleges. New disciplines—particularly economics—have forged new links between universities and Whitehall.

OXBRIDGE ON THE RUN?

Suddenly, with the sharp new interest in universities, in the early 1960s the outside world began battering on the old oak of the college doors. The colleges had kept their autonomy; the university had governed itself with its old democratic and archaic system; the vice-chancellors rotated every two years by tradition; and hardly anyone noticed Oxbridge had changed. There was a whole world of laboratories and engineering schools, doubling and tripling its numbers—but expanding largely outside the college system. A huge postgraduate population had arrived—often to lead lonely and neglected lives, falling into the Oxbridge void between colleges and university.

When administratively-minded dons at Oxbridge woke up to these problems, they appointed whole clutches of committees to look into them—committees on post-graduates, teaching methods, the curriculum, university government, the relationship between the university and the colleges. Cambridge had Annan committees, Oxford had Sutherland ones—the worldly dons worked overtime. The falling admissions number forced the colleges into some self-examination.

So, feeling they were moving as fast as possible to catch up with change, the ancient universities were furious when the Robbins Report released a spate of criticism. The report didn't deal much with Oxbridge: it analysed 'the special influence of certain universities', and suggested especially generous grants to other universities to offset this. But in one shattering paragraph, the report said: 'The number of times when it is necessary to except Oxford and Cambridge from general statements about British universities, the difficulty both universities have in reaching rapid decisions . . . and the general obscurity in which so many of their administrative and financial arrangments are shrouded are not compatible with a situation in which they, like other universities, are largely dependent on public funds. Continuance of such anomalies may well endanger not only their own welfare, but the effectiveness of the whole system of higher education in this country . . . If Oxford and Cambridge are unable satisfactorily to solve these problems within a reasonable time, they should be the subject of independent enquiry.'[1]

The wave of feeling against Oxbridge was swollen by a succession of attacks. Two young Fellows of King's wrote a frank

[1] Robbins, page 224.

insiders' view called 'Camford Observed'. Richard Crossman, MP, himself an ex-don, wrote an attack on 'educational apartheid' in *The Observer*[1] (to the fury of his Oxford contemporaries). Finally, in 1964, Oxford reacted. They set up a two-year commission of almost royal scale to look into the whole structure of the university. Lord Franks, Provost of Worcester and practised government committee man was chairman and the six members had, for Oxford, a radical look. The commission set out to let daylight into the 'general obscurity', and to suggest ways of streamlining its cumbrous organisation. But it will also clearly be concerned to maintain Oxford's pre-eminence, and the eventual report may well prove Oxford's best essay in public relations.

REDBRICK

It's absurd that four-fifths of our undergraduates should be made to feel that they're inferior for life.

Sir Alexander Carr-Saunders.

The division between Oxbridge and Redbrick—as the other four-fifths is rudely and inaccurately called—is much sharper than the separation, for instance, of the American 'Ivy League'. A Gallup Poll for the BBC in 1960 showed that 80 per cent had heard of Oxford and Cambridge, 50 per cent of London University, 8 per cent of Southampton and Reading. The more the other universities expand the greater, it seems, the centripetal pull of Oxford and Cambridge. In the civil service, politics and law there has been no visible breach in the supremacy of Oxbridge graduates. The division is essentially a class one. While over 50 per cent of Oxbridge undergraduates come from public schools, only 15 per cent of Redbrick do: many public school boys would rather go straight into business, into the services or to a foreign university like McGill, Grenoble or Harvard, than go to a Redbrick university.

In England Redbrick has been separate from the beginning. When Oxford and Cambridge were exclusively Anglican, the new Victorian universities were built to provide a liberal education for the poorer boys and dissenters of the provinces—and to give technological training. They grew up outside the old aristocratic pattern, and thus had the austere associations of self-improvement

[1] January 26, 1964.

and nonconformism. Oxford and Cambridge graduates scorned them, and London University, which was founded in 1836, was referred to as 'that joint stock company in Gower Street'.

The Scottish universities, like their schools, have avoided the rift of class which divides the English. Even in the fifteenth century there were three Scots universities and the Scots, being poorer and more ambitious, have been more convinced of the necessity of education than the English. But in England, the whole way of life in Redbrick is different. Most students live in lodgings: the building of residential halls is slower than the overall growth in numbers. Few of the students have individual tutors. Only a few universities have separate colleges, and they lack the strong corporate sense of Oxbridge. No Redbrick university or college has established the continuous relationship with politics or public service which marks Oxbridge colleges. Even the Labour cabinet can claim only three Redbrick members, Willie Ross from Glasgow and Fred Peart and Ted Short from Durham. The London School of Economics (which has produced the chairman of ICI and the chairman of the Electricity Council) has often been accused by Tories of breeding left-wing cabinet ministers: in fact the only LSE graduate to reach the cabinet—Aubrey Jones—was a Tory, and he was too radical to last long. The LSE today excels less in politics than in sociology, journalism, public opinion polls and other outsider-ish activities, and their alumni include Bernard Levin, Mark Abrams, Lord Robbins, Michael Peacock, Robert Mackenzie, Margot Naylor, Paul Bareau and nearly all the public opinion pollsters.

'Redbrick' ranges from the granite fastness of Aberdeen to the eccentric new buildings of Southampton: an idea of their range of activities and character can be glimpsed from the chart overleaf. Several are in origin 'civic' universities, founded by the mayors and corporations as the product of local pride, many of whom still maintain a town-hall attitude, regarding students' frolics as an affront to civic dignity. In terms of surroundings and architecture, there are different layers of Redbrick. There are the big, impersonal city universities like Manchester, Liverpool or Birmingham, where most students live in digs on the outskirts and commute like office workers. There are the superior provincials, like Edinburgh or Bristol, which have cleaner air and a tradition of undergraduate spirit. And there is London, in an extraordinary shapeless class of its own, with three times as many undergraduates as any other university, five hundred professors, and departments ranging from the Courtauld Institute of Art to the Imperial College of Science and Technology. The most unusual university is Wales, which has four small scattered components, at Cardiff, Swansea, Aberystwyth and Bangor (which has the distinction of owning a university boat, for the purposes of oceanography—a subject of some interest to the University Grants Committee). But the outward appearance of the universities is no clue to their scholarship. Manchester, one of the bleakest, has produced three Nobel Prize winners in a row, and for twenty years contained the most distinguished British historian, Sir Lewis Namier, while several pleasant places are classed as 'Academic Siberia'. Many Redbrick universities have established vigorous independent traditions of their own, without too much thought of Oxbridge. Some, like Aberdeen or Liverpool, which are not distinguished by their undergraduates, have strong post-graduate schools. The following section shows all the universities now in existence in Britain.

The sharp increase in government spending is at last changing the face of Redbrick. Birmingham, for instance, has moved from a scatter of blackened buildings round the town to a central campus with shops, restaurants, gleaming new faculty blocks around the redbrick Victorian Chamberlain building, and skyscraper halls of residence. Manchester—always the fourth most famous English university after Oxbridge and London—could become the English Cambridge, Mass., with a huge university sector built on land freed by slum clearance, containing the university, the new business school,[1] and the expanded Manchester College of Science and Technology.

But the external improvements have done little to alter the basic problems of Redbrick—for students, the impersonality and nine-to-five traditions, and the feeling of second-best; for dons, the hierarchical organisation, with huge faculties and all-powerful professors; for both, the surroundings, inevitably less attractive than Oxbridge and less exciting than London. The breakdown of local cultures and the spread of communications has tended if anything to strengthen the pull of Oxbridge, and rebellious dons, after a spell in Redbrick, are tempted to return to the womb. And the growth in post-graduate schools has widened the rift: Redbrick students try to move to Oxbridge for their post-graduate studies, but there is no traffic the other way.

[1] *See* Chapter 27.

NEW UNIVERSITIES

Into this muddled collection of universities, medieval, Victorian and Edwardian, there erupted very suddenly in the late fifties a group of universities that were unashamedly new. The very idea of a new university was new; for in the past it was felt that you could no more invent a university than you could invent a child; and the 'university colleges' that were built in the early twentieth century, at Leicester, Exeter, etc., were regarded as the children of London University, like colonial colleges, taking London exams and supervised by London dons—a tutelage which helped to give them their inferiority complex. The first breakthrough happened after the war, when the University of Keele was set up in 1949, in the slaggy heart of the Potteries, to provide a quite new kind of four-year course, with its own degrees. But Keele, was small, poor and—in its smoky setting—not very sought after. Fourteen years later it still had fewer than a thousand students.

But as the older universities began to split at the seams, as the empire went out, prosperity came in, and at last we became worried about the lack of higher education, so the idea gathered weight of building bigger, bolder places with real independence. Already today the idea seems obvious, and in America it is commonplace; but from the academic citadels of Oxford and Cambridge the innovation seemed outrageously radical. The new universities, like the Atomic Energy Authority or Commercial Television, were rare British examples of institutions being imposed quite suddenly on to a pattern where before things had 'just growed', and the very fact that this *could* be done was a blow to the old pragmatism.

The first and most favoured was the University of Sussex at Brighton, which had been clamouring to have a university since 1947. Brighton had natural advantages—closeness to London, enchanting surroundings, fashionability—and acquired ones. Their vice-chancellor, John Fulton, a quiet, dry Scot with a light in his eye, is a past-master at administration and committees: at Balliol, where he was both an undergraduate and a fellow, he was remembered for instituting a committee on committees, with himself as chairman, and then writing a formal minute to the chairman of another committee, who was himself. With Fulton, as pro-vice-chancellor, is Professor Asa Briggs, a dynamic but homely Yorkshireman, who is the most spectacular of the young amphibian dons, who move with equal ease in scholarship and on dry land. Briggs, whose own interests range from Victoriana to pop music, has been insistent that universities, while maintaining scholarship, must try to equip students for the modern world—a doctrine which, again, is orthodox in America but heretical in British academic circles—and he has been a main advocate of what he has called 'redrawing the map of learning'. Brighton's map is based on 'schools of studies', which enable students to escape from the rigid faculties of Oxford and Cambridge, and (for instance) to take a history course against an English, European or social studies background. Typical of Brighton are its examination papers called 'The Modern European Mind' and 'Contemporary Britain', whose questions have included:

> Do the forms and contents of pop music help us to understand contemporary Britain?
>
> Can the decay affecting a number of provincial regions be arrested solely by means of controls on the location of industry?

In spite of its many critics, Brighton established itself with extraordinary speed. An extravagant brick-and-concrete quadrangle, looking like a cross between a cathedral and a Victorian viaduct, rose up on the edge of the downs, designed by Sir Basil Spence, the most passionate of contemporary architects. Young Oxbridge dons, discontented, idealistic, or ambitious, clamoured to join the adventure, and its distinguished academics now include David Daiches (English), Martin Wight (History), Roger Blin-Stoyle (Physics) and Tibor Barna (Economics). The dons soon ceased to be refugees from the dreaming spires, and acquired a confidence and spirit of their own, mixing contemporary interests with quaint quirks: they took a special interest, for instance, in their ceremonial academic dress, and designed bizarre yellow gowns and birettas which made them look, at their inauguration at Brighton Pavilion, like Venetian villains from a Webster tragedy.

The students, too, queued to come in, and by 1964, three years after the first undergraduates arrived, *The Economist* could say: 'To have a child at the University of Sussex is beyond question the most absolutely OK thing in Britain now.'[1] The OK-ness of Brighton, with its debs and political daughters, its beauty and its comfort, is one of its difficulties as a tough academic training-

[1] 'New Learning on the Downs'. *The Economist*, November 14, 1964.

ground: but this mixture of social and intellectual snobberies has helped it to achieve the breaking up, for the first time for seven hundred years, of the Oxbridge monopoly. After three years it had over a thousand students—more than Keele had achieved in fourteen years—and however tiny this figure was by American or Australian standards, it had proved that a sudden institution can be invented without laughable results.

Other new universities followed fast, a little jealous of Brighton's fame and favour. Outside Norwich, the rich, smug old centre of East Anglia, prefabricated lecture-rooms and offices shot up round an old Jacobean mansion, with a haste that symbolised the university crisis. Its vice-chancellor, Frank Thistlethwaite is, like Fulton, an unobtrusive and patient committee-man who is adept at the first task, of raising money from reluctant local big-wigs, in a city and county that is notoriously mean. Thistlethwaite is a Cambridge historian, and has grafted some Cambridge traditions on to Norwich (half his dons are Cambridge firsts); but he is also a very American influence—he has taught at Minnesota and Pennsylvania, written a big book on the American constitution, and married an American wife. He has followed part of Brighton's new map of learning, but added more American regions of freedom and informality. He has helped to inaugurate a television 'dawn university', and TV link-ups with Cambridge lectures—thus further defying the old academic exclusiveness. And he has made use of the engaging East Anglian cultural worthies, Benjamin Britten and Angus Wilson, to bring stimulus from outside. Norwich, like Brighton, attracted distinguished Oxbridge dons, and gave them a new vigour and challenge: 'I feel ten years younger than I did when I left Balliol,' said Marcus Dick, Professor of Philosophy, 'and twenty years younger than I did when I was a scholar at Winchester.' And the attractions of Norwich will be strengthened by the bold new terraced buildings now going up, designed by Denys Lasdun. It is in the new universities that British architects have had their greatest stimulus (which neither cathedrals nor council houses could provide) to produce a bold new form to express a quite new concept.

The other universities, all competing for students, dons and fame, each offer their speciality: it is a favourite complaint against them that they are both too American and too gimmicky. York, which opened in 1963, is the most staid and conventional: it has a course in medieval history, and its degrees are more like Oxbridge ones. It has some excellent dons, including Professor Brockbank of the English School and Harry Ree, a former headmaster and resistance hero (he blew up the Renault works), who is head of the Education Department. Some of its students complain that it is run too much like a school: its vice-chancellor is Lord James, known as Lord Jim, who was for fifteen years High Master of Manchester Grammar School, and the most celebrated prophet of the meritocracy. York, like the others, is partly influenced by its strong local traditions: it owes a lot to the Rowntree Quaker chocolate family, and its medieval studies are encouraged by the archives of the magnificent York Cathedral.

The others are still in their infancy, but are already determined each to be different. The University of Essex at Colchester, the nearest to London, was only opened in 1964, with a keen young vice-chancellor from Liverpool, Albert Sloman; its particular attractions include a brilliant sociologist, Peter Townsend, and a real poet as Professor of English, Donald Davie. The University of Lancaster is more austere in its plans: it has an industrial economist at its head, Charles Carter, and offers such contemporary subjects as Operational Research and Environmental Studies. The University of Warwick, largely promoted by the late Lord Rootes, plans to be a huge, cosmopolitan technological place, and a bluff dynamo-don, Jack Butterworth, is its vice-chancellor. The University of Kent, at Canterbury, is run by a medieval historian and ex-registrar from Birmingham, Geoffrey Templeman. The youngest of all, the University of Stirling, is so far not much more than a lush prospectus and a place on the map, halfway between Edinburgh and Glasgow.

In the wake of these hectic arrivals there has followed a spate of argument, centring on the basic alarming question: 'What is a university *for*?' Before the new universities began, the question was surprisingly little asked: it was implicit in the notion of 'academic freedom' that dons should ideally be free to pursue what subjects they chose, and that their self-interest coincided with the universities', and even the nation's, interest. But once universities were started from scratch, with the government and industrialists looking over their shoulder, the question had to be asked. Should they equip their young men to be modern managers, should they give them a broad, enriching cultural background, or should they be concerned, above all, with the pursuit of fine scholarship? And if, as seemed likely, they should do all these things, where on earth should the balance rest? The arguments between the different maps of learning were quite fierce, and when Sloman of

Essex outlined his plans in the BBC's Reith Lectures in 1963, Guy Chilver, the Dean of Humanities at Kent, retorted in a review with sharp doubts: 'Can a university concerned with literature and government really afford to exclude Western Europe from its campus? . . .' 'How long is the current fashion for "comparisons" going to last?'

There were more serious criticisms, even from radical quarters, of the new universities. They were too small—many would have no more than 3,000 students—to be able to afford proper libraries, or proper equipment for engineering and science, the most needed branches of new learning. They were (complained Lord Taylor's Labour Party report) too often placed in pleasant and old-fashioned cathedral towns, and not enough in the industrial centres that needed them and could provide accommodation. They were, in some cases, too much concerned with novelty for novelty's sake. And in the face of the national predicament their buildings were too extravagant and luxurious, and still based on an élitist concept of university education.

In the ten years since the University of Sussex was first planned, the climate in the universities has already changed almost beyond recognition. The possibility of sudden, separate expansion has been opened up. Dons have been transplanted, have flourished and even blossomed. And the question, 'what are we for', though it will never be answered, has at least been faced.

TECHNOLOGY

> We must substitute a living science for dead literature, and distribute the honours and rewards of life in channels where they may fructify to the use of the commonwealth instead of being limited to the learned professions, the military and naval services, and the residents of our universities.
>
> *The Times, October 13, 1851.*

> We believe that a further striking innovation is required if this country is to demonstrate beyond all doubt that it is prepared to give to technology the prominence that the economic needs of the future will surely demand.
>
> *Robbins Report (para. 383)*, 1963.

Nowhere has the random growth of British higher education been more unfortunate than in the field of technology. Since the nineteenth century lone voices, like Prince Albert's, Lyon Playfair's, or Eustace Percy's, have campaigned for technological education and pointed apprehensively to Germany and America. British governments, industry and universities were apathetic or hostile. What is surprising is not how little progress was made in British technological education, but how much.

Since 1953, it progressed. But the Robbins Report showed how far Britain lags behind other Western countries. This table shows what percentage of all degrees in science and technology were taken in technology in 1959.[1]

Germany	68
Canada	65
Netherlands	60
Switzerland	59
Sweden	54
USA	49
France	48
Britain	36

The Industrial Revolution had very little to do with the universities. In the early nineteenth century, Oxford and Cambridge took little interest in the new sciences. The technologists, like Watt, Boulton or Newcomen, came from the factories and workshops, while the great pioneer scientists—Priestley, Dalton or Joule—taught in dissenters' academies, mainly Quaker, in the North: so that the rift between science and the humanities was widened by the rift between anglicans and nonconformists. Many modern 'Techs' developed out of the mechanics' institutes, which for much of the nineteenth century provided the only technological education available to many regions. London's first Polytechnic was only founded in 1882. It was only after France and Germany had founded their *polytechniques* and *hochschulen* for techno-managers that Britain gradually felt the need to adapt their universities to technical education. Hence the new scientifically-minded universities of the 1870s, planted in the middle of the industrial cities of the North and Midlands. They were designed not, like the continental schools, to produce a separate scientific culture, but to bring the new world of technology into the old world of liberal education.[2] Laboratories and workshops have crept up on the libraries and lecture halls—not only in the

[1] In total numbers, Britain's position looks slightly better, but with 2,600 technological first degrees, we are still well behind the US, with 38,130, France with 4,360 and Germany with 3,080.

[2] *See* Sir Eric Ashby's terse and brilliant study: 'Technology and the Academics', 1958.

new universities but in the old ones. In North Oxford and East Cambridge new scientific cities have grown up beyond the colleges, with government endowments far larger than those of the ancient foundations.

But just as the universities preferred mandarin to modern Chinese, they preferred pure science to technology. With three exceptions, technology inside the universities was only developed grudgingly, as a second-class subject. The exceptions were the great, sprawling, quasi-independent Techs—London, Manchester and Glasgow.

In 1953 the government took its first big technological step: it announced a £12 million programme for Imperial College in London. Imperial College had been a great triumph for the technological education lobby[1] when it was founded in 1907 by a merger of three London Colleges. It was given four and a half acres in South Kensington by the Commissioners of the Great Exhibition of 1851, and was financed by a curious mixture of diamond money (from Wernher, Beit & Co. and Cecil Rhodes), Rothschilds, the LCC, and interested professional groups. Although it was always part of London University, it stayed very separate with its outlandish-sounding new Chairs—like Chemical and Oil Technology, established before the Great War, and the 1919 Zaharoff Chair of Aviation, the first in the country. Imperial College, in the 1930s was already virtually a university of its own, with its own world-wide reputation. With the 1953 expansion, modern green shoeboxes were put up to replace the old Edwardian buildings—only two sentimental towers were left—and by 1964, South Kensington was the shining scientific capital of the New Britain, with Blackett,[2] the Imperial College professor of physics, as its elder statesman. Student numbers were increased from 1,663 in 1953 to 2,725 in 1961, and by 1966, they will be 3,500, almost half of them post-graduate. Imperial College has the highest professor–student ratio in the country, and many of its most brilliant men, like Professor Chain (biochemistry), Professor Lighthill (aerodynamics), Professor Buchanan (transport) or Professor Hinshelwood (chemistry), have been lured, often with whole research teams, from other places.

Manchester and Glasgow—now the university of Strathclyde—have also undergone spectacular expansions: by 1966 they will have 3,000 students. Robbins wanted to turn these three colleges,

[1] *See* Michael Argles, *South Kensington to Robbins*, Longmans, 1964.

[2] *See* Chapter 20.

BRITISH
UNIVERSITIES
1965

University	Date of first foundation (and date of Charter)	Under-graduates 1964	Post-graduates 1964	Expansion targets 1967–8	Professors 1962–3	Lecturers 1962–3
Oxford	1249 (1st college)	7,122	1,900	9,500	92	489
Cambridge	1284 (1st college)	7,500	1,760	9,600	95	823
St. Andrews	1410	2,970	302	5,300	49	335
Glasgow	1451	5,952	612	7,750	73	609
Aberdeen	1495	2,520	213	4,300	38	278
Edinburgh	1583	7,878	1,531	big	69	640
Strathclyde	1796	2,318	240	4,700	20	287
Durham	1832	1,542	369	2,930	28	176
Newcastle	1832	4,402	514	5,800	61	433
London	1836	17,134	6,452	29,000	506	3,085
Belfast	1849	4,376	746	5,170		
Manchester	1851	7,572	1,479	11,200	85	715
Manchester Tech	1827	1,689	513	2,700	19	330
Bath (Bristol Cat)	1856	763	21	1,647		
Southampton	1862 (1952)	1,708	366	4,000	31	181

Unusual subjects	Miscellaneous
Medieval and modern Greek	Almost half students public school. Post-Robbins worries about image led to Franks Commission.
Mineralogy and Petrology	Same as Oxford, except more sheltered, so worries less.
Astronomy	Really two universities. St. Andrews—mainly English, very traditionalist, students have own language, like their red gowns. Dundee—more Scottish civic, students dislike red gowns, breaking away.
Naval Architecture	Very 'Civic', large classes, angry students, good at debating. 80 per cent Scottish.
Natural Philosophy	Three-quarters of the students are local. Strong medicine. Growing fast.
Comparative Constitutions Linguistics	Powerful medical school, with professors warring about reform. 22 per cent students do medicine; 10 per cent are foreign. Once a great European university.
Industrial administration Fibre science	Quite famous as Glasgow Tech; became university in 1964, merging with Scottish College of Commerce. Bang in centre of Glasgow, 60 per cent of students live at home. 'Progressive'.
Indian civilisation	Mildly prestigious but sleepy. Eight colleges; University, the oldest and stuffiest, in castle of Prince-bishops of Durham. Newspaper called *Palatinate*.
candinavian studies and Use studies oil science	Hived off from Durham, 1963. Spence engineering building.
ou name it, they teach it	Vast federation, dozens of colleges and medical schools, professors of everything. Includes, for instance, Wye College Kent and Courtauld Institute. Big colleges, e.g. Imperial, may split off.
cholastic Philosophy	'A pub every ten yards', say students. Men-only students union, tall engineering tower.
omparative religion thiopic own and country planning	Will be huge university precinct, with tech and business school: England's Cambridge Mass. 22 per cent students from direct-grant schools. Jodrell Bank telescope, mathematics, less distinguished in arts than it was.
lymer chemistry	Lord Bowden's baby. Special paper science building. Candidate to be English M.I.T?
onomics and administration rticulture	Was Bristol Cat. Moving to Bath in 1965, when it metamorphoses into a university. Super site there, department of architecture delighted.
ructural engineering ronautics and astronautics	Nuffield theatre, like copper armadillo, best in any university. Three engineering blocks and superior wind tunnel. Lots of Spence.

University	Date of first foundation (and date of Charter)	Under-graduates 1964	Post-graduates 1964	Expansion targets 1967–8	Professors 1962–3	Lecturers 1962–3
WELSH CAT (Cardiff)	1866 (1965)	882	45	1,700		
BIRMINGHAM	1880 (1900)	3,805	1,142	6,317	81	597
LEEDS	1887 (1904)	5,324	904	8,300	75	819
BRISTOL	1876 (1909)	3,404	579	5,500	54	451
LIVERPOOL	1881 (1903)	4,121	953	6,415	64	646
BRADFORD	1882 (1965)	1,247	81	4,000		
NORTHAMPTON	1891 (1965)	1,565	84	2,750		
SURREY (Battersea)	1891 (1965)	1,082	173	1,770		
CHELSEA	1891 (1965)	706	117	1,042		
READING	1892 (1926)	1,997	389	3,000	27	346
WALES	1893	7,044	1,146	9,500	120	884
BIRMINGHAM CAT	1894 (1965)	1,380	86	2,492		
SALFORD ROYAL CAT	1896 (1965)	1,487	64	3,000		

Unusual subjects	Miscellaneous
—	Very Welsh, inter-departmental Eisteddfods. The only Cat that doesn't seem to want to become a university (see 'Wales' for reason).
3rewing Classical archeology Petroleum production engineering	High modern buildings shooting up round quasi-Byzantine Victorian ones on Edgbaston campus (Joseph Chamberlain). Good newspaper, called *Redbrick*. Richard Hoggart Mass culture.
celandic iophysics eather science hinese (Owen Lattimore)	Big university precinct, with underground roads being cleared out of slums, centring round Cemetery (to be park). Diplomatic Vice-Chancellor, Stevens. 30 per cent students do technology. TV centre planned.
rama ccounting	Fourth most fashionable; about 35 per cent public school, highest after Oxbridge. Right-wing students, cigarette building (Wills) with neo-perpendicular tower.
panish American studies atalan gyptian ceanography	Carving out precinct from slums. School of architecture, space physics block, gipsy lore.
extile design uman biology olour chemistry	Half students on sandwich courses, more than half from West Riding. Not moving out to new campus soon. Harold Wilson Chancellor-elect.
thalmic optics	Not in Northampton: 18-storey Hall of Residence near St. Paul's. Studenty students, organise art gallery, always win London-Brighton push-scooter race. 28 per cent postgraduates do management and social sciences.
ench linguistic and regional tudies tetics	Battersea was the quickest Cat off the new university mark, had site at Guildford within weeks of Robbins. 10 per cent foreign students.
—	In spite of new Kings Road buildings, still cramped and using converted warehouses. May move to Hertfordshire as university. Pure science.
rying ernetics	Very agricultural, three university farms, Sedimentology lab, and National Institute for Research in Dairying. Also moving to new campus.
Norse (Bangor) hematical philosophy technology	Uneasy federation of four colleges and one medical school, always deciding, after fierce argument, not to split up. Bangor the least Welsh bit, Cardiff the rebel.
avioural sciences ronmental health	Main building like square doughnut in city centre. 11 per cent students do Industrial administration. Boss Venables prophet of Cats.
ness operation and control	The only Royal Cat; suitably, the main building was opened by the Queen. Very close to Manchester Tech.

University	Date of first foundation (and date of Charter)	Under-graduates 1964	Post-graduates 1964	Expansion targets 1967–8	Professors 1962–3	Lecturers 1962–3
SHEFFIELD	1897 (1905)	3,189	619	5,200	63	424
NOTTINGHAM	1903 (1948)	2,600	465	4,300	45	314
LOUGHBOROUGH	1909 (1965)	1,305	26	2,653		
LEICESTER	1921 (1957)	1,613	249	2,450	21	181
EXETER	1922 (1955)	1,670	186	2,900	21	160
HULL	1927 (1954)	1,977	245	3,500	23	202
KEELE	1949 (1963)	882	41	1,600	18	126
BRUNEL	1957 (1965)	603	27	2,000		
SUSSEX	1961	810	90	2,650		
YORK	1963	216	13	1,480+		
EAST ANGLIA	1963 (1964)	87	25	1,301		
ESSEX	1964	100	20	— (3,000, 1973)		
LANCASTER	1964	270	20	1,385		
WARWICK	1964	325 (1965–6)	115 (1965–6)	1,000+		
KENT	1965	500 (1965–6)	—	1,700		

Unusual subjects	Miscellaneous
iblical History lass technology eramics with refractory technology	5 per cent students do metallurgy. Halls of residence in what J. Betjeman calls 'the prettiest suburb in England'. William Empson.
ood science nimal production	Americanised: campus life, students rarely go out. Neo-classical buildings, four film shows a week, egg and chips in the Union. Founded by Boots. Popular.
rgonomics and Cybernetics oundry technology	Four colleges, including Cat-university. 89 per cent residential, highest after Keele. Very high-level, serious sport, athletics team regularly beats AAA.
ocal history	Centres round yellow-brick ex-lunatic asylum. Spence buildings, home counties students, high proportion residential.
uropean studies	Holford *and* Spence buildings, but small and remote.
wedish mmonwealth studies uth-East Asia	Yorkshiremen and Africans. Poet-librarian, Philip Larkin. Militant union.
cial Analysis	First New University, everyone does Foundation Year to break down Two Cultures. Nearly all residential, still too small, but getting less claustrophobic. Still using Nissen huts.
—	Newest Cat, topping principal called Topping.
can and Asian studies	Most popular university of all, most competition for places. Politicians' daughters, staff called faculty, friendly and sophisticated. 16 per cent students in school of Physical Sciences, 1964.
—	Will have colleges round artificial lake. Practical, pre-fab buildings. Headmaster-vice-chancellor James; medieval history. Magazine called *Eboracum*.
—	Lovely site and buildings (Denys Lasdun) planned. Meanwhile, pre-fab student village. American-minded Vice-chancellor, Thistlethwaite; Sussexy schools of studies. Happy.
hematical social sciences	Strong on sociology, with Peter Townsend from Bethnal Green. Comparative Studies, huge language lab.
ational research ict research	Still in rented houses, will move to campus in 1966. Least known of new universities.
national ing-class history	Biggest site—417 acres outside Coventry; biggest appeal fund —£4 million; plans biggest number of students—15,000.
—	Huge mixed colleges; no students' union.

plus one CAT and one entirely new institution, into what they christened with finicky attention to initials, SISTERS—Special Institutions for Scientific and Technological Research. Sisters (which have not so far been instituted) would have 3,500–4,500 students, half post-graduate, and would specialise in ancillary subjects like social sciences, languages, operational research and statistics as well as science and technology. At least half the students should do technology, 'In making this proposal', said the committee, 'we have been much influenced by the fact that there is as yet in this country too little that compares for both scope and scale with the great institutions abroad that we visited, such as the Massachusetts Institute of Technology and the technical high schools at Delft and Zurich.' And they said: 'The main requirement is that in all five special institutions, both the three that already stand out and the two that will join them, development must be pushed forward with all possible speed. The whole group need financial support similar to that given to the Imperial College. . .'

Spectacular as was the development of Imperial College, it was only a tiny contribution in national terms. In 1955 the Ministry of Education took a further step. They gave up the universities as the promoters of technology and turned to the other stream of British technological education, the neglected practical world of the Techs. They decided to single out a few colleges and develop them so that they did only advanced work. By 1957 eight colleges had been landed with the unfortunate name of Colleges of Advanced Technology ('with its deplorable and seemingly inescapable reduction in common parlance to CATS,' complained the Cats' principals to the Robbins Committee), and by 1962, two more had been added. The final list were four London Techs, Battersea, Chelsea, Northampton and Brunel; two Northern ones, Bradford, and Salford; Birmingham and Loughborough, and in the West, Bristol and Cardiff.

The Cats operation was a typically hybrid, half-hearted one. The universities exercised their old magic so the ministry did not dare allow the Cats to give degrees, they invented a new, dreary-sounding qualification called the Diploma of Technology instead. Launched without the glamour or money needed to attract good staff, the Cats too often had to struggle on with teachers left over from the days when the colleges were ordinary techs, doing low-level courses. The contrast between the launching of the seven new universities and the ten Cats was symbolic of the apathy about technological education in Britain, and its downtrodden, second-class status.

Still, by 1963 the Cats were turning out more than 10,000 students, and by 1967 10 per cent of all university students will be in the ten colleges. They began to develop post-graduate schools (4 per cent of students were post-graduate in 1963), and introduced subjects like languages and social sciences. The growth of sandwich-courses—the sandwich is a hunk of full-time higher education between industrial jobs—were a welcome practical introduction into the rarefied atmosphere of university-level education. Two Cats in particular, rapidly added to their status: Birmingham, with a lot of local support and a proseletising principal, Sir Peter Venables, and Brunel, the last Cat to be chosen, with an impressive educationalist, James Topping, for principal. Northampton had always been a good college: under J. S. Tait it gained a high Cat reputation. Battersea and Chelsea presented the best example of the haphazardness of the planning of the Cats. Battersea was good at engineering, Chelsea at theoretical sciences. Amalgamated, they would have made an excellent college. Yet both continued to be run separately, on a shoestring—Chelsea, in spite of new buildings, was still using a converted warehouse. And even at the best Cats, the students arrived feeling second-best. 'Their first evening I always tell them "Take that chip off your shoulder",' said one principal.

Sir Peter Venables once described the difference between Oxford and a Cat. Take a nine o'clock lecture, he said. At Oxford, a handful of undergraduates arrive, in their gowns, at 9.10; the lecturer sweeps in at 9.15; 'Ladies and Gentlemen', he begins. At a Cat, the lecturer arrives at 8.45, a full class of students at 8.55. At 9.00 the lecturer begins: 'Good morning,' and they all write it down.

At last, eight years after their foundation, the Robbins Report came to the rescue of the Cats. It said what everyone but the universities had been saying for years (and the universities had come to accept): that the Cats should become universities, with self-governing status under an expanded University Grants Commission; that they should award degrees. They also said each of the new technological universities should have 3–5,000 students, at least 15 per cent post-graduate. The Cats jumped into action: Bristol acquired a beautiful site outside Bath, Battersea did a deal with Guildford, Chelsea considered sites in Hertfordshire, and may find a home at Knebworth, Lord Cobbold's home. The change in status will be crucial to the Cats: the new technological universities of Bath and Surrey may look an exciting alternative to places like Exeter, and maybe even York, when they all appear together on the UCCA form.[1]

But the battle for technology is only half-won, and whether as new universities or as Cats, these colleges will need more money to attract staff from the old universities, and to build necessary and costly plant ('You can buy a professor of Greek for three thousand a year and a Liddell and Scott, but a professor of science may cost a million pounds of equipment,' said one Tory minister). In their battle, the Cats have a formidable ally, Lord Bowden, the Minister of State concerned with universities, who was formerly head of the Manchester College of Science and Technology—which he transformed—and before that a computer salesman. A short, tough dynamo of a man, he typifies the impatience of an efficient technocrat with the amateurism and incompetence of government and parliament. He has loved to attack, with deliberately outrageous simplification, what he calls the 'Menace of the Impractical'. 'We mock at Chinese mandarins who let their finger-nails grow, to prove they never had to work'—he said to me in 1961—'but we still insist that many of our ablest schoolboys shall devote themselves to intellectual exercises which have little or no connection with the world in which they will have to live.' The arrival of this computer man into Whitehall, with his terrifying talk of 'plant utilisation factor', sent a shudder down many Oxford spines. He is, in fact, a less aggressive and philistine character than he likes to seem; but he will certainly try to advance the status and the budgets of the technological colleges, and in his north country toughness and bluntness, he accurately represents their outlook.

THE CLEARING HOUSE

By 1961 it seemed a whole new pecking order was emerging, with status distinctions that were more subtle than the old clearcut ones, but as dangerous. For all-round magnetism for dons and students alike, there was Oxbridge, of course; Sussex, and most of the newer new universities; and Bristol, which had been coming up steadily for twenty years. Edinburgh and St. Andrews were, as always, attractive to students; London, and in some departments the big civics like Manchester and Leeds, attracted dons and post-

[1] *See* below.

graduates. Imperial College was building up a new status, all its own. And right at the end of the scale, disturbingly sleepy and depressed, came the small provincial universities, like Leicester, Hull and Exeter, and, struggling to shake off their low-status origins, the Cats.

Since then two things have changed, not the basic shape of this pattern, but its rigidity. One is simply expansion and the wide new critical interest in universities, marked by the Sussex success and Robbins, which has blown a draught through all universities. The other was an administrative accident. In 1961, in the interests of efficiency, all the universities except Oxbridge set up the Universities Central Council on Admissions. UCCA was largely the work of two university administrators, Sir Philip Morris and Sir John Fulton. From then on, with a few minor exceptions, all candidates for all UCCA universities would simply fill in one form, choosing six universities in order of preference and subjects to study.

Even in the first two years, when the UCCA organisation was understaffed and struggling to work out an extremely complex system, the results were startling—and apparently entirely unforeseen. We have already noticed the startling drop in Oxbridge candidates.[1] With a formal admissions system the business of choosing a university became much more sophisticated. For the first time there was positive incentive to look at the range of universities, and compare their wares: and consumer guides (like *Which University*) were produced to help candidates choose.

More important, a gambling element was introduced into the competition for university places. Candidates heard about the 16–1 pressure on Sussex places, so they put Southampton as first choice. From 1964 the UCCA report is publishing the statistics of what competition there was for every faculty of every university, further increasing the scope for intelligent gambling. From 1965, the Cats will be brought into the system, making them an obvious alternative to other universities. And the gambling will favour the least prestigious places.

The invention of UCCA was of crucial importance to the universities; it forced them to co-operate and encouraged them to compete; it cut through secrecy, muddle and sheer lack of centralised information; it had a levelling effect, and put Oxbridge at a temporary disadvantage. Perhaps only the British could have invented such a powerful instrument by accident.

[1] *See* p. 224.

UNIVERSITY GRANTS

Who runs the universities? In Oxbridge, the heads of colleges (who take turns to be vice-chancellor) each have considerable sway: but all the other universities have professional vice-chancellors with very wide powers, for instance in deciding syllabuses, allocating funds or patronising architects. They make up a tiny profession of academic administrators. Many of the vice-chancellors meet regularly for breakfast at the Athenæum, their favourite haunt. Though much more worldly than headmasters, they are isolated men. They suffer from Oxbridge nostalgia, and operate in an uncomfortable territory between scholarship and administration. Most of their time is spent on agonising money-worries: not only finding funds, but allocating them—deciding between a new piece of engineering equipment or a secretary for a physics professor who's threatening to take his whole research team to America.

The real power behind the universities is much less heard of—the nineteen members of the University Grants Committee, who dole out the money. The first grant of government money was £15,000, distributed to universities in 1889: since then the sum has multiplied by 4,000 and in 1962–3, the UGC gave out £97 million. The committee is a very mixed bag of dons, industrialists, and public servants; among them are Alec Clegg (from local education), and Sir Alan Wilson (from industry). The committee is chosen on the favourite British principle of allowing government money to be allocated, not by the government, but by the profession concerned—a kind of 'indirect rule'. The committee thus act as a buffer between government and universities, ensuring academic freedom, and their largesse is not even inspected by the auditor-general though the Public Accounts Committee frequently criticise their spending. At the head of UGC is the chairman—the only permanent member—Sir John Wolfenden who went from being headmaster of Shrewsbury to be Vice-Chancellor of Reading university and is one of the stage army of government committee men. The powers of Sir John are enormous. His committee can, and do, bring whole new universities into being, persuasive letters beginning 'Dear Sir John' pour into Belgrave Square from ambitious heads of departments, and the Athenæum is loud with lobbying. This is another case of the divorce between the dignified and the efficient sides of Britain: while Oxbridge dons dress up in flat caps and rich robes to give honorary degrees and mumble Latin compliments to each other—all duly reported and photographed in *The Times*—their future is being settled by nineteen men in mufti, from offices in Regent's Park. The relations between the UGC and the universities are often fraught with friction and resentment. Sometimes the committee appears like a rich nephew subsidising distressed uncles, provided they pull themselves together, but sometimes more like a rich uncle, on whom young nephews can lean.

Once every five years members of the committee make a three-day visitation to each university in turn, and for a small university the arrival of this mild-looking posse of patrons produces high tension. They are met by the gowned vice-chancellor and his registrar, and shown round the premises. Some vice-chancellors like to reveal only the dingiest professors in the bleakest laboratories, to show that they urgently need money. Others display their sprucest and best, to show that they know how to use the stuff.

But the committee, though powerful, does not normally initiate new schemes: they only approve or disapprove of applications for money, and they leave the universities to spend it as they wish. There have been critics of this passive rôle, who felt the UGC should have forced the universities to develop necessary subjects like technology, using the weapon of earmarked grants. The UGC, invented as a shield between the Treasury and the universities, has stayed just that. For long too it had a staff that was too small to take any dynamic part in university planning, but with the new expansion it is being forced to look at the logistics of finance and growth.

OXBRIDGE AND POLITICS

The relations between Oxbridge and London politics are full of romantic cross-purposes. In the past the most worldly college has been All Souls, founded in 1437 by Archbishop Chichele with a constitution which other dons dream of—providing a huge endowment for sixty fellows: and the fellows and ex-fellows (called Quondams) are supposed to be the cream of Oxford intellectuals. Among their more arduous duties, at the beginning of every century, they have to parade round the college quadrangles and roofs carrying a dead duck on a pole, and singing their 'Mallard Song'. (In 1900 Cosmo Gordon Lang, the future Archbishop of Canterbury was carried by 'four stalwart fellows'—as is described in his biography—and a cable was sent to Lord Curzon, the Viceroy of India, 'an enthusiastic quondam'.) Before the war fellows included the Archbishop of Canterbury, the Foreign Secretary, the Editor of *The Times* and a partner of Lazards; and All Souls could lay some claim to be running Britain—with disastrous results.

Now All Souls still has prestige, but not much influence: their present fellows and quondams include the youngest director of the Bank of England, the Arundel Herald Extraordinary, Isaiah Berlin, Quintin Hogg and Lord Bridges: but the All Souls dinner table is much less central than it was. The Warden, John Sparrow, who edited Donne's Devotions while a boy at Winchester, is a fastidious bachelor, remaining remote from London and also from Oxford: he even refused the vice-chancellorship. And a younger generation of fellows has emerged including several left-wing rebels, a psychoanalyst, a novelist and a director of the Bank of England.

All Souls weekends have lost their close links with Downing Street and Lambeth. A more important place now is Nuffield College, founded by Lord Nuffield in 1937, with special attention to social problems, and now housed in strange cottagey buildings near Oxford station. Its fellows include several relevant and modern-minded people, such as Uwe Kitzinger, the expert on the Common Market, Mrs. Jean Floud, the educational sociologist, Margery Perham, the eminent Africanist, Sir Donald McDougall, the Director-General of the Department of Economic Affairs, Philip Williams, the expert on French politics, and the Warden, Daniel Chester, who has written authoritative works on the nationalised industries and on local government.

THE RIFT

The rift between Oxbridge and Redbrick, deepened by the rift between schools, cuts right through this book. For Oxford and Cambridge, in so far as they are geared to anything, are geared to the nineteenth century gentleman's professions—the Law, the civil service or diplomacy, which had adopted their old collegiate traditions. The powerful new professions which between them control the business corporations—accountancy, insurance, actuaries, engineering—have grown up largely outside this charmed circle, in a bleaker and more philistine air. Oxbridge has refused to adapt its curricula to take note of them while Redbrick has found itself trammelled with specialist courses—which helps to explain (for instance) the drabness of modern architecture, and underlies the whole stultifying division between two sides of British life. Here is the most exciting challenge to the New Universities, which may have huge repercussions on the pattern of Britain. For they are not trapped in any curricula, and they can construct courses which are both broad-minded and relevant.

14

CIVIL SERVICE

The Continental nuisance called 'bureaucracy'.

Thomas Carlyle.

At the very heart of British government there is a luxuriant and voluntary exclusion of talent.

Professor Brian Chapman, 1963.

When a new party comes to power in Britain, only about a hundred politicians move into Whitehall to run the 800,000 civil servants. They come with great disadvantages, fresh from opposition, out of touch with problems of organisation and management, and unused to the awkward compromises of power; and they confront a settled professional caste of sophisticated and often cynical bureaucrats. Yet this small invasion can nevertheless have a powerful psychological effect, for a time at least, on the civil service down to quite humble levels. For the British civil service—unlike the French—has been designed as a passive and obedient instrument, with a feminine need for stimulus and push. It is built round the notion of changing opposition and box-and-cox governments, to provide it with new ideas and directions. If a single party, however well meaning, remains in power for a long period, the weight of commitments, obligations, business and sheer inertia becomes so strong that only the most ruthless new ministers can cut through it. But once a new party is elected, a large premium is placed on changes of all kinds: new schemes, or old ones rejected, are brought out of drawers; new men emerge from the shadows, under the new patronage; old commitments can be repudiated; and for a time the whole character of institutions and buildings seems to be fluid.

When the Labour party returned to power in October 1964 after thirteen years, the impact on Whitehall, in spite of the slender majority, was electric. It generated the greatest institutional changes since the war. When the Socialists had been elected before, in 1945, Whitehall was being settled down, not shaken up. Clement Attlee, then prime minister, was not interested in bureaucratic reforms; and he and his ministers allowed Whitehall, to an astonishing extent, to revert to its pre-war character. The dons, businessmen and other outsiders who had occupied wartime jobs in the ministries moved back to their universities and companies. But in 1964 the mood was quite different. Demands for reform had been growing, both inside and outside the civil service, and the sense of stagnancy and inertia had been increased by the long-drawn-out pre-election period, when large areas of the civil service could make no definite plans.

The first week of changeover to a new government is a time which lights up the whole strange frontier between politics and administration; and the week following October 15, 1964 made a very sudden illumination. For weeks and months past, the senior civil servants had been making alternative plans for the two parties, but with a special eye on the reorganisations that would be required by Labour. 'Contingency planning' is a favourite occupation for Whitehall, and the files are full of schemes envisaging sudden war, drought, nuclear attack or assassination of the monarch; but this contingency was much more likely. There had been unofficial talks between likely Labour ministers and top civil servants. The Treasury had prepared alternative sets of documents and drafts, the Foreign Office was ready waiting with messages to Foreign governments, the whole infrastructure run by the Ministry of Public buildings and Works, with its warehouses, telephones and furniture, was waiting like an invading army for D-day. So that when, by the afternoon of Friday, October 16th, it was clear that the Labour Party had secured a narrow majority, the shape of Whitehall was able to transform itself, almost as suddenly as a revolving stage. By the same evening, Labour ministers were already in their offices, signing letters and making plans with their permanent secretaries. New suites of offices were mysteriously uncovered, for new ministries and departments. New staff were mysteriously available, and key men happened to have returned from abroad.

It was clear, almost immediately, that the new government would involve a major upheaval—including the splitting-up of the old Treasury into two ministries. And it was clear, too, that Harold Wilson was putting into practice his 'stage-coach' principle,[1] and was aiming to drive the Whitehall machine so

[1] See p. 105.

fast that the passengers would be too excited or too sick to complain. For some weeks after the change, senior civil servants found themselves working a seventy or eighty hour week. To many, not necessarily conservative ones, the new mood was exhilarating and full of new opportunity. 'It's like champagne', one of them said to me. 'I feel years younger', said another. And even the imperturbable Secretary to the Cabinet, Sir Burke Trend, was observed to have a new look in his eye. In some places, particularly in the Treasury, new ministers were astonished to find that civil servants were actually ahead of them in ideas for reform. There were huge areas of muddle and ambiguity, or 'blurred edges' in the Whitehall idiom, and the spattering of politicians in unlikely places in Whitehall caused confusions of responsibility and command. But with all the snags, Whitehall had been opened up, ventilated and given a new challenge. As Arthur Schlesinger, who was visiting London at that time, described it: 'London has suddenly come alive. Fresh winds are blowing. Whitehall, that once grey and depressing street, crackles with new spirit. There is the excitement which comes from the injection of new men and ideas, the release of energy which comes when men with ideas have the chance to put them into practice'.[1]

The confrontation of the new ministers with the old civil servants was full of curious cross-purposes. On the one hand, many Labour politicians, after thirteen years without office, vainly battering at the citadel of government, were apt to assume that everyone inside the citadel must be unchangeably conservative. The formalities, the hierarchies, the architecture, the continuing background of the palace and its surroundings, all seemed to belong to a single conservative conspiracy of 'they': and to find that 'they' were divided, and that many of them were reformers and even Socialists, came as the same kind of shock as missionaries might feel when they find a remote tribe already believing in Jesus. On the other side, many civil servants to whom Conservatives seemed their inevitable masters—with their confidence, their money and their Westminster clubs—found Labour ministers more interested in the workings of Whitehall, and believing in bureaucracy in a more fundamental way than their predecessors. For it is entrenched in the past of the Tory party that they have approached the civil service as a necessary evil; older Conservatives still like to use the words 'Whitehall' and 'bureaucracy' in a derogatory sense: whereas

[1] *Evening Standard*, November 17, 1964.

Socialists are much more inclined to regard bureaucracy as a positive instrument, to be worked closely with. As a result many civil servants have found themselves taken more seriously, and acquiring a new self-respect. And at the top of the Labour apparatus was Harold Wilson, ex-civil servant and ex-don, fascinated by the problems of economic organisation and, as an ex-chairman of the Public Accounts Committee, adept at the art of investigation and cross-examination. He was determined to stretch the civil service to its limits, in his 'first hundred days of dynamic action'.

But the change generated by a new government is never quite as thorough as it appears. Under the surface of movement, speech-making, and agitation there remains the solid substructure of the permanent officials. 'Do you know those electricity pylons?', one senior civil servant said to me, talking about Whitehall. 'Above ground they look quite slender and frail, and they sway with the wind. But underground there are deep holes, filled with concrete, to support them. That's the civil service.'

When new ministers arrive, the officials are very friendly and helpful, and tell them most things they want to know. But they do not tell them the secrets of the previous government's policy decisions. The filing cabinets remain firmly guarded, with combination locks if necessary, by the civil servants. If an incoming minister asks to see the files, for instance, about devaluation, or Katanga, or other politically embarrassing questions, the crucial documents will have been removed. Before the election of 1964, Treasury and other officials were carefully re-drafting important papers, with political secrets omitted. This arrangement is by agreement of the incoming prime minister, who always agrees to it, knowing that when he in turn departs he will not want to bequeath his party's secrets; when ministers or advisers complain about files being withheld—as they have done—they are quietly referred to the prime minister. The procedure dates back to the nineteenth century, before the bureaucracy was fully established, when all policy documents were removed. No party cares to question it. But these locked files symbolise the strongest weapons of the civil servants—their secret reserves of information, and their massive continuity. However much they may throw themselves into reforms and upheavals, they are still mindful that they will live to see another swing of the pendulum.

And only 35 days after their coming to office, the Labour government had already run into a financial crisis which made them acutely aware of limitations of their power and scope for reform. On the weekend of November 21st, the pound was threatened by heavy selling, and on the Monday the Chancellor felt compelled to increase the bank-rate to seven per cent. Even this drastic measure could not restore confidence, and in the next two days a vast loan of three billion dollars in foreign currencies had to be arranged by the Governor of the Bank of England and other Central Bankers to shore up sterling.[1] The humiliating rescue, and the accusations of incompetence which followed it, left the young government in a far less euphoric state of mind. The honeymoon was over, the gloomier bureaucrats had been vindicated, and the politicians settled down to a more difficult cohabitation.

WHITEHALL

We have already encountered politicians in three different spheres—in parliament, in their party organisations and in cabinet. Now we see them in their most important, but least visible rôle—running their departments in the midst of Whitehall—and here, for the next four chapters, we peer at the opaque and impenetrable regions of the bureaucracies. A journalist, accustomed to the vivid clash of policies and people in parliament, finds Whitehall a single, grey, anonymous mass, with one policy merging into another, and personalities dissolved in committees and minutes. Nothing in Whitehall is quite what it seems. Policy becomes muddled with execution, politicians with officials. The political masters in Britain can only attend to the broadest principles of policy. The rest of the administration falls on the shoulders of the permanent civil service—and in particular on three thousand men in the administrative grade. The civil service likes to depict itself from the outside as de-personalised, without opinions or policies; but behind the public face, the bureaucracies are still run by individuals, each with their own views and ideas, and as parliament and cabinet find their provinces getting increasingly out of hand,[2] so the power slips ineluctably towards the permanent officials.

Today Whitehall has powers undreamt-of by either party before the war. Public authorities (including local authories) account for over 42 per cent of the nation's investment, and a quarter of its

[1] *See* p. 419.
[2] *See* p. 136.

workers. The government can not only control the giant nationalised industries—each bigger than any private company—but by its subsidies, pressures and contracts it can exert huge influence on such industries as cotton, aircraft, agriculture, shipping or engineering. And, as everyone knows, since the war Whitehall has become the universal guardian of the individual, the provider of everything from the midwife onwards. Sooner or later, all roads lead to Whitehall.

'It's a wonderful place, this Whitehall,' said one cabinet minister: 'it has antennae all over the place. If you're thinking of doing something you can put out feelers and in a few hours you know what the reaction's likely to be.'

The outward appearance of Whitehall buildings, as a glance at the map following will show, bears no relation to their relative importance: here, once again, is a cleavage between outward show and inner reality. Many of the most important government departments are now in fact right away from Whitehall: the Ministry of Transport is in a big block in Southwark, known like so many other buildings as the biggest office building in Europe. Health is at the Elephant and Castle. Education is in Mayfair. But the tingling centre of the civil service, where the major decisions are taken, remains the half-mile of stone buildings from Trafalgar Square to Westminster Abbey, with high classical façades, tall cupolas, and heavy marble staircases. The propinquity is important: ideas, misgivings, suggestions can brush from one to another in Whitehall as casually and smoothly as dust on to a coat. In a walk through the park you can have a few casual encounters and at once sense the political attitude. And there is the telephone. When it was first invented, it was dreaded in Whitehall: 'Why, anybody could ring me up at any time, and I'd have to answer their questions,' complained one official. But since then, the civil service has taken telephones to its heart—black, green and red ones—and between them comes the dialogue of 'mmms' and 'wells' and 'up-to-a-points' and feelings and agitations, which formulate policies and decisions. (One sign of the closeness of the Whitehall machine and the like-mindedness of its operatives is the speed with which vogue-words are suddenly ubiquitous—pause, *malaise*, shopping-list, marginal, making wrong noises, stop-and-gos. The patois of the civil service emphasises the courtly protocol—going native, house-trained, knowing his way around, meshed into the machine, bowling a fast ball, agreed recommendation, imitate the action of a clam, bull in a china-shop . . .)

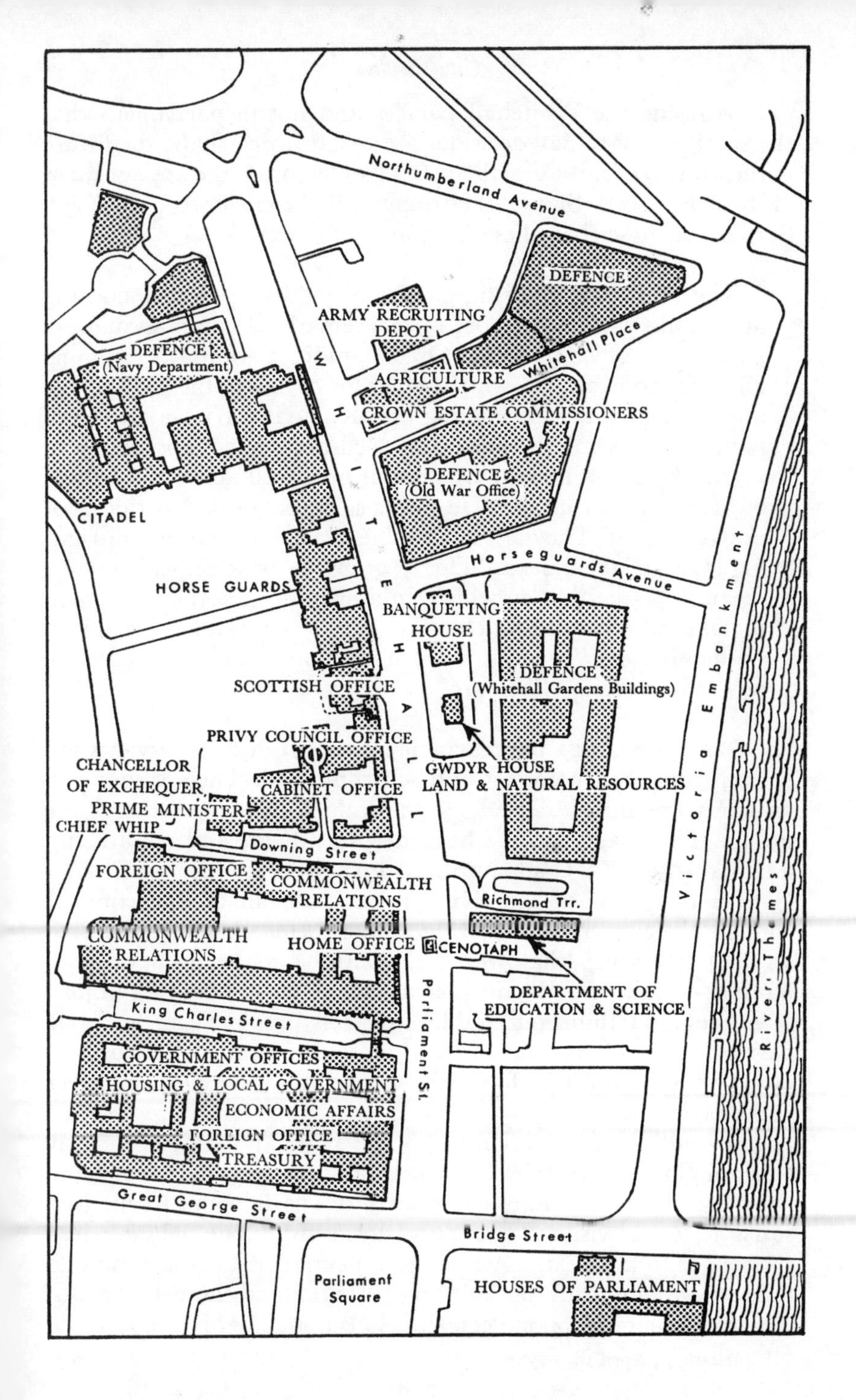
Northumberland Avenue
DEFENCE
ARMY RECRUITING DEPOT
Whitehall Place
DEFENCE (Navy Department)
AGRICULTURE
CROWN ESTATE COMMISSIONERS
WHITEHALL
DEFENCE (Old War Office)
CITADEL
Horseguards Avenue
HORSE GUARDS
BANQUETING HOUSE
DEFENCE (Whitehall Gardens Buildings)
SCOTTISH OFFICE
PRIVY COUNCIL OFFICE
GWDYR HOUSE
LAND & NATURAL RESOURCES
CHANCELLOR OF EXCHEQUER
CABINET OFFICE
PRIME MINISTER
CHIEF WHIP
Downing Street
FOREIGN OFFICE
COMMONWEALTH RELATIONS
Richmond Trr.
Victoria Embankment
COMMONWEALTH RELATIONS
HOME OFFICE
CENOTAPH
DEPARTMENT OF EDUCATION & SCIENCE
King Charles Street
Parliament St.
River Thames
GOVERNMENT OFFICES
HOUSING & LOCAL GOVERNMENT
ECONOMIC AFFAIRS
FOREIGN OFFICE
TREASURY
Great George Street
Bridge Street
Parliament Square
HOUSES OF PARLIAMENT

It is inside the Whitehall palaces and not in parliament that the sombre day-to-day decisions are taken which shape the future —the awards of subsidies, the placing of factories, the appointment of boards. Lord Snow, the romantic chronicler of the Civil Service has described these 'corridors of power':[1]

> The most characteristic picture of modern power is nothing at all sinister. It is no more or less remarkable than an office— I mean, an office building. Office buildings are much the same all over the world. Down the corridor of one of these offices, of any of them, a man is walking briskly. He is carrying a folder of papers. He is middle-aged and well-preserved, muscular and active. He is not a great tycoon but he is well above the middle of his particular ladder. He meets someone in the corridor not unlike himself. They are talking business. They are not intriguing. One of them says: 'This is going to be a difficult one'— meaning a question on which, in a few minutes, they are going to take different sides. They are off to a meeting of a dozen similar bosses. They will be at it for hours. This is the face of power in a society like ours.

Of all the world's bureaucracies, the British civil servants are perhaps the most compact and self-contained. Their values and opinions are little affected by the values of the press and the public. They have become hardened to ridicule and resentment, and like the Old Contemptibles, turn ridicule into pride. *Red Tape* is the name of the civil service trade union magazine. 'I confidently expect,' Lord Bridges (the former head of the civil service) has said, 'that we shall continue to be grouped with mothers-in-law and Wigan pier as one of the recognised objects of ridicule.' 'I think our public image is past praying for,' one permanent secretary said to me: 'we're the people who stop you doing things, who interfere, who get in the way. We can never make people *like* us.'

They still conform lovingly to the familiar caricature. They work in gloomy offices in Victorian morgues, guarded by ancient, shuffling doormen, in an atmosphere of—so it seems—contrived squalor. As a visitor, you are passed from one white-haired messenger to the next, down long linoleum corridors leading into tall ante-rooms, full of knitting, brollies and homely typists. There are long telephone conversations about 'HMG' and 'SOS'

[1] *The Listener*, April 18, 1957.

being exercised, seized, having it in mind, being agitated or embarrassed. The recurring word is 'embarrassment'—a word which signalises the dreaded intrusion of the outside world.

THE MANDARINS

The professional civil service is a Victorian invention—dating back to that dynamic third quarter of the nineteenth century when so many of Britain's institutions took shape. Its origins are so central to the character of bureaucracies, and to contemporary British education and society, that they must be recapitulated here. The civil service is the archetypal bureaucracy (though the word 'Civil Servant' dates from the East India Company, the original 'John Company'), and big businesses are coming increasingly to resemble the Whitehall which they so often mock.

The Victorian idea was that administrators should be chosen, not with special experience of government, but as intelligent, well-educated amateurs—a crystallisation of the amateur ideal which runs through English life. This crucial principle was stated by Lord Macaulay, who recommended the reform of the Indian Civil Service in 1854, in a famous and influential passage:

> We believe that men who have been engaged, up to twenty-one or twenty-two, in studies which have no immediate connection with the business of any profession, and of which the effect is merely to open, to invigorate, and to enrich the mind, will generally be found in the business of every profession superior to men who have, at eighteen or nineteen, devoted themselves to the special studies of their calling. The most illustrious English jurists have been men who never opened a law book till after the close of a distinguished academical career; nor is there any reason to believe that they would have been greater lawyers if they had passed in drawing plans and conveyances the time which they gave to Thucydides, to Cicero, and to Newton.[1]

In the late eighteenth century the civil service was incompetent, tiny and appointed by patronage: accounting was done in Latin, and the customs department alone had 150 sinecure offices. As the service grew and abuses became more obvious, various reforms were made. Then, in 1853, Charles Trevelyan (Macaulay's brother-in-law, who had spent fourteen years in India) and Sir

[1] Report on the Selection and Examination of Candidates for the ICS, 1854.

Stafford Northcote (who had been at Balliol with Jowett) were asked to report on reorganisation. They produced a sensational document. They reported that the public service was 'attracting the unambitious, and the indolent or incapable'. They criticised the system of training men by making them copy out documents (still practised in the City of London). They insisted that the public service must become a profession rather than a job to which 'the dregs of all other professions are attracted'. And they proposed recruiting from the universities by open competitive written examination—turning Greek and Latin scholars into a new race of administrators. It was a compound of Benthamite logic and Chinese experience.

This ruthless report provoked uproar. The secretary of the Board of Trade complained that it would provide 'picked clever young men from the lower ranks of society', and that 'a lower tone of feeling would prevail'. But the incompetence of the Crimean War brought Whitehall into further disgrace. Eventually, in 1870, Gladstone issued an Order in Council which embraced most of the Northcote-Trevelyan proposals. The reform was decisive. It produced, as it was meant to, a profession as dedicated as doctors or barristers, with a powerful collegiate sense, uncorrupt, clever and versatile. The new civil service became part of the core of the middle class, and it grew traditions of its own, with the sons and grandsons of civil servants becoming civil servants. The 'picked clever young men' became—within the limits of Oxbridge—the first great meritocracy, a profession to which any intelligent boy could aspire, a *carrière ouverte aux talents*. It not only reformed the civil service, but (as its framers realised) quickened the universities as well—providing a goal behind the examinations.[1]

For the past ninety-five years, the élite of the civil service, the 'Administrative Grade', have been chosen—with a few modifications—in this way. After the first world war interviews were introduced, and since the last war there have been many more promotions from junior grades: 40 per cent of the 3,000 people in the Administrative Grade now consist of promoted men. But the core of the civil service are still the recruits from the universities, chosen by careful examination and interview by the Civil Service Commissioners (the process of recruitment alone costs half-a-million a year). The recruits remain, as Macaulay meant them to be, highly-educated amateurs: though Macaulay also planned a special college (as there is in France) to teach recruits the basis of

[1] Lord Bridges: *Portrait of a Profession*, p. 9.

their job—such as Indian languages or law—which was not implemented. It is a central tenet of the modern civil service that administration is an art, which can be applied to anything, and the senior mandarins are switched overnight from running prisons to encouraging exports.

OLD BOY NET?

The senior civil servants still form a compact collegiate community. It is often said that they consist of people who have been at school together—probably at Winchester—running the country on the old boy net. Because of the large political implications, the subject has recently been much studied, more than the social background of industrialists or lawyers. In fact it is the old university tie, rather than the old school tie, which dominates the civil service. For the past thirty-five years, the civil service has been a large avenue for the grammar school boy: in 1950, out of 1,045 higher civil servants, only 23 per cent came from boarding schools, only 2 per cent from Winchester, and 1 per cent from Eton. (Even in 1929, Eton and Winchester only provided 3 or 4 per cent.)[1]

The Civil Service Commissioners lean over backwards to avoid favouring public school boys: they write a letter of congratulation to every grammar school headmaster who produces a successful candidate, and they were very excited when their first successful candidate from a comprehensive school appeared in 1960. Between 1948 and 1956, only 30 per cent of the young men selected for the Administrative civil service came from boarding schools; 40 per cent from local authority schools.[2] (But the proportion of boarding school men in the higher reaches in twenty years' time will be much less—because half of the Administrative class are now promoted from junior ranks.)

The civil service is not a public school preserve; but it is very much an Oxbridge—and particularly an Oxford—affair. In 1950 out of 332 civil servants above Assistant Secretary, 60 per cent were from Oxford or Cambridge, compared to 69 per cent in 1929 (Oxford's proportion had gone down, and Cambridge's had gone up). Between 1948 and 1956, no less than 50 per cent of the young recruits were from Oxford, and 30 per cent from Cambridge —leaving only 20 per cent from other universities. Fifty-three per

[1] R. K. Kelsall: *Higher Civil Servants in Britain*, p. 124.

[2] Recruitment to the Administrative Class: Cmd. 232 of July, 1957. p. 25.

cent of the recruits had studied classics or history: only 1 per cent had studied science.[1] In the 1964 examinations, out of 51 successful candidates, 15 had taken degrees in classics, 18 in history, *one* in mathematics and *none* in science or technology. These proportions will later be diluted by promotees from junior ranks, and by a few scientists changing over: but the Oxford humanist tradition in Whitehall is virtually as strong as ever it was. 'It's partly that the best people are creamed off to Oxbridge at sixth-form level,' explained one commissioner in 1961, 'but also that the life at Oxford and Cambridge gives people wider interests and more developed ideas. At the other universities so many students have never even left home.'

The old boy net of Whitehall is not the net of Eton or Winchester, but of New College or King's. (The net has a wide spread, and can cut across party barriers so that opposition politicians can have links with the civil service through their old college friends.) Some colleges—such as Selwyn, Cambridge, or Pembroke, Oxford until 1962 (when they produced a burst of civil servants)—hardly ever produce a candidate, but others have a very consistent record among successful candidates. Between 1956 and 1961:

27 were from New College, Oxford
26 „ „ King's, Cambridge
25 „ „ Balliol, Oxford
19 „ „ Magdalen, Oxford
19 „ „ Trinity, Cambridge
16 „ „ Christ Church, Oxford

Is the civil service maintaining its standard of recruits? Since the war the big industrial corporations have been competing heavily for the best men, and offering larger eventual prizes. 'But it's not industry which is jeopardising our recruitment so much as the universities,' one of the commissioners said: 'It's the academic types who tend to try for the civil service, and these are now finding the idea of an academic career more attractive, especially as the new universities make more jobs.' Where industry does compete heavily is in the special departmental classes, where there is now less enthusiasm to become postmasters or inspectors of taxes.

Oxbridge moulds the character of Whitehall, and senior civil

[1] Cmd. 232. pp. 26 and 27.

servants look back to colleges with nostalgia. 'We are unfortunately lacking,' Lord Bridges has said, 'in those expressions of corporate life found in a college. We have neither hall nor chapel, neither combination room nor common room.'[1] But the favourite civil service clubs—such as the Oxford and Cambridge or the Cabinet Office Canteen—take the place of college dining-halls. In contrast to industry, it is not difficult for civil servants to spend most of their life in the company of Oxbridge men. The civil service, in the words of one American observer, is one of the 'forms of corporate social existence which flourish widely in England and the origins of which often ante-date the era of individualism'.[2] To quote the Fabian Report of 1964 'the administrative hierarchy is as closed and protected as a monastic order. A young man enters at twenty-one or so and is virtually locked in until sixty.'[3]

SPECIALISTS

But while the amateur collegiate tradition remains, the whole character of the civil service has changed. It has not only increased in size twentyfold since 1870: it has found itself involved in technical and commercial problems which Macaulay never dreamt of. The old civil service was mainly concerned with regulating people—collecting taxes, running a police force and prisons; what the Victorians wanted was 'a corps of reliable umpires'.[4] The new civil service is occupied in directing industries, allocating vast research programmes, building airports, supervising railways, constructing roads—in fact running half Britain: and the administrators are now entangled in an undergrowth of specialists—engineers, scientists, economists, accountants, agronomists. The Ministry of Aviation is much more like ICI than the Home Office, and it employs 3,000 scientists. All but three of ICI's fifteen executive directors joined the company as scientists or technical people;[5] but much of the Ministry of Aviation is run by Latin and History scholars. In 1964 the Estimates Committee of the House of Commons took the trouble to interview the deputy-chairman of ICI, Sir Ronald Holroyd, to give his views about the use of specialists: 'With us the boundary line between the specialist job and an administrative job is a very thin one. It is really a

[1] *Portrait of a Profession*, p. 32.
[2] S. Beer: *Treasury Control*, 1957. p. 114.
[3] Fabian Society: *The Administrators*, 1964. p. 15.
[4] *ibid.*, p. 2.
[5] *See* Chapter 26.

permeable membrane . . . I think you do need people in the civil service who speak the industrial language. One hears a lot about the employment of more scientists in government departments. I do not think myself that what you want is more Scientists, with a capital S, the sort of super-specialist type; you really need the sort of man that we try to synthesise in industry, who has a much broader base than just scientific knowledge, who knows quite a bit about economics and the commercial side of things, and can discuss an industrial problem in a very wide sense. They are very difficult to find. I mean, they are not produced by any university. You have really got to make them inside industry.'[1]

The experts in the civil service not surprisingly resent this *apartheid* between them and the administrators, and in the last twenty years a cold war has existed between the two sides. The specialists do not believe that administration is an art in itself, while the administrators insist that trained minds can deal with any problem. This conflict between amateurs and professionals, between gentlemen and players, runs through many British institutions—more than on the continent or in America—but has its most troubled frontier in the civil service. 'In an age when the importance of science and specialised knowledge has increased so much,' said the Fabian Report, 'the perpetration of this kind of class distinction is indefensible.'[2]

Many senior civil servants are worried about their relationships with specialists. Some departments, like the Ministry of Transport, are notoriously hostile to experts, while others, like Aviation, are trying to come to terms. 'I don't think we've got the right answer yet,' one permanent secretary said to me: 'we don't take enough account of the ambitions of professional people.' 'We don't give our engineers enough scope, or enough money,' said another: 'you can't expect first-class men to be happy as simply *advisers*.' 'What we must avoid,' said another, 'is having a dual structure all the way up—with administrators on one side and advisers on another, coming up on their own narrow pinnacle. That's terribly wasteful.' Since the war the specialists in the civil service have increased sixfold.

SILKY MINDS

'They have very silky minds,' R. A. Butler said to me, about

[1] Fifth Report of the Estimates Committee, 1964 § 908 965.
[2] *The Administrators*, p. 36.

higher civil servants: 'they've Rolls Royce minds. In fact, the civil service is a bit like a Rolls Royce—you know it's the best machine in the world, but you're not quite sure what to do with it. I think it's a bit too smooth: it needs *rubbing up* a bit.' This image has stuck in my mind throughout this book.

The existence of a strong, professional civil service has immense advantages—often envied by Americans and others. But like most professions it is jealous of its position and self-absorbed. Bagehot predicted that men selected as bureaucrats would 'imagine the elaborate machinery of which they form a part, and from which they derive their dignity, to be a grand and achieved result, not a working and changeable instrument': and his fears were well-grounded. Since the war, it has had to face a vast area of administration which needs new kinds of talent. The old caution and scepticism of civil servants can be disastrous when dealing with dynamic industries of the future: witness the running of British airports, which has been determined not by the excitement of vast expansion, but by the horror of new expenditure and a new shock every year when passengers mount up: or telephones, regarded as a distressing extravagance rather than as an essential tool (the increase in British telephones has been among the lowest in Europe). Both telephones and airports have recently been loosened from the civil service control: but in other fields—transport, aviation, works or stationery—old attitudes remain. It is not only dynamism, and a sense of the future, that these departments have needed: it is the whole process of opening up and rubbing up—coming to terms with salesmanship, exhortations, public relations, and above all with the public. The conditioned reflex of the civil service has been to imitate the action of a clam, and retire into its shell.

In the war there was much opening-up. Economists, scientists, journalists, businessmen, future politicians, were all imported into Whitehall, to plan the economy, organise rationing, run research, exhort the public. Whitehall was rubbed up by the stimulus of outside connections—particularly industry. But after the war they went back to their peacetime jobs, and the senior civil servants heaved a sigh of relief, and adjusted their beautiful machine.

Can this mandarin profession continue unchanged? In the last fifteen years it has made some concessions—absorbing an occasional economist, promoting scientists, commissioning accountants. But rather than incorporate specialist administrators on a permanent basis, it has built up a second ladder of advisers —scientific, economic or engineering—and a whole web of advisory committees. There has been mounting criticism of the civil service amateurism, with broadsides such as Professor Chapman's booklet *British Government Observed*, (1963) and the Fabian Report of 1964; and there has been growing unease inside the civil service itself. In April 1964 the First Division Association, the club of the Administrative Class, organised an essay competition on the subject of civil service reform; these were some of the more provocative criticisms by civil servants themselves:[1]

> The trouble with us is not that we are gifted amateurs in a professional world, but that we are narrow professionals working in one of the less technical of professional fields.
>
> The administrative class is trying to achieve what is not possible outside Utopia; a body of integrated individuals who are all exactly alike in being capable of quickly acquiring enough deep knowledge and understanding to advise on policy, negotiate and take decisions on any technical, professional or specialist subject to which they are set.
>
> A further manifestation of arrogance in the administrative class carrying amateurism too far is in the 'do it yourself' attitude whereby the service sets its members to do or to instruct and supervise others to do the most highly specialist jobs for which in outside bodies expert professionals would automatically be employed, or staff trained specially.
>
> Surely the distinction between the executive and the administrative classes should be abolished . . . If the change proposed were to result in an increase in the highest posts of those who take training for their profession seriously, this would be no loss.
>
> Administrative civil servants do not typically think of themselves as managers. By training and inclination they are fitted to regard themselves as advisers to ministers and to the small group of very senior officials who help to fashion ministerial policies. This is, they feel, the essence of their function. This is where the excitements lie. This is the field where brilliance may be displayed and advancement won.

Among many of the younger civil servants a more sceptical approach can be found. Here—as in other fields, including the 'apparatchiks' of the BBC,[2] or the young tycoons of industrial management[3]—a significant rift can be found between the pre-war

[1] Reprinted in *The Economist*, August 8, 1964.
[2] *See* Chapter 36.
[3] *See* Chapter 27.

and post-war generations, in their attitudes to power. As one eminent permanent secretary, in his 'fifties, put it to me:

> When I went into the service it was because there wasn't anything much else to do. I'm too busy to be conscious that I'm exercising much power—as soon as I go home I don't think about it. I think the idea of the enlightened amateur allows people to have disinterested power—which is important. The young people in Whitehall are very able, but they're actively looking to see how power is being exercised—they're much more aware of their power. When they were recruited, they knew they could get other jobs, and they saw Whitehall as a field to exercise power. They've read their C. P. Snow and their Theodore White.

The criticisms of civil service amateurism have become increasingly insistent. A small step was taken in 1963 when a 'Centre for Administrative Studies' was opened in Regent's Park, to give an eighteen-week course in economics and statistics for young assistant principals in their third year. It was designed as a kind of miniscule version of the *Ecole Nationale d'Administration* in Paris, but without anything approaching its intensity and breadth. Another step was taken in 1964, when a course at the Royal Institution (a kind of plain man's Royal Society, in a fine pillared building in Mayfair) was introduced to teach senior civil servants some of the rudiments of scientific thinking, of the kind that Lord Snow is constantly advocating ('this scheme has Snow on its boots,' one Treasury man commented). But neither of these did more than to peck at the problem.

Harold Wilson had bolder notions of civil service reform than his predecessors as prime minister—though still tempered by his instinctive caution.[1] In 1963 a small committee was set up by the Fabian Society, to prepare recommendations. Their members included Shirley Williams, then secretary of the Fabians; Dr Thomas Balogh, later Harold Wilson's economic advisor; Michael Shanks, the economist and author of The Stagnant Society; David Henderson, an economics don; Anthony Crosland, later Secretary of State for Education; and most importantly, Robert Neild, now economic advisor at the Treasury. They prepared their report with the help of several senior civil servants, and in consultation with Harold Wilson, George Brown and James Callaghan. It was published in the summer of 1964, and it made some powerful criticisms of the mandarin structure of Whitehall. It

[1] See for instance the incident with his permanent secretary in 1945, p. 91.

recommended, among other things, the splitting of the Treasury and the creation of an enlarged Civil Service Commission, to look after the problems of staff, structure and management that had been the responsibility of the Treasury. The report served as a kind of unofficial blue-print for the new Labour Government, and some of its proposals, including the Treasury division and the freer use of economists, were quite quickly achieved. But how far the Labour government will succeed in breaking into the 'monastic order' of Whitehall, it is still too early to say.

THE DEPARTMENTS

Opposite are the principal home civil service departments, with their permanent heads, and their number of employees in 1939 and 1964. It is interesting to compare the comparatively small increase in the administrative class with the vast increase in the total. The operation of Parkinson's Law—which we shall see more of later—may not be as extreme as it seems, for the scope of the departments has enormously increased: but it gave great concern to the Estimates Committee in 1963, who observed that in four years the number of non-industrial civil servants had gone up by 34,500, or nine per cent.[1]

'They spend so much time fighting each other,' said one civil servant, 'that it's difficult to remember that they're all supposed to be serving the same government.' Each department has what it likes to call its own 'departmental philosophy'; once inside the building, the rest of Whitehall can seem as remote as Scotland. Most civil servants spend their whole lives in the same department, and only the most senior are switched round. A man at the Board of Trade will talk about 'those Min of Ag people' as if they were serving a foreign power. 'The most time-consuming and distracting subject in Whitehall,' said Lord Eccles in the House of Lords in 1963, arguing against having two Ministries of Education, 'is the dispute over the frontier which divides one department from another. Nothing more delights the professional, nothing diverts his energy more, than the struggle to gain or defend some little bit of power.'

The departments are much less separate than they were. Before the 1870 reforms they were private empires with no common recruitment policy or salaries. Gradually, as their circles widened

[1] Ninth Report from the Estimates Committee, July 1963.

Department	*Number of Staff employed* April 1, 1939	April 1, 1964	*Permanent Secretary*
Post Office	196,206	376,687	Sir Ronald German
Inland Revenue	24,974	58,944	Sir Alexander Johnston
Defence	—	111,741	Sir Henry Hardman
Pensions and National Insurance	—	38,761	Sir Clifford Jarrett
Aviation	—	24,391	Sir Richard Way
Labour	28,338	21,473	Sir James Dunnett
Customs and Excise	15,017	15,800	—
Agriculture and Fisheries	2,653	14,620	Sir John Winnifrith
Works	6,274	20,810	Sir Edward Muir
Transport	2,968	7,706	Sir Thomas Padmore
Board of Trade	4,845	7,863	Sir Richard Powell
Dept. of Agriculture for Scotland	658	2,514	Sir Matthew Campbell
Dept. of Scottish Home and Health	—	2,952	Ronald Johnson
Health	6,676	5,293	Arnold France
Home Office	2,493	15,144	Sir Charles Cunningham
Housing and Local Govt.	—	3,409	Dame Evelyn Sharp
Education and Science	2,079	3,252	Sir Herbert Andrew
Power	461	1,627	Sir Dennis Proctor
Treasury and Depts.	356	2,747	Sir William Armstrong Sir Laurence Helsby
Economic Affairs[1]	—	—	Sir Donald MacDougall
Technology[1]	—	—	Sir Maurice Dean
Land and Natural Resources[1]	—	—	Frederick Bishop
Welsh Office[1]	—	—	Goronwy Daniel

and touched, their overlapping segments have become apparent, and the business of 'interdepartmental consultation' or (as Winston Churchill called it) 'interdepartmental slush', set in. 'The interdepartmental committee,' (wrote the Fabian Report of 1964) 'is so much a characteristic of government as to make it difficult to imagine its absence.' It is a surprise to find Whitehall decisions resulting not from anyone taking a broad look at the country, but from a difficult compromise between four rival departments. These rivalries may be essential expressions of democracy, but departments often acquire a self-centred momentum of their own. When Commonwealth Relations begins fussing about the rights of Rhodesian settlers, you can never be sure how much of the fuss is self-generated: and when the Ministry of Agriculture makes noises about tomato-and-cucumber growers, they sometimes seem to be anticipating rather than representing market gardeners. The most notoriously self-centred department is the Home Office, who regulate and badger aliens and visitors with little consideration of Commonwealth or foreign interests, or even of human decency: the intense conservatism of the Home Office

[1] Created by the Labour Government, October 1964.

has trapped nearly every would-be-reforming Home Secretary. The over-riding aim of the Home office, like Bournemouth landladies, is to avoid trouble, however much trouble that may cause elsewhere.

The departments have very different metabolisms. The GPO, with a quarter of a million employees—more than twice the numbers of ICI—is a kind of industry. The Cabinet Office or the prime ministers secretariat are like private offices, with great power but a small staff. Like colleges or schools, the civil service has its time-honoured hierarchy: and, as usual, there is no real substitute for age. The three most-favoured home departments are the oldest—the Treasury, the Home Office and the Board of Trade: while new important places like Transport or Aviation come at the end of the queue.

Departmental psyches remain curiously unchanged. The passion for un-reform of the Home Office or the laissez-faire philosophy of the Board of Trade remain intact through political swings to left and right. Most departments are much more afraid of interfering than not interfering. Some departments—notably Education, Transport and Housing—work at one remove from the public through local councils, maintaining a delicate advisory rôle which inhibits any suggestion of national planning.

Even the smaller civil service departments have an astonishing scale of activity. The Stationery Office, for instance, is the biggest publisher in Britain: it publishes 20 million copies of 5,000 books and pamphlets, and 60 periodicals, every year. Their books range from *The Density of Residential Areas* to museum publications which include such oddities as Fossil Birds, Raphael's cartoons or even Edward Lear's Nonsense Alphabet. And they have recently branched out into more daring presentation of government reports—such as the lushly produced Buchanan Report, or the midnight publication of Lord Denning's Report on the Profumo Affair.

The hierarchy of Whitehall succeeds in making some of the most important ministries seem like dustbins. Traditionally the Ministry of Works has been a kind of parliamentary joke, but it has been by far the biggest patron in the country, in charge not only of ancient monuments and parks, but of the architecture and design of all government buildings: and in the past this power has been dreadfully abused. Pompous embassies and gloomy post offices have been in the rearguard of public taste, and their traditional safe taste is exemplified by the Ministry of Defence building in Whitehall—'this monument of tiredness and distrust of the world of the twentieth century'—as Nikolaus Pevsner called it. Recently there have been signs of change; the ministry has been enlarged, renamed the 'Ministry of Public Buildings and Works', and given much larger powers: it has begun to show more architectural daring—as for instance in the Post Office Tower in Bloomsbury. But in the perspective of Whitehall it is still an underprivileged ministry, and 'he's been moved to Works' still has an ominous ring. Likewise the Ministry of Transport, another powerful and potentially exciting ministry which is changing the face of the country, is still apt to be regarded as an infra-dig job, like Transport Command during the war.

With some ministries, like Transport and Works, the job in hand is quite clear, and very exacting; but with others their rôle is much more advisory and nebulous. The Ministry of Labour, which was founded by Lloyd George in 1916 and achieved central importance in the two wars, when labour was almost a more important commodity than money, now only becomes crucial in rare moments of strike crisis, and there are some (including *The Economist*) who advocate its abolition; it is certainly unclear why its minister needs to be in the cabinet. Perhaps the most nebulous is the Board of Trade, in its big new air-conditioned building in Pall Mall. 'It was blown up like a balloon by Cripps after the war,' said one senior civil servant, 'and it's never really gone down again. Nobody really seems to know what goes on inside there.' It is supposed to act as a spur to British industry, but it has always fought shy of dynamic attitudes, and in spite of efforts by Edward Heath to make it the instrument for 'modernising Britain', it still lacks aggressive power. As one well-informed commentator, George Cyriax, has written: 'The Board of Trade, speaking very broadly, has been content to keep the industrial show running. In doing so, it has missed the opportunity to promote the growth policies that would have been good both for industry and for the department's own prestige. Indeed, it can be argued that the formation of the National Economic Development Council was really an effort to fill the gap that the Board of Trade left so wide open . . . Despite its virtue of working hard, it is a department that, in the last resort, lacks the required intellectual calibre.'[1]

In a special, rather cosy world of its own is the Ministry of Education, in a bleak building in Mayfair, just opposite the

[1] *New Society*, October 24, 1963.

Mirabelle and looking, with its concrete wall, like an embattled fortress in the middle of deb-land. It has an austere and missionary dedication, and an insistently democratic atmosphere.[1] Traditionally the Ministry has been cautiously advisory, gently influencing local authorities and coaxing teachers; but with the national concern with education, it has become—to use current jargon—more 'purposive' and confident. At the head of the civil servants is one of the most likeable of the permanent secretaries, Sir Herbert Andrew, an alumnus of Manchester Grammar School who was one of the 'heroes of Brussels'—the group of knights who undertook the testing and exhausting negotiations with the Common Market. Sir Herbert sums up the modern senior civil servant—observing the red-hot political issues with perceptive and tolerant detachment.

MINISTERS

> Political heads of departments are necessary to tell the civil service what the public will not stand.
>
> *Sir William Harcourt.*

> Ministers can be divided into those who run their departments and those who are run by their departments. I believe parliament finds out jolly quickly into which category ministers fall, and civil servants know within 48 hours of the minister putting his foot over the doorstep.
>
> *Iain Macleod, January 1964.*

The two heads of each department—the minister and the permanent secretary—are from two different worlds, and their relationship is the vital joint in Whitehall—the elbow of government, between decision and execution. On the one hand is the minister—famous, extrovert, politically committed. In the waiting-room there is no photograph of the permanent secretary, but a row of photographs of past ministers, from proud bearded Victorians in faded daguerrotypes, gradually changing—with the pressure of universal suffrage—to the beaming and plausible men of the present. The minister embodies the whole public personality of his ministry, and he alone is blamed for its public faults.

He must defend and explain his department to parliament: and this public accountability remains in theory the over-riding difference between a civil service department and private industry. It takes its most obvious form in parliamentary debates and the

[1] *See* Tyrrell Burgess in *New Society*, September 12, 1963.

parliamentary question—the 'PQ'. The PQ, in theory at least, is the eye of the public, and it affects the whole character of the ministry: rooms-full of filing cabinets, overflowing with trivial correspondence, are preserved for fear of some future awkward question. Many a civil servant will dream of the peaceful opaqueness of Unilever and ICI, where millions can be lost and no questions asked. The traditional caution of civil servants, their dislike of publicity, their obscurantism, all derive from the dread of the public. The PQ produces a flurry of activity before parliament. 'We've got sixty-two questions coming up on Monday,' says a private secretary, rushing through with an armful of files: 'How did the questions go?' asked a permanent secretary, as if awaiting news of a distant battle. But the PQ is a much less seeing eye than it used to be: with the complexity and secrecy of many departments, enormous incompetence can be perpetrated and never come to light.

Listening to cabinet ministers talking with their refreshing indiscretion—behind their big leather-topped desks, leaning back on their chairs or resting their legs on the desk—my main impression was how much, in spite of all the pressure and overwork, they are engrossed and sustained by their power. I began to understand why they are always reluctant to resign. Compared to the other two parts of his job—parliament and cabinet—a minister is here is own boss, able to do what he likes, with the whole structure of the department built round him, and a private office next door with a handpicked staff at his beck and call. It is here that the manager-ministers come into their own, away from the bothers of speech-making: and in their ministries they have quite a different *persona*. In parliament every blunder and anxiety is exposed. In the ministry—where they may spend nine-tenths of their time—they have the whole staff to support and defend them. This is what some ministers, both Conservative and Labour, said about their civil servants:

> Running a civil service department is like playing an organ—you can do almost anything with it. No industrialist gets the same kind of service. A minister can ring a bell, ask for a report on anything, and get it.
>
> Boy, those people next door are wonderful! I tell you, my speeches are going to sound a lot better from now on!
>
> The trouble with the civil service is that it is overstaffed at the bottom and understaffed at the top.

You know, they've got a wonderful political sense, without themselves being political. They can get the feel of your ideas very quickly.

They often give you advice based on assumptions of government policy which turn out to be quite wrong.

Of course I know their tricks: they fill up your in-tray so that you're too busy to make any changes. But I keep a check on things I've asked to be done and make sure they've done them. They're wonderful people really.

They can ruin a minister if they want to, you know.

There's no real rule about policy being left to ministers and execution to civil servants. Often civil servants' decisions can have an important effect on policy.

They're extraordinarily adaptable. I remember when we (Conservatives) took office in 1951, the same civil servant who had been looking after nationalisation had already got out a plan for denationalisation. He went about it with just the same enthusiasm.

Civil servants aren't passive by nature. They're do-gooders, they're Benthamites at heart. They want to reform the world.

Part of the point of the civil service is that people don't take decisions. There are only two or three people who are really meant to take decisions.

If the civil service departments are too strong, that's the politicians' fault as much as the civil servants'.

Any fool can find the answers to the questions. The difficult thing is to find the questions to the answers.

Whoever the minister, a great deal of the power rests with the bureaucracy. In business, as well as in Whitehall, a chairman may *imagine* he is running a company—like a pianola-player, sitting on the music-stool, varying the speed and volume, while the tune is being played by the motor. In the past the minister was held responsible for things he knew nothing about: Austen Chamberlain resigned over the medical supplies to Mesopotamia, and Sir Thomas Dugdale resigned over the Crichel Down affair. 'The one thing a minister must never be able to say,' said Sir Richard Hopkins, 'is "why wasn't I told?".' But in the more technical and managerial ministries, it is impossible for the head to know everything: once he started asking 'why wasn't I told?' there would be no end to it. Every minister nowadays finds himself signing minutes he knows nothing about. Inevitably, like a good chairman, a minister must delegate to his juniors—and the frontier between politicians and civil servants (in some ministries at least) is lost.

Moreover, the long time-span of so many government projects ensures that, when a scandal or mismanagement *does* come to light, the minister, and probably the permanent secretary too, is a quite different man to the one who was in charge when the scandal occurred. The most spectacular example of this was in the Ferranti scandal of 1964,[1] which was concerned with events of four years before. The scandal had occurred at a time when Peter Thorneycroft was Minister of Aviation, and Sir William Strath was permanent secretary; but since then there had been two new ministers, and two new permanent secretaries; so that when the scandal came to light, it was defended in front of the Public Accounts Committee by Sir Richard Way, and in front of parliament by Julian Amery—who was able to shoulder the blame and act as a convenient scapegoat for the public anger, while being obviously innocent to his colleagues—a typical example of Whitehall's contempt for the public. 'The time factor,' commented one very senior civil servant to me afterwards, 'provides a real element of doubt as to the viability of the concept of ministerial responsibility.'

PERMANENT SECRETARIES

> Wise men have always perceived that the execution of political measures is in reality the essence of them.
>
> *Sir Henry Taylor, 1832.*

> I was once asked what was the function of the civil servant in relation to the House of Commons. I replied that he sat in a dark seat and listened to his minister dropping bricks.
>
> *Lord Attlee.*[2]

Next door to the ministers, in less spectacular rooms, are the permanent secretaries. The contrast with their 'masters' is immediately obvious. The secretaries are, above all, anonymous. Their comings and goings may revolutionise departments, but they are unproclaimed: it is not until their obituaries that their contributions are fully appraised. With many senior civil servants

[1] *See* p. 284.

[2] *The Civil Service in Britain and France.* Hogarth Press, 1956. p. 20.

anonymity is a passion as gripping as fame is for their masters, and as they hear a politician proudly produce a phrase that they invented, they feel a thrill of non-recognition. The names of the permanent secretaries—Cunningham, Powell, Winnifrith, Hardman or Sharp—are rarely heard outside Whitehall.

An encounter between a veteran permanent secretary—inhibited and cautious—and a new young minister—unorthodox and idealistic—provides a sharp antithesis. Ministers—particularly Labour ministers—are full of stories of how they have been told 'it's impossible', 'it's never been done before', 'but it's always been done like this'. Very rarely the permanent secretary is discreetly removed to another ministry: but 'it's very difficult to get rid of 'em, you know,' said one present minister, 'things have to get pretty desperate.' More often the conflict is resolved in compromise. For the permanent secretary is the repository not only of caution, but of the armoury of facts, which have a habit of winning ('facts that seem to live in the office,' said Bagehot, 'so teasing and unceasing they are').

The frontier between the civil servants and politicians induces the occupational disease of the civil service—cynicism. Much of their time is spent working out perfect-looking schemes, about roads, welfare, housing, which then disappear into the minister's room, and from there to the cabinet—and then come back mangled and muddled, full of nasty political compromises or stipulations about 'what the public will not stand'. After thirty years watching closely the inner workings of politics, devising schemes for nationalisation and de-nationalisation, most civil servants end up with a profound scepticism about any scheme for improvement, and a few develop a hankering to be rid of the whole business of democracy. And many of them resent the assumption by the politicians that only they are qualified to take bold decisions and face up to responsibilities, and that the civil servants are (as one of them put it to me) 'only half-men'.

Permanent secretaries are at the top of the gently-sloping pyramid of the civil service hierarchy. This is how the 'Administrative Class' is graded:

Permanent Secretary	£8,285—£8,885
Deputy Secretary	£5,885
Under-Secretary	£4,785
Assistant Secretary	£3,135—£3,985
Principal	£2,036—£2,810
Assistant Principal	£885—£1,423

Most administrative civil servants stop at the Assistant Secretary level: the next jump, as to Flag Officer in the Navy, is the difficult one. But the bottleneck is not, perhaps, as agonising as it might appear from outside. Many men's ambition has worn out by the age of forty, and the senior jobs are much more burdensome and less financially rewarding than the peaks of private industry.

There are fifty-two men in the service earning over £8,000 a year—not all of them in Britain, and not all heads of departments (the Treasury, for instance, has five of them). They are less well-off in real money terms than they were in 1871, when the head of the Home Office earned £2,000 a year. Their backgrounds are varied: of thirty heads of departments in January, 1961, eleven went to public school, twenty-six to Oxbridge, seven to Scottish universities (five went to Oxbridge afterwards), but none to an English Redbrick university. Thirteen had been in the Treasury. All but two began their careers in government service: (Sir Henry Hardman and Sir Laurence Helsby began as economics dons). Sir Dennis Proctor left for three years to go into Danish business. Nearly all of them had moved between several departments—an average of 2·5 each.

Their status relative to ministers—or at least to Conservative ministers—has risen in the past thirty years. 'There's much less caste difference,' R. A. Butler told me in 1961: 'In the old days it used to be thought that the minister was chosen by God, and the permanent secretary was just an official. Now they're much more equal.' Some ministers are on easy terms with their permanent secretaries, and dine with them regularly: others remain impersonal and avoid Christian names.

'Establishment is the right word to use about senior civil servants,' said one cabinet minister. They form a close-knit homogeneous group. Most of them live either in London, S.W., or in Surrey: their favourite club is the Oxford and Cambridge. 'They mostly go straight home to dinner, and don't meet many people outside Whitehall,' one minister said: and this social seclusion brings the permanent secretaries closer to each other. For most of their time they are immersed in their departments, but they keep in touch through the quick antennae of Whitehall. When the permanent secretaries are opposed to something—for instance, aid to under-developed countries—an invisible wall takes shape in Whitehall. Somehow or other things mysteriously fail to get done, difficulties prove insuperable. Then perhaps a lever at the top is pulled, and the wall equally mysteriously dissolves:

the gap between policy and execution, between cup and lip, which is the source of the permanent secretaries' power, becomes bridgeable after all. In theory the permanent secretaries do not have attitudes about anything. In practice it would be absurd to expect thirty highly intelligent men to be all politically castrated, and the attitudes they do have can be decisive.

Permanent secretaries are more articulate, more literary, more questioning, than most company chairmen. Industrialists are often reluctant to talk about their job, lacking in professional introspection and curiosity: I often had the feeling that they were, after all, simply making nuts or bolts or soap. If you ask them about generalities, trends, or even how they reach decisions, they seem genuinely puzzled. But permanent secretaries enjoy talking about their rôle: in their approach and background they are half-way to dons. They like to see their job less as a trade than an art. 'The work provides,' wrote Lord Bridges, the son of a poet-laureate, '. . . an intense satisfaction and delight in the accomplishment of difficult tasks, a delight which has much in common with that felt by artists on completion of some outstandingly difficult task.'[1] They do not have the same edginess as businessmen: they will often agree that things are far from perfect. On the other hand, they lack the same capacity to *change* things that the industrialist has. They are more intricated in a machine, with committees, balances and gradual modifications.

Yet they remain individuals. Their arrival can transform a ministry more drastically than a minister's—though the minister will always take the credit—and their influence on the minister is often paramount, though they will never say so. This is what some of them *did* say:

> The person is more important than the job. Some people can get away with much more than others. Its a question of *esteem*.

> Some people seem to think that we've got a lot of power through the advice we give: but I can't say that I've ever noticed it.

> It's our job to provide the brake rather than the spur. A lot of our time is spent pointing out the snags.

> You have to spend so much time understanding what other men think that you sometimes forget what you think yourself. But I don't think that matters too much.

[1] *Portrait of a Profession*. p. 32.

You can't delegate things here as company chairmen do: you have to know all the important things that go on.

I think we may have to change the whole system before long. It wasn't designed to run big business.

Beeching has made quite a difference. Since he has put forward his own policies and defended them in public, a lot of people have said that senior civil servants should stand up and be counted.

Some permanent secretaries are more permanent than others. In some ministries—most notably Aviation[1]—the turnover in secretaries has been as rapid as that of ministers. But in others they have become formidable fixtures, who have seen the politicians come and go. Sir Charles Cunningham, a Scotsman, has had his firm hand on the Home Office since 1957. One of the most permanent, and influential, has been a woman, Dame Evelyn Sharp, who has been at Housing for nine years. The presence of senior women in Whitehall comes as a surprising feature after the male preserves of the Church, the Bench and Oxbridge colleges: the civil service is one of the rare fields where women enjoy equal power and pay. They first made their way in the first world war: and by 1925 the civil service—always aiming to be 'model employers'—admitted them to the Administrative Grade. Miss Mary Smieton and Miss Evelyn Sharp, both from Oxford, came into the civil service that year, and both rose to be Dames and permanent secretaries. Dame Evelyn is one of the most formidable characters in Whitehall, the daughter of a political clergyman, a keen walker and hiker. She is an expert on town and country planning, a fierce opponent of litter and defender of green belts, and she has a reputation—very rare in Whitehall—for calling a spade a spade. She insists that being a high-ranking civil servant is not really unlike being secretary to any important man, and that women are just as good at that as men, if not better. 'You serve your minister whoever he is. I always feel a man would secretly rather be the minister.'[2]

A permanent secretary can be, by temperament, anyone from a don to a tycoon. An example of the don-type is Sir Richard Powell at the Board of Trade, a quiet and very articulate bachelor who came from a Lancashire grammar school. One of the most tycoonish is *another* Scotsman, Sir James Dunnett at the Ministry

[1] *See* p. 273.

[2] *The Guardian*, October 12, 1959.

of Labour. He appears more like a businessman than a civil servant; he is outspoken, informal, and draws firm lines with his pencil on blotting paper. He became a permanent secretary (at Transport) at only 45. He is one of those many prominent sons of the Indian Empire (including Professor Tawney, Lord Beveridge, Robert Birley, R. A. Butler, Hugh Gaitskell). His father was an administrator in India and his elder brother is also a civil service knight.

Dunnett is one of the few permanent secretaries who feel strongly about the need to reform—particularly for engineers, scientists and economists to be brought closer into administration. He said in a sensational lecture in 1961:

> I think we have got to face the fact that increasingly government departments are doing much more than merely advising ministers. Many of them are, in effect, running his business . . . We are in the civil service perhaps inclined to be a little conservative; once an organisation has been set up in a certain way we are perhaps inclined to let it run on in that way without too much self-examination . . . the Administrative class has not been without a certain intellectual arrogance of its own . . . We are just a little bit inclined in this country to think we know more about administration than anybody else and that we have little or nothing to learn from other countries. I do not believe this to be true.[1]

All permanent secretaries are overworked: it is almost a point of pride in the profession that they should stagger home laden with papers after what is termed 'a hard day's toil'. They must not only advise the minister, but manage their department and supervise promotions. Like their masters, they feel they have to know what's going on everywhere, in case it might suddenly explode in parliament. They cannot, like Paul Chambers of ICI, go home for tea and thought. They are tied to their departmental machine. 'If you sit and think,' said one permanent secretary, 'you find that the world has gone past your thoughts.' 'So the brain of a great administrator,' wrote Bagehot in 1856, 'is naturally occupied with the details of the day, the passing dust, the granules of that day's life; and his unforeseeing temperament turns away uninterested from reaching speculations, vague thought, and from extensive and far-off plans.'

[1] Reprinted in *Public Administration*, Autumn, 1961.

The same kind of view has come from Sir Charles Snow, in his book *Science and Government*, though Snow here seems to be (strangely) equating foresight with scientific knowledge:

> I have the greatest respect for the English professional administrators. They are extremely intelligent, honourable, tough, tolerant and generous. But they have a deficiency..
>
> By temperament active men, the nature of their job tends to make them live in the short term, to become masters of the short-term solution. Often, as I have seen them conducting their business with an absence of fuss, a concealed force, a refreshing dash of intellectual sophistication, a phrase from one of the old Icelandic sagas kept nagging in my mind. It was; 'Snorri was the wisest man in Iceland who had not the gift of foresight.'

The three thousand administrators of the civil service include many of the best brains in the country—a unique intellectual corps: but few in Whitehall have disengaged brains, with time to think about long-term problems. Compare, for instance, the human architecture of Whitehall with the structure of Shell—which has seven men at the top, deliberately detached from day-to-day decisions, spending their time travelling, thinking, planning and considering sums over a million pounds.[1] It might be argued that 'long-think' is the job of the politicians: but there are many departments, like Transport, Aviation or Power where planning is often a technical, not a political, business. And politicians are, if anything, closer to the grindstone than their secretaries.

INSTITUTES

Some of the long-think is being undertaken by the new institutes, which provide a kind of shadow civil service, and which deserve a brief digression. There are more than 130 institutes in the London telephone directory, including the Institute of Breathing, the Institute of Certified Grocers and the Institute of Sewage Purification: no sub-profession is complete without one. But the institutes that concern us here provide a kind of academic, non-party *doppelgänger* to the state departments. Many have been set up with the help of American money—institutes are a favourite American idea—and supplemented by funds from British big business. The first was the Royal Institute of International Affairs, usually known as Chatham House after Lord Chatham's old house which it inhabits in St. James's Square: it was founded in 1920 by

[1] *See* Chapter 26.

a group of rich benefactors including Lord Astor and Sir Abe Bailey, and is now heavily augmented with American money. After the war it accumulated a lot of dead wood, and was even slower than the Foreign Office in realising the importance of Black Africa and the Common Market: but recently it has shown interesting signs of revival. Since the war, new institutes have followed. These are some of them, with their directors (three of whom were formerly on *The Observer*) and their governmental counterparts:

Royal Institute of International Affairs (Kenneth Younger, Andrew Shonfield)	Foreign Office
National Institute for Economic and Social Research (Christopher Saunders)	Treasury
Institute for Strategic Studies (Alastair Buchan)	Ministry of Defence
Overseas Development Institute (William Clark)	Ministry for Overseas Development

Relations between the institutes and Whitehall are often tricky: in some respects they encourage criticism, by providing ammunition and expertise that political opposition cannot afford. The NIESR, for instance, is a collection of 25 economists, with as many assistants, within a few hundred yards from Whitehall. They include several ex-Treasury men, who enjoy firing off salvoes in the direction of Great George Street. They specialise in short-term economic forecasts, and are actually subsidised by the Treasury. Whitehall, inherently suspicious of research, does not always enjoy the feeling of being overlooked by ghost-bodies, but the more adventurous civil servants appreciate this new competition. While Oxford and Cambridge have remained proudly aloof from most contemporary studies, the institutes are beginning to provide an academic circumference to Whitehall.

HEAD OF THE CIVIL SERVICE

At the head of the network of permanent secretaries is the official Head of the Home Civil Service (the 'Home' is carefully inserted to make clear that he does not have direct jurisdiction over the Foreign Office). He sits on one of the three peaks of Whitehall, alongside the Head of the Treasury and the Secretary to the Cabinet. Up till 1956 the first two peaks were occupied by the same man—Sir Edward (now Lord) Bridges; and from then until 1962 the Secretaryship of the Cabinet and the Headship of the Civil Service were both occupied by that greyest of eminences, Sir Norman Brook—now Lord Normanbrook, Chairman of the BBC. But whenever a very strong man retires from the Civil Service, his job—by the inexorable processes of Parkinson's Law—is apt to be split in two, and thereafter no one can imagine how the jobs were ever done by one man. Many people—particularly junior ministers—complained that Sir Norman was too powerful, and that his extra unofficial post of the prime minister's closest adviser gave him more influence than all but top politicians; but his range of activity and contacts also gave him scope to break through interdepartmental slush and to get things done quickly and boldly.

When Brook retired, Sir Burke Trend became Secretary to the Cabinet, and Sir Laurence Helsby came from the Ministry of Labour to become Head of the Civil Service, based on the Treasury. He is also known as 'Joint Permanent Secretary of the Treasury'—the other half of the joint being Sir William Armstrong who (as we will see in the next chapter) is in charge of the economic and financial activities of the Treasury. But Sir Laurence is concerned with the running of Whitehall, the moves on a human chessboard, the training, salaries, organisation and promotion of the 800,000 civil servants in Britain. He thus, in the midst of all the shortcomings and criticisms of Whitehall, occupies a job of central importance.

Sir Laurence is unobtrusive, even in a street of unobtrusive men. He is thoroughly grey—grey suit, grey hair, grey voice. He puffs a slow pipe. He has the civil servant's gift—so invaluable in committees—of making all things sound dull. He is informal, relaxed, quite prepared to talk about anything, but stands on his dignity. He commutes from Dorking, and belongs to the Oxford and Cambridge Club.

It is tempting to depict him as an archetypal civil servant, but in fact he did not come into Whitehall till he was thirty three—shaken up, like so many others, by the war. When he left Keble College, Oxford, he became a lecturer in Economics, first at Exeter, then at Durham. In 1940, he took the job of temporary senior clerk in the House of Commons, and began to show his talents in the zones of power. A year later, he moved to the

Treasury, where he spent the rest of the war, becoming (in that gruesome Whitehall phrase) 'meshed into the machine'. Then, in the Labour government, he had his great opportunity; he was appointed to be Principal Private Secretary to Attlee, and thus became part of the inner network, and earmarked for special promotion. Number Ten under Attlee was not as pivotal as it had been under Churchill or became under Macmillan; but it gave plenty of scope for Helsby's detached and analytical mind. After three years, he moved from there to the Ministry of Food, and then to become First Civil Service Commissioner, in charge of recruitment. He moved to the Ministry of Labour and then—to many people's surprise—to the top job. His qualifications were sound; he was expert in economics, he knew the workings of politics, he had seen how people came into the service, and what happened afterwards. He had the open mind of a good don, and the selfless dedication of a good administrator. He was quite aware of the faults of the civil service, and the importance of managerial expertise. There were some who complained that he was too resigned in his attitude, too much part of the machine, too much a stickler for protocol, too apt to leave innovation to the politicians. But in those respects he accurately personified his service. This is how he described the problem of the administrator, talking to me in 1964:

> Public administration is a profession which is second to none in the rigour of the demands which it puts on its members, and it is quite as skilled as any other. Part of the skill of the administrator lies in an ability to isolate very quickly the point that really matters from a tangle of unrelated or irrelevant material. But it is not easy to provide an exact definition of the skill. One distinguishing feature of our profession, as compared with other kinds of administration, is its dependence on the written word. The discipline of the written word is a part of our official lives to which we grow accustomed from very early days.
>
> But if public administration has some special needs of its own, much of the work of a senior civil servant calls for just those qualities of 'management' that are needed in business. We in Britain have a lot to learn about good management, and it is salutary that the setting up of the new 'business schools' will in itself make us more conscious of the professional skills of the good manager: they are as necessary in the public service as in private enterprise and broadly of the same kind.
>
> It is sometimes suggested that the administrator is a mere amateur, with no skill of his own if he has not been trained as a lawyer, an economist, a scientist, and so on. It may well be that members of our profession do increasingly need some specialised skills, but they are to

a great extent additional to effective administration, which has a positive skill of its own. Certainly as the functions of government go on changing and the subject matter of public administration becomes more varied and complex, we have to be ready to face changes. Increasingly the administrator, however skilled, does need some specialised skills, such as those implied in a knowledge of economics. Most other professions have had to do a great deal of thinking in recent years about recruitment, basic qualifications, and training. Most of them have introduced important changes. It is not to be expected that we in the civil service should be able—or want—to stand still.

PUBLIC ACCOUNTS COMMITTEE

How can parliament and the public hope to keep an effective eye on all these intricate and secretive ramifications of Whitehall? It is one thing—quite difficult enough—for a minister to be able to control and understand his department; it is quite another for the rest of parliament to find out what is going on.

The most formidable weapons of parliament in dealing with the civil service are the committees, made up of members from both sides of the House who are empowered to co-opt and question anyone they wish. The 'select committees' periodically produce their verbatim reports which, unnoticed by the public, are full of interesting glimpses of the workings of government. The most effective committee is the Public Accounts Committee (PAC), instituted by Gladstone in 1861, with powers to scrutinise all government accounts and to criticise them on behalf of parliament —a committee of which Harold Wilson was chairman for several years. For their scouting, the committee make use of the most important watchdog of Whitehall, the Auditor-General, or (to give his full title) the 'Comptroller-General of the Receipts and loans of Her Majesty's Exchequer, and Auditor-General of the Public Accounts'.

The Auditor-General is a unique civil servant; he is appointed for life, in theory by the Crown, and like a judge he can only be sacked by an address from both Houses of Parliament. Although he comes from the ranks of civil servants, he is kept deliberately separate; he works in 'Audit House', a building looking over the river, symbolically placed half-way between the Bank of England and the Treasury. It is part of his job to underwrite the cheques drawn by the Bank of England on the Treasury Account, to make sure that the money is properly spent; but the more important part of his business is the auditing of the accounts, for which he has a staff of 460 auditors—men in the Executive class of the civil service, who are given a special eighteen months training under the City of London College. They audit £8,000 million worth of accounts every year, together with another £6,500 million of the Inland Revenue. Only fifty of the auditors work in Audit House; the rest of them are sitting at desks inside government departments: 'the ferrets are down their holes'.

The present Auditor-General, Sir Edmund Compton, comes from a fairly conventional Treasury background;[1] New College; first in Greats; keen musician (three daughters sing in the Bach Choir); lives in S.W.7; married a magistrate's daughter. He worked in the Treasury until 1958, when he was appointed Auditor-General. 'A wretchedly poor use of a first-class public servant,' commented Hugh Dalton; and many people thought that if he had stayed in the Treasury, Compton would have become its head. But he is well suited to the Auditor-Generalship; he has a very independent mind, detachment and scepticism, and has not been too conditioned by Whitehall attitudes. He is a modest, informal man with bright eyes, no pomp and a strong Church of England background.

Much of the auditor-general's job is dull and routine, like that of any company auditor, but from time to time a large scandal is unearthed in Audit House. Soon after Sir Edmund took over, he discovered from the Inland Revenue accounts the practice of 'hobby farmers'—rich men who evaded taxes by running expensive farms at a loss—and his report produced an uproar, and new regulations to prevent the evasion. Then, in 1964, he exhumed from the books of the Ministry of Aviation the extraordinary discrepancy in the contract with Ferranti Ltd.[2] for producing Bloodhound missiles—a contract which, it turned out, enabled Ferranti's to make a profit of £5,400,000, or 113 per cent on the capital employed. Sir Edmund's initial report was taken up by the Public Accounts Committee under Douglas Houghton, MP, who questioned Sir Richard Way, the permanent secretary at the Ministry of Aviation, and Sebastian de Ferranti, the chairman of the company. One of the Committee, Cledwyn Hughes, MP, questioned Sir Richard about the system of contracts: 'You are in no position to say to the Committee this afternoon that there are not similar cases?' 'I am in no position,' answered Sir Richard, 'to say that I am sure that there are no similar cases.'

[1] *See* p. 293.
[2] *See* p. 273.

The Ferranti affair produced a public roar. A committee of inquiry under Sir John Lang was appointed to look into the case; at first Ferranti's refused to open their books to the committee, but eventually they agreed; and it was eventually made known that Ferranti's would repay a large part of the profits. The case marked an important achievement for the Auditor-General and the PAC; but it also raised questions as to whether this system of watchdogs should not be extended. For the only effective check that the Auditor-General has on government departments is through the accounts; and it was only by accident that the Ferranti discrepancy came to light. The Auditor-General cannot investigate what a department *does*, how efficient it is, or whether its staff is justified; and with departments who have no measurable output, such as the Board of Trade, which is advisory and exhortatory, there can be no effective check on their competence.

There is a strong argument for extending the powers of the Auditor-General, to allow him to investigate not only accounts, but work in progress, organisation and systems, and to deal not only with extraordinary situations but also apparently ordinary ones; so that he could make spot checks into any kind of contract or large expenditure. The usual civil service retort is that this is not parliament's job but the Treasury's; that the Treasury already has the necessary powers; and that to increase the powers of parliament would merely create an extravagant new 'anti civil-service' (as in Washington) and cause much greater friction and non-co-operation between politicians and civil servants. As against this, there is little sign at present of effective Treasury supervision of departmental blunders and waste. Moreover it is doubtful whether a parliamentary secretariat, to deal with larger inquiries, could cost more than a fraction of what would be saved.

The Ferranti case marked both the usefulness of parliament, and its limitations; for it showed how large an area of government spending had passed outside parliament's ken, and how hard it is for MPs, with their present machinery, to uncover the matters which should concern them most.

15

COMMITTEES

The English way is a committee—we are born with a belief in a green cloth, clean pens and twelve men with grey hair.

Walter Bagehot.

The ideal committee is one with me as chairman, and two other members in bed with flu.

Lord Milverton.

A camel is a horse designed by a committee.

Anon.

IN Whitehall, sooner or later, individuals always become lost into committees. It is in committees that personalities appear to evaporate: the essence of committeemanship is de-personalisation —gradually getting your own way by avoiding any kind of emotional conflict. 'A government department,' it has been said, 'is a collection of people, but if they are to do their work effectively they must try so far as possible collectively to resemble a *thing*.'[1] The committee is the embodiment of that thing.

As departments grow in size, and as their problems become more interlocked, so interdepartmental 'committees' grow up between them—trying to reach agreement between different points of view, and to avoid 'departmentalism'. Men from the Board of Trade, the Treasury, the Home Office and the Min of Ag will come together with an agenda and a chairman to produce a decision in no-man's-land. 'Interdepartmental consultation'—that deadening phrase—is the bugbear of Whitehall: liaison breeds liaison and committees breed committees. 'It's terrifying, the man-power it uses up,' said one minister: 'Some of our best men spend most of their time in liaison.' Committees are the inescapable penalty of democracy. This is a characteristic problem of modern organisations: the senior men in the mammoth corporations seem to be—and are sometimes called—co-ordinators. Bishops, judges, admirals or scientists are all entangled in committees, all needing the same

[1] C. H. Sisson: *The Spirit of British Administration*, 1959.

qualities of patience and compromise—'all Gerald du Maurier in the end'.[1]

Beyond the civil servants there is a wide untidy fringe of committees connecting with the outside world. There are now more than *five hundred* standing advisory committees attached to Whitehall departments, usually containing a mixture of civil servants and outside people: the Ministry of Agriculture alone has fifty of them. The more cut-off Whitehall becomes, the more advisory committees spring up, to provide the eyes and ears of the world: and this penumbra has produced its own race of committee men, nipping in and out of Whitehall from business, farming or trades unions. Once a man is established as a 'good committee man'—'house-trained' as they say—he will move from one committee to another: in 1960 it was found that 34 people occupied 85 places in Home Office committees, while 30 individuals filled a total of 154 places—over five each—on government bodies.[2] 'Round how many ministerial tables are to be found the same convex waistcoats and bloodshot eyes?' asked the *New Statesman*.

What are committee men like? This is one romantic description, by William Cooper, who—like Lord Snow—is a novelist-civil-servant-scientist:

> A dozen men are standing about in a nondescript room that contains a carpet, a desk, a glass-fronted book-case, possibly a picture, and a big table: a dozen men of *not* all shapes and sizes. Of all sizes possibly, but of a family resemblance in shape, heavily muscled, substantial, pretty masculine men, men who probably played games well in their youth and have certainly enjoyed sustained robust health ever since. The committee man is characterized by energy and stamina; he can go on for hours—he will never get his way if he cannot. His facial expression is sharp and intelligent but not given to sudden changes, least of all changes indicating passing emotion. His voice is loud—the committee man does not have to be asked to speak up. He stands around chatting genially, possibly jocularly, about one of that morning's letters to *The Times*, until the chairman's voice sounds unhurriedly above the rest: 'Well, gentlemen, shall we get round the table?'
>
> The committee man loves his job. It would not be unusual to hear two members of our type of committee reminiscing nostal-

[1] *See* page 172.

[2] Advisory Committees in British Government. *PEP*. 1960. pp. 53–54.

gically about the days during the war when life was really being lived to the full—when they went home at half-past nine instead of six! . . .

Is the committee man who governs us a ruthless seeker and wielder of power? asks the beady-eyed, non-committee, governed man. The answer is that he may or may not be, but in any case, *that is not how it seems to him.*[1]

The 'good committee man' is one who patiently lets others speak, guides the discussion, gradually infiltrates his viewpoint, accepts a few compromises, but eventually produces a solution that is nearer his than other people's. An important chairman's technique, when faced with a disagreement on principle, is to discuss not *whether* something should be done, but *how*—to lose the ends in the means, until the question of principle imperceptibly disappears—as happened in the cabinet, one suspects, over Suez and over the Common Market, and as happened in R. A. Butler's masterly handling of the dissolution of the Central African Federation. One of the men who, by training and temperament, perfectly understands the ends and means problem in committees[1], is Harold Wilson.

To swing a committee effectively involves a good deal of hard work: 'The man who reads his agenda properly,' said Lord Hill, 'has a tremendous advantage. You can't really impress a committee unless you've done your homework.' To be a bad committee man is not necessarily an overwhelming drawback in Whitehall. At least one influential man in the Treasury quite often loses his temper, and Sir Solly Zuckerman, the chief scientist in Whitehall, is well-known for his offhand committee behaviour and his habit of suddenly going off to the zoo. But many brilliant, first-class men have been ousted by second-raters because they were 'bad at committees': and for most men, the path to power is through the quiet and patient handling of a group of colleagues.

Depersonalisation is emphasised by the minutes—the links which convert committees into actions. A careful memorandum circulates through Whitehall, describing the art of minute-taking, explaining how to play down personal conflicts, to avoid ascribing particular views to particular men, and to compose a corporate committee-view.

The horrors of committees are notorious. They not only waste

[1] William Cooper: The Committee Man and the Technician. *Twentieth Century*, October, 1957.

time and energy: they are apt to produce camel-like decisions which may look sensible inside the committee room, but are absurd in a larger context. The camel image is quite exact, for when given the problem of an awkward hump, like a dromedary's, a favourite committee device is to resolve it by adding *another* hump. In this way the BBC resolved the problem of the dwindling Third Programme by adding a half-hearted extra one, Network Three; and the Home Office, faced with the absurdities of an expensive passport, invented a second kind of passport. Similarly, when faced with a conflict between two or three people, a committee will always tend to resolve it by bringing in a fourth. Committees dread 'having a row', however legitimate the row may be. They can often acquire a life and vested interest of their own, continuing with chairman, secretary and agendas long after their original purpose is finished.

Committees are masters of muddle, in their closed world of cross-purposes. Muddle is the extra unknown personality in any committee. This is how one commentator has described it:

> It comes from people not doing what they were expected to do, or doing what they are not expected to do, or simply not bothering to say they have not done what they were expected to do. It springs from the exchanges of memoranda in which everybody puts his position too strongly, from the conference at which complete agreement is reached and which everyone leaves with a different idea of what has been decided, from the order half understood but instantly executed, from the stand on dignity . . .
>
> The most engaging feature of muddle at its best is that it proliferates like yeast in a warm room, and every attempt to explain it gives rise to a new and more complex muddle.[1]

'If our society comes to an end,' wrote William Whyte, writing about America, 'it will not be with a bang or a whimper. The sound track will be the soft tinkle of rimless glasses on a conference table.'[2] But in spite of all the apparent deadness and de-personalisation of the committee world, decisions are still pushed and swung by strong individuals: a man with 'fire in his belly' (a good Treasury phrase) can still activate and enthuse other people: and the vital decisions of our time are the result of not green cloth and

[1] Patrick White: Not-so-plain Muddle, *The Guardian*, October 6, 1961.
[2] W. H. Whyte: *Is Anybody Listening*, p. 223. New York, 1952.

clean pens, but of one or two men making up their own minds, tempering and trimming them to the needs of committees, but never fooled into thinking that satisfying a committee is an end in itself.

16

TREASURY

Whichever party's in office, the liberals are in power.

Harold Wilson.

Like inverted Micawbers, waiting for something to turn down.

Winston Churchill.

It is a grave administrative mistake to concentrate this massive power of negation in the hands of, relatively, a small number of officials who have no other function but the forthright utterance of the Everlasting Nay.

Harold Laski.[1]

AT the end of Whitehall, where it turns into Great George Street, is a huge and ugly building, with cupolas at the corners and a circular courtyard in the middle. It contains—so one messenger assured me—a thousand rooms and nine miles of corridors. It is officially known as 'The New Public Offices'—the name it was given when it was planned in 1908. More commonly it is known as 'the Great George Street Front'. The labyrinthine corridors inside, which curve and converge like an underground railway, are high and dark, painted with the hospital colours—greens and creams—favoured by the civil service; and above the corridors hangs a mass of piping and wiring, like the lower decks of a battleship.

This is the Treasury building, central citadel of Whitehall. If anyone were to wish to bring the British administration to a halt, it is on this building, rather than on parliament opposite, that he should drop his bomb.

Of all government departments, the Treasury is the most abused, mocked and disliked: for it is their job to say No. They are responsible not only for taxing the public, but for cutting down government expenditure, and for questioning every new project. They are abused, not only by the taxpayers, but by every Whitehall department—and most of all by the scientists, who regard the Treasury with venomous incomprehension. 'The Treasury can never be popular among Depart-

[1] *Reflections on the Constitution*, 1951. p. 184.

ments in every way',[1] Sir Laurence Helsby said, 'and indeed it would probably denote a serious failure on the Treasury's part if it ever did become popular.' Faced with this odium, the Treasury adopt, like judges, an attitude of resigned immunity. In the waiting-room of the Chancellor of the Exchequer is a framed quotation, intended, no doubt, to placate angry deputations demanding money:

> Friends and neighbours, the Taxes are indeed very heavy, and if those laid on us by the Government were the only ones we had to pay, we might more easily discharge them; but we have many others, and much more grievous to some of us—we are taxed twice as much by Idleness, three times as much by our Pride, and four times as much by our Folly; and from these Taxes the Commissioners cannot ease or deliver us.
>
> *Benjamin Franklin, 1758.*

No question of government has been more debated over the past few years than the proper rôle of the Treasury, in a succession of speeches, pamphlets, seminars and books. For the organisation of the Treasury involves the duality that has been at the heart of all governments since the impact of Keynes—that they should on the one hand save and control, but on the other hand lead the country towards expansion and growth. It is a conflict that lies inside every company, and every family, and there can never be a solution to it. But since October 1964 a new, or revived system has been operated in Whitehall—a major 'Department of Economic Affairs', to supervise expansion and planning. And this innovation, muddling and awkward though it seems, has brought out into the open, and into the political forum, the necessary conflict which before was concealed in the womb of the Treasury. The DEA, with the Deputy Prime Minister, George Brown, at its head, became in many respects more important and powerful than the Treasury: but the Treasury is so much part of the history and structure of government that it looms much larger in Whitehall.

TREASURY MEN

> The good Treasury man, I have always thought, ought to be very like a first-class common law barrister conducting a rigorous, but fair, cross-examination of an expert witness.
>
> *Sir John Woods, 1956.*

The most distinct species in Whitehall are the Treasury Men,

[1] *The Civil Service in Britain and France*, Hogarth Press, 1956. p. 114.

for they are the mandarins among mandarins. There are only about 1,400 people at the Treasury (compared to 7,000 at the Board of Trade and 57,000 in the Inland Revenue), but of those only about 150 are members of the Administrative Grade, and it is they who run the country's finances.[1] They are the pick of the civil service; the Treasury can take the cream of recruits, and later can steal men from other departments, or send its own men to run departments. Treasury men are known to be members of a chosen race, and apart from their actual power, this gives them an edge over the un-chosen.

The compactness of the Treasury astonishes American enquirers, compared to the complexity of Washington. The hundred-and-fifty all know each other, and information and reputations run through Great George Street as through a school. In the Treasury the literary, Oxbridge character of Whitehall has had its quintessence, exemplified by its previous head, Lord Bridges, son of a poet-laureate, Old Etonian, Fellow of All Souls. In the past ten years this atmosphere has been diluted by economists, grammar school men and war-time accretions: but some of the literary mystique remains. The Treasury is still half-way between a university and a business, and caught awkwardly between the two—without the academic standards of the first, or the practical engagement of the second.

The Treasury is an intellectual, not a social, élite; none of them belong to the world of interlocking relationships mentioned in the first chapter, and few are likely to be seen in the drawing-rooms of 'Society'. Most of them live in suburbs, and retire in the evening, with a bulging brief-case on a late train, to a simple meal and perhaps washing up. At lunch time they will either go to the Treasury canteen or walk across the park, down the Clive steps and up the Duke of York steps, to, probably the Reform Club. In one fortnight I had lunch with three Treasury men. Each of them said: 'Where shall we lunch—what about the . . . er . . . Reform?' I found Treasury men accessible, straightforward and with few pretensions. No group could be further from the power-hungry men of popular nightmares. Lord Snow has described in his novel *Corridors of Power* the cross-purposes between the two worlds of rich country houses, typified by Diana Skidmore's house, Basset, and of austere suburban houses of top Treasury men, typified by Douglas Osbaldiston.

[1] Even this is a huge increase over previous numbers: in 1914 there were only 35 Administrative Treasury men.

'Just as some men of Douglas's origins or mine set themselves up as country gentlemen, Douglas did the reverse. It was done out of deliberate unpretentiousness, but, as with the bogus country gentlemen, it was becoming a little of an act. When, over dinner, we told him that we had been at Basset for the weekend, he whistled cheerfully, in excellent imitation of a clerk reading the gossip column and dreaming of social altitudes inaccessible to him. Yet Douglas knew—for he was the most clear-headed of operators—that just as he suspected that places like Basset still had too much effect on government decisions, so Diana Skidmore and her friends had an identical, and perhaps stronger, suspicion about his colleagues and himself. Neither side was sure where the real power rested. In the great rich house, among the Christian names of the eminent, there were glances backwards, from the knowledgeable, in the direction of suburban villas such as this.'

The corporate spirit of the Treasury is still expressed by its legendary passion for music, which seems to fit with its withdrawn world, and un-musical men in the Treasury have an uneasy feeling that music is important to promotion. There is no longer, as there once was, a quartet of Treasury knights singing madrigals: but there is still a flourishing Treasury choir, which rehearses in a conference hall inside the building. 'The Treasury isn't as *establishmenty* as it was', said one of its political masters, 'but it's still rather cut-off: I think music has something to do with it.' Music also seems to be connected with the quiet detachment of Treasury men. As Samuel Brittan has put it: 'It is not done to show enthusiasm for any idea, or to take too seriously the national objectives discussed in the newspapers. The worst thing that can be said about a proposal is that it is "political", and the next worst that it is journalistic. The words "there is nothing new under the sun" seems to be written on the walls in invisible ink'.[1]

Sitting in offices round the central circular courtyard are the heads of the Treasury, the two 'joint permanent secretaries'. Until 1956, when Sir Edward Bridges, now Lord Bridges, retired, there was one man at the top; but since then the two provinces have become very separate. One joint is Sir Laurence Helsby, who, as we have already seen,[2] is Head of the Home Civil Service, in charge of the administrative machine. The other is Sir William Armstrong, who deals with the whole financial mechanism of the Treasury.

[1] Samuel Brittan: *The Treasury under the Tories*, 1964. (Penguins). p. 33.

[2] *See* p. 281.

Few men could better symbolise the political detachment of the Treasury than Sir William Armstrong. He is a quiet, very courteous, unassuming man who took over his job in 1962, with a spectacular leap-frog, at the age of only forty-seven. His background and career have been remarkable; his parents were officers in the Salvation Army, and he spent his childhood travelling round with them through the poor quarters of England, and carrying the banner for the processions—he was not musical enough to play an instrument. From this austere background he was suddenly dropped into prewar Oxford, with a scholarship to Exeter College. His mind was superbly efficient; he took firsts in Mods and Greats, and acquired an easy mastery of logic. But he was quite uninterested in politics, unmoved by the questions of unemployment or the Spanish Civil War, and he has maintained his political neutrality without any difficulty during his twenty-seven years in the public service. After the war—when he worked in the office of the War Cabinet—he became private secretary to the Chancellor of the Exchequer, always a key job, and served Cripps, Gaitskell and Butler. By 1958 he was running the Home Finance Department of the Treasury—a department of great complexity—where he was able to show his capacity for detached analytical thinking. When in 1961 plans were afoot to reorganise the structure of the Treasury, Armstrong submitted his own ideas; much of his scheme was accepted, and he himself was appointed to the top job, to institute the reorganisation of November 1962.

The reorganised Treasury is divided into two 'Sides' (the word 'side' is a favourite civil service category, reminiscent of school life) and four or five 'groups'. The chart overleaf shows how the Treasury was (in theory) organised at the end of 1964.

Sir Laurence's territory is reasonably self-contained, almost entirely concerned with running the civil service. Helsby reports direct to the prime minister, rather than the chancellor, on critical questions of reorganisations, dislodging permanent secretaries or expanding departments; under Sir Alec (who had little occasion to alter the machinery of government) such direct contact was rare, but under Wilson it has been much more frequent. Both the Pay and Management groups are mainly involved in internal problems, settling wage disputes, or discussing superannuation and perks; but the Management group has more scope for enterprise, in (for instance) putting forward schemes for reorganising ministries, and in recommending the promotion of 'high-fliers'.

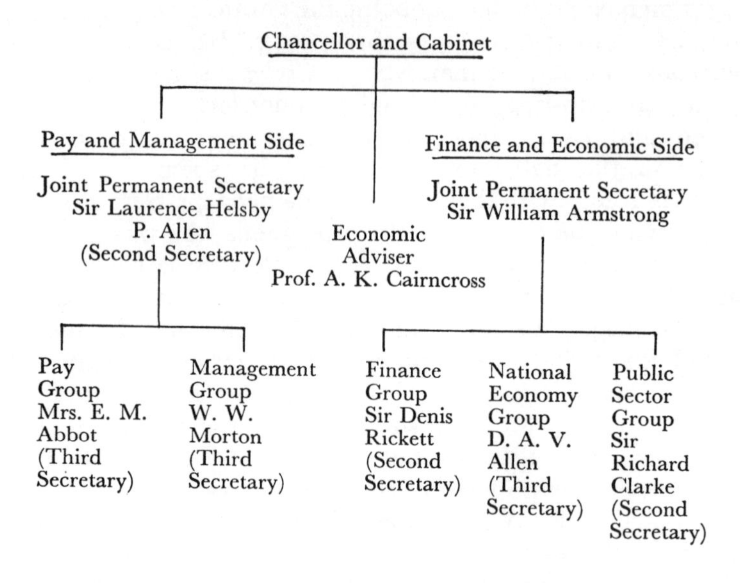

Sir William's side is more complex, and much less easy to chart, for it interlocks with other departments, with the outside world, and now with the Department of Economic Affairs. And it depends a great deal on the personalities of the Treasury Knights. The Finance Group is under Sir Denis Rickett, a suave and impressive mandarin from Balliol and All Souls, who has awed more than one chancellor. His field includes the whole field of monetary policy, relations with the Bank of England, and the defence of the pound; the group is proverbially conservative and cautious, and perpetually blamed for high bank rates and drastic budgets. The public sector is under Sir Richard Clarke, better known as Otto Clarke, a Cambridge mathematician who after a spell of financial journalism went into Whitehall during the war; he is known in Whitehall for his independent views and outspokenness in committees. His group is the hard core of the Treasury, concerned with controlling government expenditure in all the ministries and all the nationalised industries; and as such it is the butt of all argument about mean-ness, candle-ends and non-co-ordination.

THE TREASURY'S POWER

The traditional task of the Treasury has been to save the

government money: the chancellor must enforce the ancient parsimony of parliament, and this still makes up the largest part of the Treasury's job. It finances not only every Whitehall department, but also Covent Garden Opera, the National Theatre, the Royal Society, the Science Museum, the Tate Gallery, the Arts Council, the University Grants Committee: in all these places the Treasury, as their pinchpenny patron, is mentioned with special dread. Among the more picturesque items which appeared in the 1961–2 estimates were:

Salary of the Pursuivants, at £16 13s. 4d.—£50.
Engrossing and copying patents of Arms—£350.
Grouse Ecology Unit—£1,000.
£89 9s for the bishop of Sodor and Man to distribute among the incumbents and schoolmasters of the Isle of Man.
Creation money to Trinity College, Cambridge, for the counties of Cambridge and Huntingdon—£5 6s. 8d.
£1,000 compensation to Oxford and Cambridge for the loss of the privilege of printing and vending almanacs.

The time-honoured Treasury attitude to spending is summed up by 'candle-ends'—the phrase used by Gladstone to describe minute saving of detail. (In the eighteenth century, the stumps of Foreign Office candles were a perquisite of the housekeeper, who sold them to the gentlemen clerks to light their homes.) Much of the candle-ends attitude survives: Treasury men still enjoy 'teasing' other ministries, particularly the Foreign Office—forbidding an embassy refrigerator or a new coat of paint. 'The Treasury can argue for months on end with all the subtlety of Duns Scotus about what a day's subsistence allowance ought to be for Bogota', said a former Economic Secretary, Nigel Birch, 'but when really large sums are at stake there tends to be a certain withdrawal of interest.' This is always an ominous sign (as with Lord Avon at the time of Suez)—the swallowing of ends in a multitude of means.

While the Treasury have continued counting the pennies, the whole nature of their task has changed. In the nineteenth century the Treasury had to control the two fighting services and a handful of Whitehall departments. In 1886 Lord Randolph Churchill resigned because the cabinet would not approve a budget of £100 million (equivalent to about £500 million today). In 1964 the cabinet approved a Budget of £7,500 million. The Treasury found itself in a position to influence the whole character of the country, to discourage some industries and encourage others. 'Instead of worrying about candle-ends', said one ex-Treasury minister, 'they should have asked themselves the question "in what sense should Britain still be a great power?" ' But with their old aloofness from trade, the Treasury have been astonishingly slow to realise that they are, in fact, the holding company for the biggest group of businesses in Britain. The drastic techniques of investigation used by the big business corporations—for instance in the reorganisation of Shell[1] have filtered very slowly into Whitehall; the whole new science of 'organisation and management' was for a long time regarded—as one Treasury man put it—as 'third rate witchdoctory'. Gradually since the war the Treasury have been adjusting their methods. Since 1949 they have given more self-government to departments; they have paid less attention to candle-ends and more to investigation, and 'asking questions' about projects; and they have begun to make use of management consultants, computers and accountants to analyse their departments. A new wave of decentralisation followed the Plowden Report of 1961, which recommended (among other things) that the Treasury should leave the details of economics and costings to the permanent secretaries. Parliament, at the same time, has become less querulous, and has come to regard government expenditure less as a necessary evil, and more as an essential investment. 'Before the war both sides of the House were really against public spending', said one Treasury man: 'since the war they've both been *for* it.'

But the Treasury have never fully faced up to their vast new responsibilities. The common complaint about the Treasury's stranglehold is misleading: they cannot be more powerful than their Chancellor is in Cabinet. They have preferred, like Lord Lugard with African tribes, to practise 'indirect rule'—avoiding putting one of their own men in charge, controlling large spending through the local chieftain—while still keeping petty restraints—the relics of candle-ends. The reluctance to rule directly can be seen in their curious relationships with the Court of the Bank of England—regarded essentially as a foreign tribe—in their tolerant attitude to Parkinsonian tendencies, and in their astonishing cat-and-mouse games with the nationalised industries.

WHITE PAPERING

A persistent feature of the Treasury is secrecy: and this can be well observed in the character of White Papers—which are meant

[1] *See* Chapter 26.

to explain changes, but are in fact carefully devised to conceal them. Pronouncements about fundamental policy changes are made to appear as vigorous endorsement of previous policies. 'The Treasury is like the Vatican'—as one ex-Treasury economist explained to me—'whenever it says something new, it has to pretend that it's really just the same as before. Like the Pope, it must appear infallible.' When a White Paper appeared in April 1961, about the financing of nationalised industries, few laymen could guess that this marked a revolution in government policy. The Plowden Report of July 1961, was a revolutionary and critical document: but it appeared as a piece of amiable congratulation—'treading with such extreme delicacy'—in the words of *The Times*—'that its footsteps are scarcely audible'. This is a *locus classicus* of Treasury style. Here are some of its phrases, with what I have understood to be their actual meaning:

We hope that it is fully appreciated that . . .

You completely fail to realise that . . .

Greater emphasis should be laid on . . .

You haven't bothered to notice . . .

We have the impression that insufficient study has been given to . . .

No one has considered . . .

Our enquiry seemed to provide a welcome opportunity for discussions of problems of this kind . . .

No one had thought of that before . . .

We do not think there is sufficient awareness . . .

There is ignorance . . .

There has been a tendency in the past to overestimate the possibilities of useful short-term action in public investment . . .

You should look ahead . . .

There should be an improvement in the arrangements to enable ministers to discharge their collective responsibility . . .

The cabinet should work together . . .

This obscurantism is deep-rooted. It comes partly from the traditional 'kid glove language' of Whitehall, which always disguises instructions as suggestions, and instinctively prefers 'not inappropriate' to 'appropriate'. Departments are never *ordered* to do anything: they are 'invited to submit proposals . . .' Learning this language is part of the process of becoming 'house-trained' in Whitehall; and anyone who says straightforwardly what he thinks is likely to be labelled as a bull in a china-shop. Obscurity is encouraged, to avoid offending previous ministers and officials. I asked one Treasury man why, since the White Paper on nationalised industries was so important, it did not say so: he said 'But what would all the previous ministers think, if it appeared that they'd been doing it all wrong?'

Much of the fog conceals disagreement. When a report is unanimous, like the Devlin Report on Nyasaland, it is translucent: when it is a compromise, like the Radcliffe Report on the Bank of England, it is opaque. Important Whitehall documents all go through the process of toning down, passing from department to department, 'papering over the cracks' (in the Treasury phrase), until much of the original force—or even sense—has vanished. 'By the time the civil service has finished drafting a document to give effect to a principle', said Lord Reith, 'there may be little of the principle left.'[1]

Treasury men insist that this process is part of the machinery of democracy, and that the ambiguities stem from the chief committee of all—the Cabinet. The muzziness of White Papers expresses the muzziness of twenty men each trying to get his own way. But in the Treasury, fogginess has long ceased to be a temporary smoke-screen, and has become a permanent camouflage. To compare the Northcote–Trevelyan report, with its hard-hitting language about 'the unambitious, and the indolent or incapable', with modern White Papers, is to see how far the civil service has become turned in on itself. At a time when the Treasury, much more than ever before, needs to exhort and enlighten the public, the idea that White Papers are meant to inform the public and parliament has been virtually forgotten. They are written from one department to another, full of mandarin language, and in the process of fooling the public, one suspects that civil servants begin to fool themselves.

Another Treasury characteristic is the reluctance to abolish anything, or to cut down down anything which has become long-established. Anything once started acquires its own momentum, and (as Lord Plowden pointed out in his 1961 report) subsidies which were begun as a temporary 'pump primer' to revive a languishing industry have continued long after the purpose had faded. Few people can seriously doubt that the preposterous ramifications of the Ministry of Defence could not be cut down in

[1] J. C. Reith: *Into the Wind,* 1949.

size. Parkinson's Law seems to have become accepted as having a comic inevitability (it might even be said that the Professor himself, by showing how widespread it was, has encouraged acceptance of the Law). This acceptance would matter much less if ours was an age of unemployment and surplus funds. But the grim corollary of the Treasury's love of antiquities is their reluctance to launch anything new, and it is here that the Treasury's lack of imagination has been most alarming.

The Treasury's suspicions of novelties are most acrimonious in their relationships with science. They have still not quite recovered from the early days of the Atomic Energy Authority when the scientists—as is their way—asked for *carte blanche*, and to their astonishment got it: since then the Treasury have reacted with a special scepticism towards scientific ventures, and scientists and mandarins have been at odds.[1] The Treasury's contact with any scientific project, from jet fighters to Concord, is embarrassed by the fact that they have no scientists on their staff. Scientists angrily complain that their projects are turned down by Treasury committees containing not a single scientist, and they counter-attack by making outrageous demands for money, knowing that they will be cut by half—but finding them sometimes suddenly accepted. It is in scientific fields—the most foreign tribes of all—that the Treasury's indirect rule can be most dangerous.

Treasury men insist that in choosing between rival projects intelligent laymen, like cross-examining barristers, are just as competent as experts—who anyway never agree. But a huge new doubt about the Treasury's methods of control was raised by the Ferranti scandal of 1964 which, although blamed on the Ministry of Aviation, showed a hopelessly inadequate supervision by the Treasury. For in the Ferranti affair, millions of pounds were found to be authorised by middle-ranking civil servants, without any effective check on their methods of costing. Nothing more clearly illustrated the Treasury's schizophrenia.

THE BUDGET

The core of the Treasury's traditional rôle is the annual ritual of the budget. The Treasury's year revolves round the budget, as shops revolve round Christmas: the process begins months beforehand—preparing estimates for the departments, calculating the effect of taxes, working out priorities for future spending. At the

[1] *See* Chapter 20.

end of July a secret 'Budget Committee' (so secret that no one is supposed to know about it) starts meeting, including Sir William Armstrong, the Economic Advisor, and the chairmen of the Inland Revenue and Customs and Excise. At the end of November departments send their estimates to the Treasury and the Chancellor adds up the claims, and decides on the cuts he wants to make. 'I do not know whether you can visualise what the Treasury is like in December and January', one witness told the Select Committee of 1959, 'but it is absolutely chaotic.' By early February the chancellor begins to solidify his plans, in consultation with the prime minister and one or two other cabinet ministers; but the rest of the cabinet is only told on the day before the speech, when it is said to be too late for a change. Finally the tattered black box appears, held up in the air by a smiling chancellor in front of the photographers, and there is the marathon speech itself.

This is how the sum of £7,455 million, which was allocated in 1964, was raised and spent:[1]

REVENUE	£m.	EXPENDITURE	£m.
Income Tax	3,043	Defence	2,126
Surtax	195	External relations	199
Death Duties	310	Roads and Transport	340
Profits Tax, etc.	415	Employment, industry and trade	105
Tobacco	958	Industrial research and research councils	125
Petrol, Oil and Motor	801	Agriculture, fisheries and forestry	373
Alcohol	551	Housing and environment services	127
Purchase Tax	605	Arts	9
TV Advertisements and Betting	39	Law and order	139
Other Duties	252	Education	229
Non-Tax Revenue	286	Health and welfare	796
		Children's services	272
		Benefits and assistance	584
		National Debt, Sinking Funds, etc.	702
		Administration, etc.	375
		Total	7,388
		Surplus	67
	7,455		7,455

[1] Based on 'Financial Statement (1964–5)' pages 11 and 20–22, and 'Estimates 1964–5, Memorandum by the Financial Secretary to the Treasury' (Cmnd. 2290) pages 7–8.

ENTER PLANNING

Planning has become an emotional word. For myself, I have always rather liked it. *Harold Macmillan, December, 1961.*

The purpose of planning is to make things change. It must expose the consequences of doing nothing, show what must be done, and awake the will to get it done. *Sir Harry Douglass, September, 1964.*

But while the Treasury has been engaged in these traditional activities, it has uncomfortably become aware of a new situation. It is as if a rich man in a small country, running his estate in a thrifty and meticulous way, gradually realises that he is the only rich man left, that he accounts for half the country's wealth, and that he is printing money with one hand and spending it with the other. This is how direct government spending ('supply expenditure') has swelled, compared to Gross National Product:

1870	..	4 per cent
1910	..	6 per cent
1930	..	12 per cent
1960	..	22 per cent[1]

Including spending by local authorities, by the nationalised industries and by national insurance funds, the spending in the whole 'public sector' amounts to 42 per cent of the Gross National Product. And while their spending has grown, the government has accepted a much greater responsibility for the well-being of the country. In the words of the historic White Paper of 1944: 'The Government accept as one of their primary aims and responsibilities the maintenance of a high and stable level of employment after the war.' These new responsibilities have altered the whole significance of the budget. As the Plowden Report puts it: 'The budget is seen, not as a simple balancing of tax receipts against expenditure, but as a sophisticated process in which the instruments of taxation and expenditure are used to influence the course of the economy.'

This sophisticated process has brought the Treasury knee-deep into the mysteries of economic policy—the pressures, examples, incantations, exhortations and warnings which generate the economic climate. And with their massive new involvement in spending, they have found the initiative for monetary policy passing inevitably from the City of London to Great George Street. Like a large ship in a narrow channel, they have discovered to their alarm that the waves and currents are being created as much by

[1] *See Plowden Report* (Cmnd 1432), p. 6.

themselves as by the tide. Inflation has repeatedly undermined their plans for control: 'While they're arguing about messengers with one hand', said one critical former chancellor, 'they're printing millions of bank notes with the other . . . In one year wages have gone up by as much as the cost of three navies . . . In the last resort, the Treasury don't borrow money, they *print* it.'

The awareness of this new situation has brought with it the most controversial word in Whitehall—planning. The idea has ebbed and flowed since the war. Its first high tide was in 1947, under a socialist government, when Sir Edwin Plowden (later Lord Plowden of the Report) was Chief Planning Officer. Even before the end of Socialist rule, planning fell into disrepute, discredited by miscalculations and economic crises. Then, after a long lapse, thoughts of planning seeped back in 1961, and came in with a rush in October 1964.

Several factors changed the tide. The nationalised industries had obviously come to stay and, since they involved vast government spending, the Treasury had to forecast the needs of transport and power in ten years' time. The Federation of British Industries, a traditional stronghold of free enterprise, had come round to believe in the usefulness of planning. The government was deeply involved in research projects, most in defence, which might take a decade to fructify and which affect the future of whole industries. ('Can I see your plans for the next five years,' one Minister of Defence asked, on moving into the department. 'I'm afraid we haven't got any,' replied the civil servant.) And all kinds of government investment demanded longer periods of gestation. The building of teacher-training colleges now will affect the cost of education in *eight* years' time. 'It's like one of those balloons on Hampstead Heath, with bits sticking out', as one Treasury man explained it: 'it takes a very long time to blow up, and it comes out a very odd shape.' This big balloon has compelled the Treasury to think more in terms of five-year plans, and less in one-year budgets. Gradually the Treasury—and the cabinet—have been coming round to considering all government expenditure together, as a single plan.

But the government has become aware that it must not only co-ordinate its own finances and production, but those of private industry too. In the course of 1960 and 1961 the French idea of a *Commisariat au Plan*—of industrialists and civil servants together setting targets for economic growth—slowly filtered into Great George Street, stimulated by the Federation of British Industries and the National Institute of Economic and Social Research. The Treasury, in one of its slow corporate changes from one dogma to another, began to abandon old notions of non-interference, and new words like 'guide', 'pause' and 'regulator' began to be murmured. Late in 1961 a National Economic Development Council—generally known as Neddy—was set up with the help of the trade unionists and industrialists, to act as a mild British equivalent to the French *Commisariat*—to help to map out the industrial future of Britain. Its director-general was Sir Robert Shone, an enthusiastic planner from the Iron and Steel Board. Other members included six trade unionists, the chairmen of the Coal Board, and several of the more analytical tycoons—including Reay Geddes of Dunlops, Francis Cockfield of Boots, J. N. Toothill of Ferranti, and Maurice Laing, managing director of the Laing construction group, and one of the most forward-looking people on the Council. The economic director was Sir Donald McDougall, a widely-travelled Oxford economist.

It was the most important feature of Neddy that it should not be a part of the government, so that it could enjoy the trust and outspoken views of trades unionists and businessmen. It was (as Samuel Brittan has put it) to be a 'pressure group for growth', liberated from the Treasury in a separate place. Shone and McDougall set up a small staff of fifty, to act as the planning secretariat—some loaned from the civil service, others brought in from the universities. By the middle of 1962 Neddy had settled on the magic figure of four per cent per annum for their target for growth—to produce a fifty per cent increase in ten years. By February 1963 Neddy produced its first major report, the historic survey of 'Conditions Favourable to Faster Growth', the result of nine months' work and £100,000. The report proclaimed the four per cent growth rate over a five-year period, analysed the possible growth in seventeen key industries, and gave strong recommendations as to how greater growth could be achieved. They proposed higher unemployment pay, more government contracts to industry, a drastic change in the apprenticeship system, and more State spending in education and research. They also recommended the setting up of business schools, on the Harvard pattern, which was accepted in the following year.

DEPARTMENT OF ECONOMIC AFFAIRS

Neddy's separate career was short-lived, for by the end of 1964 its tentative moves towards national planning had become caught up in the great tide of planning generated by the Labour government, and its staff and functions were absorbed in the new 'Department of Economic Affairs' which became in essence a Ministry for Planning: it was known as 'DEA', or 'George Brown's Goddess'. The idea of the new ministry was not as new as it looked. It had been tried before, under the Labour government in 1947, when Sir Stafford Cripps became for a few weeks the Economics minister, with his own staff of economists and planners, to supplement the Chancellor of the Exchequer, Hugh Dalton. But soon afterwards Dalton leaked news of the Budget and had to resign, so that Cripps took over the Treasury, bringing with him his section of economists—which has stayed there ever since. The plan for a separate ministry subsided, but did not quite die; it depended a great deal on political personalities. But then, in 1963, the influential Fabian committee[1] on the reform of the civil service again took up the idea; and the desire for a new ministry coincided conveniently—though painfully—with Harold Wilson's problem of two political rivals,[2] George Brown and James Callaghan. Callaghan, the conscientious and popular, became Chancellor of the Exchequer, the job for which he had been 'shadow'; while George Brown, the 'human tornado', as Callaghan described him, was put in charge of the new Department, with immediate and widespread repercussions.

There were several definitions of the difference between the new Department and the Treasury. The DEA was to be concerned with long-term developments, the Treasury with short-term; the DEA was concerned with capital expenditure, the Treasury with current expenditure; the DEA was concerned with physical planning, the Treasury with financial planning. But in fact, of all the 'blurred edges' in Whitehall, this is the most blurred, and the outcome depends more on personalities than demarcations. Originally, George Brown had insisted that his department should be in a quite separate building, away from the atmosphere and influence of Great George Street; but the DEA was in fact accommodated in one corner of the Treasury building, previously occupied by the Ministry of Defence. Between the two ends of the building, George Brown's and James Callaghan's, the borderline, almost physically, moved to and fro. 'With George Brown over there, it's like having a bulldozer in the building,' a Treasury man complained.

Each side had strong support. With Callaghan at the Treasury

[1] *See* p. 265.
[2] *See* p. 112.

was the Chief Secretary, Jack Diamond, MP, a wealthy, sophisticated accountant from Leeds who brought with him a tough businessman's mind. Sir William Armstrong looked after the financial machine; and as Economic Adviser came Robert Neild, the radical economist from the National Institute of Economic and Social Affairs. On Brown's side were three of the ablest young politicians; Anthony Crosland, as Economic Secretary to the Treasury, was soon succeeded by Austen Albu, a former engineer and works manager; Maurice Foley, an under-secretary concerned with incomes policy, is a persuasive Irishman who (as director of the Ariel Foundation) has been much involved with Africa; while Bill Rodgers, parliamentary under-secretary in charge of regional planning, is frequently tipped as one of the most likely Labour leaders of the future. As his chief officials, Brown had Sir Donald McDougall, from Neddy, as his Director-General, who brought most of his staff with him; and as permanent secretary Sir Eric Roll, a subtle and cosmopolitan civil servant of extraordinarily varied experience. He came from Hungary, wrote books about money and politics, became Professor at Hull University, joined the civil service, played a key part in the British negotiations at Brussels, and then, after a spell at Washington as British financial representative, came back to Whitehall. Under the aegis of George Brown, Neddy was reconstituted, retaining many of its old members, but bringing in some new ones, including Sir Ronald Edwards of the Electricity Council; Kenneth Keith, the merchant banker; and Sir Peter Runge, president of the Federation of British Industries—all of whose names will recur elsewhere in this book.

Between the clusters of able and ambitious politicians, it is not easy to map the division between long and short-term plans, or to detect exactly where the central decisions are taken; and part of the complexity is indicated by the chart shown overleaf. For some time after October 1964 the reports from Great George Street indicated uncertain boundaries and nebulous functions. The critics of the new scheme maintained that it divided responsibility and created further confusions; its defenders maintained that it brought the disagreements that were inherent in the Treasury right up to the top, to be aired in cabinet; and that (in the words of Clement Leslie, a former Treasury PRO) 'an administrative symbiosis is coming into being'.[1] But what is clear is that the combination and interlocking of the two ministries had made the Treasury building more powerful than ever before in peacetime.

[1] *The Statist*, November 6, 1964.

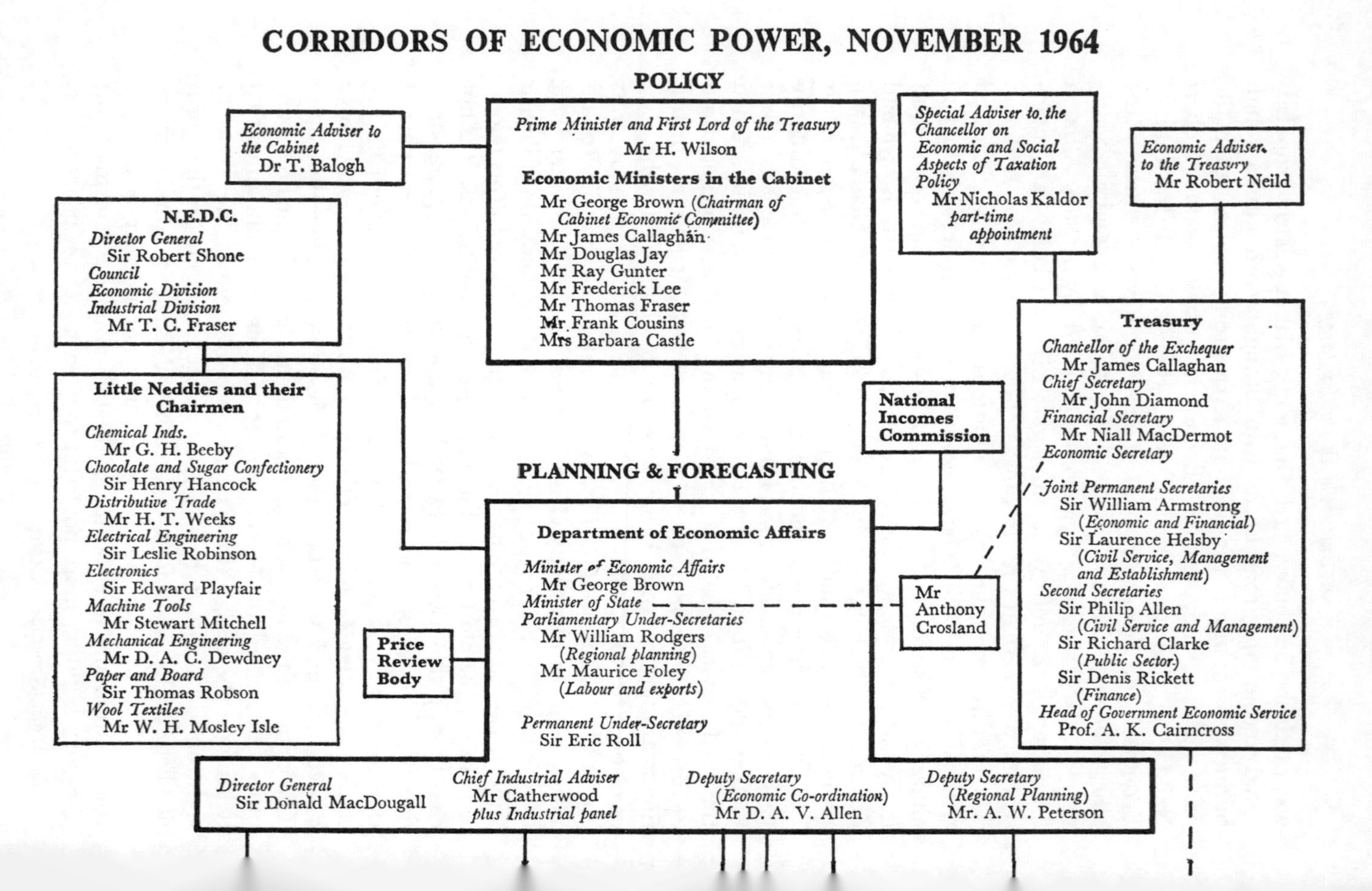
CORRIDORS OF ECONOMIC POWER, NOVEMBER 1964
POLICY
Economic Adviser to the Cabinet
Dr T. Balogh
Prime Minister and First Lord of the Treasury
Mr H. Wilson
Economic Ministers in the Cabinet
Mr George Brown (Chairman of Cabinet Economic Committee)
Mr James Callaghan
Mr Douglas Jay
Mr Ray Gunter
Mr Frederick Lee
Mr Thomas Fraser
Mr Frank Cousins
Mrs Barbara Castle
Special Adviser to the Chancellor on Economic and Social Aspects of Taxation Policy
Mr Nicholas Kaldor
part-time appointment
Economic Adviser to the Treasury
Mr Robert Neild
N.E.D.C.
Director General
Sir Robert Shone
Council
Economic Division
Industrial Division
Mr T. C. Fraser
Little Neddies and their Chairmen
Chemical Inds.
Mr G. H. Beeby
Chocolate and Sugar Confectionery
Sir Henry Hancock
Distributive Trade
Mr H. T. Weeks
Electrical Engineering
Sir Leslie Robinson
Electronics
Sir Edward Playfair
Machine Tools
Mr Stewart Mitchell
Mechanical Engineering
Mr D. A. C. Dewdney
Paper and Board
Sir Thomas Robson
Wool Textiles
Mr W. H. Mosley Isle
National Incomes Commission
Treasury
Chancellor of the Exchequer
Mr James Callaghan
Chief Secretary
Mr John Diamond
Financial Secretary
Mr Niall MacDermot
Economic Secretary
Joint Permanent Secretaries
Sir William Armstrong
(Economic and Financial)
Sir Laurence Helsby
(Civil Service, Management and Establishment)
Second Secretaries
Sir Philip Allen
(Civil Service and Management)
Sir Richard Clarke
(Public Sector)
Sir Denis Rickett
(Finance)
Head of Government Economic Service
Prof. A. K. Cairncross
PLANNING & FORECASTING
Department of Economic Affairs
Minister of Economic Affairs
Mr George Brown
Minister of State
Parliamentary Under-Secretaries
Mr William Rodgers
(Regional planning)
Mr Maurice Foley
(Labour and exports)
Permanent Under-Secretary
Sir Eric Roll
Mr Anthony Crosland
Price Review Body
Director General
Sir Donald MacDougall
Chief Industrial Adviser
Mr Catherwood
plus Industrial panel
Deputy Secretary
(Economic Co-ordination)
Mr D. A. V. Allen
Deputy Secretary
(Regional Planning)
Mr. A. W. Peterson

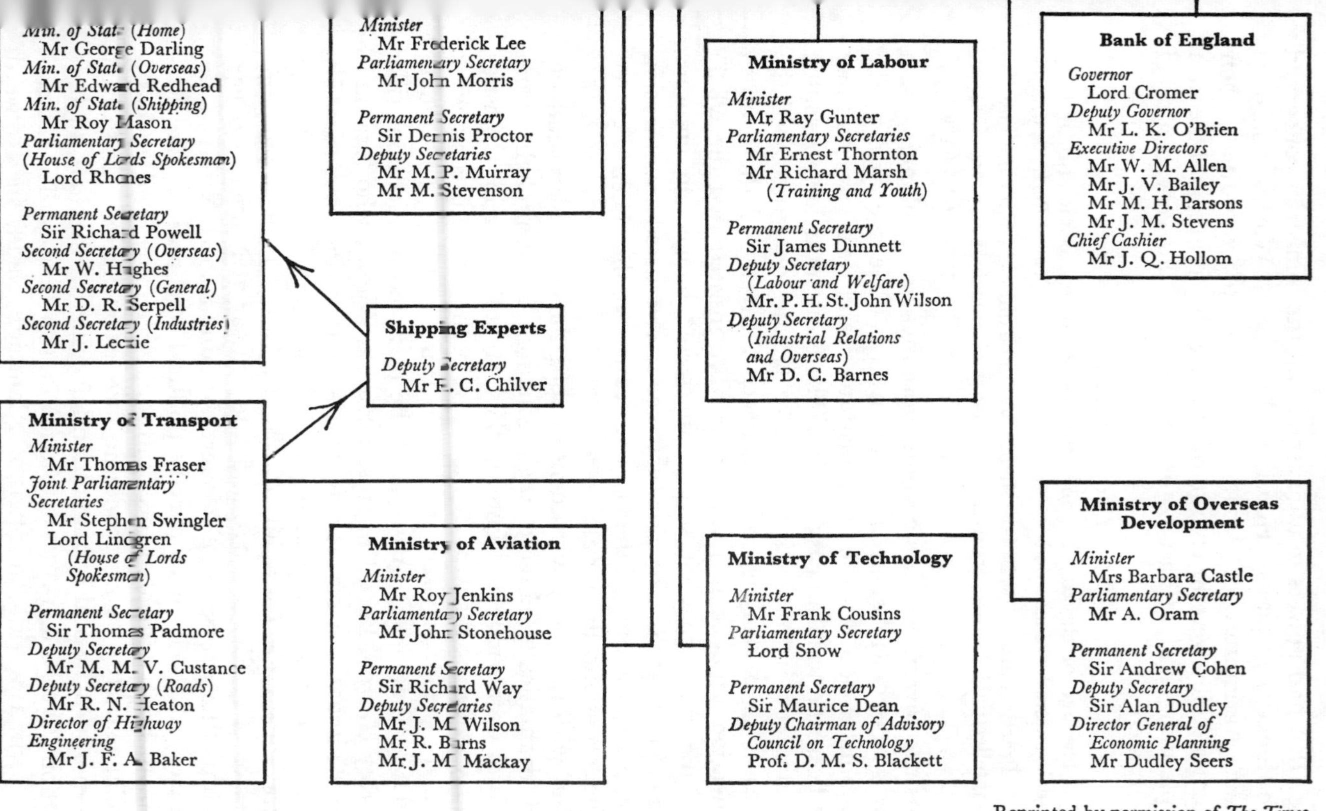

Reprinted by permission of *The Times*

The pattern of organisation of new and old economic departments, Ministries, and other related bodies is beginning to become clearer. The chart above traces the connections between them and shows who wields the ministerial and administrative power. The Department of Economic Affairs will, it appears, be the co-ordinating centre of the work of individual economic Ministries. It in turn will be guided by the economic ruminations of the Cabinet. * Mr Anthony Crosland although holding an official position in both the Treasury and the Department of Economic Affairs, will, it is believed, be solely concerned with the latter. † Mr Brown has stated that bodies will be established to study the structure of both wages and prices.

The DEA had powers to intervene in all the ministries concerned with long-term plans—Housing, Transport, Works, Board of Trade, Agriculture or Aviation—in order to co-ordinate their schemes. They were in charge of shaping the future, and the idea of planning had at last come to roost, in the very centre of government.

ECONOMISTS

The age of chivalry is gone; that of sophisters, economists and calculators has succeeded. *Edmund Burke, 1791.*

Practical men, who believe themselves to be quite exempt from any intellectual influence, are usually the slaves of some defunct economist. *Lord Keynes.*

As the government has become more involved in planning, so a new species has begun to settle in Great George Street—the economists. Between the 'administrators' and these experts there has been the usual uneasy rivalry. The economists have resented the amateur, ivory-tower aura (Lord Keynes once described the Treasury as being 'suspended between Heaven and the Scottish Education department'), and some have insisted that the whole machinery of the civil service must be changed to embrace economic thinking. The Treasury men have resisted any intrusion by experts, and only in the last few years have they been expected to be 'economically literate'.

But with the new government of 1964 the economists suddenly and dramatically entered their kingdom in Whitehall. From Oxford, Cambridge and London they came flocking in, almost as thickly as during the war. At the centre of the economists' network were the senior advisers in the Treasury building. Sir Donald McDougall at the DEA is one of the many economics dons (like Sir Roy Harrod, Lord Robbins or Harold Wilson) who first came into Whitehall during the war, and who have since moved easily between the two worlds of academics and administrators; he was a statistician for Churchill during the war, became economic director of OEEC in Paris, and later bursar at Nuffield College, Oxford—the All Souls of Modern Britain. Robert Neild, at the Treasury itself, is more overtly political and radical; like McDougall he is dedicated to expansionist planning, and he has a special expertise as an economic forecaster: he belongs to that group of urbane and cosmopolitan left-wing intellectuals, such as Anthony Crosland or Andrew Shonfield, who temper their radicalism with a worldly scepticism. Alongside Neild, in awkward partnership, was the economic adviser appointed when the Tories were in power in 1961, Professor Alexander Cairncross, a realistic, cautious Scot from Glasgow who had quietly strengthened the Treasury's economic contingent.

But apart from these more conventional appointments, Harold Wilson bravely introduced into the midst of Whitehall two spectacular and controversial Hungarian economists from Oxford and Cambridge. Dr. Thomas Balogh and Dr. Nicholas Kaldor had for years been favourite bogymen for the right, and although rivals and often at loggerheads, they had been associated firmly together, and nicknamed 'Buda' and 'Pest'. Like the two great Hungarian nuclear scientists in America, Teller and Szilard, they had helped to set the pace for each other: a definition that Teller enjoyed quoting is that 'a Hungarian is one who goes into a revolving door behind you, and comes out in front of you.' Balogh and Kaldor had been at the same model gymnasium in Budapest, and had emigrated in the twenties; their impact on Britain was astonishing; Balogh at Balliol, Oxford, and Kaldor at Trinity, Cambridge, had established legends as political dons, with their courts of admirers and periphery of angry critics.

In fact, they are very different characters. Kaldor is the quieter, the more academic, an expert on tax reform, for which he has advised many foreign governments boldly and controversially. He is a strong believer in fiscal weapons, and has advocated a capital gains tax and corporation tax. He moved into the Inland Revenue in Somerset House—under the umbrella of the Treasury—to advise on long-term plans for tax reform, with surprisingly little resentment from permanent civil servants. Balogh is a more political and unpredictable prophet, fascinated by power and its workings, and closely and loyally involved with Harold Wilson over the last ten years, all through his time in the wilderness. He came into the Cabinet Office with the special brief of Overseas Development, but he was in effect the prime minister's personal adviser. In Whitehall he was a startling apparition. He is a strikingly handsome man, crowned with tufts of white hair. He has vast charm, and a disarming habit of calling a lot of people 'darling'. He talks richly and persuasively, so that Oxford dons refer to three kinds of conversation: dialogue, monologue and Balogh. In economic policy he is a passionate believer in centralised planning to achieve faster growth. To many civil servants and conservatives, including the *Daily Express*, the arrival of the two Hungarians was an opportunity for excited xenophobia.

But it is very doubtful how far, in Whitehall, any single

economist or school of economists holds sway. Under the Conservatives, various academic economists had their say—Lord Robbins, Sir Roy Harrod, Professor Paish, apart from the Treasury experts. But their influence ebbed and flowed, and any two pundits very rarely agreed. It was an old joke that 'for every five economists there are six opinions—two of them Keynes's'. With the arrival of left-wing economists, there is a general agreement about some measure of central planning, but every kind of disagreement about methods of expansion and control: and on top of their arguments are the arguments inside a government bristling with economics dons—including the first-ever economist prime minister. The economists' invasion will certainly produce feuds and ructions throughout Whitehall, and economists' feuds can be almost as fierce as theological ones. But it has brought new air and new horizons into the mandarin world, and encouraged civil servants to think more in economic terms. And Wilson, with his cabinet and advisers, has the same kind of common economic language as Kennedy had with his Harvard dons.

TREASURY NETWORK

In any speculations about 'The Establishment' or 'They', the Treasury will always be the favourite target, for its complex combination of powers could easily become a conspiracy. It not only decides on economic and financial policies, and regulates the whole civil service; it has also a large influence on honours and quasi-government appointments (ranging from a director of the Tate Gallery to a director of British Petroleum), is the centre for the process of talent-spotting and approval of all the hundreds of men from outside the civil service who serve on committees and commissions. A secret tome of *The Great and the Good* is kept,[1] listing everyone who has the right, safe qualifications of worthiness, soundness, and discretion; and from this tome come the stage army of committee-people who are scattered through this book. The Treasury, like any school or college, has its grapevine, which records who is in, who is out; and for anyone who feels neglected, persecuted or underestimated it is not difficult to imagine his name in a Book of the Bad. The arrival of the Labour Party, with its new army of dons, outsiders and oddities, has done something to shake up the complacent isolation of the Treasury, and many hope that it will cause new and more daring names to be added to the tome.

[1] *See* Samuel Brittan, *The Treasury under the Tories*, p. 58.

But in some respects the Labour occupation has strengthened the notion of a Treasury network, though of a different kind to the earlier one. For between the politicians, the dons and the civil servants there is a greater like-mindedness, with the common background of the Oxford Economics School. And the strengthening of centralised planning inevitably puts a larger range of decisions into the hands of a few people at the top.

With the progress of planning, the Treasury has gradually come closer to industrialists and, at the same time, the influence of the traditional 'Treasury men', with Treasury attitudes, has been extended by the growing exodus since the war of senior mandarins into top industrial jobs—a process parallel to the 'parachuting' of the French *inspecteurs des finances* into private industry. The exodus began in 1951, when Sir Henry Wilson-Smith left to become Deputy-Chairman of Powell Duffryn, and Sir John Woods left the Board of Trade for English Electric; Sir James Helmore left the Ministry of Supply in 1956 for Warburg's Bank; his successor, Sir Cyril Musgrave, left to become Chairman of the Iron and Steel Board. In 1960 there was a greater shock when Sir Leslie Rowan, one of the Treasury knights, left for Vickers; and the next year Sir Edward Playfair, the head of Defence, became chairman of International Computers. In 1964, Sir Timothy Bligh, the prime minister's principal private secretary and a former Treasury man, left to become a director of the Thomson organisation. One firm, Tube investments, contains two formidable ex-Treasury men—Lord Plowden, the chairman and former chief planner in the Treasury; and Sir William Strath. Then there has been the steady migration from the Inland Revenue—a Treasury annexe—including Sir William Coates and Paul Chambers to ICI, and Francis Cockfield to Boots.

The main cause (as in France) is money. Permanent secretaries can earn more than twice £8,000 in industry: and since the war they have been allowed to keep their pensions if they leave after the age of fifty (they can now keep them earlier). The life of a tycoon is easier—there is less pressure of work, no parliament watching you, no minister in the way. There are fewer committees and less frustation, and some civil servants, like Sir Leslie Rowan, had become visibly impatient with the Whitehall machine. The powers in Whitehall insist that they are not much worried by the exodus, and regard it more as a compliment to the excellence of their senior civil servants than as a reflection on working conditions.

Until 1964 there was no corresponding flow of industrialists into

Whitehall; but after the election George Brown imported a group of businessmen into the DEA headed by Frederick Catherwood, formerly managing director of British Aluminium. After leaving Cambridge, Catherwood joined Costain's, the building firm, and quickly established himself as a 'whizz kid' of industry, with a ruthlessly analytical eye on costing and planning, in an industry which was notoriously pragmatic. He had also a Christian interest in social services and education, and became involved with Fabians and Labour politicians. In a book on 'The Christian in Industrial Society', published in 1964, he expounds his stern views on business behaviour and taxation, and advocates an expenditure tax: 'luxurious expenditure takes a disproportionate and unnecessary share of goods and services: it is both depraving and a social evil'. In October 1964 he was invited by George Brown to join the new Economic Ministry, at the age of only thirty-nine. Catherwood is a further link between Whitehall and Tube Investments, under the benign aegis of Lord Plowden.

The exodus has certainly helped to encourage a new closeness between the separate worlds of Whitehall and industry. Industrialists like to choose civil servants partly because 'they know their way around Whitehall'—which has growing powers over industry: but also because the industrial giants, as they develop from pioneering and brigandage into vast, settled corporations, feel the need for the patient, analytical intellects of Whitehall.

This cosiness between government and industry, and the spread of the Treasury net, is bound to cause a twinge of alarm. One can imagine a clutch of chairmen, from ICI, British Aluminium, Tube Investments, Powell Duffryn and Vickers (all of which have, or will have, ex-Treasury bosses), all talking their house-trained language, meeting at the National Institute, exchanging a few mathematical jokes, and then quickly settling the country's future with the dons, economists, Labour Oxford-type politicians, and a few tamer trade unionists. To anyone inclined to the conspiratorial view of history, it is a credible nightmare; and even to someone who is not, the exclusive like-mindedness of the mandarins looks like something which can easily turn into complacency and arrogance, of the kind so evident among the French *mandarinat*. But there remain powerful centrifugal forces keeping the groups apart, and there is not much sign as yet of a pact between the Treasury, the City, Industry and the Labour party. Each sector has suffered in the past from too narrow and blinkered a view of the others.

17

DIPLOMATS

If you are to stand up for your government you must be able to stand up to your government.

Sir Harold Caccia.

Dining is the Soul of Diplomacy.

Lord Palmerston.

A STONE's throw from the Treasury, between Whitehall and St. James's Park, is the oddest of all the Whitehall palaces, the Foreign Office. You come at it through an arch in Downing Street, opposite the prime minister's house, and into a great square Italianate courtyard surmounted by statues. At the north-west corner of the palace is a tall square tower, looking over the lake in St. James's Park. Inside, the building is still odder. It has the atmosphere of a provincial Italian museum. You walk through a hall of purple wallpaper, along long arched corridors and mosaic floors, past a room filled with ancient pneumatic tubes, till you come face to face with a marble grand staircase, with two tall alabaster statues at the bottom (one of George Villiers, Earl of Clarendon: one of the first Marquess of Salisbury). At the top of the staircase are huge faded frescoes: one of them, 'Britannia Sponsa', apparently depicts a rape, though called 'The Sea-farers claim Britain as their bride': another called 'Britannia Nutrix' shows a young mother suckling a disagreeable baby: a third shows a buxom girl pointing with a flourish to the word 'Silence'.

In the middle of the frescoes a high heavy door leads into a room, twenty feet high and thirty feet square: the walls are of pale green dotted with gold stars, and above the marble mantelpiece is a life-size romantic portrait of King George III. Round the room are distributed bits of Victorian furniture, deep leather armchairs, lamps, tables, and an old clock. In the middle is a big desk, covered with boxes, telephones, a reading-lamp, and writing paper. Inside this well-preserved museum a live Foreign Secretary works. From this desk, for the past hundred years, British Foreign Secretaries have watched the rise and fall of the

British Empire, two world wars, and the eclipse of Britain's international power.

How potent, one wonders, is the influence of architecture? The Foreign Office was designed by Sir Gilbert Scott to be a tall Gothic castle until the plans were turned down by Lord Palmerston. Will the attitudes of British diplomats become more enterprising when the Foreign Office is rebuilt, as it soon will be, in a more glassy and airy style? Certainly the architecture, with its high indivisible rooms which junior diplomats must share, has influenced the organisation of the Office, producing the boarding-school ethos of the 'Third Room'.[1] But it seems also to have encouraged the diplomats to assume that Britain's rôle, like the building, is aloof from the realities of the sixties. Nevertheless, when a choice had to be made between revamping the present building and putting up a new one the 'Office' came down firmly for the new.

Between the Treasury and the Foreign Office, the twin peaks of Whitehall, there is an old, unfriendly rivalry: they live in worlds as separate and unequal as the army and the navy. You can see both kinds walking across St. James's Park at lunch-time, both with bowler hats and umbrellas, but the Treasury men make for the Reform, while the diplomats go into the Travellers' next door—known in the Foreign Office as the 'works canteen', but with a more pretentious atmosphere than the Reform. The grandest diplomats go farther on to the St. James', with its backgammon and port.

Diplomats, alone of the civil servants, are independent of the Treasury in matters of promotion and policy, and they talk with special scorn of the *Home* Civil Service. Diplomats call themselves the 'F.O.', 'The Office' or simply 'The Service'. They used to be less separate: from 1919 to 1956, Sir Warren Fisher, Sir Horace Wilson and Sir Edward Bridges were Heads of the whole Civil Service, including diplomats, and they liked to interfere. But when Brook took over in 1956 he was announced as head of the *Home* Civil Service, and the Foreign Office were left to themselves, with their own private pyramid. The Treasury still have their revenge in 'teasing' the Foreign Office over their expenses.

The diplomats, though usually less important than Treasury men, are more self-important. Diplomats are aware of being, if not aristocrats themselves, the heirs to an aristocratic tradition: not clerks, but knights. Only since 1919 has it been possible to enter the Foreign Office without a private income, and there is still a

[1] *See* Lord Strang: *Inside the Foreign Office.*

family-circle feeling. Diplomats know each other by Christian names, exchange chatty telegrams, or cosy letters beginning 'Dear Chancery' and ending 'Yours ever, Far Eastern Department'. Unlike permanent secretaries, who remain anonymous to the end, diplomats write *belles lettres*, or little monographs concluding, after mature reflection, that British diplomacy is the best. Two books of diplomats' memoirs were called *The Inner Circle* and *The Ruling Few*. (Sir David Kelly wrote *The Ruling Few* and *The Hungry Sheep* —sometimes unkindly confused as *The Ruling Sheep*.) Diplomats abroad are inclined to regard themselves as representing not the United Kingdom but the Foreign Office; and in London (one civil servant complained) they regard every other department—including 10 Downing Street—as a Foreign Power, to be bullied or cajoled according to their strength.

Many diplomats marry foreign wives, often well-to-do, as a result of spending their lives in expensive society abroad. They have to have the consent of the office to marry a foreigner. Iron Curtain wives, or Jewish wives in Arabic countries, cause difficulties, but American wives are often a diplomatic asset.

About a thousand people (including women) serve in the senior branch of the Foreign Service, 'the size of a large public school'—as one of them put it. They are bound together by their Oxbridge background; by the intimacy of Third Rooms; by the perpetual round of embassy parties; and by the flow of telegrams which provide a school magazine, welcoming contributions. Everyone's ambition is to get 'into print'—so that their despatches are circulated to all posts abroad. This corporate spirit—like the Treasury's—has advantages. Members speak the same (Oxbridge) language and understand each other quickly and subtly. The Foreign Office can transact business more quickly and with many fewer cross-purposes than the Americans, for instance. British diplomats are intelligent, hard-working and dedicated: at seven p.m. most lights are still on in the palazzo. They give some evidence of being what they so often claim to be—the best foreign service in the world.

But this closed, collegiate society, like the Treasury's, has serious snags. 'A young man who goes into the Foreign Office at twenty-one,' one ex-ambassador has said, 'has a change of life at twenty-seven.' Several factors induce this social menopause. The intensity and isolation of embassy life and entertainment—the nightly round of cocktail parties, the formalities and protocol—all contribute to the diplomat's lassitude: 'Diplomacy is easy on the brain,' one American remarked, 'but hard on the feet.' 'Depends which you use more', said another. Young British diplomats soon lose their curiosity, usually after their third posting, and achieve a lack-lustre expression, an immunity to new experience and new people, and above all an absence of zeal: young recruits are still reprimanded with a reminder of Talleyrand's famous instruction —'*pas trop de zèle*'.

'Some reduction in the extent of national day celebrations is desirable,' said the Plowden Report of 1964, wistfully. This list of celebrations in the second half of June gives some idea of the growing burden:

June 17—Anniversary of the establishment of the Republic of Iceland.
German day of Unity.
18—Battle of Waterloo.
19—*Dia de Artigas* (Uruguay).
Kuwait National Day.
20—Independence day of the Republic of Senegal.
21—Luxembourg National Day.
22—National Tree Day (El Salvador).
24—Soviet aviation day.
25—Proclamation of the Independence of the Malagasy Republic.
27—Buddhist festival of POSON.
28—Canadian Army day.
Treaty of Versailles anniversary.
29—Name day of the King of the Hellenes.
Polish Navy day.
30—Anniversary of the Revolution of Guatemala.
Independence Day of the Republic of Congo (Leopoldville).

Behind its façade of an aristocratic club, the Foreign Office has changed more than it likes to be known. Firstly, in one man's lifetime it has expanded fifteen-fold. In 1914 there were only 176 people in the Office in London, including forty doorkeepers and cleaners, and only 450 in the diplomatic and consular missions abroad. By 1964 there were over 10,000 people, and the annual cost of running the whole overseas services (according to the Plowden Report) was about forty million pounds—nearly half what the government spends on universities. This colossal expansion, at a time when Britain's power has steadily diminished, exercises the Treasury. Diplomats blame the complexity of modern embassies—the tiresome need for financial, military, technical experts, the growing involvement of the state with economic affairs, the sheer increase in numbers of countries.

Secondly, diplomacy is no longer a question of negotiating secret agreements only between the chancelleries of the 'Inner Circle': it has become sullied with much more vulgar and technical matters—helping exports, negotiating loans, propaganda and salesmanship—where *zèle* is all-important. And diplomats have had to come to terms with *publicity*. Journalists and diplomats are traditional enemies—the Montagues and Capulets of foreign affairs—and if asperity is detectable in this chapter, this may explain it. Diplomats regard journalists as backstairs intruders, liable at any moment to wreck negotiations. Journalists divide diplomats into two classes—those who tell but don't know, and those who know but don't tell: and the matter is complicated by the repressed desire of many journalists to be diplomats, and of diplomats to end up as journalists.

NEW DIPLOMATS

How far has a new kind of diplomat appeared to meet the new situation? Diplomacy has always been the most aristocratic of all government professions, and in the nineteenth century foreign policy was described by John Bright, in a famous phrase, as 'neither more nor less than a gigantic system of out-door relief for the British aristocracy'. Until 1919 wealth was vital, intellect suspect; Sir David Kelly described how when he went before a selection board in 1914, he overheard the examiners saying, 'Good Lord, he got a first!'

Then in 1941, in the worst part of the war, Sir Anthony Eden, with support from diplomats, set up a committee to advocate reform. One wonders how Britain found time then—and so little time now—to think about so many future problems? It was the time of the Beveridge Report, the Colonial Development Corporation, the Fleming Report on public schools, and other radical thinking ('When a man is about to be hanged,' Dr. Johnson said, 'it concentrates his mind marvellously'). A revolutionary White Paper eighteen months later said (in language which itself has a war-time, Churchillian flavour):

> Among the criticisms which have been brought against the Diplomatic Service, the view has been expressed that it is recruited from too small a circle, that it tends to represent the interests of certain sections of the nation rather than those of the country as a whole, that its members lead too sheltered a

life, that they have insufficient understanding of economic and social questions, that the extent of their experience is too small to enable them properly to understand many of the problems with which they ought to deal, and that the range of their contacts is too limited to allow them to acquire more than a relatively narrow acquaintance with the foreign peoples amongst whom they live . . .

These criticisms are often overstated (the White Paper went on): it is, however, true, that the conditions which the Diplomatic Service originally grew up to meet no longer exist unchanged in modern international affairs.

As a result, the 'Eden-Bevin' reforms emerged after the war. Four separate branches—diplomatic, consular, commercial, information—all became interchangeable. Men could be promoted from consulates, or from junior grades, to become ambassadors. Recruits were to be chosen not simply by written examination and interview, but by thorough psychological tests—based on the war-time WOSB tests. A second language was no longer required. Older diplomats who had not come up to scratch could be discreetly retired with a pension before the age of sixty; and in the next twenty years ninety actually *were*. And *women* were to be admitted to the senior grade. (The arrival of senior women has been smooth, but has produced regional problems. 'If a girl diplomat asks you to dinner in South America,' said one foreign office man, 'you naturally bring your toothbrush and pyjamas.') Although there has been no great rush of women into the Foreign Service, the innovation has been quite successful. 'We received no evidence,' said the Plowden Report of 1964, 'which would suggest that women in the Foreign Service have proved "tender plants".'

The reforms seemed impressive enough: and yet the complaints in the 1943 White Paper—about the narrow circle, the lack of specialists, the seclusion—are still to be heard, even in Whitehall. The Foreign Office is still lacking in economists, and diplomats are still reluctant to talk to non-diplomats. In 1963 there were still only 27 members of the Foreign Service with degrees in Science.[1] Diplomats have been inclined to be too busy mixing with the ruling circles, like Farouk or Batista, to notice potential new rulers, like Nasser or Castro. Their social narrowness, one suspects, helps to explain the insensitivity to new frontiers. The Office is full of experts on nineteenth-century history, but when the Congo be-

[1] Plowden Report, para. 361.

came independent in 1960 hardly a single man in London knew the difference between the two factions, or could make sense of the stream of crisis cables.

The question of specialisation was one of the matters considered by the Plowden Committee, set up in 1962 to have a look at the overseas services, under the chairmanship of the ubiquitous Lord Plowden, and including two former diplomats (Lord Inchyra and Sir Percival Liesching), two MPs (Arthur Henderson and Sir Charles Mott-Radclyffe), a banker (Lord Harcourt) and a director of Unilevers (A. D. Bonham Carter). The committee were much more cautious and circumlocutory than their predecessors twenty years before; but they were clearly sensitive to the charges of amateurism in British diplomacy, and, in 1964 they reported, in kid-glove terms, that 'the reformers of the Foreign Service in 1943 were less successful in dealing with the problem of specialisation than they were in most other directions,' and concluded 'that the pendulum was allowed to swing too far away from specialisation in the post-war years, that the readjustment now taking place is necessary, has some way to go and should be pressed ahead vigorously.'[1]

The Committee were also surprised by the lack of actual training for diplomats: 'Training in the overseas services has cost remarkably little,' they said, with a hint of a Treasury smile, 'partly because not enough has been done';[2] and they revealed that the Foreign Office spent less than £45,000 a year on training programmes (including their share of the Middle East Centre for Arab Studies); while the Commonwealth Relations Office spent only £4,200 a year. The Committee went so far as to suggest that a further £50,000 a year should be spent on training, and that (among other things) diplomats should spend up to three months learning about a country and its language before being sent there.[3] They also decided that it would be sensible for diplomats to stay in one place for four or five years.[4] (Why, one wonders, has it taken so long for the Foreign Service to reach this obvious conclusion?)

Some diplomats seem to imagine that they are in the midst of a tremendous social upheaval: 'Today it is as difficult for an aristocrat to enter the Foreign Service,' said Sir Harold Nicolson

[1] Cmd. 2276, para. 188.
[2] *ibid.*, para. 403.
[3] *ibid.*, para. 418.
[4] *Ibid.*, para. 190.

in 1961, 'as it would be for a camel, loaded with the bales of Eton and Balliol, to pass through the eye of a needle.'[1] But in fact, Eton provides more diplomats than ever. Between 1935 and 1938, six successful candidates came from Eton, six from Rugby and five from Winchester: between 1958 and 1961, seven came from Eton, five from Rugby and seven from Winchester.[2] True, twice as many men go in to the Foreign Office as before the war, and the extra numbers are partly made up by grammar school men. But the Plowden Committee showed that, between 1952 and 1962, 70 per cent of the successful applicants for the Senior Branch came from independent public schools, 8 per cent from direct grant schools, and 20 per cent from maintained schools. The range of universities was even narrower; during the same period, 94.2 per cent came from Oxford or Cambridge, and 59 per cent from Oxford alone: 'the rather wider spread of recruitment from schools,' they reported, 'has not been matched by a comparable spread of recruitment from universities.' They found no evidence of a bias against 'non-Oxbridge' candidates, and decided regretfully that 'if the Foreign and Commonwealth Services want, as they do, recruits of high quality, they are bound to find a high proportion of them at Oxford or Cambridge'; they also suggested, rather surprisingly, that one reason that more Redbrick graduates did not apply was because 'the ambitions of a large number of able men who graduate from universities other than Oxford or Cambridge are deterred just as much by the '*misères*' of Foreign Service life as by its supposed '*grandeurs*'.

Out of 78 ambassadors and senior Foreign Office officials in 1961, 63 had been to public school, and with the exception of a deputy secretary, Ralph Murray, the others were all in smaller embassies. Very few ambassadors have had outside jobs: D. A. H. Wright was once an advertising man for Senior Service; Con O'Neill has resigned from the Foreign Office twice—once to become leader-writer on *The Times*. Fifty-nine of the ambassadors went to Oxbridge, seven to London, and none to any other English university.

The new flow of grammar school men has been disguised by the influences of the Office—the pressure of the 'Third Room', the cocktail parties, the social menopause; and the powerful influence of the old-style ambassadors, suppressing zeal, recommending the Travellers' Club, has confused new men with the old. Nor has the

[1] 'The Old Diplomacy and the New.' David Davies Memorial Institute, March 1961.
[2] *Daily Telegraph*, July 12, 1961.

merging of the diplomatic and the consular services been as complete as it appears. The old diplomats soon detected an unease among ex-consuls, did little to alleviate it, and called it *consulitis.*

Gradually those double-barrelled names which move through the pages of diplomats' memoirs—Sir Hughe Knatchbull-Hugessen, Sir Eugen Millington-Drake, Sir D'Arcy Godolphin Osborne, have diminished. A few names would still look well in a romantic comedy—Sir Herbert Gamble, Sir Roderick Barclay, Sir Geofroy Tory, Sir Moore Crosthwaite—and ambassadors still have a remarkable faculty for emerging with bizarre Christian names when they are knighted; but there are now many more Sir Johns, Sir Pats, or Sir Franks.

Old diplomats also complain that the new men are bringing with them a new conformity; and that, in their unease, they are *plus royaliste que le roi.* They like to reminisce about the grand eccentrics, like Sir John Balfour, the witty former ambassador to Madrid with a bushy moustache, who had a large repertory of risqué songs about Franco and Peron: or Sir Andrew Gilchrist, the bearded and brave ex-ambassador to Iceland, who placated an angry crowd by playing bagpipe music, and sent back witty, important, cables about cod; and who has since acted with similar panache in Djakarta.

There is still a good deal of variety in the Foreign Service. I found diplomats much more willing to talk freely about their service than home civil servants, and events like Suez or Katanga arouse widespread discontent, and stimulate the Office rebels. But inevitably the growth of bureaucracy, committees and telephones has given foreign ambassadors—like judges or tycoons—less scope for eccentric individuality. The greatest blow to eccentricity came when Burgess and Maclean disappeared. In the next four years nine hundred senior diplomats were examined and checked; four were asked to leave the service and six others moved to less important jobs. Nowadays the Foreign Office is much more security-minded: every few weeks a notice appears in the arched corridors, to warn people not to leave papers on their desk, even though the doors are locked:

SECURITY NOTICE

WINDOW CLEANING TODAY

AMBASSADORS

An ambassador is an honest man sent to lie abroad for the good of his country.

Sir Henry Wotton (Ambassador to James I).

The Foreign Office itself is a 'department' of state: but it is divided into 38 sub-divisions, ingeniously called 'departments'. There are ten political departments, each dealing with different parts of the globe. The 'Northern' department includes Russia; the 'Eastern' department includes Persia; the 'Central' department covers Iceland and Turkey. Most people, from the Foreign Secretary downward, are called secretaries (there is a Principal Private Secretary to Her Majesty's Principal Secretary of State for Foreign Affairs). A young man works his way up from being third secretary to second secretary to first secretary (no relationship to a first secretary in the Treasury), to 'counsellor' and then—if he is lucky—to 'minister'.

The old-style ambassadors, whatever their nationality, live grandly in surroundings which since the eighteenth century have become deep-frozen so that, like Oxford colleges, they and their families have become a temporary subsidised aristocracy, leading more ducal lives than most dukes, and popping in and out of the gossip-columns, as part of the fantasy-life of Britain. They are called 'Your Excellency' and half are knighted, with a KCMG. Abroad, they represent the Queen and thus have precedence at table over cabinet ministers. As a status-symbol, they remain unbeatable—witness the names of night-clubs, cosmetics, hotels, cigarettes, all over the world.

But they are not what they were. Firstly, there has been a spectacular inflation: before 1914 there were 9 British Ambassadors: in 1939 there were 17: by 1965 there were 84 (including the ambassador to the Common Market). Some smaller states (such as the Vatican) are still allowed only 'ministers plenipotentiary', but they feel increasingly insulted if they do not have an ambassador. Iceland for instance actually has an ambassador with a staff of four, and a consul and two vice-consuls, for a population of 170,000—rather less than Croydon's. Secondly, the grandest ambassadors are no longer necessarily the most important. The august ambassadors of the 'inner circle', in Paris, Bonn, Rome and Madrid are no longer very crucial. Their diminution began with the electric telegraph (the telegraph to Constantinople was built as early as 1870), but it has only recently become more apparent, accelerated by jet planes and telephones. 'The Paris embassy isn't really so important now,' said one former Foreign Secretary, 'if anything serious happens, you can get over there in an hour. It's some of the smaller places, in the Middle East or South America, where the ambassador can play a really important rôle.' This situation has produced a discrepancy between the dignified and the efficient parts of the Foreign Office. On the one hand are the ancient embassies, with pomp (codified by the Congress of Vienna), chandeliers and colossal '*frais de representation*', but dwindling political importance. On the other hand are the small new embassies in remote capitals, without protocol but with perpetual crises. Gorgeous but unimportant posts are useful to the Foreign Office, for they provide a dignified upstairs, a kind of House of Lords. On the other, dumping deadbeat diplomats in remote capitals is now very dangerous: for the most unlikely countries, like Cuba or Laos, can suddenly prove troublesome. 'No more Nicaraguas now,' as one diplomat said.

A new kind of ambassador has emerged with the boom in new countries—mostly in Africa—in the past six years. Odd-sounding capitals suddenly appeared on the map—Conakry, Tananarive, Yaounde, Abidjan, Mogadishu. This explosion of independence sent a breeze through the Foreign Office: they found themselves called upon at a few weeks' notice to provide complete new embassies, and a new kind of diplomacy. Young diplomats, instead of arranging *placements* for dinner parties, or writing witty marginalia, were faced with finding an office to work in, paper to write on and discovering who was running the country—without even a *chef de protocol* to help them. Some of them even had to cope with several countries at once, like country vicars with their parishes. Thomas Shaw must have his hands full as Ambassador to four places—Ivory Coast, Dahomey, Niger and Upper Volta.

In the young countries ambassadors have to be reporters as much as negotiators, watching for signs of trouble and change, and often salesmen and PROs as well. In Iron Curtain capitals the scope for negotiation is tiny and the embassy is largely a listening post to register the tremors of summit opinion. In the past, it was part of the arrogance of the ruling classes to send out ambassadors who couldn't speak the language. Now, all the senior men in Moscow speak Russian, and most in Tokyo speak Japanese.

PARIS AND WASHINGTON

Theoretically the twin peaks of the profession are Paris and Washington. The Paris embassy is the grandest of all: the ambassador occupies a superb mansion, bought from Napoleon's sister and inhabited by the Duke of Wellington, and now jealously watched by the Treasury. It has a courtyard in the Faubourg St. Honoré, a hundred yards from de Gaulle's Elysée Palace, and a long garden leading down to the Champs Elysées. There is a large ballroom, a row of reception rooms full of *boiserie*, flunkeys and bits of the English set in Paris. It is a far more lavish establishment than 10 Downing Street, and it induces folie de grandeur in its incumbents. The Paris Embassy is more practical and down-to-earth than it was, but it still suffers from the kind of illusions and emotions that go with the architecture. After the collapse of the Common Market negotiations in 1963, a wave of ineffectual bitterness swept through the Embassy; Francophiles suddenly turned Francophobe, enormous rumours were circulated about de Gaulle's next intentions, and the pique reached its silly peak when Princess Margaret was advised to cancel her visit to Paris. Afterwards the Embassy recovered some of its sang-froid, but remained sadly isolated from the centres of French affairs. Some expectations of change attend the new ambassador, Sir Patrick Reilly, a quiet shy man with a steep head who was once ambassador to Moscow. He is not a bold showman or salesman, and he comes from a quite orthodox background: his father and father-in-law were both out in India, and he went to Winchester, New College and All Souls. But he is realistic, cool and very clever, and well able to keep pace with the subtleties of French diplomacy.

In a class by itself is Washington: for since the war the one central plank of British foreign policy—albeit a wobbly one—has been the maintenance of the Anglo-American alliance. The Washington embassy has a staff of no fewer than 500, including five diplomats with the rank of minister, and not including the web of consulates and information offices spread over the States. The Washington embassy itself, a huge pillared palace designed by Sir Edwin Lutyens, is (as one ex-Foreign Secretary put it) a kind of microcosm of Whitehall, with a big office block attached to it. The total cost of the embassy and consulates is £1,692,000 a year—more than half the total grant to the Arts Council.

The new ambassador to Washington, Sir Patrick Dean, is a career diplomat—unlike his predecessor Lord Harlech, who was appointed by Harold Macmillan, and who belonged to the close network of interlocking families of Macmillans, Cecils, Devonshires and Kennedys. Dean, like so many other top diplomats, comes from a donnish background. His father was Master of Trinity Hall, Cambridge, and he himself taught law at Cambridge, and practised as barrister for five years in London. He came into the Foreign Service as a legal adviser during the war, and was part of the prosecuting team at Nuremberg. After the war he spent most of his time in back-room posts in London, and had his first ambassadorial job at the United Nations in 1960. As an official in London, he had been involved in the Suez operation in 1956 which has (unfairly) been held against him; but at the U.N. he was popular, modest, and visibly sensitive to the views of Afro-Asians. He is a tall, untidy, vague-looking man, still with a touch of the don about him. He is not a great projector of personality, but he has kept the capacity (rare in older diplomats) of friendly listening.

As the senior ambassadors have become less influential so the London headquarters have become more so, and diplomacy has found itself mixed up with bureaucracy. Only since the first world war, in fact, has the permanent under-secretary and his London staff emerged 'from clerkly bondage'[1] to become important advisers: Lord Salisbury, for instance, in the 1890s, never consulted his PUS on any matter of importance. But it is arguable that the most influential diplomats today are not the ambassadors but the group of senior men in London—Sir John Nicholls, Sir Geoffrey Harrison, Sir Bernard Burrows, Lord Hood, Sir Charles Johnston, Sir John Coulson. And there is also the most unknown influence of all, the Foreign Secretary's principal private secretary (at present Nicholas Henderson, a witty and independent character) who can by his sheer closeness to decisions often out-influence everyone else.

Probably the most important is the permanent under-secretary, the chief official adviser to the Foreign Secretary. In 1965 part of the job was taken by the new 'Head of Her Majesty's Diplomatic Service', Sir Saville Garner, who came from the Commonwealth Relations Office to look after the unification of the services. But that job is purely administrative, and the permanent under-secretary remains the policy adviser. The new PUS is Sir Paul Gore-Booth, a striking man with huge ginger eyebrows, and a

[1] *See* Lord Strang: *The Foreign Office*. p. 147.

powerful nose. Sir Paul comes from an orthodox diplomatic background, Eton and Balliol, and went straight into the service. Like Dean he made his reputation largely as a back-room thinker and organiser, particularly in international organisations: during and after the war he took part in the formative conferences about food, UNRRA, international finance, and the United Nations. Later he became ambassador to Burma, and then (after an interval in London) to New Delhi, which he left in 1965 to take up the top job. Sir Paul is a reflective man, a Christian Scientist, with quite strong political views of his own, particularly on Afro-Asian questions; he can sometimes appear pompous, but he is original, conscientious, and very aware of the future.

The PUS, like his opposite numbers in Whitehall, is proverbially overworked; he is, as Lord Strang (a former incumbent) has put it, at the top of a gently-sloping pyramid: 'the apex of a pyramidal structure of the administrative kind becomes the more uncomfortable to occupy, the more gently the sides of the structure slope.'[1] In the Foreign Office there is the same grindstone attitude, the same dislike of unattached thinking, as in the Home Civil Service, but intensified by the extra pressure of telegrams—which give to the Foreign Office, as to a TV studio or the Stock Exchange, a perpetual atmosphere of haste: 'If there is one sense that rules in the Foreign Office,' wrote Lord Strang, 'it is a sense of urgency.' (It is symbolic of the urgency that the library is tucked away in a dingy block south of the river.) World events provide the constant stimulus of diplomacy. 'The most important decisions,' wrote one diplomat, Sir J. Headlam-Morley, 'are often made, not as a part of a concerted and far-sighted policy, but under the urgent pressure of some immediate crisis.' Decisions which might from the outside look bold, from the inside look merely inevitable. In Lord Strang's words: 'Events are very strong.'

The Foreign Office have always had an aversion to long-term plans. Bevin, when he was Foreign Secretary, started up a planning department, but this lapsed, and has only recently been revived, and long-term ideas still find great difficulty in making themselves heard above the daily din. In the long chain-reactions of the past ten years—the collapse of Middle East régimes, the retreat from one base to the next (from Suez to Cyprus to Aden to Kenya) the emergence of independent Africa, the wave of unrest in South America, the officials have always thought it mildly improper to put up bold, five-year plans to their political

[1] *The Foreign Office*, p. 198.

masters. 'I distrust anyone who foresees consequences and advocates remedies to avert them,' said Lord Halifax before the war; and this old English pragmatism is still glorified. It is not easy, it is true, to imagine what a British five-year plan for the Middle East would look like: if events are strong, they are also volatile. But there were many outside the Foreign Office who could and did predict the collapse of bases and régimes.

Here again we find Rolls-Royce difficulty. 'The Foreign Office is like a very sensitive octopus,' said one of its members: 'It's superbly equipped to receive impressions from all over the world, and to react to them with speed and efficiency. But it's not designed to make positive moves.' Only when a new party is elected, and a new set of ideas and attitudes is imported, does the octopus come fully to life, and show itself capable of movement.

In these surroundings, the permanent under-secretary has little opportunity for thinking about the future of the world. One has the impression that much of the time he is more like a nannie, trying to keep his difficult children happy, and keeping the office running smoothly. In this respect he is not unique: many company chairmen, as we will see later, spend most of their time as nurse-maids, and to think of top people perpetually sitting, like Law Lords, on abstract problems, is misleading. But in the touchy world of diplomacy, nannie-qualities seem particularly valued. Men with strong, far-seeing ideas are apt to find themselves *not* becoming permanent under-secretary, and in this fine-ground, well-oiled machine, smoothness is all.

FOREIGN SECRETARY

The frontier between politicians and officials, as in the Treasury, is a shifting and fine-drawn one. But diplomacy is a more thoroughly political business than Treasury control, and amateurs have more scope and more confidence. A Chancellor need not have a view, or understand the finer points of the sterling area or the Bank Rate, but every Foreign Secretary must have a line about the cold war; and each bend in his policy will affect the cabinet. The assessments of his officials will influence his decisions, but a Foreign Secretary is less likely to be trapped by his diplomats than a Chancellor by his financial advisers.

The ability of a cabinet to defy official advice was established with dreadful clarity on the afternoon of October 30, 1956, after Israel had invaded Egypt. While a Foreign Office spokesman was explaining to journalists in London that Britain's policy was to invoke the Tripartite Agreement opposing the use of force in the Middle East, Sir Anthony Eden was announcing in the House of Commons that Britain had issued an ultimatum to Egypt, and insisting that the Tripartite Agreement was irrelevant.[1] The Suez invasion broke like a bomb on the Foreign Office. Only one diplomat (so far as is known) was privy to the government's plans —Sir Ivone Kirkpatrick, then Permanent Under-Secretary. The Foreign Secretary, Selwyn Lloyd, had flown in and out of Paris without even visiting the embassy. Nearly all the ambassadors were against intervention, and had to defend a policy which none of them had been told about. Suez was an uncomfortable reminder that in spite of the mechanism of consultation, crucial decisions could still be made by a tiny cabal.

The arrival of a Labour politician among the conservative surroundings of the Foreign Secretary's drawing-room is the subject of intense speculation in every office in every embassy. Ernest Bevin, who moved in in 1945, became more popular within the office than his predecessor Eden, who seemed so completely to epitomise the British diplomat to the outside world, and Bevin alone, of this century's ministers, has a bust amidst the frescoes. The legend of Bevin still haunts the Foreign Office. 'Of course, I got my education in the hedgerows of experience,' he liked to inform his officials. His directness, his courage and his regard for officials made him respected and loved; and, most important of all, he could win his wars in the secret battleground of the cabinet.

The arrival in 1964 of Patrick Gordon Walker was a less spectacular innovation, for he was an experienced diplomat, who had run the Commonwealth Relations Office under the earlier Labour Government; and he was a man of conservative instincts of whom his radical colleagues complained 'he's the best Conservative Foreign Minister we've got'. But his period was short. He came into the job in an awkward situation, having lost his seat at Smethwick, where coloured immigrants had aroused anti-Labour feeling. Three months later, contesting the apparently safe seat at Leyton, he lost not only the seat but his job, and after quick consultation Wilson appointed in his stead Michael Stewart, the former Minister of Education.

Stewart entered the Foreign Office without warning, and with almost as little experience of diplomacy as Ernest Bevin. But (like

[1] *See* Brian Crozier: The Role of the Foreign Office. *Twentieth Century*, October 1957.

Bevin) he had great prestige inside his party. He is an austere, quite puritan person, quiet, reserved and very self-contained. He is shortish, with white hair, a lantern jaw, direct and penetrating eyes, and a very shy manner which makes personal contact difficult. But he is one of those politicians whose whole personality seems transformed when he speaks in public. He can think on his feet, and can frequently state his opponent's argument better than he did, and then demolish it.

His rise in politics has been slow and dogged. His father was a scientist, he went to Christ's Hospital (a public school for the sons of less prosperous parents), and then to Oxford, where he took a first. He became a schoolmaster and lecturer, contesting seats in the meantime, and writing thorough Fabian pamphlets. After the war (which he spent in army intelligence and education) he went into Parliament, and had minor jobs in the Labour Government. In opposition he showed his mastery of briefs and in the October government he was given the key job of education. He was not quite as effectual as many people expected—he seemed too bogged down slowly reading reports—but he pressed ahead with his main objective of comprehensive schools. He was, said *The Economist*, 'just about the only cabinet minister to emerge from Labour's hundred days with more credit than he went in with'.

Stewart's direct experience of foreign affairs had been slight. He spent some time studying the League of Nations in Geneva in 1929, and was impressed by the ideas of Arthur Henderson (then Labour Foreign Secretary) on collective security and disarmament. He had travelled in Europe, been to Moscow with Wilson and had opposed Britain's entry to the Common Market. He speaks French, and some German. He was scarcely known in Washington. But he brought to foreign affairs a tougher mind than his predecessors, Gordon Walker and Butler, great confidence in his own careful judgment, and a strong position in the Cabinet.

Under the Foreign Secretary, Wilson put five ministers, including George Thomson, the Fabian Scots member from Dundee, Walter Padley, the former trade unionist, and Lord Walston, the wealthy Etonian farmer. But the two major ministers were both brought in from outside Labour circles, both with Liberal backgrounds which caused some rumblings of complaint. Both are men of unusual independence and fire, who have made their mark on diplomacy. The first, Lord Caradon, Minister of State concerned with the United Nations, was formerly Sir Hugh Foot, who has been called the colonial governor who ran out of colonies. After a heroic career as governor of Cyprus in the height of its troubles, he became the British Representative to the Trusteeship Council of the United Nations, until he resigned in indignation over Britain's ambiguous policy towards Southern Rhodesia, when he joined the UN itself. He returned in 1964 to head the British delegation, superseding his previous boss, Sir Patrick Dean. His life peerage confused his Afro-Asian friends, who christened him instead U Foot. Caradon, like Sir Andrew Cohen,[1] is an exciting mixture of gubernatorial dignity with radical independence. He has magnificent eyebrows and a rich, grave voice, but he also has an original modern mind and a powerful sense of Britain's proper rôle in the developing world. Lord Chalfont, the other importation, is equally original. As Alun Gwynne-Jones, he served as a regular soldier, rising to be a Lieutenant-Colonel in the War Office, and then boldly switched to become Defence Correspondent to *The Times*, where, to the astonishment of his colleagues, he proved to be one of the most daring and outspoken journalists in Fleet Street, writing long denunciations of muddled thinking which were both well-informed and funny. He even defied the traditions of *The Times* itself by appearing on television as a defence commentator of unshakeable smoothness. The appointment of this intellectual journalist to the job of Minister for Disarmament was one of the boldest of Wilson's strokes.

COMMONWEALTH AND COLONIES

One of the most tragic mistakes of British diplomacy since the war has been to leave the Commonwealth—one of the most important and exciting fields of influence—in the hands of a service which was visibly second-rate, and which was kept quite separate from the Foreign Service, thus producing internal rivalries almost as complicated as international ones. 'We must kill the crow!' Ernest Bevin used to say at the Foreign Office—referring to the Commonwealth Relations Office, or CRO. Set up in 1947 to provide a special relationship between Commonwealth countries, it has had its own network of 'High Commissioners' (the equivalents of ambassadors), and its own permanent secretary. CRO, being new, suffered lower status than the Foreign Office, who openly despised it, and regarded it as a post office or letterbox; many high commissioners in the past have been frequently inferior

[1] *See* below, p. 336.

to ambassadors, a fact much resented by Commonwealth countries. The existence of two organisations side by side has duplicated experts and bureaucracies, and given great scope for inter-departmental muddle: at the United Nations they have each had their separate groups, thus ensuring that the Foreign Office didn't know enough about the Commonwealth, and vice versa. Their separate organisation seemed to make the influence of Commonwealth countries *less* rather than *more* potent, and it has helped to shield the Foreign Office from African influences, rather than expose it to them.

At last, in 1964, the Plowden Committee recommended that the two services should be amalgamated, into a single 'Her Majesty's Diplomatic Service'. But while the Committee agreed that the 'logic of events points towards the amalgamation of the Commonwealth Relations Office and the Foreign Office', they 'hesitated' (a very typical Whitehall verb) 'to recommend the establishment of a single Ministry of External Affairs as an opportune step to take at the present time, although this is the practice in all other Commonwealth countries'. The two ministries, with their separate ministers and separate policies, will thus continue to confuse the pattern of British diplomacy.

And for some time to come Commonwealth diplomats will retain the characteristics of the old CRO, and the vague awareness of being second-best. There are some outstanding exceptions, including the High Commissioner in Pakistan, Sir Morrice James, a former farmer and a career diplomat with a real interest and feel for the Commonwealth. Recently the Commonwealth Service has been stiffened with men from outside, including John Freeman, formerly editor of the *New Statesman*, now the High Commissioner in Delhi. But there remains a sleepiness and slowness in many High Commissions, which has transmuted the challenging job of Commonwealth diplomacy into an anxious drudgery, with a perpetual sense of *embarrassment* about the local inhabitants; indeed many British diplomats, with their fussy periphrases, seem to find the very existence of their temporary country an embarrassment, like a drunken wife, rather than a challenge.

Perhaps the most depressing and backward area of Commonwealth diplomacy is the information services, now being merged with the Foreign Office information services. Both sides have tended to regard information—a kind of euphemism for propaganda—as a department which, though separate, is not separate enough to be manned by experts. As a result the information services are frequently run by men who, while dealing all day with journalists or broadcasters, have never worked on newspapers or television; and they operate, in the middle of this jungle territory, in a stately and long-winded way, like clergymen in a brothel. They succeed in being neither journalists nor diplomats, and while dispensing enormous and expensive quantities of information, they are apt to forget what the point of the information is: 'the information service,' said the Plowden Committee, 'must not come to regard themselves as purveyors of information as an end in itself.' The Committee recommended that the information services should be incorporated with the diplomatic service as a whole, thus making it more aware of policies and points. But I find no sign of any more expertise or drive.

Another awkward residue of the Empire is the Colonial Office. No institution in Britain has seen such rapid change. In 1946 the Colonial Secretary was responsible for 65 million people and 37 separate territories. By 1962 he had 31 million people under him, and by 1970 the number will be nearer 4 million. In the five years to the end of 1963 the staff at the Colonial Office dropped from 2,000 to 700—'A very run down office,' commented *The Times*. But it still had some very thorny problems, including Aden, the Persian Gulf, Gibraltar and the South African protectorates.

With the colonies are departing the remarkable breed of governors. Twenty years ago there were thirty-four of them. They were monarchs, prime ministers, judges rolled into one. They lived in vast, draughty palaces and castles, called 'Government House', and teams of flunkeys and gardeners waited on their guests and trimmed their lawns. Their bold, tall, cocked hats were covered with swan-plumes—bought for £20 from Moss Bros.—and they toured their colonies to the sound of brass bands. Their lives were punctuated by old-fashioned hazards: they were liable to be shot at, or to have their palaces stormed by settlers.

After 1947, with considerable sang-froid, the governors set about liquidating their powers—imprisoning the revolutionaries one moment, making them prime minister the next, and then retiring to the English countryside. Governors will soon be almost extinct. A few outposts will remain, mostly Pacific or Caribbean islands, too small or undeveloped for self-government. They include the Seychelles (population 41,452), Ascension Island (418) and the Falkland Islands (2,800) of which one ex-governor said 'the only memorable thing about the Falkland Islands is the wind.'

Also, according to the *Colonial Office List*, 'various islands and rocks throughout the world are British territory but are not included in any country . . . Many of them have no permanent inhabitants'. Some of the surviving governorships, like the Bahamas, Bermuda, or Gibraltar, are virtually 'grace-and-favour' appointments, ideal for retired generals, admirals or monarchs (the Duke of Windsor governed the Bahamas during the war).

The scope for muddle between the three departments involved with external affairs—the FO, CRO and CO—can be remarkable, and not helped by the traditional rivalries and snobberies. One awkward place, like Aden or Southern Rhodesia, can involve all three. The co-ordination was not improved in 1964, when Wilson appointed three cabinet ministers in these three jobs who were known to have very different political viewpoints. Gordon Walker was the most conservative: while Anthony Greenwood, who became Colonial Secretary, represented the left-wing, inclined towards unilateralism and anti-Americanism. And in the uncertain middle was Arthur Bottomley, the amiable ex-Mayor of Walthamstow, known to his friends as 'Bumley', who went to Commonwealth Relations. Returning British diplomats were confused by the multiplicity of views. 'Soon we'll have Greenwood's volunteers going out to fight Gordon Walker's troops,' commented one politician. But in this as in other 'blurred edges' there were signs that the prime minister enjoyed acting as mediator.

ODM

Out of the messy ashes of the Colonial Office has grown the new and exciting 'Ministry of Overseas Development' or ODM,[1] with the task of allocating financial and technical aid to developing countries. (The uneasy euphemisms for the word 'poor' have gradually changed, from 'backward' to 'undeveloped' to 'underdeveloped', to 'developing'). It began in 1961 as the 'Department for Technical Co-operation', launched without panache and with a forgettable name, soon shortened to 'Co-op'. But under the Labour government in October 1964 it was renamed, enlarged and promoted to a Ministry, with the extra responsibility of handling the £200 million worth of capital projects, taken over from the Treasury. Among its responsibilities is the organisation of 'Voluntary Service Overseas'—the corps of young ex-schoolboys and graduates who spend a year in Africa, Latin America, or Asia

[1] Not to be confused with the Ministry of Defence (MOD).

working on projects ranging from schools to relief camps. The VSO is the British equivalent of the American peace corps; but half deliberately and half accidentally, the British volunteers are much less publicised and organised than the Americans, and they are able to slip into useful jobs without ballyhoo or resentment.

The extension and rejuvenation of the ODM has been one of the most interesting results of Wilson's Labour government, and the new stimulus has released new energies—not least in the permanent head of the ministry, Sir Andrew Benjamin Cohen, who is one of the most unusual and unconventional of the senior civil servants. He is an enormous shy man, given to long, disconcerting silences, with a large appetite and untidy hair. He belongs to a distinguished Anglo-Jewish family; his sister is Principal of Newnham College, Cambridge; he had a brilliant Cambridge career and married the daughter of a don. In the Colonial Office in London he had a strong and radical influence on post-war policies: then in 1952 he was sent out to the stormy post of governor of Uganda—where he first exiled the Kabaka, then welcomed him back. After a spell at the United Nations in New York, he came back to London to build up the new department. A characteristic story is told of Cohen in Malta—where he served for a time during the war. The dockyard workers had made angry complaints about the bad food: their leader insisted on an interview with Cohen, and sent in as an exhibit beforehand a piece of mouldy bread, which had been served at the dockyard canteen. But by the time the angry worker arrived, the exhibit had disappeared. Cohen had absentmindedly eaten it. Cohen is an appropriate symbol of the transition from gubernatorial pomp to practical technical aid. He is an intellectual idealist, with strong views on Britain's continued rôle in poor countries. Though he has spent his life as a civil servant, he maintains an open-ness to new ideas and new people.

To reorganise the ODM, there burst in as minister the ebullient figure of Barbara Castle, the most explosive member of the new Labour cabinet—a provocative and outspoken fighter from Bradford, firmly aligned with the left, and with enduring sympathies with underdogs of all kinds. Polemic and argument are part of her blood; her father was a Yorkshire tax-inspector who worked as a part-time radical journalist; she married a *Mirror* journalist, and herself wrote for the *Mirror* and the *New Statesman*. Her passionate, sentimental speeches sweep up her followers and sometimes carry her away into rash statements, and from time to time she has dropped loud clangers. But behind her display of emotionalism she has, too, quite a critical mind. The combination of this whirlwind with the solider weight of Sir Andrew Cohen is both important and picturesque, and the Ministry has already been nicknamed 'The Elephant and Castle'.

The ODM represents the opposite kind of diplomacy to the stately irrelevance of the Paris embassy and the old 'Inner Circle'. It is the main outlet for the idealism and enthusiasm of the post-imperial Britain, freed from overlordship or paternalism. Compared to the vast cost of conventional diplomacy and international showmanship, it is still a very junior partner. But it represents a far more exciting aspect of Britain's rôle in the world.

18

HONOURS

When everyone is somebodee
Then no one's anybody—
W. S. Gilbert (later Sir William Gilbert).

Even now, the number of those who are not knighted exceeds the number of those who are. Time doubtless will reverse these figures.
Max Beerbohm, 1899 (later Sir Max Beerbohm).

TWICE a year, a few weeks before January 1 and June 6, about 4,000 letters, marked Urgent, Personal and Confidential, arrive at British homes from a private secretary at 10 Downing Street. A typical letter reads:

Sir,
I am asked by the Prime Minister to inform you that he has it in mind on the occasion of the forthcoming list of Birthday Honours to submit your name to the Queen with a recommendation that she may be graciously pleased to approve that you be appointed a Companion of the British Empire (CBE).
Before doing so, the Prime Minister would be glad to be assured that this mark of Her Majesty's favour would be agreeable to you.
I should be obliged if you could let me know at your earliest convenience.
I am, sir,
Your obedient Servant.

The expression 'has it in mind' (one honorand pointed out to me) is an invaluable piece of civil service phraseology. It infers that the prime minister can quite easily put it *out* of his mind, if the offer is rejected: but that in the meantime all those potential earldoms or Orders of the British Empire are revolving slowly and quietly in the back of his head, waiting to be crystallised. But nearly always the offers are accepted. In official lists at international gatherings foreign dignitaries appear simply with their names: but British delegates will be cluttered with GCBs, GCMGs, KBEs, CHs. However odd they may seem to foreigners, these initials still have magical importance to the British, with faint emanations from the monarchy and the Round Table, and they have become part of the very fibre of the civil service.

The multiplicity of the 'orders of chivalry' is enough to baffle the most loyal Englishman: Queen Victoria, King Edward VII, King George V all founded new orders—each with slightly different nuances of glory. The grandest order is the Garter, founded in 1348, as a reward for skilful jousting: it has not more than twenty-six members who at their investitures wear dark blue velvet garters bearing the inscription 'Honi soit qui mal y pense'. Lord Melbourne (who never accepted the Garter) said 'there's no damned merit in it', but nowadays the Garters are an odd mixture of merit and birth. On the one hand are royal favourites, such as the Duke of Beaufort, with a tiny band of six fellow-monarchs, including the Emperor of Ethiopia; the Emperor of Japan was sacked for unchivalry during the war, but allowed to wear the insignia in time to meet Princess Alexandra in 1961. On the other hand are genuinely illustrious leaders, such as Lord Ismay and Earl Alexander. Other very cosy orders are the Royal Victorian Chain, mainly for royalty, but including President De Gaulle (who has not yet been sacked); and the Imperial Order of the Crown of India, for Maharanis and ex-Vicereines of India. There is also the Royal Victorian Order, awarded personally by the Queen, in varying degrees from GCVO to MVO, for faithful service, to such people as the Keeper of the Privy Purse, the Extra Groom in Waiting, and the Keeper of the Swans.

In contrast to the Garter are the twenty-three members of the Order of Merit whose name itself suggests a side-swipe at other orders. OMs have no association with royalty or jousting, and are merely distinguished; they never even meet together, and if they did it is doubtful if, for instance, John Masefield and Lord Russell would have much to talk about. The OM is an impressive little band, from poets and painters to dons and boffins: divorce, promiscuity and atheism are no bar to the OM. Another side-swipe is the Companionage of Honour—founded in 1917—which likewise suggests that other companions are not wholly honourable. Their sixty-five members include an equally mixed band, from Lord Attlee, Henry Brooke and Lord Malvern to Somerset Maugham, Benjamin Britten and Sir Osbert Sitwell. The distinction between honour and merit in the two orders is sometimes rather obscure.

But most orders are much more mundane, mainly concerned with rewarding civil servants, and it is here that inflation is rife.

The most senior of the civil service orders are the Bath (CB, KCB, GCB), mainly for military men and civil servants; and the St. Michael and St. George, whose motto is 'token of a better age', which was originally established in 1818 for the natives of the Ionian Islands and Malta, but is now distributed to diplomats, colonial servants and overseas officials; members rise from CMG (known sometimes in Whitehall as 'Call Me God') to the KCMG ('Kindly Call Me God') to—for a select few governors and super-ambassadors—the GCMG ('God Calls Me God'). The number of CMGs awarded has nearly doubled since the war.

To these older orders was added in 1917 the Order of the British Empire, invented by King George V with the motto 'For God and the Empire'. As the British Empire has dwindled, so its orders have multiplied, until now there are over 75,000 people who belong to its various grades, from the MBE to the OBE to the CBE to the KBE to the GBE. Each department is allocated a maximum number of members each year; for CBEs the Admiralty are allowed fourteen, the Air Ministry twenty-one.[1]

	1935	1961
CBE	50	170
OBE	110	400
MBE	140	700

(The inflation is not as acute as in France, where Napoleon's 2,000 members of the Legion d'Honneur have grown to hundreds of thousands, each with their ribbon in their coat lapel.) The Commanders of the British Empire now include an extraordinary mix-up of people; the New Year's list in 1964 included Professor Colin Buchanan, the traffic expert: Lynn Chadwick, the sculptor; John Lehmann, the writer; the general manager of the Chatham Dockyard; and Alderman J. V. Floyd Bottomley. It is a pleasant fantasy, to think of the Commanders all belonging to a single unified order, embracing aldermen, sculptors and dockyard managers, all jostling among each other, discussing imperial questions and occasionally raising a glass and muttering 'for God and the Empire!'

CBEs, CMGs and CBs have become part of the equipment of the bureaucratic machine. To the public their meaning is vague, but in Whitehall they are pregnant with status, and together with carpets, hat-stands and desks they define a man's place on the ladders. This is the rough code of awards that civil servants can expect to receive:

[1] *See* Peter Nichols: *Patronage in British Government*. 1963, p. 181.

Permanent Secretary	KCB
Deputy Secretary	KBE
Under Secretary	CB
Assistant Secretary	CBE
Principal Chief Executive Officer	OBE
All lower grades	MBE

Honours are always said to be a cheap substitute for higher salaries; the CBE for instance, might be worth £500 a year in terms of status. But there is a price to be paid, for the prospect of honours enhances conformity. A civil servant hoping for his CBE is as careful not to put a foot wrong, or to chance disfavour, as a Tudor courtier to escape beheading. 'Poor George still hasn't got his C,' they will say, and George will make his memoranda still more cautious and inoffensive. The minor honours also provide an unscrupulous method of rewarding political services without resorting to more expensive methods: in the Conservative honours lists, a quota of about a tenth of the MBEs, OBEs and CBEs have gone to Conservative party workers,[1] and the aura of the palace and peers which they convey are an essential incentive to constituency parties.

The most visible recipient of honour—apart from a peer—is a knight: overnight Mr. J. M. Smith will be transformed into Sir John and—more important—his wife will become Lady Smith. Through all Britain's social revolutions, the charms of knighthood have remained undiminished: echoes of Sir Lancelot and Sir Galahad mingle with more practical advantages: 'Expect clients to pay sir charge' cabled one witty architect after his knighthood had been announced. Nor has the knightage swelled quite as Max Beerbohm forecast: there are about 3,500 knights today—about the same number as in 1935—though there are now fewer Empire knights, and more inside Britain. This chart (from Debrett) shows how new creations of peers (excluding life peers) baronets and knights have varied over the last fifty years:

	1911–15	1916–20	1921–25	1926–30	1931–35	1936–40	1941–45	1946–50	1951–55	1956–60
Peers	41	79	51	54	57	51	71	67	67	69
Baronets	96	192	132	74	52	44	40	6	33	41
Knights	955	1770	1026	856	952	902	1098	1099	1040	924

[1] Andrew Roth in the *New Statesman*, December 29, 1961.

The bulk of the knighthoods still go to civil servants and to party hacks 'for political and public services'. But the field of knight-worthy activities has been enlarged, albeit in an erratic fashion. There are several acting knights, but no TV knights: two cricketing knights, one football knight. City men,[1] advertising men and publishers all feel aggrieved at their lack of recognition; but honours nowadays are awarded for services to motoring, horse-racing, or fashion.

Theoretically anyone can recommend anyone for an honour, and thousands of people write to the prime minister suggesting their friends or themselves. But the weighty recommendations come from Whitehall departments, from the Conservative Central Office or Transport House, and from the parts of the Commonwealth which still care about honours. They are sifted and weighed by Sir Laurence Helsby (who takes a keen interest), and scrutinised by the indefatigable Sir Robert Uchtred Eyre Knox, who has been secretary of the Political Honours Scrutiny Committee for a quarter-century. Only the more important recommendations are passed on to the prime minister. Occasionally unfortunate mistakes are made, as when before the war they meant to knight a distinguished theatrical figure and knighted an obscure man with the same name. Recent prime ministers have not taken a fervent interest in honours. Sir Anthony Eden, with some advice from his wife, took a lively interest in the honouring of the arts, and was prepared to weigh in the balance the rival claims of a ballet dancer and a managing director for the CBE. Harold Macmillan did not take much interest in honours below a peerage. Before Harold Wilson came to power there were many Labour MPs who hoped that the honours system would be abolished, like William Hamilton, who complained that it aroused 'cynical hilarity' in millions.[2] But when Wilson took office he found it far too useful—and too much fun.

How many people reply that Her Majesty's favour would *not* be acceptable? There is no reliable information, of course, about the refusal rate, since publicly to refuse an honour is at least as vain as to accept it, but there are some signs that honours are becoming more, rather than less, acceptable. 'Fourteen out of fifteen of the people who write back to refuse are obviously annoyed because they weren't offered something better,' said one man who had been concerned with honours: 'it's a relief when

[1] *See* p. 394.
[2] *The Guardian*, December 16, 1964.

you come to the fifteenth who really honestly doesn't want it.' Before the war many leading intellectuals, including Professor Tawney, Bernard Shaw and H. G. Wells, refused honours and Rudyard Kipling never accepted one. A few people still clearly refuse honours, such as Ted Hill, J. B. Priestley or Evelyn Waugh; but today most prominent artists and intellectuals have accepted honours of some kind. Even Oscar Kokoschka, the eccentric Czech painter, who made a lifesize wax model of an ex-girl-friend, has accepted a CBE, and nearly all the former Labour leaders have accepted peerages. Most politicians, and some palace officials, would agree that honours have got out of hand. But neither party —confronted with queues of civil servants waiting for their Cs and Ks—dare suggest abolition.

The more uprooted and complex our society becomes the more, it seems, these handles of status are grasped. And at a time when Britain is having to adapt herself quickly to a more commercial and technological age, the honours system helps to perpetuate Victorian values for which most of them were invented. Inevitably, honours have social repercussions. The extension of CBEs to include industrialists—particularly exporters—has done something to widen the field, but the bulk of the honours still reflect a Victorian world. Could the system be reasonably brought up to date? The *Daily Mirror* once suggested a new 'Order of Elizabeth'[1] for 'achievement particularly in keeping with the spirit of the age'. But who can possibly decide what *is* the spirit of the age? Should knights of Elizabeth be football-pool knights, take-over knights, or power-station knights? At a time when Britain is becoming more involved with the rest of the world, why should we only honour Britons serving Britain? No possible new system could be devised which did justice to all the spirits of the age, and the multiplication of honours involved would soon become still more difficult. In the end, surely, the only real judges of a man's achievement can be his immediate friends, who will honour him with a K or without.

[1] *Daily Mirror Spotlight:* Honours and Awards. p. 16.

19

ARMED FORCES

Army, Navy,
Medicine, Law,
Church, Nobility,
Nothing at all.

Cherry-stone rhyme.[1]

The British Army should be a projectile to be fired by the British Navy.

Lord Grey of Fallodon.

No limb of Britain has had such sharp and sudden jolts as the fighting services. The civil service has come up against problems almost equally pressing, but less spectacular and visible. All three fighting services have been faced with inventions which have challenged their core, and confronted by these revolutionary situations they have not been able to say to themselves 'it may seem odd, but it works'. After the afternoon in Hiroshima of August 6, 1945, it seemed as if they might virtually cease to exist. Since then, with the re-emphasis on conventional warfare, they have continued in uncertainty, hovering between H-bombs and rifles, missiles and fighters, aircraft carriers and nuclear submarines. The navy is being forced further under water, for longer times; the air force must envisage planes without pilots; the army is becoming a mobile police force. The old idea of defending the British Isles has become virtually meaningless, and the three services have all become involved in elaborate and tricky alliances.

'The boffin', too, has come into their midst. The services, like civil servants, have always liked to keep experts at arm's length. 'Never let the engineer on to the bridge,' has been a naval maxim, and the most technical branches of the army, like REME or Signals, have been the most junior. Military technology—more than in most other countries—has been regarded as something separate. Naval engineers used to have purple between the gold rings on their sleeves, to mark them off from executive officers. Reluctantly the services are accepting the importance of

[1] Oxford Book of Nursery Rhymes, p. 110.

specialists; engineers are still not allowed on the bridge, and the Board of Admiralty still consists entirely of executive officers. But there is now no badge except a Scots accent to distinguish the engineer.

In spite of their contraction and changes, the cost of the services still accounts for a quarter of the budget, or eight per cent of the national income—second only to America among NATO countries. This was the percentage of the national income spent in NATO countries in 1963, from lowest to highest:[1]

Portugal	3·0
Belgium	4·6
Canada	4·7
Netherlands	6·3
Germany	7·0
France	7·1
United Kingdom	8·3
United States	10·6

Britain spends nearly twice as much on defence as she does on education: the cost of a single new aircraft carrier—about £50 million—could build five universities the size of Brighton's. The air force costs as much in a year as the entire gross national product of Ghana. This is how the (estimated) defence budget was divided in 1964–5:

Army	£525 million	190,000 men
Navy	£496 million	100,000 men
RAF	£503 million	134,000 men
Ministry of Defence	£26 million	
Ministry of Aviation	£275 million	
Ministry of Public Buildings and Works	£164 million	
Atomic Energy Authority	£6·8 million	
Civil Defence	£24 million	
TOTAL	£2,019·8 million	

THE ROYAL NAVY

> Pray state this day, on one side of a sheet of paper, how the Royal Navy is being adapted to meet the conditions of modern warfare.
>
> *Winston Churchill to First Lord, 1941.*

The most dramatic post-war change has been the diminution of the Royal Navy—the arm which, most of all, has been associated

[1] Institute for Strategic Studies: *The Military Balance, 1964–5.*

with Britain's imperial grandeur. To a schoolboy before the war, the navy on cigarette cards, in news films or in the Spithead review, was a visible symbol of 'red on the map'. In 1914, when the navy was at its peak, it had 389 ships, including 71 battleships and battle-cruisers and 148,000 men. In 1939, it was still the largest navy in the world, with 300 ships and 161,000 men. By 1964 it was the third largest navy, with 194 ships, no battleships, but still 100,000 men.

These were the navy's ships in 1964–5:[1]

4 aircraft carriers	3 aircraft direction frigates
2 commando ships (carriers)	33 anti-submarine frigates
2 cruisers	1 nuclear submarine
4 guided missile destroyers	38 conventional submarines
10 other destroyers	61 minesweepers
4 fleet pickets	7 patrol and despatch vessels
14 general purpose frigates	8 landing vessels
3 anti-aircraft frigates	93 fleet support ships

The old symbol of naval glory was the battleship, the grey floating fortress which was Britain's ultimate weapon. It had the infinite protocol of a floating court, and it provided its own grand mythology of rum, beards and quarterdecks. There are some who say that the battleship was obsolete by the time of the Battle of Jutland, in 1916: but its doom was sealed on May 24, 1941, when the biggest of them all, HMS *Hood*—pitifully unprotected—was sunk by the *Bismarck*. Battleships lingered like dinosaurs until 1960, when HMS *Vanguard*, the pride of the post-war fleet, was towed to the scrap-yard. With it went a way of life. The new kind of navy is as different as porpoises from whales: aircraft carriers and submarines, with eccentric designs, have penetrated under and over the water. In a modern submarine, jammed with pipes, wires and electronic equipment, there is no room for protocol or even for admirals.

The precipitate change has brought agonising adjustments. Young naval officers trained before the war for a life of seamanship have found themselves in the sixties with not a ship in sight. Only one in six senior naval officers is now attached to a ship. At the age of thirty or so, naval officers are divided into a wet list and a dry list. A sea-captain ashore remains a fish out of water.

The enormous numbers in the navy (particularly the eighty admirals) compared to the ships, have aroused a good deal of

[1] Source: Institute for Strategic Studies.

comment: it was the navy which caused Professor Parkinson to formulate his famous 'Law' (which we will encounter several times in this book) that 'work expands so as to fill the time available for its completion'. Parkinson observed that the fewer the ships the larger the numbers in the Admiralty; and his theory was fully supported, as it happened, by the Select Committee on the Estimates, who published a report in September 1960. They observed with anxiety that although the number of ships between 1952 and 1960 had fallen from 376 to 235, the number of headquarters staff in the previous year had actually *risen* by twenty-eight. They even dared to criticise the navy's conservatism—'Noble traditions of loyalty and service must be jealously preserved', they wrote, 'but they must not be permitted to form a barrier against experiment and reform.'

The Admiralty still shows itself as remarkably accident-prone—particularly in relation to secrets. Its record of losing secrets is remarkable, culminating in the case of Vassall, the spy who was employed in the Admiralty for fifteen years, as a junior official but with access to quite secret documents, until he was discovered in 1962 and sentenced to 18 years imprisonment. Even in smaller matters the incompetence of Admiralty security has persisted, and in 1962 some secret naval documents were found in the drawer of a desk that had been sold to the public. 'The desk was searched', explained Mr. Orr-Ewing, then Civil Lord of the Admiralty, who was questioned in parliament by Leo Abse, 'but it appeared that these papers must have stuck, either under the drawer or at the back . . . I am very sorry for it. We are trying to tighten up our procedure.'[1]

The navy often appears trapped in tradition. At the Royal Tournament in 1961, the navy's two exhibitions showed cutlass fighting and hornpipe dancing at the time of Nelson, and field-guns at the time of the Boer War. Ships, cut off from the mainland, acquire a strange way of life of their own. The navy has always been conscious of being the special and Senior Service (it has the least difficulty in finding recruits) and the unique flavour of the naval officer ashore can be sampled at the Goat Club in Bond Street, or at the RNVR Club in Mayfair, where the bedrooms are cabins, and taxis are called alongside.

But the navy has always had a tradition of radicalism tinged with eccentricity alongside its conservatism. It can suddenly be extraordinarily unconventional—as when in 1915 Lord Fisher had

[1] *Hansard*, January 30, 1963.

two battleships stripped of their guns to carry aeroplanes, thus inventing the aircraft carrier. The navy has a contact with foreign countries which induces a sense of diplomacy, and a certain vulnerability to other ideas; navies are closer to each other than armies or air forces, and they develop a salt-water comradeship. Outside the services, British naval officers are regarded as the smoothest and most adaptable of the three arms—which reflects itself in the ease with which they find jobs in industry.

At the top of the navy, there has always been a mixture of radicalism and conventionality. The first has been most strikingly evident in two recent First Sea Lords, Lord Mountbatten, the regal ex-Viceroy, and Sir Caspar John, the outspoken and witty son of Augustus John, who retired in 1963 ('There's too much top hamper, Sampson, that's the trouble', he told me, 'we need drastic changes. I had to tell people: "if you can't keep up with the times, please leave the Navy".') But the current First Sea Lord, Sir David Luce, a shy withdrawn person, is in a more orthodox mould. He is the son of an admiral, and one of his sons is a naval officer. He lives in Hampshire, the admirals' county, and was soaked in seamanship from the age of thirteen, when he went to the Royal Naval College at Osborne, the navy's prep school. He went through the stiff and formal training of the stately old navy, starting as a midshipman ('the lowest form of marine life') on the famous battleship the *Iron Duke*. But he broke into the more adventurous world of submarines, and commanded one, the *Cachalot*, for two years in the war, before serving in Combined Operations under Mountbatten. After the war he commanded cruisers, directed the Staff College at Greenwich, and commanded with distinction, the Far East station—including the army and air force—for three years, until he came back to be First Sea Lord. Like all senior sailors, he has moved from a self-centred service into a strange new world where airmen and soldiers are no longer enemies but allies.

After the war, with the domination of the air force, the invention of the H-bomb, and the disappearance, one by one, of British bases abroad, it looked as if the navy's day was done. (I remember cleaning an Oerlikon gun on a cruiser, the day after Hiroshima, and wondering how it could possibly be needed again.) But with the nuclear deadlock, and the development of nuclear submarines, navies reasserted themselves. After a long depression, the British navy began about eight years ago to feel itself important again. And as the Empire dwindled, leaving fewer safe bases for armies and navies, so the idea grew up that the navy itself might constitute a floating base in the Far East, like the American Sixth Fleet, complete with its own air force, commandos, missiles, tankers and depot-ships—capable of remaining at sea if necessary for months on end. This has become the navy's dream, and if it comes true it will mark a full circle. For the navy was first built up to protect British shipping and interests abroad; then helped to establish Britain's military strength in the great bases of the Empire; now it is retreating from the shore bases, back to the safety of the sea.

THE ARMY

> Conscription may have been good for the country, but it damn nearly killed the army.
>
> *Sir Richard Hull, 1962.*

'Britain's a very tribal nation', said one major-general at the War Office: 'that gives the army tremendous moral strength, but it has snags.' The tribal basis of the infantry is the regiment, which is (far more than a ship or a squadron) the repository of loyalty. Regiments in their modern form were invented—like the civil service—in the dynamic 1870s. They were devised by Colonel Cardwell, the secretary of state for war, as a way of ruling the empire: there were seventy-five regiments, each with two battalions—one at home, the other guarding a distant outpost—and in their static isolation they developed powerful and splendid characters of their own. 'Regiments are not like houses', said Winston Churchill in 1904, 'they cannot be pulled down and altered structurally to suit the convenience of the occupier or the caprice of the owner. They are more like plants: they grow slowly if they are to grow strong . . . and if they are blighted or transplanted they are apt to wither.'

Like most other British institutions, the regiments acquired their strict 'peck-order'. The richer ones insisted on private incomes, and through bequests and private enterprise they acquired large funds (the Grenadiers supplement their funds by sending their band round the world). The younger, poorer regiments fell behind. At the top of the peck-order are the six regiments (four of foot guards, two of cavalry), known as the Household Brigade, or simply 'The Guards'. They are entrusted with guarding the Queen, including marching outside Buckingham Palace in black bearskins, and with the most prominent rôle in royal occasions, such as the State Funeral of Sir Winston Churchill.

The Guards are the epitome of the tribal strength of the army. The three oldest foot regiments—the Grenadiers, the Coldstream and the Scots Guards—all date back to the Civil War, when they helped to restore King Charles II to the throne (though the Coldstreamers, the oldest of the three, had originally been raised as part of Cromwell's New Model Army). The Irish Guards were founded in 1900, to commemorate the Irish bravery in the Boer War, and the Welsh Guards (whose Colonel is Prince Philip) in 1915.

Since the war, the Guards have modified their requirements; officers need no longer buy their own headgear, and men need only be five-foot-eight. Like ordinary regiments, the Guards have had to drum up their recruits as best they can: the Irish Guards have little difficulty, but the others have had to roam the country to recruit their seven thousand. The tribal pattern is beginning to dissolve, and some of their best recruiting areas—Nottingham, Lincolnshire or Bristol—are in very unguardsmanlike areas.

But the 550 regular Guards officers form a tightly-knit group which—more even than merchant bankers or the Inns of Court—have resisted the democracy around them. Half the officers (I was told) are sons of Guards officers: all went to public schools, a large proportion to Eton, and most still have a private income. ('Officers commanding regiments', says the recruiting pamphlet, 'discourage parents from giving their boys more than £200 a year at the most when they first join.') They have their own club in Mayfair, their own polo club, cricket club, saddle club, flying club, shooting club. They have a network of ex-officers all over the country, who help in recruiting and providing employment. Guards officers can even, through the Guards Employment Society, arrange to have their houses built, or their suits made, by ex-Guardsmen. Guards officers like to cultivate careful snobberies and, like courtiers, a rigid code of what is and is not said, of a Nancy Mitford kind—like not saying 'cheers' before drinking. You must say servant, not batman; bearskin, not busby; telephone, not phone; go to London, not up to town (the distinctions were proudly explained in the film *The Queen's Guards*). They thrive on the nice distinctions of mess behaviour. They can be rude, idle, self-satisfied and unintelligent. But they remain what they are supposed to be, a superb fighting force: and it is in the army that tribalism and lack of social mobility—so damaging in other fields—have their greatest justification.

OFFICERS AND TECHNICIANS

In the post-war years the regiments, magnificent though they are, have become an awkward problem, for they hamper the army in the most crucial modern quality—mobility. Units invented for long campaigns in distant colonies are much less useful for quick flights to unpredictable crises. While the air force and navy can cross-post their men to any ship or base, the army must deal with units of 800. And there have been too many regiments. Between 1958 and 1961 twenty-three pairs of regiments were merged, painfully and with bitter resentments which are still smouldering. Regiments, like the Inns of Court or Oxbridge colleges, produce endless complications of rivalries and non-collaboration. 'A military system so old, so involved and so set about with traditions is cram full of complications and special circumstances; particularly where the various land reserve forces are concerned, the heirs of the Elizabethan trained bands, the Georgian militia and the Victorian volunteers.'[1]

The caste tradition of army officers is followed by most fighting countries. In Russia the officers are much more segregated: the sons of private soldiers cannot become officers, and the highest ranks earn 115 times as much as the lowest (in Britain they earn twenty times, in America fifteen times as much). But tradition and segregation often comes into conflict with innovation, and in the British army, where technologists have always been regarded as an inferior race apart, the synthesis is difficult. The old separation between the teeth and the tail—the fighting men at the front, and the technicians at the back—is dangerous at a time when the tail must often be swallowed by the teeth. Regimental traditions are apt to encourage officers to believe that they have some ancient moral right to lead men into battle, while the modern army demands technical and professional, as much as moral, qualifications.

The army college at Sandhurst has tried since the war to produce more technical officers, but between its traditions of conformity and discipline and the need for enterprise and innovation there remains a difficult gulf ('A troublesome and erratic figure', said the Sandhurst report on Cadet Montgomery, with a mixture of prescience and narrowness, 'far too self-opinionated and grievously lacking in the polished manner one would like to see in a Sandhurst cadet').[2] And Sandhurst cadets are still

[1] M. R. D. Foot: *Men in Uniform*, 1961. p. 129.
[2] Hugh Thomas: *The Story of Sandhurst*, 1961. p. 173.

recruited from a tiny sector of society. The Estimates Committee of parliament reported in August 1964 that sixty per cent of the men at Sandhurst came from Headmasters Conference schools;[1] they criticised the Director-General of Army Training, Lieut.-General Sir George Gordon-Lennox, for being unduly complacent in his attitude to wider recruitment and decided that 'there is need for considerably more understanding of the reasons for the army's continued failure to attract school-leavers from maintained schools'. The army, they were surprised to learn, did not, like the other services, require two 'A levels' for their entrants to Sandhurst.

The position has changed remarkably little in seventy years. These were the schools which supplied more than ten cadets in the years 1891 and 1961:

1891		1961	
Wellington	37	Wellington	54
Eton	29	Haileybury	21
Clifton	19	Eton	20
Marlborough	16	Ampleforth	17
Harrow	16	Marlborough	16
Haileybury	14	Downside	15
Charterhouse	14	Rugby	12
Cheltenham	12	Cheltenham	11
Westward Ho	11	Sherborne	11
Bedford	11	Bedford	10

The most powerful spokesman for the intensive education of officers is Lieutenent-General Sir John Hackett, now deputy Chief of the General Staff. Hackett himself, though a great advocate of equitation, is a striking example of a new, rare, egg-head officer. The son of a diplomat, he was a scholar at New College, Oxford. He joined the army—one of very few graduates at that time—and rose quickly, with persistent courage, in the war. 'Fully to justify a position of superiority for the officer', Hackett said in 1960, 'we must make him in fact a truly superior person . . . Is the service of the Crown in this country's land forces to be left in the hands of those whom industry would reject, young men too dull to get into Shell, or ICI, or Glaxo?' He foresees a future army in which all senior officers will have taken degrees or their equivalents: 'The army', he said, 'cannot be allowed to become a cloistered enclave of privileged idleness.'[2]

[1] *See* p. 202.
[2] Paper to the Royal United Services Institute, November 23, 1960.

Since the decision to end conscription in 1962, the recruitment of infantry has been a mounting problem. The Labour Party's defence policy requires many more conventional forces, but is not clear how to get them. The more warlike parts of the kingdom—Northern Ireland, Scotland and Wales—still provide a steady supply of soldiers; but full employment, affluence, television and motor-cars and mobility have made soldier-families harder to find, while affluence has widened the gap between home life and army life: 'The new kind of council-house life, with washing machines and TV, isn't the obvious background for a soldier,' said one general.

The army has tried to attract men with more comfort, higher wages and less harsh discipline, and they have launched a massive TV advertising campaign, showing contradictory images of jungle warfare and girls on the beach. 'We're competing with industry now', said one man at the War Office, 'and we have to take a different attitude: it's no longer a question of "you're behind the barricades now—go and get your 'air cut".' This 'TV Army' has been mocked by the navy, who have no difficulty in finding recruits. 'They're going about it the wrong way', said a senior naval man: 'telling them that they can have a bedside lamp and a free pass, and see mother every Thursday. Men like to think of themselves as being tough—that's what impresses the girl-friend.' But the television tactics have met with some success, and each time there is another skirmish or landing in Aden or the Far East, recruiting figures jump up.

This is how the British army was made up in 1964–5:

65 infantry battalions (including 8 Gurkha)
3 parachute battalions
22 tank and armoured-car regiments
31 artillery regiments
Various engineer and signal regiments.

The army remains very tribal, and its senior officers inhabit a world that is full of military dynasties. An example is the top soldier of all, Lieutenant-General Sir Archibald Cassels, the Chief of the General Staff (the word 'imperial' has been quietly dropped): his father, General Sir Robert Cassels, was commander-in-chief of the Army in India, and married a colonel's daughter; and Sir Archibald married a brigadier's daughter. He rose up through conventional paths, from Rugby to Sandhurst to the Seaforth Highlanders; he began the war as a captain and ended it as a temporary major-general, and then, like the other service chiefs, entered the amphibious world of liaison, between the three services and between the Commonwealth countries.

THE AIR FORCE

Within the lifetime of many airmen, the Royal Air Force has been born, has struggled for survival, has saved Britain from conquest, and then once again has had to struggle for survival. In 1945 it seemed that the air force was the most secure of all the services. Twenty years later, with missiles, H-bombs and nuclear submarines, it seems possible that the manned fighter and bomber —the very soul of the air force—may become extinct. The main business of future airmen may be to carry the army, and the navy is steadily encroaching on the air.

The RAF, unlike the other two services, has never had a settled existence. Born in the first world war, it was jealously resented by the army and still more by the navy. The RAF fought bitterly for its independence: 'The air mentality', wrote Lord Templewood (political head of the air force in the twenties) 'required a special atmosphere of its own if it was to infuse its full power into a new and revolutionary service . . . The very weight and glory of the naval tradition would have prevented the full recognition of the sovereign power of the new service.'[1]

Airmen were looked down on by the others as upstarts, non-gentlemen, raffish and undisciplined. They reacted by being aggressively air-minded: the new 'university of the air' at Cranwell instilled the spirit of independence, and distrust of the navy. The separateness of the RAF is reflected in its clubs: while generals, admirals and even other professions mix at the United Service Club or the Army and Navy, the RAF club—to which most air marshals belong—is reserved for airmen.[2] The air force, on the other hand, has a broader intake of officers than the army or navy, with fewer from public schools and a much larger recruitment from the Commonwealth; in 1961 three out of seven members of the Air Council, and five out of twelve of the Commanders-in-Chief were from other Commonwealth countries.

In forty years the temper of the air force has been transformed. In its 'string-and-glue' period it was a service of daring individuals. Courage and skill were essential, and air squadrons were capable of extraordinary carelessness. The air force hero of the last war was

[1] Lord Templewood: *Empire of the Air*, 1957. pp. 272–4.

[2] De Witt C. Armstrong: *The Changing Strategy of British Bases*, 1959. p. 115.

still the brilliant individualist, called to his fighter at a moment's notice. But after the war, jet planes became faster, more expensive and complex, and discipline and technical certainty became much more crucial. The Meteor jet-fighter, a much more difficult plane than its predecessor, brought reappraisal. Several Meteors crashed through carelessness, and the RAF stiffened its discipline and precautions at airfields. The picture of flying as a way of triumphant self-expression soon faded.

The new kind of pilot is a different animal from the old Flying Officer Prune, and the training of one bomber-pilot costs £100,000. More than the others, the air force has found the glamour taken out of it. A pilot is likely to find himself, not alone in the clouds, but flying in a bomber like a power station, watching a row of black boxes, always in touch with his base: he may not even—as in the latest American bombers—have a glimpse of the air. A pilot is a technologist—the kind of person so insistently wooed by industry and commercial airlines. But he must still have courage and devotion, and in peacetime and full employment the mixture is doubly difficult: at the training station at Hornchurch (the Chief of Air Staff told me) 700 people applied to become pilots in a six-month period in 1961, and only 126 were accepted—half what the RAF needed.

The air force today needs equally daring and expertise. (The RAF has proportionately more graduates than the other services, and more officers to men.) The combination of qualifications is apparent at Cranwell, where cadets fly at 40,000 feet in the morning, and come down for Plato and mathematics in the afternoon.

After forty years the RAF already has strong traditions. A large proportion of Cranwell cadets are the sons of air force men. The backbone of the air force is still the group of men, now in their forties, who flew in the Battle of Britain. But unlike the other two, it is far bigger than it was before the war. In the twenties it had 20,000 men: in 1964 it had 134,000.

This was how the RAF was composed in 1964–5:[1]

Bomber Command: 180 medium bombers, led by Mark II Vulcan and Mark II Victor bombers, with Blue Steel air-to-ground missiles. Also Valiants, Victors and Canberras.

Fighter Command: Javelin and Lightning 1 and 2 interceptors, and Lightning 3 interceptors with Red Top air-to-air weapon. Bloodhound 1 and 2 surface-to-air guided weapons.

Source: Institute for Strategic Studies.

Coastal Command: Shackleton aircraft for reconnaissance and anti-submarine.
Transport Command: 23 Britannias and 11 Comets, 11 VC10s, 10 Belfasts, 116 medium-range aircraft. Also helicopters.
RAF Germany: Canberra strike squadrons, and Hunters and Javelins.
Near East (*Cyprus*): Canberras, Javelins and Whirlwind helicopters.
Middle East (*Aden*): Shackletons and Hunters.
Far East: Shackletons, Canberras, Hunters, Pioneers and helicopters.

The Chief of Air Staff, Air Chief Marshal Sir Charles Elworthy, the professional head of the air force, is regarded in Whitehall as the most impressive of the service chiefs, and his career has been in keeping with the new sophistication of the service. He was born in New Zealand, the son of a Guards captain, went to Marlborough school and Trinity, Cambridge, where he took a law degree, and was later called to the bar. He learned to fly after leaving Cambridge, and three years later took his commission in the RAF. He was twenty-eight when the war broke out, and he already had long experience of flying bombers. He spent the war with bombers—commanding a squadron, bombing German ships and bases, earning medals for bravery, and then running the bomber base at Doncaster. After the war be became further involved in Commonwealth liaison, first touring the Far East, Australia and New Zealand, and then for two years commanding a station for the Pakistan air force. Back in Britain he became caught up in the administrative machine, looking after personnel at the Air Ministry, and later running the staff college at Bracknell. In 1960 he went for three years to Aden, as Commander-in-Chief of Middle East Command, and then returned as Chief of Air Staff. He is a man with flying in his blood—one of his sons is a flight-lieutenant—and in his mixed experience of flying, the law, the Commonwealth and administration, he is typical of the new airman-diplomat.

SECURITY SERVICES

> He that has a secret should not only hide it but hide that he has it to hide.
>
> *Thomas Carlyle.*

The most obscure parts of Britain's defence, as one might expect, are the 'Security Services', concerned with espionage and counter-espionage. Unlike the Americans—who have two apparently open organisations, the FBI and the CIA, with well-known premises in Washington and well-known people at their head—the British cloak the whole operation in secrecy. It can safely be revealed that there are two organisations which were once called MI5 and MI6 (MI stands, rather misleadingly, for military intelligence): the first deals with protecting Britain's own secrets against other countries' spies; the second—whose existence is never officially acknowledged—deals with Britain's own spies. But nobody is supposed to know who is at the head of them, or where he and his staff have their headquarters. A previous head of MI5, Sir Percy Sillitoe, did emerge from anonymity, and became a famous—perhaps too famous—public personality; but since then all newspapers are asked to refrain from publishing the names of security chiefs, and they are referred to by cryptic initials, such as 'M', or 'C', or simply as 'The Director-General'.

One of the most mysterious questions about the secret services is; to whom exactly are they responsible? Their organisation is outside the neat hierarchies of the new Ministry of Defence. Each ministry in Whitehall which is involved in secret work has its own security service, and as far as possible, in accordance with the old British tradition, the Director-General likes to leave Ministries to guard their own secrets. However unsatisfactory this may prove—as with the Admiralty—the alternative of having counter-spies within the departments, responsible to an outside authority, is abhorrent. But MI5 itself remains a very separate and nebulous province, and its full mystery emerged after the Profumo affair; here again, we are in the wake of Christine Keeler. The mystery revolved round the fact that, although Profumo told the Director-General of the Security Services (or 'M') that he was involved with Christine Keeler, 'M' did not pass on this information to the Prime Minister, who was assumed to be in charge of security, and who might be expected to be interested in his minister's doings. When one of Macmillan's secretaries upbraided an MI5 man for not doing so, he replied blandly 'this isn't a police state yet you know'. 'M', as Lord Denning's report revealed, was very much concerned with the Profumo affair; he knew that Profumo was seeing Stephen Ward, who was known to be close with the Russian naval attaché, Ivanov: and having learnt this, he suggested to the Secretary to the Cabinet, Sir Norman Brook,[1] that he might warn Profumo of this dangerous connection; he also daringly suggested that Profumo might possibly persuade Ivanov to join the British side. It was 'M' to whom Profumo admitted his liaison with Christine, and

[1] Now Lord Normanbrook, Chairman of the BBC (*see* p. 648).

'M' then decided that it was not his business to find out whether Christine had actually been Profumo's mistress—in keeping with the principle that the Security Service should not investigate minister's private lives unless a clear security issue was involved. What was mysterious about 'M's' behaviour was that he did not pass on his information to the Prime Minister, who is generally assumed to be in charge of security, until the full scandal had broken; and when Macmillan made his long speech of exculpation on June 10, 1963, he blamed the Director-General, and the Secretary to the Cabinet, for not keeping him informed. In the subsequent debates there was widespread confusion as to who *was* 'M's' boss: according to a directive of Maxwell Fyfe (later Lord Kilmuir) in 1952, he should be responsible to the Home Secretary; but the Home Secretary seemed as uninformed as the Prime Minister, and Macmillan briskly passed the blame on to subordinates.

But what seemed to emerge from Lord Denning's report was that 'M' has no boss, that he can roam anywhere, and deal with any ministry. Having been appointed, he must decide for himself to whom he should report. He makes large use of the Home Office, for MI5 works closely with Special Branch of the Police, which comes under the Home Secretary, and also of the C.I.D. But in extraordinary matters, including the carelessness of ministers, he is a free agent, and uses his own discretion as to whether to report to the Prime Minister. As Sir Findlater Stewart wrote in 1945, 'Having got the right man, there is no alternative to giving him the widest discretion.' This misty position is exasperating to parliament, who naturally expect to have a minister they can blame for security mistakes; but in fact parliament is never privy to the workings of security, and their questions are always fobbed off. Security, by its nature, must always go against parliamentary traditions, and much of the oddity of the system can be justified by Carlyle's dictum. But the trouble with all Whitehall is that they never know where secrets should end; secrecy soon becomes an invaluable excuse for avoiding any kind of accountability.

DEFENCE

'I suppose we'll all end up in a mud-coloured uniform' is a recurring service phrase. The three services are finding themselves, with amphibious modern warfare, more and more entangled. The air force carries the army, the navy protects the air force, and a joint operation of all three—such as the smooth and rapid landings in Kuwait—can find itself commanded by an air marshal. Sea and air still demand and mould different characters, but using missiles, commando-carriers or landing craft, the arms can no longer be separated limbs; they stand or fall together.

If Britain had no fighting traditions, and her forces were invented from scratch, she would probably choose one big service for land, sea and air, for the services now spend a great deal of energy fighting each other for money and jobs. Gradually the British services are coming closer together—trying to compound their individual loyalties and rivalries with the 'tri-service outlook'.

As Sir John Hackett has described it:

> As the profession grew more professional, first at sea and then on land, the sailor and the soldier moved farther apart from each other and the functional area in which both operated, the military, grew more sharply distinct from the non-military. . . . The movement of the military away from the civil has now been reversed. They have come closer together. Military skills are less exclusively specialist. The military community lives less apart. Uniforms are less worn in civilian society. The working clothes of a general are very like those of a machine minder, though he still has something rather more grand put by for special occasions.
>
> How far will this tendency to reintegration go? Not, I am sure, as far as a complete merger. The special nature of the military calling will persist, and although the threshold between civil and military has in recent years got lower, and may get lower still, it is unlikely to disappear. The task of those in charge is to determine its optimum height, or, to put it another way, to see how close the military can be brought to the civilian without destroying the value of the soldier to society. One thing is particularly important: to facilitate reintegration when the soldier wishes to cross the threshold and become a civilian.[1]

Since the last war, several attempts have been made to bring the services closer together, and in 1946 the Ministry of Defence was first created, to co-ordinate and control the three services. Its power was tactful and discreet, hidden away in one corner of the 'New Public Offices'; but by controlling the money, it kept the services in check. The three service ministries, however, remained very separate and at constant cross-purposes, and successive governments stopped short of any basic reorganisation in the

[1] From 'The Profession of Arms': Lees Knowles lectures at Trinity College, Cambridge, November, 1962.

style of the Pentagon in Washington. At last, in July 1963, a massive reorganisation was announced, one of the most important achievements of Harold Macmillan. Beginning from April 1, 1964, it brought the heads of all three services into one 'Main Building' (sometimes called the Quadrigon), the big stone office block between Whitehall and the river, formerly inhabited by the Air Ministry and the Board of Trade. The political heads of the three services still have the rank of minister, and access to the prime minister, but they have much less autonomy. The post of 'First Lord of the Admiralty', first held in 1673, no longer exists: in its place is the 'Minister of Defence for the the Royal Navy', alongside his counterparts for the Army and Air Force. And at the head of them is the Minister himself, renamed the Secretary of State, the overlord of the three services. 'The Secretary of State for Defence', said the White Paper of July 1963, 'must have complete control both of defence policy and of the machinery for the administration of the three services. The line of authority and responsibility from the Secretary of State will run unbroken through military, scientific and administrative staffs, throughout the Ministry.' The elaborate and largely incomprehensible organogram of the new set-up is reproduced on the opposite page.

The new proposals met angry criticism; Lord Attlee protested that 'by destroying these old landmarks they may destroy the spirit of the services'; and Lord Teynham complained that they were creating 'a post for a superman'. The House of Lords even went so far as to vote against the government on the proposal to call the top naval committee the 'Navy Board', and insisted instead (successfully) that it should be called the 'Admiralty Board'. The uprooting of admirals and generals from their historic offices was bitter and painful; and the day before the new scheme came into force, the Navy held a special ceremony at the Horse Guards to haul down the Admiralty Flag. It was hard to imagine a Britain without a First Lord.

The Quadrigon is full of new dangers. The power of the Secretary of State is unparalleled in a peace-time ministry. He regulates not only £2,000 million a year, but a force of 400,000 servicemen and women, and another 400,000 civilians—more than the total employees of British Railways. The job requires not only mastery of the problems of strategy and nuclear chess, but also a real insight into the workings of large bureaucracies—made far more complex by continuing inter-service rivalries. It calls less for the traditional ministerial and parliamentary talents than for

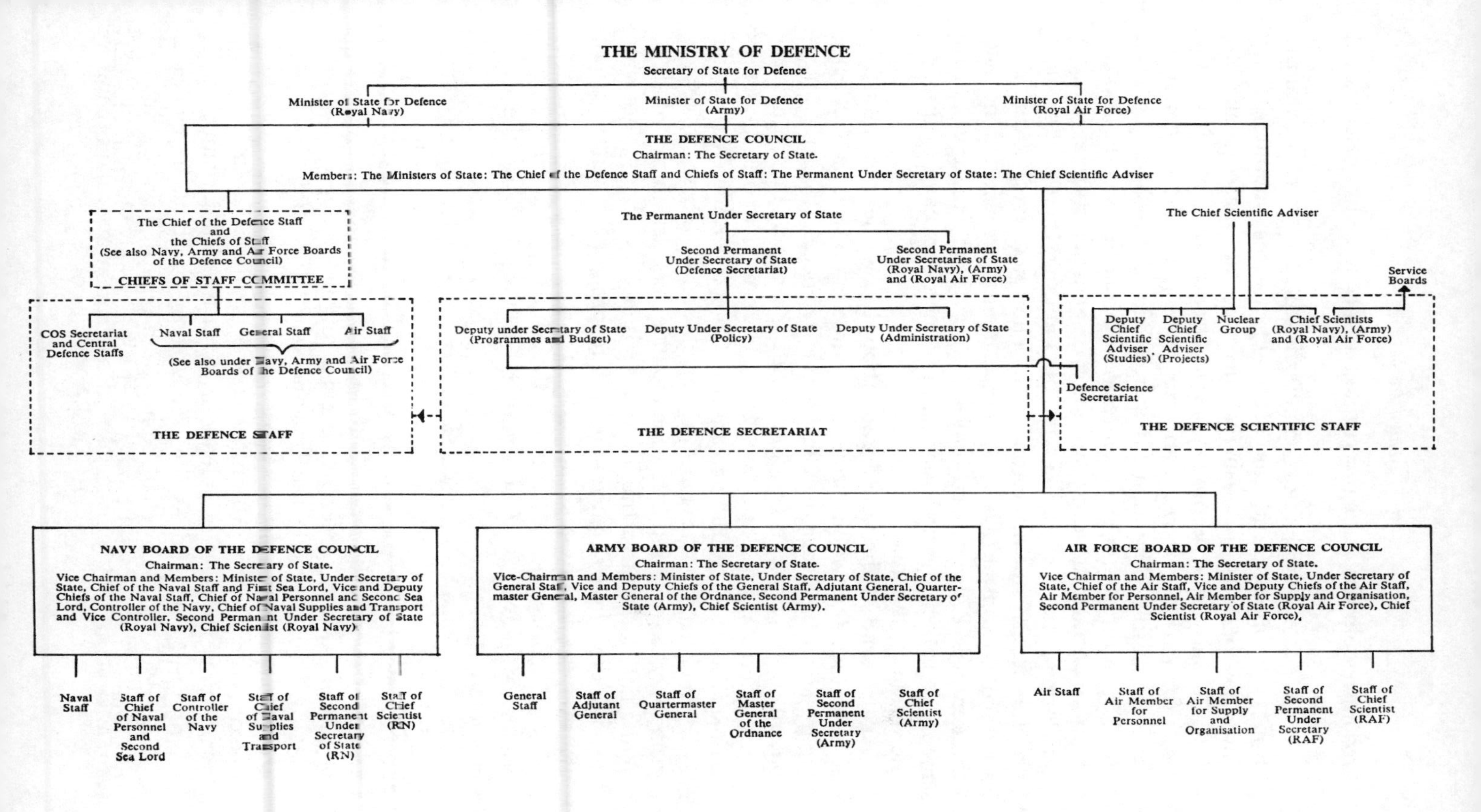
THE MINISTRY OF DEFENCE
Secretary of State for Defence
Minister of State for Defence (Royal Navy)
Minister of State for Defence (Army)
Minister of State for Defence (Royal Air Force)
THE DEFENCE COUNCIL
Chairman: The Secretary of State.
Members: The Ministers of State: The Chief of the Defence Staff and Chiefs of Staff: The Permanent Under Secretary of State: The Chief Scientific Adviser
The Chief of the Defence Staff and the Chiefs of Staff (See also Navy, Army and Air Force Boards of the Defence Council)
CHIEFS OF STAFF COMMITTEE
The Permanent Under Secretary of State
Second Permanent Under Secretary of State (Defence Secretariat)
Second Permanent Under Secretaries of State (Royal Navy), (Army) and (Royal Air Force)
The Chief Scientific Adviser
Service Boards
COS Secretariat and Central Defence Staffs
Naval Staff
General Staff
Air Staff
(See also under Navy, Army and Air Force Boards of the Defence Council)
THE DEFENCE STAFF
Deputy under Secretary of State (Programmes and Budget)
Deputy Under Secretary of State (Policy)
Deputy Under Secretary of State (Administration)
THE DEFENCE SECRETARIAT
Deputy Chief Scientific Adviser (Studies)
Deputy Chief Scientific Adviser (Projects)
Nuclear Group
Chief Scientists (Royal Navy), (Army) and (Royal Air Force)
Defence Science Secretariat
THE DEFENCE SCIENTIFIC STAFF
NAVY BOARD OF THE DEFENCE COUNCIL
Chairman: The Secretary of State.
Vice Chairman and Members: Minister of State, Under Secretary of State, Chief of the Naval Staff and First Sea Lord, Vice and Deputy Chiefs of the Naval Staff, Chief of Naval Personnel and Second Sea Lord, Controller of the Navy, Chief of Naval Supplies and Transport and Vice Controller, Second Permanent Under Secretary of State (Royal Navy), Chief Scientist (Royal Navy)
ARMY BOARD OF THE DEFENCE COUNCIL
Chairman: The Secretary of State.
Vice-Chairman and Members: Minister of State, Under Secretary of State, Chief of the General Staff, Vice and Deputy Chiefs of the General Staff, Adjutant General, Quartermaster General, Master General of the Ordnance, Second Permanent Under Secretary of State (Army), Chief Scientist (Army).
AIR FORCE BOARD OF THE DEFENCE COUNCIL
Chairman: The Secretary of State.
Vice Chairman and Members: Minister of State, Under Secretary of State, Chief of the Air Staff, Vice and Deputy Chiefs of the Air Staff, Air Member for Personnel, Air Member for Supply and Organisation, Second Permanent Under Secretary of State (Royal Air Force), Chief Scientist (Royal Air Force).
Naval Staff
Staff of Chief of Naval Personnel and Second Sea Lord
Staff of Controller of the Navy
Staff of Chief of Naval Supplies and Transport
Staff of Second Permanent Under Secretary of State (RN)
Staff of Chief Scientist (RN)
General Staff
Staff of Adjutant General
Staff of Quartermaster General
Staff of Master General of the Ordnance
Staff of Second Permanent Under Secretary (Army)
Staff of Chief Scientist (Army)
Air Staff
Staff of Air Member for Personnel
Staff of Air Member for Supply and Organisation
Staff of Second Permanent Under Secretary (RAF)
Staff of Chief Scientist (RAF)

tycoonish qualities, and the ruthless inspection of organisational diseases.

At the same time the new complex is still more cut off from the public, parliament and the press. The secrecy about defence plans has become increasingly effective, and fiascos, like the TSR2, usually only become apparent after it is too late. Now, the scope for parliamentarians and the press (with the exception of the irrepressible Chapman Pincher, of the *Daily Express*) is even less. For in the past a large source of information was the leakage of information from angry admirals or generals warring against each other; and now, in the same big building, there will be more watchfulness, if not more solidarity. The Quadrigon is the most spectacular example of a bureaucratic monster growing up beyond the ken of MPs; you need only read a defence debate in parliament to realise how little opportunity members have to discover the inside arguments.

At the head of the new organisation, below the four ministers, is the triumvirate who represent the three main strands of defence organisation. They are the Chief of the Defence Staff, Earl Mountbatten, who represents the three fighting services; the Permanent Under-Secretary of State, Sir Henry Hardman, who is the senior civil servant in the building; and the Chief Scientific Adviser, Sir Solly Zuckerman, the most powerful boffin. These three are probably the most important men, outside politics, in the whole of Whitehall; for their attitudes and decisions reverberate not only through the whole defence budget, but through the whole pattern of Britain's scientific and industrial development. In hundreds of offices, factories and laboratories, the Ministry of Defence—or its creature, the Ministry of Aviation—is the chief, or the only, customer.

The top job in the services, called the Chief of the Defence Staff, is held (in theory at least) in rotation by a soldier, sailor, airman. But for six years it has been held by the same dominating and controversial figure, Admiral of the Fleet Earl Mountbatten of Burma, whose career has been a unique example of royalty making a mark inside the bureaucracies of Whitehall. He is a great-grandson of Queen Victoria, and his nephew Prince Philip married the Queen. Mountbatten's own life has kept a quasi-royal aura. He lives in splendour, with liveried servants, at his Hampshire seat; and as the last Viceroy of India he evokes a vanished age. In Whitehall he has been regarded with a mixture of pride and envy, and known as 'El Supremo', 'Burma' or 'The

Earl'. He maddened many of his colleagues, with his vanity, his brisk authoritative gestures and his dominating manner; and he was constantly suspected by his rivals of empire-building. But he also had courage and determination, and a radical desire to reform the navy and to integrate the three services, which helped to leave the Quadrigon a much more rational and workable place.

His successor, as from July 1965, is a much quieter and less regal man, Field Marshal Sir Richard Hull, the former Chief of the General Staff. Like his successor as CGS, Cassels, and his two predecessors, Festing and Templer, Hull is the son of a soldier, and comes from a thoroughly military family—his father was a major-general, and his sister is married to one. He has a fine military moustache and a thin, lined face; he is an excellent horseman and a good shot. But he belongs too to the new breed of graduate soldiers; and he was the first graduate CGS that anyone can remember. He went to Trinity, Cambridge, joined the Lancers and was thirty-two when war broke out. Three years later he was commanding a special striking force in North Africa called Bladeforce, with calm daring, and by 1944 he was commanding the 1st Armoured Division in Italy. He had the enterprise and resourcefulness of a good cavalryman, and a special interest in the mechanics of tank warfare. After the war he was caught up, like his colleagues, in the ring of administrative jobs reserved for promising men—running the staff college at Camberley, directing staff duties at the War Office, teaching at the Imperial Defence College. He commanded British troops in Egypt and in the Far East, where he earned a high reputation for his interest in troops' morale and welfare. In 1956 he played a central rôle in planning the future of the army, acting as chairman of a War Office Committee; and it was Hull's report (never made public) which set the figure of 200,000 men. By the age of fifty-four he was at the top of the army, facing all the awkward problems of a rigid army in the changing post-Suez world, but regarding them with detachment and flexibility. In Whitehall he has been widely respected for his mixture of military authority, with bursts of frank outspokenness and drastic realism.

The other two triumvirs come from very different backgrounds, and there is always speculation in Whitehall about the encounters of these disparate men. Sir Solly Zuckerman—who will appear in the next chapter in the realm of science—is essentially the adviser from the foreign territory of boffins, and his influence depends on his being—at least apparently—detached and non-political.

Between him and Mountbatten there was quite a close relationship, known as the 'Zuckbatten Axis', based on a common interest in technological innovation: a large part of Sir Solly's rôle is the injection of scepticism into the solid assumptions of defence policy. The civil servant, Sir Henry Hardman, the 'eminence grise' of the building, is a formidable person (as his name suggests), not afraid of politics or large decisions. He came from Manchester Central High School, went to Manchester University, and became a lecturer in economics to the Workers' Educational Association. He did not join Whitehall till the war—like so many other successful civil servants—when he came into the Ministry of Food. At the Ministry of Defence, the civil servants have in the past been regarded rather as mufti adjuncts to the fighting men, and expected, if they have power, to conceal it doubly—both from the politicians and the soldiers; and this awkward situation has been reflected by the reluctance of young civil servants to join the defence ministries. But now, as the Quadrigon becomes more professionalised and both generals and politicians become more donnish, the division is less acute; and the civil servants are well aware that their ministry is responsible for a quarter of the budget.

On top of this intricate jumble of soldiers, sailors, airmen, civil servants and boffins are the politicians, trying to make some pattern of purpose, and to impose the will of their cabinet. There are four ministers in the Quadrigon, three of them confusingly called 'Ministers of Defence', for the army, navy and air force respectively. But the only cabinet minister is the Secretary of State for Defence. Into this job came in October 1964 Denis Healey, a quiet and unassuming Yorkshireman with large black eyebrows and strong eyes, facing probably the most intellectually demanding job in Whitehall. Healey is one of the lone wolves of the Labour cabinet; he has no definite or enthusiastic political following and he is not associated with groups or movements. Before and after the war, he was on the far left of his party, but now he is well to the right of centre, firmly anti-Communist, and on close terms with Washington. His main interest has always been in foreign affairs and defence, and he is one of the few people in politics who can fully master the convoluted problems of international nuclear strategy. He first showed his agile mind at Bradford Grammar School and Balliol, where he became involved in very left-wing politics (though not with the Union) and, in 1940, took his double first. In the war he became a major in the

Engineers, and then went into parliament, where he was soon involved in committees and delegations on foreign affairs. He remains a solitary, mysterious man ('He's one of those people who go to the cinema alone,' a Tory complained), and he is not an obvious political leader. He is not an exciting or well-ordered public speaker. But he can talk and write with wonderful lucidity, and brings to problems of defence a mind trained and attuned to all the ifs and buts of nuclear chess. It is too early to see how far he has the qualities of a Macnamara, to grapple with organisational muddle, and to bully, wheedle or cajole the warring factions into submission and collaboration. But he has a quickness and incisiveness, tempered with wit, which make him a formidable opponent. Socialist ministers have always been thought to be at a disadvantage in dealing with the military, for even if they have been majors, mentioned in despatches, they are yet suspected of being unsoldierly people, liable to scuttle whole navies for the sake of their principles. The association between war and Conservatives is a strong one, and Tory television programmes are apt to bear a resemblance to films for promoting recruitment. But in the new, more intellectual atmosphere of the ministry, as much concerned with the arts of organisation and costing as with fighting, the arrival of a new team of politicians, fresh from a long study of defence problems, was welcomed by quite conventional soldiers. Apart from Healey, the Minister for Defence (Army), Fred Mulley, is an expert on western defence and NATO; and Christopher Mayhew, the Minister for Defence (Navy), is a student of foreign affairs and co-existence. Lord Shackleton, the son of the explorer, the Minister for Defence (Air), was a former wing-commander in the air force.

WAR LORDS?

Politicians remain firmly in control of the services. Britain has never had a very separate fighting caste. The younger-son tradition, it is true, has now virtually died out and has given way to a tradition of fighting families: in 1961, out of seventeen full generals, admirals and air chief marshals who listed their fathers in *Who's Who*, two-thirds were the sons of fighting men. But most service chiefs have (in contrast to Americans) remained part of a broader society: they belong to Boodle's and White's as well as the United Service. They have never had the chance to develop *folie de grandeur*, and they have become used to being cut down and bullied by politicians in peacetime. They have realised that the only way to get money, in the hectic scramble of Whitehall, is to please the politicians. 'It's a kind of miracle in Europe,' said an African leader after the mutinies of 1964, 'that the armies take orders from civilians.'

The men at the top are not at all typical fighting men: they are chosen with an eye to their skill in negotiation, and the services are beginning to develop a special race of Whitehall soldiers. The Chiefs of Staff are unobtrusive, unpublicised men. In war-time a dozen generals are known: but now few people could recite the names of Hull, Elworthy or Luce. Half their careers have been behind desks, and their battles are intricate arguments with the politicians, and with each other, in the corridors of Whitehall. The making of defence policy is one of the most secret and guarded activities of Whitehall, and of the clashes between services and personalities it is hard for any observer to get a glimpse. Parliament has to debate £2,000 million a year with very little knowledge of the arguments behind it.

They are far from the 'war lords' of Marxist imagination. Ever since Cromwell's major-generals, Britain has fought shy of giving soldiers too much power. There has been no General MacArthur or General Challe, who can defy political leaders, and there is no powerful military lobby at Westminster like Washington's. Since Haig effectively withstood Lloyd George in the First World War, no warrior has had much political strength. Nor has Britain chosen a general to run the country—like de Gaulle, Eisenhower, Nasser or Khan. The last and only military prime minister was the Duke of Wellington.

20

SCIENTISTS

> There are millions of people — trained, skilled, professional — for whom these phrases about class are becoming more and more meaningless. The white coat, the growing technological character of modern industry, is making some of the old battlegrounds seem unreal.
>
> *Harold Wilson.*[1]

> How can we become the masters, not the slaves, of technological change?
>
> *Richard Crossman.*[2]

THERE is no greater, or more difficult, challenge to modern governments than the integration and organisation of scientists into the fabric of the administration. Britain has excelled in producing these awkward, independent men; but has kept them insistently apart from the traditional institutions of her government — so that scientists seem almost to operate as an underground movement, popping up in dangerous unexpected places, and sabotaging the neat calculations of mandarins and accountants. Since the war the problem of absorbing scientists has grown steadily more acute, and the more the scientists are ignored, the more awkward they become. Every government has tried, to some degree, to comprehend and grapple with the problem, with expedients ranging from Lord Cherwell to whole clusters of committees. But the Labour Government of 1964 was specially pledged to lead the white coat workers into their kingdom, and in particular to 'wave a wand over Whitehall' (in Professor Blackett's phrase), to bring scientists into the heart of the administration. The Labour cabinet, it is true, is no better qualified in education than its Tory predecessor; among its thirteen graduates there is only one Fred Peart, with a B.Sc. from Durham—with a scientific degree. But the Labour Party, in seeking for its lost soul, has found a new cause, and a new rallying-cry, in the mastery of

[1] Conversations with Kenneth Harris. *The Observer,* June 16, 1963.
[2] Scientists in Whitehall. *Encounter,* July, 1964.

science; and ever since the speech by Harold Wilson and Richard Crossman at Scarborough in 1963, speaking of the 'white-hot technological revolution', the Labour Party has become identified with the advancement and integration of scientists. As with schools and universities, they faced an immense problem of jumbled and disparate bodies, which had 'just growed', and which seemed to defy rationalisation. It was another classic case of planners and co-ordinators coming up against a beguiling jungle.

THE TRIUMPH OF SCIENCE

Already early in the century the scientists were changing the shape of the future, but up to the last war their importance was largely unacknowledged. 'This war was the turning point. Whereas previously scientists were seen, according to the interests of the observer, either as dedicated scholars, or as the source of invention, or as the technical guardians of the social service on which an urban civilisation depends, today they also appear in a number of new guises—as the backbone of national defence; as pioneers of outer space; and even as the counsellors of presidents and prime ministers.'[1]

The suddenness of the change has been as bewildering for the scientists as for the others. Men accustomed before the war to scrounge for equipment as government 'boffins' or university pariahs, have found themselves wooed by government and industry, with new labs, vast equipment, nervous respect and multiplied staff. 'The feeling of being a depressed class has quite gone,' said one science knight: 'When I told my father I wanted to read physics at Cambridge he said "surely you want to be well off: if you read science you'll never be able to have a car." I remember in 1940 the young naval officers all had nice girl friends and the scientists had plain wives. Now the scientists are the privileged class. I suppose the arts people actually have to live on their *salaries*.' At schools and universities the old 'stinks' departments have become a status symbol, and the output of scientists has raced ahead: three-quarters of the scientists and technologists who have ever lived, one of them has calculated, are alive and practising today.[2] This table shows how immensely the numbers of new scientists has increased since 1938:[3]

[1] Sir Solly Zuckerman: Liberty in an Age of Science. *Nature*, July 18, 1959.
[2] *See* Lord Bowden: Too Few Academic Eggs. *Universities Quarterly*, November, 1959.
[3] From Report of the Advisory Council on Scientific Policy, 1962–3.

Honours degrees in	*1938–9*	*1961–2*
Biological sciences	159	618
Chemistry	408	1,339
Geology, etc.	21	228
Mathematics	246	739
Physics	151	1,055
General science	432	1,412
Total honours degrees	1,117	5,081

But the scientists remain a separate breed, and particularly separate from parliament. 'It would be impossible to name a dozen members of the House of Commons,' wrote *The Times*' political correspondent in July 1963, 'who can claim to have had anything better than a rudimentary training in the sciences or who feel the least assurance when they examine or judge the pronouncements of the scientists.' In 1961 Martin Madden, one of that handful of scientific MPs, pointed out that:

> Of 36 heads of Oxford colleges 2 were scientists;
> 24 heads of Cambridge colleges 6 were scientists;
> 31 vice-chancellors (or their equivalent) 10 were scientists;
> 20 members of the cabinet 1 was a scientist;
> 22 permanent heads of government departments 2 were scientists;
> 20 editors of national newspapers 0 was a scientist.[1]

In the seventeenth and eighteenth centuries, science was still a gentlemanly pursuit: the first President of the Royal Society was an Irish peer, Lord Brouncker, who was the first man to give a series for quadrature of a portion of the equilateral hyperbola. The Marquess of Rockingham, when not prime minister, whiled away his time trying to turn coal into oil. But the fragmentation of science, its narrow educational syllabus and exclusion from the 'humanities', made it a less fashionable subject. Arts men still take pride in not knowing how motor-cars or jet planes work, and science has come to be regarded as a career for ambitious, single-minded men, not for the wordly all-rounder or talented amateur. A scientist who *does* become part of the politico-literary world—like Lord Snow, Professor Bronowski or Sir Solly Zuckerman—is regarded as an ambassador from a distant territory, and invited to talk endlessly on the problems of being a scientist. Scientists have begun to produce their own dynasties—the Huxleys, Braggs,

[1] *See The Times*, August 26, 1961: 'scientists' here includes engineers, mathematicians and doctors.

Thomsons or Darwins—but they have remained surprisingly separate; in 1964 a young Huxley married a young Darwin. The current 'swing' towards science may help to bridge this gap in fifteen years' time, but the educational rift is a deep one, for the English fondness of the amateur is biased against the specialised scientist. And the scale of scientific experiments has become so large that scientists have lost some of their apparent individuality. Few men have the intellect to grasp the implications of new inventions and frontiers. 'In this great scientific age,' said Sir Solly Zuckerman in 1964, 'we haven't produced, pro rata, more alpha-plus minds.'

The 'innumeracy' (to use Sir Geoffrey Crowther's phrase) of British politicians is a weakness of which both political parties are aware, but neither are well qualified to put it right. 'This is not the first time this kind of educational inadequacy has characterised the ruling class in British history,' wrote Richard Crossman, MP in 1964.[1] 'At the beginning of the modern age (say, in the fifteenth century) literacy was just about as rare in parliament as numeracy is today. In those days, the sound, sensible men of affairs who ran the country regarded the clerks, on whose reading and writing they relied, with a mixture of envy and suspicion and were determined to maintain them as a small élite circle so as to keep them well under their thumbs. In due course that changed; and the modern state came into being when it was found necessary to require literacy of the ruling class. We shall only be able to talk of a modernised Britain when numeracy as well as literacy becomes a requirement of the ruling class.'

Scientists, on their side, have resented the supremacy of arts graduates in politics and the civil service, and have felt ostracised from decisions and influence. The expressions 'They' and 'the Establishment' are often muttered by scientists. 'There's a kind of war between the two sides', one scientific civil servant explained: 'sometimes I begin to feel that they are determined to keep us down, and that they put their narks in everywhere.'

In spite of this rift, the scientific achievement of Britain, particularly in physics and chemistry, has been out of all proportion to her size: in radio astronomy or molecular biology Britain is pre-eminent. One index (though not a significant one behind the iron curtain) is the number of Nobel Prizes, awarded by the Swedish Academy of Science. These were the leaders between 1901 and 1963:

[1] 'Scientists in Whitehall'. *Encounter*, July, 1964.

	Physics	Chemistry	Physiology or Medicine	Total
USA	20	13	27	60
Germany	13	20	9	42
Britain	15	14	13	42
France	7	6	3	16
Holland	5	2	2	9
Sweden	2	4	2	8
Austria	3	1	3	7
Switzerland	–	3	4	7
USSR	4	1	2	7

I found my conversations with scientists a relief after the more guarded dialogues with managers and bureaucrats. They talk freely and wittily, and maintain a buccaneering attitute to the Treasury. They are used to fighting for recognition and they love describing the subterfuges involved in raising a million pounds. Most of them remain unpompous,do-it-yourself people with boyish enthusiasms and little snobbery; not all the most eminent have knighthoods. Several answer their own telephones, and get straight down to business: there is not much amateur rigmarole. They are nearly all—in keeping with their image—badly dressed, in reach-me-down suits with baggy trousers. Many enjoy fast cars, gadgets and music—louder music, one suspects, than Treasury men. Their new involvement with power and destruction has worried many of them, as it has worried Americans and Germans, but in face of the blandishments of government, most of them have retained a stubborn independence.

Yet the enormous new involvement of British government with research is inevitably transforming the situation of scientists and their institutions. These figures from the OECD show the rough increase in spending on scientific research between 1950 and the early 1960's, in terms of the percentage of the gross national product.[1]

United States	from	1 per cent	to	3 per cent
Britain	from	·8 per cent	to	2·7 per cent
Japan	from below	·5 per cent	to	1·5 per cent
Holland	from	·3 per cent	to	1·2 per cent
France	from	·7 per cent	to	1·1 per cent

[1] From *Science, Economic Growth and Government Policy*: OECD, Paris, October 1963. 'The figures are notional,' the *Economist* warns, 'and some of them are inspired guesses.' The British figure of 2·7 per cent is from the government estimates for 1961–2.

The flow of money into scientific research is changing the whole balance of power in government, industry and the universities. This was how spending on research and development has changed in six years:

	(£ million)	
	1955–6	1961–2
Government (Defence)	177·5	245·7
Government (Civil)	44·7	139·3
Public Corporations including GPO	5·8	22·7
Private industry	68·3	213·0
Other	3·7	13·3

THE ROYAL SOCIETY

The new largesse in the first place has affected the scientists' own most ancient and venerable institution, the Royal Society. 'The Royal' is a society of all Britain's most distinguished scientists. King Charles II founded it, and its tercentenary was celebrated in 1960, culminating in a rally at the Albert Hall. In the seventeenth century the Society was the hub of scientific discovery, Newton, Halley, Dryden, and Pepys gathered to chat about inventions and even though Pepys (who was President) couldn't understand Newton's *Principia*, they could all enjoy telescopes and comets. Since then specialists have learnt more and more about less and less, and the renaissance ideal of the 'universal man' has faded. It was in 1901 that the Fellows decided to exclude altogether the 'human' sciences—economics, for instance, or philosophy—and their proceedings have become steadily less intelligible to the layman. The Society has been split into two sides—the 'A' side (mathematics, physics, chemistry, etc.) and the 'B' side (geology, botany, physiology, etc.), and one side has great difficulty in comprehending the other.

The Fellows are elected by a series of sub-committees, with extraordinary care; the initials FRS are often more coveted than a knighthood. There have been persistent complaints about the narrowness and caution of the elections, and many Fellows have not been elected until after their time of active research is over. At last, in November 1964, the Society decided to extend its annual quota from 25 to 32, to allow the inclusion of applied scientists and technologists. In a lively anniversary address to his Fellows, the President, Howard Florey, the co-discoverer of penicillin (who became a Life Peer in 1965), suggested that 'with the passage of time they begin to detect signs that the scientific attainments of newly elected Fellows are not quite what they were in previous generations'. He went on to say that technology, not science, was changing our lives: 'is it wise for the Society at this time not to have among its Fellows those skilled in demographic work or anthropology, or even a substantial representation of psychology and psychiatry?' and he warned his colleagues not to adopt the frame of mind 'of our illustrious founder who, you will remember, made fun of those who weighed air'.

Past presidents include Wren, Newton, Davy, Huxley, Kelvin, Thomson, Rutherford, Bragg, Dale, Adrian. Florey sits once a month on an old leather throne under a portrait of King Charles II, with beside him a treasurer (Lord Fleck), three secretaries (Sir William Hodge, Professor Arnold Miles and Sir Patrick Linstead) and sixteen councillors.

The Royal Society has all the dignity of a scientific parliament: over three centuries it has grown up alongside monarchy, government and Church. But, like the House of Lords or the Court of the Bank, it is not as decisive as it looks. Many Fellows suspect that, in vast new scientific oceans, the Royal is becoming increasingly irrelevant. The rebellious Fellows—quite a large segment—regard the Society as pompous and obsequious to government. 'The only important thing the Fellows do is elect other Fellows,' said one radical one. 'It's like one of those marine organisms which has lost every faculty except that of reproduction.'[1]

The Royal has many indirect contacts with government. Nearly every important scientific adviser is an FRS, and the initials open the door to government and industry. The Society elects members to committees; provides the cabinet with advice when asked; and acts as a kind of scientific Foreign Office, maintaining a network of international connections (science is the same kind of *lingua franca* as Latin was in the middle ages, and remains determinedly international in spite of the cold war). As a body the Royal has never been closely involved in major government decisions, but its aloofness has become much more apparent with the vast new expenditure since the war; it has fought shy of the government who in turn have sometimes found it too fussy and pure. 'They had a pathological and unnecessary horror of being controlled by government,' one eminent Fellow said: 'They had the choice after the war of remaining a mutual admiration society, or really taking

[1] e.g. the Pacific Palolo Worm (Eunica Viridis).

part in the control of science. They chose the former. They threw away the handles of power.'

SCIENTISTS AND INDUSTRY

Science is no longer simply an academic pursuit but, primarily, a matter of national survival.

'We are entering now upon the most serious struggle for existence to which this country was ever committed. The latter years of the century promise to see us in an industrial war of far more serious import than the military wars of its opening years.' That was written by T. H. Huxley in 1872. Most of British industry has never taken kindly to scientific research. The industrial revolution, as we noted in Chapter 13, owed nothing to the universities or the government: spinning jennies and steam engines were built by practical factory mechanics (though several, like Arkwright—a classical scholar—were well educated). Already in the 1860's and 1870's, when continental technical colleges were establishing close relationships with industry, Britain was lagging behind. The English exhibits at the Great Exhibition in Paris in 1867 were described as 'slovenly extruded heaps of raw materials mingled with pieces of rusty iron.'

In the light of these warnings, repeated over the past ninety years, it seems surprising that British industry has survived at all, and the monotony of these Cassandras encourages some people to think that Britain can always 'muddle through'. But in the 'second industrial revolution' of automation, science-based industries and mass-production, the integration of research with industry has become far more important, and this awareness has increasingly involved the government in industrial science.

It was to counter the research effort of German industry that in 1916 the government established the 'Department of Scientific and Industrial Research', to coax British business men into more research. Newer 'science-based' industries—chemicals, electrical, aircraft—have from the beginning been deeply involved in research: they know that without it they could not survive, and in 1958 these three employed 65 per cent of the scientists in industry. But in older industries—shipbuilding, machine tools, coal, laundries, building and even motor-cars—research has been, and still is, relatively tiny, and a far smaller proportion of turnover in Britain than in America. For forty-nine years the DSIR has been trying to persuade these industries to adopt new methods, usually working gingerly behind the scenes, terrified of publicity. 'It's no good criticising industrialists in public; they just button up their coats: we want them to come into the party and join us. We hate fuss and headlines. What we're doing is missionary work, introducing scientific ideas to the factories.' But occasionally they have come out into the open, publishing papers—on machine tools or shipbuilding, which both caused a large furore. Soon after he became Minister of Science, Lord Hailsham complained in an explosive interview about the difficulties of the DSIR in encouraging builders to use a better kind of hod. 'That they should have to try and persuade a major industry to accept such a development in this modern age is pathetic.'[1]

Another large industrial weakness is the 'development hump'—the obstacle between discovering things and developing them. All too often inventions are left to be developed in America, from lack of interest or finance. One device to fill this gap is the National Research Development Corporation, founded after the war to allocate money for promising inventions. One NRDC project, the 'Hovercraft', has proved exciting and fruitful, but the inventions coming forward have so far been disappointing. Another scheme has been the idea of 'developing contracts', placed by the government with industrial firms to experiment with new devices—computers, for instance, or new kinds of ship. But it has so far been difficult to place contracts without any particular customer in mind—like not knowing what gun to design when you don't know who the enemy is.

This is part of the nub. For nearly all the major engineering and scientific advances—jet planes, atomic power, ball-point pens, radar, transistors—have been precipitated by war, or the fear of it. The most destructive inventions produce constructive by-products, and even missiles can launch satellites for radio-communications. To provide a substitute for war, giving the same stimulus and financial incentive to industry, is the heart of the government's problem. Americans achieve it partially by giving a wide interpretation to 'defence', using it as a pretext for subsidising computers, electronic devices, new kinds of aircraft: the USAF even sponsors research into grasshoppers. But in Britain defence is less popular, and the solution less easy.

In March 1962 a committee was appointed to look into the organisation of civil scientific research, under the chairmanship of that polished committee-man Sir Burke Trend, secretary to the

[1] Interview with the *Financial Times*, November 4, 1960.

cabinet. Their recommendations, somewhat amended by the government in 1964, resulted in the DSIR being split up into new bodies, with confusing and un-memorable names, showing their dissociation from the public. Firstly, the Science Research Council (SRC), to support research at universities and observatories—spending about £20 million a year; and a Natural Environmental Research Council (NERC), to supervise research into geology, fisheries, nature conservancy, etc.—spending £3 million a year, and described later as 'encompassing almost everything mentioned in the first chapter of *Genesis*'. But the Trend committee were prevented by their terms of reference from discussing, 'either the scale or the content of the research programmes', and its recommendations produced further complications. 'It was,' said Professor Blackett, the architect of the forthcoming Labour scheme, with characteristic shortness, 'the wrong committee, with the wrong terms of reference, reporting at the wrong time.'[1]

ENGINEERS

The profession of Civil Engineer, being the art of directing the Great Sources of Power in Nature for the use and convenience of man.
Charter of the Institution of Civil Engineers, 1828.

Of all countries I know, this country respects engineers least.
Lord Snow, December 1964.

Some people suspect that the insuperability of the development hump is partly due to the decline in the influence of engineers. Compared to engineers on the continent, or in Russia (where they are one of the most respected professions) British engineers are not much in evidence. In Victorian times names like Brunel, Naesmith or Telford were national heroes: in the railway boom, ambitious engineers set up their offices in Victoria Street, close to parliament where they pushed through their bills. The consultants are still there, several of them earning as much as £20,000 a year: but they are far less noticed by parliament or the public. The Institute of Civil Engineers, a stately palazzo off Parliament Square, still evokes the grandeur of Victorian technocrats, with rooms full of portraits of past presidents, including Bidder, the mathematician who could multiply twelve figures by twelve figures in his head. It has a council room with a horseshoe table,

[1] *New Statesman*, September 11, 1964.

holding the names of present councillors—Manzoni, Baker, Owen Williams, Skempton, Bugsby.

Hundreds of contemporary engineers, including these and men such as Sir George Edwards (who designed the Viscount), or Sir Christopher Hinton (who planned the first nuclear power stations) have had a large effect on British life. But engineering has become much less associated with individual names. Partly this is because much exciting British engineering takes place abroad, for such projects as the Indus dam in Pakistan or the Kariba dam on the Zambesi. But the men behind new projects in Britain, like the M1 or the Forth Road Bridge, have become much more anonymous. Since Victorian times engineers have no longer dealt with single patrons like the Duke of Bridgewater, but have become involved with teams and committees, and this has helped to weaken their influence. Many engineers feel that they have lost their initiative to the businessmen—particularly accountants.

Engineering has lost a good deal of its panache: it is sad to compare the astonishing speed and boldness of Victorian projects —the Crystal Palace took a few months from drawing board to completion, and the first fly-over, the Holborn Viaduct, was built a century ago—with the delays, committees and qualifications of modern engineering: the extension of the Victoria underground was at the discussion stage for over ten years. Much of the slowness is due to the delays of democracy, and the sheer *poverty* of modern Britain: but it is partly, too, due to the lack of powerful engineers at the top.

Compared with the continent, the *average* British engineer is as well trained, but there is no British equivalent for the rigorous two-year course of the French *polytechniciens* who have had such a large influence on their industry and civil service, and the British schools lack their high standing. Continental engineers have a strong schooling in theory, which helps to give them a daring and enterprise, shown in the French monorail, Orly airport, or Nervi's Olympic stadium at Rome. Initiative for the Channel tunnel has come from the French engineers, with less interest from London.

The scope of engineers has been further limited by the fragmentations of the profession which, like the Inns of Court, has produced complicated internal rivalries. These were the technological institutes with their memberships (excluding overseas members) in 1962:[1]

[1] From Report of the Advisory Council on Scientific Policy, 1962–3. p. 47.

Institution of	Chemical Engineers	449
	Civil Engineers	1,254
	Electrical Engineers	1,671
	Gas Engineers	102
	Marine Engineers	406
	Mechanical Engineers	2,501
	Metallurgists	354
	Mining Engineers	102
	Mining and Metallurgy	18
	Municipal Engineers	163
	Naval Architects	91
	Production Engineers	521
	Radio Engineers	663
	Rubber Industry	60
	Structural Engineers	295
Textile Institute		123
Plastics Institute		71
Royal Aeronautical Society		386
Total		9,230

The oldest of the institutes, the 'Civils' (bridges, roads, dams) took a high-handed line with newcomers, and actually refused to elect George Stephenson a member, which led to the foundation of the 'Mechanicals' (trains, cars, aeroplanes). Others, the Electricals, Chemicals, etc., followed, so that by 1929 there were already more than a hundred societies for engineers. And since 1900 the architects have stolen some of the engineers' thunder: the two professions have been at daggers drawn, and much more separate than in Europe. But the different branches of engineering are now, more than ever, interdependent; a dam can involve Civil, Mechanical and Electrical—and engineers are aware that this fragmentation has weakened their scope: 'a multiplicity of bodies and an attitude of mind which seems to elevate the importance of the part above that of the whole.'[1] Is not the status of the engineer badly hampered,' asked Lord Hailsham in May 1963, 'by the whole alphabet of letters and too-narrow syllabuses imposed by the present structure of the profession?'

A brave new bid for unity was made by Sir George McNaughton, chief engineer to the Ministry of Housing, in his presidential address to the Civils on November 7, 1961. 'If engineers are to gain their old position of policy makers and financial controllers in the work they undertake,' he said, 'they must be able to express

[1] J. G. Orr, General Secretary of the Engineers Guild: *The Times*, November 13, 1961.

views on wider fields than the purely technical.' He criticised the fragmentation of the profession, and suggested that there should be a high-level co-ordinating body between the Civils, Mechanicals and Electricals, 'so powerful that other chartered bodies could not afford to stand aside' (which produced an angry retort from the Chemicals). Talking about the decline in engineers' influence, he said: 'One can only speculate as to the cause of the present position. Can it be the absence of a higher standard of education in the humanities and the social sciences amongst the entrants to the profession?'

As a result of this and other criticisms, in 1962 twelve of the professional engineering bodies formed a joint organisation to represent the views of the professional engineer, to enable engineers to speak with one voice. But the basic troubles of the engineers remain, and a further attack came in July 1963 with the publication of the *Feilden Report on Engineering Design*, under the chairmanship of G. R. B. Feilden, the group technical director of Davy-Ashmore. The report made strong criticisms of the professional institutions—particularly the Mechanicals—with their narrow attitudes and lack of interest in design. It reported the decline of Britain's trade in engineering goods and recommended that 'if Britain is to conquer the proportion of a competitive world engineering market necessary to maintain our standard of living, quite drastic alterations will be needed to the present arrangements. A much greater number of first-class people must be recruited, trained and kept in the field of mechanical design.'

SCIENTISTS AND WAR

Nearly half the scientific research in the country is undertaken by the Ministry of Defence, who in 1964 employed 5,270 scientists with degrees or equivalent qualifications, out of the 12,000 employed by the government. This is the murkiest region of all, for what happens to the money is known to only a handful of people. Most of the scientists work in isolated stations, scattered over the country, knowing little about each other. Secrecy is anathema to scientists. Discovery depends on communication. Scientists have, since the end of the seventeenth century, been internationally-minded. Science knows no real frontiers; and a Russian scientist can soon find himself at home in the Royal Society. The creeping expansion of *secret* research, largely devoted to means of destruction, has depressed scientists all over the world.

Defence inevitably is an area of preposterous waste. Extravagant projects can take seven or eight years to complete, rolling on with their own massive inertia, only to find themselves hopelessly unwanted, for either political or technical reasons. 'Research' still conjures up test-tubes or microscopes, but more often it means gigantic engineering contraptions, lumps of radio-active hardware, and intricate electronic devices—enough to build a whole town, and all likely to be scrapped. Only momentarily does parliament and the public glimpse the waste—as when the government abandoned the military project for the Blue Streak missile in 1960 after it had cost £100 million. 'The trouble with controlling expenditure,' as one senior scientist said, 'is that you're dealing with crises which only surface when they're already heavily charged politically.'

The decisions for these vast outlays are taken by the Chiefs of Staff, the Minister of Defence, and ultimately by the cabinet. But a key position—probably the most important scientific job—is held by the Chief Scientific Adviser to the Ministry of Defence. He lies in the centre of the committee-web: and he is the main link between science and war. The title 'adviser' is misleading, for he is in effect the boss of five thousand scientists, and on his yea or nay projects can prosper or collapse. And since October 1964 he has had the extra position of adviser to the Cabinet Office and, in effect, to the prime minister.

The occupier since 1960, Sir Solly Zuckerman, is a surprising person to find in this sombre position. He is a gay ex-South African (he has not been back there since his youth), with a restless, overflowing mind. He is an expert on baboons and thirty years ago wrote the standard work on the social life of monkeys. He is a gregarious, drawing-room man: he married the daughter of Lord Reading and unlike most scientists moves in several unscientific circles. In spite of his Whitehall commitments, he still goes to Birmingham, where he is still Professor of Anatomy, once a week, and remains tremendously excited by the London Zoo, of which he is secretary.

Since the outbreak of war, Sir Solly has been involved with government science: he studied the effects of bombing and blast, and belonged to the school opposing the wholesale bombing of homes. His perceptive mind, charm, and persuasiveness brought him into the midst of committee-country; he made easy friendships, and remains the confidant of ministers on both sides. He enjoys the corridors of power, but he remains a sensitive intellectual, well aware of his social responsibilities. Some people in Whitehall complain that he is not sufficiently interested in war.

'While essential in matters of defence, the business of secrecy also has great drawbacks,' Sir Solly said. 'It makes it most difficult to get cross-fertilisation between the different branches: and the lack of communication is demoralising for scientists. You get too many people retreating to scientific establishments in the provinces, soaking themselves in their specialised subject, without knowing how it relates to some other subject, or how it will be applied. With the growth of science and specialisation, the isolation is getting worse, everywhere in the world. Scientists nowadays don't think much about the social consequences of science—they're only interested in their specialised fields. When I deliver lectures about the social responsibilities of science, the young scientists regard me as an old square.'

Sir Solly is often criticised for having too much power. He is the funnel through which most scientific ideas pass into government, and in dealing with a cabinet who are so innumerate, his views—like those of Lord Cherwell's during the war—could well be too unquestioned. But he insists that on major issues there is no special magic in the scientific approach. 'The big issues of strategy,' he said to me in 1964, 'like the MLF, disarmament, the Western Alliance, can't be put down like a set of algebraic equations. The basic arguments don't have numbers in them. If you ask an interested scientist for his views about disarmament, he might do his little sums, but he'll also end up with the same comments as a politician about threats of mutual destruction, and so on.'

ATOMIC ENERGY

> Rarely has an industry run through an apparently bottomless fund of public goodwill as rapidly as atomic power.
>
> *The Economist*, July 1963.

The most expensive part of defence research is concerned with atomic energy: and here the ministry delegates its task to the mammoth nationalised industry, dealing both with peaceful and warlike applications—the Atomic Energy Authority. It is the most inpenetrable industry: even to enter their London headquarters in Charles II Street, a visitor has to wear a yellow 'V' badge. The annual report of the 'Atomic Iceberg' reveals little about how its

£35[1] million from the Treasury has been spent. It is divided between two main clients—the Ministry of Defence, for whom it makes weapons, and the Electricity Generating Board, for whom it designs power stations. Between them the AEA manages to be accountable to no one.

It was founded in 1954, full of high promise, as an off-shoot of the Ministry of Supply, which had made the first atomic bombs. The American AEC farmed out all its nuclear research to universities and companies, but the British decided to have it all in one rich national organisation, separate from industry or universities. The new Authority was full of enthusiastic scientists, headed by Sir John Cockcroft, and Britain seemed on the verge of leading the world to cheap nuclear power. The AEA was determined to free itself from the civil service, to become a flexible organism, run by scientists for scientists.

But the excitement wore off. Nuclear power turned out to be far more expensive than coal or oil. Building power stations produced unsuspected problems, and large losses for the contractors. 'Zeta', which it was hoped might produce power from fusion, did nothing of the kind. And AEA grew from exciting youth to corpulent middle age. In seven years the assets increased from £155 million to £250 million, and by 1964 the staff was 36,000. Scientists complained that the administration became top-heavy, bureaucratic and cluttered with protocol—that it was becoming just a bureaucracy with a small eccentric fringe—a BBC of science. For a time the scientific knights wouldn't talk to each other. The administration of research has appalling problems: for often there is no obvious output like broadcasts or oil sales, no clear distinction between means and ends, and the spending of millions may depend on one uncertain hunch. The ups and downs of public excitement have their effect on morale: 'First they put us on a pinnacle withich was much too high,' said Sir William Penney, in 1961, 'then we went down into a hole which we never deserved: in five years they may regard us as quite a reasonable bunch of men.'

At the head of the Authority is Sir William Penney, the man who, more than anyone, was responsible for the British A-bomb and H-bomb. He is the epitome of the self-made, dedicated scientist. He has a boyish-looking face with a thatch of hair, large glasses and an ambling walk. He lives a quiet, suburban life. He talks in a

[1] Estimate for 1964–5. This includes £9½ million for the National Institute for Research in Nuclear Science.

sing-song, almost apologetic way, and has a matter-of-fact attitude to questions. Penney is one of the 'new men'—the race of scientists growing up with a background quite separate from the old class-structure. He was the son of an army warrant officer, and went as a boy to Sheerness Technical College where he discovered his mathematical flair. He became assistant professor at the Imperial College, and during the war (like Sir Solly) he investigated bombing effects. In 1944, as one of the most brilliant of Britain's young scientists, he was invited to America to study the atomic bomb; and on August 9, 1945, he was one of two Englishmen to watch the explosion on Nagasaki. Since then he has been bound up with nuclear research, perfected the A-bomb in 1952, and the H-bomb in 1957.

He is known for his unpretentious approach to problems. A story is told of Americans in the New Mexico desert discussing expensive methods for measuring atomic blast. 'Why can't you try,' said Penney diffidently, 'putting a row of tin cans across the desert, to see how they get dented by the blast.' It worked perfectly.

Penney remains ultimately responsible for all Britain's nuclear research. The centre for basic research is at Harwell in Berkshire, the most expensive of the AEA's establishments, which claims to be the biggest atomic research establishment in the free world—employing 6,000, including 1,500 scientists.

Like so many modern research centres, Harwell is remote and isolated. It looks like, and was, a war-time air force base, sitting by itself in the Berkshire countryside, with rows of married quarters, a high fence all round, and inside, a mass of fantastic ironmongery, like a deserted fairground. It is dominated by the reactors, built inside great concrete cubes and surrounded by strange noises—beeps, tapocatas, boinks and pssts. Thick double doors lead into a jungle of engineering round the central reactor. It is a world on its own: there are TV screens, dashboards of dials, and a travelling crane. Bits of radio-active metal are taken out of the reactor and carried in lead caskets to laboratories where scientists in rubber gloves study them behind glass screens.

Harwell is a long way from the conversaziones at the Royal Society and the idea of the universal man. It is typical of the fragmented state of science, where one man can spend a lifetime experimenting with one vast, possibly quite fruitless, contraption. No one yet knows whether Harwell will become a forgotten white elephant, or the forerunner of the dawn of a new age. For at

Harwell a layman realises with apprehension what in his own awe of science he can well forget, that scientists are not omniscient or prophetic, but groping in the dark like anyone else.

GOVERNMENT AND SCIENTISTS

The relationship between the freedom of scientific institutions and the controlling power of government finance is a problem in all Western democracies, made more pressing by the immense concentration of Russian scientific effort. In Britain the problem is complicated by the low science quotient among the administrators—notably in the cabinet and the higher civil service; and here the Whitehall division between specialists and mandarins is most serious of all. The introduction of 'scientific advisers' to provide the link between Whitehall departments and research organisations has not been very effectual, since the advisers do not often become closely involved in policy-making: 'Unless this type of integration is assured,' said Sir Solly Zuckerman's report in 1961, 'we do not think that many good scientists would find the job attractive in certain departments; they would have few staff and would have no direct responsibilities for research, and they would be uncomfortably placed between the main body of the department and the research establishments of other organisations.'[1] 'Young scientists aren't so interested in the business of government,' Sir Solly told me: 'It was the war that pushed many of the old ones into government service, and they're getting older.'

Between the Treasury and scientific departments there remains a wide distance: Sir Solly's report pointed out in kid-glove language some defects—the lack of 'forward looks', the arguing in a 'financial vacuum', the way projects 'drift on from one state to another without strict control at critical points', and the preservation of old projects through inertia: 'Lay officials in the Treasury . . . must inevitably tend to focus their attention on new major projects, on new fields of research, or on unforeseen increased expenditure on old projects, and less on the elimination of existing items because they have declined in importance.'[2] Since his report appeared, Sir Solly has noted some improvement. 'I think we have slowed down the process whereby we make mistakes,' he told me in 1964; 'and we can check ourselves more frequently than we did before.'

[1] *Management and Control of Research and Development.* HMSO 1961, p. 80.
[2] *Ibid*, p. 44.

Differences in background exacerbate the relationship—inevitably bitter—between science and politics. 'You pursue a thing up to a certain point and then the whole thing disappears into a higher political level, and the decision is taken—and nobody quite seems to know why,' as one leading scientist put it: 'The people who take the decisions really don't know anything about them. You might just as well toss a penny—in fact that would be better than not deciding at all, like Blue Streak. They tend to put off decisions until *nature* decides.'

The integration of scientists into government is obviously not easy. Many are naturally radical, dis-organisation men, not 'house-trained' and quite enjoying their battles with Whitehall. And very often—as civil servants love explaining—they fail, like economists, to agree among themselves. But the present exclusion of scientists from the centre only makes things worse: it is here that the closed collegiate tradition of Whitehall, and the amateur tradition in politics, is most obviously hopeless. When politicians *do* take science seriously, there is the danger that they adopt a court 'prof.', like Lord Cherwell, taking his advice as more infallible than any scientist's could possible be; and laymen are often too easily overawed by scientific technicalities. 'The trouble is, I suspect,' said Stephen Toulmin in 1964, after the OECD conference on science in Vienna, 'that we in Britain are inclined to exaggerate the technicality of science policy questions, and that we are unduly pessimistic about the value of public debate in this area.[1]

THE BRAIN DRAIN

Many of the complaints and disabilities of British scientists emerged more sharply during 1963, when startling figures were published showing the scale of emigration of British scientists to America. The subsequent political row about the 'brain drain', as it was called by Peter Fairley of the *Evening Standard*, produced a lot of jingoistic reactions, and neglected to take into account the drain *towards* Britain, from the Commonwealth and South Africa. But the figures were certainly alarming for a country which wants to 'live on its wits'. The Royal Society published a report in February, followed by a memorandum in May to the Minister for Science from the Advisory Council for Scientific Policy, headed by Lord Todd. The memorandum (which patronisingly criticised the

[1] *The Listener*, June 11, 1964.

Royal Society's report) reckoned that 'there has been a definite increase over the past ten years in this loss, which at present amounts to 7 to 8 per cent of our annual intake of newly-qualified Ph.Ds.' The attractions were 'salary, opportunity, escape from a social order which they feel undervalues them relative to others, and better facilities'. It found that, while chemical concerns in Britain pay fresh Ph.Ds. £1,000 to £1,200 a year, their equivalent in America would be paid between $9,000 and $10,000: 'It is generally agreed that salaries of scientists (notably in the academic sphere) have not achieved comparability with the general post-war level of incomes.' On the score of opportunity, the memorandum went on, 'It is generally held that the scientists in American industry has a much better chance to rise rapidly in an organisation with no positions barred to him provided he shows ability and aptitude.'

Discussing the social factors the memorandum suggested, 'There is a fairly general feeling among scientists, especially in industry, that they are usually undervalued in relation to others with less obvious qualifications. Phrases like "back-room boys", and "on tap but not on top" are themselves indicative of a feeling which is widespread and has many ramifications. It is widely held that the social status of the scientist in the United States is higher although, again, such matters are hard to evaluate. What does appear to have some real basis is the relative lack of vigour and enterprise in research in wide areas of industry and of intimate and stimulating contacts between academic, industrial and government institutions. In this matter, faults are not confined to one group and lack of enterprise can readily be found in all three. But it is probable that a greater degree of vigour in these directions would, coupled with the gradually changing public image of the scientist and engineer, in due course lead to a healthier situation more akin to that found in the United States.'

WAND OVER WHITEHALL?

Whitehall, partly because of the lack of scientists in its midst, partly because of its healthy democratic respect for the independence of other institutions, has approached the control and co-ordination of research with great hesitation. As far as possible, the government has left the scientific dons to themselves, while giving them large grants: 'In our view,' wrote the Zuckerman report, 'pure basic research is best carried out in the environment of a university rather than in that of a government research establishment. It is characteristic of universities that they provide their members with the necessary freedom to pursue any line of enquiry they wish to follow and, broadly speaking, at whatever pace their inclinations dictate.'[1]

The aristocrats of science remain the university dons: of the 616 Fellows of the Royal Society in 1960, 126 were at London University, 107 at Cambridge, 50 at Oxford, 16 at Edinburgh, 13 at Manchester, 13 at Bristol, 11 at Birmingham and 60 at all the other universities.[2] Cambridge remains the phenomenal seed-bed of British science, as it has been, off and on, since Newton's day: and the most concentrated area of scientific talent in the world.

But applied government research is controlled by a whole cluster of councils—committee-country with a vengeance. A single scientist may sit on a score: 'I *loathe* advisory committees: there are far too many,' one of them said. 'If only committees had actual control over spending, they'd be much more responsible.' 'There's a small group of committee-people who the civil servants have got used to,' explained another scientist: 'it's not so much that they've got *confidence* in them, but they know they won't make a nuisance of themselves, by telling things to the *Daily Mail*.'

Some of the councils have clear-cut powers, with definite annual budgets to allocate for research projects. These are the main government councils, under the post-Trend system, with their executive heads and annual allocations

Science Research Council (£20 million)	Sir Harry Melville
Natural Environmental Research Council (£3·5 million)	Sir Graham Sutton
Medical Research Council (£8·8 million)	Sir Harold Himsworth
Agricultural Research Council (£8 million)	Sir Gordon Cox

These main councils are run on the same principle as the Universities Grants Committee, of allowing 'indirect rule' to the academics. But at a lower level there are webs of committees who can only advise civil servants and ministers, and it is in this tangled region that scientists have felt most cheated and wasted. Here is the basic cross purposes and frustration between science and government. The most persistent critic has been Patrick Blackett, Professor of Physics at Imperial College, who, in the past few

[1] Zuckerman, p. 26.
[2] From *Discovery*, July 1960.

years, became the most effective political spokesman among the top scientists, and who has set himself to cut through this muddled undergrowth. He is a tall, ruggedly handsome man with a strong steep head and a clipped and articulate voice, which can be devastatingly brusque. His career has been probably the most distinguished of all Britain's living scientists; he began as a regular naval officer—he still has that quarter-deck authority—and became a fellow of King's, Cambridge and part of Rutherford's glittering team of young physicists, who split the atom. He was known for his strong left-wing views and his suspicions of America, but during the war he played a key part in atomic research, and after it was closely concerned with the relations of government and scientists, helping to set up the Advisory Council for Scientific Policy. He became passionately interested in the consequences of the nuclear bomb, and its effect on East-West relations, making sharp attacks on the American 'war game experts' and 'cold warriors'; and at the same time was emotionally involved in helping poorer nations.

Blackett has kept close links with the Labour Party, and in spite of his intolerance and brusqueness he has understood the problems of government as few other scientists have done. In an important article in the *New Statesman*, just before the election of 1964, he analysed the uselessness of the advisory committees—'so beloved of Whitehall, I suspect, just because of their relative ineffectiveness'. The Whitehall system, he said, 'seems almost designed to ensure the giving of advice without the responsibility of action and the taking of action without real knowledge'. He compared the advisory councils to the story of the FAO Bull:

> Once upon a time, not long ago, the Food and Agricultural Organisation of the United Nations sent a prize bull to some developing country to improve the local breed of cattle. When the bull arrived it showed amiable interest but no more in the cows presented to it. When asked why he did not get on with his job, the bull replied: 'You forget that I am an FAO bull—so my rôle is solely advisory.'

To create this 'wand over Whitehall', the Labour Government in October 1964 reorganised once more the structure of scientific policy-making, with a new alphabet of forgettable initials. On the one side, the Department of Education and Science, under its Minister, was given responsibility for the SRC, the

NERC, the MRC and the ARC[1]—the bodies most involved with universities and pure research—and took charge of the whole field of scientific education and expansion. The Education Ministry, too, was to appoint a new Council for Scientific Policy, as advocated in the Trend report, but with greater powers. The CSP is the closest thing to a 'Scientists' Cabinet' and is designed to be (in Blackett's words) 'the main decision-making body for matters scientific'. It is the successor of the Advisory Council for Scientific Policy, which was likewise intended to be decisive and influential; but without a staff, or a full-time chairman, or time to discuss long problems, it had become something of a joke among scientists. How far the new CSP will be allowed teeth, to carry its wishes against the Ministry, is still too early to see; but this council is likely to be the main battleground between scientists and politicians.

On the other side, a new 'Ministry of Technology' was set up, in the glass Vickers Tower on the Thames, to supervise the industrial research, and to act as the ginger-group to push industry into innovation. It took over the research stations and industrial side of the DSIR, and the embarrassing responsibility for the Atomic Energy Authority. And it had a *new* Advisory Council on Technology, made up of industrialists, scientists, economists and trade unionists, with the Minister as Chairman, and with none other than Professor Blackett himself as vice-chairman. The other members were:

Sir Leon Bagrit, chairman, Elliott-Automation, Ltd.
Wilfred D. Brown, chairman, The Glacier Metal Co. Ltd.
Sir William Carron, president, Amalgamated Engineering Union.
Charles Carter, Vice-Chancellor, University of Lancaster.
Dr. Samuel Curran, FRS, Vice-Chancellor, University of Strathclyde.
Sir Arnold Hall, FRS, managing director, Hawker Siddeley Group.
Frank Kearton, FRS, chairman, Courtaulds Ltd.
Professor Michael Lighthill, FRS, Imperial College of Science and Technology.
Lord Nelson of Stafford, chairman, English Electric Co. Ltd.
Hugh Tett, chairman, Esso Petroleum Co. Ltd.

The new Ministry has a fascinating conjunction of personalities. For as the minister, Wilson appointed Frank Cousins, the militant left-wing trade unionist; and as his parliamentary secretary came Lord Snow (novelist–scientist–civil servant) who had acquired public fame both as the propounder of the 'Two Cultures' of

[1] *See* p. 387.

Science and Arts, and as the chronicler of the 'Corridors of Power'. Snow's was as controversial an appointment as Cousins': this big, bald man, with his flare for publicity and his romantic optimism has set himself up as a modern prophet, and his adulation of Russia has made him an easy target for intellectuals, particularly *Encounter*. But he has done more than anyone else to increase the self-respect of scientists, and to state their case; and his absorption into Whitehall was a symbolic gesture of recognition. Snow gives a bold outward flourish, but it is likely that Blackett will emerge as the more influential figure in the ministry.

The problem of combining vast Government spending on science with individual opportunity remains an insoluble one—both for democracies and for totalitarian states. How to co-ordinate research without directing it, how to keep universities separate, yet not too separate, how to have variety without jealousy—all these are familar problems in other spheres, but made harder by the special unpredictability of scientists and their discoveries. No government can avoid vast wastage and muddle. The most that can be hoped for is a structure and relationship between the two sides which breeds confidence and enthusiasm; and for that, the appearance is as important as the reality.

Anatomy of Britain Today

PART TWO

21

THE CITY

I believe that our system, though curious and peculiar, may be worked safely; but if we wish so to work it, we must study it.

Walter Bagehot (Lombard Street).

There was an Old Person of Bow,
Whom nobody happened to know;
So they gave him some Soap,
And said coldly, 'We hope
You will go back directly to Bow!'

Edward Lear.

LONDON is two cities—the city of Westminster, and the city of London, each with its own cathedral. Although the green fields and river banks between them have long ago been built over, the difference in character remains: Whitehall and Bishopsgate are at the opposite ends of Britain's affairs—government in Westminster, and finance in the city. Here we enter a territory much less mapped than Whitehall, and harder to report accurately. Only three documents since the war—the astonishing Bank Rate Tribunal of 1957, the Radcliffe Report of 1959, and the Jenkins Report of 1963—have helped to open up the interior: there are no royal commissions, select committees or parliamentary debates to throw light on its activities, and city men are very unreflective about what they are doing. But as Britain begins competing more hotly with Europe and America so the character of the city becomes more central.

The city is still almost as concentrated as a hundred years ago: it breathes a far more restricted air than Westminster. It is still bounded by the 'square mile', which can be crossed in twenty minutes, and which contains most of the important financial institutions in Britain. In the middle of this square is a still smaller area, a quarter-mile across, centring on the Bank of England and the Lord Mayor's Mansion House, which forms the heart of the city: it includes the stock exchange, several insurance companies, the commodity markets and nearly all the banks. Concentration is the most important characteristic of the city:

within the square mile, although only 5,000 live there by night, 400,000 people work by day. Apart from the newspaper industry on the Western edge, none of them makes anything except money. The propinquity of the financial offices, their steady rubbing, shaping and polishing, has provided the 'sensitive mechanism' (to use the favourite city phrase) on which their reputation rests.

The inner square has an intense atmosphere which no visitor can fail to notice. Nearly everyone wears a dark suit and carries an umbrella, and discount brokers or gilt-edged stockbrokers still wear top hats. The restaurants are crowded with rows of pale-faced, black-coated men. Since the war tens of thousands of girls have strayed into the city, to work on the adding machines, typewriters and files, and their short skirts and jaunty walk contrasts with the solid lope of city men: but they are kept well apart, and have giggling lunches at the tea-shops while the men have beer and steaks. 'The city is a village' is a favourite saying: the streets and bars are full of people meeting, recognising, discussing each other. They are pressed closely together by their work, and isolated from the rest of London or the country. But even the different sectors of the city are very introverted: few stockbrokers have even been inside Lloyd's. The city is really a group of villages, with a moat round them all.

The moat, like that round other professions, has grown wider in the past thirty years. In spite of the inter-marriages and politico-financial dynasties, the city no longer enjoys very close connections with the Conservative party. There are still strong bonds between right-wing Conservatives and the more imperialistic city companies, such as the British South Africa Company and Tanganyika Concessions, and city companies still subsidise the Conservative party. But the new generation of professional Tory politicians have no love for the world of EC2; Heath and Maudling have joined the boards of merchant banks, but with no obvious enthusiasm. The distance between the Tory party and the city is reflected by the singular lack of city honours conferred during the Tory administration. In the New Year's Honours of 1963, not a single city man was honoured.[1] The rift no doubt has mixed causes. The landed interest have always liked to be aloof—or at least seem aloof—from trade, as at White's club: but the professionalisation of politics has increased the distance, and the Conservative Central Office look more anxiously to the electors and their subscriptions than to the city.

[1] *See* Nigel Lawson in the *Sunday Telegraph*, January 6, 1963.

But this new aloofness from the Conservative party has not noticeably resulted in a new closeness to the Labour Party. 'You could work for years in the city as a director, and lunch out every day, without meeting a recognisable Socialist'[1] wrote Lord Longford, the Labour politician who, as chairman of the (Irish) National Bank, *did* work for years in the city. He was made aware of the deep anti-Socialist feeling, not least when he was black-balled from a city club on account of it.

When the Labour party took office in 1964, there seemed at first a good chance of friendly relations between the city and the Government. Many city people were resigned beforehand to a Labour victory, and some even looked forward to a change. *The Economist* was able to report ten days after the election that 'the city has quickly reconciled itself to living under Labour; that Labour has a majority of only four has made the reconciliation all the easier. The money broker who felt the result "could have been a damn sight worse" and the two merchant bankers who considered the Tory defeat was a "damn good thing" were fairly representative of city opinion . . . The city is increasingly passing into the hands of professional men who may be discreetly socialist or whose conservatism springs from intellectual conviction rather than inherited wealth.'

Two months later, the city's mood had degenerated into a selfish and destructive sulk. The Labour party's moves had not, in fact, been at all radical: they responded to the financial crisis which they inherited with traditional methods—introducing an emergency deflationary budget, raising the bank rate, and creating a credit squeeze. George Brown, from his new department, James Callaghan, from the Treasury, and Douglas Jay, from the Board of Trade, had all stressed their respect for private industry and profits. But the new Government's plans for a capital gains tax and a corporation tax, the reactions of investors and speculators abroad, and the aftermath of the sterling crisis—all of which depressed the stock market—caused a wave of bitterness and recrimination through the city. Bankers and brokers spread damaging rumours—that the Governor of the Bank of England was going to resign, that a merchant bank was going into liquidation—which further reduced confidence abroad. The city, whose contact with the rest of London was always tenuous, began to talk about the new Government, as they had in 1945, as if it were some foreign army of occupation, which could

[1] Lord Longford: *Five Lives*, 1964. p. 21.

only be ousted by sabotage. By Christmas, the city's feud had become embarrassing even to Conservative newspapers. 'The city has got into a state that I can best describe as hysterical semi-paralysis,' wrote Kenneth Fleet in the *Sunday Telegraph* on December 20; 'in measuring out doses of gloom and misery it is outstripping the Government and compounding the doubts and fears of British industry.' 'The City of London has already allowed itself to drift too far away from the rest of national life . . .' wrote William Rees-Mogg in the *Sunday Times* on the same day: 'it has lost its old contact with the political life of the country . . . To mistake this modest, inoffensive, cautious, co-operative and proper-minded administration for a menace to the welfare of business and to the peace of mind of financiers is as absurd as to mistake one's maiden aunt for the Merry Devil of Edmonton.'

Several attempts have been made to bring the city and the Labour party closer together; enterprising banks and stockbrokers, like Rothschilds' and Warburg's, often have Labour leaders to lunch, and Harold Wilson has been quite assiduous in reassuring the city about Labour's sound financial views. A few individuals, like Siegmund Warburg or Sir Leon Bagrit, help to serve as bridgeheads between the two worlds; but the ravine remains. Probably the most influential of the left-wing city men is Sir Jock Campbell, the dynamic and outspoken chairman of Booker Brothers, the group of companies based on sugar in British Guiana. Sir Jock is a gay and humorous tycoon with a love of fast cars, but he is one of those enigmatic characters who cut across most classifications. He is both a very shrewd practical businessman and an intellectual, with a sharp, analytical mind, expert (for instance) at crosswords. He belongs to the sixth generation of a family of sugar-planters, whose firm was absorbed into Booker's; but very early in his life he identified himself with West Indians and Africans, which has led him to become an unrelenting opponent of apartheid. Much of his sympathy for the underdog is also good business policy; like the anti-slavery movement in the last century, the anti-apartheid movement is a blend of passionate do-gooders with far-sighted business interests; but Sir Jock combines both, and unlike the heads of other ex-colonial companies, he has kept ahead of the wind of change, and barged into politics with extraordinary daring—most notably during the Nyasaland crisis of 1959. In his moral beliefs, his intellectualism, and his political daring, he is the antithesis of most city men, who look on him with puzzlement.

TRADITION AND PROGRESS

It is the pride of the city that it can combine formality with adaptability, tradition with enterprise—the first giving security to the second. Much of the paraphernalia is still Dickensian; the shiny Victorian drinking saloons, down small alley-ways; the ancient mahogany offices with worn brass-plates beside the front door; the liveried uniforms of waiters and butlers. But city men point out the electronic apparatus alongside their aged butlers, and ancient offices furnished with teleprinters. 'Tradition and Progress' is a recurring heading to articles about the city, in annual surveys about steady advance.

In training its people, too, the city is traditional; much of it is still run on the 'fagging system'—the habit rejected by the civil service in 1870, of employing young men, often intelligent and expensively educated, at menial tasks for several years, copying transfers, writing in ledgers, or checking figures. The docile 'public school proletariat' are employed on jobs which for some years may need no part of their expensive education except simple arithmetic. The analytical Oxbridge mind of Whitehall is noticeably absent in the city. There is a City University club, founded in 1885 (Oxbridge only, of course), but social and other ambitions centre round the city companies—the Fishmongers, Stationers or Haberdashers, and the grand premises of Armoury House. It is the loyal unquestioning spirit of the regiment rather than the enquiring approach of universities which pervades the city, which contains whole light brigades of men at their desks, not reasoning why. The repression, like that of fags at school, achieves an awful continuity, with the older men remembering their own young drudgery, and although since the war the city has seen a large influx of graduates, much of the old discipline survives.

'It doesn't matter *what* you know, but *who* you know', they say in the city: personal contacts, and the personal background which provides them, are still decisive. This helps to account, perhaps, for the fact that the city remains the unchallenged bastion of the minor public schools, and within the square mile you hear more talk about men's schools, background, and above all their families, than anywhere else except perhaps in the Guards. The waves of the meritocracy, of examination wallahs and managerial revolutions which have swept through the civil service and industrial corporations, are only now lapping into the city. The 'Old Boy

Net' which has become a sheepish or satirical phrase in other areas, remains a venerable concept.

The justification is that the city is based on *trust.* 'My word is my bond' is the motto of the stock exchange: 'Fidentia' is the motto of Lloyd's. The speed of the city's operations depends on acceptance of verbal promises, and this has been increased by the invention of the telephone—which allows hundreds of thousands of promises to be made every day. This quick trust, it is argued, depends on knowing to whom, or to what kind of person, you are talking—knowing he is 'one of us'. Unlike New York or Paris, which have a less homogeneous tradition, the city of London has a tribal past, and this eliminates—as in the Foreign Office—fuss and lawyers. The public school proletariat help to provide the lubricants to the sensitive mechanism.

But it is often thought that trust is the *only* requirement. What-you-know is gradually gaining over who-you-know. Since the war many clever young men with no connections have made fortunes and reputations. Stockbroking, insurance and banking are becoming increasingly specialised, and with specialisation the expert enters his kingdom. But it is still surprisingly possible to build a city career by knowing everyone, and knowing very little. The city, like the conservative party, still loves the ignorant but reliable amateur, but even the most calculating professionals often like to appear as amateurs in the end.

Most English institutions are weighed down with Victorian furniture, but none so heavily as the city. For every part of the city is conscious of its glorious past: from 1815 to 1914—the 'English Era'—London was the undisputed financial capital of the world. Since 1914 the city has suffered a series of shocks—the shift of power to Zurich, the dwindling of foreign loans, the growth of nationalism, the Labour government, the loss of Empire, the disappearance of China. The city has survived these buffets with a resilience which has surprised many critics; the Dickensian-looking men in their mahogany parlours have turned from financing foreign governments to devising hire-purchase schemes; the Lloyd's underwriters have continued sitting in front of dog-eared ledgers, but now insuring atomic power stations and jet planes. The city (which is full of self-praise) congratulates itself on remaining the leading international market for commodities, chartered shipping, foreign exchange or insurance, and above all on providing the 'invisible earnings' which help to redress Britain's balance of payments; and this last fact alone has been enough to dissuade Labour governments from trying to tamper with that sensitive mechanism. City people justify their curious archaisms—the ceremonial of discount brokers, the fagging, the ritual of Lloyd's—with the phrase so often used of the House of Lords, the election of bishops, or the gobbledigook of barristers: 'It may seem odd to you', they say, 'but there is one thing to be said for it—it *works.*' But the phrase 'it works' is of course inadequate: Liberia works, avoirdupois works. The city is never likely to collapse suddenly, with a broken mainspring; its danger is that it might, like the Hapsburg court, gradually become irrelevant to the modern world.

STOCK EXCHANGE

In the city
They sell and buy
And nobody ever
Asks them why.

But since it contents them
To buy and sell
God forgive them!
They might as well.

Humbert Wolfe

The city of London is full of exchanges, buying and selling *things*—wool, meat, gold, metals, rubber or spices, each with their own special smell—but since the joint stock system was invented in the seventeenth century, allowing the public to buy shares of companies, the most important market has become the market for shares. There are no fewer than twenty-two stock exchanges in Britain, from Aberdeen to Exeter, but by far the biggest is in London. The London stock exchange is the main market for 55 billion pounds' worth of investments, in 9,000 different kinds of shares. £18 billion are in government stock, representing part of the National Debt. The rest are shares in anything from banks and shops to steel-mills and shipping companies. The centre of the market is the big block of offices, shaped like the bow of a ship, just next to the Bank of England. Round the block and in neighbouring buildings are stockbrokers' offices, each with their ticker-tapes and white plastic boards showing the latest prices. In the middle of them is the dingy Victorian hall of brown marble, filled with two thousand men in dark suits, which is the stock exchange itself.

The building has been described by the senior deputy chairman,

Henry Murray Owen Knox, as 'absolutely out of date and grossly inadequate', and in 1964 plans were drawn up for rebuilding a skyscraper on the same site, by a socialist peer architect, Richard Llewelyn Davies.

The hall is essentially a market-place, with men—no girls—busily buying and selling, and it is the nerve centre of the city of London. The stock exchange is dingier and rowdier than the insurance 'Room' of Lloyd's—which may reflect its seedier origins: the 'rascally' stock-jobbers of the eighteenth century who clustered round 'Change Alley' were much less solid citizens than the insurers at Lloyd's coffee-house. The stock exchange has the atmosphere of a superannuated schoolroom. On an afternoon when I was there, one lugubrious-looking broker was walking round the room with a feather duster, tickling the other side of men's bald heads, so that they looked round to discover nobody; another broker was kicking a newspaper, crunched into a football, round the hall; another was throwing paper-pellets, with careful marksmanship, at his colleagues.

Looking down on the 'House', you can see the different parts of the market at work. Government stock ('gilt-edged') on the right is usually sedate, with a few men in silk hats—the gilt-edged uniform. On the left are Mines; in the middle are Oils and Industrials. In each section are the 'jobbers', the middle-men (who provide the market and quote the prices)—a unique English profession, whose necessity is often questioned. Weaving round the jobbers are the stockbrokers, the agents of the public, trying to buy or sell their shares. From time to time a bell rings in the House, a notice is put up on a board, and yellow words begin to move across a big screen on the wall. They may announce an important dividend or a new industrial issue, and now the activity on the floor becomes more comprehensible: brokers rush to the jobbers, trying to buy or sell stock after the news, while the jobbers try to decide how the news will affect their prices.

Several changes have impinged on the conservatism of the stock exchange since the war. In the first place, the 'small investor' has loomed larger: a survey carried out by the Wider Share Ownership Council in 1962 reckoned that about 3·5 million people—or 7 per cent of the population—in Britain now invest in stocks and shares; a Gallup Poll five years before showed that 18 per cent were manual workers, 45 per cent were women, 16 per cent were under 34.[1] The proportion is not so high as in America (10 per

[1] *See* 'The Private Investors'. Gallup Polls, February, 1960.

cent) or in Japan (18 per cent), but the British total has almost doubled in 15 years, and is still rising by about 100,000 a year. Private individuals and trusts probably hold between a half and a third of quoted equities. In the past few years, in order both to attract investors, and to counter political attacks, the stock exchange has tried to endear itself to the public. Since 1953 a public gallery has been opened behind a glass screen, from which visitors can look down on the astonishing spectacle beneath. Gay-looking girls in uniforms (which change colour each year) answer questions; a pamphlet explains 'Why the Stock Exchange is Indispensable'; and films called 'My Word is My Bond' and 'The Launching' are shown every three-quarters of an hour. Stockbrokers are touchy about their reputation. 'Just how well are they—the public—getting to know you?' asks a writer in the *Stock Exchange Journal*: 'more important: when they know you, do they *like* you?'

The present Chairman of the Council is Lord Ritchie of Dundee. He is a handsome, rather theatrical-looking stockbroker with a monocle and pearl tie-pin, and three two-tone green telephones in his panelled office above the main hall. 'We're trying to dispel the Victorian idea that the stock exchange is something mysterious, doing fiddles on the side,' he said: 'we're showing that it's a straightforward job, and part of the nation's business. But we've avoided approaching the stock exchange with advertising like "you want the best shares, we've got them".'

Stockbrokers, like joint stock bankers, are still not *very* keen on widening their custom: they want to be liked, but they do not welcome a rush of new small customers. They look aghast at the activities of American stockbrokers, who advertise in newspapers and sell shares over the counter at Grand Central Station. The ban on individual advertising makes stockbrokers far more anonymous than their American counterparts. The public only sees the names of those who handle new issues, and firms with hundreds of employees are practically unknown save to their private and institutional clients. British stockbrokers sometimes explain that it is wrong to sell shares like soap, but one suspects that the real objection is that it is not worth the *bother*; they are much less mechanised than the Americans, and the cost of arranging a small share transfer often exceeds the profit. One recent survey showed that 17·5 per cent of all bargains carried out at the stock exchange involved amounts of a hundred pounds or less.

The Stock Exchange Council, headed by Lord Ritchie, has been cautious in trying to break down the wall of secrecy that surrounds British companies. But in 1964, following belatedly after the advice of the Jenkins Report, the Council issued quite bold 'recommendations' to the 4,500 public companies quoted on the stock exchange. They asked them to disclose their holdings in other companies, to issue quarterly or half-yearly interim reports, to analyse their trading results, and to reveal their turnover—though in this last case there was no attempt to enforce the disclosure. The recommendations came just at the time of the collapse of John Bloom's washing machine company—a company shrouded in secrecy and muddle—when small fortunes had been lost, and the prestige of the stock exchange was at its lowest point for years. The proposals did something to restore public confidence, but companies are still well able to baffle the ordinary investor with incomprehensible accounts.

The major new influence on stockbrokers has been not the small investors but the new giants of the city—the 'institutions'.[1] The one-and-a-half millions a day that come from the insurance companies, demanding to be invested, have influenced the market much as the arrival of the SS *Caronia* in an African port. When the insurance companies buy, they buy in tens of thousands: by favouring some kinds of shares, they can push the price up steeply, so that the whole market turns round. But the insurance companies, like rich men, are fussy, and demand much more information and service than individual investors. Stockbrokers, like solicitors, have watched since the 1880's the eclipse of rich private clients by the new corporate wealth. Like lawyers' firms they have had to become bigger, more concerned with statistics and research, and have begun to acquire independent information about industry. The big firms have become regarded as the intelligence service for the city, at the centre of the telephone network of 'mmms' and 'wells' and meaningful grunts. 'Better ask Cazenove's', a banker will mumble, and the answer will come back with the authority of the market-place.

Stockbroking has become a more specialised, organised business: the big firms no longer rely entirely on relations and friends to provide their young men, but recruit university graduates of proven intelligence—a new idea for the city. Here, at last, we see the upthrust of the professional meritocrats against the ingrained English respect for the amateur. The institutions have had the effect of institutionalising their brokers, too. Many stockbroking

[1] *See* Chapter 25, p. 449.

firms have their own department of 'investment analysts' who watch trends in share prices, and even visit factories and offices—however unwelcome that may be. Many brokers never go near the rowdy hall, or throw darts or play with feather dusters, and the 3,400 stockbrokers and jobbers have become a rather more respected clan. In Victorian times they were looked down on as a get-rich-quick trade, with vulgar Gothic mansions in South London for pretentious dinner parties. Today, coming closer to industry and insurance, brokers, like admen,[1] are becoming expert agents, not private profiteers.

But one suspects they are apt to exaggerate the extent of their professionalism. The attraction of the stock exchange remains, as it always was, its closeness to the roots of money, and the information and scope it provides for augmenting personal capital. The opportunities which built those stockbrokers' mansions in Victorian times are still at work, and a clever and lucky young stockbroker can still make £10,000 a year by the age of thirty, and a fortune before forty. However much it may have the appearance of a profession, dedicated to service, stockbroking remains close to money-making. Most stockbrokers have their 'peck-order' of clients to whom they will pass on quick tips. Near the top will be close friends, important contacts, large clients, perhaps a duke or an earl; for a client interested in making money, it is always important, through friendship or favours, to be near the top of his broker's list. But usually at the top of his list is '*self*': and it is this first peck at the corn which gives the stockbroker the chance of his fortune.

GREED AND TRUST

The greedy basis of the stock exchange may seem sordid and deplorable, compared to the ideals of public service or the dedication of teachers: after spending two months talking to people in the city, I felt oppressed and dispirited by its narrowness and bleakness, the quasi-sexual fascination with money concealed behind large layers of humbug and ritual, and the sheer boredom of it. And yet (it seems to me) it would be disastrous if the city were to become *genuinely* professional—with aims over-riding the making of money. But if one accepts the necessity for stock exchanges then money-making must surely be the inspiration: Western capitalism has not yet discovered a dynamic substitute

[1] *See* Chapter 35.

for the self-advancing entrepreneur. Only the prospect of personal gain can provide the lively eye on the future, the gambler's skill, the restless awareness of what industries are finished and what still to come, on which the city's reputation must eventually stand or fall. This might seem trite: and yet I found myself surprised how often the city seemed to have turned its back on its money-making origins, and to have become, not too greedy, but not greedy enough.

'The rough and vulgar structure of English commerce is the secret of its life', wrote Bagehot too, 'for it contains "the propensity of variation" which, in the social as in the animal kingdom, is the principle of progress': and Bagehot went on to emphasise how much of the enterprise and progress of the city came from the self-made men, who did not have the protective instincts of the already rich. Does the city still have this 'rough and vulgar structure'? The protective instinct has certainly grown stronger since Victorian times, providing a vast haven of non-competition. There has grown up a thick web of 'gentlemen's agreements' arranging for banks, insurance companies or lawyers not to steal each other's business, and the phrase 'it's not done' is always lurking to console the mediocre and frighten the newcomer. The city, it is true, has an old trick of being first appalled by a newcomer—as we will see—and then accepting him as soon as he is obviously unsquashable (perhaps the same instinct which allowed Britain to jail prime ministers one moment, and invite them to Buckingham Palace the next). Several rough and vulgar men have come up since the war, and behind some stately boardrooms of doddering peers you will often find a few clever upstarts from the suburbs running the business on long-distance telephones. The city, like so many other places, instinctively maintains the gap between dignity and efficiency.

But with protective tariffs, the collapse of foreign governments, and the strictures of exchange control, the roughness and vulgarity have had less scope, and much of the city has become entangled in the 'Old Boy Net'. To a surprising extent, the big new developments of the last fifty years—hire-purchase, building societies, industrial life assurance, property development—all of them keyed to the future—have been exploited by men outside the square mile, and outside the Net.

What the city can do will depend eventually on its balance between those two contradictory strains in the British character—trust and cunning. All the odd totems and mumbo-jumbo which we will find in the next chapters—the scarlet robes, the brokers' top hats, the Governor's ritual—can be justified as the trappings of trust, the badges of a stable and confident machine. Businessmen like a certain fustiness in their bankers, and impatient young men in the city are sometimes appalled to find Wall Street even more pompous. But the city must operate, behind that misleading ritual, with cunning and speed: it must adventure abroad with the same ruthlessness that it showed before its Antonine Age. For the survival of the city as an international financial centre depends in the end not on tradition, or a Conservative government, but on the ability to see into the world and the future and supply its needs more quickly than anyone else.

22

BANK OF ENGLAND

Lord Radcliffe: It is very deep in history that bankers have been regarded with suspicion?

Lord Brand: And always will be by people who cannot get credit.

Memoranda of the Radcliffe Report. Question 10739.

In the centre of the city, next door to the Royal Exchange and facing the Lord Mayor's Mansion House, is the massive quadrilateral of the Bank of England. Its appearance aptly symbolises its famous secrecy. Round the whole building at street level is a blank windowless façade broken by corinthian pillars, above which rise six storeys of offices. Inside the Bank has the look of an eccentric court; tall men stand in the hall wearing long brown overcoats and top hats with gold bands; other men, in black trousers, pink morning coats and red waistcoats, escort visitors into high-ceilinged rooms perfectly air-conditioned at 67 degrees. Few people would think that this was the home of a nationalised industry.

The Bank is proud of its nickname of the 'Old Lady of Threadneedle Street': in the exhibition room there is the original cartoon by Gillray called 'Political Ravishment or The Old Lady of Threadneedle Street in Danger', in 1797, showing Pitt as prime minister assaulting an aged hag sitting on a trunk labelled 'Bank of England', shouting 'Murder! Murder!' (the fear of financial rape has haunted the Bank ever since). 'The Old Lady' is the title of the Bank's own house magazine, with the crinkly cover favoured by nineteenth-century quarterlies, and the Bank is fascinated by its own past. In the 'Court Room' there is a weather-vane so that the directors can see if their sailing ships are in difficulty. Until 1963 a troop of guardsmen in bearskins and scarlet tunics marched through the streets in the height of the rush-hour, to guard the building against rioters; now they arrive in a truck, wearing battle-dress.

The secrecy is obsessive—particularly compared to other central banks. 'We are after all a bank', said Lord Cobbold, the previous Governor, 'doing business for customers, and nobody wants their bankers to talk too much'; the idea that they should try to enlighten the public is quite foreign to them, and their secretiveness rivals that of the Treasury. Nationalisation in 1946 made little difference; the Bank has never accepted the notion of public accountability, and over the past hundred years its activities have become more, not less, shrouded. For this book they would not commit themselves as to the names of the Committee of Treasury who are thought to be the Governor's advisers on monetary policy. When the committee headed by Lord Radcliffe published their Report in 1959 on the monetary system, it let some light into the darkness, but the members were politely exasperated by the lack of information: they mentioned the Annual Report, 'the meagreness of which has become a byword', and even made the wild suggestion that there should be 'a revival of the 1844 idea that the Bank should publish certain key figures exposing its operation in the monetary system'. Since then the Bank *has* begun issuing quarterly reports, which have let in some more light. 'It isn't so much that they don't *want* to tell you what's going on', one banker explained it: 'It's more that they don't know how to explain it: they're like a Northumbrian farmer.'

THE COURT

On the ground floor is an interlocking set of rooms reserved for the Governor and Directors, decorated in the twenties' Adam style, with the splendour and peace of a rich man's country house. A wide carpet leads past the green dining-room, past a pillared hall full of bankers' portraits, into the heart of the Bank—the long white room, known as the 'Court Room', flanked with columns and filled with an ornate, hundred-and-fifty coloured carpet. A blue-cloth table stands in the middle, with nineteen chairs round it: here, every Thursday morning, sit the eighteen members of the 'Court'.

These eighteen are chosen to run the Bank, and to advise the Treasury on financial policy and 'feeling in the city'. Before the war they consisted predominantly of city men—a phenomenon which helped to explain the appalling insensitivity of the government to unemployment. Today (partly because of that criticism), they are more diversified: six are full-time members of the Bank of England; four from banks, seven from industry and commerce; and one from a trade union. These, in March 1965, were the eighteen directors with their most important other position:

Lord Cromer	Governor of the Bank
Leslie O'Brien	Deputy Governor
Lord Sanderson	Director, Shaw Savill & Albion (Shipping)
Lord Kindersley	Director, Lazard Brothers (Merchant Bankers)
Sir George Bolton	Chairman, Bank of London & South America
Michael Babington Smith	Director, Glyn Mills (Clearing Bank)
Sir Geoffrey Eley	Chairman, Richard Thomas & Baldwin (Steel)
Lord Bicester	Managing Director, Morgan Grenfell (Merchant Bankers)
William Keswick	Chairman, Matheson Ltd. (Eastern Merchants)
Sir Harry Pilkington	Chairman, Pilkington Brothers (Glass)
Maurice Parsons	Bank of England, full time
Lord Nelson of Stafford	Chairman, English Electric
Sir Maurice Laing	Managing Director, Laing's (Builders)
Sir William Carron	President, Amalgamated Engineering Union
Sir Henry Wilson Smith	Chairman, Powell Duffryn
James Vincent Bailey	Bank of England, full time
William Maurice Allen	" " "
Jeremy Morse	" " "

Many of these names will recur in the next hundred pages. The Directors of the Bank are conservative, traditional men, most of them sons of bankers or industrialists. Of the eighteen, 13 are 60 or over, 11 went to public school, and 5 to Eton. At least six of their surnames have been well known in the city for a hundred years.

At the head of the Court is the Governor of the Bank of England, the headmaster of the city. (The title 'Governor' itself is curiously evocative. There are governors of prisons, schools, the BBC, Colonies and the Bank of England: they have a grim affinity.) In the square mile the Governor of the Bank is known as 'Grandma', 'the little white father', or mysteriously as 'the Authorities': and it is his job, among many others, to enforce the unwritten laws and codes of city behaviour—with the same kind of unstated rule as the Lord Chancellor has over barristers, but with larger powers. His weapons seem mild enough: he will 'drop a hint', 'make observations' or 'frown'; but in the closed society of the city, his disapproval can—and very occasionally does—mean ruin.

BARINGS

To the authority of the job the present Governor, Lord Cromer, brings an extra command, for he is not only an earl, but the head of the Baring family—the oldest of all the British banking dynasties. The family are all the descendants of a deaf clothing manufacturer, Sir Francis Baring, who was known as the 'first merchant in Europe' when he died in 1810, leaving seven million pounds. The Barings established themselves as one of the most powerful and richest of the great Whig families: in 1818 it was said that there were six great powers in Europe—England, France, Russia, Austria, Prussia and Baring Brothers. Since the slump in South America in 1890, when Baring Brothers collapsed and had to be rescued by the Bank of England, their power has been much less visible. But the influence and wealth of the family has remained: in 1964 a Baring bought back one of the family houses they had earlier had to sell. They have footholds not only in the city, but in the Palace and in Whitehall—a rare combination. There are no fewer than five separate Baring peerages—Cromer, Northbrook, Revelstoke, Ashburton and Howick. They have provided two Chancellors of the Exchequer, a Governor-General of India (first Lord Northbrook), a poet (Maurice), a Lord Chamberlain (second Lord Cromer) and a Governor of Kenya (Lord Howick). 'Nothing is more like itself, nothing less like anything else, than a Baring', wrote Lord d'Abernon: 'Strong, sensible, self-reliant men, with a profound belief in themselves, their family and in their country . . . not subtle or mentally agile, but endowed with that curious combination of character which lends authority even to a doubtful decision.' Part of the Baring family tree is shown on the following page.

THE GOVERNOR

The present Lord Cromer has followed a Baring pattern of moving between private banking and public service. After Eton, Cambridge and the Guards in war-time, he spent ten years as a managing director of the family bank, and then two years as Economic Minister in Washington, where his combination of ability, charm and title made a large mark, and he was even talked of as a possible president of the World Bank. (He had married a daughter of the present Lord Rothermere, chairman of the *Daily Mail*—of which he was for a time a director.) The appointment of an earl to the Bank of England, after a long period of speculation (during which time Lord Franks was offered the job and said no), produced the same kind of mixed reactions as greeted those other earls then at the Foreign Office and the Ministry of Defence. There are many who thought that a charming and clever Baring, of 'Kennedy's age', with American connections, was the right man to induce confidence in the city. Others insisted that Cromer's lack of experience in industry, economics and general banking were serious drawbacks: the previous Governor, Lord Cobbold, had spent his life in the Bank before his appointment, and to bring in a young Baring, however well qualified, was interpreted as a setback to the city's very tentative managerial revolution.

But there have been some signs that the new Governor, without being at all obviously bold, has tried to stir the city up from its long complacency. He is a large stooping man with the kind of slow, cautious talk which distinguishes most bankers; but he has inserted some carefully placed bombs into some of his stately speeches. In particular he has tried very gingerly to urge city institutions towards a little more competition. As he said in his speech to the bankers of Newcastle in March 1964:

> I have never been able to discover to what extent the Great British public believes in competition. It is always something that is good for the other fellow but rather mean if applied to oneself. Such is the British love of the under-dog, entirely commendable as a humanitarian principle, that there tends to be greater commiseration over those who are unsuccessful in their ventures rather than admiration for those who are successful.

He has tried to encourage bankers to take an interest in the international capital market: 'this entrepôt business in capital, if I may so describe it,' he said at the Lord Mayor's Dinner in November 1962, 'would not only serve this country well, but would fill a vital and vacant rôle in Europe in mobilising foreign capital for world economic development.' He has also suggested that the insurance companies, with their huge capital sums, might take more interest in more enterprising investments: 'too narrow an interpretation of policyholders' interests could militate to the disadvantage of the country and policyholder alike'.[1] And he has even dared to suggest that the joint stock banks might try to attract more new customers, and might even consider opening at a time when working people could use them. In a notorious speech at the 400th anniversary of Martins Bank, in April 1963, he said:

'There is, of course, I know, competition amongst banks and, in the matter of service, I am frequently informed the competition is intense. But the question this leaves in my mind is whether the competition is really for existing bank customers or whether it is in the sphere of seeking new depositors which, from my point of view, seems infinitely more important . . .

[1] September 27, 1962.

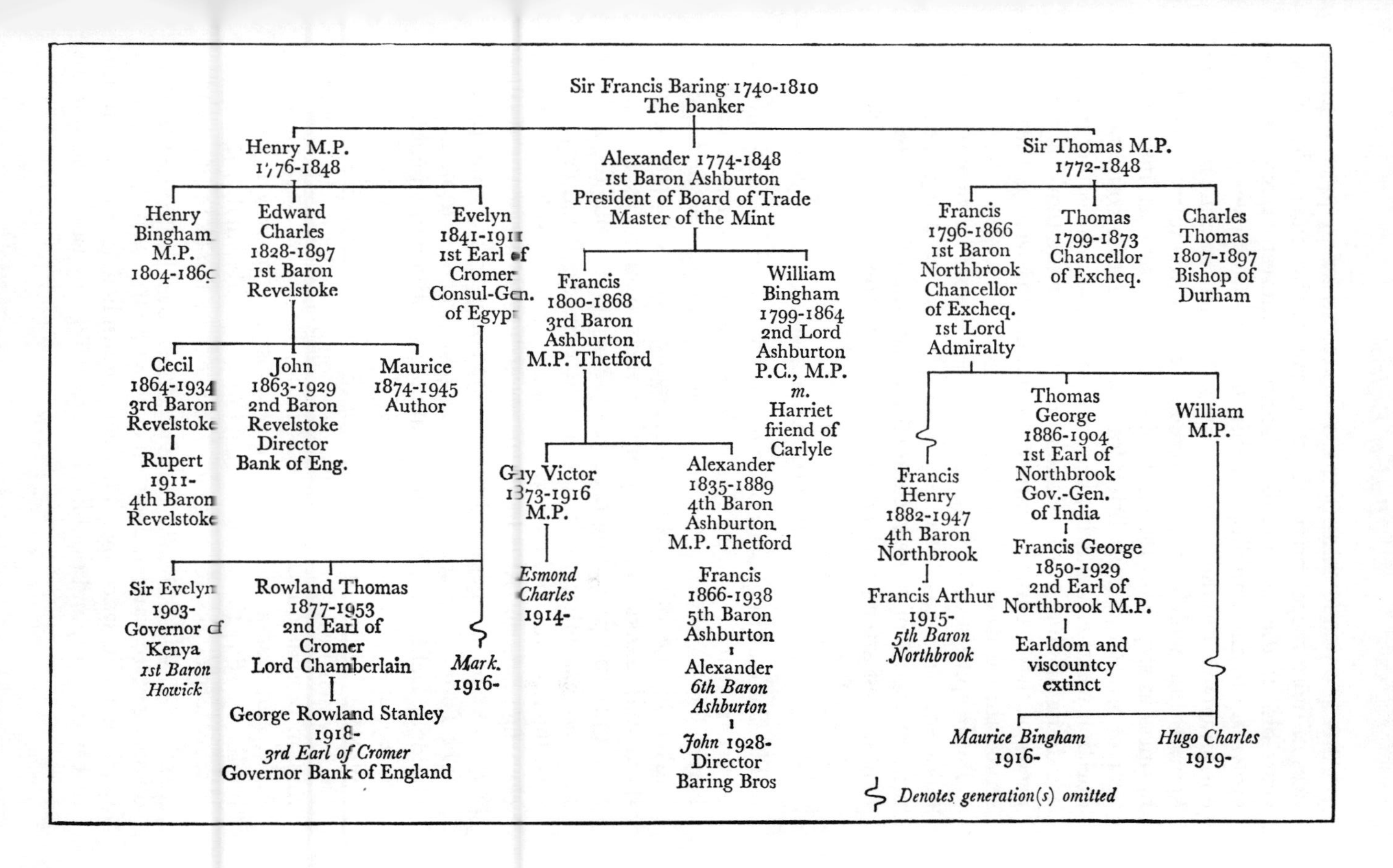
Sir Francis Baring 1740-1810
The banker
Henry M.P.
1776-1848
Alexander 1774-1848
1st Baron Ashburton
President of Board of Trade
Master of the Mint
Sir Thomas M.P.
1772-1848
Henry
Bingham
M.P.
1804-1869
Edward
Charles
1828-1897
1st Baron
Revelstoke
Evelyn
1841-1911
1st Earl of
Cromer
Consul-Gen.
of Egypt
Francis
1800-1868
3rd Baron
Ashburton
M.P. Thetford
William
Bingham
1799-1864
2nd Lord
Ashburton
P.C., M.P.
m.
Harriet
friend of
Carlyle
Francis
1796-1866
1st Baron
Northbrook
Chancellor
of Excheq.
1st Lord
Admiralty
Thomas
1799-1873
Chancellor
of Excheq.
Charles
Thomas
1807-1897
Bishop of
Durham
Cecil
1864-1934
3rd Baron
Revelstoke
Rupert
1911-
4th Baron
Revelstoke
John
1863-1929
2nd Baron
Revelstoke
Director
Bank of Eng.
Maurice
1874-1945
Author
Guy Victor
1873-1916
M.P.
Esmond
Charles
1914-
Alexander
1835-1889
4th Baron
Ashburton
M.P. Thetford
Francis
1866-1938
5th Baron
Ashburton
Alexander
6th Baron
Ashburton
John 1928-
Director
Baring Bros
Thomas
George
1886-1904
1st Earl of
Northbrook
Gov.-Gen.
of India
Francis George
1850-1929
2nd Earl of
Northbrook M.P.
Earldom and
viscountcy
extinct
William
M.P.
Francis
Henry
1882-1947
4th Baron
Northbrook
Francis Arthur
1915-
5th Baron
Northbrook
Sir Evelyn
1903-
Governor of
Kenya
1st Baron
Howick
Rowland Thomas
1877-1953
2nd Earl of
Cromer
Lord Chamberlain
George Rowland Stanley
1918-
3rd Earl of Cromer
Governor Bank of England
Mark
1916-
Maurice Bingham
1916-
Hugo Charles
1919-
Denotes generation(s) omitted

'After 400 years I think perhaps we are entitled to question practices of more recent origin, be they, say, twenty years old or 200 years old. Is the considerable rigidity in interest rates which has grown up in the banking world in the last twenty years or so an encouragement to the growth of bank deposits? Are the traditional hours within which bank customers are expected to transact their business in step with demands of potential bank customers in the year of grace 1963? In brief, for time runs out, I would pose the question whether we as bankers, and speaking as a banker myself, are doing all that can be done to ensure that the banks serve the needs of the twentieth century community as well as they have served the needs of past centuries.'

But in spite of this strong talk, and the uproar in the city which followed, there has been very little sign—as we will note in the next chapter—of a new competitiveness among the joint stock banks, or of attempts to attract the new custom.

NATIONAL DEBT

The Bank of England's basic rôle is not very different from that of other central banks. Firstly it is the government's banker, borrowing money for the state when required. Secondly, it is banker to the other banks—arranging free exchange between them and banks abroad, printing their bank-notes (except in Scotland) and providing their reserve of money. But the Bank of England has other duties. It has to regulate Britain's overseas investments—the highest per head of any country. It has to enforce exchange control. And it has to act as custodian of the sterling area, holding balances on behalf of the other sterling countries.

The Bank's largest service to the government is to manage the National Debt, which occupies about two thousand people in a crescent-shaped building facing St. Paul's called 'New Change', built since the war in ugly neo-Georgian style. It was the National Debt which brought the Bank into being: William III needed a million pounds quickly, to raise money for his war against Louis XIV, and was advised, very ingeniously, to borrow it from the public. In 1694 the Bank of England was established, with a staff of seventeen clerks, to fix the loan. Since then, the Debt (it is usually given a capital D) has never looked back: governments have gone on using it to raise money quickly without waiting for taxes—particularly in war-time. The Debt multiplied seven times in the first world war, and doubled in the second—by raising such loans as 'Victory Bonds' or 'War Bonds'. By March 31, 1964, the Debt stood at £30,224,000,000.[1]

Some people, including Ted Hill of the TUC, find the idea of a government in debt rather shocking, and a few have even helped to pay it off: in 1929 Lord Inchcape gave half a million pounds towards reducing it. But it has gone on growing, and no Western country has managed to do without this handy device.

The Debt is made up of about three million separate accounts, and six million payments a year are made to stockholders from New Change. New government loans—known as 'gilt-edged stock' because of their thorough reliability—are floated by the Bank with the help of Peter Daniell, who occupies the semi-hereditary post of Senior Government Broker; the families of Daniell and Mullens have been government brokers since 1829. Mr Daniell provides the main link between the Bank and the stock exchange. He is surrounded with feudal dignity—like most gilt-edged people, he wears a top hat in the city—so that it is difficult to remember that he is actually making money. Officially (and rather hopefully) he is known as 'Broker to the Commissioners for the Reduction of the National Debt': he inhabits the offices of 'Mullens and Co' in Moorgate, only a few yards from the Bank of England, where portraits of Mullenses look down from tall panels. The other seven partners include Robin Peppiatt, son of a former chief cashier of the Bank of England, and David Bewicke-Copley, heir to Lord Cromwell. (Gentlemen prefer bonds, they say in the city.) Being privy to the government's plans, Mr. Daniell is the object of immense interest in the city, and his selling of bonds can generate panic in the stock exchange. His 'tap'—the price at which he will sell one or more key gilt-edged bonds which the government is using to raise money—sets the whole structure of the gilt-edged market.

The Debt is no longer regarded by the Bank as a regrettable consequence of wars, to be reduced as quickly as possible. It has become so vast, and so involved with the country's economy, that its management affects the whole circulation of money. By adjusting the interest and the quantity of new government stock—and by the curious operation of 'funding'—changing the debt from short to long term loans—the Bank through Mr. Daniell regulates the money situation. Controlling the money supply is the most

[1] But this figure does not bear much relationship to the real indebtedness of the government to the public—which was estimated by Professor Victor Morgan at £17,000 million in 1955 (see *The Structure of Property Ownership in Great Britain, 1961*).

important rôle of the Bank, and it is here that the Bank's goings-on are most intricate and obscure. For in the city, money becomes (in Sir Oscar Hobson's phrase) 'two dimensional'—varying in character according to interest rates and time of repayment. The Bank deals in all kinds of money—cheap money, dear money, liquid money, frozen money, long-term money, short-term money, safe money, risk money, dollar money, sterling money, and even with 'moneyness'.

MONEY MARKET

Among these odd kinds of money are the short-term loans raised for the Treasury, through 'Treasury Bills'. These Bills—invented by Bagehot in 1877—are government IOUs for sums ranging from £5,000 to £100,000, to be repaid (usually) in 91 days. They allow the government to raise money quickly, later to be repaid from taxes and long-term loans: every Friday afternoon the Treasury announces how much money it will raise by these Bills the following week—usually between £200 and £300 million.

These huge sums of money are in effect borrowed largely from the only people who can afford them—the bankers, with their enormous deposits. But as intermediaries between the joint stock banks and the Bank of England there exists one of the most astonishing professions in Britain—the Discount Brokers, or 'Bill Brokers'. They are not numerous or important, but they are so much part of the extraordinary 'sensitive mechanism' of the city that they deserve a special mention. Their job is to borrow large sums from the joint stock banks and then lend it, through Treasury Bills, to the government. Every Friday they lodge their tenders at the Bank of England to buy the Treasury Bills, at a price agreed beforehand by the brokers' syndicate, and 'deliberately manipulated' (in the words of the Radcliffe Report) to try to exclude outside tenders.

The Treasury Bills are the largest quantity of floating funds in the city, and round them revolves the 'money market'. The ease with which one can borrow a few million pounds for a few days is one reason why sudden trades come to London. With such large sums involved, the difference between a sixteenth and a sixty-fourth becomes crucial. The discount brokers nibble their tiny percentage from the Treasury Bills, and grow prosperous on it. On days when 'money is scarce', the top hats can be seen rushing from bank to bank—just before 2.30 when the Bank of England stops lending—trying to find a million pounds or so with which to balance their books. Here we might pause to note the indifference of the city to the decimal system: the first strong official recommendation for decimalisation was made in 1841, but only in 1961 was a decisive enquiry instituted. ('These things take time,' said a Treasury man.)

The discount brokers—only about eighty in all—are unique, not surprisingly, to the city of London. They lead lives of antique formality: every morning they call *in person* at the joint stock banks, to discuss the weather, cricket, and perhaps the money market. No other country makes use of them: *their* Treasuries go direct to the banks. Since the discount brokers fix prices between themselves, they cannot be said to make the money market any more competitive. The city's justification for them is partly that they provide a kind of cushion—a pet city word—to the money market, making it less volatile and neurotic than Wall Street; and partly that the brokers, by constantly scrabbling around for cheap money, make sure that there are no 'idle lakes' or even 'puddles' of money which aren't being used. Also (of course) that 'it works'. The discount brokers awaited the verdict of the Radcliffe Report with some trepidation, but they need not have worried. 'It would not be beyond human ingenuity', Lord Radcliffe concluded, 'to replace the work of the discount houses; but they are there, they are doing the work effectively, and they are doing it at a trifling cost in terms of labour and other real resources.'

BANK RATE

The Bank can influence the supply of money in three principal ways. First, it can adjust the operations and requirements of the National Debt. Secondly, it can bring pressure on the joint stock banks to restrict loans to their customers. Thirdly, it can wield its most controversial weapon, the Bank Rate—the rate of interest at which it lends money, and hence (by tradition) the interest rate of the joint stock banks to their customers—which affects the cost of borrowing all through the country. Every Thursday morning the Court considers Bank Rate, and at about 11.45 Mr. Daniell, accompanied by a stock exchange waiter, walks in his top hat from the Bank of England to the stock exchange—a journey which takes exactly two and a half minutes—enters the hall, gets up on a chair, and announces Bank Rate. From 1932 till 1951, which marked the era of 'cheap money', it was nearly always two per cent. Since then it has been used by successive governments to control the rate of activity, oscillating between seven and three per cent.

The efficacy of the Bank Rate is fiercely debated. Several factors have weakened its power. Firstly, the great industrial corporations now largely finance themselves out of profits: a succession of industrialists—including Lords Godber of Shell, Fleck of ICI, Heyworth of Unilever—explained to Lord Radcliffe that their investment plans were virtually unaffected by Bank Rate.[1] Secondly, government spending has enormously increased: 'nearly half the total volume of investment is now financed by public authorities', wrote the Report (para 49), which 'does not respond in the same way as private investment.' Thirdly, the hire-purchase business has multiplied, thus allowing the government to stop public spending much more quickly by changing hire-purchase conditions and decreasing the sales of cars or refrigerators.

The techniques for influencing spending are still shrouded in mystery, as much psychological as economic. It is reassuring to the layman to find in the Radcliffe Report the economy frequently described in homely terms—'stoking up the boom', 'spitting into the wind', 'going off the boil'. The uncertainty about Bank Rate was vividly expressed by Professor Cairncross,[2] questioning Lord Cobbold, then Governor of the Bank, in the Radcliffe Committee:

> PROFESSOR CAIRNCROSS: There is an old saying that prayers and incantation, with a little arsenic, will poison a flock of sheep. I wonder whether the Bank Rate plays the rôle of the incantations here. If I may put the question in a slightly different form, just how do you visualise a change in the Bank Rate as affecting the demand in the economy?
>
> MR. COBBOLD: This is a very arguable subject and anybody can have his own opinion. My own view is that it has still quite a considerable effect both in its general psychological influence, and on reality. On reality it has a far higher effect when you get towards the higher rates. I regard the seven per cent Bank Rate, particularly in conjunction with the trend of emphasis of policy in general, as being in its own right a very effective weapon in reducing demand.

The Radcliffe Committee concluded that, without control of public spending or hire-purchase terms (which rest with the Treasury, not with the Bank), an increase of Bank Rate would be —in the Governor's phrase—like 'spitting into the wind'.

[1] *See* p. 488.
[2] *See* p. 311.

TREASURY AND BANK

Who is really responsible for Britain's monetary policy? The answer is characteristically obscure. In the first place the Court of the Bank of England is not quite what it seems: 'There's a lie in the heart of the Bank', as one banker puts it. For while the Bank retains the trappings of a joint stock company, as it once was, its reality is quite different—not primarily because of nationalisation, but also because of the huge rôle of the Treasury, and the personal authority of the Governor (who is appointed not by the Court, but by the prime minister). The Court, for all its splendour and dignity, is not a very decisive body. 'It would be unrealistic', said the Radcliffe Report in its kid-glove language, 'to regard the meetings of the Court as the source of effective decisions on policy made by the Bank.' The Court delegates many decisions to the 'Committee of Treasury' consisting of the Governor, the Deputy-Governor, and five other nominated directors. 'It is in the Committee of Treasury', wrote the Report, 'that the Bank's views are formulated on matters of central banking.' But even the Committee of Treasury 'is and must be in essence advisory to the Governor'. The most crucial decisions are taken by the Governor in consultation with the Chancellor of the Exchequer (who, by the Act of 1946, has power to give directions to the Bank). The Radcliffe Report urged that Bank Rate, the most important decision of the Bank, should be announced in the name of the Chancellor, not of the Governor—thus making it clear where the responsibility lay. But the suggestion was not implemented, and Mr. Daniell still stands on his chair.

Is the Bank of England the city arm of the Treasury, designed to impose the government's policy on the banks? Or is it still, as it was, a part of the city—a bank which happens to have one huge client, the government? In its internal character, with its secrecy and splendour, the Bank is much more like an old-fashioned business enterprise than the civil service. The relationship between the Bank and the Treasury is one of the most peculiar of all, complicated by the personal contrast between bankers and Treasury men, a mile away. As one commentator put it, 'men who have never been to boarding-school often feel that they are dealing with men who never left it'.[1] The Bank embodies the unquestioning regimental spirit of the public school proletariat, and only about six graduates are recruited each year. Clean-

[1] *Time and Tide*, April 6, 1961.

limbed young men show visitors round the building with the reverence for trophies and pillars shown by schools or regiments. Their spirit is at odds both with the introspective musicians of the Treasury, and the blasé graduates of the Foreign Office. The men in Threadneedle Street are on top of the day-to-day abrasive mechanism of the city, in the midst of sixty-fourths, fine rates, moneyness, etc. They are inarticulate but confident, tilling the financial fields with an almost agricultural rhythm, and their senior men are held in some awe by Great George Street where the mandarins work in their ivory tower surrounded by abstractions. Treasury men nowadays visit the city more often, but exchanges between bankers and mandarins can still be difficult and stiff.

The Treasury, too, regards the Bank, more than any other parts of its empire, as a foreign tribe who must not be interfered with, and here the doctrine of indirect rule is very evident. The Court of the Bank, odd though it is, is apt to be regarded as voicing 'city opinion', and the Governor is expected to carry the Court with him. Even the Labour party, though it nationalised the Bank and Sir Stafford Cripps said jokingly 'the Bank is my creature', dreaded any kind of outright clash with Threadneedle Street, and the mystique of the city remains a powerful influence on Westminster. The British government is not alone in not wanting to interfere with the central Bank. The American Federal Reserve and the German Bundesbank can both openly contradict their governments, but Britain prefers to keep the relationship obscure.

The balance of power between the Governor and the Chancellor varies with personalities and policies. In November 1964 the relationship became acute, when the financial crisis, and the run on sterling, produced sharp conflict between orthodox bankers and the Labour government. By early in November, the Bank of England had become worried by the loss of confidence in sterling, and the Governor was urging that the bank rate be increased from five per cent to six per cent. But Wilson and his Chancellor were determined to avoid such a restrictive measure, and speaking at the Guildhall on November 16th, Wilson seemed quite confident about the pound. The bank-rate, to the city's surprise, remained the same on the following Thursday. On that day the real crisis began: dealers suspected imminent devaluation, and began selling sterling so fast that the Bank of England was forced to start buying, to keep up the price—at the cost of over £20 million. By the Friday night, when the cabinet was on its way to a defence conference at Chequers, the financial crisis dominated everything else. All over the weekend Callaghan, Brown and Wilson conferred by telephone with the Governor and the Treasury knights: the Governor insisted that by now only an increase in the bank rate of two per cent would satisfy foreign financiers, and the politicians reluctantly agreed. On the 'Black Monday' Peter Daniell, the government broker, arrived at the stock exchange and announced the increase to seven per cent—the first change on a Monday since 1931.

The Chancellor seemed confident that this would restore confidence, but it did not: selling continued, and the next day the Bank of England again had to start buying pounds. At that point, the Governor had to resort to his last and unbeatable line of defence—the mustering of support from central bankers abroad. The American and European banks could not afford to watch the collapse of sterling. Cromer, with his deputy Leslie O'Brien and his co-director Maurice Parsons, spent the night in discussions with central bankers, led by Al Hayes, the head of the New York Federal Reserve Bank. The Americans agreed to lend $1,000 million, and another $2,000 million was lent by ten other central banks. By Wednesday evening the deal was announced, and with this colossal loan the position of sterling was, at least for the time being, restored. The earlier warnings of the Bank of England had been grimly vindicated, and the balance of power had shifted noticeably towards Threadneedle Street. 'We have seen into the abyss,' said the Governor the following February: 'it is an uninviting prospect.'

23

BANKERS

Most bankers dwell in marble halls,
Which they get to dwell in because they encourage
deposits and discourage withdralls,
And particularly because they all observe
one rule which woe betide the banker who fails to heed it,
Which is you must never lend any money to anybody
unless they don't need it.

Ogden Nash
('Bankers are just like anybody else except richer'.)

With a group of bankers I always had the feeling that success was measured by the extent one gave nothing away.

Lord Longford.

WHEN ordinary people talk about a bank, they mean one of the 'joint stock banks' or 'clearing banks' whose names are to be seen, above stone façades, in every high street in the country. They have become, like town halls or public libraries, part of the face of town life; and their character is almost equally institutional, for they exist in a strange limbo between nationalisation and free enterprise. They long ago reached a truce between each other, about the limits of gentlemanly competition. Being among the richest financial institutions in the country, they are carefully watched and controlled by the Governor of the Bank of England, who prints their banknotes, acts as their master-bankers, and keeps an eye on their reserves. The joint stock banks are in the midst of that curious city world, so difficult for the outsider to comprehend, where competition only exists between small but unwritten limits, where 'it's not done' lurks behind every counter, with a headmaster in the background.

THE BIG FIVE

There are only eleven joint stock banks in England, and those are dominated by the 'Big Five', which are, in order of size:

Bank	*Deposits* (June 1964)	*Chairman*
Barclays	£2,076 million	John Thomson
Midland	£1,895 "	Sir Archibald Forbes
Lloyds	£1,557 "	Harald Peake
Westminster	£1,162 "	D. A. Stirling
National Provincial	£1,031 "	David Robarts

The remaining six banks—Martins, District, Williams Deacon's, National, Glyn Mills and Coutts—are much smaller, and half of them are subsidiaries of other banks. But each of them has its specialities; the Royal Bank of Scotland even has a drive-in branch in Trafalgar Square.

The Big Five are among the biggest banks in the Western World: before the devaluation of the pound, in 1949, the Midland was *the* biggest. American banks are restricted by law to a single state, while the British ones have national coverage: Barclays, Lloyds and the Midland each has more than 2,000 branches. These giants took their present shape, after a succession of swallowings of smaller banks, at the end of the first world war, after which the Treasury became worried, and 'made it known' that they would disapprove of any more amalgamations—one of the first cases in Britain of monopolies being prevented—although in 1963 the National Provincial acquired the share capital of the District without much fuss.

The Big Five had their roots not in the city, but in the provincial banking families, most of them Quakers, who grew up in the seventeenth and eighteenth centuries: many old banking names still survive on the boards. The Quakers were a close-knit, persecuted community, who were used to helping each other with money, and they soon became trusted by others as money-keepers. After some early disasters the banks settled down into cautious, conservative businesses with a strong public conscience and an emphasis on trust over enterprise: the last bank to get into difficulties was the military bank of Cox and King's in the Haymarket, now absorbed by Lloyds and still with a military tradition. The banks regard themselves, first and foremost, as the guardians of the public's money. They insist that they cannot lock up money in long-term ventures, and five years is (in theory but not in practice) their longest loan. They do not invest in industrial companies, and by tradition they keep around thirty per cent of a bank's deposits 'liquid'—available for immediate recall. The vast deposits of the banks are invested in government stock, Treasury

Bills, hire-purchase companies, or loans to industrial or private customers.

It is the forty per cent which is lent to customers, amounting to over four billion pounds, which affects the social life of the country: this web of credit, largely controlled by the branch managers, can provide a new dress, a new house, or a new factory. This credit clearly concerns the government, for by ordering the banks to restrict their lending, the Treasury can reduce the amount of money in circulation. For nearly twenty years, from 1939 to 1958, this is what they did, to the vexation of the bankers and the borrowing public. Overdrafts were restricted and banks imposed their 'self-denying ordinance', promising not to compete for customers by offering better loans. The main business of banks—lending money for profit—became uncompetitive and the Big Five were united in their unwillingness to lend. 'The banks were anaesthetised', as one banker said, 'it was like driving a very powerful car at twenty miles an hour.'

In July 1958 the 'credit squeeze' was quite suddenly relaxed: the banks, to their astonishment, found themselves able to lend more money and they began competing. Anthony Tuke of Barclays had already astonished his fellow-bankers by taking a share in a hire-purchase business: but soon after the end of the squeeze Lord Monckton of the Midland announced a new kind of 'Personal Loan' for customers, and other banks followed with mild counter-attractions. The freedom was very limited, but since 1958, in spite of a renewed credit squeeze, a slight competitiveness has remained between banks: 'They have been able to stand up,' to quote the same banker, 'to breathe—and even to walk.'

But the banks often still seem to regard progress as something rather vulgar and regrettable, which requires apology; for instance, Coutts' bank, the Queen's bankers (now owned by the National Provincial) who have ancient premises in the Strand, began one of their advertisements with: 'The idea of a firm such as Coutts' and Co. going over to a computer might strike some as unlikely, some as slightly reprehensible, some as positively dangerous . . .'

BARCLAYS AND MIDLAND

The walking-pace is set by the two biggest, Barclays and Midland; the others—even Lloyds—are apt to follow behind. Their competition is a little more vigorous, and their characters more different, than one might suspect from their uniform architecture, scratchy pens, or rates of interest. Their chairmen, though they meet once a month to discuss banking problems and blossom out into long, philosophical reports every January, are quite keen to steal a march.

The biggest in terms of deposits is Barclays, which still retains something of its old Quaker family character. Twenty banks, Quaker and mostly in East Anglia, came together in 1896 to avoid being swallowed by other combines, and they determined to keep their character by a system of 'local directors'. They still have old family names—a Barclay, a Bland, a Bevan, a Seebohm—on their board. The present chairman, John Thomson, is also from a banking family, though not Quakers. Barclays are proud of the fact that their board (which meets weekly) is largely composed of professionals: in 1964 the chairman claimed that twenty-five of the thirty-four directors 'could properly be described as professional bankers'.

The Midland, sometimes known as the 'small man's bank', has a less gentlemanly past than Barclays, with Midlands roots and a reputation for thrusting methods and 'gimmicks'—including a bank on the *Queen Mary*. It has smaller deposits than Barclays, but more branches, and the largest number of industrial customers. The Midland, like other big banks except Barclays, is largely run by its general managers, but with a less heavily titled board; as chairman, since Lord Monckton retired in 1964, they have had an austere Scots accountant, Sir Archibald Forbes, who has moved between the worlds of government and big business for the past thirty years.

NEW CUSTOM

In spite of the occasional competitive gestures of the joint stock banks, their most surprising trait to outsiders is their lack of competition for new kinds of custom. 'There have been two important changes in the field of banking,' one chairman told me, 'one is the development of medium-term credits for British export —which has the effect of locking up more of the banks' capital. The other is the growth of banking for the weekly wage-earner. We're still feeling the effects of the post-war social revolution. What's happened to money in Britain since 1948 means that now there's often very little difference between the wage of a secondary school headmaster and a man on the line at the Nuffield works:

this has meant that huge sections of the population have become bankable. We're slowly moving towards the weekly wage-earner, and this will probably mean a new kind of bank—looking less frightening and less like a magistrates' court—and a new kind of bank manager.'

But so far there is little sign of such transformation, and American tendencies which have appeared in journalism, business or shopping have not penetrated to banks. Few Anglo-American contrasts are more striking than this: in the newest banks in New York the customer goes up to a long open counter without glass in a vast open hall, containing an expanse of young crew-cut men behind desks, with hardly a single private room. Banks may have floral displays, dog-shows, ice-skating exhibitions, or chamber music to attract their customers, and tempting booklets describe the easy arrangements to borrow money. In Britain, despite some gay new buildings, the puritan, nonconformist conscience of the early days still hangs over the banks.

Traditionally the banks—even the 'small man's bank'—were the custodians of the rising middle class; and they are as sceptical about small savings as stockbrokers about small investors. Their hours of opening (from ten to three) do not exactly encourage working men, and their advertising and the placing of their new banks is designed for the middle class. 'The clearing banks', in the words of the Radcliffe Report, 'have broadly, as a matter of deliberate and concerted policy, stood aside while small savings have fed the development of building societies, savings banks and other specialised financial intermediaries.' Working men and their wives have preferred the Post Office Savings Bank, where money can be paid in or out at any Post Office counter, with a fixed interest of 2½ per cent.

BANK CLERKS

The social revolution is most apparent among the staff of the banks themselves: for the 126,000 bank employees—most of whom work in joint stock banks—are white-collar workers whose wages are being overtaken by the working-class. An average bank clerk in 1964 would start work at sixteen with £315 a year, rising to £960–1015 at the age of thirty-one—by which time he may still be earning less than a docker or factory worker. Some bank managers earn as little as £1,750 a year. Bank clerks work long hours, including Saturday mornings, under strict conditions—

their own bank balance is regularly inspected. But they are reluctant to join a trade union and press for better wages: The National Union of Bank Employees (NUBE—pronounced Newby) can only claim 40 per cent of the bank workers, and only Barclays and the National Bank, of the eleven, recognise it. Most clerks prefer the 'Staff Association' of their own bank, which enjoys the patronage and subsidy of the management. The rift between the Staff Associations and NUBE is symptomatic of the predicament of the modern clerk—suspended between his middle-class aspirations and proletarian wages.

In the unthrusting atmosphere of the banks, opportunities for quick advancement are small. At the Midland some years ago a local manager wanted to upgrade a brilliant young man; but this would have meant breaking the normal promotion arrangements, and his request was refused. He resigned, decided to read for the bar, and found himself, fifteen years later, a leading expert on Trust Law, earning £10,000 a year and advising the joint stock banks.

Meanwhile, new intruders are affecting the bank clerk—machines, computers and women. The banks find that women work better with machines than men; at the Midland (with a total staff of 20,000) the proportion of women, I was told, has risen by 5 per cent in ten years, to 40 per cent. These regiments of women are liable at any moment to marry. 'After the first war, there was a rush of young men into the banks', said one chairman in 1961, 'which tends now to produce some frustrated men in their fifties, with not enough managerial jobs to go round. But I'm afraid we may be leaving our successors with the opposite problem—of not enough young men to provide managers for the future.'

The banks, like insurance companies, maintain a rigid and semi-feudal division between the board and the managers, which has often been attacked and which may help to explain their difficulties in recruitment. This is how one former bank chairman, Lord Longford, the Socialist former chairman of the (Irish) National Bank, describes it:

'The top-level structure of our commercial banks is fundamentally wrong. There is a fundamental anachronism in the whole division into board members on the one hand and general managers on the other, with the latter "running" the bank. This division stems from, and to an extent perpetuates, a quasi-feudal era in which boards, drawn primarily from outside commercial banking, are the first-class citizens. The rest of the staff, even though some of them will be receiving very high pay, in one sense at least are hewers of wood and drawers of water. The biggest decisions, on paper at least, are taken above their heads. The point remains true even though sometimes the top helots (chief general managers) themselves become first-class citizens (members of the board) when they retire. I feel sure myself that the commercial banks, as distinct for example from the merchant banks, will never attract their share of the ablest and most ambitious young men while the present demarcation continues. I am aware that the chief general managers if "polled" today would probably disagree with me. They prefer the substance of power without the shadow, but for all their well-earned reputation for efficiency and prudence they are a very conservative race.'[1]

The rumblings of complaint about this archaic demarcation have grown louder in the last few years. 'More banks should follow the lead of the Westminster in putting their chief general manager on the board while he is still in harness,' wrote *The Economist* in an outspoken supplement on banking in June 1964: 'and they should lose their inhibitions about translating able managers below the level straight into executive directorships. The real work of the board should then be delegated to small and carefully chosen policy committees. As it is, policy making in the great British banks goes largely by default. General managers know too much about banking, the directors too little'.[2]

The scope for initiative among joint stock bankers is not large. With their customers they try to neutralise themselves as far as possible: bank managers are taught never to use the words 'I think', and in their approach to loans (as Ogden Nash suggests of American banks) they favour the big battalions and the status quo. Industrial giants, like Hawker Siddeley, have colossal overdrafts, but the British banks do not, like the Americans, have their own big investigation department to discover which smaller firms are deserving of credit. Only occasionally do the banks appear in controversial fields (Lloyds lent money to Charles Clore to help him try to take over another of their customers, Watneys, and the National Commercial Bank of Scotland helped Lord Fraser to take over Harrods). In their dedication, their lack of greed, and their sense of quiet service, the joint stock bankers provide a placid, safe centre to financial Britain: one can no more imagine a bank going bust than the monarchy falling. But for

[1] Lord Longford: *Five Lives*, 1964. pp. 30–1.

[2] *The Economist*, June 6, 1964.

large opportunities and an eye on the future, we must look elsewhere in the city—to merchant banks and financiers.

HIRE-PURCHASE

Two new kinds of bank have grown up during this century—building societies and hire-purchase. Both have had enormous social consequences: the 'incentive goods revolution' has brought men back into the home, strengthened the position of women and 'deproletarianised' working-class homes.[1] Both of them are essentially extensions of banking, geared to the future, and building societies are really a kind of hire-purchase. But both fields have been ignored and often scorned by the old joint stock banks, and have grown up from quite different roots, with peculiar histories.

Building societies began as poor men's clubs during the early nineteenth century: the first recorded was in Birmingham in 1781, when subscribers arranged to meet once a month at the Fountain tavern, paying half a guinea a share towards a building scheme.[2] Houses were chosen by ballot, and 'ballot-and-sale societies', often based on pubs, grew up all over the Midlands. At the same time the Nonconformist Churches in the Midlands and Yorkshire began thrift clubs and sick benefit clubs, which expanded into house-building: and the movement had great support from social reformers, like Bright and Cobden, who saw property as a key to the franchise. The Abbey National Building Society with its big white tower, sometimes thought to be the site of Sherlock Holmes' rooms in Baker Street, represents a merger of chapel and pub—the Abbey Road Baptist Chapel, and the National Society, which met in the London Tavern. Forty years ago the combined assets of the two societies were two million pounds: by the end of 1963 they were £559 million, and a computer has been installed to deal with the book-keeping. The biggest of all is the Halifax, still based on Halifax, and patronised since 1853—when it was founded—by the Halifax family. It keeps its North Country independence—nearly every member of its board comes from the West Riding—and until December 1964, it remained separate from the Building Societies Association.

In spite of their vast expansion, the building societies have kept much of the character of Nonconformity and self-help. The building society knights are earnest, moral men, who have seen a

[1] *See* Norman Macrae: The Incentive Goods Revolution: *Credit*, March, 1961.

[2] *See* Sir Harold Bellman: *Bricks and Mortals*, 1949, p. 14.

movement becoming an institution in their lifetime; Sir William Cash, chairman of the Abbey National, is related to John Bright: Sir Bruce Wycherley, the President, comes from a methodist family.

The co-existence of the building societies with banks is odd. 'Borrowing short and lending long is anathema to the banker', said Sir Harold Bellman, the former chairman of Abbey National, who died in 1963; 'but we know that default by our members is very rare. There's no hostile competition between banks and building societies—we regard our work as complementary.' The building societies occupy a very curious place in the British financial world; in the words of the *Financial Times*: 'Few institutions in Britain are more hybrid than the building societies. They do not work obviously for profit and yet must throw up a growing surplus if they are to expand; they do not obviously compete—indeed the Building Societies Association is the vehicle for keeping the terms of smaller societies as attractive as those of the large—and yet the big societies, year by year, take a growing share of the total business. They are heavily circumscribed in their activities by statute, and yet are in no sense a part of the public sector. The building societies and their management in fact exist in a curious half light between private and public sector, between competition and cartel'.[1]

There have been some glimmers of movement in this half-light; in 1964 the Chief General Manager of the Abbey National, S. W. G. Morton, dared to raise the question of whether building societies should make a profit, and whether the old musty atmosphere of their offices, which stems from the old cautious ideas of self-help, should not be invigorated by more competition. But most of the 700 building societies will resist any hotting-up of the pace; like the banks fifty years ago, competition would mean amalgamation. Already half the total assets of the building societies are held by 'the big seven', and amalgamations are proceeding steadily—in the ten years from 1951 to 1961, the total number dropped by 101.[2] The big societies are not inclined towards an all-out fight, and they are likely to remain for some time in this uncertain limbo.

Hire-purchase has a more commercial and less moral origin than building societies, and for a long time it was regarded as disreputable. It began, rather oddly, with the invention of the

[1] *Financial Times*, May 27, 1964.

[2] *See The Times*, April 24, 1963: 'Are 700 Building Societies Needed in Britain?'

sewing-machine in the mid-nineteenth century. The machines were expensive, long-lasting and productive; the Singer company began selling them by hire-purchase, and their idea was followed by piano-makers and furniture makers. The Civil Service Mutual Furnishing Association was founded in 1877, by a group of senior civil servants—a surprising activity for deputy secretaries—to assist their juniors to furnish their homes.[1] Meanwhile during the 1860's 'wagon companies' had been formed in the North of England, to provide hire-purchase for railway trucks (which the railways did not provide) to take coal from the mines to the merchants. From filling this gap, the companies expanded to cars and equipment: the 'North Central Wagon and Finance Company' and the 'British Wagon Company' became two of the biggest hire-purchase concerns.

The idea of hire-purchase, unlike that of building societies, often outraged the Nonconformist conscience: and the companies, like the insurance collectors, could be ruthless in enforcing 'snatch-backs' if payments had lapsed. Not until 1938 was a Hire-Purchase Act passed which partly protected the hirer. Further legislation, long overdue, was passed in 1962. The prejudice against hire-purchase has largely dissolved since the post-war boom: TV, washing machines, refrigerators and cars have all multiplied under the never-never. The total hire-purchase debt has risen steeply. By the end of 1964 the debt was £1,094 million, or over £20 per head.

Like the building societies, hire-purchase firms have grown up outside the city nexus, looked at askance by most bankers—until in 1958 Barclays took a share in UDT, and other banks followed. The companies vary widely in stature: the great boom of 1958, when hire-purchase shares rocketed, was followed by heavy losses. The biggest and most belligerent is the omnipresent United Dominions Trust, with a huge white building in Eastcheap.

It began as an American idea, established in 1919 by a young Scots barrister, J. Gibson Jarvie, as a branch of the Commercial Investment Trust in New York. By 1923 it had become a British company, with Jarvie as chairman. Mass-production of cars made hire-purchase much more respectable and, after a long period of disapproval, by 1930 UDT was sufficiently regarded for the Bank of England themselves to buy half-a-million pounds' worth of shares.[2]

[1] *See* Hire-Purchase in a Free Society, Institute of Economic Affairs, July 1959.
[2] The UDT Group of Companies, 1960.

Jarvie saw his business grow from an upstart lender into a major city institution. Its letterhead says firmly at the top 'United Dominions Trust Ltd. Bankers', and it even has Sir Brian Mountain, a dignified city pluralist, on its board. The group now have huge ramifications in industry, for they provide not only the capital for hire-purchase, but expert advice for farmers, engineers and small businessmen, and like other bankers have found themselves increasingly involved in industrial problems (they have lent money for the steel balls used in making the Kariba dam, or for engines for trawlers). The UDT, in spite of the setbacks of bad debts, continues to be the most aggressive of the hire-purchase companies, and in 1962 it caused a new flurry by outbidding others with a new bonus system for its agents—a step which caused a furore in the city, but which forced other companies to follow. When Gibson Jarvie retired in March 1963 (he died in December 1964), to become president, his place as chairman was taken by a New Zealander, Alexander Ross, who had begun his career in the National Bank of New Zealand. (New kinds of institutions in Britain tend to be run by people from newer countries.) Ross, a keen oarsman and sportsman, has brought with him a less aggressive attitude than his predecessor, and the UDT, like hire-purchase in general, is beginning to settle down to a respectable middle-age.

MERCHANT BANKERS

Who hold the balance of the world? Who reign
O'er congress, whether royalist or liberal?
Who rouse the shirtless patriots of Spain?
(That makes old Europe's journals squeak and gibber all)
Who keep the world, both old and new in pain
Or pleasure? Who make politics run gligger all?
The shade of Buonoparte's noble daring?—
Jew Rothschild and his fellow-Christian, Baring.

Byron: Don Juan. Canto V. 1823.

The merchant banks stand with relationship to Barclays or the Midland rather as a barrister to a firm of solicitors, or a bookie to the tote. They are much smaller (they employ between them less than 4,000 people) and most are privately controlled. They do not have cheque books or counters for small customers: they deal with big firms and rich individuals. 'You live on your deposits,' Lord Brand used to tell his joint stock banking friends: 'we have to live on our wits.' The merchant bankers are wealthy, usually hereditary, and are still widely regarded as the princes of the city. They are the inner bastions of private enterprise: 'if you want to observe the profit motive at work, a good merchant bank is the place'.[1]

They are the descendants of seventeenth-century merchants, most of them from Germany, who developed into bankers—selling their signatures instead of their goods. They found it more profitable to deal in credit than materials, and they made money both by guaranteeing other people's credit (accepting houses) and by raising loans (issuing houses). In these delicate operations, their integrity and judgment became their chief asset—their justification for hereditary bias. Ever since the Medicis of Florence, the merchant banks have been dynastic, passing down know-how, wealth, and sometimes brains.

In the early nineteenth century the London merchant bankers were richer than governments; Rothschilds financed whole armies, and Barings developed South America. The first heavy setback came with the South American slump of 1890, when Barings had to be rescued from ruin by the Governor of the Bank of England (who ordered the other bankers to come to their assistance). But a new decline in foreign business came after the first world war, when nationalism and the rise of Nazi Germany made foreign loans far more risky. Since then the London bankers have turned more to advising industry at home—a connection once considered undesirable.

In the meantime the wealth of the merchant banks was being eclipsed by the Treasury, the industrial corporations, and the provincial institutions which were pushing their way up—insurance companies, building societies and joint stock banks. New financiers, working through investment trusts, had become more powerful, if less respectable, than the bankers. The city, which can be dazzled by romance, often credits merchant bankers with more influence than they have. Many have lived on their names, and clung to old business instead of looking for new. But their connections and knowledge still give big opportunities, and a few banks have had a visible effect on the pattern of trade.

A 'merchant bank' corresponds roughly to an American 'investment bank' and a French *banque d'affaires*. The élite of the merchant banks are the seventeen 'acceptance houses', who have the backing of the Bank of England to accept other people's bills—to guarantee payment by one firm to another. The 'acceptance business' is less

[1] Kenneth Fleet in the *Sunday Telegraph*, December. 8, 1963.

important today, when many firms are richer than their banks, and can finance themselves; and most banks are more active as 'issuing houses'—floating new issues of stock. But the partners (about 140) of the acceptance houses, backed by the Bank of England, are regarded as part of the city 'Establishment'. These were the sixteen banks of the Accepting Houses Committee, in February 1965, with their date of foundation and committee members:

1763	Baring Brothers	Sir Edward Reid (Chairman)
1804	N. M. Rothschild	Edmund de Rothschild
1804	J. Henry Schroder, Wagg	H. W. B. Schroder
1805	Wm. Brandt's Sons	W. A. Brandt
1808	Antony Gibbs	Lord Aldenham
1810	Brown Shipley	Angus McKinnon (Deputy Chairman)
1830	Kleinwort, Benson	Ernest Kleinwort
1831	Hill, Samuel	Lord Bearsted
1833	Arbuthnot Latham	S. R. Allsopp
1836	Guinness, Mahon	H. S. H. Guinness
1838	Morgan Grenfell	Viscount Harcourt
1839	Hambros	C. E. A. Hambro
1853	Samuel Montagu	Louis Franck
1877	Lazards, de Stein	R. H. M. Kindersley
1896	S. Japhet	R. A. Harari
1946	S. G. Warburg	Geoffrey Seligman

BANKING FAMILIES

The merchant bankers work in a formal atmosphere, conditioned by trust and steeped in tradition. In many banks the partners still work together in one large room: in at least one of them all partners' letters are opened every morning, and put on a table for the others to see. Mahogany, black-coated waiters and grandfather clocks set the tone of privacy. Nearly all are hereditary firms, and only two were founded since 1900. All but two of the senior partners are sons of bankers, and families dominate the boards. This, for instance, is the list of partners in Wm. Brandt's Sons:

W. E. Brandt
H. A. Brandt
W. A. Brandt
J. M. Brandt
P. A. Brandt
F. D. O'Brien Newman

In merchant banking hereditary privilege remains unassailed. But several family banks, while maintaining control, have introduced able outsiders to enliven or run their businesses, like Sir George Erskine of Morgans, Gordon Richardson of Schroders, or Louis Franck of Samuel Montagus. This is part of the recurring pattern of the city—helping to provide the balance between trust and enterprise—solid, long-established families in control, with clever outsiders, often from the Continent or Scotland, providing the dynamic.

The banking families have an influence beyond their own banks. Many of the partners of the accepting houses are directors of insurance companies, and a growing number have become directors or chairmen of industrial firms, or powers behind them: 'I've sacked a dozen chairmen in my time,' one banker told me. And since the eighteenth century, bankers have repeatedly intermarried with the aristocracy, and with the other bankers. Their connections with the political and ducal families are perhaps not as close as they look, but they help to give merchant bankers wider horizons and contacts than other men in the city.

The family with probably the most remarkable financial ramifications is the 'Financial Smiths' (not to be confused with the bookselling Smiths, headed by Lord Hambleden, or with the descendants of F. E. Smith, later Lord Birkenhead). Every summer a lunch is given by the Smith Family Club, presided over by Sir Alexander Smith, which is confined to the descendants of Thomas Smith, born in 1631, who founded a bank in Nottingham. In 1959 17 descendants were reported to hold city appointments: between them they held 87 directorships in 75 companies, including 6 chairmanships and 3 managing directorships. They included the heads of two merchant banks—Lord Bicester of Morgan Grenfell and Reginald Abel Smith of Arbuthnot Latham—partners of two others, Hambros and Schroders, and directors of two joint stock banks, Coutts and the National Provincial (which absorbed the original Smith family bank at the end of the last century). The Smiths have traditionally favoured Eton, Cambridge and the city, but recently young Smiths have gone into industry, and one, Brian Abel Smith, is a radical economist at the London School of Economics.

Some of the more prominent Financial Smiths[1] in 1959 are shown on the following page.

Apart from Barings who maintain enterprise as well as authority

[1] *See The Economist*, March 28, 1959.

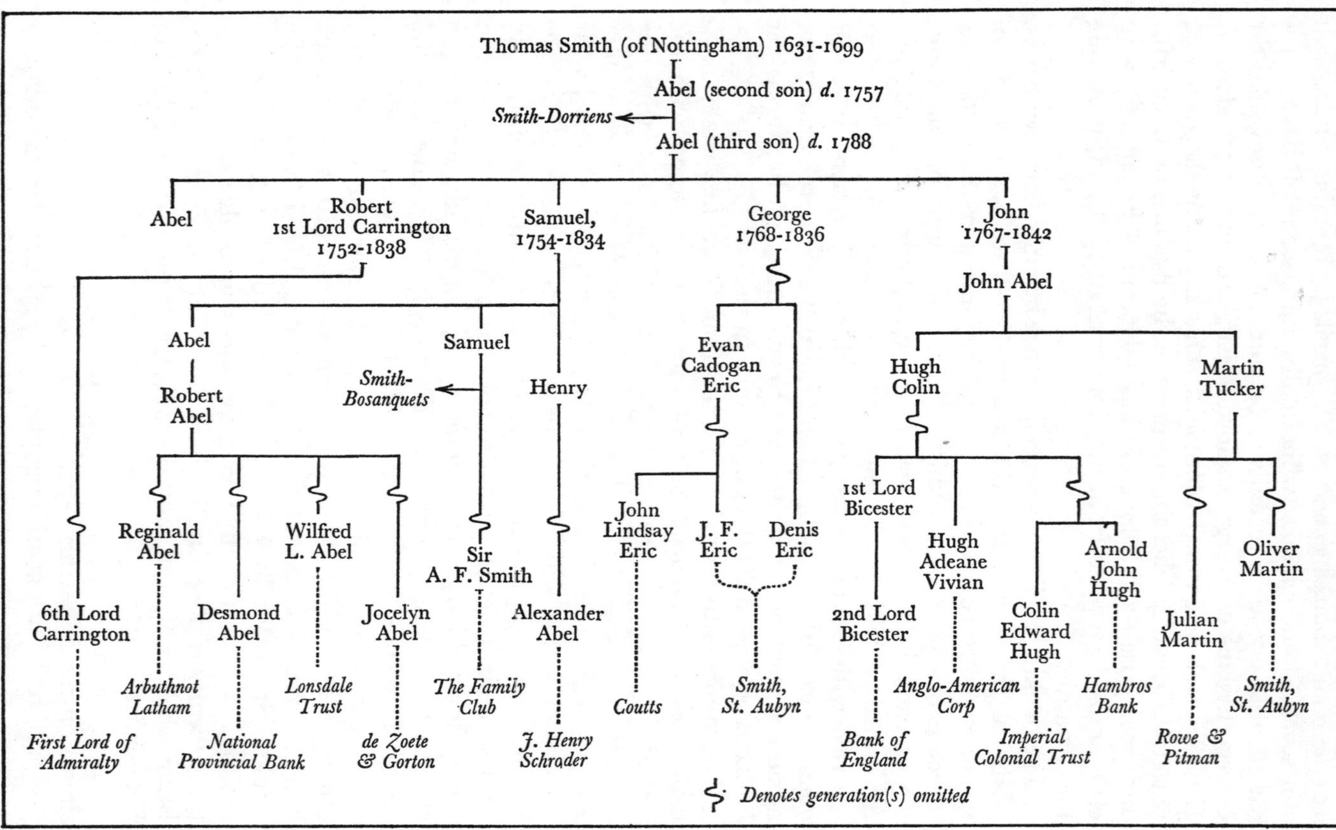
Thomas Smith (of Nottingham) 1631-1699
Abel (second son) d. 1757
Smith-Dorriens
Abel (third son) d. 1788
Abel
Robert
1st Lord Carrington
1752-1838
Samuel,
1754-1834
George
1768-1836
John
1767-1842
John Abel
Abel
Robert
Abel
Samuel
Smith-
Bosanquets
Henry
Evan
Cadogan
Eric
Hugh
Colin
Martin
Tucker
6th Lord
Carrington
Reginald
Abel
Desmond
Abel
Wilfred
L. Abel
Jocelyn
Abel
Sir
A. F. Smith
Alexander
Abel
John
Lindsay
Eric
J. F.
Eric
Denis
Eric
1st Lord
Bicester
2nd Lord
Bicester
Hugh
Adeane
Vivian
Colin
Edward
Hugh
Arnold
John
Hugh
Julian
Martin
Oliver
Martin
First Lord of
Admiralty
Arbuthnot
Latham
National
Provincial Bank
Lonsdale
Trust
de Zoete
& Gorton
The Family
Club
J. Henry
Schrader
Coutts
Smith,
St. Aubyn
Bank of
England
Anglo-American
Corp
Imperial
Colonial Trust
Hambros
Bank
Rowe &
Pitman
Smith,
St. Aubyn
Denotes generation(s) omitted

(specialising in South America and beer), the oldest, and certainly the most famous is Rothschilds. Their symbol is the sign of the five arrows, to commemorate the five Rothschild brothers who first scattered to London, Paris, Vienna, Naples and Frankfurt. The English house was founded by Nathan, a cotton merchant in Manchester; three of his great-great-grandsons and one of his great-great-great-grandsons are now partners. Rothschilds is now less romantic: no longer does the Rothschild pigeon bring in the news, the Rothschild boat lie waiting off Folkestone, or Rothschild couriers leave daily for the capitals of Europe. Armies (such as Wellington's in Spain) no longer need wait for Rothschilds' support. But they continue to be enterprising in less romantic fields, such as founding hire-purchase firms and unit trusts, and developing Labrador. And they have recruited clever young outsiders, like Philip Shelbourne, from the bar, and Rodney Leach.

Rothschilds are very *haute banque*, and the visitor feels the full weight of family tradition—particularly in the unique ritual of the bankers' lunch. Bankers' lunches, in quiet panelled rooms with silver platters and crested china, help to bring their country-house life into the middle of the city. They entertain clients or guests in a hushed Victorian setting, well away from ticker-tapes or telephones, and they can use prestige as a weapon. One or two banks have up-to-date lunch rooms (the Ionian Bank, an unorthodox place, has a row of three modern dining-rooms, a fish-shaped table and specially designed cutlery). But most banks prefer to evoke safe nineteenth-century glory.

GENTLEMEN V. PLAYERS

At first glance the merchant banks, each with their lunches, insurance companies, butlers and discretion, might seem to be a united club. But since the war—and probably since their beginnings—they have been divided into two rough groups, sometimes described as Gentlemen v. Players, where the two spirits of the city, the protective and the aggressive, have come into conflict. The two sides have often skirmished, and often made truces: but the sharpness of the conflict was revealed in the most extraordinary affair in the recent history of the city—the 'Aluminium War' of 1958-9. 'It was a watershed,' said one banker, 'the city has never been quite the same since.'

On the one side are the gentlemen, or as the American magazine *Fortune* describes them, the 'Old Freddies', who 'quietly partition the city's vast business among themselves—which is why the city can put over a huge money deal in half the time it takes Wall Street'.[1] The most prominent of them is Lazards—descended from the French-Jewish *Lazard frères*, but now wholly and emphatically British. Lazards lies at the heart of the hereditary banking nexus. They have four important peers on their board—Lord Poole, a former Chairman of the Conservative Party; Lord Hampden, now the senior and probably the ablest partner, related to the Dukes of Buccleuch and Devonshire; Lord Kindersley; and the man who owns two-thirds of Lazards' shares, Lord Cowdray. Lazards is an interesting example of the blending of old wealth with new—of ducal and mercantile. They are capable of being both stuffy and ruthless, and they represent the British aristocracy at its toughest—though not necessarily at its shrewdest.

Behind the bank is the legendary personality of Lord Cowdray, a cousin of Churchill and one of the richest and most formidable men in Britain. He is the heir to the oil fortune of his grandfather, Westman Pearson, who founded the Mexican Eagle oil company, later merged into 'Shell-Mex'. The present Cowdray interests include three important trusts (Whitehall Securities, S. Pearson and the Cowdray Trust, which work at the top of the Vickers skyscraper), the Westminster Press chain of provincial newspapers and the Financial News Ltd., which owns the leading financial papers in Britain, headed by the omnipresent *Financial Times*. Cowdray is a man of relentless energy, with the reputation of making money out of everything he touches—even polo, which he organises on Sundays, with a good profit from spectators. He lives in two big Victorian houses in Sussex and Wales, and (although he has only one arm) goes shooting with an energy which wears out his guests. Once a year he tours through Texas, where he has large interests, exhausting Texans with questions. He is one of those aristocrats who have never lost their ancestor's urge to make money. Although he touches political circles, he is hardly interested in politics. His actual intervention in Lazards or Whitehall Securities is infrequent but important: he appears for lunch with the managing directors, but leaves most day-to-day decisions to his representative, Lord Poole.

For the last decade the dominant influence in Lazards has been Lord Kindersley—a tall, confident banker with a military moustache, and the quiet, superior manner of hereditary bankers, who resigned from the senior partnership in 1965. He gave way to a

[1] *Fortune*, June 1959—to which I am indebted to some of the facts in this section.

younger man—a year younger—Lord Hampden, nephew of the late Lord Brand. It was Kindersley's father (then Sir Robert) who gave Lazards their high reputation for shrewdness, and in those days it was Lazards who were regarded as upstarts. ('I remember when Baron Schroder crossed over the streeet to avoid meeting Sir Robert,' one banker told me, 'because Sir Robert had pinched the Brazilian coffee business from him.') But his son has been the personification of the city insider (as vividly emerged in the Bank Rate Tribunal of 1957)—director of the Bank of England, Governor of the Royal Exchange Assurance, Chairman of Rolls-Royce.

Working closely with Lazards is the stately establishment of Morgan Grenfell, still associated with the Morgan Guaranty Trust Company of New York, and founded by the American philanthropist, George Peabody (builder of model Victorian dwellings). The partners of Morgans include Lord Harcourt (related to the Morgan family and brother-in-law of Lord Ashburton, of Barings), who is also chairman of the huge Legal and General Insurance Company; Lord Catto, a son of a former Governor of the Bank of England; Lord Rennell, a former diplomat; and his brother-in-law Lord Bicester (one of the Financial Smiths), senior partner and director of the Bank of England, who pops up all over the place. 'Morgans and ourselves', Lord Kindersley explained to the Bank Rate Tribunal in a famous and revealing passage, 'are probably closer than any other two issuing houses in the City of London; we discuss intimate details of every kind and description. I do not think Lord Bicester would find it in the least surprising that I should come to him and say to him: "Look here, Rufie, is it too late to stop this business or not?" '

Other 'gentlemen' banks are Hambros, entirely controlled by the Hambro family, who came from Copenhagen in 1814 and still have a large Scandinavian connection; and M. Samuel, founded by Marcus Samuel, the East End trader who later founded[1] the colossus of Shell. Samuel's has been run by Samuels, headed by Lord Bearsted, who have a family director on the board of Shell, but compared to the Royal Dutch-Shell annual turnover—more than £3,000 million—the bank which helped to create it is now tiny—symbolic of the change in financial power over the last century. A small stir was caused in March 1964 when Charles Clore, the master of take-overs, joined the board of Samuel's, with a 14 per cent stake in its equity; but his presence did not visibly change the banking scene. More importantly, in 1965 Samuel's merged

[1] Or helped to form it: *see* p. 481.

with Philip Hill (*See* below) to make the second biggest acceptance house (next to Hambros).

The traditional bankers move in similar circles: they meet at the favourite bankers' clubs—Brooks's, Boodle's, White's—stay at each others' country houses at weekends, and shoot each others' grouse in Scotland in August. Some have more cultural habits: Barings and Rothschilds share a permanent box at Covent Garden, and Lazards and Morgan Grenfells share another. Most of their business has been inherited, and has not much expanded in the past ten years: 'The position of the traditional banks', one of them said to me in 1961, 'is rather like the British Empire after the war. There's nothing much more to gain, and a lot to lose. But it's a bit less of a closed club than it used to be; newcomers are always coming along, and seem like strangers until they're not new any longer. It's rather like a village.'

Confronting this club have been a small band of strangers, with very little to lose and a lot to gain. The most unusual intruder was Lionel Fraser, who became chairman of Helbert Wagg, which merged with Schroders in 1962, for he was that rare phenomenon—the self-made banker. He was the son of a butler, and at the age of sixteen he answered an advertisement for a job with a small banking firm, now part of Helbert Wagg's. 'The city meant precious little to me, for I was completely without background or connection. It was just somewhere to scrape a living.' Before he died in 1965 he had risen to be not only chairman of Wagg's, but head of a very diversified industrial holding company, Thomas Tillings.

Another intruder is Kenneth Keith, formerly managing director of Philip Hill, now chief executive and deputy-chairman (under Lord Bearsted) of the merged merchant bank of Hill, Samuel. Keith, though he served in the Guards, comes from an unbankerlike profession—chartered accountancy: after the war he was brought into Philip Hill's by Sir Brian Mountain of Eagle Star Insurance (who have a large interest in the bank); he became managing director in 1951, at the age of 35. He is a tough, casual, feet-on-the-desk banker, with swept-back grey hair and a brisk way of talking. He has found new fields in the Commonwealth and set up a branch in Nigeria: and he is determined that London should become the financial centre of Europe. 'We're all rather jealous of him,' said one prominent banker. Keith was the first city man to be appointed (in 1964) to 'Neddy', and he has not been afraid to speak up. 'I think Britain's problem is that we've had it too good for too long,' he said in December 1964: 'Fundamentally we don't believe in competition; we always hope for some easy way out.'[1]

The merger of Philip Hill's with M. Samuel in 1965 provided a spectacular example of the mingling of outsiders with insiders. Twenty years ago Philip Hill's was only a 'West End finance house', right outside the City Establishment. Keith built up the assets of Philip Hill's from £2 million to £74 million in 18 years. Samuel's had the kind of respectability and connections which, in the City, can only come with age. Between them, the two firms could combine stateliness with drive, and could boast £162 million of assets. But as one of the Samuel's directors, Lord Melchett, explained to the *Sunday Times*: 'compared with our real rivals on Wall Street, we are still in the tiddler class.'

But the most spectacular newcomer is Siegmund Warburg, from an old Hamburg banking family, who came to England as a refugee, and established his bank in 1946. Cultured and sensitive, with dark, deep-set eyes and a quick intuitive mind, Warburg has fluttered the city since the war. He perceived very early the new trends in British banking—particularly the importance of industrial mergers. He advised Associated Television, Roy Thomson in his buying of the *Sunday Times*,[2] and the *Daily Mirror* in buying Amalgamated Press and Odhams. More recently, he has pioneered the raising of foreign loans in London, including the 15-million dollar Italian Autostrada loan in 1963, and the 20-million dollar City of Tokyo loan. Warburg has recruited his staff and partners from a wider range: they include two ex-civil servants (Sir Andrew McFadyean and Sir James Helmore), a former journalist (Ronald Grierson) and the former ambassador to Paris (Lord Gladwyn). In the city Warburgs are notorious for hard work and perpetual travel. They work in a new building in Gresham Street, furnished in bankers' contemporary, with a grandfather clock and old prints, and electronic devices.

THE ALUMINIUM WAR

These were the main city forces assembled on each side of the extraordinary 'Aluminium War' of Christmas 1958 which, in one dazzling fortnight, illuminated the workings of the city and in-

[1] *The Observer*, December 7, 1964.
[2] *See* p. 147.

dustry. It was a conflict between old and new banks, between American and British approaches to industry, and between shareholders and directors. The new won.

The seeds of the war were sown in 1957, when the American Reynolds Metals, run by four aggressive brothers, had decided to try to buy British Aluminium (the *only* British aluminium company) in order to acquire their new plant in Quebec. Reynolds were advised by their bankers, Kuhn Loeb and their London correspondent, Siegmund Warburg, not to antagonise British nationalism by an outright American bid, but to operate with a British company. After much exploration, they went into partnership with Sir Ivan Stedeford of Tube Investments, a self-made engineer from the Midlands[1]—whose adviser was the other maverick banker in the city, Lionel Fraser. Stedeford was at first anxious about an Anglo-American take-over of a sedate British company: but eventually he was persuaded. Through Warburgs, Tube Investments and Reynolds secretly began buying British Aluminium shares.

By October 1958 TI had bought about 10 per cent of the shares, and Stedeford arranged a meeting with British Aluminium, headed by Lord Portal, the war-time Chief of Air Staff, to say that his firm would like to have an association with British Aluminium. Stedeford made a definite offer for BA shares two days later. Portal, in a second encounter replied that he had already reached an agreement with Alcoa, Reynolds' American rivals, and could not pass on Sir Ivan's offer to shareholders. Sir Ivan, furious, summoned a press conference revealing the whole story, and the terms of his offer to BA shareholders (which was far more attractive than Lord Portal's arrangement). The press sided quickly with Sir Ivan, and the big insurance companies who held shares in BA were annoyed at not being consulted. Portal (replying to suggestions that he might have consulted shareholders) said in a classic phrase—'those familiar with negotiations between great companies will realise that such a course would have been impracticable'. On December 14 TI sent a formal bid to shareholders of 78/- for each BA share. Five days later BA's board announced that they would increase the dividend. But it still seemed likely that the BA shareholders would hang on to their shares.

Then, on New Year's Eve, the bombshell came: fourteen august financial institutions wrote to BA shareholders, in a letter signed by Lord Kindersley and Olaf Hambro, to announce that between

[1] *See* p. 539.

them they were holding two million shares in BA, that they were prepared to buy shares at 82/– each, and that the TI take-over bid must be resisted in the 'national interest'. The consortium included Lazards, Hambros, Morgan Grenfell, M. Samuel, Samuel Montagu, the Whitehall Trust, and the British South Africa Company. Between them they made up the heart of the interlocking city establishment. Lionel Fraser, to the fury of Lazards, replied with an interview in the *Evening Standard*:

'It all seems like Alice in Wonderland when really calm judgment is called for. How my friends on the other side can say their proposals are in the national interest astound me.'

Looking back on the incident, it seems astonishing that such a group, with so many able men, should have behaved so unwisely: the consortium's appeal to 'the national interest' ('saving British Aluminium for civilisation' as one banker put it) had little support, since both schemes involved equal American participation. Reynolds retorted easily to the consortium by buying 1,300,000 BA shares in the first two days of the New Year, and by making an improved bid on January 5. In the meantime the Governor of the Bank of England had tried to patch up the row by inviting the parties to talks on January 1 and 2, but without success. By January 9, Reynolds and TI held 80 per cent of British Aluminium shares. The war was won, but the victors soon found that they had paid too much—as often happens after hectic take-overs.

Afterwards Lord Portal and Geoffrey Cunliffe resigned from the board, with compensation of £88,000 between them, and Lord Portal was appointed as charman of the British Match Corporation—an 'Establishment' job previously held by Lord Kindersley: while Lord Plowden, the nominee of Sir Ivan and later his successor, moved in to inject new life into British Aluminium.

Recriminations soon followed. Olaf Hambro wrote to *The Times* on January 12, to complain that 'it is very unclear why the majority of city editors of the press seemed to be against city opinion and openly wrote in favour of the take-over bid'. Anthony Crosland, the Labour MP, writing about the consortium, said 'their outlook appears about as contemporary as the architectural style in which the city is now being rebuilt—both make one shudder'.

AFTER ALUMINIUM

Behind the allegations about the national interest lay a deeper resentment—that the new bankers, by their secret buying and bypassing of boards, were undermining the network of trust and authority on which the city rested, and (a subsidiary charge) were coming too close to industry, in a continental, un-British way. For some months the two sides in the city would not speak to each other: but then, as happens in the city, out of the sharp antithesis a synthesis emerged. Warburgs, after other successful deals, began to be accepted as part of the 1960's, and soon to acquire a *haute banque* flavour, while Lazards rapidly increased their home industrial business. Only two years after their patriotic appeals in the Aluminium war, Lazards were engaged in buying British Fords shares for the American company. Meanwhile in the quieter old banks amateurism since the war has been slowly giving way to professionalism. Bankers have been arriving at 9.30 instead of 10.15, moving from Hampshire into London flats, and talking shop at lunch. "People are no longer *ashamed* to work", Siegmund Warburg said to me in 1964; "they're no longer trying to pretend to be country squires".'

'I believe that the British Aluminium affair provoked a remarkable transformation in the city', wrote Lionel Fraser afterwards: 'Old citadels crumbled, traditional strongholds were invaded, new thought was devoted to city problems, there was a freshness and alertness unknown before, dramatic to watch. Now the merchant bankers are more on their toes; they vie with one another to give a better service to industry and their clients, some even advertise the facilities they can offer; there has been a girding of loins, resulting in more enterprise and competitiveness and less reliance on the "old boy idea". Of course, these advances might have taken place anyhow, but I do not believe I am exaggerating when I say that most of them date from the British Aluminium episode and that the effects have spread beyond just banking and have included the whole city'.[1]

The two extremes—the hereditary Old Freddies and the thrusting upstarts—have become less obviously irreconcilable as the banks have become more enterprising; and there are many prominent bankers who belong to neither camp. Such, for instance, is Sir Mark Turner, one of the managing directors of Benson, Lonsdale, a formidable but unobtrusive financial expert, who is chairman of the hire-purchase company Mercantile Credit, and a director of the Commercial Union. He is a liberal and broad-minded banker (although on the board of Tanganyika

[1] *Sunday Times*, April 28, 1963.

Concessions) and he has worked his way up through the city. Another impressive self-made banker is Gordon Richardson, the chairman of Henry Schroder, Wagg, who began his career as a Chancery barrister and, finding that too exhausting, switched at the age of 39 to merchant banking, in which he had a rapid success (as in other fields, the city has a greater respect for outside expertise than for its own skills). Richardson is a highly professional banker, ruthless but fair, opposed to nepotism, and his directorships range from the Royal Ballet to Lloyds Bank; he was an outspoken member of the Jenkins Committee on Company Law (though he did not go so far as to advocate the publication of banks' accounts).

There is still a suspicion—partly a residue of the 'Bankers' Ramp' of 1931—that bankers are plotting the economic future of the country. But most of them, while invoking the national interest, are too absorbed in the day-to-day worries of the city to call on the Chancellor or nobble the Treasury. In spite of their family networks, the old bankers appear to spend much more time weekending between themselves than with politicians or industrialists. Ever since the first post-war Labour government—when more than one merchant bank made preparations for moving their headquarters out of England—there has been a simmering distrust between bankers and the Treasury. And in 1964 the simmering came close to boiling point.

24

FINANCIERS

Avarice, the spur of Industry.
David Hume.

All over the city, men in small offices are buying and selling little bits of industry. They range from 'bucket-shops' which make a living out of speculating in shares, to imposing investment trusts, which raise money from the public and invest it, at a profit, in hand-picked companies.

Historically the city, though closer to industry than the Wall Street bankers, has been separate from industrialists. The bosses in the North and Midlands have nursed a bitter (and sometimes well-founded) suspicion of bankers and financiers. There are many city stories about the encounters between bluff Yorkshiremen and smooth Bishopsgate bankers. Many big firms like ICI, Courtaulds or Unilever have prided themselves on their independence from EC2. 'We are suspicious of banking,' said Samuel Courtauld in 1942, 'because we think it is often overpaid for its services, and also because we doubt its efficiency. Historical development has given it a privileged position on which it is apt to trade. We are suspicious of company promoters and gamblers in stocks and shares, because they want something for nothing, and do far more harm than good.'[1] In a time of crisis, as when ICI threatened Courtaulds, they become very aware of the city and shareholders; but in their normal operations the industrial Leviathans have become virtually independent of the city.

But Britain remains a country of small businesses: and for thousands of them, particularly the fast-growing ones, finding money is still crucial and very difficult. The city, like the joint stock banks, used to operate on the principle of lending large sums only to those who have large sums. It was easy enough for big companies to go to the stock exchange and insurance companies, but for smaller firms there was a gap in the city machine—known since the Macmillan committee of 1931 as the 'Macmillan Gap'. Since then, the city has become interested in their pet small

[1] Quoted in *The Boss*—by Roy Lewis and Rosemary Stewart, 1958.

companies, and various industrial holding companies have grown up to help smaller firms with finance. Among them are the Charterhouse Group, under the chairmanship of W. F. W. Ram, which owns ten companies, including a merchant bank (S. Japhet), and has shares in seventy-five others, including a publishing group (Associated Book Publishers, including Methuen and Eyre and Spottiswoode); and 'Credit for Industries Ltd', a subsidiary of the hire-purchase firm United Dominions Trust. Others are Tillings, the 'family of companies' built up by Lionel Fraser; Firth Cleveland, the engineering group run by Charles Hayward; and Norcros, the 'club' of firms controlled by John Sheffield.

Two more philanthropic groups have been set up since the war. One is the 'Finance Corporation for Industry' (FCI), subsidised by the government. The other is the 'Industrial and Commercial Finance Corporation' (ICFC), known as 'Icky-ficky', set up by the joint stock banks and run by Lord Sherfield, the tall, booming ex-Ambassador to Washington.

The word financier is one which city men nowadays avoid: it brings back memories of thirties scandals, and names like Clarence Hatry, the financier who financed United Steel but then crashed and went to jail. With their talk about 'families of companies', 'nurseries', 'clubs', 'filling a gap' and 'providing services', financiers provide an impression of paternal—almost maternal—care of industry. They, too, have been influenced by the vogue for professionalisation, and the fact that they make private fortunes out of industry is sometimes forgotten. The independence of the industrial Leviathans, run by their own managers, sometimes suggests that the city entrepreneur is a dodo-person, killed off by the war and the managerial revolution. But among the hundred biggest companies in Britain, as we shall see, there are still more than a score which are controlled by such entrepreneurs. There is no chance in this book of dealing with all their various characters: here I pick only one—perhaps the most spectacular—Harold Charles Drayton, usually known as Harley Drayton.

117 OLD BROAD STREET

At number 117 Old Broad Street is a door with a list of 48 companies printed on metal strips, beginning with 'Alcoy and Gandia Railway and Harbour Ltd', and ending with 'Vector Securities Ltd'. Upstairs, the offices have the usual musty city smell, and sense of historical standstill. These are the headquarters of Harley Drayton, chairman of twenty-three companies, led by British Electric Traction, which owns 12,000 buses in Britain and 60 per cent of the shares in the biggest TV company, Associated-Rediffusion. He controls, among others, Mitchell Cotts, the African traders; Advance Laundries; the Antofagasta and Bolivia Railways; Provincial Newspapers Ltd, with four newspapers; and a group of twenty investment trusts. The 'Drayton Group', as this is usually known in the city, is probably the most striking example of a group of industries financially controlled from the city.

Into these offices comes every morning a big, bucolic man with a red face, white hair brushed back, a monocle dangling over his pin-stripe suit, and tall, laced boots. He looks, as he is, a strong man from country stock who has somehow strayed into the city and applied laws of tough common sense. Drayton likes to gaze out of the window in his old leather chair, puffing at a cigar, philosophising about the world and the city, and quoting the Bible: 'The twenty-fifth chapter of Leviticus is the only economic system which ever worked. It tells you how to run a sinking fund, how to manage a business, how to make an issue.' At weekends he retires to his 1,400-acre farm in Suffolk, and reads the lesson at Plumton parish church. In the country he loves his country-squire life, walking and shooting, and his greatest pride is to have been High Sheriff. He collects illuminated manuscripts, and lives in 'Millionaires' Row' in London (one of the last three private residents to do so). His interests outside his companies are not large, and his political attitudes are antique. He stood as a Liberal candidate after the war, but largely because he thought the Conservatives were becoming too Socialist; and the Liberals have since disillusioned him. He belongs to the Council of the Institute of Directors, and to the London Committee of the South African Foundation (the organisation founded to put South Africa into a favourable light in the world outside); and he has put a lot of money into South Africa since the war. He operates almost entirely from the city, only occasionally going out to inspect his interests in Africa, Canada or South America, or Television House in Kingsway (he goes there when his nephews want to look round). 'You have to pick your man and give him final responsibility for the day-to-day management. My job is the final financing, picking of high executives. You have to make yourself available when they're in a hole. Otherwise I don't interfere. Sometimes I just give them a bit of advice like "Boys, be careful, copper's going up".'

Drayton is a self-made man. His grandfather was a Lincolnshire farmer, and his father was a gardener who settled in Streatham. At fifteen he answered an advertisement for an office boy, and joined 'Government Stock and Other Securities Ltd'—a group of very successful investment trusts then run by Lord St. Davids, who had built up a large business in South America. Young Drayton's ambition and quickness with figures soon made a mark on Lord St. Davids' associate Jack Austen—a pioneer in transport who had expanded British Electric Traction. When Austen died in 1942, he left Drayton the running of the business, and his house, Plumton Hall in Suffolk: and Austen's portrait now hangs above Drayton's fireplace, between two paintings of the Bank of England. 'All that I am', Drayton said to me in an expansive conversation, 'I owe to him. When I was young, you had to catch the eye of someone who would help you—and there were only eight or ten people who would do that. Nowadays it's much easier—there are far more people who can help you—about thirty or forty: and you can make profits much quicker. But in the old days they helped you out of kindness: nowadays they all want their cut from you.'

Drayton never thought, 'it just isn't done', and the name Drayton, even though it now appears on the board of the Midland Bank, can still cause grunts in the city. But like other ex-rebels in the city, he has become respectable; he is proud of having Angus Ogilvy, husband of Princess Alexandra, as one of his protégés and directors. I asked Drayton what had distinguished his own career from others':

> Most of the city has the idea that you must conform. What stops most people in the city is snobbery. You don't have to worry about being popular. You have to take risks and stick your neck out. If you're an artist, nobody worries if you're a failure: but in the city it's regarded as a crime almost against the Holy Ghost to make a mistake.
>
> Some people are born with a bug inside them: if they are, they can do anything: if they're not, they might as well settle down to be a clerk—it's like the parable of the talents. You have to have a burning belief in what you're doing, and sell it to people who will back you. I'm still prepared to see people in my bath at eight in the morning, and I'm ready to do a deal at midnight. Before the war, when business was difficult, you really had to *sell* things. We used to say: any damn fool can make electricity; it takes a genius to sell it.
>
> The city by and large lost its position after the first world war

and still more after the last war—but most people didn't tumble to it. Between the wars, big money was still in the hands of merchant banks—Lazards, Rothschilds, Barings, Morgans—each with one, two or three million. But with inflation, and the rise of the new financial institutions, one or two millions became chicken feed. The big people were either the ones who had a great deal of money of their own, or the industrialists. I think it was the new industrialists who proved themselves to be the descendants of the great old adventurers, like Drake or Raleigh.

Drayton showed his independence from city opinion in 1955, with the arrival of commercial television. While nearly the whole of the city was sceptical, Drayton had a hunch that it would make large profits; British Electric Traction bought a large share in Associated-Rediffusion, in partnership with Lord Rothermere's Associated Newspapers (*Daily Mail*, *Daily Sketch*, etc.). Drayton reckoned to lose one-and-a-half million: in the first nineteen months BET lost £3,719,000. But he stuck to his hunch. When Lord Rothermere decided that the losses were too high, Drayton's representative casually suggested that he might be able to find a buyer, and Rothermere thankfully sold out. The buyer turned out to be none other than BET. Very soon afterwards the television tide began to turn and the advertising rolled in. 'I thought it would make two-and-a-half million a year,' said Drayton: 'in fact, it's making seven million . . . I think I've always been more enterprising than most. But there was quite a lot of wear and tear on the tummy.'

25

INSURANCE

By means of which Policies of Assurance it cometh to pass upon the loss or perishing of any ship there followeth not the undoing of any Man, but the loss lighteth rather easily upon many than heavily upon few.

Act of Elizabeth, 1601.

When you want *really* big money, you usually find yourself talking to people who *didn't* go to Eton.

A banker.

Democracy, in finance as well as in government, has put power into bureaucracy. It is a parallel to the shift of power from parliament to the civil service. The financial giants of the city today are not the bankers or financiers, but the great anonymous bureaucracies of the insurance companies, and their cousins, the pension funds. In investment the insurance companies, trustees for millions of individuals, have taken the place of the magnates, dukes and Rothschilds who dominated the city a century ago. 'The Institutions'—as the insurance companies and pensions funds are enigmatically called—play with about eight hundred million pounds of new money every year, enough to finance a new ICI; in five years the new investments of insurance companies went up from a million a day to one-and-a-half million.

The power of the institutions is one of the most important developments of the mid-century. But it has grown up outside the traditional mythology of Britain: there are no good novels about insurance, no fashionable memoirs of forty years with the Pru. Decisions are taken by clerkdoms much more remote than the civil service, away from parliamentary questions, and the institutions emerge into the headlines even less than bankers.

Insurance is split into two species. Firstly, insurance against accidents—ships sinking, buildings burning, cars running over people. Secondly, insurance (or technical 'assurance')—of a man's life against a *certainty*—death. The first kind is hazardous, based ultimately on a calculated gamble. The second is largely predictable, for the average span of men's lives—when hundreds of thousands are involved—can be quite accurately calculated.

The first kind, gruesomely called 'Non-Life Insurance', has the oldest origins. Insurance of ships followed Vasco da Gama's voyage, and the first recorded British policy was for the vessel *Santa Cruz*, in 1555. The 'Fire Office' was founded by Nicolas Barbon, son of Praise-God Barebones, in 1680, fourteen years after the Great Fire of London. Insurance followed the path of new inventions—against railway, car, or aeroplane accidents, or the indisposition of prima donnas. International insurance was a British development, and in the eighteenth century the symbols of British insurance companies—suns, phoenixes or globes—spread over Europe as the marks of trust in British money. In nineteenth-century Germany, villagers saw the Sun symbol—the face of a man inside a radiant sun—and knelt down to worship it.[1] London no longer dominates insurance in Europe, but it remains its biggest insurance market.

The traditional heart of 'non-life' insurance has been the collection of rich individuals and their friends known as 'Lloyd's'—the city insurance market, containing 'The Room', which claims to be the biggest air-conditioned room in Europe. It is a curved hall of green-and-white marble 340 feet long, like a Danish-blue mine, surrounded by a gallery: a sedate and sedentary version of the stock exchange. It contains sometimes as many as four thousand people, all selling or buying insurance. Unlike most city activities, what is happening is quite clear; Lloyd's still keeps its simple seventeenth-century routine, when men gathered in Edward Lloyd's coffee-house to offer insurance for ships. Sitting on medieval-type benches, four-in-a-row, in front of shelves and leather-bound ledgers, are the 'underwriters' of insurance, looking like overgrown schoolboys. Wandering between the 'boxes' (as the desks are called) are the 'Lloyd's brokers', holding long folded cards, or 'slips', representing a ship, fleet, cargo or pair of legs to be insured. The brokers queue up in front of the underwriters, to ask them to add their name on the slip. If the underwriter agrees, he puts his signature, and the proportion of the risk he is prepared to take, under the name of the proposition (hence 'underwriter') The broker then goes round The Room until the signatures and the proportions add up to 100 per cent.

The Room contains a typical city mixture of new and old devices. In the middle is a raised rostrum containing a man known as the 'caller', in a big red robe with a wide black collar, looking

[1] *See* P. G. M. Dickson: *The Sun Insurance Office*, 1710–1960.

like a town-crier, reciting the names of brokers through a microphone. About him is the old 'Lutine Bell', which is rung once for overdue news about ships, twice for good news, and below it an electronic notice board, showing names of brokers. When a broker is wanted, one of the 'waiters' (who stand round the room in scarlet uniform) writes his name on a 'telewriter', and the name is reproduced by an electronic hand in front of the 'caller', who then calls for the broker. There are no typewriters, computers, dictaphones, teleprinters or girls in The Room. Clerks inscribe the details of premiums and clients in their crowded, dog-eared ledgers. The system looks medieval, but in its simplicity and lack of paper-work it is not unlike some of the newest Marks and Spencer ideas of office efficiency. Round The Room are ante-rooms, dining-rooms and committee rooms, all built since the war in a heavy style which emphasises the country-gentleman image of Lloyd's: the Adam committee room has a ceiling and chimney-piece brought almost intact from Bowood, the Marquess of Lansdowne's house in Wiltshire.

The financial backbone of Lloyd's is made up by the five thousand 'names', grouped in 275 'syndicates', who provide the capital and must pay up for disasters—with unlimited liability. Each of the outside names has to be worth at least £75,000; these two-thirds are sleeping partners or 'back-woods-men' who never go near The Room. Working Names need only produce £10,000 to £12,000, the rest being guaranteed by their firms. The Names form a proud club. To be elected you must be sponsored by six members, and cross-examined by the Committee, and the list includes large numbers of old city families. Old school ties dominate The Names; people working at Lloyd's who are not members—known as 'substitutes'—are kept severely separate, and they even have their own 'substitutes' lavatory'.

Lloyd's, like merchant banking, depends on a mixture of trust and daring. Syndicates vary enormously in their profits: several, helped by the inflation of the fifties, have made spectacular post-war profits, but the majority make not much more than 10 per cent on their business. The pride of Lloyd's is its foreign trade (it was estimated that in 1964 well over half the £340 million annual premium income came from overseas): American film-directors, Italian ship-owners, Chilean wool-growers, have all come to Lloyd's. Their reputation depends not only on their reliability, but on their readiness to insure almost *anything*, all in one big room, very quickly and without fuss: the speed is part of the justification of the club. But with the growing insurance centres in New York, Paris or Frankfurt, many underwriters doubt if they can maintain their proportion of international business, particularly marine insurance.

Two-thirds of non-life insurance now comes not from Lloyd's but from 'The Companies'—the big joint stock insurance companies, which stand to the 'Lloyd's Boys' as a bus to a taxi: they are bureaucracies, run not by free-lancers but by salaried managers. Most of them (the biggest exceptions are Eagle Star and General Accident) belong to 'The Tariff'—fixing the minimum premium for common objects like cars. The competition between Lloyd's and the Companies is an interesting contest: Lloyd's (like barristers) have low overheads, quick decisions and personal connections, while the Companies have the advantage of mass-production. But Lloyd's are gradually developing fewer and bigger syndicates, more specialists, and mechanised statistics in separate offices: they even reinsure companies' policies. Competitors, here as elsewhere, grow like each other.

Most big companies handle both life and non-life, and are thus called 'composite', although the two businesses are kept separate. These are the biggest non-life companies, with their total 'premium income' in 1963, and their chairmen.

Royal Group	£218,506,027	F. Leslie Orme
Commercial Union Group	£116,548,336	R. C. Brooks
General Accident	£95,526,716	Sir Stanley Norie-Miller
Northern & Employers	£93,552,343	Lord Knollys
Royal Exchange	£56,402,063	Lord Kindersley
Guardian	£53,957,371	Lord Blackford
Sun Alliance Group	£53,643,053	T. D. Barclay
Phoenix	£46,645,312	Sir Edward Ferguson
London (& Sea/Beacon)	£40,301,681	Harald Peake
Norwich Union	£35,336,911	D. E. Longe
Eagle Star	£34,823,103	Sir Brian Mountain
Prudential	£25,810,641	Sir Frank Morgan

Most insurance companies are old-established city institutions, with head offices within the Square Mile. Their boards are part of the network of interlocking city directorships, usually with close connections with one or two merchant banks. Like the joint stock banks, they are made up almost entirely of outside directors, including peers, generals and admirals and old city surnames, who meet once a month for discussion and lunch. In 1959 it was calculated that out of 182 Insurance Directors, 59 had titles, 33 were bankers and only 29 had worked in insurance companies. A cartoon in the *Insurance Guild Journal* once showed a decrepit old man staggering through the office: 'No, that's not an accident claim, Clogg', said one clerk to another, 'that's a Director.' Many managers, on the other hand, insist that they welcome a board of outside directors. 'The managers have more influence than anyone on the board,' one of them told me: 'but management is a lonely occupation, and we appreciate the moral support of the board: they're a comforting and valuable part of the machine.'

The Companies, of course, have their peck-order. The most aristocratic—'the Eton of insurance'—is The Alliance (now merged with an even older company, the Sun) founded by Nathan Rothschild in 1824, and still with a Rothschild on the board. Their chairman is T. D. Barclay, a Suffolk landowner from the banking family. It specialises in high-class clients and ducal estates, but also enjoys taking exotic new risks: they were the first company to insure radioactive isotopes. In 1964 they appointed no fewer than three Tory ex-ministers—Selwyn Lloyd, Hugh Fraser, and the Duke of Devonshire—to their board. One of the oldest surviving companies is the Royal Exchange, granted a royal charter in 1720, with its head office beside the tall portico of the Royal Exchange itself. Lord Kindersley is their 'governor', and in 1964 their twenty-seven directors included a duke, two earls, four viscounts, two barons, a field-marshal and a major-general (a much heavier load of blue blood than in 1961). They meet once a month: 'It's just a jolly good club,' one banker chairman explained, 'hardly any of the directors know anything about insurance. All the real decisions are taken by their sub-committees.'

Some companies prefer chairmen who have actually worked in insurance, like Sir Stanley Norie-Miller and Sir Edward Ferguson. Lord Knollys (who was chairman of the Vickers industrial combine until 1962) was an insurance managing director for fifteen years. Sir Brian Mountain of Eagle Star (which has a marquess, an earl and three Mountains among its directors) is a former general manager, son of the founder of the company, and a member of an old Lloyd's family. Other large companies keep provincial roots: the Yorkshire in York has a local landowner, Lord Middleton, as its chairman.

The biggest company for general insurance (where non-Life business predominates) is the Royal, with strong roots in Liverpool and the slave-trade. It originated in 1845, when Mersey businessmen decided that London rates were too high, and it still has several Liverpudlians on its board, with a Liverpool cotton merchant, F. Leslie Orme, as its chairman; it was only in 1960 that it moved its boardroom to London. The directors include such recurring and variegated nobs as Lord Derby, Paul Chambers and Lord Cornwallis, but like most insurance companies it is effectively run by its chief general manager, T. H. Smeddles. Smeddles, too, is a Liverpool man, with a no-nonsense approach and a sceptical eye on London pretensions; his special expertise is the North American business, from which the company gets most of its premium income, and most of its problems.

In the last three years insurance companies, like other businesses, have been merging, and familiar old names like the Sun, the Atlas and the Sea have been absorbed with others. The numbers of competing offices, behind their frosted glass in the high streets, are diminishing. The mergers are partly the result of the particular hazards of insurance in America, where, since the end of the Civil War, the big British companies have been well established. The companies draw 70 per cent of their income from overseas, much of it from North America. But American claims are heavy: the San Francisco earthquake and fire in 1906 (when fifteen American companies could not pay up) cost eighteen British companies £11 million: and hurricanes in America in the last few years have been heavy. When General Motors lost £12 million in the great fire of Detroit in 1953, half was paid by London companies. One or two companies have recently decided to give up their American business, but most are waiting for better days, and strengthening themselves by mergers and 'rationalisation'. British fire and accident business has become less profitable, too, and the companies are actually beginning to try to prove, instead of guessing, that some risks are greater than others. (If only they could charge insurance by the mileage . . .). Larger volumes and smaller profits have made the insurance companies, like joint stock banks, settle down into big and staid institutions.

THE MANCROFT AFFAIR

The predominance of 'outside' directors on insurance boards, without apparent knowledge of insurance, has been the subject of mounting criticism. The practice is defended by many general managers, and of course by the directors themselves; this is how

Sir John Benn, the Chairman of the U.K. Provident Institution, has described the rôle of the outside director:

> The chief function of the non-executive director, as I see it, is to advise on overall policy and trends. Except in the field of investment, where to some extent a board may assume executive responsibility, it is definitely not his function to do the job of the management. Moreover, he can speak his mind more freely than those who are solely dependent on the company for their living.
>
> Another important function of the directors of any business is to ensure the proper succession of the management. This is one of their most responsible duties and one in which an inefficient board is apt to fail. A good general manager is helped by feeling that he can, and should, refer all appropriate matters to his board. A good board will, *per contra*, see that the general manager does not become autocratic or out of touch with current realities.
>
> The non-executive director who comes for a few hours a week or fortnight into the insurance board room brings a trained mind and wide judgment to bear on the problems of a different type of business. He is wise enough to realise that the actuaries or accountants know much more than a director can ever hope to do about the techniques of insurance. His function is to judge whether a particular step or recommendation is likely to be best for the business in the widest sense and to ensure that proposed actions are reviewed from outside before they are implemented. This means that the executives are not judges in their own right—a most difficult thing for anyone to do in any sphere where the same person is responsible for policy as well as management.

But the value of outside directors was abruptly called in question after the extraordinary affair of Lord Mancroft and the Norwich Union, in December 1963. The crisis arose after the Arab states had brought pressure on the Norwich Union—as they had brought pressure, with varying success, on many other companies—to sack Lord Mancroft, a prominent Jewish businessman and director of Sir Isaac Wolfson's Great Universal Stores, from its London board, where he held the not-very-important job of Vice-President. The Norwich Union gave in to the pressure, and Lord Mancroft offered his resignation. An uproar followed: the Norwich Union was accused of anti-semitism, weakness and incompetence, their Jewish clients threatened to cancel their business, and its board, largely composed of Norfolk dignitaries, suddenly came into the limelight. The president was Sir Robert Bignold, a 72-year-old Norfolk brewer and author of 'Five Generations of the Bignold Family', and other directors included the Marquess of Townshend, the wealthy Norfolk landowner descended from Turnip Townshend, and the veteran diplomat Sir Hughe Knatchbull-Hugessen.

The board held anxious meetings, and Sir Robert appeared on television. The British government made a public statement condemning the Arab pressure. Eventually Sir Robert invited Lord Mancroft to resume his position, an invitation which he (not surprisingly) refused. Even quite conservative circles in Norwich—a city of profound conservatism—were critical of the Norwich Union's embarrassing *faux pas*; and soon after the incident was over Sir Robert resigned his position as president, to be succeeded by D. E. Longe, also from an old Norfolk family, one of a huge parson's family.

The affair left its mark not only on the company, but on the city in general; for it appeared to show the incompetence of directors in just the field in which they are supposed to be most useful—in advising on broad matters of policy, world affairs, and public opinion. The whole justification for the 'all-round amateur' seemed to fall apart, if a board of outsiders could make such a blunder of judgment and common sense. The *Financial Times* commented: 'This raises the whole question of the way in which insurance companies recruit their boards. Insurance is one of the few remaining preserves in British business life of the non-executive board. One of the criteria of an insurance company director is the amount of outside business he can bring in. One wonders whether this practice can be maintained very much longer.'[1]

THE LIFE COMPANIES

But the most spectacular new insurance power lies with the life companies, whose backgrounds are more humble and provincial. The life companies (with relatively small initial capital) receive their money week after week, month after month, and pay back their lump sums only after a lifetime: and so they have funds ten times bigger than the non-lifes'. The largest life companies, like so many of the new powers of the last century, originated not from the city but from nonconformist movements of lower middle-class men in the provinces. That these poor men's clubs should have become the giants of the city is one of the ironies of twentieth-century finance. These are the ten biggest life companies (most of which also do non-life business), with their premium income.

[1] *Financial Times*, December 11, 1963.

	Life Funds	*Premium Income*	*Chairman*
Prudential	£703,991,041	£89,229,333	Sir Frank Morgan
Legal & General	£562,762-810	£64,210,280	Viscount Harcourt
Standard	£404,843,236	£45,584,600	Sir James Campbell
Norwich Union Life	£283,547,706	£34,383,958	D. E. Longe
Sun Life	£216,399,560	£26,750,883	C. G. Randolph
Eagle Star	£207,832,376	£21,935,428	Sir Brian Mountain
Pearl	£152,606,766	£18,826,554	Geoffrey Kitchen
Scottish Widows	£200,641,171	£18,132,364	Sir Arthur Porritt
Guardian	£170,627,864	£18,002,845	Lord Blackford
Royal	£165,705,231	£11,277,631	F. Leslie Orme

THE PRU

By far the biggest is the legendary Prudential, with the motto 'Fortis Qui Prudens'. To the public, 'the Pru' is best known for its 12,000 'men from the Pru', the army of local travellers, many with small cars, dark suits and little books, who call at three hundred doors a week collecting the weekly insurance contributions. But to the city of London, the Pru presents a different face, for it is the largest single investor in the country: its *total* assets (a sixth of the assets of all life companies) amounted in 1964 to 1,300 million pounds. Though this is less than the deposits of Barclays Bank, the Pru does not need to keep its money ready, like a bank's, for quick withdrawal: it can invest the whole sum, for a whole generation, without the need to call it back. Every week, the Pru has another two million pounds to invest—pouring into government stock, industry, or property. Pru and her colleagues, with their massive wealth, have stolen the thunder from the bankers. One city story tells how an industrialist called on his merchant banker to discuss raising some money. 'Can I discuss it with my colleagues?' said the banker. 'All right,' said the industrialist, 'but don't pinch my taxi to go round to the Pru.'

The Pru is the biggest and oldest of the 'Industrial Life Companies'—those life companies which grew up from the weekly savings of industrial workers. It originated as a company in 1848. In June 1852 a deputation of working men called on the secretary of the new company, and two years later a director appointed agents, to collect weekly savings from the Potteries and the weaving districts of Cheshire and Lancashire. Eager for thrift and self-help, and determined to avoid state aid, the artisans and workers embraced the new security of life insurance; by 1886 the Pru had more than *seven million* policies, with three-quarters of all the industrial life business.[1] The proud Victorian character of the Pru is expressed in its towering Gothic castle in Holborn, just west of the city. (The topography is significant, for like its rival the Pearl up the road, the Pru stands at arm's length from city influences.)

The castle is an astonishing fantasy: outside there is a jumble of pointed windows, pinnacles, gables and steep roofs (in contrast to the plain red glass slab of the *Daily Mirror* opposite, which Pru men deplore). In the hall are walls of polished yellow tiles, Gothic pillars spring up between stained glass windows, and black-letter notices, like hymn-boards, announce the managers' offices.

Through the hall every morning 3,000 clerks and typists stream in to file, check and transcribe thirty million policies. In long, vault-like offices rows of teenage girls write on cards behind wooden desks, or feed facts into punching machines. On the top floor is the Pru theatre, for amateur theatricals; in the basement are the diesel engines; on the second floor is the ecclesiastical board-room, with a square throne in the middle. In one corner a big glass goblet engraved with aeroplanes, trains and pylons, by Laurence Whistler, commemorates an unusually big sale of government stock from Messrs Mullens and Co. But in spite of the Gothic surroundings, the Pru people are very down-to-earth: lunch there is much less pretentious and formal than lunch at a merchant bank, and the surroundings are more like a liner than a country mansion. Drinks are served on the sideboard, there is lager instead of wine, waitresses instead of butlers, and plain English food. The conversation is matter-of-fact and professional.

The Pru tries to compose its board equally from three elements—the management, the old Prudential families (Deweys, Harbens, Hornes, Lancasters, Reids), and the outside directors. But nowadays fewer come from the families, and more from the managers. The chairman, Sir Frank Morgan, is a self-made man who has spent his whole life in the company, and so have the triumvirate who run the Pru (who are not on the board, but sit in on board meetings): K. A. Usherwood, the General Manager; Leslie Brown, the Secretary and Chief Investment Manager; and F. M. Redington, the Chief Actuary.

[1] Dermot Morrah: *A History of Industrial Life Assurance*, p. 53.

ACTUARIES AND CLERKS

It would seem that the dictum of Rabelais that 'l'appetit vient en mangeant' applies to the employment of actuaries in many capacities.

K. A. Usherwood, FIA[1]

Nearly all the senior managers of the Pru—and of other life companies—carry after their names the initials FIA—Fellow of the Institute of Actuaries[2]—and at this point it is necessary to pause to look at the sequestered and powerful profession of actuaries. There are only eight hundred of them in Britain, nearly three-quarters of them employed in life insurance offices; and ever since the Institute of Actuaries was founded in 1848—the same year as the Pru—the stability of life insurance has depended on them. One of the earliest fellows of the Institute, Dr. William Farr, wrote in 1853 with great prescience (and much greater clarity than most actuaries since): 'The whole of the commerce of the country turns on contingencies which demand the application of scientific observation and calculation; as English agriculture has its chemists, English commerce must—to keep pace with it—ultimately employ actuaries, to calculate risks, which are now roughly guessed at; and thus extend the useful sphere of an important scientific class of men at present almost peculiar to this country.' Dr. Farr was right, and in the next hundred years actuaries spread, not only into insurance, but into government service, pension funds and the stock exchange.[3]

Actuaries are basically highly specialised mathematicians who, after a course of six years or more, are versed in the intricate study of probabilities, on which the success of life insurance depends. Their name, 'adopted largely as an antiquarian whim',[4] is very misleading, and in Germany and Sweden they are more sensibly described as 'insurance mathematicians'. The profession had its beginnings in 1662 when John Graunt, FRS (who was falsely charged with being privy to the Great Fire of London), wrote his 'Natural and political observations made upon the bills of mortality', which began the study of expectation of life, and remained a thoroughly British invention. It is an odd profession, both highly commercial and highly academic, and the Institute of Actuaries

[1] Presidential Address to the Institute of Actuaries, 1962, p. 11.

[2] Or FFA (Fellow of the Faculty of Actuaries, in Scotland).

[3] In 1962 there were 28 actuaries on the London Stock Exchange, and 34 in Government Service; *see Transactions of the 17th International Congress of Actuaries*, 1964, Vol. 1, p. 169.

[4] *Transactions*, Vol. I: review by J. B. Dow, p. 312.

are 'at the same time a learned society and a professional organisation'; for the last eighty years the Institute has inhabited the often-rebuilt Staple Inn, appropriately enough just next to, and owned by, the Pru.

Actuaries have a very large influence on the city and hence on the country; not so much by their actuarial work, as by the access this gives them later to most of the top jobs in insurance; they can influence not only investment and social patterns, but also—to a spectacular extent—architecture. They are very highly-paid; the graph opposite, from the Pilkington Report on Doctors' Salaries, shows the incomes of various professions in 1960. But in spite of this long-established affluence, these powerful decision-makers emerge from a training which is narrow and bleak; most of it is done by correspondence, with a few lectures and classes, and there is a large proportion of failures. Life insurance draws its meritocracy from a self-made, specialised world from outside the universities—a very different world from the board-rooms of merchant bankers, or Lloyd's. Only about a quarter of the Fellows of the Institute are graduates, though the proportion among younger men is now one-half. Many actuaries are sensitive to the charge of narrowness: 'The man who immures himself in his professional castle deprives himself of much,' wrote K. A. Usherwood, in his presidential address to the Institute in 1962. But there are still very few points of contact between the actuarial profession and the larger, older worlds that revolve beyond it.

The other 80,000 insurance workers (life and non-life) are less well placed: like bank clerks, they are caught between trade unionism and professionalism, and there is similar friction between the trade union, the 'Guild of Insurance Officials' (with 18,000 members), and the staff associations which they call 'the yellow union'. Since the war the wage of many insurance workers has slipped below manual workers', and at twenty-one their wage is much less: 'a marrying wage at a marrying age' is a union slogan. But their bargaining position, like bank clerks', has been partially weakened by the intrusion of mechanisation and women. The Pru, for instance, have installed a computer called Orion, which eventually will do the work of hundreds.

The industrial life companies have often been attacked for the expense of their weekly collections, and their ruthless attitude to 'lapsed' policies. Among critics have been Mr. Gladstone in 1864, who set up an alternative and abortive Post Office system; Sir Benjamin Cohen's report of 1931; and Lord Beveridge's report of

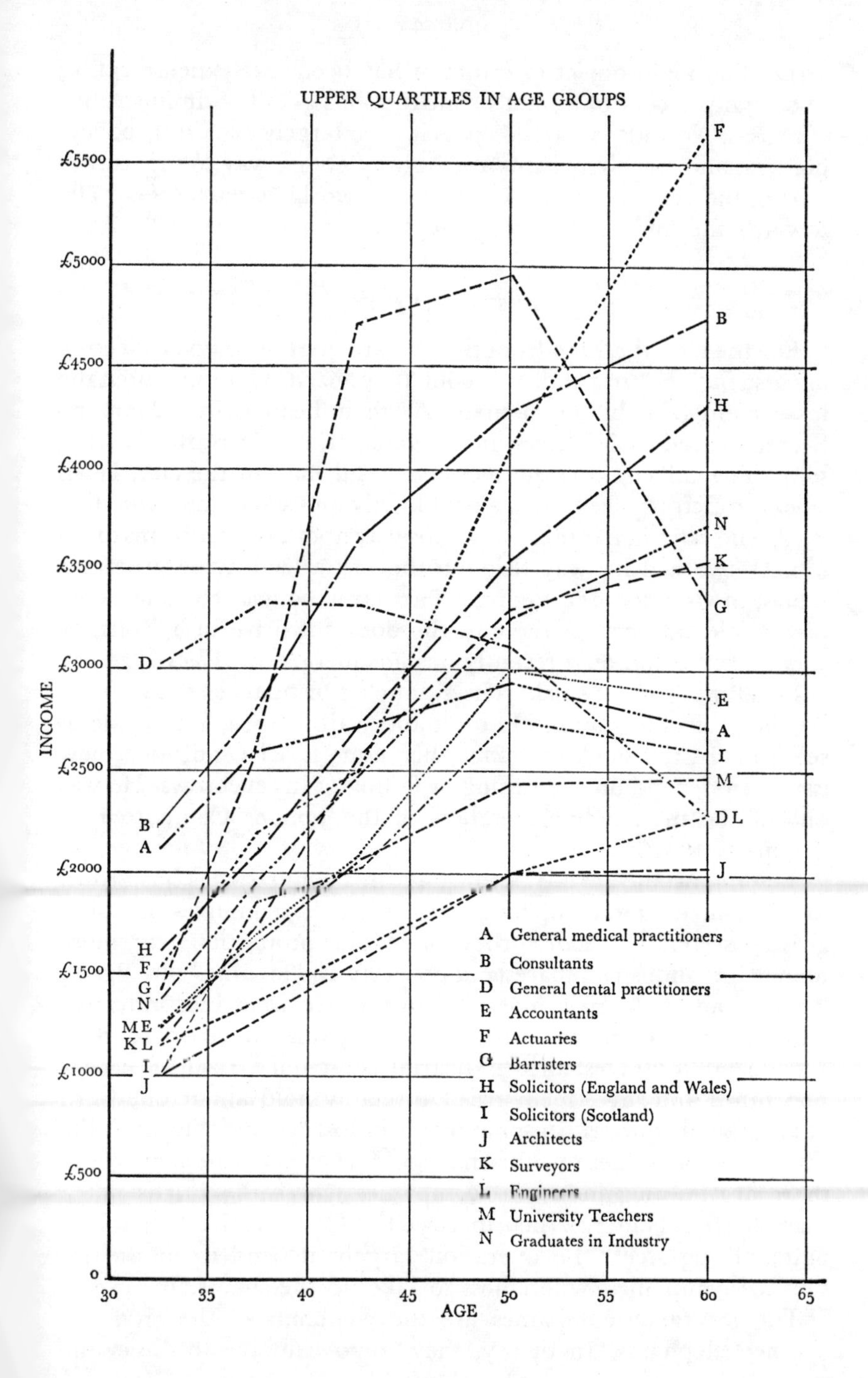
UPPER QUARTILES IN AGE GROUPS
INCOME
£5500
£5000
£4500
£4000
£3500
£3000
£2500
£2000
£1500
£1000
£500
0
30
35
40
45
50
55
60
65
AGE
A General medical practitioners
B Consultants
D General dental practitioners
E Accountants
F Actuaries
G Barristers
H Solicitors (England and Wales)
I Solicitors (Scotland)
J Architects
K Surveyors
L Engineers
M University Teachers
N Graduates in Industry

1942. The main object of criticism has been the 'expense ratio'; about 30 per cent of a man's contributions goes to administrative expenses. Nowadays 'lapsed' policies are largely repaid to policy-holders, and weekly policies are anyway giving way to monthly—part of the general trend away from the working-class week-cycle, towards the middle-class month-cycle.

LESLIE BROWN

For the city, the Men from the Pru are not the 12,000 collecting agents, but the tiny staff of about two dozen who look after the investment of a billion pounds. At their head is the Company Secretary and Chief Investment Manager, Leslie Brown, FIA—sometimes talked of as the most powerful man in the city. He is stocky, quietly-spoken, with a neat bristly moustache and twinkling eyes, who talks in a frank, humorous way about the problems of his job. He worked his way through the Pru after leaving grammar school in Croydon and taking his actuarial course. He is not part of the 'old boy net' of the city: he does not drive in a Rolls, or shoot grouse, and only recently has he emerged in *Who's Who*. He is sometimes seen at stockbrokers' lunches or financiers' banquets, but he prefers to stay in Holborn and wait for people to come to see him. In the stock exchange, his name is a legend, for a new issue can depend on the raising or falling of his eyebrows. He was one of the most active members of the Jenkins Committee on Company Law.

The importance of Mr. Brown and his counterparts has grown steadily since the war, firstly because their share in investment has grown, secondly because they have put proportionately more money into industrial shares and property and less into 'gilt-edged'. Nearly half of the new money from the Pru went into industry; and between them the insurance companies have more than £2,000 million invested in industrial companies. Insurance pension funds and investment trusts probably hold about one third of all quoted equities. In some major industries, notably steel, the insurance companies together now hold nearly half the shares, and there are few big industrial companies where the Pru is not a sizeable shareholder. When in 1953 the Conservatives began de-nationalising steel, the operation largely depended on the insurance companies' willingness to take up the shares.

The insurance companies are the elephants of the city, but chained elephants. In theory, they could combine to direct the

Steel Company of Wales, and appoint its chairman; in practice, they carefully avoid entanglements with management. This shyness has several causes. Firstly, their money is not their own, but held in trust for their millions of policy-holders: their job is to obtain the maximum interest, not to run Britain's industry; insurance men murmur the word 'fiduciary', and (like civil servants) talk about 'those whom we serve'. Secondly, they know that if they tried to exercise their financial power, it could soon be circumscribed or nationalised. Thirdly, they don't *know* anything about management or industry.

Brown tries not to buy more than 7 per cent of the shares of any one industrial company: but even so, the Pru often finds itself the biggest single shareholder, and occasionally has to exercise its power. 'There was one small company where two groups of directors—one young, one old—were equally divided,' Brown told me, 'and they came to me to ask what view the Prudential would take.' The idea of the Prudential taking a view was essentially repugnant, but eventually Brown did express his opinion—in favour of the older directors, who found a compromise.

Something of the potential influence of the Pru emerged in the dispute in the BSA company in 1956. A group of directors, led by John Sangster, opposed the sitting chairman, Sir Bernard Docker. For two months there were accusations and counter-accusations. Sir Bernard bought time on television to appeal to the shareholders. Lady Docker told the *Daily Telegraph*: 'We just had not got a Daimler any more. This has been the hardest day of my life.' But behind the battle between the Dockers and the directors, the Pru suddenly stood out as the most important factor. They were by far the largest shareholder, with 260,000 ordinary shares compared with the Dockers' 100,000, and they had recently approached Sir Bernard with a demand for an independent investigation into the company's affairs.

The climax came at the wild and noisy shareholders' meeting of August 1, 1956. Docker made an emotional appeal, and accused the directors of revealing the company's private affairs to the Pru behind his back: it transpired that Sangster had gone to the Pru as early as January with his worries. An anonymous 'Man from the Pru' explained its rôle, and told of the meeting with Sangster: 'I then learned about his own particular anxiety about the company. The action which the company took was in no way sponsored by the Prudential . . . It is our clear policy in the Pru not to interfere in the management of industrial companies in which we invest. In this case, when there were no other large shareholders whom we might consult, we came to the conclusion that we had a duty to all the shareholders as well as ourselves to take some action.' But it became clear that wherever the initiative lay, the revolt could not have happened without the Pru's support. By the end of the meeting Sir Bernard had been defeated, and John Sangster confirmed in his place.

The insurance companies (they insist) never compare notes about making investments: they normally only come together on the 'investment protection committee' (IPC), which meets once a month. Occasionally, when a company proposes a change of articles affecting shareholders' rights, the committee recommends companies to withhold their approval: without their support, a new share issue has small chance of success. Their most evident objection has been to the extension of 'non-voting' or 'A' shares, enabling families to retain their control through ordinary shares.

Can the insurance companies, with their growing investment, maintain this aloofness from industry? Should the biggest shareholders in the country be sleeping ones, only wishing to be woken in moments of outrage? It seems likely that the Pru will play a less passive rôle as it becomes more accustomed to its power, and already they are beginning to take rather more than a purely accountants' view. At the same time, insurance companies are becoming more aware of the responsibilities of their wealth and investment. One interesting innovation camc from Sir John Benn, Chairman of the United Kingdom Provident Institution, one of the insurance chairmen, who has philanthropic interests. In 1961 he persuaded various insurance companies and other city institutions to provide capital for a new company to exploit inventions and to help fill the 'development gap' to which the Radcliffe Report had drawn attention.

PENSION FUNDS

Since the war, an even more sudden wealth has emerged in the city—pension funds. Nearly all big firms now have their own pension schemes and, though many are administered by insurance companies, the biggest are independent. The accumulation of savings has risen so fast in ten years that the biggest pension funds invest more than all but the top insurance companies. In 1958 the total investment of pension funds in all shares amounted to

£1,625 million (for 'internally administered schemes and nationalised industries'). Since then (the Radcliffe Committee were told) the increase has been about £150 million a year.

The pension fund controllers are not a spectacular cabal: they have their own association, with an office above an ironmonger's shop in Kensington, and a twice-yearly journal called *Superannuation*. But they do not see much of each other. To the stock exchange, the names of the investment managers are more important than the chairmen of the companies: each of them controls millions of new money a year. Probably their most prominent spokesman is Ross Goobey, an actuary who runs the Imperial Tobacco pension fund in Bristol; like other investment experts, he does not like to be too close to the city, but he has taken on more directorships, notably in M. Samuel.

Many pension funds are heavily restricted by their constitution: some can only invest in gilt-edged, others have 50 per cent of their money in industry. In a few, such as Marks and Spencer's, the provident fund comes near—in theory—to controlling its own company (in America the Sears Roebuck mail-order firm is virtually controlled by the Sears Roebuck pension fund).

The biggest pension fund belongs, as one might expect, to Britain's biggest employer, the National Coal Board. Its investments are run by an unobtrusive former stockbroker, P. D. Johnstone, who administers three funds, one for staff, another for mineworkers' pensions and a third to supplement benefits under the Industrial Injuries Act. These schemes produce about £19 million of new money a year, and will amount to about £450 million of investment by 1975. He is responsible to 'investment committees', consisting of members of management and the mineworkers' union. But apart from occasional objections (such as an unwillingness to invest in oil shares) the miners do not interfere with investment policy. Johnstone doesn't see much of the other pension funds except at such functions as stockbrokers' lunch parties. The Coal Board prefer to paddle their own large canoe.

PROPERTY

The most visible part of the wealth of insurance companies is their ownership of land in the centre of cities, and it is here that their rôle has been most striking and most controversial. In five years several of Britain's biggest cities have been face-lifted: they have changed from horizontal to vertical skylines. Steel and glass cliffs have pushed up between old churches; rows of Victorian shops have given way to big white office buildings; skyscrapers have grown up round St. Paul's. The relaxing of controls (after twenty years of restrictions) and the booming value of metropolitan land have turned the centres of London, Birmingham or Manchester into miniature Manhattans. Office space in the middle of London is now more expensive than in New York, and in Cheapside it can cost £3 per square foot. The land itself in most cases is owned by the only people who could possibly afford it—the insurance companies. In property they have found an apparently safe resting place for part of their money-gusher. But the buying-up of the land, the planning, designing and leasing of the buildings has been largely put into the hands of a handful of speculator entrepreneurs—the property developers. There are few more astonishing collaborations than those between the cautious insurance bureaucracies, preoccupied with trusteeship and security, and the flamboyant self-made millionaires who, by borrowing huge sums from the insurance companies, have changed the face of the cities, and made their fortunes many times over.

Property is a difficult commodity: it involves assessing and visualising the potential of sites, patiently bargaining and buying up clusters of old buildings, negotiating with local councils, planning new blocks to cram in the maximum office space. In New York, which was laid out from the beginning in large criss-cross blocks and where laws are more cut-and-dried, the operation is easier. But the very jumble and messiness of London, its zigzags, curves and old buildings, yield great prizes for those who can disentangle it.

In London and other cities surprising amounts of land are still owned by the old aristocratic families who first developed it—the Dukes of Bedford and Westminster in Bloomsbury and Pimlico, of Lords Cadogan and Howard de Walden in Chelsea and Harley Street. Other large tracts are owned by the Crown and the Church Commissioners and other bits are still owned by individuals, department stores to British Railways. But it is the property developers—subject to the wayward controls of local councils—who are taking over the rôle of master townplanners, which was once the prerogative of dukes, earls or the monarch himself.

The exploitation of property has helped to produce quick profits in other businesses; shops, breweries, or department stores which own sites in city centres have found their value multiplied.

The property boom has helped to enrich the financier Charles Clore—who, for example, after buying the shoe-shop chain of Freeman, Hardy and Willis, sold the freeholds to insurance companies with a large capital profit: and tried to do the same by bidding for Watney's breweries, which has pubs on precious corner sites. Lord Fraser, the Glasgow draper who owns Harrods and Eskimo Foods, has made large profits by selling his freeholds—such as John Barker's and D. H. Evans. It might seem odd that so many English businesses sit on precious sites without exploiting them, and so fall an easy prey for take-overs; the loyalty to freeholds runs deep in the English character.

The property tycoons have been nearly all self-made millionaires, from modest middle-class families; mostly Jewish, a few Scottish or Canadian. Among them are Harold Samuel, the unobtrusive chairman of Land Securities Investment Trust, in partnership with his cousin Basil, Max Rayne, of London Merchant Securities, Maurice Wohl of the Wohl group, and Charles Clore of City Centre Properties. But the man who developed the property business most thoroughly and effectively, and who set the pace for others, was Jack Cotton, the flamboyant and hectic tycoon from Birmingham who died in 1964. His life at suite 120 at the Dorchester was an extraordinary contrast to the gloomy caution of the insurance offices, which provided him with the capital for his development. Cotton worked always from the hotel, surrounded by Renoirs, vivacious secretaries, brisk surveyors, maps of London, press cuttings, and a stream of visitors. He sat talking, drinking and laughing at the long table in his drawing-room, sometimes till two in the morning, occasionally striding jauntily to the telephone to talk to Charles Clore, Erwin Wolfson, or somebody. He exuded the atmosphere not of a businessman but of an impresario: in an age of conformity, Cotton's exuberant Dorchester life became a legend.

Cotton was the son of a Birmingham Jewish export agent, who had South African connections. After school, first at King Edward's, Birmingham, then at Cheltenham College, he set up an estate agency business at the age of twenty-one. He soon began developing valuable sites, and by the end of the war (which he spent partly in America, organising Jewish immigration to Palestime) he had several important Birmingham properties. He acquired a public company in 1946, to develop London and Birmingham properties with insurance companies—which grew enormously in the following ten years. In 1956 Geoffrey Kitchen of the Pearl, noticing that Cotton was making large profits from property, suggested that the Pearl and Cotton should go into partnership. After that Cotton formed a host of subsidiaries with insurance companies (notably with the Pearl and the Legal and General) and also with industrial giants, including ICI, Shell-Mex, BP and Barclays Bank DCO—who all felt the need of Cotton's expertise in developing their properties. In 1960, when Cotton's company merged with his friend Clore's City and Central Investments, they created the biggest property development group in the world, with assets of £67 million.

The scale of property development steadily grew. In the fifties fortunes were made by Cotton and others, by buying up small sites and selling them together. When small sites began to be scarce, whole areas were developed—as in Hammersmith or Birmingham, costing as much as ten million each. Finally, Cotton and Clore took to buying up whole companies (like the Royal Exchange in Manchester) and developing the developers.

In Britain Cotton's most celebrated project was his scheme to rebuild half Piccadilly Circus, in conjunction with Lord Harcourt's Legal and General Assurance; and it was this scheme which brought to light the enormous powers and freedom of property developers. The plan came to light only by accident, because Cotton showed his plans on TV. A rumpus followed, culminating in a public hearing in December 1959. It not only exposed the haphazard approach to London's town-planning, and the uncertain hand of the LCC: it showed, too, how far the ownership of new buildings had become divorced from responsibility. The freehold owners of the Piccadilly site were the Legal and General, but they had little say in the design of the building, which was planned by Cotton, his architects, and his surveyors (Jack Cotton and Partners). The eventual tenants would have no control over the architecture. The owner and the occupiers were equally irrelevant. The decisive planner—the 'paraproprietor'—was the go-between, Jack Cotton.

By 1965, after more than ten years wrangling, planning, unplanning and re-planning, Piccadilly Circus still remained unchanged, its offices let on short leases, its façades fading, its traffic increasingly jammed—a monument to the muddle and cross-purposes of the 'irresponsible society', and a kind of grim microcosm of the problems of national planning.

For fifteen years Cotton's career continued to soar; £100 invested in his company just after the war would have produced

£200,000 twelve years later. But as his operations became vaster, so his showmanship and passion for bigness gradually overwhelmed his financial shrewdness. After 1960, when the merger with Clore took place, there were growing rumours of rows and extravagance, and City Centre Properties began slipping: in 1963 their shares dropped to half their previous value. Cotton himself, who had been running the business in his highly personal way, became seriously ill, and had to retire from the chairmanship in 1963. His place was taken by a far more cautious financier, George Bridge, the deputy chairman of the Legal and General, the company who held six per cent of the shares of City Centre. Bridge was a complete contrast to Cotton: he was the son of a Lancashire borough treasurer, and has been in the Legal & General since 1919. He made no secret of the fact that he had inherited a mess; he set about economising and rationalising, and in his first bleak review he said: 'Several major developments have not matured as quickly as anticipated, and others have not come up to expectations, or have been deferred.' The next year Cotton died. The fat, spectacular years of property companies were over: shares had slumped, and the prospect and later the fact of a Labour government further depressed them.

Cotton was a unique and eccentric operator who, with engaging rashness, became lost in the grandeur of his visions. But his surprising partnerships with the insurance giants set the pattern for many others. The insurance companies are usually content to leave the building to the developer, and this delegation of responsibility has a depressing effect on patronage, for the speculator, using the money of an anonymous insurance company to build for anonymous tenants, tends towards anonymous architecture—squeezing in the maximum possible floor space. The building will not express the personality of the owner, or the tenants; it need only be a safe investment. Some big firms—such as Shell, AEI, or English Electric—still commission their own buildings. But most office blocks are designed for no one in particular. Whether this is worse for the architect than designing for a wilful and tasteless client, like English Electric or AEI, is debatable: the Vickers skyscraper, owned by the Legal and General, is a much more up-to-date and exciting affair than Shell's.[1] But at least the company's buildings express some kind of personality, with someone to take the blame.

[1] *See* p. 558 for theories about the interrelation of architecture and profits.

THE PARAPROPRIETORS

The British insurance companies are more powerful, and more free, than their counterparts in most western countries. In America insurance firms, after scandals early in the century, were restricted in many states to investing only 5 per cent of their money in industrial shares: and they received a sharp shock in the slump, when Manhattan was full of half-empty buildings owned by insurance companies. In Britain there have so far been no such disasters.

The most persistent critic of insurance is Richard Titmuss, Professor of Social Administration at the London School of Economics, who helped to frame the Labour party's pension plan: he has the distinction of having *worked* in an insurance company—the County Fire Office—before becoming a don. In his pamphlet *The Irresponsible Society* in 1960 Titmuss attacked the secrecy of the insurance companies (they refused to disclose the value of their assets to the Radcliffe Committee), their untrammelled freedom, and the narrow social attitudes of the 'Pressure Group State'. He maintains that this concentration of investment leads to centralisation and social irresponsibility. 'It is power concentrated in relatively few hands, working at the apex of a handful of giant bureaucracies, technically supported by a group of professional experts, and accountable, in practice, to no one.' The insurance companies reply that they are acting simply as the honest trustees of their policy-holders. 'We are not at all *eminences grises*,' said Geoffrey Kitchen, chairman of the Pearl: 'it is not our policy to approach the government. We never try to use our influence—except when we are attacked, as with nationalisation. We're always trying to get the best possible return for our policy-holders. We have a very active and lively investment policy. We made almost 7 per cent on our investments last year—that's not bad.' But the insurance companies, after attacks on their methods of collection and their irresponsibility, and threats of nationalisation, are aware that their image is not too good: and they have spent some money on advertising their service to the public, with coy fables about animals and bees and a TV hero called Fred.

The economic power of insurance and pension funds is a phenomenon not only in Britain, but in the whole of the West, and its consequences are still unresolved. Father Harbrecht[1], a Jesuit economist, has compared the new financial institutions to

[1] Pension Funds and Economic Power. New York, 1959.

the 'Great Domains' of eighth-century Europe—when feudal landlords, without actually owning property, had property vested in them by their occupation, and by the services and armies they provided. Similarly, Fr. Harbrecht suggests, 'control over property has gravitated to the managers of the financial institutions because they perform a function which is valuable to society. This function is to distribute among the generality of people the wealth which the corporations (that is, the big industrial companies) are creating.' To this new system he gives the name 'the paraproprietal society', 'because in it the connection between men and things, which is another way of saying property, is so attenuated that the fundamental function of property is not dominant . . .' He concludes that 'a man's relationship to things—material wealth —no longer determines his place in society (as it did in a strong proprietary system) but his place in society now determines his relationship to things. This is the consequence of the separation of control over property from individual ownership.'

The growth of insurance companies marks the latest stage in the divorce between property and power, which we will note in the ownership of the industrial Leviathans: the men whose money is used by the Pru and the Pearl to invest in ICI or Unilevers have no say in the running of those companies. 'Divorce between men and industrial things is becoming complete,' wrote Adolf Berle: 'a Communist revolution could not accomplish that more completely.'[1]

In Britain this new power of the paraproprietors has grown up suddenly and obscurely, away from traditional institutions. However much they may see themselves as mere intermediaries, the investment managers, in their narrow funnel between the wealth of millions of policy-holders and the corporate wealth of industry, have a scope for patronage, for enterprise and social improvement scarcely equalled by any other group. But it is one of the tragedies of contemporary Britain that this powerful group has grown up in a narrower, more etiolated atmosphere than the old estates—with few of the cultural and social influences that play round the old professions and the universities. The failure of the old humanist world to come to terms with the new corporate institutions has had melancholy consequences.

[1] Adolf A. Berle, Jnr: *Power Without Property*, 1960. p. 76.

Anatomy of Britain Today

PART THREE

26

CORPORATIONS

As the banker, as a symbol of economic power, passed into the shadows, his place was taken by the great industrial corporation.

J. K. Galbraith: American Capitalism.

As the twentieth century moves into afternoon, two systems—and (thus far) two only—have emerged as vehicles for modern industrial economics. One is the socialist commissariat; its highest organization at present is the Soviet Union. The other is the modern corporation, most highly developed in the United States.

Professor Adolf Berle.

Along these lines from toe to crown
Ideas flow up, and vetoes down.

Anon.

WE come to a new and crucial sector of British life which is ostensibly unconnected with earlier institutions—the industrial corporations and their professions and managers. The world of country-house amateurs, though it has influenced their way of life, has little relevance to the provincial factories and offices of corporation scientists, salesmen, technicians, accountants. Since the last war, the corporations have bothered little with parliament and few now employ a member as their spokesman, for they prefer to lobby direct with Whitehall bureaucrats. The old professions of the universities, the Law and the Church, have few points of contact with them, and the press, busy with the romantic regions of politics, parliament or diplomacy, do not often penetrate inside their walls and pyramids, except on missions of congratulations. The boards and managers of Shell or Unilever are less known than the obscurest backbencher.

The bankers and financiers, who helped to give birth to some of the industrial giants, have seen their offspring becoming far richer than themselves. Even politicians now accept their inevitability. The biggest corporations have become supra-national bodies, with interests far wider than those of the British economy, involved in an elaborate balancing trick with rivals and governments all over the world. And as European countries come closer to each other and to the Americas, so the corporations (it seems) will grow to American dimensions.

THE NEW LEVIATHANS

The names of ICI, Shell, Unilever or Imperial Tobacco dominate hundreds of thousands of Britons. To visit the headquarters of a big industrial corporation is like visiting a foreign country, and talking to their managers one becomes aware of a complex, self-enclosed microcosm, held together with oil, soap or steel. These industrial organisms, inside and outside the organism of a nation, are one of the most mysterious phenomena of the western world. Shell-land or Unilever-land are kingdoms without kings. When in 1651 Hobbes wanted to depict the nature of the modern State, he showed on the frontispiece of his book *Leviathan* a sceptred king whose body was entirely made up of small men. In the twentieth century the industrial corporations—both publicly and privately owned—have taken over much of the rôle of Leviathan. But they have no kings. No one man controls or owns them; and at their head are committees of men who are themselves an organic part of the body of the whale.

Their nebulous characters are aptly expressed by the French word for limited company—*société anonyme*. Their palaces staring at each other across the Thames, like those of seventeenth-century dukes, are different universes, and to the conformity of work is added the conformity of their home life—with Shell suburbs and ICI suburbs crystallising over the country. They have bureaucracies in many ways similar to Whitehall's or the Pru's, but much more self-contained and all-embracing, with their own factories and territories and international ramifications.

There are many features of these new Leviathans which are disturbing—their conformism, their introversion, their secretiveness, the narrow limits of their competition, and, above all, their endemic elephantiasis. But few critics can suggest any alternative system for running an industrial economy. The difference between private corporations and nationalised ones is diminishing, as also in Russia and America. It is difficult to visualise the great corporations being replaced in the next fifty years; they have begun to achieve the staying power of nations themselves. It is hard to imagine the big diversified companies, like ICI or Unilever, losing their supremacy, although the giants at the beginning of the century—Bradford Dyers, Fine Cotton Spinners, J. & P. Coats—are no longer the biggest.

Before considering British giants, we must take a glance at America, for there the corporation is most developed and most thoroughly studied, and British companies are rapidly approximating to the American pattern. For the past thirty years American professors of economics and law have been observing, with unconcealed bewilderment, the inexplicable growth of big business. Since the thirties, about 130 corporations have been responsible for half the manufacturing industry of America; the *number* of giants has hardly changed during that time, but their power has steadily increased. Though they certainly compete in salesmanship, advertising and research, their competition in prices is narrow; and the classical economists' free-for-all competition, with firms subjected to the 'judgment of the market-place', is not evident when a few vast firms make up an oligopoly.

What is uncanny is the manner of their development. For as Professor Berle and Dr. Means first explained thirty years ago, their nominal owners, the shareholders, have no effective control over their policy; and more recently ownership has separated still further from control, through the emergence of the insurance companies (the 'paraproprietors') as the principal shareholders.[1] The days of autocratic heads, such as Henry Ford, John D. Rockefeller, or Lord Nuffield, are largely past, and most of the Leviathans have broken away from the families and financiers who first founded them. It is the absence of controlling owners which makes the corporations such an odd development in western economic history. 'The capital is there', Professor Berle has written, 'so is the capitalism. The waning factor is the capitalist.'

The board of directors, except in cases of spectacular mismanagement or feud, when shareholders unite to rise in revolt against them, are responsible to no one but themselves. They are managers without bosses, and they elect one another. They are (like so many other ruling groups) 'tiny self-perpetuating oligarchies'. The extent to which the corporation can be controlled from outside the firm is severely limited. Economists are led to the confusing conclusion that the corporations, like perpetual clocks, run themselves—a conclusion which many of them reach with obvious distress and alarm. As Professor Berle has put it: 'The young lad mastering the technique of his bicycle may legitimately

[1] *See* pp. 470–1.

shout with pride, "Look, Ma, no hands", but is that the appropriate motto for a corporate society?'

In the terms in which left-wing critics were accustomed to regard capitalist organisations in the thirties, the existence of this small group of giants would be hardly short of a nightmare. But even quite radical economists have been surprised to discover that the corporations behave better, and more in the public interest, than they had ever expected. Several factors have brought this about: the development of a managerial class, concerned as much with prestige as profits; the competing pressures of specialist departments; the growth of a 'countervailing power' from the trade unions or retailers; even the emergence of a corporate conscience. With all these, and above all with the disappearance of the single, autocratic boss, the behaviour of the big corporation and its managers has changed out of recognition. Anthony Crosland has fulminated about this:

> Leverhulme, Rhodes, Morgan, Rockefeller, 'the malefactors of great wealth' (as Theodore Roosevelt called them)—these were the disagreeable stuff of a true power-élite or Marxist ruling class. Not so the other-directed organisation men of Shell and ICI. Jelly-fish where their predecessors were masterful, they are slaves to their public relations departments, constantly nervous lest some action may provoke a parliamentary question, frowns in the Board of Trade, trouble with the unions, or criticism in the press. Suburban where their predecessors were feudal, the summit of their business ruthlessness is an occasional take-over bid; and even this is sometimes an ignominious failure. Apologetic where their predecessors were haughty, the height of their political ambitions is the stand-pat conservatism of an Eisenhower or a Macmillan, a defensive holding operation against the forces of democracy and change.[1]

The rôle of the corporation in modern America is the subject of heated and anxious debate. Should they stick firmly to making profits (as the British are inclined to prefer) leaving the individual, the state and local communities to look after the rest? Or should they face up to new responsibilities of patronage, of building up new communities, of culture and education? Some critics have found the last alternative more alarming than the first: 'Our ancestors feared that corporations had no conscience' (to quote

[1] *The Conservative Economy*, 1962. p. 55.

Berle again): 'We are treated to the colder, more modern fear that, perhaps, they do.'

In Europe since the war industries have tended to the American pattern: instead of a mass of local or family firms competing, there are now often only three or four huge rivals. In Britain the concentration has increased rapidly in the last few years. In 1953 (according to Sigmund Prais) the hundred largest companies in Britain, measured by net assets, accounted for 31 per cent of the total industrial profits:[1] since then, with take-overs, mergers and growth concentration has spread.[2] Like the Americans, the British giants have become independent of financiers and the city. They, too, are often without single dominating heads, and are ruled by tiny self-perpetuating oligarchies: they, too, have continued much the same under different governments. European firms have found themselves competing increasingly with Americans, and competition, whether between firms, nations or newspapers, often makes competitors resemble each other.

There are big differences. In Britain the amalgamation is still continuing. The British managerial revolution is less developed than in America. The nationalised area of British industry is much larger, and all industry has been influenced by the threat of nationalisation. British corporations are apt to be less ruthless, more tolerant than the Americans, and perhaps more prone to administrative corpulence and gout. The very biggest firms in Britain—notably Shell and Unilever—are bigger in proportion to the country than their American counterparts and belong more to an international, than a national, economy.

And the British corporations are much less known to the public than the Americans. Many firms since the war have spent large sums on prestige advertising, but that has been designed to divert rather than to inform the reader, with eccentric dialogues, joke drawings, or photographs of children; perhaps to show the corporations not as important, but as unfrightening. When Shell celebrated their golden jubilee in 1957, they sent a superbly illustrated book to all their shareholders—not about oil, but about sea-shells.

To generalise about corporations is dangerous, for their histories, products and managers have moulded very different personalities.

[1] *See* S. J. Prais: The Financial Experience of Great Companies. *Economic Journal*, June, 1957.

[2] *See* pp. 551–2.

I have therefore tried to describe the three biggest firms in Britain, which are not only important in themselves, but also show patterns into which other industries are shaping.

In terms both of sales and assets the three largest are Shell, Unilever and ICI (excluding British Petroleum, which comes just above ICI, but has 56 per cent of its shares owned by the British government). These three are enormous even by world standards: Shell is the fourth biggest, by sales, in the world, and Unilever sixth. These were the world's largest companies in 1964, as calculated by *Fortune* magazine:[1]

	Company	*Headquarters*	*Sales* ($ 000)	*Assets* ($ 000)	*Net Profits* ($ 000)	*Employees*
1.	**General Motors**	Detroit	16,494,818	10,784,872	1,591,823	640,073
2.	**Standard Oil**	New York	10,264,343	11,996,691	1,019,469	147,000
3.	**Ford Motor**	Dearborn, Mich.	8,742,506	5,948,782	488,547	316,568
4.	**Royal Dutch/Shell**	London/The Hague	6,521,292	10,651,001	601,292	225,000
5.	**General Electric**	New York	4,918,716	3,015,131	270,639	262,882
6.	**Unilever**	London/Rotterdam	4,297,384	2,720,250	156,478	290,000
7.	**Socony Mobil Oil**	New York	4,352,119	4,659,543	271,852	79,700
8.	**U.S. Steel**	New York	3,599,256	5,139,329	203,549	187,721
9.	**Chrysler**	Detroit	3,505,275	2,123,714	161,595	120,447
10.	**Texaco**	New York	3,415,746	4,455,095	545,668	55,040

SHELL

By far the biggest in Britain is Shell, fourth in world sales after General Motors, Standard Oil and Ford Motor, and the largest industrial concern outside America. Its size is difficult to comprehend. It produces 14 per cent of the free world's oil. Its annual income, of £3,338 million in 1963, is bigger than the entire national income of Switzerland, and nearly three times that of Greece. Its annual expenditure is more than the whole annual investment of Britain overseas. Its tankers alone, amounting to twelve million tons of shipping, form by far the biggest fleet in the world—four times the tonnage of the biggest passenger group (P and O). The towering importance of Shell in the British economy—and its conservatism—is aptly symbolised by its stone skyscraper block on the Thames, containing 5,000 people and dwarfing the Houses of Parliament opposite. The building, too,

[1] Reprinted by permission from the July and August issues of *Fortune*. Copyright 1964. Time Inc. All rights reserved.

sums up the self-sufficiency of Shell. It has its own restaurants, swimming-pool, exhibitions and underground entrance, and it is quite possible to work there without ever leaving the building.

Shell is the most inscrutable of the corporations in Britain. Oil has its own complex, convoluted problems, and oilmen have been sufficiently harassed and attacked in the past to be defensive and touchy about their affairs and their size. 'Groupthink' is a noticeable characteristic. The outsider might see Shell as a single, solid force with firm opinions. But inside, the picture is much more fragmented—like the inside of Whitehall—with hundreds of smaller Shells interacting, engrossed in technical problems.

Shell is not strictly a British firm. More properly known as 'Royal Dutch/Shell', it was the result of the spectacular merger of 1907 between Henri Deterding, the brilliant little Dutch financier, and Marcus Samuel, the trader from Whitechapel who began by importing sea-shells from the Far East—which gave their name to his vast oil empire. The resulting combine of Royal Dutch/Shell—generally referred to as 'The Group'—is controlled by two parent companies, and the British parent—confusingly called 'Shell Transport and Trading'—controls only 40 per cent. But the financial headquarters of the Group are in London, and it is there that, twice a week, the managing directors meet. The British have 39 per cent of the shares, Americans 21 per cent, and Dutch only 17 per cent. Correspondence is in English, finance in sterling, and the whole Group is English-speaking. The collaboration between English and Dutch, with their complementary characteristics, is difficult but workable.

But to speak entirely in terms of English and Dutch is misleading, for Shell in its staffing is probably the most international firm in the world, and its internationalisation over the last fifteen years has been an operation without commercial parallel. Shell, more than any other giant, has found itself on the angry frontiers of nationalism and race; and unlike its American rivals it had no safe home oilfields to which it could retreat. The word nationalism sent a shiver down its spine, and as early as 1938 it experienced its first great trauma, when the Mexican Government expropriated the rich oil wells of the Shell subsidiary, El Aguila. Its overseas branches were then run largely by British and Dutch graduates, with benevolent paternalism of the District Commissioner kind.

The fate of El Aguila showed that paternalism was not enough. And so, after the war, the seven managing directors instituted a vast scheme for 'regionalisation'. They realised that their only chance of retaining their vast and valuable empire was to make every possible concession to local nationalism. They pushed through—*ahead* of politics—the quick recruitment and promotion of Asians, Africans or South Americans, giving them as much independence as they dared. They tried to avoid choosing local managers by Western or 'old boy' standards, and to accept the values of local communities. For many of the old-style administrators the change was appalling. (I remember seeing their bewilderment in East Africa in the early fifties when inexperienced Africans were promoted.) But it was carried through, helped by Shell's hard international experience, and the geographical detachment of the seven men. In tricky countries such as Ceylon or Egypt, they tried to recruit key political figures—to 'buy in the bell-wether', in their own phrase. They became deeply involved in local problems—subsidising education, creating a 'commercial class', bringing Africans to London. It was a painful operation, full of disappointments and mistakes, but it achieved quickly and relentlessly—and in striking contrast to BP—the obliteration of the imperial idea alongside which Shell had been built. As regionalisation progressed, so Shell was able to have a hundred different nationalities on their various staffs. In 1964 they had Trinidadians in Nigeria, Indians in Germany, Venezuelans in Brunei, and a Tanganyikan in Norway.

The regionalisation made it not only international but looser. 'The Group' now has about 500 separate and apparently autonomous Shells all over the world. In many countries the Group holds only a proportion of the shares (69 per cent in America, 79 per cent in France). When one looks at the headquarters or house magazines of West African Shell, South American Shell or Shell Française, one could well be unaware that any other Shell existed: for the employees it is this local entity, rather than the shapeless mass of the Group, which commands their loyalty. Likewise the British subsidiary, jointly owned with BP and awkwardly called 'Shell Mex and BP', has a quite separate existence, in its own big squat building on the north side of the river. Like Shell Française, or Shell Italiana, it is purely a marketing organisation.

Regionalisation has made the Group's job more subtle, more specialised, and needing relatively fewer metropolitan people. In ten years, though Shell's output has nearly doubled, the numbers of British and Dutch recruited to the Group has remained the same, and the need for the old-style administrators, as for district commissioners, has virtually disappeared. But the hard core remains the 4,000 'expatriates', of whom 1,618 are British—of whom in turn about 1,000 are administrative, as opposed to technical. These thousand can be compared roughly in their numbers and in their jobs with the Foreign Office, and in most Asian or African capitals Shell men have a status second only to the diplomats. They are the earliest corps of industrial graduates. Shell was the first firm to recruit systematically from the universities: in 1910 it gave £10,000 to set up an Appointments Board. Four-fifths of the young Shell administrators are now graduates—and they are recruited widely from Redbrick.

Shell is less formal than the Foreign Office and less bound by hierarchies and titles, but for that reason Shell men are apt to be very *protocolaire*. They have been immersed in oil abroad, living in Shell houses, or in Shell compounds, going to Shell parties at Shell country clubs, travelling in Shell planes to visit Shell towns in Shell oilfields. They talk about oil and the Group in the same tone diplomats use for HMG. 'I wish the administrators wouldn't talk about oil as if it was a *faith*,' said one senior Shell rebel: 'Anyone would think it was a church. At least the technologists aren't fooled by that.' Shell deals in a single commodity, but many executives have never actually dirtied their hands with oil. One told me how he was once attending a conference about marketing naphtha. 'By the way,' he asked half-way through, 'has anyone actually *seen* any naphtha?' Nobody had.

SEVEN MEN

At the head of the Group, meeting twice a week in the skyscraper boardroom are the managing directors, 'The Seven Men'. They are a legend within Shell and in the city. Their (secret) salaries are each around £50,000 a year—over three times the prime minister's. Much of their lives is spent flying in private Shell aircraft between London, The Hague, and foreign Shells; luxury planes, with beds, dressing-rooms and arm-chairs are waiting at two hours' notice. At their London meeting they do not bother themselves with sums of less than half a million pounds.

The seven are very much a product of the managerial revolution. All of them have worked their way through the firm, without any considerable shareholding. They have a smoothness in sharp contrast to the founders, and are distinctively committee-men—though they dislike the word: ('Only a committee,' one Shell man remarked, 'could have commissioned that South Bank building.')

Four of the seven, as stipulated by Deterding's agreement, are Dutch. They are Jan Brouwer, an ex-geologist in charge of exploration and production; Willem Starrenburg, director of chemical co-ordination; Gerry Wagner, the youngest of them, who had previously been running the Compania Shell de Venezuela; and the chairman, John Loudon. The three British directors are led by David Barran, the deputy-chairman of the committee, a Winchester-and-Cambridge man who was president of the Asiatic Petroleum Corporation in New York; John Berkin, a quiet engineer considered by many to be the most brilliant; and Frank McFadzean, a tough Scot who joined the seven in 1964 at the age of forty-nine, and who had come in from the civil service twelve years before: he is suspected of being the most formidable of the seven.

The most obviously international is the chairman, John Hugo Loudon, who has a house in Holland, a flat in Grosvenor Square, speaks five languages and spends 150 hours in the air every year. Although born and brought up in Holland, he speaks polished, slightly nasal English, which sounds more American than Dutch. He is tall, elegant, with wavy grey hair and restless eyes. He has the manner of a diplomat, not a tycoon, and he comes from a Dutch diplomatic family. His grandfather was a governor-general of the Dutch East Indies, his uncle was Foreign Minister, his father was chairman of Royal Dutch, and he himself is a Jonkheer—a kind of Dutch baronet—and a KBE. He has a fine collection of paintings in Holland, including a Rembrandt self-portrait.

John Loudon thus grew up in a statesmanlike home, at a time when much of the oil business was still rough and tough, but international tact was beginning to be valued. He showed his diplomatic gifts in Venezuela, when he went as general manager in 1944 and pushed through rapid Venezuelisation. Three years later, at forty-one, he became one of the Seven Men—taking over as chairman ten years later.

'Most of my job', Loudon told me, 'is strictly commercial . . . I'm concerned far more with inside problems than with outside ones.' The diplomacy, he insisted, is in the hands of the local general managers. He is, like most chairmen, concerned with public relations—'I don't know why, but oil always seems to me to have a smell to it'—and he spends much time trying to dispel damaging ideas. 'The dogs may bark, but the caravan moves on.'

SHELL RESHAPED

Shell's managerial revolution after Deterding's departure produced massive problems, and large areas of bureaucratic muddle. The Dutch-British sides, entrenched in London and The Hague, gave wonderful opportunities for cross-purposes and duplication, and private princedoms still lingered.

Loudon took a sensational step. In 1959 he and his board engaged the celebrated American firm of efficiency experts, McKinsey Inc., to recommend changes of organisation. It was by far the biggest investigation ever commissioned in Britain. A team of crew-cut graduates flew over to London and The Hague, sat on a committee with Shell experts, interviewed managing directors, tramped round the offices. After nine months—the usual gestation period—they gave birth to a drastic and largely secret report, which was almost totally accepted. Many of the ideas indeed were thought to be Loudon's own, and McKinsey provided timely corroboration.[1]

London and The Hague were to have a single organisation, and the two centres were to be run as one. Several senior men were discreetly declared redundant. A big and growing subsidiary of the Group, Shell Chemicals—which deals with a rapidly expanding line of business—was to be hived off as a separate company. The Seven Men were to have more time for thought and were told to detach themselves (as the Cabinet signally fails to do) from day-to-day problems (one of them had to be ticked off for taking too much interest in detail). To relieve them a new race of 'Co-ordinators' or 'Solomons' was devised.

The new scheme was an attempt to produce the 'perfect pyramid' which is every efficiency expert's dream. In Shell, as in most companies, there were bound to be bumps in the pattern where personalities obtruded, and Parkinsonian tendencies successfully defeated a good deal of the reorganisation of the chemical side. But the McKinsey plan was an example of self-analysis more drastic (though no more necessary) than anything in Whitehall. Shell claim that since 1960, as a result of the reorganisation, the staff of the central offices organisation fell by more than a quarter; but there was still a good deal of continuing chaos. Four years later, Loudon called for a review of the post-McKinsey changes—'not to start a further revolution but to see if, by sound evolution, further improvements can be made on the base already won'.

[1] *See* Professor Parkinson, p. 510.

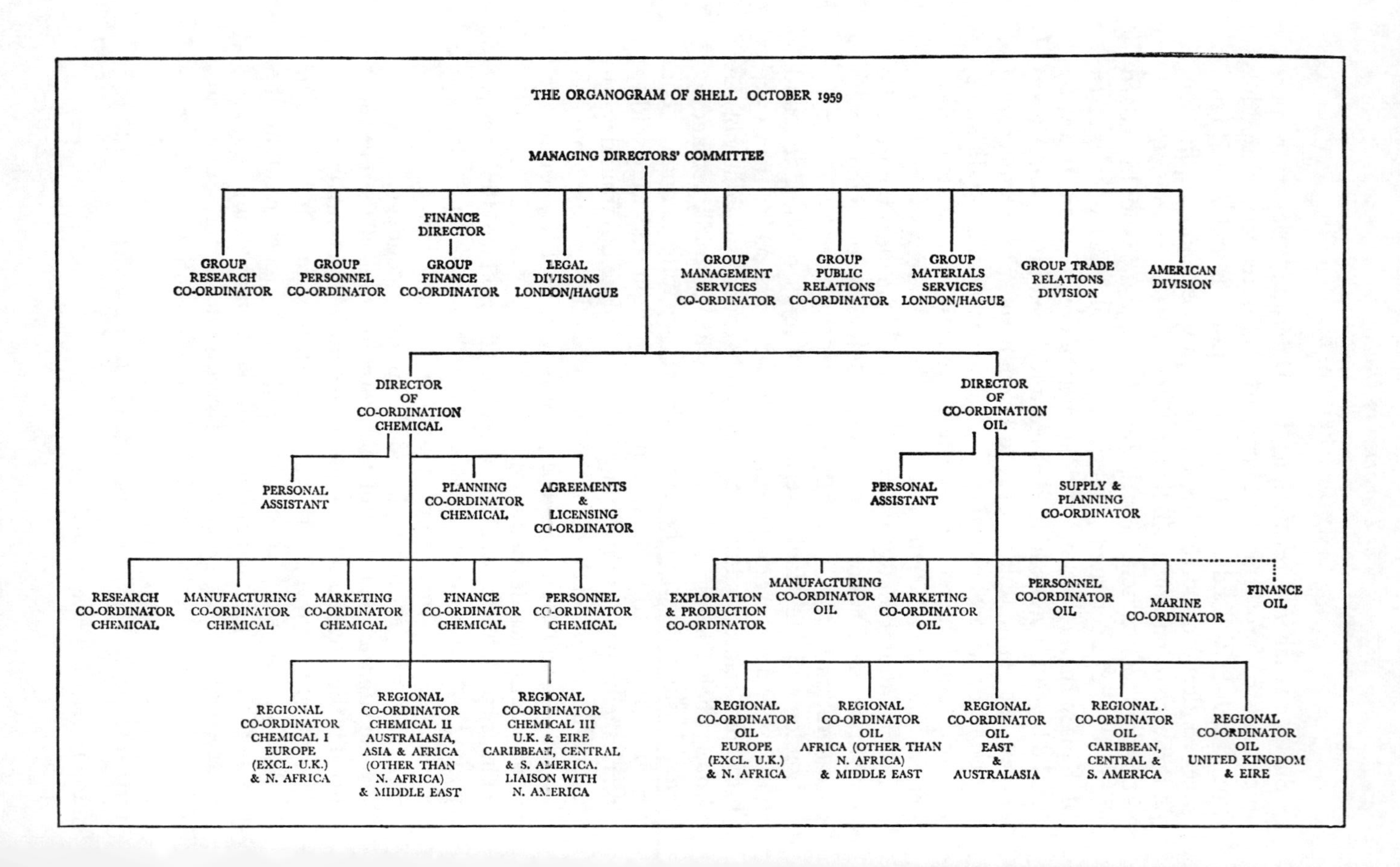
THE ORGANOGRAM OF SHELL OCTOBER 1959
MANAGING DIRECTORS' COMMITTEE
GROUP RESEARCH CO-ORDINATOR
GROUP PERSONNEL CO-ORDINATOR
FINANCE DIRECTOR
GROUP FINANCE CO-ORDINATOR
LEGAL DIVISIONS LONDON/HAGUE
GROUP MANAGEMENT SERVICES CO-ORDINATOR
GROUP PUBLIC RELATIONS CO-ORDINATOR
GROUP MATERIALS SERVICES LONDON/HAGUE
GROUP TRADE RELATIONS DIVISION
AMERICAN DIVISION
DIRECTOR OF CO-ORDINATION CHEMICAL
PERSONAL ASSISTANT
PLANNING CO-ORDINATOR CHEMICAL
AGREEMENTS & LICENSING CO-ORDINATOR
RESEARCH CO-ORDINATOR CHEMICAL
MANUFACTURING CO-ORDINATOR CHEMICAL
MARKETING CO-ORDINATOR CHEMICAL
FINANCE CO-ORDINATOR CHEMICAL
PERSONNEL CO-ORDINATOR CHEMICAL
REGIONAL CO-ORDINATOR CHEMICAL I EUROPE (EXCL. U.K.) & N. AFRICA
REGIONAL CO-ORDINATOR CHEMICAL II AUSTRALASIA, ASIA & AFRICA (OTHER THAN N. AFRICA) & MIDDLE EAST
REGIONAL CO-ORDINATOR CHEMICAL III U.K. & EIRE CARIBBEAN, CENTRAL & S. AMERICA. LIAISON WITH N. AMERICA
DIRECTOR OF CO-ORDINATION OIL
PERSONAL ASSISTANT
SUPPLY & PLANNING CO-ORDINATOR
EXPLORATION & PRODUCTION CO-ORDINATOR
MANUFACTURING CO-ORDINATOR OIL
MARKETING CO-ORDINATOR OIL
PERSONNEL CO-ORDINATOR OIL
MARINE CO-ORDINATOR
FINANCE OIL
REGIONAL CO-ORDINATOR OIL EUROPE (EXCL. U.K.) & N. AFRICA
REGIONAL CO-ORDINATOR OIL AFRICA (OTHER THAN N. AFRICA) & MIDDLE EAST
REGIONAL CO-ORDINATOR OIL EAST & AUSTRALASIA
REGIONAL CO-ORDINATOR OIL CARIBBEAN, CENTRAL & S. AMERICA
REGIONAL CO-ORDINATOR OIL UNITED KINGDOM & EIRE

There is something inherently baffling about finding at the top of a huge department a boss with the evasive title of co-ordinator: but this is, of course, part of the discreet rôle of Shell headquarters which, like the Treasury, prefer to issue advice instead of instructions. Its activities are incomprehensible to the outsider, as the chart opposite suggests, for it is turned tightly in on itself, with its own commercial ambassadors negotiating between one Shell and another.

Between the distant outposts of Shell and the London headquarters lies the same contrast of improvisation and formality as exists between African embassies and the Foreign Office. But the bureaucracy of Shell headquarters—as of other Leviathans—is more opaque than anything in Whitehall. No parliamentary questions or select committees disturb *its* workings, whose deadening fatuity is terrifyingly conveyed in Thomas Hinde's novel about Shell, *For the Good of the Company*. The cream of Oxbridge graduates find themselves confronted with the rules of a third-rate clerkdom, and a jargon of 'Shellese' more fatuous than Treasury language: 'the price is going down' is transformed to 'we would think the price is going down' and finally to (since 'feeling' is regarded as more democratic than 'thinking') to 'we would feel that in view of the depression in the general market level'. One Shell graduate recorded for me a selection of the actual changes that superiors had made on various people's letters:

urgent	a matter of some urgency
we hope you will let us know	we would ask you to let us know
please let us know if you need further help	we would be pleased to assist on receipt of your detailed advice
uneconomical	anti-economical
also	a further complication is the fact that . . .
without a precedent	. . . lacks an established historical background
will lower the prices	will have a depressing effect on the general market level
we would prefer to defer alteration of these prices until the necessity occurs	we suggest that the question of possible alterations to the present transfer prices should be considered in the event of competition arising when they may be reviewed in the light of the situation at that time

The vital question for Shell is the price of oil, and on this point most oil men are sensitive. For although the cartel arrangements of the thirties are now broken up, the oil giants, or 'seven sisters'—

Standard Oil of New Jersey, Socony Mobil Oil, Shell, BP, Caltex, Gulf and Compagnie Française des Pétroles ('Total')—still dominate the western world, all selling petrol at very similar prices. Shell is insistent that the closeness of prices at the retail pumps (which is only 17 per cent of its business in Britain) does not represent any lack of competition, and that the intrusion of 'pirate' companies selling cheaper petrol (like 'Jet') keeps them on their toes. But the British retailers' profit at the pump can be as much as 8d. a gallon—twice as much as in France. In other respects their competition is fiercer, though often depressing and defensive—buying up service stations, clubbing together to keep a new man out. The fight of the seven sisters can be seen all through Europe—in the clamour of advertising from the shells of Shell, the flying horses of Mobilgas (Socony Mobil Oil) or the blue-and-red ovals of Esso (Standard Oil of New Jersey). At the pump, they compete with wash-basins, maps, motels, radio commercials or special ingredients—with almost everything except cut-rate prices.

The fight is dominated by Standard Oil and Shell, and their world-wide duel—involving sheikhs, geologists, garages, prime ministers, universities, café-owners—has transformed deserts, created cities and modernised countries. In the last ten years, mainly because of its large share of the markets of Asia and Europe, Shell has been catching up on Standard Oil; but Shell has been unlucky in the race to find cheap new oil, and it has faced more aggressive competition from (for instance) BP in Germany and Italy, or smaller American companies which are selling cheap oil from Libya.

Both Shell and Standard Oil, with their colossal wealth, have cut themselves loose from outside finance. Shell have invested £3,300 million of capital into expanding the business over the last ten years (up till 1964); but less than 5 per cent of that money comes from outside the Group. 'The capital requirements of the international oil business,' said Lord Godber to the Radcliffe Committee, 'have outgrown the money markets of the world.' Probably more than half Britain's income from overseas investments comes from her two oil companies, Shell and BP.

Some oil experts maintain that, however much the giants liberalise themselves, their day is done, and that the forces of nationalism will defeat them. One of their most aggressive critics was Enrico Mattei, the free-booting head of the Italian state-owned oil company, ENI, who died in 1962. He broke into the field of the sisters, bought oil from the Russians, undercut them by a fraction in Italy, outbid the traditional fifty-fifty agreements between oil companies and Middle Eastern rulers, and arranged to build refineries in North Africa and Ghana. But since Mattei's death, ENI has become more friendly to the international companies, which have themselves become more adventurous.

Shell men insist that they provide a necessary buffer between producer and consumer countries, that the alternative to the orderly squabble of the seven sisters is a hopeless free-for-all of two hundred sisters, scratching one another's eyes out, never secure enough to make long-term investments. They like to quote the oil economist Jack Hartshorn that 'if the international oil companies did not exist it would be necessary to invent them'. Undoubtedly Shell and the other six face a difficult future—with an over-supply of oil, and a surge of economic nationalism. In the last decade Shell has shown that it can change its attitude and strip off some of its superfluous fat. But it is still possible that Shell, like Hollywood film studios, may disintegrate from sheer out-size. In the next ten years it will need all the ingenuity of the seven men to keep their five hundred Shells intact.

UNILEVER

> Avis Unileverensis (managerialis).
>
> Plumage: highly variegated; habits: too numerous to list; habitat: the world; distinctive characteristics: a high flyer. The birds who run Unilever come in many shapes and sizes. For a marketing man, for example, a spell in a sales team in Yorkshire may lead to experience in an advertising agency in London. Later, from London, our man may go to Brazil—or Pakistan, or Australia, or to one of many overseas stations. The Parent Board of Unilever itself and the Management of our 400 companies are peopled by men like this. So if you are bird that likes a varied habitat, above all, if you're feathered for flight into the higher realms, Unilever's atmosphere may be congenial to you.
>
> *Unilever advertisement for recruits.*

> Business History has as yet been but little studied in Britain and the inquiring reader still has to choose between what are virtually two sorts of propaganda: an heroic mythology on the one hand and a kind of economic Crime Club on the other.
>
> *Charles Wilson: History of Unilever*, 1954.

Unilever has many likenesses to Shell. It is Anglo-Dutch, international, decentralised (with four hundred separate companies). It, too, has come to terms with nationalism: as the expropriation of the Mexican company shook Shell, so was Unilever shaken in 1948 by the looting of the Kingsway Stores in Ghana. But one need only step inside the Unilever building, half a mile down the river, to notice the contrast. In Shell you sense an unchanging hierarchy of men in pin-stripes discussing pipelines or South-East Asia. In Unilever House a salesman might stroll down the corridors discussing frozen doughnuts. While Shell is concerned with its one holy commodity, Unilever sells a fantastic range of stuff, including Lux Soap, Stork Margarine, Gibbs Toothpaste, Walls Sausages and Ice Cream, Birds Eye Frozen Foods, MacFisheries, Atkinsons Perfumes, Omo, Vim and Persil. Shell men talk reverentially about 'The Group', but Unilever people have been heard to refer to 'Dear Octopus'. They keep their central identity in the background, and do not shout too much about the connection between Stork and Omo. One of their mandarins told me that when years ago, as an undergraduate at Oxford, he saw a Unilever careers advertisement, he assumed that Unilevers had to do with cantilevers.

While Shell is one big pyramid, Unilever is a collection of small pyramids, constantly changing their size and position and forming zigzag routes to the peak. A man in Unilever can (and has) become managing director of Walls Sausages at the age of twenty-eight, and from there might move through soap, timber or toothpaste up to the central board.

Unilever is probably the most sophisticated corporation in Britain, and also one of the least pretentious. It still has something of the character of the institution from which it grew—a cosy, efficient grocer's shop. But it has also developed psychological selection, computers, ergonomics, elaborate costing, and scrupulous care for its 23,000 managers. It has even had its history objectively written—a kind of corporate psychoanalysis.

It is rash to generalise about the Dear Octopus. Its biggest limb of all, the United Africa Company, is engaged in quite separate activities, including making cement, beer and plastics. But Unilever is concerned above all with salesmanship. There is no sense, as in Shell, of purveying a noble and indispensable product. 'The kind of problem we're facing at the moment', one senior Unilever executive explained to me, 'is whether you can sell collar studs in fish-shops.' Unilever is mixed up in the social change of Britain and forty-nine other countries and while Shell's ultimate strategy might be said to depend on handling a sheikh, Unilever's depends on handling a housewife.

LORD LEVERHULME

All this is implicit in Unilever's tempestuous past, and in the character of the founder of the British side of the business, the brilliant and impulsive first Lord Leverhulme. It was William Lever (as he then was) who first introduced mass-advertising to Britain, in the soap business in 1885. He repeatedly quoted the old American jingle:

> If you whisper down a well
> About the goods you have to sell
> You will not make as many dollars
> As the man who climbs a tree and hollers.

By 1920 Lever controlled more than three-quarters of the British soap trade. But he had also embarked on other rash and eccentric enterprises. He fell in love with the Western Isles; to help the fishermen there he set up companies to process their fish. To sell the fish he founded a chain of high-street shops, called MacFisheries; to sell alongside the fish he bought Walls Sausages; and Walls, to keep themselves busy in the summer, had started making ice-cream. The original fishery business in the Western Isles was a total flop, but MacFisheries, Walls and the food business which grew around them are now the third largest section of Unilever's business.

Still more rashly, Lever decided in 1920 to buy a company which traded in oil-seeds for his soap and margarine—the Niger Company in West Africa. It nearly ruined him. But it survived as the United Africa Company to become by far the biggest of all Unilever's subsidiaries, with a large chunk of the trade in Ghana and Nigeria.

When Leverhulme died in 1925, Francis D'Arcy Cooper, who had been his accountant, became chairman. He was one of the first of many cases of accountants rescuing crumbling companies, and without him Lever's would probably have collapsed. The firm was then in hot competition with Continental rivals—notably the margarine-and-soap firms of Jurgens, Van Den Berghs, and Schichts, who had merged in 1928 into the 'Margarine Unie'. The two rivals, the *Unie* and Lever's, opened talks, and in September, 1929, they merged as the Anglo-Dutch firm of Unilever, with two holding companies and twin boards, called 'Unilever Limited' and 'Unilever NV'. It is an arrangement similar to Shell's, but more centrally based on London. This huge and awkward conglomeration, through the slump, went through a time of agonising 'rationalisation'; for a time, in the D'Arcy Cooper era, there was an attempt to centralise the whole outfit until, as one Canadian executive complained, 'you had to cable London before you went to the bathroom'. But later Unilever took on an opposite tendency, leaving its local managers largely—and sometimes too much—in control.

HEYWORTH'S MANAGERS

> I don't think you'll find many men at the top of this company who've got there because of an acquisitive instinct.
>
> *George Cole, 1963.*

In 1942 Cooper was succeeded by Geoffrey Heyworth, later Lord Heyworth, who ruled the British end of Unilever for the next eighteen years. Heyworth is a quiet, thoughtful man, a self-made intellectual given to long pauses and meaningful but ambiguous grunts. He has now retired from the chairmanship, but he left a decisive mark on the character of Unilever and much else. He embraced the new problems of marketing and growth with an un-English enthusiasm: the idea of change, of one product pushing out another, of detergents pushing out soap, stimulated him. He told me how he had urged the young Unilever men to 'make change your ally'. He generated a sense of un-complacency in Unilever, welcoming anything which was new.

He pushed ahead schemes for training graduates, and took a close interest in universities, sitting on the University Grants Committee, becoming a fellow of Nuffield. His speeches at annual general meetings have since become a model—choosing each year one main theme, on advertising, managers, or investment. Above all, Heyworth pressed on with the managerial revolution which D'Arcy Cooper had initiated, building up a new 'meritocracy' of managers from inside the firm, watching their training, and encouraging 'cross-fertilisation' between the different Unilever companies, 'keeping the fences low'. As Unilever decentralised and diversified, so the managers became more important. 'The firm isn't really run by the board, it's run by five hundred managers,' Heyworth said to me. Unilever came to see itself more as a central management service. 'You can raise ten million pounds in two days,' one Unilever man said to me, 'but it takes ten years to produce ten managers.' They built up an 'industrial civil service', almost as a-political as Whitehall; they are 85 per cent Conservative, according to one estimate, but two of the Unilever board are said to be Socialists and several are Liberals.

Unilever managers come from two strains—the graduates, and the promoted clerks or salesmen, from the 'University of Hard Knocks', as Lever called his own education. Since the war Unilever has tried to introduce a more dignified, civil service atmosphere—graded carpets, canteens and morning tea (tea-and-cake for senior managers, tea-and-biscuit for middle managers)—and to dispel the undergraduates' prejudice about super-grocers. Today about half the senior managers are graduates, and the proportion is still rising.

The 'royal families' of the founders gave way to self-made and self-perpetuating managers. Old Leverhulme luckily had no truck with nepotism: 'The surest way to annoy the old man', said Lord Heyworth, 'was to promote one of his relations beyond his merits.' Today, of the twenty-four members of the Unilever board, all have been in the business all their lives, and only three belong to 'royal families'. Lord Leverhulme, grandson of the founder, comes up from his Cheshire farm once a month, as an 'advisory director', but his share in the company, like that of the Dutch descendants, is tiny in proportion to the total shareholding. The final stage in Unilever's managerial revolution was reached a few years ago, when it was announced that directors no longer had to have any financial stake. None of the present directors are from the city, insurance companies, or other firms. Unilever has, in fact, become entirely self-perpetuating, virtually independent of the city. Like those of Shell, the financial operations of Unilever are dictated, not by the stock exchange or by the financiers, but by the necessities of international competition. 'If we feel that we must keep up with the Joneses,' Lord Heyworth explained to the Radcliffe Committee, 'whether we have to pay 8 per cent or 6 per cent doesn't make much difference. It is a horrible business, keeping up.'[1]

THE CHAIRMAN

The present chairman of Unilever Limited, George Cole, took over from Heyworth in 1960, at the age of fifty-four: he thus belongs to the new generation of bosses, too young to fight in the first world war, less isolated and perhaps more competitive. In a gathering of businessmen, Cole seems unobtrusive, and not part of the intimate confident circle of the city's Old Boy Net: he is shy and hates public speaking. But within Unilever he is regarded as

[1] Proceedings of the Radcliffe Committee, 1960. Q. 11479.

something of a superman. He went to the 'University of Hard Knocks'; he comes from North Country stock and went to school in Singapore. He joined the Niger Company as a junior clerk, at the age of seventeen, and worked his way up through the West African business. In his boldness and down-to-earthness he remains basically an African trader; he has described how, at the age of twenty-one, he went on an African tour:[1] 'Out there, going from one little town on the river to another, one had a chance to see the workings of a primitive economy. Though I didn't realise it at the time, I was given a wonderful lesson in basic economic principles. The central problem for each outfit was the same, to say how much it would be worth our expanding—what investment to recommend, the balance of risks and advantages—to the bosses back at home. This meant arriving at all kinds of simple judgments and making simple predictions. Analysis was relatively simple in these primitive situations. Even if you didn't arrive at the right judgments you were able to see the kind of judgments that have to be made in the most complex economies. That's all business is, after all, if you can see it through the complexities: judging risks, making predictions, framing policies accordingly. Another thing: some of these outfits were making rather a mess of things, and you can learn a great deal from other people's mistakes, as well as your own. Also, it was good to learn to work so young with other nationalities. More than ever useful today.'

He is a large, broad-shouldered man—high bald head, humorous deep-set eyes, unpompous manner, soft voice. He became a Life Peer in 1965. I was tempted to divide British businessmen into those who sat behind their huge bare desks, and those who come forward to relax on a chair or a sofa: Cole belongs to the second, Chambers of ICI to the first.

Cole rules Unilever jointly with his Dutch co-chairman, F. J. Tempel, whose office has a communicating door, and most of the day-to-day decisions are taken by a special committee, a triumvirate of the two chairmen and a vice-chairman, Dr. E. G. Woodroofe, a scientist and ex-head of the research division. To help them they have 'mandarins'—not unlike the co-ordinators of Shell—each in charge of a division: technical, personnel, marketing, finance and tax, company secretary. Recently, to this already complicated structure there have been added other co-ordinators, supervising the different products—detergents, toilet preparations or frozen foods.

[1] Conversation with Kenneth Harris: *The Observer*, January 13, 1963.

Cole's main preoccupation is with managers: when I asked him what was his most important job, he said immediately, 'finding successors'. The special committee only considers sums above £25,000, but they try to ensure that their subsidiaries are not becoming involved in businesses they don't understand. That is a central tenet of Unilever's: 'We are not an investment trust', wrote Heyworth,[1] 'concerned to find capital and leave management to others. We normally go into businesses we can run ourselves.'

Cole has described his own method of operation with his colleagues and directors: 'I think I spend most of the time talking . . . Looking in on people in their offices. Conversation between two people, mostly. The board discusses matters of general policy when they've come to the point of decision . . . Most of the important decisions are arrived at outside the boardroom. Directors talk to one another in small groups. I talk to colleagues on the board, one or two at a time. We lobby one another, persuade one another, sound one another. By and large, I think the process of decision-forming is carried out outside the board meeting as a result of a very large number of man-to-man talks. The Unilever board has had to divide on a formal vote only once in living memory.'[2]

Both Heyworth and Cole have tried to leave their companies to themselves: like Shell, they believe this gives Unilever an advantage over American competitors. But the balance between centre and perimeter is difficult to keep, for there is always a danger (as Heyworth put it) that 'the business might fly apart by centrifugal force'; and under Cole, Unilever has become more centralised, particularly in Europe in the past two years.

How will the Octopus grow in the future? The pattern of 'diversification', first set by the eccentricity of Leverhulme, has proved an immense advantage in the sixties: while other 'one-track firms' have been shopping around for new and different businesses, Unilever already had its eggs in several different baskets. But in 1943, under Heyworth, they took a decision which was just as bold as Lever's buying of MacFisheries, and which led them into a vast and important new territory. They bought Birds Eye Frozen Foods—the invention, amazingly enough, of Mr. Clarence Birdseye. Unilevers had reckoned that the post-war years would bring greater prosperity, and that more women would go out to work, and would thus need the kind of food that

[1] Lord Heyworth: *Capital Investment*, 1960.
[2] *The Observer*, January 6, 1963.

was quick to prepare. They developed the new business with spectacular success. In 1946 housewives spent around £150,000 on frozen food, which was only available in a hundred shops in the whole country: in 1964 they were spending £75 millions, in 115,000 shops, and about two-thirds of those frozen foods were made by Birds Eye.[1] This extension of their food business had large new implications. It brought Unilevers into a profitable but uneasy relationship with farmers, linking them with big business in a quite new kind of way. It took them still further into the insides of the kitchens. And it involved them more deeply in the world of advertising and market research.

Marketing, motivational research, depth interviewing and mass advertising lie at the heart of Unilever's operations. The process which began with William Lever's hoardings for Sunlight Soap has culminated in the huge apparatus of modern advertising. Unilever is spending about £100 million on advertising, of which probably about one-fifth is spent in Britain—the biggest single advertiser. The annual cost of Unilever advertising is roughly the same as its annual profits. Unilever products—1,200 different brand names throughout the world—advertise not only against their rivals but against each other—Gibbs against Pepsodent, Summer County against Stork. Unilever men discuss the tooth-paste war as intently as if it were an international crisis: in the belly of the Octopus groupthink and conformism are rife, and managers easily become absorbed in the tiny limits of their competition. But at the higher levels there is some worry about Unilever's responsibility for strident and misleading advertising. As Cole has said[2]: 'I think some advertisements on television have been embarrassing. And in the press. I'm not making any special claims for Unilever advertisements, either. The trouble is that because it's so terribly expensive to *start* advertising, your advertising experts tend to set a good deal of store on the kind of advertisements that they know—from research—are at any rate *selling* products. Very often they are not the kind of advertisements that commend themselves from the point of view of the image of the company they present. But, if it sells, you're naturally reluctant to throw out the advice of the experts for that reason. Moreover once you've made a start, it doesn't do any good to chop and change your story. You may not like our advertisements, but I can tell you we are giving plenty of thought to this problem:

[1] *See Investment in Food*, Unilever, 1964.
[2] *The Observer*, January 13, 1963.

combining advertisements that sell with advertisements that don't give an embarrassing image of Unilever.'

The pace—and the embarrassment—has been quickened by commercial television, which can bring Birdseye or Lux on to the screen in the housewife's home on the same day all over the country. And TV breaks down the British loyalty to established products—'brand loyalty'. In the past, while Americans have enjoyed changing their soaps, toothpastes and cars, the British have stuck to Sunlight, Persil and other established brands, and have mocked the Americans' fickleness. But now we too are becoming more changeable. Unilever is urging us on, pushing out one product with another, analysing the housewife's subconscious desires, and stimulating them into spending. TV and supermarkets (Cole told me) have made the old-fashioned huckster-salesman out of date, and the television screen has taken over the function of the foot-in-the-door. Instead of the brash salesman in a van, talking an old grocer into buying more soap than he wants, Unilever now has subtle executives planning a nation-wide advertising campaign, plotting when to move in Omo, or pull out Vim. The marketing men have always been the top dogs of Unilever. Scientists, who resent the grocer-image, are becoming more important, and research now looms much larger. But marketers remain the mainspring: they have been paid more and sacked more. With the complexity and centralisation of advertising, their value grows; they are on the profitable frontier between industry and salesmanship.

'Keeping up with the Joneses' is the centre of Unilever's business To some idealists who join it, the operation may seem narrow: 'It's difficult to feel very serious', said one Oxford recruit, 'about making a housewife buy two sausages when she needs only one.' But Unilever is proud of what is is doing. 'Some people, who have spent years castigating the evils of poverty', to quote Lord Heyworth again, 'now seem disconcerted by prosperity, and they make very sour noises about it. We cannot follow their logic. We like to see people well off, and although we realise that mass prosperity brings new and unfamiliar problems we would much rather face those than poverty's ancient curse.'

ICI

On board the RMS *Aquitania* in October, 1926, Sir Alfred Mond, Sir Harry McGowan and other chemical industrialists sketched out an agreement on Cunard notepaper. Thus Imperial Chemical Industries was born. In the following thirty-eight years ICI has come to be regarded as Britain's industrial superman. It has tripled in size since its birth and ridden high on the post-war chemical boom, proliferating new factories, new products and new ways of life. Today it employs about 93,000 people, but this number (which has been diminishing) belittles it, for the proportion of capital to men in ICI is enormous (four times, for instance, the ratio of AEI). If one wanted a symbol of ICI, it might be a huge clean chemical plant with a mass of pipes and towers, and one technologist standing by a gauge.

In the World Series, ICI was (by sales) thirty-third from the top in 1964. Though it has big overseas subsidiaries, it is much less international than Shell or Unilever. But in Britain it is the biggest of them all, and wholly British. 'People talk about *us* as a sinister Anglo-Dutch concern', said one of the Unilever mandarins, 'but they regard ICI as part of their patriotism, as if it were the army or the navy.' In some important products—caustic soda, soda ash—it has a monopoly, which leads to some unreal and uncommercial attitudes; ICI salesmen go through the motions of persuading customers who have no option but to buy from them. But monopolies have also made it unusually aware of public opinion; it has been a sensitive giant, and taken its responsibilities seriously, looking after its people, awarding research fellowships to universities, and anxious to do the right thing by the country. It is afflicted with the usual problems of giants. There is a macabre story about a director of British Railways arguing with a director of ICI as to whose organisation was biggest. 'Of course we're bigger—look at our turnover!' said the Railways man. 'Aha,' said the ICI man, 'but we've got more *passengers*.'

ICI does not have the same closeness to the customer as over-the-counter companies like Unilever. Most of its products are sold to other firms: only an odd mixture of things, like paint, zip-fasteners, drugs or cartridges are sold direct to the public. Scientists, not salesmen, are the key men of ICI: out of the fifteen executive directors—though all have long ceased to be specialists—only three (Chambers, Clapham and Todhunter) are non-scientists. But between specialists and administrators there is (as not in Whitehall) a 'permeable membrane', as Sir Ronald Holroyd called it.[1] The preoccupation of ICI with scientific research has been helped by its monopolies, and partly because

[1] *See* p. 262.

of this ICI men have often been uncommercial. But in the past few years, as we shall see, the personality of ICI has changed. The old heavy industries—such as explosives or alkalis—have remained relatively static, while new, more domestic ones have brought ICI closer to the customer, generating competition. Shell, in 1960, broke into the old monopoly of nitrogenous fertilisers—bringing a change of ICI's personality as significant as the more famous Courtauld fiasco of 1962. And ICI, in the past years, have devised bold, cheap, new ways of making traditional products.

The roots of ICI are in the sprawling chemical factories of the provinces, and it is still essentially a group of big provincial companies, bound together by common finance. The merger was a federation rather than a union; although McGowan built a great imperial palace on the Thames, with tall nickel doors, much of the power of ICI remained in the manufacturing divisions. The early slump years of ICI saw bitter resentments from the divisions, rivalries, feuds, axings and suspicion of London. But gradually, with enlightened directors and paternalism from Alfred Mond, later Lord Melchett, the components got together as a single company, and the letters ICI became a source of pride. The character of the company was formed by two men—McGowan the shrewd Scot, and Mond the benign German Jew.

But the separate divisions—now nine—remained strong. 'You'll never understand ICI', one veteran scientist told me, 'until you realise how *different* the divisions are—as different as parts of the United States.' From the country-squire aura of Winnington Hall, (the port-drinking club in the Mond Division of Cheshire) to the self-made, no-nonsense atmosphere of Dyestuffs in Manchester, they are all worlds of their own: few of the chemists or managers move outside their division. They are immersed in the family atmosphere of their chemical towns—the alkali town of Winnington, the Terylene town of Harrogate, the ammonia town of Billingham (where I was born). Some divisions, like Harrogate, are young and expanding; others, like Winnington, have settled down to a comfortable middle age. There is not much contact, either between the divisions or with the outside world. They have their own clubs, sports, theatrical and charabanc tours, and they quite often marry company wives.

These provincial roots have given the combine its strength and weaknesses. The strength has lain in its vigour, its capacity for advancing self-made men, its lack of pomp, its closeness to the workers. Since the days when Mond and Brunner encouraged the trade unions, ICI has been a model of labour relations and works councils, and later of profit-sharing. ICI has had, too, a provincial dislike of the city; many ICI men in divisions still like to talk disrespectfully about the world of high finance and stocks and shares. ICI does not normally deal through a merchant bank, but direct through stockbrokers; and some directors have taken a pride in *not* knowing the morning's stock market quotation of their shares. They think of themselves as enlightened industrialists, rather than businessmen. Directors are expected to spend a good deal of their time in the provinces, and British Railways are proverbially full of ICI men. ICI has been able to feel independent of the city and such matters as Bank Rate: in the ten years from 1953 to 1962 it spent the staggering sum of £475 million on new plant and projects—of which £366 million has come out of its own profits. 'It would be wrong to say that Budgets are of no interest', Fleck told the Radcliffe Committee in 1959, 'but I cannot recall any of them that made any significant change in our approach to what we were thinking of doing.'

From the provinces, and from its monopoly, come some of its weaknesses—its insularity, its complacency, its old-fashioned approach to organisation, its resentment of metropolitan and non-scientific intruders. It has a conservative respect for hierarchies and an almost medieval attitude to women, who rarely get promoted above secretaries. And there is its smugness: anything less than unqualified praise—for instance this chapter—ICI is liable to regard as a stab in the back, and their public relations still has an old-fashioned blustering, threatening quality. A great deal of money and energy goes into the business of self-congratulation. When they celebrated their thirty-fifth birthday, ICI arranged for a twenty-two page supplement in *The Times* devoted to untarnished admiration, including an article on 'South Africa: Need for Faith', and accompanied by a congratulatory editorial.

In spite of their smugness ICI are sensitive to the old attacks on 'merchants of death', and their large involvement in the explosives business. In Britain this has ceased to be an emotional issue, but in South Africa ICI have become heavily compromised in ammunition factories; they have a half-share, with de Beers, in 'Africans Explosive and Chemical Industries' which have embarked on a large programme of expansion, for military purposes, with the heavy backing of the South African government; and this has caused misgivings both among shareholders and directors—though so far with no effect. At the 1964 annual meeting one worried young shareholder, Mr. Haley-Dunne, appealed to the company to withdraw from South Africa, because it was no longer possible to separate the 'system of racial discrimination, known as apartheid, existing in South Africa, from the company's continuing policy of investment in South Africa'. He received some applause, but the chairman, Paul Chambers, replied that the explosives were used for industrial, not military purposes, and that ICI's investments were doing much to 'raise the standard of living of the African peoples'.[1]

Invention is the life-blood of ICI. Its long-term future depends less on capital and managers than on research. It spends roughly £18 million a year on 'research and development'—more than is spend by all the universities put together. The 10,000 research and development workers are ICI's spearhead to the future, producing such inventions as 'Polythene', 'Perspex', 'Paludrine', 'Procion' dyes or 'Terylene' (bought from Calico Printers), which have changed our pattern of living. But research brings the insoluble problem of running a commercial civil service side-by-side with difficult eccentrics. Every organisation scientist is aware that individualists such as Rutherford, Whittle or Fleming, who do not take easily to organisation, are supremely important.

Holding a balance between discipline and eccentricity is one of ICI's hardest tasks. In its early years its scientific achievement was impressive: before the war it built a whole school of research chemists, with a sense of freedom and challenge and close contact with universities; they had a fair record of inventions, and still have an FRS as senior deputy-chairman. But some of their scientists are doubtful whether they will have such a free rein in the future, and whether the organisation men may not be winning over the individualists.

As its factories become more mechanised and automated, ICI is becoming increasingly a firm of technologists. In 1964, 5,000 of its employees—about five per cent—had university degrees, made up of:

2,500 chemists	250 physicists
1,000 engineers	280 other scientists
230 chemical engineers	500 other graduates.[2]

The total number of ICI employees (in spite of its vast expan-

[1] *The Guardian* (Third Manchester edition) April 29, 1964.

[2] From Sir Ronald Holroyd's evidence to the Fifth Report from the Estimates Committee, 1963–64.

sion) has fallen, while the number of 'staff'—or monthly-paid people—has risen: the ratio of weekly-paid to monthly-paid has fallen in ten years from 2·7 to 1, to 2 to 1. This huge heavy industry, in fact, is quite rapidly becoming an industry of white-collar workers.

Into their technological jungle ICI has recruited since the war hundreds of an unfamiliar species—the arts graduate. The meeting of test-tubes with the humanities has been painful; the two sides have found themselves staring across the deep divide between the 'two cultures', almost equally illiterate in each other's subjects. Several young graduates have described to me the frustration of leaving university to do drudgery work in an alien atmosphere, and ICI has been accused of recruiting first-class brains, and then wasting them on workaday jobs. In some fields, particularly selling, arts graduates have reached top positions rapidly; the chairman of the metal division and a managing director of dye-stuffs are both arts men, and in the next few years, as the first post-war generation comes to the top, the company will probably acquire a more humanist character. But it remains predominantly a technological firm. ICI has the particular problems of a company thirty-eight years old—an awkward age, when the first young men have grown old, and pioneering opportunities are fewer. It is a pyramid with a square base—an awkward bulge of men in the middle, and not enough jobs at the top.

The provincial (and particularly Scottish) roots are apparent in the succession of chairmen. After Mond (the first chairman), McGowan, Bain (his deputy), Rogers and Fleck were all self-made Scots boys, two of them from the same street in Glasgow. Fleck, a rugged man with huge bear-like shoulders and a rich Glaswegian accent—who retired in 1960—embodied the most attractive ICI qualities: he rose from being a Glasgow lab-boy at fourteen to being not only chairman but also a Fellow of the Royal Society.

PAUL CHAMBERS

But in 1960 ICI made a clean and dramatic break with this scientific tradition, appointing Paul Chambers, who joined the board straight from the civil service in 1947. Chambers is a Londoner, an intellectual, a graduate of the London School of Economics, the son of a city wine-merchant. He has spent half his life in the Inland Revenue—where he invented the PAYE system and reorganised Indian taxation. He is short, articulate, quick-thinking, with a photographic memory. In Whitehall he had the reputation of a wonderman, and had even been tipped by some as an eventual head of the Treasury. He has kept in touch with cabinet ministers, who tend to regard him as 'Mr. Big Business'—rather as Lord Chandos once was. Since he became chairman, Chambers has emerged (unlike Cole of Unilever, or Loudon of Shell) quickly into the political foreground: he has criticised budgets, urged lower surtax, attacked Britain's 'sentimental softness towards inefficiency' and insisted that the profit motive must prevail in nationalised industries. He was in the van of the movement into Europe: 'for too long sections of British industry have been becoming increasingly insular, introspective, restrictive, reactionary and inflexible'. Chambers has nothing of the amateur about him: he is a single-minded and uncompromisingly professional man, not afraid to talk about taxation and rationalisation all through a cocktail party. He belongs to the new unflamboyant school of chairmen; he can travel up in one of the grand nickel lifts of ICI house without being recognised (McGowan would have had the lift cleared for him). He lives unpretentiously in a big house in Bishop's Avenue, Hampstead, with his second wife—who worked in ICI—and three daughters; he has a brother who is a stores clerk in an Acton electrical firm. He likes going home early, enjoys gardening and mending greenhouses, and plays bridge or scrabble in the evenings. He has firm, unsophisticated views about Britain and the world, dislikes pop singers and votes conservative. He earns £50,000 a year.

His arrival in the ICI boardroom caused a flutter. Chambers did not try to conceal his cleverness, loved talking and was quick to point out the mistakes of his colleagues; with some of the unmoney-minded senior scientists there were some difficult scenes. But Chambers had the mastery of the intricate financial affairs of the giant, which the scientists lacked, and by the time Fleck had become due to retire in 1960 it was clear to most—though not to all—directors that Chambers must be chairman.

The transition showed how dangerous it is to personalise a company by 'Mr. ICI', for whatever Fleck is, Chambers isn't. But the change of chairman *did* represent a shift of emphasis in the company's character—away from the provinces and scientists, towards the city and finance. Not only Chambers but the finance director and treasurer also came from the Inland Revenue (all introduced by a former treasurer, the late Sir William Coates).

ICI veterans soon noticed—sometimes with sadness—a new concentration on financial expertise. Helped by its monopoly position, ICI had managed, like other manufacturing companies, to reach a position of colossal financial strength with a surprising indifference to finance. But all that was now changing. Special courses in finance and taxation were introduced, an investment committee was set up, and more 'outside' directors were introduced—including the head of the National Provincial Bank, David Robarts. The pure scientists became less confident that science was supreme.

Chambers' position as non-scientific head of a chemical giant was not easy, but he had a gift for quickly absorbing new situations, following the threads of his complex organisation and talking about chemical compounds accurately and enthusiastically. He brought to ICI a broader view of economic trends and world trade—which was shown in his successful negotiations with Russia.

Chambers presides over the twenty directors of the main board —fourteen of them full-time, each earning £24,000 a year. The control of finance is in the hands of a quadrumvirate of the chairman and three deputy-chairmen (Holroyd, Allen, Williams). But the main board has delegated most of its control to the divisions. The balance between headquarters and the divisions, as with so many other giant companies, remains a continuing problem for ICI. In 1962, following the example of Shell, the board called in the McKinseys to advise them about their organisation. 'A number of very stimulating ideas' resulted from the studies, and the Board decided that 'increased responsibility should be in the hands of individuals, rather than of groups of individuals acting collectively; and, similarly, that greater authority also should be given to individuals who, given clearer descriptions of their jobs, will know what is expected of them and where they fit in with others'. In January 1964 a new scheme came into force, in which division chairmen (instead of the division boards collectively, as before) became directly responsible to the main board, with the main board directors no longer sharing responsibility for the divisions. This meant both that the division chairman had more proconsular powers—a step away from committeemanship; and also that the main board directors were less involved in day-to-day management problems and (like the Seven Men of Shell) were (in theory) able to spend more time on long-think and 'overall direction'. The reorganisation, and the dynamic of Chambers, had a visible effect on profits and efficiency; and since 1961 (when profits fell by 30%) there has been a sharp improvement in profits and a fall in the number of employees.

In such a disparate empire, it might seem that no single head could dominate. And yet, in two astonishing months of 1962, Paul Chambers transformed the public personality of ICI by trying to take over a rival Leviathan, Courtaulds. This is not the place to tell the complicated story of that frustrated effort, which has been dramatically chronicled by Roy Jenkins.[1] But the take-over illuminated the changed character of the company with a clarity which appalled many of its employees.

A company known to the public primarily for its care for workers and research, associated with profit-sharing and university fellowships, suddenly emerged as one of the most relentless of all big businesses, prepared to enlarge its monopoly to the point of embarrassing even a Conservative government, and disturbing thousands of its managers. The bid for Courtaulds affected not only the two companies, but all British business: for it revealed that in an extreme crisis (like men in love or war) the conventional trappings, the opaque annual reports, the secrecy, the smugness, become suddenly ridiculous, and are thrown overboard in the desperate need for help. To read ICI's articles in *The Times* in 1961, or Courtaulds' 1961 annual report in the light of the subsequent events, is to see how far large companies are prepared to ignore their shareholders, and the public—until they need them.

The frustrated take-over had a sequel that was almost equally astonishing. ICI were left with 37 per cent of Courtauld's shares, and still shared with Courtaulds the ownership of British Nylon Spinners, which has 85 per cent of the nylon market in Britain. In 1964 the two companies agreed that ICI should give back their shares in Courtaulds in return for Courtaulds giving up their shares in BNS—while ICI would also pay Courtaulds 2 million pounds a year for five years, to provide capital for developing nylon. This bold agreement for industrial alimony finally divorced the two rivals. As Mr. Justice Pennycuick, who sanctioned the scheme in the High Court, remarked: 'very large figures and a very simple scheme'.

[1] *The Observer*, March 18-April 1, 1962.

27

MANAGERS

The last word on how we may live or die
  Rests today with such quiet
Men, working too hard in rooms that are too big,
  Reducing to figures
What is the matter, what is to be done.

W. H. Auden: The Managers.

Management, like war, is made up of long periods of routine divided by short bursts of intense activity and peril.

John Tyzack.

EVER since James Burnham's book was published in 1941 the phrase 'the managerial revolution' has become something of a bogy-word, conjuring up those anonymous men in huge rooms, running vast industries by means of some unspeakable expertise. The word manager, like general or permanent secretary, has acquired its own mystique. In clubs or in the old professions—where there is not much contact with managerial men—the phrase is full of dread: managers represent the antithesis of the old knightly ideals. It is sometimes difficult to remember that the managers are ordinary men doing very ordinary things—selling soap, finding oil, making chemicals—and that the senior managers are simply junior managers promoted. This shock confronts many young graduates going into large companies. They expect to be led into a *métier* as intricate and challenging as Greek iambics, and they find themselves selling kippers in the high street, slowly moving up to selling more kippers in more high streets, until they find themselves regarded as 'managers'.

When the Acton Society Trust conducted a survey of managers in thirty-seven large firms,[1] they found that the median ratio of managers to employees was about two per cent. The status of this two per cent has risen spectacularly since the war. The post-war export crisis, the collapse of imperial jobs in the Indian Civil or Colonial Services, the reaction against the civil service with its associations of rationing and the new attitude to big corporations

[1] *See Management Succession:* Acton Society Trust, 1956.

as being themselves a kind of public service—all generated a new respectability, and an inrush of able young graduates into industry. These figures show the numbers of Oxford arts graduates going into industry, introduced by the appointments committee:

1906	6
1926	39
1936	77
1946	49
1956	277
1957	291
1958	275
1959	292
1960	291
1961	273
1962	228
1963	218[1]

'For ambitious young undergraduates,' C. E. Escritt of the Oxford Appointments Committee told me, 'industry and the foreign service are now the twin tops.' The universities now send more men into industry than into any other occupation. In 1961-62, 20 per cent of arts men and 40 per cent of scientists and technologists went into industry, or 31 per cent overall.

Many are reluctant recruits. Dr. Mark Abrams has analysed the results of a Cambridge survey of 927 undergraduates in 1959, which showed that though 17 per cent were choosing a career in business management or advertising, only 8 per cent would have chosen it if other professions—notably teaching, writing or social work—were equally remunerative. Analysing the replies of the reluctant majority, Dr. Abrams concludes: 'Their leisure activities suggest that they have comparatively little taste for individualistic competition, and less than average liking for the responsibilities of leadership and organisation. When they take part in group activities they show a preference for anonymous and passive rôles. They find information more satisfying than ideas, and entertainment more attractive than controversy . . . Business might regret ever having recruited them.'[2]

In the fifties the Leviathans began to tumble over each other to

[1] The recent decline is due partly to the decline in arts graduates, partly to the demise of National Service, which has caused many graduates to postpone their choice of a permanent job.

[2] Mark Abrams: Business Aspirants from Universities. *The Manager*, September, 1961. For further complaints of graduate trainees, *see* Anthony Lejeune's study in *The Director*, May 1963: 'Is the board to blame for the graduate who flops?'

recruit the cleverest young graduates. 'Each year the courtship grows a little more feverish,' wrote J. G. W. Davies, of the Cambridge Appointments Board in 1956, 'every device being exploited to acquire prestige in the university.' Several pressures induced this new interest in graduates. One was the 1944 Education Act, which businessmen believed would scoop up nearly all the able young men into the universities, leaving less talent on the shop-floor. Another was pure fashion; bosses like to have graduates in the firm, even if (as so often) they don't quite know what to do with them. But the main pressure was the obvious shortage of 'manager material', and the urgent need to buy the best brains quickly.

The new scramble for managers can be seen in the pages of appointments advertisements in the quality newspapers—particularly on Sundays—where the variety, salaries and habitat of managers and technocrats can be observed. The growth of this 'market-place' in the past five years has caused a minor business revolution, for here are large and dignified firms publicly bidding against each other for senior men, stating quite plainly the kind of salaries—even five-figure salaries—which they would pay. To many of the old school, the clamour from this market-place is horrifying, for it cuts across two old industrial traditions—secrecy and lifelong loyalty.

The manager market began quite suddenly with the foundation of selection specialists in London, offering to serve as 'job brokers' for managers and technicians, otherwise known as the 'head-hunters'. The first and biggest—responsible for more than half the appointments—is Management Selection Limited (MSL). Others are:

Personnel Administration (PA),
Associated Industrial Consultants (AIC),
Executive Appointments (EA).

In discreet West End offices they interview managers, to marry them with new employers. These selection firms have set a new pace by providing shop-windows, generating curiosity, ambition and envy. This, for instance, was the 1960 Christmas Message of MSL:

> On Christmas Day . . . we send our greetings to all who read these columns regularly. We would not exclude, of course, those who are merely curious to see how their lot compares with others, those who

feel compelled to keep a watchful eye on their competitors, or even those who find it a diverting weekly exercise to speculate on the identities of our clients . . .

There are now about 18 separate consultant firms in London, and the big corporations have stepped up their own advertising for staff, with large spaces, more romantic headings, and more challenging requirements. In 1961 I collected a small anthology, of which this is one:

PROMETHEUS UNBOUND

As Shelley interpreted the Greek myth, Prometheus was released by Hercules. His crimes, in the eyes of Zeus, were making man from clay and teaching him the use of fire. We need neither to be made nor exactly taught.

Morgans—104 years old—make more foundry crucibles from clay and graphite than anyone in the world and know a good deal about their uses.

We now seek a man—AN EXPERIENCED CERAMIST—who can join us as a Technical Manager, take charge of technical control and development for both our large crucible factories and, by planning an ambitious programme of new uses for our traditional materials, qualify for the post of Technical Director within two years.

This Prometheus (yes, a demi-god) must have creative urge restless curiosity, leadership, the talent for choosing good men, initiative, strength of personality and youth—say 35 years.

Many of the management consultants, apart from advising and placing individual managers, provide a service to companies, recommending re-organisation and changes in structure. The consultancy business in Britain began as early as 1926, when a French-American, Charles Bedaux, opened an office in London; but there was heavy resistance to American methods, and it was not till the post-war years that consultancy became generally accepted. Since then, the expansion has been spectacular, and in 1964 the Management Consultants Association (with only nine members) claimed a total staff of 1,476; their chairman, Coutts Donald, was even appointed to the reconstituted Council of Neddy.[1] Probably the most formidable in the field is McKinsey's, the high-powered American firm who set up an office in London in 1959, and who specialise in basic probings of large companies; in Britain they have not only advised Shell[2] in their massive

[1] *The Times*, March 18, 1964.

[2] *See* p. 485.

re-vamping, but also Dunlop's and ICI. Their ruthless examinations have become a by-word in British business, and (as with other American newcomers, Emerson and Booz-Allen) they have helped to set a new pace and depth to other consultants.

Inevitably a good deal of mumbo-jumbo surrounds this new profession of consultancy; already in 1963 an Institute of Management Consultants had been set up, with its own code and rules. But their investigations are not always what they seem. 'A careful survey has now established the fact that the clients who approach a business consulting firm do so with one of two motives', wrote Professor Parkinson: 'On the one hand they may want scapegoats for the reorganisation upon which they have already decided. On the other they may want to prevent such a reorganisation taking place.'[1]

The consultants are the shock-troops of industry, and they have succeeded in storming the walls of companies, increasing the flow of ideas between them. On the careers of managers they have had a noticeable effect. They have helped to push up salary scales, and have increased the mobility of managers between firms. The consultants have exhaustive punch-card systems to match the right man to the right job, and some executives, even after having been placed in one firm, keep their names on the books.

Till recently, British managers were more obviously loyal to their companies than Americans, more likely to stay in one firm all their lives. The zigzag career of an American executive, hopping from one firm to another up to the top, was frowned on, and 'poaching' for staff on other companies' land was not done. 'We like to grow our own timber,' said a Shell personnel manager, and most of the timber is still home-grown (though even the biggest companies now try to keep the doors open for senior outsiders). Many senior pension schemes are still non-transferable; a married man in his forties knocks away a large prop if he leaves his firm. He is bound to it (in Lord Heyworth's phrase) by 'chains of gold'.

But since the early fifties, this pattern has been changing. The loss of empire, the invasion of American firms, and full employment have all encouraged managers to try moving around; and although the big companies still encourage the corporate spirit, the man who zigzags is not as suspect as he used to be. In the last few years company attitudes to their managers have become more ruthless and realistic. This is how John Tyzack, one of the most

[1] *The Director*, June, 1960.

penetrating of the management consultants, described the situation to me in 1964:

> Starting between two and three years ago, British industry generally speaking has really begun to cut out some of its fat, and is perhaps facing the drastic change imposed by the swing over in 1958–59 from a seller's to a buyer's market. We are at last beginning to realise that we have got to fight in a hard, tough, competitive world. This I believe is changing, perhaps rather too slowly, many of our attitudes. We are at last coming back to accepting that the job of management is to manage, and we are looking much more critically at many of the expensive fringe activities which have blown up our overheads since the war.
>
> One of the consequences of this change in industry has been the very high managerial unemployment in the upper age bracket. I think that this now is beginning to level off, but it does of course present an acute social problem. It is very much more difficult today than it was even a few years ago for the manager of fifty or over to get another job if he has been made redundant. In parallel with this, there is, I believe, a strong trend towards putting appreciably younger men into more senior jobs. In a sense I believe we are instinctively, not consciously, trying to jump over a generation, and to put into senior management young men who have been conditioned since the war to the new world in which we are living. There is no doubt at all that there is a sharply increasing demand for able, risk-taking younger men and that the shortage of such men is very great. I find it hard to come to any conclusion as to whether the supply is stationary and the demand is increasing, or whether we are no longer breeding enough of this type of man.
>
> I strongly suspect that the young man who is now emerging, that is, in his twenties, is very different from the last few generations. He is not willing to spend a long time learning a job: he demands the opportunity to learn quickly and to climb the ladder quickly. If he cannot get both in a company, then he is very much more willing than his predecessors to throw up his job and look elsewhere. He is quite unwilling to face a future which will give him a senior job in twenty years' time. He wants it by his middle thirties, and is going to do his best to get it. There is of course an increasing clash between this attitude of the young man and that of the very much older man who claims that nothing can take the place of experience, and that judgment must be based on long experience. I think that we, the older generation, are tending to ignore the vital factor which is essentially post-war, and that is the incredible rate not only of technological change, but social change, and it is only the young and the truly post war generation that is growing up conditioned to this rate of change.
>
> Another factor which is also I think facing managers and the type of man one needs is that once again, profit has become not only respectable but desirable—even for the publicly owned industries. Quite rightly, since the war we have placed great emphasis in our manage-

> ment training on producing men who were cost-conscious. Now we want managers who can be profit responsible. I think perhaps we all may accept that the true *entrepreneur* cannot be predicted or trained. On the whole he is rarely a man of any managerial competence, but he employs managers. I think we are really looking for a third category for which there is no descriptive title. I call him the 'business man'. He is a competent manager, but more than that he also has the touch of the *entrepreneur*, that quality of judgment which enables him to identify and back new ideas, but at the same time is also a reasonably good manager. He may not be an exceptionally good manager. It is rather like the salesman: the brilliant salesman rarely makes a good sales manager, but every good sales manager has on the whole been a competent salesman. All the new developments in automation and techniques will not in my opinion make any difference to the need for very high quality business men to run companies; they may well reduce the number of managers we need.

Why do managers change jobs? 'It's like divorce,' said one personnel consultant: 'money only comes into it when the marriage has already collapsed.' Advertisements often lay more emphasis on 'The Challenge of Tomorrow', 'Rapid Expansion' or 'a pleasant part of Southern England' than on the actual salary. A recurring motive for change is frustration—because of a bottleneck, a hide-bound board, a lack of appreciation of technical skills, or simply overpowering boredom and absence of challenge. The situation of politicians who often apparently need a new challenge to bring out new energy, is often echoed in industry. But money (and the status that goes with it) is becoming increasingly important to the manager: 'Whether we like it or not,' said John Tyzack, 'the younger man is in this context a good deal more materialist than his predecessors.'

Big firms compete hotly for first-class managers, but do they make full use of them? The impact of unqualified, analytically-minded graduates on the provincial, home-grown world of industry has often been painful: in some firms after the war as many as 75 per cent of the graduate recruits had left after a few years. The Leviathans are full of able young men doing crosswords and watching the clock; if they were coming to grips with factories and shop-stewards the wastage might be more forgivable, but all too often they are learning nothing except patience, and how to live with frustration. The older men resent the young 'management trainees' without technical knowledge, while the trainees feel the lack of a definite job or stimulus. The Acton Survey in 1956 found that:

> The creation of an élite corps tended to spoil the trainees and to antagonise other employees. Trainees became bored because they had so little opportunity for exercising responsibility, and because so much of their time was spent watching other people and being given useless information, such as that 'the pink slips go in this tray and the yellow in that'. And finally, at the end of the training period, companies were apt to find themselves landed with too many 'nice' people not suited for any particular job.[1]

But recently the big corporations have tended to adopt a more informal and less irksome approach to recruits. The idea of a 'management trainee' has—at least on the surface—become disguised: graduates are given definite workaday jobs and 'unobtrusively earmarked' for quick promotion.

THE MIND OF THE MANAGER

Industrial managers are a very mixed bunch. It has been roughly reckoned that there are 450,000 of them in Britain, of whom less than one per cent have had any formal training for the job.[2] Among the 3,300 analysed by the Acton Society Trust, average age 46, over half began as manual and clerical workers, one in two went to elementary or secondary school, one in five to a public school, one in five had a degree. But graduates and qualified men were much commoner among the younger ones, and by the mid-sixties the first post-war inrush of graduates will be reaching senior jobs—which is likely to bring industrial corporations closer in character to the other graduate professions of Whitehall, the law and the universities themselves.

Old businesses which have stopped growing, like railways or shipbuilding, can easily defeat scientific managers with what John Tyzack calls the 'law of maximum mediocrity': conformity and loyalty press managers to the toleration of the same second-rate uniformity. But in expanding firms—chemicals, electronics, television—there is more scope. Special managerial diseases (according to the Acton survey) afflict firms between twenty and thirty years old, where young men have grown old together—leaving a gap in the middle age-group. The go-ahead company of one generation—like Distillers' or Dunlop's—can often become the laggard of the next: and to a remarkable extent corporations behave like individuals, becoming middle-aged, corpulent, and

[1] *Acton*, p. 45.
[2] *Towards a Management Elite*, by Stephen Aris: *The Listener*, June 18, 1964.

sometimes just dying from old age. But some old-established firms, faced with threats or opportunities, have succeeded in reorganising themselves efficiently (Wallpaper Manufacturers, Ind Coope beer, South West Gas Board) and even the threat of take-over can transform a complacent firm—as ICI, without buying it, transformed Courtaulds.

The main opportunity for a modern manager comes with size. However conservative or ancient, big companies find themselves having to establish a proper management structure, or else disintegrate. A pyramid is built, with 'lines of responsibility' and layers, and once a firm grows beyond the ken of the board, managers enter their kingdom. In the industrial giants, the managers evolve their own values, and the social problems of the American manager are becoming visible here. The career of a corporation manager cuts across traditional societies and local communities; he is a 'spiralist'—moving towards the top in narrowing circles, from one community or country to another, gathering local experience before he settles in the head office as a senior executive. He has no local obligations, and is preoccupied with his company. 'The young business executive in Wigan', wrote William Watson, 'is likely to have more interests and friends in Manchester and London, or even in New York, than he has in Wigan.'[1] The British manager, like the American organisation man, becomes a 'free loader on the body politic'.[2] Taxation increases the enveloping influence of the corporation: the lunches, cocktails, chauffeur-driven cars and cigars inside the corporate womb contrast with the shepherd's pie in the suburban home. High income tax makes it hard for an individual family to compete against the neopaternalism of the company.

The impact of corporate communities on the traditional communities, centred round the squire, the church and the small town, has so far been very little studied in Britain: as the corporations become more international, revolving their 'spiralists' in wider circles, so they will presumably cut across local societies more sharply, substituting for the old landed aristocracy and its values the new aristocracy of the company managers (as in America). But so far this conflict, like others, has been blurred by the amateur tradition, and the reluctance of managers to appear to be managers.

Bigness creates vast new problems. The more layers there are, the longer a man takes to reach the top, and the less he can see all

[1] William Watson: The Managerial Spiralist. *Twentieth Century*, May, 1960.
[2] *See* Norton E. Long: *above*.

sides of the business. A young graduate taken on for his 'broad horizons' (a favourite management cliché), will find himself in a thicket of specialist problems, with no glimpse of horizon in sight; and specialisation is worse for the young technologist, moving from a university lab to a works lab, with little scope for handling people. ('The arts graduate needn't worry about competition from the scientists', said one personnel expert: 'they're like pygmies. They treat people as if they were chemicals: they want to wait until all the variables have been eliminated.') Thousands of scientists escape from laboratories to become managers—helped by the frequent weakening of scientific curiosity at the age of thirty. 'It was as easy as getting up in the morning', said Lord Fleck, of his change from research to management. But the Acton survey suggested that arts graduates were more likely to reach top management than scientists.[1] A PEP survey in 1961 showed that though arts men began with salaries on an average £70 lower, four years later they were more successful than scientists.[2] According to two American writers, Harbison and Myers, in an international survey in 1959, in Britain 'recruitment in top management is still biased in favour of the former public school boy and the Oxford and Cambridge graduate, and against persons with other educational qualifications such as engineers'.[3]

The Leviathans have developed an intricate mechanism of management, like the hierarchies of the civil service, geared not to parliament but to profit. 'Management by exception' has spread, defining the day-to-day responsibilities of junior managers, beyond which exceptional cases are passed to middle managers, with *their* defined responsibilities, who pass *their* exceptions to senior managers, and so to the board. Each manager can authorise expenditure up to a standard figure: he will evolve from a hundred-pound man, to a thousand-pound man, and eventually (like the directors of Shell) to being a half-million-pound man. The amount he can authorise, like his carpet or his desk, can define his status.

COMPUTERS

Into this intricate pyramid an alarming new master-manager has entered: a brain which can remember everything about everyone, which can check figures, write cheques, calculate turn-

[1] *Acton*, p. 24.

[2] PEP: *Salaries of Graduates in Industry*, March 1961.

[3] Frederick Harbison and Charles A. Myers: *Management in the Industrial World*, 1959. p. 314.

overs and notice exceptions in every factory and shop. No manager can ignore the influence of the neat grey machines, with their menacing names—Leo, Pegasus, Orion—silently working in their air-conditioned rooms, disgorging their ticker-tapes of figures. The computer is still only in its infancy in Britain, but clearly computers will eventually have a drastic effect on managers. A big one—like the £2 million machine installed by the Atomic Energy Authority —can discover quite new kinds of information, and every computer provides a brain-box of centralised knowledge which must strengthen the central management—and the accountants, who can unravel it. A computer can report on monthly sales from hundreds of shops a few days after the end of the month and can analyse changes and qualifications of staff. It can organise 'management by exception', by letting out a mechanical scream when the figures go wrong. As one consultant put it: 'A big computer can put a giant corporation back into being a one-man firm.' If the computer is properly exploited, a company must be 'bent round' it, and the pyramid changed in quite painful ways.

Computers will certainly encourage centralisation, allowing managers to control branches at a distance. In Boots or Marks and Spencer, computers will enable headquarters to keep count of every article sold, to have it automatically replaced, and to note the daily trend of sales. 'It will put the shop manager into the position of being not much more than a housekeeper,' said one management consultant. This centralisation may make it harder for junior men to gain the experience—particularly the scope for mistakes—which can train them for senior management. The emergencies which have given so many office-boys their first lucky break, revealing them to the boss, are in danger of being eliminated. The computer cannot usurp the rôle of the *senior* managers: a man must still assess the problem in the light of the facts, through his own instinct. But, rather as television can by-pass the small salesman, so computers may by-pass the small manager.

A MANAGERIAL PROFESSION?

> I do not believe that business is the only career in this country for which no formal intelligent preparation is called.
>
> *Lord Franks, November, 1963.*

Are managers a profession? 'The difference between industry as it exists today and a profession is, then, simple and unmistakable,' wrote the late R. H. Tawney, forty years ago, in *The Acquisitive Society*: 'the latter is organised, imperfectly indeed, but none the less genuinely, for the performance of *duties*.' Tawney saw the new managerial class and the 'gradual disengagement of managerial technique from financial interests' providing the beginnings of professionalism. 'It marks the emergence within the very heart of the capitalist industry of a force which, both in status and in economic interest, is allied to the wage-earners rather than to the property-owners.'

Tawney also believed that the new managers could only be rescued from preoccupation with money-making by nationalisation. But in the forty years since, without wholesale nationalisation, managers have become much more professional-minded, in Britain as in America. 'In a short thirty years we have passed from a corporate order whose managerial style was derived from the so-called "robber-barons", the divine-right Bayers, and the public-be-damned Vanderbilts, to the business-school-trained, public-relations-conscious professional of the highly complex corporate bureaucracy of today.'[1]

In Britain, professionalisation has been the catchword since the war, in this as in other occupations. The British Institute of Management produces papers and awards diplomas in management. The Administrative Staff College—a big country house on the Thames near Henley—provides gentle three-month courses for middle-managers. On the other hand, in America, there have been signs of a reaction against the mystique of management, with its 'elaborate witchcraft replete with high priests (public-relations experts and public-opinion testers) with rituals (brainstorming, market research), with incantations (business serves the public) and with a vast literature of holy writ'.[2] 'Management is a means to an end, not an end in itself,' William Whyte pleaded: 'The rôle of the manager is quite tough enough without being saddled with theology.'[3]

But bigness, specialisation, computers and the tools of scientific management have all tended towards the formation of a much more defined race of managers separated, discreetly but firmly, from the rest. 'The experience of those who have paid most attention to management development,' wrote the Acton survey, 'suggests that such early selection and training is essential if

[1] Norton E. Long: Chapter in *Corporation in Modern Society*, 1959.
[2] Bernard D. Nossiter: *Management's Cracked Voice*. Harvard Business Review, 1959.
[3] Eric Moonman: *The Manager and the Organisation* (Introduction), 1961.

managers are to have the necessary variety of experience, and if they are to be given opportunities to develop while they are still flexible enough to do so. To those who object that this creates an élite, the answer is that this is inevitable.'[1] Although much of industry is still concerned with ordinary people doing ordinary things, the Leviathans are beginning to evolve their own breed of mandarins, like the Whitehall ones, and with the same dangers of separation and unconscious arrogance. Much of the argument about the professionalisation of management boils down, in the end, to how far such an élite is desirable: and the argument flared up again when in June, 1961, Balliol College announced that they were establishing a research fellowship in Management Studies, endowed by the Institute of Directors. 'The same services that Balliol has rendered to the civil service, to politics, diplomacy, the Law and the Church,' said the Master of Balliol, with characteristic Balliol smugness: 'it is capable of rendering to business. In the last century the Northcote-Trevelyan Report transformed the civil service into a model of integrity and efficiency. A similar reform has long been overdue for recruitment into business administration. The universities have been slow to respond, and where they have responded the result has not always been what is needed. But we believe that we should make a start here and now.'[2]

But Balliol's blessing was not welcomed with unmixed enthusiasm, and a long *Times* correspondence ensued. 'One can see it clearly,' said Dr. V. L. Allen on the BBC: 'Not a new struggling discipline but one sumptuously provided for, dominating and dominant, with the rest of the social sciences serving it from odd corners, basements and attics . . . Universities which run management training schemes are helping to rationalise the present power structure in industry. They are, therefore, providing a service for the controlling élite . . . Perhaps the possibility of serving the country's centres of economic power is irresistibly attractive when compared with the task of investigating the underdog, the unemployed, the pathological case, a task which has so often been their lot.'

'The universities must come to terms with management,' replied J. H. Smith in a broadcast the following week: 'I think Dr. Allen finds it difficult to accept this because he has little enthusiasm for managers, or for élites. I can sympathise, but feel bound to draw his attention to an authority whom I am sure he respects: more

[1] *Acton.* p. 49.
[2] *See The Times,* June 2, 1961.

than forty years ago, Sidney Webb wrote: "Under any social order from now to Utopia a management is indispensable and all-enduring . . . The question is not: 'Will there be a management élite,' but 'What sort of élite will it be?' " '

Between the values of universities and those of industry there continues to be acrimonious cross-purposes. 'What distresses me,' said Donald Stokes, the managing director of Leyland Motors in August 1964, himself apprenticed at the age of sixteen, 'is the number of boys with academic training who are completely useless.' And a controversial broadside was fired by Paul Chambers of ICI in June 1964, who said to the National Union of Teachers: 'How often have I met men of unblemished character, of high academic achievement, but whose life, sheltered from the harsh need to make important decisions, has left them timid and irresolute, or stubborn because of the fear of making a mistake . . . I have too often attended meetings chaired by dons who have been pathetically indecisive and have allowed discussions to drag on and to wander in the most undisciplined manner into wholly irrelevant bypaths.'

The old universities have continued to resist the idea of management as an academic study (which had begun at Pennsylvania University as early as 1881), but by 1963 there were strong demands that Britain should have some kind of equivalent to the Harvard Business School and its many offshoots. Early in 1963 a 'Neddy' report recommended a management school in the interests of productivity, and later in the year the Robbins report on higher education proposed 'at least two major postgraduate schools associated with a well established institution'. Several groups of businessmen devised rival plans for management schools, and in August 1963, Lord Franks, the Lord-High-Everything-Else of the British Establishment, was asked to mediate. His report, published three months later, and almost immediately accepted, advocated two new schools, one at Manchester University and one in London, jointly run by the London School of Economics and Imperial College. The schools would each cost about a million pounds, and would provide a year's course for both postgraduates and 'post-experience' students from industry.

The establishment of these new colleges marks a new stage in the growth of a managerial élite. But controversy still rages as to how far management can, and should, become an authentic profession; for professionalisation brings with it all the perils of the 'organisation man', and the effective yardstick of business will remain, not professional standards, but ability to make profit, which must always be unconventional and unprofessional. Profit will always be the criterion of success, and the manager's prestige is identified with profits as a civil servant's is with CMG's. 'Not only his corporate loyalty to the firm,' Anthony Crosland has written, 'but all his personal motives—professional pride, ambition, self-realisation, desire for power and prestige—find their fulfilment in high output and rapid growth, and hence high profits.'[1]

[1] *Corporation in Modern Society*, p. 266.

28

ACCOUNTANTS

Accountants are the witch-doctors of the modern world and willing to turn their hands to any kind of magic.

Lord Justice Harmer, February, 1964.

Cold, passive, noncommittal, with eyes like codfish . . . minus bowels, passion or a sense of humour.

Elbert Hubbard (describing the typical auditor in America).

THE accountants, the fastest-growing profession in Britain, stand to the world of corporate business much as the lawyer stood to the nineteenth-century world of rich men's property. They are the priesthood of industry: the more fragmented and diversified a company becomes, the more important becomes the man who can disentangle the threads of profitability that hold it together. Few people in a vast company are in a position to see over the tops of the trees. An able accountant can, and from his knowledge comes his power. The telegraphic address of the Institute of Chartered Accountants is the word UNRAVEL.

The growth of the profession has been spectacular. In 1940 there were about 34,000 accountants: by 1963 there were over 68,000—three times the number of lawyers and thirty times the number of barristers. Their power has been enormously enhanced by taxation, which can mould the shape of a corporation, of which few people except accountants can make sense. The 'innumeracy' (as Crowther called it)—the ignorance and fear of figures—of the average British businessman has added to the accountants' mystique. 'It's pathetic,' said one management consultant, 'to see how accountants pull wool over the eyes of the engineers.'

Accountants or former accountants play a decisive rôle in British industry. In the slumpish times of the twenties and thirties, several large firms were rescued by accountants, as Lever Brothers was rescued by Francis D'Arcy Cooper, and since the war there has been a massive flow of accountants into industry.

According to one estimate, they quadrupled in 25 years, reaching 10,000 by 1958.[1] Among the most powerful present-day accountants are Sir Ellis Hunter, chairman of Dorman, Long: John Davis, the managing director of the Rank Organisation; Sir Halford Reddish, chairman of Rugby cement; Philip Shirley, finance director of British Railways; and Henry Lazell, chairman of the Beecham Group. Paul Chambers of ICI comes from that sanctuary of the priesthood, the Inland Revenue. In politics, thirty-seven accountant candidates stood for parliament in 1964, of whom only seven got in. But they included Ernest Marples and Jack Diamond, the influential Labour accountant from Leeds, who became Chief Secretary to the Treasury.[2]

The accountants, however powerful, have been a pariah profession. They are a striking example of the British reluctance to accept new occupations; like actuaries or scientists, they have come in through the back door. Their beginnings were squalid. The first accountants, who began practising in the city about 1840, were invariably associated with bankruptcy and liquidations; like undertakers, they had an aura of gloom. With the passing of the Companies Act of 1862 and the Bankruptcy Act of 1869—which provided for the appointment of an accountant for creditors—the occupation became much more important, but still associated with calamity. Ernest Cooper, a founder of Cooper Brothers, has described their position when he first went to the city in 1864: 'We could hardly, south of the Tweed, claim to be a profession. There was absolutely no organisation or co-operation, no Institute or Society, no examinations, very few articled clerks, no newspaper, no library, no benevolent fund, and not even a dining club or golf club. Our social position was not enviable . . . I well remember that to be seen talking to, or having your office entered by, an accountant, was to be avoided, particularly in the stressful times of 1866.'

In 1880 'The Institute of Chartered Accountants in England and Wales' was founded, and the job became a profession with its own rules of conduct. With the expansion of the joint stock companies, which required independent auditors by law, and the advance of taxation, accountants multiplied, and soon became associated with normality, rather than disaster. But they never acquired the dignity of lawyers or doctors. Their education

[1] *See The Future Rôle of the Accountant in Industry*, by W. W. Fea, Institute of Chartered Accountants in England and Wales, 1958.

[2] *See The Accountant*, October 24, 1964.

remains stark: there are few university courses, no Inns of Courts, little sense of brotherhood. Most accountants are taught at evening classes or at 'crammers', run by commercial firms for profit—a bleak initiation. Their training, like that of actuaries, neglects the broader aspects of their job: 'For an accountant to have no knowledge of fundamental economics is rather like a doctor who knows nothing of chemistry or biology or an engineer who is ignorant of physics,' said Professor Eden, who has the chair in accountancy at the London School of Economics; 'I think the system of training accountants is about a hundred years behind the times.'[1]

In Scotland the status of accountants, as of teachers and engineers, is higher—partly because the courts made earlier use of accountants: Sir Walter Scott, as early as 1820, recommended that his nephew 'cannot follow a better line than that of an accountant'. Edinburgh had its society of accountants in 1854, thirty years before England. The Scots training for accountants is broader, and insists on higher preliminary qualifications.

More than half the 68,000 accountants work in accountants' firms, run by partnerships, like lawyers or doctors—varying from single men advising on taxation, to international institutions. Four firms dominate the profession: one or other of their names can usually be seen above the annual reports of any industrial giant. This is their likely order of size (they are much too secretive to divulge the size of their staff):

Peat Marwick Mitchell
Deloitte, Plender Griffiths
Price Waterhouse
Cooper Brothers

In the city, their incantatory names have acquired a respectability equal to Barings or Freshfields. The arrival of their senior partners, in bowlers and black coats, far from suggesting calamity, brings calm and confidence.

Their main job is still auditing, and once a year their emissaries arrive at their clients' offices to check through last year's ledgers. It is a job of massive tedium, checking the past rather than visualising the future; though nowadays with the mechanisation and standardisation of accounting, auditors must concentrate on checking systems, rather than go through all the figures. The

[1] Quoted in 'Accountants in Power' by Stephen Aris: *Twentieth Century*, Spring, 1964.

auditor is the key to the company system—the representative of the public's interest, the licensed spy for the shareholders. His essential quality is independence: if figures are wrong or misleading, he must say so. For Deloitte's or Cooper's to 'qualify their report'—to suggest that sums have not been accounted for—is worse than an 'observation' from the Governor of the Bank.

Auditing occupies about 80 per cent of most accountants' time, but as the large partnerships have grown in resources, so they have provided other services. After checking through a company's books, they can know more about its workings than most directors; they can advise on taxation problems, systems of costing, pension schemes, capital structure—and more recently on office organisation, for which the big firms have special departments, rivalling the management consultants. The 'Big Four' have broader international connections than most bankers and consultants, with networks of branches, and their services and advice are much cheaper than the banks'.

As corporate business has grown more complex, so the advice of accountants has grown weightier: they can analyse not only honesty and competence, but general health and prospects. Travelling from one corporation to another, they can compare their problems—acting as business doctors and specialists on industrial anatomy, putting their stethoscopes near the heart, checking the blood stream, diagnosing the curious diseases and intestinal troubles of Leviathans. In a crisis their advice can be at least as valuable as bankers'—for instance Binder Hamlyn's advice to Courtaulds in 1962.

A very heavy weapon is the 'special investigation'. A large company planning a project, a bridge, or a take-over, will often commission accountants to report on its feasibility, and (in accountants' words) 'generally to introduce a sense of realism'. After engineers have drawn up plans for a dam, a group of accountants will fly out, peruse the figures, compare them with other projects, cross-examine the engineers, and produce their own—often more pessimistic—report. Broad investigations are now beginning to be used by the government and even the Treasury: in 1961 Ernest Marples, the Minister of Transport, commissioned Peat Marwick's—often regarded as the Establishment accountants—to prepare a report on shipbuilding contracts, as part of his campaign to stimulate the industry. But the Treasury is only beginning to make use of outside accountants as an instrument of control: it is now clear that if a full investigation had been made into the British Railways modernisation plan before it was approved, scores of millions could have been saved.

This kind of accountancy is concerned not with the past but with the future, and it requires from the accountant what he (like a solicitor or a bank manager) most shrinks from—an opinion. 'Clients are not impressed by a report,' wrote Sir Henry Benson, senior partner of Cooper Brothers and son-in-law of D'Arcy Cooper,[1] 'however detailed or painstaking, unless it is concluded by a firm opinion. I do not suggest that the accountant's traditional attitude of caution should change or that he should cease to be impartial. The point I am seeking to make is that if we are to be of real use to our clients, we must be prepared to give a common-sense judgment on the facts that we have discovered.'

This new scope depresses some other businesses—particularly engineers. For, in so far as accountants are known to make decisions, they are liable to say No. To a team of engineers, no nightmare is worse than a group of men arriving to introduce realism (= pessimism), to envisage bad weather, floods and 'contingent liabilities' —that menacing accountants' phrase—to shake their heads and ask awkward questions. Accountants indignantly deny that they are habitual no-men: 'a true and fair picture' is their object, and some accountants, certainly, can become quite romantic about vast and risky expenditures. But their whole history, beginning with bankruptcies and flourishing in the age of slump, has filled them with a vivid sense of disaster. Imagination and daring are not their first requirements; and the business doctors are sometimes unable to diagnose the most deadly of diseases—the creeping caution and hypochondria induced by some of the doctors themselves.

TAX

The strongest source of power for the accountant is tax. Since income tax was introduced by Pitt in 1799, taxation has influenced the pattern of society. It helps to account for the spate of weddings in March, the generosity of fathers to children, the number of authors living abroad, the boom of life assurance, the largeness of businessmen's lunches and the smallness of their dinners. While in America taxation has become the province of lawyers, in Britain it has been largely taken over by accountants.

[1] Paper to the Institute of Chartered Accountants in 1958.

Company tax brought the accountant into the industry, income tax and surtax brought him into the home. Tax avoidance, juggling with schedules, covenants, domiciles and beneficiaries, have made the accountant as important to the middle-class family as a dentist or solicitor; avoidance is regarded no longer as a nasty trickery, but as a private duty—a perpetual and inevitable war.

'No man in this country,' said Lord Clyde, President of the Scottish Court of Session, 'is under the smallest obligation, moral or other, so to arrange his legal relations as to enable the Inland Revenue to put the largest shovel into his stores. The Inland Revenue is not slow . . . to take every advantage which is open to it under the taxing statutes for the purpose of depleting the tax-payers' pocket. And the tax-payer is, in like manner, entitled to be astute enough to prevent, so far as he honestly can, the depletion of his means by the Revenue.'[1]

At the centre of this great tax web is the much-abused Board of Inland Revenue. 'The Revenue' itself maintains a corps of 3,752 inspectors and 22,075 tax officers, at a cost of £31 million for 1964–5.

Tax-collecting is not very popular, and since the war the Revenue have had difficulty in recruiting—and keeping—enough people: by 1961 they were 300 inspectors short. Tax experts have become more and more in demand by industry, moving from one side of the fence to the other—from gamekeepers to poachers. As the rules have become more intricate, so both sides have come to talk a private language—like burglars and safe-makers, progressing from new evasion devices, like 'scissors' or 'share-stripping', to new attempts at safeguard.

The Revenue successfully preserves an impassive façade. But it is not entirely rigid in its methods of extortion. If it cannot obtain money from someone who is visibly broke, it is quite capable of making a bargain, and settling for a monthly payment—keeping the cow alive in order to milk it. In the field of show business—where large sums of money are made, spent, and then demanded—the relationships with the Revenue are most bitter. Actors and musicians, unable to pay taxes, find themselves bonded for life to the Revenue, like Elizabethan spendthrifts to usurers.

[1] Quoted in *The Tax Gatherers* by James Coffield, 1960, p. 98.

But the Revenue are not wholly inhuman. Sir Alan Herbert once wrote a cheque, duly stamped and crossed, in this form:

Dear Bankers, PAY the undermentioned hounds
The shameful sum of FIVE-AND-EIGHTY-POUNDS £85.0.0
By 'hound', of course, by custom, one refers
To SPECIAL (INCOME TAX) COMMISSIONERS
And these progenitors of woe and worry
You'll find at LYNWOOD ROAD, THAMES DITTON, SURREY.
This is the *second* lot of tax, you know,
On money that I earned two years ago
(The shark, they say, by no means Nature's Knight,
Will rest contented with a single bite:
The barracuda, who's a fish more fell,
Comes back and takes the other leg as well).
Two years ago. But things have changed since then.
I've reached the age of three-score years and ten.
My earnings dwindle: and the kindly State
Gives me a tiny pension—with my mate.
You'd think the State would generously roar
'At least, he shan't pay SURTAX any more'.
Instead, by this unChristian attack
They get two-thirds of my poor pension back.
Oh, very well. No doubt it's for the best;
At all events, pray do as I request:
And let the good old customs be enforced—
Don't cash this cheque, unless it is endorsed.

The cheque was cashed and an official reply came back from the Office of the Special Commissioners of Income Tax:

Dear Sir, it is with pleasure that I thank
You for your letter, and the order to your bank
To pay the sum of five and eighty pounds
To those here whom you designate as hounds.
Their appetite is satisfied. In fact
You paid too much and I am forced to act,
Not to repay you, as perchance you dream,
Though such a course is easy, it would seem.
Your liability for later years
Is giving your accountants many tears:
And till such time as they and we can come
To amicable settlement on the sum
That represents your tax-bill to the State
I'll leave the overpayment to its fate.
I do not think this step will make you frown:
The sum involved is only half-a-crown.

Yours faithfully,
A. L. Grove.

Sir Alan replied:

> I thank you, Sir, but am afraid
> Of such a rival in my trade:
> One never should encourage those—
> In future I shall pay in prose.

29

CHAIRMEN

I wish I knew if I was chairman of this company,
It would make a lot of difference at conferences:
Gorgeous conferences we have, simply gorgeous,
Finest in the City, I imagine.
I am always in the top chair, but the boys will never
let on if I'm chairman or not.

D. B. Wyndham Lewis: Lament.

WITH all the talk in the past twenty years about the 'managerial revolution' it is often assumed that the revolution is virtually complete—that most of industry is run by committees of managerial men, divorced from ownership or inheritance. This is far from the truth. Only in a few giant companies which have outgrown their families, such as Shell, Unilever or ICI, has the revolution been achieved; at the top of most companies an individual or a family still wields large influence. The old race of managers, who worked their way up through the factory without special training or outside experience, like insurance or bank managers, have not often been strong enough to break into the board and achieve a dominant position. Only since the war have the new race of graduate professional managers had the confidence and all-round experience to challenge the old boardroom traditions, and most will not be reaching the boardroom age for another ten years. The conflict between the old family tradition, still with shades of the amateur squire, and the new professional managers, though often confused, is fundamental. It is the few hundred top industrial managers, rather than, for instance, a few hundred MPs, who will determine the economic strength of Britain.

The typical British business is not the anonymous corporation, but the family firm. In 1959 a third of the profits in the manufacturing, building and distribution industries were earned by private companies, not quoted on the Stock Exchange.[1] Even after private companies have 'gone public', as we shall see, family interests remain dominant. When Dr. Copeman in 1955 conducted a

[1] *See* Radcliffe Report, p. 82.

survey of 1,243 directors in public companies with assets over £1 million, he found that 28 per cent of the directors had succeeded their fathers in the same firm and no less than 8 per cent had succeeded as the fourth or fifth generation.[1] In the older industries, such as shipbuilding, cotton or printing, many firms are still run by the great-great-grandsons of the founders, descending from the industrial revolution.

FAMILY FIRMS

The old family firm has a character as different from the managerial corporation as a tree from a house, and over the decades it has taken on some curious organic characteristics. Portraits of the bearded founder and his progeny hang in the front office, retainers reminisce about the chairman as a schoolboy, the chairman's secretary looks after tomatoes from the kitchen garden or the children's return to school after the holidays, between filing invoices for machinery. The sense of family spreads out from the boardroom to the whole factory, and in a small town the company can dominate the social life; at Richard Clay's printing works in Suffolk (where I once worked) a sixth of the population of Bungay worked for the firm, and nearly everyone had a son, a brother or a husband in the company.

To the workers in the smaller companies, the family *is* the firm. They may resent young Mr. Charles, straight down from Cambridge, being introduced round the factory, to become a director over their heads in a few years' time; or doing odd shopping jobs for the chairman's wife; or the patronising airs of Mrs. Peter, Mrs. Tom and Mrs. Alan at the annual staff outing. But the family represents a simple embodiment of something which is impersonal and complicated, and young Mr. Charles is its continuity. Compared to a managerial corporation, a family firm is like a monarchy compared to a republic:[2] it is more interesting and more comprehensible. The mystique and inertia which can gather round a family chairman after a few generations may eventually bring the whole company to disaster, but in the meantime it is very reassuring, for trade is insecure and restless, while a family is secure and continuous, loyal and visible.

Some family firms have achieved equilibrium over generations, settling to a convenient size, gathering subsidiary families round

[1] *See* G. H. Copeman: *Leaders of British Industry*, 1955. p. 97.
[2] *See* Bagehot, Chapter 2.

them—of book-keepers, factory hands, craftsmen, each handing down jobs from father to son. In the smallest firms—shops or builders—there may be no incentive to grow beyond a single boss.

A few family firms have grown to international dimensions, while still remaining private companies. Probably the most celebrated is Wedgwood's, founded in 1759 by Josiah Wedgwood —who himself came from a long line of potters. He personally invented most of the designs and processes which made Wedgwood famous: he was an extraordinary mixture of eighteenth-century dabbler, technician, businessman and Fellow of the Royal Society. Since then Wedgwood's have maintained a continuous family tradition; not only the board, but many of the workmen are descended from the original eighteenth-century people. The present chairman, Josiah (author of *The Economics of Inheritance*), belongs to the sixth generation, and by 1920 the tenth generation of Wedgwoods was already in the company. The *Wedgwood Review* has such headings as 'Mr. Josiah on the US recession', or 'Brush up your Wedgwood', a quiz about the firm's history. But the Wedgwood family have branched out into barons, historians and artists, intermarried with the Cambridge intellectual dynasties: recently there has been a shortage of young Wedgwoods interested in business, and the family tradition seems likely to dwindle.

Pilkington's, the glass makers at St. Helens, are much the largest private family firm. Their founder, William Pilkington, made a success of the family wine business, and invested some money in the St. Helens Crown Glass company in 1826. Two years later the firm ran into trouble; William bought out all the partners except his brother-in-law, and set up as Greenall and Pilkington. His four sons were equally dynamic and fascinated with new processes: they experimented with electric light and installed a telephone as early as 1880. In the next decade the experimental instinct waned, and they were slow to develop safety glass, but later they did a deal with Triplex, and now control safety-glass factories in Australia and South Africa and South America, with large shares in Canada's biggest firm, Duplate. By the 1950's, with the help of an enterprising young Pilkington, they had caught up again technically, and spent £4 million on the new 'float glass' process.[1] Their chairman, Sir Harry, is not only a very successful businessman, but has been a director of the Bank of England (to which he bicycles) and chairman of the royal commissions on doctors' salaries and television.

[1] *See* J. C. Barker, *Pilkington Brothers and the Glass Industry*, 1960.

Family firms can break up in several ways. The family may lose interest, or die out. They may encounter such powerful competition that—like the components of Barclays Bank, Imperial Tobacco or ICI—they have to merge with other families. They may find death duties insuperable. They may need extra capital for development and be forced to 'go public' on the stock exchange. The change-over from a family firm to a managerial corporation is a recurring drama of our time. Instead of the loved and hated old name, like Morris or Austin, there are initials—BMC, AEI, BAC. Instead of an impossible old boss there are committees and 'they'. The workers who cursed the old man now have only a committee to blame, and reminisce gloomily about the rough old days of the bicycle shop.

The British readily feel sentimental about family firms. Where the firm revolves round one dynamic personality, the transition to a committee can mean a loss of vigour; but many second or third generations of a family are more likely to be complacent than dynamic. Not many families—even of bankers—are ruthless enough to exclude nitwits from the succession, or fecund enough to produce enough first-class managers. The drawing-room privilege which hangs about the boardroom can easily act as a disincentive to ambitious outsiders. The chairman himself, who must be moderately efficient to survive, is not the main obstacle: it is the periphery of nephews, cousins and particularly sons-in-law who so often clog the wheels of management, and by the assumption of privilege damage the dignity of professional managers.

In the more backward industries, family complacency must take much of the blame. The incompetence of shipbuilding, the obstinacy of machine-tool companies, the medieval habits of many printers, often emanate from grandsons and great-grandsons of founders: the company is handed down, with the furniture, the heirlooms and the country house, and the ships and machines become part of the family estate. The undeniable charms of the family firm, like those of the palace or the squire, are dangerous for a country that must come quickly to terms with change.

TWENTY-SIX CHAIRMEN

Among the largest firms in the country, there is still often a family or an individual with a dominating influence on the board: even among American giants, Fords and du Ponts are still controlled by Fords and du Ponts. The managers may be in control of the day-to-day running, but in major investment decisions—which can make or break the company—the family can still be decisive. Below are the twenty-six companies which in 1964 qualified for the 'hundred million club'—having (British) assets of over £100 million. (Assets are not a satisfactory guide to size, but the other two yardsticks, profits and turnover, can be equally misleading, and turnover is still frequently secret.) Below are brief notes on the twenty-six firms and their chairmen.

Company	*Headquarters*	*Assets* (£ million)
Shell	London	1,003[1]
ICI	London	893
British Petroleum	London	659·3[2]
Unilever Ltd.[3]	London	384·4
British-American Tobacco	London	370·5
Imperial Tobacco	Bristol	322
P and O	London	259·4
Courtaulds	London	238·9
Distillers	London and Edinburgh	226
Guest, Keen and Nettlefolds	Smethwick	217·9
Esso Petroleum	London	210·8
Bowater Paper	London	197·7
Great Universal Stores	London and Manchester	196·8
Tube Investments	London and Birmingham	184·4
AEI	London	174·4
Steel Company of Wales	Port Talbot	173·2
Vickers	London	166·9
Dunlop Rubber	London	145
Stewarts & Lloyds	Glasgow	140·4
United Steel	Sheffield	138·8
Allied Breweries	London	134·9
Reed Paper Group	London	132·1
Ford Motor	Dagenham	127·9
J. & P. Coats, Patons & Baldwins	Glasgow	116·8
British Motor Corporation	Birmingham	108·9
Turner & Newall	Manchester	106·9

1. *Shell Transport and Trading (Assets £1,003 million)*
(*See* pp. 480–9.)

[1] Shell Transport & Trading (British holding Company)
[2] Group assets.
[3] Including interests in Commonwealth countries.

2. *Imperial Chemical Industries* (*Assets £893 million*)
(*See* pp. 497–505.)

3. *British Petroleum* (*Assets £659·3 million*)
Half-owned by the British government—though its influence is small: the two government directors are regarded as having 'gone native', and they both find that their apparent involvement with the British flag can be embarrassing in their negotiations abroad. BP, like Shell, is a vast oil concern, owning 50 per cent of Kuwait oil, 40 per cent of the consortium in Iran, and 24 per cent of the Iraq Petroleum Company. BP (formerly Anglo-Iranian) were at first less crafty and sensitive to post-war changes than Shell, as they learnt to their cost in 1951 at Abadan—since when they have quickly put on a more international face, and given Shell a run for their money. Like Shell, they long ago grew beyond the control of one man. Their present chairman, Maurice Bridgeman, belongs to the civil-service school of oilmen; he has spent his career in BP or in government service, but he has an Eton-and-Whites background and banking connections. His father was Lloyd George's Home Secretary; his brother, Lord Bridgeman, is a director of Warburg's Mercury Securities, his daughter married a Baring.

4. *Unilever Ltd.* (*British part*) (*Assets £384·4 million*[1])
(*See* pp. 489–497.)

5. *British-American Tobacco* (*Assets £370·5 million*)
Formed in 1902 to grow and sell tobacco abroad (it still sells no cigarettes in Britain) with the rights to the export business of Imperial Tobacco (see below), which owns some of its shares. It employs 100,000 people with 100 factories in 50 countries, but has only 4,000 employees in Britain. Its American subsidiary is estimated as the third largest tobacco company there. Their chairman, Sir Duncan Oppenheim, is a very civilised solicitor who came from the city firm of Linklaters and Paines—a comparatively rare example of a lawyer-chairman. He has exhibited an action painting, and is chairman of the Council of Industrial Design, and of the Council of the Royal College of Art.

6. *Imperial Tobacco* (*Assets £322 million*)
An extraordinary example of continuing, rather sleepy family

[1] Including interest in Commonwealth countries.

influence in a giant firm. It was formed in 1901, as a protection against American invasion, out of three big family firms—Wills, Players and Churchmans—and several smaller ones. Together with Gallahers—of which it owns 37 per cent—it produces 90 per cent of British cigarettes. Its headquarters is a great red-brick palace in Bristol, from which it directs its various Branches—which are left to compete with each other on a narrow but hectic territory. The parent company, known as 'IT Co' maintains an aloof, mahogany attitude to the sales race, but it benefits from its monopoly position by its influence with shops. Wills has always been the dominating influence, and Lord Dulverton, head of the family, is on the board. The last chairman, Roger Clarke, came from one of the family firms (William Clarke) which made up Imperial. But John Partridge, elected chairman in March 1964, went straight into Imperial Tobacco from a local school in Bristol, and worked his way up from the bottom, as a junior clerk at five pounds a month. He helped to start the statistical section, and became company secretary after the war. He has become the main spokesman and dogged defender of the tobacco industry against charges of dealing in death. He smokes about twenty cigarettes a day.

7. *P and O Steam Navigation* (*Assets £259·4 million*)

The biggest shipping line in the world, with about 350 ships and a large interest in the biggest private airline (BUA). Shipping, like the navy, faces extreme changes, but has been slower to face up to them. Cunard is run by Brocklebanks and Bates's, Union Castle and Clan lines are run by the Cayzer cousins. P and O, though a huge public company, has strong family traditions: there are two Geddes on the board, plus an Earl and a Viscount. But the company is largely run by two Etonian brothers, Sir Donald Anderson, the chairman, and Sir Colin, an art-collector who lives in a big old house in Hampstead. They are the sons of a previous chairman of Anderson, Green, part of the P and O empire. They have helped to change the face of P and O, with comparatively daring ship-designs and some civilised décor by Sir Hugh Casson.

Sir Donald has made tough statements about the shipping industry, and has rejected the idea of government subsidies as 'a form of artificial respiration for the half-drowned' (1960).

Like other companies, P and O has suffered heavily in the shipping depression of 1961–2, which produced painful self-examination and some modernisation, particularly in salesmanship. It has also spread into the field of oil tankers, and is now the biggest independent tanker owner. But it is wary of diversification, and loyal to the sea: 'The company's purpose, established position and experience lie in shipping,' said Sir Donald in 1963: 'The company is receptive to other investment possibilities outside shipping. Any growth in this direction is, however, not to be hurried.'

8. *Courtaulds* (*Assets £238·9 million*)

Up till January, 1962 Courtaulds seemed, and in many respects was, a stately company of the less aggressive kind. The chairman, Sir John Hanbury Williams, belonged to the courtier tradition—son of a general, born in Windsor Castle, married a princess. Courtaulds was secretive, public-spirited, afflicted with troubles in textiles, and not much interest in its shareholders. The chairman-elect, Sir Alan Wilson, F.R.S., had the reputation of being an outstanding scientist, but not primarily a businessman.

Two months later ICI had tried and failed to take it over, and Courtaulds emerged with a very different face: it spent £250,000 on ruthless advertising, effectively accused ICI of a poor research record compared to its own, and convincingly revealed its own programme of expansion and future profits; it also displayed an impressive director, Frank Kearton, an F.R.S. who began with ICI, who did much to save the company from absorption. He and his colleagues swept away reticence and protocol, and gave an impression of both scientific and commercial enterprise. 'When we fought, we stuck our necks out,' said Kearton afterwards: 'A lot of people thought we were mad. And that made us much more ready to take risks and tread on toes.'[1]

Afterwards Sir Alan Wilson left Courtaulds, and an aged baronet Sir Dallas Bernard was elected chairman, succeeded in November 1964 by Frank Kearton, whose prestige had shot up after his aggressive intervention. The company has succeeded in keeping up the stimulus produced by the threatened takeover: 'The spirit throughout is entirely different', said the finance director, A. W. Knight, 'and although this change is largely an attitude of mind, it has loomed large in our profits.'[2] The change has been compared to the change in British generalship in the two world wars; it needed a war to make the change.

[1] *Business Week*: December 31, 1963.

[2] *Business Week*, February 8, 1964.

The board of seventeen still includes two Courtaulds and two former Tory cabinet ministers, Lord Eccles and Aubrey Jones; but the company is now effectively ruled by the triumvirate of Kearton, Knight, and H. R. Mathys, all deputy-chairmen, who together fended off the ICI bid.

9. *Distillers* (*Assets £226 million*)

A near monopoly of Scotch whisky, including most of the well-known names: it was formed from a group of family distillers in 1877, based on Edinburgh. Since then, its whisky profits have been so huge that it has expanded first into industrial alcohol then into petro-chemicals, plastics, etc. It also owns both Gordons and Booths gin. But Distillers, like Imperial Tobacco, shows signs of monopolitis, and is less enterprising than before the war. Between the whisky and the industrial sides is a strange contrast: the whisky people are mellow and family-bound, entrenched in Edinburgh society, each brand with its own board, competing with other brands. The industrial people are much more technical and self-made. The two converge on the main board, which includes Major Macdonald-Buchanan of Black and White, Lord Forteviot of Dewars. The chairman, Ronald Cumming, whose family has been in Scotch whisky for four generations, is a former Scottish rugger international who for much of his career has been concerned with exporting Johnny Walker's.

10. *Guest, Keen and Nettlefolds* (*Assets £217·9 million*)

Made up of nearly ninety steel and engineering firms, making things from traditional fasteners to welding equipment. They are run from Smethwick in Staffordshire, with a modern office in Kingsway, London. Parts of GKN go back to the industrial revolution, but they are not atrophied by old age, and have been expanding suddenly. GKN has become largely a managerial company. Their chairman, Sir Kenneth Peacock (also a director of the Steel Company of Wales) is the son of a former managing director, and went into GKN from Oundle. He is an adept committee man, skilful in dealing with his scattered companies, and keeping quite a strict hold on investment.

11. *Esso Petroleum Company* (*Assets £210·8 million*)

A subsidiary of Standard Oil of New Jersey, and Shell's main competitor, both outside and inside Britain. Its London office is allowed fair independence, but the parent company keeps it on its toes; its most striking Americanisation was the building of the Fawley refinery near Southampton—the biggest in the Commonwealth—in record time. Managers arrive at the same time as the workers. Its chairman, Hugh C. Tett, often assumed to be American, is in fact a Redbrick technocrat, in contrast to nearly all the other twenty. He took a science degree at Exeter university, did research at London on tetra-ethyl lead, and worked his way up through Esso technical sales. He became a petroleum expert, looked after Esso's research in Europe, and became London chairman in 1959.

12. *Bowaters* (*Assets £197·7 million*)

Britain's biggest newsprint producers, which also supplies 20 per cent of American newsprint: 70 per cent of Bowaters profits come from America, and they own the biggest mill in the United States, in Tennessee. The firm was founded by a Bowater in 1881, but it was built up to its present size by Sir Eric Bowater, who was chairman for 35 years, until he died in 1962. Sir Eric was one of the last great actor-managers of British big business. He was a man of great daring, and great vanity; he gambled, and usually won. When he became chairman, he bought out his uncles, who wouldn't agree with his expansionist policy, and went into partnership with Lord Beaverbrook *and* Rothermere—later advantageously buying both out. He bought plants and timber in Newfoundland and Scandinavia, and after the war expanded into America and Europe. He ran his empire with great panache; he broadcast to his Canadian employees on Christmas Day, and presided over his shareholders meetings with a theatrical flourish. He had 75,000 shareholders, half of them with £200 or less in the company, and most of them women; he gained their confidence, but never really reassured the bigger investors, the 'institutions'. His monument was Bowater House, the big black palace in Knightsbridge, with a sumptuous thirteenth floor from which the chairman can look over London.

Bowater was brilliant but rash, and by the time he died the huge company was in a tricky condition. He gambled on inflation, and triumphed while inflation continued; but by the time he died world conditions were less comfortable. He had made no allowance for a successor, and did not even bother to hold board meetings for his directors. His was an astonishing example of the autocratic powers of a chairman in a big public company.

He was succeeded by Sir Christopher Chancellor, the former

head of Reuters and Odhams (before it was taken over by Cecil King of the *Daily Mirror*), who had joined the board only ten months before. Sir Christopher is a quite shrewd Etonian, the son of a Colonial governor and more subtle than Sir Eric. He moved into the uncertain empire with evident surprise, and set about trying to rationalise and decentralise, with careful ruthlessness, the imperial court. He cut the headquarters staff by half, let four floors of the building, and re-formed the extravagant hierarchy, with the help of a vigorous young managing director, Martin Ritchie.

13. *Great Universal Stores* (*Assets £196·8 million*)

The largest giant created by a single entrepreneur, who still controls it. Sir Isaac Wolfson, by a series of take-overs (when they were still unfashionable), built up the shop empire called Gussies. It includes the biggest mail-order business in Europe, with lush catalogues which rival Sears Roebucks' (which provided his original inspiration); a merchant bank; a travel agency; and about 120 separately incorporated companies, trading under as many separate names including Weaver to Wearer, Jax women's clothes, Easiephit shoes, Boyds TV and radio stores and Woodhouse furniture.

Gussies still revolves round its dynamic founder, a tireless teetotal tycoon, and master planner of the empire. His desk, adorned only by two paperweights—one labelled 'Big Deals', the other 'Little Deals'—is uncluttered; and his 'filing cabinet' is a small yellow metal wastepaper basket. His 36-year-old son was appointed as joint managing director with his father in 1963, and will almost certainly succeed him as chairman. By issuing non-voting shares[1] the Wolfson family retain complete control, as Marks and Spencer remains with Markses and Sieffs.

14. *Tube Investments* (*Assets £184·4 million*)

Another mixed engineering group, with products from scaffolding to hypodermic needles. Based on Birmingham, where it has an ugly, Cotton-and-Clore building and a Midlands accent, but with a growing back-base in London. 'Tubes' has been built up by its chairman, Sir Ivan Stedeford, a Methodist engineer from Birmingham who married the boss's daughter (he has a son and a son-in-law in the business). He preserved an autocratic Midlands independence, as emerged in the Aluminium War

[1] *See* p. 546.

against the 'Old Freddies' of the city.[1] He is now an elder tycoon-statesman for government committees. He has been able to choose good men and leave them alone—notably his successor, Lord Plowden.

Plowden is an interesting new-style chairman—formerly chief planner at the Treasury, and head of Atomic Energy. He is a quiet Treasury man, precise and very influential: an intellectual, with an analytical approach. Behind his mild exterior he can be bold and critical, particularly of Old Freddies and family firms. He has chaired a succession of government committees, with kid-glove tact, which have left large and controversial results in Whitehall. And in Tubes he has been rationalising—closing down plants, new management structure, more profits—rather like Chancellor.

15. *Associated Electrical Industries* (*Assets £174·4 million*)

The biggest electrical company, making everything from electric light bulbs to power stations and railway engines ('We have both elephants and rabbits in our zoo,' said Lord Chandos). The result of several mergers, absorbing such famous names as British-Thomson-Houston, Ediswan, Henlys, Siemens and Metropolitan Vickers—names that in the end it ruthlessly suppressed, imposing a new corporate personality with the help of glamorous advertisements. The divisions remain separate, dominated by by engineers—except for Hotpoint (refrigerators, etc.), run by Brian Bonfield, an able young lawyer from Oxford. But the main board is very un-managerial, including the omnipresent Lord Bicester. The chairman, Mike Wheeler, went into steel from St. Paul's School, and worked with Lord Chandos (his predecessor) during the war. After the war he rose to be chairman of a division of GKN, until he was invited by Chandos to AEI. He is quiet, professional, son of a GWR manager, Master of the Beagles in Bucks. But he is a tough, incisive man, capable of making shrewd decisions quickly on the telephone and not bothering too much with subordinates; and in the past two years AEI have become rather more competitive, and more concerned with profits than prestige.

16. *Steel Company of Wales* (*Assets £173·2 million*)

An unusual company invented from scratch in 1947, with no family traditions: it was started by, among others, Richard Thomas and Baldwin and GKN[2] to produce sheet-steel and tin-

[1] *See* pp. 439–41.
[2] *See* p. 537.

plate in South Wales, and now has the largest integrated steel-works in Europe, producing 3 million ingot tons a year—the 'City of Steel which never sleeps'. It was nationalised and denationalised, and now is likely to be renationalised. It is part-owned by GKN, and the chairman of Metal Box is on the board. The company is run by a triumvirate who were largely responsible for building up the steel-works (the first two both came from Guest Keen's), Sir Julian Pode, the chairman, an ex-accountant who breeds horses; Frederick Cartwright, the managing director; and David Young, a Scots financial expert. Like most steel companies, SCOW is close to the factory, proud of its provincialism and not showy, and in the past its relations with unions have been friendly. But in 1963 it was involved in a six-week strike by the Amalgamated Engineering Union, which left a wake of bitterness, and it has become a favourite target for accusations of overmanning in British steel.

17. *Vickers* (*Assets £166·9 million*)

Engineering giant, originated in Sheffield 150 years ago, now with four big divisions—aviation, shipbuilding, engineering and steel. All are headed by engineers and are kept separate: the enterprise of the aircraft division (which produced the Viscount) does not cross-fertilise the more somnolent shipbuilders: though a Vickers research company does span all divisions. The head office, in its glass skyscraper (owned by the Legal and General Insurance Company) is becoming more of a holding company, and in some of its satellites, like the British Aircraft Corporation or Vickers overseas, it shares ownership with others. Vickers, the biggest armament company, has become very close to the government after two world wars. People sometimes talk of 'the army, navy, air force and Vickers'.

Vickers has difficulty in finding enough engineers with enough breadth of experience for top jobs: their board includes Sir Sam Brown, the city lawyer, Lord Bicester (of course) and a vigorous Treasury knight, Sir Leslie Rowan, as managing director. As chairmen they have preferred generals or peers: the two previous chairmen, Lord Weeks (a general from Pilkington's) and Lord Knollys (an insurance peer, page of honour to two kings) were both brought from outside the company, and the chairman, Major-General Dunphie—son of a courtier and banker, married a general's daughter—was brought into Vickers by his friend Lord Weeks.

18. *Dunlop* (*Assets £145 million*)

Founded by John Boyd Dunlop, a vet, who invented an inflatable tyre for his son's tricycle: but since then it has become less dynamic, and has tended to rest on its rubber, without much diversification. Its territory stretches from Malayan plantations to Midlands factories—making tyres, rackets, tennis balls, cushions, etc. Its chairman, Sir Edward Beharrel, is the son of a former chairman (who worked his way up from being Assistant Goods Manager to the LNER). Most of the day-to-day running is done by Reay Geddes, the managing director, whose father, too, was chairman of Dunlops. He read economics at Cambridge, went into the Bank of England, and then joined his father's company. He is a transport enthusiast, one of the early agitators for the Channel tunnel, and now heading a Government enquiry into shipyards. He is also an important member of the Treasury's 'Neddy'.

19. *Stewarts and Lloyds* (*Assets £140·4 million*)

A steel giant, merged in 1903, with a Lloyd on the board until 1961, James Peech as another director, and Graham Stewart as their chairman. He is a vigorous Wykehamist who has been in the forefront of the campaign against nationalisation which he explained in 1958, was 'a long step towards the setting up of communism . . .' He was again on the warpath before the 1964 election. Much of the company is run by managing directors, but Stewart flies 35,000 miles round England a year, and takes a large hand in investment decisions. United Steel, Stewarts and Lloyds, and John Summers have all been interlocked with directors—making up the 'Holy Trinity' of steel.

20. *United Steel* (*Assets £138·8 million*)

A merger of family steel companies in 1918: like other steel companies, it has a superstructure of old families, with self-made managers and numbers of Oxbridge graduates. Its bosses, like other men of steel, have developed from the days when Lord Nuffield described steelmasters as 'gentlemen with fat cigars and nothing to do, except grow fat on a ramp'. It is technically very advanced, but maintains a wide divide between managers and the board of fifteen, which is largely hereditary. James Peech, the chairman is (as usual) less flamboyant and political than his predecessor, Sir Walter Benton Jones, but he also comes from a steel family. He went from Wellington and Oxford to the city, and joined the company in his thirties.

21. *Allied Breweries* (*Assets £134·9 million*)

The biggest of the breweries, formerly called Ind Coope, Tetley, Ansells', was created as a result of a merger arranged at two Derbyshire picnics in February 1961 ('that infamous patch of grass'—*Daily Worker*). 'This is not a take-over', said the chairman, Edward Thompson: 'it is a commonwealth concept—and a new one to the British brewing industry.' The group controls an eighth of the pubs in England, and is the most spectacular of several recent mergers which, by January 1965, had concentrated half the British pubs in the hands of ten companies:

	No. of Pubs
Allied Breweries	8,500
Watney, Mann	6,862
Courage, Barclay & Simonds	4,850
Whitbread	4,760
Charrington & United	4,753
Bass, Mitchells & Butlers	4,500
John Smith (Tadcaster) & Assoc.	1,690
Greenall Whitley & Assoc.	1,500
Truman, Hanbury, Buxton	1,250
Scottish & Newcastle	1,000
Total for 'Top Ten'	39,665
Total number of pubs in UK	75,000

Much of the recent drive in brewing has come from men outside the brewing families or 'beerage', including Alan Walker of Bass, Mitchells, and the Canadian E. P. Taylor. Ind Coope's has no Inds or Coopes on the board; Thompson is a former solicitor who became managing director of Ind Coope in his thirties, a follower of American methods and a believer in high-pressure marketing and branding (Double Diamond, Skol, etc.). He has been described as 'a man who could as easily be running a chain store or a steel combine', and unlike most other brewers he is very interested in international affairs, particularly world government, where he has shown immense energy and enthusiasm.

22. *Reed Paper Group* (*Assets £132·1 million*)

Bowaters' paper rival, making newsprint, paperboard, packaging, tissues, etc.; run from a shining new building in Piccadilly.

Forty-four per cent of its shares are owned by the International Publishing Corporation—the Daily Mirror newspaper group—and the chairman of both companies is thus Cecil Harmsworth King. Reed's was originally set up with the help of King's uncle, Lord Northcliffe, but it led a fairly independent existence until 1963 when, after an epic boardroom struggle, the previous chairman, Lord Cornwallis, was ousted by King.

The Cornwallis-King conflict followed a classic pattern. Lord Cornwallis is a tough old dreadnought, Lord Lieutenant of Kent and Custos Rotulorum, laden with city directorships; he moves in stately style between Tunbridge Wells, London and Perthshire, and accumulates directorships as other men collect parking tickets. For years he ruled Reed's with apparent ease; but it was clear that King was becoming increasingly restive with the company which IPC half-owned. Dealings between Cornwallis and the IPC directors became increasingly strained; relations were not improved by the fact that King was a socialist intellectual, and Cornwallis was a soldierly Tory. Eventually, in 1963, the directors made it clear that they thought Cornwallis should go. In June it was announced in the annual report that he would not seek re-election, and that Cecil King would become chairman.

The annual meeting in July was an extraordinary example of how little the smaller shareholders take part in their company's affairs; of the 20,000 or so shareholders, only about forty turned up, and none of them asked questions about the major upheaval on the board; nobody asked why Philip Walker, who had been managing-director for twelve years, had vacated his job—to be succeeded by Sydney Ryder, a former financial journalist and businessman from the Mirror group. And there was not even a vote of thanks for Lord Cornwallis. As *The Times* reported: 'A fundamental change has taken place in the boardroom of the second largest paper-making company in the country with substantial international interests, and the stockholders' reticence on this occasion is baffling. Only a little less baffling is that the chairman also failed to refer to this matter and the short proceedings ended as they began as if nothing whatsoever had changed.'

23. *Ford Motor* (*Assets £127·9 million*)

The biggest car company by assets, although BMC produces more cars. Since 1961 wholly owned by Fords in Detroit: its vast Dagenham works are Britain's most spectacular example of American 'vertical integration'. In many ways very American in its approach—ruthless, quick-changing, cosmopolitan—using American and German inventions freely. A visit from Henry Ford is preceded by weeks of worry. Its chairman, Sir Patrick Hennessy, is a tough Irishman who began his career making Model T Fords in their Cork factory—one of the tiny group of vigorous Irish businessmen in England (compare C. O. Stanley, chairman of Pye's). In 1963 he retired as chief executive and was succeeded by Allen Barke, an engineer from the Manchester College of Technology who worked his way up Ford's over thirty years—one of the few engineers at the head of a big company.

24. *J. & P. Coats, Patons & Baldwins* (*Assets £116·8 million*)

Founded by James Coats in Paisley in 1824, producing a large dynasty: between 1910 and 1930 nine Coatses and two Clarks died millionaires. In 1910 it had the biggest profits of any company in Britain.

Since the war Coats has lost ground, and has been slow to diversify into more expanding fields: but in 1960 it merged with Patons and Baldwins, which gave it a big holding in wool. Its board used to be full of family. Now they have only two Coatses, and its chairman, Sir Malcolm McDougall, is a self-made Scot who walked into Coats at the age of 14, and got a job in the accounts department as an office boy.

25. *British Motor Corporation* (*Assets £108·9 million*)

The result of the merger, in 1952, between the two rival car companies, Morris and Austin, now producing more cars than any other British company, its cars include not only Morrises and Austins, but Wolseleys, Rileys and MG's.

Since the death of its two autocratic founders, Lord Nuffield and Lord Austin, the British car industry has passed swiftly but painfully into the managerial phase. The first chairman of the merged company was Leonard Lord, now Lord Lambury, who worked his way up from being an engineering apprentice to become chairman of Austin's. The present chairman, George Harriman, had a very similar career; he began, like Lord, as apprentice in the Hotchkiss factory of Morris Motors, where Harriman's father was works manager: he was befriended by Lord and rose quickly, reorganising the Cowley works and then, like Lord, moving over to Austin's.

Harriman, like other car men, lives in the self-contained world of the Midlands, with its own practical values, and without much natural contact with Europe or America; but under Lord and Harriman the BMC has begun to break out of its provincial background—with the particular help of its technical director, the brilliant Greek Alec Issigonis, who designed the Mini Minor.

26. *Turner and Newall (Assets £106·9 million)*

A scattered empire, based on asbestos, out of which it makes all kinds of things including asbestos cement and Ferodo brake linings; it has large mines in Africa and Canada, and factories in America and all over the Commonwealth. The company is well known for the secrecy of its public statements. It is run from 'Asbestos House' in Manchester.

Its chairman, Ronald Soothill, belongs to an early generation of graduates in business; the son of a minor public school headmaster, he went to Cambridge, then into chocolate, then into asbestos.

FAMILIES AND FIRMS

All these twenty-six companies have thousands of shareholders, often headed by the Pru, but the 'managerial revolution' is far from uniform or complete. Although committees of managers and technicians make up their middle ranks, at the top of many there continue to be individuals whose bold decisions—as with ICI or Courtaulds—can change the character of the company: some, like Chambers, have succeeded in imposing their character on vast concerns; others, like Wolfson, have virtually created their concerns; others, like the heads of breweries or shipping companies, have inherited a special authority.

In some companies, such as Great Universal Stores, Marks and Spencer, or the House of Fraser, families can keep control by issuing non-voting shares: young Fraser, young Wolfson, young Sieff are all likely to succeed as chairmen. But even without a majority of voting shares, families can often dominate Leviathans. Among thousands of small shareholdings they may own the biggest block, or enjoy the tacit support of the biggest shareholders, usually the Pru and the Legal and General; or the other directors may have such a strong hereditary loyalty—particularly when the firm carries a family name—that they loyally elect a family chairman. Sons-in-law, too, remain an enduring phenomenon, as in the Conservative party, the court and banking.

The position of families varies widely. Some chairmen have

virtually private sheikhdoms with their own miniature court which cuts right across the managerial pyramid. Others are more like a constitutional monarch, chosen by a board of executives as a personification of the company, and a wise adjudicator in times of crisis: as the Queen's most critical function is to choose a prime minister, so the chairman's may be to choose a managing director. Often big businesses experience the ambiguous condition of the eighteenth-century government, with power somewhere between the king and the cabinet. The firm gets more complicated, the managers more indispensable, the family's holding proportionally smaller: the balance gradually—sometimes suddenly—shifts from the family to the managers, from a court to a committee. Often an autocrat retires, like a Caesar, leaving a disorganised empire to be run by a triumvirate: the end of the pioneer generation, like Leverhulme's, is nearly always difficult. Lord Nuffield and Lord Austin, two heirless pioneers, left the jumbled inheritance which became the British Motor Corporation—only now achieving a tidier pattern: the aircraft companies, built up by brilliant pioneers like de Havilland or Sopwith, are passing painfully into an era of accountants and organograms.

THE CHAIRMAN'S JOB

> The most distinctive characteristic of the businessman—the thing that most sharply distinguishes him from the lawyer, college professor or, generally speaking, the civil servant—is his capacity for decision.
>
> *J. K. Galbraith: American Capitalism.*

What does a chairman's power amount to? 'Ninety per cent of the time I'm just a superior nursemaid,' said one of the chairmen: 'I spend my time deciding to move Mr. Smith to replace Mr. Brown, trying to find another place for Mr. Brown by persuading Mr. Robinson that it's time for him to retire. The other 10 per cent of the time is spent deciding about capital investment: and a lot of these decisions are forced on you by the competition. That's what I was told when I took over—but I didn't believe it then. Most of your time is spent in the engine room. Only occasionally do you go up on to the bridge: then you lash the helm and go down again.'

'The most important change that has come with the managerial revolution is the need for good communications,' said another: 'More and more the man in the centre is left with nothing to do except sit and write: that's one of the ways in which British business is falling behind—they're not used to the idea of presenting business to the community, and the gift of the gab is still suspect in the boardroom. Not that American businessmen are much more articulate than we are: the main difference is that they hire ghost writers and we don't.'

'The difference between politics and business,' Lord Chandos has said, 'is that in business you finish something. If you spend £10 million and employ, say, 3,000 or 4,000 people, and the project produces a profit of 25 per cent you can safely go home and leave criticism to Michael Foot or anybody else who likes to have a go at it. The work has been finished and is in being. That's the attraction of business.'[1]

'Businessmen are on the whole kinder, nicer and more straightforward than intellectuals and professional men', said Sir Geoffrey Crowther, the intellectual ex-editor of *The Economist*: 'they pay more regard to people's feelings.'[2]

Businessmen remain, in spite of the encroachment of bureaucracy, much freer to decide things than Whitehall committees. 'In the civil service,' said one ex-Whitehall tycoon, 'most decisions came up from below: you might not always take the advice of junior men, but you always expect them to give an opinion. But in business, I was surprised how often decisions come straight from the top.'

But the decisions are not perhaps quite so far-sighted and wide-ranging as they sometimes appear in chairmen's philosophic reports. 'How did you find the tycoons?' asked one cabinet minister, 'I find they've got minds like searchlights: they light up a narrow strip very brightly, but that doesn't mean that they can see all round. I'm often surprised how little they understand about other things,' After talking to chairmen, I found myself abandoning images of ships and tillers, and visualising instead roundabouts and swings in a foggy fairground. As Bagehot described it in 1872:

> Most men of business love a sort of twilight. They have lived all their lives in an atmosphere of probabilities and of doubt, where nothing is very clear, where there are some chances for many events, where nevertheless one course must be determinedly chosen and fixedly adhered to. They like to hear arguments suited to this intellectual haze.

[1] Interview with Malcolm Muggeridge. Granada TV, July 25, 1960.

[2] *Sunday Telegraph*, December 13, 1964. Interview with Donald McLachlan.

Or, in the description by Lord Heyworth, to the select committee on nationalised industries in 1953:

> No one can tell at the point of having made a decision whether it is going to prove right or wrong . . . The point is that decisions have got to be taken. That is the thing which matters. It is dynamic. You have got to do something. As I always put it, I look upon myself as someone who is perpetually in a fog; you get used to being in a fog. Occasionally you think the fog has lifted while you have made a decision; and then it obscures again.

Yet in spite of all the apparent limitations of a chairman's scope—the fog, the muddle, the committees, the sheer effort required to counteract centrifugal force and Parkinsonian tendencies—there is no doubt that even in the most intractable managerial corporations, a dynamic chairman can have a crucial effect. Many of the companies with the most spectacular growth since the war have a single dominating man at their head. Any chairman must spend much of his time in nursemaid duties, but his moments of decision remain crucial. Many companies may find it agreeable and reassuring to have a constitutional head, leaving most decisions to managing directors. But when a vigorous chairman does appear—a Chambers, a Plowden, a Kearton—the change can affect every limb of the company.

30

COMPANIES

One of the curses of the political atmosphere of Britain is the sentimental softness towards inefficiency.

Paul Chambers, October 1961.

BRITAIN has traditionally been a country of small businesses, but the past ten years have shown a rapid concentration. The trend is not new: at the turn of the century many giants arose, such as the Bradford Dyers' Association, Imperial Tobacco, or Calico Printers, and another crop came with the depression of the twenties, when ICI, Unilever, AEI were all formed. During and after the war there was a lull:[1] but then came a new wave which has changed the whole pattern of business.

In some fields, such as chemicals (largely due to ICI) and entertainment (due to Ranks and the TV companies) giants already prevail. In building, small firms are well entrenched (in Britain as in America). But in other trades—cars, cotton, printing, shops or beer—small firms have been quickly swallowed by big ones. All of them except cars are old industries and have faced cold winds—foreign invaders, decreasing demand, or rising costs. Beer has been traditionally very secure, protected by the system of 'tied houses'. But the drift from pubs to TV, the rising costs, and the arrival of an invader (E. P. Taylor from Canada) and a would-be invader (Charles Clore) have produced a flurry of mergers. In the words of Colonel Whitbread: 'We must integrate, or disintegrate.'

TAKE-OVERS

Jungle red in tooth and claw, and particularly Clore.

Lord Attlee (House of Lords, 1961).

Many mergers have been voluntary, but several have been the result of take-overs, which have often transformed the characters of firms, by-passing the old directors. Several factors have en-

[1] *See* P. E. Hart: Business Concentration in the UK, *Journal of the Royal Statistical Society*, Vol. 123, Part I, 1960.

couraged the raiders, and the situation has been not unlike America at the time of Coolidge. The boom in city property increased the potential value of many companies; the ploughing-back of profits gave companies tempting hoards; the combination of high income tax without a capital gains tax made quick capital appreciation very attractive; and the issue of non-voting shares enabled single entrepreneurs to keep control of huge public companies. A small group of raiders—most notably Sir Isaac Wolfson, Charles Clore, Lord Fraser, Lord Thomson—became the heads of colossal empires within ten years. The most celebrated and successful of the raiders is Charles Clore, the son of a Russian-Jewish refugee who had built up a small textile business. Clore began his property career by buying the Cricklewood Ice Rink at the age of twenty-two: now, at the age of sixty, he owns among other things half the shoe-shops in Britain, Furness shipbuilding yards, the Hampstead Garden Suburb, Loch Ness, and 16,000 acres of Herefordshire, where he occasionally leads a country-squire existence. He also has a large share in City Centre Properties, the biggest property company in Britain. He is restless, single-minded and secretive (he refuses to see any journalists). His business philosophy was tersely expressed when he told the Jenkins Committee that it did not matter if a director could read or write, provided he maximised the returns.

In the early fifties, when Wolfson and Clore were most active, take-overs were rare and frowned on. Even in late 1959, when the Aluminium War[1] burst on the city, they were still thought disgraceful by half the city; but by 1960 ICI itself was trying a take-over. The raiders transformed whole areas of business: sleepy and comfortable firms have been rationalised, combed and costed, their properties sold up, their products standardised, their managers re-valued, with unsuspected thrusting men emerging from the undergrowth. Some take-overs aimed only at quick plunder, but many have brought greater efficiency as well as exploitation. The attitude of the city remains ambivalent, as it was in the Aluminium War. 'Generally speaking, bidders have created new employment rather than the reverse,' wrote the authors of one study of take-overs.[2] 'There may be occasions', said Anthony Tuke in 1960, 'where something more drastic than a gentle kiss on the brow from a Prince Charming is needed to awaken the sleeping beauties. It may even be necessary sometimes to tip them right out

[1] *See* p. 439.
[2] *See* George Bull and Anthony Vice: *Bid for Power*, 1958. p. 24.

of bed. But it can seldom be wise to pull down the whole house or even to sell it as it stands to a stranger.'

'THEY'

Giant firms have similar problems. Their mergers bring together proud separate units, with the same kind of agonies as those of federated countries or amalgamated regiments. Some component companies appear independent and competing—Players against Wills cigarettes, White Horse against Johnny Walker whisky. Some federated firms like Unilever or Imperial Tobacco keep their central organisation in the background. Others, like AEI or ICI proclaim their unity. The amalgamation is often painful, and new giants have to make great efforts—by advertising, tours or house magazines—to persuade their workers that AEI, ICI or English Electric really *exist*. 'When a previously independent business becomes incorporated into a group,' wrote H. P. Barker, chairman of Parkinson and Cowan, 'a change of atmosphere often occurs . . . The executives feel that some measure of responsibility has been lifted from their shoulders, the carrot seems further away, the stick less frightening, and an entirely new factor has appeared on the scene. This factor is the arrival of "they".'[1]

Many giants are still working out the relationship between centre and circumference. But most are tending towards greater decentralisation of units, while maintaining shrewd financial checks—preferring to regard themselves more as a holding company or a family bank. British business is still unaccustomed to bigness: most giants have not been giants for long, and the nationalised industries have produced quite new dimensions.[2] The relationship between the parent and its subsidiaries is still an unresolved problem—how to control without stultifying, how to advise without interfering—and even the words 'parent' and 'subsidiaries' are begging the question. The rôle of a modern industrial headquarters is subtle and complicated: 'Headquarters', said Lord Heyworth, 'always seems a half-crazy place anyway.'[3] But how this problem is solved—how 'they' appear to the men in the factories and local branches—is a question more important to millions of workers and managers, whose life is bound up with their company, than the workings of Whitehall or Westminster.

[1] Quoted in *Business Enterprise* by R. S. Edwards and Harry Townsend, 1958. p. 199.
[2] *See* p. 572.
[3] *See* Select Committee on Nationalised Industries, 1953. Q. 705.

DIVERSIFIERS

Business has become both bigger and more mixed, and 'diversification' has become a craze. Some companies, such as Unilever or Beechams (pills, Brylcreem, Lucozade, etc.) have gathered a gallimaufry half by mistake, but others have deliberately 'gone shopping'. Courtaulds were worried about rayon, bought their way into chemicals, engineering, paint and packaging, and then bought up one third of Lancashire's spinning capacity. The Ross trawler-fishing business, headed by Carl Ross of Grimsby, were faced with a shortage of fish, and went into printing, lorries, hire-purchase, chickens, crop-spraying and frozen foods. De La Rue expanded from bank-notes and playing cards to formica, oil heaters and computers. Charles Clore's empire, Sears Holdings, not only owns half Britain's shoe-shops, but also makes ships, pumps, laundries, pipes and jewellery. Imperial Tobacco, disturbed about their cigarettes, bought their way into potato crisps and teaching machines.

Even stubbornly one-track firms have branched out. Ever since 1799, Guinness have concentrated with fantastic success on one product, stout, but they have now turned to selling butterscotch and Irish salmon. Some companies have extended into an adjacent territory: Booker Brothers have moved from shipping to shopping. Many mixed groups have a common denominator: all Beechams' stuff is very dependent on advertising, all ICI's revolves round research, all Vickers is concerned with 'making big things out of metal' (as Lord Knollys put it). But several groups, like Sears, Tillings or De La Rue, have no perceptible common thread—except profit.

This hectic mix-up has changed the outlook of the top businessman. He need no longer be a brewer, a shoe-maker, a shipowner or a printer, with the smell of a dock or a print-shop: but he must be a master-manager. Paradoxically, in an age of specialisation, big firms—like country trading stores—often specialise in everything. Many find the implications disturbing, widening the gap between the factory, with its technicians printing or brewing, and the headquarters, dominated by finance, controlling their shoes and ships and sealing wax purely through their profit and loss account. This, it seems, leads both to a more mandarin headquarters élite and also, at the same time, to an exaggerated dependence on the men-on-the-job.

Bigness has strengthened the lure of London. In the nineteenth century the centres of industrial power were Manchester, Birmingham or Glasgow and the directors lived and worked near them. But as companies merge and grow, their headquarters need to be close to Whitehall, the city, their rivals, lawyers, advertising agents, London airport. Now most of the giant companies have their board meetings in London. The big steel companies are still run from the North, and the car firms from the Midlands: but as with insurance companies, building societies or banks, the drift is still towards London. Britain is less centralised than France, where Paris is the dominating centre. But compared to Chicago or Los Angeles, Hamburg or Dusseldorf, British provincial centres are depleted, and the trend is threatening to turn London into a nightmare megalopolis.[1]

Provincial companies suffer a transmogrification when they reach the metropolis. Who would guess that the new English Electric building in Aldwych, with its portland stone, second empire boardroom and ornate executive suites, was the centre of a rugged provincial empire? The décor and architecture of London headquarters seems to represent a conscious desire to be part of an imaginary immemorial London with emanations from Buckingham Palace and the Bank of England.[2] But to the men at the factory, the London palace is the physical embodiment of 'they' or —as headquarters are sometimes called—'the Kremlin'.

GIANTS AND PYGMIES

The main pressure to bigness has come from foreign invaders, who can afford to take large risks, draw on international experience, and regard Britain as a suburb; while in the reverse direction, international British companies need huge resources for their battles in America and Europe. The invasion of American tobacco, as early as 1901, produced Imperial Tobacco; German chemicals helped to give birth to ICI; continental margarines produced Unilever. Since the war the international battle has intensified—for instance the detergent war between Unilever and Procter and Gamble; the oil war between Shell and Esso; the car war between American Vauxhalls and Ford, and British BMC and Leylands. In many fields like typewriters, cameras, sewing machines, vacuum cleaners, razor-blades, tinned soups, cornflakes, foreigners dominate the field.

[1] *See* London Diaspora? *The Economist*, January 13, 1962.

[2] *See* below, p. 558.

Canadians have a special aptitude for invasion, for they combine aggressive North American attitudes with an evident fondness for Britain. Garfield Weston (Allied Bakeries ABC teashops, Fortnum and Mason, etc.); Lord Thomson following Lord Beaverbrook; E. P. Taylor (United Breweries); Sir Billy Butlin (holiday camps); they have all helped to disturb the placid stream of British business. For some, like Weston or Taylor, their British business is only an extension: 'Remember, a bad year for United Breweries is just a bad *day* for Mr. Taylor,' one brewer was told. But often, as with Thomson or Beaverbrook, the British business becomes the major interest, with much greater scope for exploitation and glory than on the Canadian side. 'There must be *something* wrong with this country,' Thomson is reported to have said, 'if I can make money so easily out of it.'

Where, in this Brobdingnag, is the place for Gullivers? There is still no lack of small firms: in 1963 there were no fewer than 460,000 private companies in Britain, as opposed to 16,080 public companies and 4,500 quoted in the stock exchange.

Some kinds of firms refuse to grow in size—notably builders and civil engineers: apart from a few big contractors whose names stare out from the tops of new buildings—Laings, Taylor Woodrow, Cubitts, etc.—the building trade remains defiantly fissiparous, in Britain and also in America. Between the Leviathans, small fish can still swim and grow without being gobbled.

The self-made businessman is now less likely to make his fortune in manufacturing than in 'service' industries—a shop, a launderette, a window-cleaning business. As Britain becomes more prosperous, so these services increase, and by 1960 more people were employed in services and distribution than in manufacturing. Britain's centre of gravity is moving away from mines and factories, towards shops, hairdressers (100,000 of them), lorry-drivers, or TV technicians: and like an Arab bazaar, we are busying ourselves with persuading and entertaining each other.

Britain, following America, is slowly moving away from a steel-based economy, with motor cars and washing machines among the most precious possessions, towards an economy where services predominate. Spending on travel, food, security, hygiene, medicine is rising, and it is in providing services—particularly for comfortable leisure—that the large opportunities for the self-made businessman will occur. The one-man success stories will be not so much about engineers, aircraft designers or inventors—those fields are developed by laboratory teams or committees of managers—but interior decorators, grocers, pop singers, supermarket owners. The era of Nuffield and de Havilland is being succeeded by the age of Charles Forte and the Beatles.[1]

GROWTH

The most important attribute for companies, in terms of the future prosperity of the country, is not their size, their shape or their profits, but their ability to *grow*: in the past ten years the word growth has spread through industry, economics and politics like a magic password, propagated above all by the National Economic Development Council, or 'Neddy'. The question 'What makes a company or industry grow?' has passed from the board rooms into the senior common rooms and Whitehall corridors.

Neddy set the national target of an increase in output of 4 per cent a year which, set against a labour force increasing by only 1 per cent, implies a large improvement in efficiency and productivity. The expected increase varies, of course, enormously with different industries. These were the predicted annual percentage increases between 1961 and 1966 in the seventeen industries classified by Neddy:[2]

	%		%
Agriculture	+ 3·3	Electronics	+ 9·7
Coal	+ 1·0	Motor vehicles	+ 9·5
Electricity	+ 10·0	Wool textiles:	
Gas	+ 6·4	Yarn	+ 1·3
Petroleum	+ 7·6	Woven fabric	+ 2·0
Chocolate, etc.	— 0·1	Paper and Board	+ 2·6
Chemicals	+ 7·6	Combustion	+ 4·4
Iron and Steel:		Post Office	+ 5·4
Crude Steel	+ 4·6	Distribution	+ 3·7
Iron Castings	+ 2·5	17 Industries	+ 4·8
Machine tools	+ 8·0	Rest of Economy	+ 3·5
Heavy electrical	+ 12·6	Gross domestic product	+ 4·0

But within industries, the capacity and desire to grow vary hugely between different companies. In 1962 Dr. Tibor Barna (one of the formidable group of Hungarian economists in Britain) published a study of growth in British firms, which analysed the factors that made some companies grow, and some stay still.

[1] *See* New Patterns of Affluence: *Financial Times,* December 27, 1961.
[2] NEDC: The Growth of the Economy, March, 1964. p. 11.

Dr. Barna analysed eighty-one firms in two industries, electrical engineering and food processing—the first a growing industry, the second a stable one. He discovered that in the fast-growing electrical field, it was both new firms, and new people who had been most successful[1]: 'Although it is obvious that new firms should enter new industries, it is surprising that none of the older firms has gained a dominant position in a new field. It is not the makers of telephones who dominate the field of radio communications, nor makers of cookers who make washing machines, nor makers of stoves who make electric fires. The bulk of the market for each domestic electrical appliance (except cookers) goes to one or two firms; all these are either first-generation firms (that is, still controlled by the founders) or subsidiaries of foreign firms established in the British market since the 1930's . . .

'It is also interesting to observe,' continued Dr. Barna in a much-quoted passage, 'that among the new firms, and among the successful firms in general, a large proportion is controlled by foreign firms, by immigrant firms or firms founded by immigrants, and by members of minority groups such as Jews or Quakers. Again, it is obvious that newcomers should concentrate on new industries and new developments; but that is not the whole explanation. The "outsider" is likely to be more strongly activated by the profit motive; for him accumulation of wealth may bring social recognition.[2] He may also see more clearly the unsatisfied wants of consumers and he may be more ready to experiment with new products, new techniques and new forms of organisation. He does not share the attitudes of the established native firms.'

Dr. Barna concluded that companies vary much as individuals do: 'A corporate business may therefore be possessed of the drive to grow and to make profits; and if it is successfully organised, the drive may be stronger and more sustained than in the individual. But corporate business may also be used by its members as an organisation for resisting change.' He found that Harold Laski's findings of 1932 were still applicable: that many firms showed 'a disbelief in the necessity of large-scale production in the modern

[1] Tibor Barna: Investment & Growth Policies in British Industrial Firms. Cambridge University Press, 1962. pp. 56–57.

[2] Dr. Barna adds the footnote: 'The rôle of outsiders in supplying entrepreneurship is of course recognised by sociologists, for instance by Weber. In an earlier age, the Huguenots are an example. It is to be noted that the social position and the personality rather than the racial origin of the outsiders is the relevant factor. Minorities, like the Chinese in Malaya, the Indians in East Africa or the Syrians in West Africa, play an important rôle in the trade of their adopted country, but are not particularly noted for enterprise in their country of origin.'

world; just as the gentleman would rather lose his income than his uniqueness'.[1] 'The management which resents the purchasing power of the working classes,' writes Dr. Barna, 'which resents the increased rôle of women as consumers and which equally resents technological innovation in production and in distribution, is unlikely to be successful,' and he adds the illuminating footnote: 'It is unwillingness to accept change, and the feeling of insecurity which this unwillingness reflects, that seems to manifest itself in the architecture of head offices of some firms, with emphasis on massiveness and inner courtyards. It is not accidental that among firms in the sample those whose architecture has been criticised are low-profit firms, and those whose architecture has been praised are high-profit firms.' This apparent correlation between high profits and good architecture was corroborated in a humorous article called 'Buildings Don't Lie', by 'Actaeon' in *The Statist* in January, 1963. The author suggested an amendment to Parkinson's Law, to state that 'Good buildings go with good companies, and bad with bad'; and taking the criticisms of the *Architects' Journal*, he found that when the journal praised the head offices of companies such as Thorn Electric or Castrol, the shares subsequently went up; while if it condemned them (as with English Electric or Shell) the shares fell—with the exception of the *Financial Times*, which has one of the most-criticised new buildings in the City, but whose shares nearly quadrupled their value in four years.

JOHN BLOOM

The most spectacular example of the sudden success of a new man in a new business was John Bloom, the master-salesman of washing machines who in six years built up a £15 million company, revolutionised selling and advertising methods, and then crashed at the age of thirty-two in July 1964. The fall of Bloom was held by many of his enemies to indicate the irresponsibility and wildness of his business methods; but in his short career he had forced his competitors to follow his suit, shaken up the complacent giant companies, and reduced the price of washing machines by as much as thirty pounds. His enterprise compelled his conservative rivals to abandon the gentlemanly pursuit of small markets with large profit-margins in favour of the more risky but lucrative pursuit of mass markets with small margins. There are others besides John Bloom who have been breaking

[1] H. J. Laski: *The Danger of being a Gentleman*, 1932.

through this gentleman's enclosure (another spectacular example has been Max Wilson, the young South African *entrepreneur* who launched cut-price cruises, in collaboration with big shipping lines). But Bloom, with his youth, his daring and relentless salesmanship, became a figure in folk-lore, a symbol of bold free enterprise, to be loved or hated.

Bloom comes from a Jewish family in the East End of London, and he had the drive and directness of the classic outsider. As a young man he tried several unsuccessful business schemes until in 1958, on a trip to Holland, he came across a twin-tub washing machine which was far cheaper than British models. He found he could buy it for £29 and sell it for £44, and he immediately set about a bold, simple scheme to undercut the shops. He simply put a strident advertisement into the *Daily Mirror*, which received 7,000 replies. He began by buying the components for washing machines from Dutch and British manufacturers, assembling them in his factory and delivering them direct to the buyers; he built up, with ruthless hiring and firing, a high-powered sales force of tireless young men who followed up the replies to advertisements with insistent salesmanship. Bloom was, and remained, essentially a salesman, who was able to identify himself with the housewife, and produce what she wanted, in a way that does not come easily to old British businesses. As his sales increased, he started making his own washing machines; he bought up Rolls Razor Ltd., a languishing company that made old-fashioned strop razors, and gradually built it up into a company mass-producing washing machines.

As his success grew, so Bloom accumulated influential allies: he recruited to his board Sir Charles Colston, a former managing-director of Hoovers and an expert on domestic appliances; he made a spectacular deal with Alex Abel Smith of Pressed Steel, which exchanged shares with Rolls Razor and made Rolls washing machines in their factory at Swansea. He obtained large financial support from Barclays Bank. He chose as chairman of Rolls Razor a Tory MP, Richard Reader Harris. And he arranged with Sir Isaac Wolfson, the powerful head of 'Gussies', to handle his hire-purchase finance. Wolfson for a time was clearly impressed by this young tycoon, and saw him as a young Wolfson—a picture which Bloom enjoyed propagating.

But Bloom was very soon in difficulties. In the first place his rivals, however sleepy they had been before, were not slow to perceive his impact. They too began direct selling and heavy advertising, and introduced new, more effective products, culminating in the fully automatic washing machine. The prices fell, and the market began to be satisfied: Bloom had to step up his advertising at enormous expense—in 1963 Rolls Razor was the biggest single advertiser in the country[1]—and his young bearded face stared out, week after week, from full-page advertisements prepared by four competing agencies. He loved to depict himself as the 'housewives' friend', the David taking on the Goliaths. With his washing-machines he advertised fan-heaters, all kinds of household appliances, and even Belgian and Bulgarian holidays; he emerged as the 'cut-price king', ready to do battle on any front. But as his advertising and fame grew, so the profit-margins dangerously diminished.

Not only was the washing-machine business waning; Bloom was also unable to extend his methods to other products. He tried refrigerators, heaters, home movies, male cosmetics, trading stamps, but in none of them did he have the same touch. He was a super-salesman, without a financier's caution, and after his first success he thought he could sell anything to anybody; but he had been unusually lucky in washing machines—which were ripe for revolution—and his own success had helped to shake up the whole electrical business. From the middle of 1963 Bloom's fortunes began to slip. The alliance with Pressed Steel broke up; Sir Isaac Wolfson withdrew further support; Bloom's ventures became increasingly hectic and unrewarding. The Rolls Razor shares, which had been as low as 4½d. before Bloom bought the company, had gone up to 47/9d. at their peak (in November 1963) but thereafter they steadily fell down, down, down. Bloom himself seemed unaware of impending disaster; surrounded by his family and loyal associates, he seemed as jaunty and dynamic as ever—flying to and from his yacht in the South of France, devising perpetual schemes for enlarging his empire. He seemed to be insulated by his fantasy personality; in the words of *The Economist*, 'He was unable to come to terms with two forces with which his success brought him into contact, that of mass publicity and of the City. To the popular press and television he was no more than a phenomenon. The thoroughness of exposure of any new 'personality' gave him an image more tycoonish and businesslike than the reality, at the same time insulating him in many ways from some harsh commercial realities.'

But the creditors were rapidly closing in. In June 1964 his

[1] *See* p. 637.

merchant bankers, Kleinwort, Benson and Lonsdale, insisted on installing a 'company doctor', Claude Miller, to inspect the books of Rolls Razor; he found vast debts and no hope of recovery, and on July 16 told the directors that the company was insolvent, and that no more cheques should be issued. Bloom himself was away in Bulgaria, but the next day the other directors met and announced that the company would be wound up. Bloom flew back in a fury, tried to save the company, but was soon disillusioned. The shares collapsed to 1/3d., then to 6d.

The moralists and investigators moved in. The Secretary for Trade, Edward Heath, ordered an inquiry. The City pundits enjoyed saying 'I told you so.' New trading stamps were quickly printed without the famous bearded face. But behind the *schadenfreude* and recriminations, the importance of Bloom in his heyday was not forgotten. 'If the British economy is not sufficiently competitive,' wrote Harold Wincott in the *Financial Times*, 'if established industry is too solidly wedded to price maintenance, we need more John Blooms, not fewer of them.' 'As the wreckage is exposed,' said *The Economist*, 'it is easy to forget what a lasting impression Mr. Bloom made on the retailing of household durables in this country. Before his arrival manufacturers tried to sell at the highest possible price thc appliances they found it most convenient to make, competing mainly on advertising claims of better performance and new technical tricks. Over a time, the consumer gets more performance for his money, at each conventional price level: what he did not get was the chance to buy a given grade of machine cheaper. Now, five years later, the customer is king, of price as well as design.' And in a provocative letter to *The Times*, Ralph Harris, the Director of the right-wing Institute of Economic Affairs, wrote: 'Mr. Bloom has already done more for economic growth in Britain than many of its verbal champions in NEDC and elsewhere.'

31

DIRECTORS

England is the last home of the aristocracy, and the art of protecting the aristocracy from the encroachment of commerce has been raised to quite an art,
Because in America a rich butter-and-eggs man is only a rich butter-and-eggs man or at most an honorary LL.D. of some hungry university, but in England he is Sir Benjamin Buttery, Bart.

Ogden Nash.

'FOR the first time in English History, the businessman has reached the Top', wrote a left-wing critic, Ralph Samuel, in 1959. 'It has not always been so. It is scarcely two decades since business was in disgrace, business leaders suspect, and the capitalist system, to all appearance, disintegrating . . . How are the fallen mighty! Today the Businessman is everywhere. Whoever you are, where-ever you are, it is hard to miss him. If you're a writer, he's probably bought out your publishers, or holds important interests in them. If you're an artist, his commission will certainly be the best that comes your way: perhaps you already work for him, designing his products or his "packaging", laying out his advertising, his brochures, his "House" magazine . . .'[1]

The new acceptability of the businessman can be detected everywhere: in the cosy gossip-paragraphs in newspapers; in photographs in *The Times* of boards of directors staring at their blotting paper; in the university 'Magnates Club' at Oxford; in advertisements showing lovable chairmen on winter cruises. The old aristocratic prejudice against trade—always hypocritical—has weakened: 'When I was a boy,' said Sir Miles Thomas, chairman of Monsanto, 'I was always told that the gentry didn't want to soil their hands with trade: nowadays it's very different. I'm a member of White's for instance, and people like Lord Dudley and his brother are very proud of their place in business.'

The British attitude is a long way from the American enthusiasm. A detergent salesman or a cornflakes tycoon is still something of a joke in St. James's Street, and businesses are socially classified

[1] The Boss as Hero: *Universities and Left Review*, Autumn, 1959.

not by their profits or size—as in America—but by their respectability, with books and beer near the top and scrap metal near the bottom. Nor have tycoons come nearly as far out into the open as in America. The British approach of 'please address all communications to the secretary' remains well entrenched.[1] 'There's still a hole-and-corner tradition in British business'—to quote Sir Miles again: 'The British businessmen still hate being criticised: they like to present a front of constant achievement and progress.' Secrecy is still deep-seated; the annual reports, with phrases like 'taxation equalisation account', remain incomprehensible to the lay shareholder compared to American or even Japanese reports. Only when a company desperately needs the support of its shareholders, as Courtaulds did in 1962, does it begin to publish serious information.

But in the sunnier post-war climate, directors have been coming out of their holes, stretching their limbs and basking. One sign of their new confidence can be seen in the company reports in newspapers: ten years ago most of them were grey rivers of text, usually beginning with an obituary ('his ability and wise counsel will be greatly missed'), following with bare trading figures, and ending with a tribute ('long and loyal service of which I think we can all be proud'). Now each year a few more chairmen look out benignly from a photograph, explaining their progress in stirring language.

DIRECTORS' BACKGROUNDS

What kind of men are directors? The *Directory of Directors* lists over 35,000, of companies with assets of more than £25,000.

A sidelight was shed by the Institute of Directors which in 1959 sent out 5,000 questionnaires, of which 60 per cent were completed. According to this directors' picture of themselves:

14 per cent	have a university degree
61	depend on experience alone
68	drive to work
21	arrive before 9 a.m.
38	work every Saturday
59	take three weeks holiday a year, or more
34	have lunch every day without discussing work
19	have only a snack lunch
40	think they are overweight
4½	are teetotal

[1] Roy Lewis and Rosemary Stewart: *The Boss*, 1960. p. 221.

70 per cent never smoke cigars
20 have over $\frac{3}{4}$-hour of exercise a day
63 have no voluntary commitments at week-ends or evenings.

In 1965 the Institute published another survey, in which 10,000 directors were asked about their qualifications, of whom 60 per cent replied. The replies showed that smaller companies had a much lower percentage of graduate directors than big ones, and that in companies with a capital of over half a million pounds, arts graduates were nearly twice as common as science or engineering graduates.

Among the directors as a whole

13 per cent went to secondary modern schools
15 " " " " technical schools
31 " " " " grammar schools
13 " " " " private schools
48 " " " " public schools[2]
23 " " " " universities

Of the directors between 26 and 35, 75 per cent went to public schools, but among directors who held Ph.D degrees (only ·7 of the total) only 20·5 per cent went to public schools.

This is an (anonymous) description of the life of a provincial director:

'He will probably drive a Jaguar to the office every day, in a large industrial town; he will live 15 miles out in a modern house with eight bedrooms and five acres. His wife will be as old as he, but ageing faster and will look rather exhausted with the effort of keeping up with him. He may well conduct a few unserious affairs, probably when he visits the Head Office in London. He will be well-preserved and extremely well-turned out; he will take *The Times*, but read the *Express*; his staff will be devoted to him; his wife will run an Austin; he will have children at boarding school. There will be very few books in the house; holidays will be taken in Spain; he will be drinking rather more whisky than he should and will rely on television for relaxation more than he should; he will be well up in the supertax class, but not saving very much. In the home, talk will be seven-eighths of his colleagues at work and about his friendly but lethal struggles with them; he

[1] This contrasts strikingly with senior American executives of whom (according to a *Fortune* survey) more than half took part in civic or charitable activities.

[2] The figures do not add up to 100 per cent, because many directors went to two kinds of school.

will know his job backwards, despise outside experts, but be secretly worried about the prowess of his junior colleagues. At 50 he may well have a heart attack, perhaps in the bath, and after that will have to work at half-speed.'

Directors' salaries are surrounded by secrecy: by law only the total salaries paid to directors need be published. When the government revealed that Dr. Beeching, the chairman-elect of the British Transport Commission, was earning £24,000 as a director of ICI, the news came as a bombshell to the civil service. The highest paid director is thought to be Sir William Lyons, founder-chairman of Jaguar Cars, said to earn £100,000 a year. Other prosperous bosses are Paul Chambers of ICI, with £50,000 a year, and the 'seven men' of Shell, also (it is believed) earning £50,000. Salaries above £20,000 are becoming commoner.

How do British directors compare with others? According to F. X. Olanie, of McKinsey's, managing directors of smaller companies (turnover about £1 million) compare favourably with their continental counterparts: but in firms with turnover around £40 million, they are paid less than in France, Germany, Italy or Belgium.[1]

INSTITUTE OF DIRECTORS

One pointer to the new self-confidence of bosses is the Institute of Directors, in three mansions in Belgrave Square. After the war it was moribund, and then was revived by a ginger-group led by Lord Chandos and Sir Edward Spears: it aimed to become a 'Bosses Trade Union', and to encourage a 'warm family feeling' among directors—a kind of counter-revolution to the Socialists. Since then it has multiplied a hundredfold, and in mid-1964 had over 40,000 members, including 400 women and over 250 members of both houses of parliament who (according to the brochure), 'Can be counted upon to see that the views of directors are adequately voiced in parliament and their interests protected whenever occasion demands it.'

The Institute presents a kind of caricature of directors, as in satirical films or George Gross cartoons. Its club is called 'The Number 10 Club'. A long bar is filled at lunch-time with large and leisurely men, who progress to the dining-room for big long lunches (some of the best in London), served by Italian waiters on Wedg-

[1] Deciding the Executives' Salary: *Financial Times*, December 20, 1960.

wood Napoleon Ivy plates (as used on Elba), followed by endless cups of coffee. At three-fifteen directors are still in the coffee-room, while the chauffeurs wait in Jaguars and Zephyrs. A thick, glossy magazine, *The Director*, with a very enterprising editor, E. D. Foster, and quite provocative articles, is sent monthly to members. Every November the Institute holds a jamboree of five thousand directors, addressed by speakers who in 1964 consisted of Lord Robens, George Woodcock, Sir Alec Douglas Home, the Russian Ambassador and Peter Scott.

A formidable critic of the Institute was Lionel Fraser, the merchant banker and former Chairman of Thomas Tilling (who died in 1965). In his candid autobiography, *All to the Good*, published in 1963, he wrote:

> It seems to me to be quite unnecessary to have this colossus of a Directors' trade union—a caucus of Right-wing business men—for the protection of directors as a class. If you are a member of a board of directors you should be able to look after yourself, even if the company is a small family business in the provinces.
>
> Surely directors do not need the Institute of Directors to nurse them, to stand by them in face of the Inland Revenue, for instance, to show them how to avoid a heart attack or how to conduct themselves in their relations with their employees. I know the working man has his trade union, and quite rightly so, for he has had to fight for his present satisfactory position. But why do directors require a trade union? To protect them from what? They should be leaders.
>
> Members of the council of the Institute have flatteringly suggested I might rejoin, but most ungraciously I have replied that I would only do that in order to resign again, so underlining my distaste for this organisation. Perhaps I am unreasonable, but their gigantic annual meetings, the swank and pomposity of these jamborees, bring out only the worst of me.
>
> Again, I was at a loss to comprehend their rush to intervene in the political sphere in December, 1962, at the time of Dean Acheson's criticism of Great Britain's rôle in world affairs. This self-appointed guardianship of our country's greatness by the Institute, as somebody said, seemed to me precipitate and inappropriate.

The Institute encourages a mystique of directorship as opposed to managership, and stays aloof from the British Institute of Management, their less effective rival, which they describe as 'madly serious'. The Director-General of the Directors is an Etonian baronet, Major Sir Richard Powell—bluff and amiable, with wavy grey hair, a humorous moustache and (still) enormous charm: he inhabits a big office with a coal fire, murky paintings, a row of gadgets on the desk, and a patio outside. 'There are three different classes in industry—labour, managers and directors,' said Sir Richard: 'The board itself doesn't have to be experts: technicians and accountants should be available, to be consulted by the board. We believe that directors are a kind of aristocracy: they should be men of parts, and they should have interests outside their business. Directors have become noticeably less selfish in the last seven years: it's easier now to find men to join committees.' 'I know it is a dangerous phrase,' Sir Richard has said, 'but you could say we were a gigantic Old Boy network.'[1]

Among the more influential members of the Institute's council are three powerful backers of commercial television: Harley Drayton[2] of British Electric Traction (whose matter-of-fact and authoritative statements are held in some awe); Lord Renwick, the tough baronial stockbroker, and C. O. Stanley, chairman of the Pye Group—both co-founders of Associated Television.[3] The chairman of the Council is Sir Edward Spears, a veteran of the first world war and Chairman of Ashanti Goldfields, known as 'Beaucaire'. For many years the High Priest of the Institute was their former President, Lord Chandos, who stood as a kind of director-hero, and an important symbol of bossmanship; a long study of him went through three issues of *The Director*. Chandos represented that rare phenomenon, the aristocrat in business, with an intellectual's as well as a businessman's mind; he was one of many people who have been called 'Mr. Establishment', and he helped to give directors a new sense of dignity and importance.

The new President, who took over in January 1964, is Paul Chambers,[4] the chairman of ICI, representing a more thrusting and meritocratic type of industrialist then Chandos. Chambers has set out to improve the public image of directors, both by informing the public and by improving the directors. He explained to *The Times* that, whereas people can count on professional conduct from doctors or chartered accountants, anybody can become a director by registering a company and spending a little money.[4] He maintains (with his own experience as a former tax commissioner) that directors' behaviour is better than it was twenty or thirty years ago, but he thinks there is still room for improvement, and that the Institute can have an important influence, for instance, by expelling outrageous directors (three

[1] *See Daily Mail,* November 9, 1961.
[2] *See* p. 445.
[3] *See* pp. 653–4.
[4] *The Times,* December 10, 1963.

were expelled in 1962).[1] Chambers may knock some of the amateur nonsense out of the Institute, for he is not himself a man to disguise his intense professionalism; but there is not the slightest sign of the Institute developing into any kind of public-spirited organisation.

DIRECTORS AND POLITICS

The Institute should not be taken too seriously. To become a 'Fellow', as members are called, requires no more than any kind of directorship: 40 per cent of the Fellows come from companies with assets of less than £100,000. Fellows can be divided into those who use the letters 'FInstD' after their name and those who don't: 'When somebody writes to me using those initials,' said one management consultant, 'I'm inclined to discount him: it suggests that he doesn't realise how meaningless they are.' Most Fellows use the Institute less as a trade union than as a handy hotel, a car-park and a club.

Few Fellows are politically active, or take any part in the Institute's affairs: but the politically minded officials, like trade unionists, are not afraid to invoke their whole membership, and they have their own '10 per cent democracy'. The Institute has assembled large funds from industry, and has a special 'Free Enterprise Fund' for advertising and other campaigns against nationalisation: before the 1959 election they put out a good deal of anti-Labour propaganda, and publicised a list of doomed firms. Many modern Tories, conscious of their new image, see the Institute as either a joke or an embarrassment, and many modern-minded businessmen, such as Lord Nelson of English Electric, refuse to join it. The Institute's political support, with its aura of expense-accounts and amateur boardrooms, is not an unmixed blessing. 'The idea of a businessmen's lobby isn't altogether attractive,' said one former Conservative chairman: 'The Institute aren't a particularly *nice* collection of people.' But the Institute do have some political influence with the Conservative party. Before budget-time they are always very active and vocal, and after the surtax relief in 1961 there were special celebrations.

The Institute of Directors has done something to educate and professionalise their directors. It stresses the importance of labour relations ('without that, nothing goes right, it's like sex in marriage'), provides an advisory service, holds courses on management

[1] Interview with Derek Hart on *Tonight*. BBC, December 12, 1963.

and mass meetings about exports, publishes a book on 'Standard Boardroom Practice', and endows a fellowship in management studies at Balliol. But in their country-squire cult (business documents, as at White's, are regarded as *de trop*), they confuse the real priorities of business, the images with realities. 'They are,' as one chairman put it, 'a kind of rearguard action against the managerial revolution.'

The more serious, and less political directors' organisation has been the Federation of British Industries (FBI), regarded as the main spokesman for British industrialists, together with the British Employers' Confederation (BEC) and the National Association of British Manufacturers (NABM). The FBI has often been regarded as a sinister capitalists' lobby, and before the war it successfully intervened with the government over tariffs in 1931, and over the amalgamation of the coal mines in 1938. But since the war it has carefully adopted a less political and committed attitude. The 300 members of its Grand Council, who met once a month, were too many and varied to have very unified views, and some businessmen complained that the FBI was more on the side of the government than industry. 'The notion of the FBI as the eminence grise of British politics must be abandoned' wrote Professor Sam Finer in 1956: 'even with a Conservative government in power the FBI is but one voice—albeit a very powerful one—among many.' Compared to continental employers' organisations, like Confindustria in Milan, which has a bevy of MPs and its own daily newspaper, the FBI has been very unpolitical. 'It's a typically British institution,' said one of its more radical staff: 'rather grey, nothing to get hot under the collar about, but not very exhilarating either.'

In February 1965, after previous attempts, the three organisations eventually agreed to merge into a single 'Confederation of British Industries', following a report the year before by Sir Henry Benson (of Cooper Brothers, the accountants) and Sir Sam Brown (of Linklaters and Paines, the solicitors). As its first president the CBI has Maurice Laing, the managing director of the Laing building companies, who has been one of the most public-spirited of the employers' representatives, and who was active in promoting George Brown's 'statement of intent' on incomes policy. Laing is a director of the Bank of England, a member of 'Neddy', and a prominent churchman—the very model of the reconstructed businessman. The Director-General of the CBI—the executive head of the organisation—is John

Davies, a Welsh accountant who had been chief executive of Shell-Mex and BP, the oil marketing company. Davies, too, represented the British businessman in his most sophisticated and international state: he is only 49, and he belongs to the new generation who went into business after the war. He is said to speak French, German and Swedish. He spent some time in France, where he much admired French planning techniques. He is a strong advocate of joining the Common Market. He is an unashamed salesman. And he is said to have both a Welsh eloquence, and a Welsh diplomacy. He is thought by the *Financial Times* to earn about £20,000 a year.

Not all businessmen, or conservatives, were keen on the merged organisation, at a time when the Labour Party was in power. Enoch Powell, the most effective advocate of free enterprise, attacked the rôle of the industrial organisations in *The Director*, just before the CBI came into being: 'They start more than half beaten by the very fact that they are, or claim to be, the spokesmen and representatives. It has been their pride and occupation to "represent" industry to the Government. Yet the safest posture for any industry confronted with Socialism would be not to have an organisation or spokesman at all . . . Remember Caligula, who wished the Roman people had one neck, so that he could cut it off? The Association of These, and the Federation of That, present just that one neck to the Socialist garrotter, (and now, not content, these employers seem to be bent on all amalgamating into one great, soft, vulnerable neck!).'

32

NATIONALISED INDUSTRIES

If you keep pulling up the plant to see how the roots are getting on, it does not grow very well.

Lord Heyworth (Select Committee 1953. q. 723)

It may be regrettable, but it seems to be a fact that people's enthusiasm about almost any group to which they belong is enhanced by competition.

Hugh Gaitskell: Socialism and Nationalisation, 1956.

NATIONALISED industries are the major innovation of post-war Britain; unlike most British institutions they have not grown slowly out of the past, but have been deliberately imposed, appearing fully armed, like Athene from the head of Zeus. Ever since they disappeared from the stock exchange, they have become a battleground of theory—a rare thing in so pragmatic a country—crossed and recrossed by armies of commissions, select committees, politicians, dons and consultants, all trying to decide what to do about them. Only in the last few years have they begun to acquire more definite personalities.

They are an odd jumble of properties. The state has been landed with many of the most unprofitable estates in the country, in most cases because they have apparently become unworkable by anyone else. The full list includes the Sugar Corporation, Cable and Wireless Ltd., the North of Scotland Hydro-Electric Board, Short Brothers and Harland Ltd., the Atomic Energy Authority, and, of course, the Post Office—a nationalised industry in every country, but which in England has grown to become a banker, telephone company, tax-collector and pension agent. But the Post Office is a separate case, run directly by the civil service. The core of the state industries is made up by the great national utilities—coal, gas, railways, electricity and airways.

They all have exciting histories: they represent, in that order, the layers of Britain's industrial revolution. It was on coal that the industrial revolution was based: the invention of gas (in 1798), of railways (in 1829), and electricity (in 1881) built up the urban industrial country which we know. Today they have grown from daring pioneers into ancient, reviled and unwanted retainers. And as Britain becomes more involved in affluence, cars and private property, so the fabric of public services becomes increasingly taken for granted, like rivers, and only noticed and cursed at when strikes interrupt their flow.

Their most obvious characteristic is size: they make the private industrial giants look like midgets. British Railways employs six times as many people as ICI, and the Electricity Board devours enough capital to build a new ICI every three years. Each of the Coal Board's nine divisions is bigger, in turnover, than English Electric. These are the six leading public corporations, with their numbers of employees, profit, and date of nationalisation:

	Employees 1964	*Surplus or Deficit 1963 £M*	*Date of Nationalisation*
British Railways Board	442,000	−133·9	1947
National Coal Board	564,000	+·1	1946
Electricity Council and Boards	210,000	+42	1947
Gas Council and Boards	123,119	+4·9	1949
BOAC	20,650	−12·5	1939
BEA	17,108	+3	1946

Their size, as much as their ownership, has made them problem children, for when they were nationalised in quick succession, no one had had experience of running huge concerns except generals; and industrial corporations are not at all like armies. In retrospect, perhaps the most surprising fact about the nationalisation was how, in spite of all the theorising and discussion that preceded it, hardly any of the nationalisers had any idea of how large corporations could, or should, be run; this was part of the price of the divorce between parliament and the world of managers. As the problems grew, several of the heads of private firms were called in: Lord Heyworth from Unilever, Lord Fleck and Paul Chambers from ICI, Sir Ivan Stedeford from Tube Investments—they all gave their diagnosis and prognosis, but none had had experience of malaise on such a massive scale. As Lord Heyworth put it to the Select Committee in 1953: 'Anyone can find out what is wrong at any moment of time, but very few people can get it better . . .' The problems of the big corporations have been compounded of size, old age, service and neglect, for which there is no quick cure.

While cabinets were slow to understand the organisational problems, the Treasury were slow to realise the economic implication. The industries added enormously to the government's responsibilities, not only in appointing their heads and directing their policies, but in allocating their capital. And nationalisation changed the whole balance of economic power. Between them, in 1961, they invested £740 million, compared with some £1,200 million spent by the whole of private manufacturing industry. In its responsibility for regulating this sum, Treasury policy can drastically affect and alter the country's economy, but it has come to this realisation slowly and reluctantly.

Though nationalisation is associated with socialism, these industries had been moving steadily towards state control since the nineteen-twenties. The nationalisation of coal was first proposed by the Sankey Commission of 1919. BOAC was created by a Conservative government in 1939. Nationalising electricity was considered by Lord McGowan in 1936, and nationalising gas was recommended by Lord Heyworth in 1948. The state had been intervening in railways and coal as they declined through the twenties and thirties: and vigorously though their nationalisation was opposed by Conservatives, few openly advocate de-nationalisation.

The concept of the public corporation was first fully expounded by Herbert Morrison, who was responsible for creating the London Passenger Transport Board. 'The public corporation must be no mere capitalist business, the be-all and end-all of which is profits and dividends,' wrote Morrison in 1953: 'Its board and officers must regard themselves as the high custodians of the public interest.' But the 'high custodians' have been caught between the ideals of service and the demand for profitable running. We have seen how the whole dynamic of private industry is provided by the profit motive—how their structures, hierarchies, prestige and self-respect only make sense in terms of profit. The socialist founders of nationalisation wished to substitute the service motive as the driving force, but profits and service are bound to be at loggerheads. Telegrams, airways to the Hebrides, country electricity and branch-lines all lose money but are all essential services. No one likes to be associated with losing money. 'Our chaps hated our making a loss,' said Lord Douglas of Kirtleside, the former chairman of BEA: 'they used to go into the pub and someone would say, "Well, Bill, how much money have you lost today?" When we started making a profit, the whole atmosphere was different.'

NATIONALISED CHAIRMEN

And who should run these corporations? Morrison insisted that the public corporations should be largely independent of government interference: they would not, like civil service departments, have a minister sitting in the building. Their boards would be left to get on with their job, like the boards of private companies, with parliament, as shareholders, occasionally surveying the scene, and the appropriate minister maintaining contact with the board. But the relationship has not worked out that way. At first, ministers left the corporations pretty much alone: 'I think they were too ready to abdicate to the Frankensteins which they'd created,' one ex-minister said to me. Then, as things began to go wrong, parliament became restive, and ministers and civil service departments (who have often resented the freedom of the corporations) intervened more in running the industries.

It is perhaps not surprising that these bodies have no strong personalities of their own. Their names are elaborately confusing: the electricity people have changed three times—from BEA to CEA to (now two names) EC and CEGB: who now knows the difference between CEGB—which employs 64,000 people—and EC, which employs 600? The two million people who work for these organisations, from the SWGB to BR (ER), appear as a single government army. The nationalised managers, like insurance managers or accountants, are largely separate from the public school nexus and the old boy net: they have their roots with provincial engineering schools or branch offices.

In this unhappy no-man's-land between government and commerce are placed the chairmen of the nationalised boards. They are not much envied and, compared to the chairmanship of a joint stock company, they are very vulnerable. They are appointed for five years only—not long enough to see the fruits of their capital investment: and though one chairman survived fifteen years, many resigned before the end of their term. They have to run their vast and complex properties with an inquisitive parliament and often a determined minister looking over their shoulder. There must always be disagreement between a chairman trying to run a commercial business and a minister trying to placate the public—whether the chairman wants to raise the price of coal or fares, to make large capital investments, to buy American aircraft, or to give in to wage demands. The argument is not usually settled by open directives from the minister, but by the 'fireside chats' or 'old boy messages'—the traditional British technique. The outcome of the chats is the secret test of the chairman.

The chairmen have at last appeared as an identifiable species. Most of them have come from outside their industries—from the armed forces, from private industry or politics. The four major chairmen all come from outside the traditional civil service background:[1] they include a professor, an engineer and a scientist. Here, as in insurance or hire-purchase companies, new institutions are run by new men.

These were the chairmen of the major nationalised industries in January 1965, with their salaries:

Railways	Dr. Richard Beeching	£24,000
British Overseas Airways	Sir Giles Guthrie	£15,000
Coal	Lord Robens	£12,500
Electricity—		
Council	Sir Ronald Edwards	£12,500
Generating Board	Stanley Brown	£12,500
Atomic Energy	Sir William Penney	£12,500
Gas	Sir Henry Jones	£11,000
British European Airways	Anthony Milward	£11,000

When the corporations were created, it was hoped that a new kind of manager would emerge—someone half-way between a civil servant and a businessman, between the world of budgets and the world of profits—a new 'industrial civil service'. The salaries followed this pattern: most of the chairmen earned £10,000 a year—more than the civil service heads, but much less than the private tycoons. Many chairmen and some of their boards, had accepted large cuts of salary. The ideal of public service showed itself in the austerity of the dingy corridors, bleak offices and chipped cups of tea on the civil service pattern, with little of the expense-account splendour of private industries.

But into the midst of these assumptions was dropped in March, 1961 the 'Beeching Bombshell'—the announcement that the new head of British Railways, Dr. Beeching, would earn the same salary as he had as director of ICI—£24,000 a year. It happened that in the following week, I was interviewing three chairmen of

[1] *See* p. 260.

nationalised industries. Their reaction was immediate: 'Absolutely deplorable', 'thoroughly demoralising', 'tremendous repercussions'. It was almost as if it had been announced that the Royal Navy had sold out to Shell.

Behind this furore lay the whole proud history of the public service—which in Britain, unlike in America, has in the past been more highly regarded than private industry. The nationalised industries—particularly coal and electricity—still have many managers who have an idealistic dedication to state service, and a fixed dislike of private industry. But since the war the private industries have become more concerned with prestige, and the public ones with profit, while the public corporations, at a time of full employment, have had to compete strongly for their managers. The Beeching bombshell seemed to imply that public and private service were indivisible, and that service was no longer its own reward.

Meanwhile a fundamental force had pushed all the corporations in the direction of private industry—competition. When first nationalised, they were indispensable services at a time of shortage, sure of their market, in danger of producing too little rather than too much, and all basically dependent on coal. But road transport, natural gas, airways and oil have made all of them less secure, setting coal against oil and natural gas; gas against electricity; railways against cars, and lorries and airways; airways against foreign airways. The fights have not only made the industries more cost-conscious; they have gradually made them emerge as separate entities to the public eye, as more aggressive, positive bodies. The desirability of competition has, of course, been emphasised by the Conservative government; an important White Paper in April 1961 (suitably disguised in Treasury language) on the 'financial and economic obligations of the nationalised industries' said: 'They are not, and ought not to be regarded as social services absolved from economic and commercial justification.' This is the antithesis of Herbert Morrison's high custodians.

One pointer to competition is provided by advertising, to which parliament has often objected. The public corporations have increasingly advertised not only to attract people from roads to railways, from oil to coal, from electricity to gas, but also to improve their labour relations and present a better image to the public. Expenditure rushed up until in December 1964 the new Minister of Power, Fred Lee, resolved to restrict it: 'Competition,' he said, 'has reached a daft level.'[1] These figures[2] show spending on advertising:

	1950	*1960*	*1963*
National Coal Board	£732	£700,658	£979,938
British Railways	239,834	646,513	679,995
Electricity Council and Regional Boards	42,788	358,256	631,036
Gas Council and Regional Boards	65,755	1,242,828	1,338,144
BEA	33,700	127,396	162,759
BOAC	62,240	304,357	253,234
GPO	2,934	161,082	602,758

COAL

The miners never had a better friend than Alf Robens.

Lord Robens, April 1964.

Coal is the oldest, most basic industry of all. Deep mining began in Britain three hundred years ago, and by Dr. Johnson's time all the present coalfields were being worked. Coal production reached its peak—like the navy and the city—in 1913, with 287 million tons a year, when a third of the coal was exported and the mines employed over a million men. Today, with 200 million tons a year, Britain is still the fourth biggest coal-producer, next to America, Russia and China.

Coal mining is part of the life of the country: the black pit heaps and pitheads which jut out of the landscape in South Wales or Durham have grown their own villages and communities. In many ways coal mining, like some family firms, is closer to agriculture than industry, rooted in local communities, cut off from the towns, dependent on manual labour. In spite of mechanisation, 56 per cent of the cost of coal is the cost of labour. It is the mining village, with the lodge, the pub, the club, the union branch-office, which still determines the character of the industry.

Coal has an unhappy history—exploitation, child labour, unemployment and strikes, which reached a climax in 1926, when the miners continued on strike for six months after the rest of the country had gone back to work. The mines had been built on cheap labour and the coal-owners faced the twentieth century

[1] *Sunday Times*, December 13, 1964.

[2] Source: *Legion Statistical Reviews*.

with reluctance, little research, poor labour conditions and no co-ordination.

The nationalisation of this sad run-down industry in 1946 was an operation without parallel in British history: the new 'National Coal Board' bought 640 former colliery owners at the cost of £388,000,000. The new board established itself in Hobart House, a big rabbit-warren near Victoria. For the miners, the day of nationalisation was a day of triumph—the end of a twenty-year war. Hobart House still has an atmosphere of dedication, partisanship, and bitterness about oil, quite different from other corporations. The forging together of these scattered collieries was a gigantic task. Few men had experience in large-scale management, and many who did left the industry on nationalisation. The separate collieries were proud of their independence, and the colliery managers were often a law to themselves. The industry remains dominated by the mining engineers, whose training is primarily concerned with machines. 40 out of 41 of the area general managers, the 'barons of the industry', are mining engineers. The impact of a national organisation on these rugged communities was bound to be difficult: 'It was such an upheaval,' one observer said, 'that there was no humus left: there was nothing on which managers could grow.' The Coal Board was accused of a stifling centralisation, and Hobart House became a favourite Tory symbol of Socialist bureaucracy. But when the Fleck committee reported in 1955, they said that there had been too *little* centralisation, and that separate divisions were given too much freedom in staffing, organisation and capital expenditure, with some area general managers allowed to authorise projects up to £100,000: 'This degree of delegation cannot be matched in any well-run industrial undertaking within our knowledge.'

The Coal Board maintains a vast subterranean empire, including 1,300 railway engines and 14,000 miles of roadway under the surface. They are one of the biggest brick-makers in the country, and one of the biggest landlords (130,000 houses and 210,000 acres of farmland). They maintain a vast private railway system, with 78,000 wagons and 4,000 miles of track.

The coal industry has reluctantly come round to the idea of competition. For nearly twenty years after 1938 there was no alternative to coal—for gas, electricity, blast furnaces, central heating or railway engines. In the post-war years the government urged the Coal Board to produce as much coal as possible, without too much regard to cost: salesmanship was not needed, and quantity had to come before quality. The consumption went steadily up, from 186 million tons in 1946 to 218 million in 1956. And then, in 1957, against all predictions of economists, it went down. It continued to go down for the next three years. Between 1958 and 1960 the Coal Board had to cut production by 28 million tons; they cut their manpower by 120,000—equivalent to the whole of ICI, and in 1961 they were still losing men at the rate of 80 a day. Several unexpected factors created this slump. Industry had a recession, the use of coal became more efficient, railways began to turn to diesels, there had been three mild winters and a brilliant summer. The use of oil had increased—for power stations, central heating, road transport. Oil consumption doubled in two years, and the Coal Board found itself with international new enemies—Shell, Esso, BP—armed with the menacing slogan 'anything coal can do, oil can do better'. And above all, the spectre of cheap gas, piped in from the North Sea, loomed over the whole coal industry.

Grappling with this new situation is the head of the Coal Board, Lord Robens, a big welcoming man with a comfortable Lancashire accent and long legs which sprawl over the chair. Alone of the nationalised chairmen, he is a politician: he left school at 15, worked his way up through the Co-op, became a Labour cabinet minister at forty, and took over the Coal Board in 1961, at fifty. If he had not taken that job, and a life peerage, he might well now be prime minister, for after Gaitskell's death he would have been a natural compromise candidate between Wilson and Brown. He has the toughness, the fluency, the expansive gestures of a politician—wagging a finger, shrugging big shoulders. In Hobart House he is known as the Chairman, but still answers to Alf. He has identified himself with the new situation of coal, and projected a new vigour; he was the first nationalised chairman to have a private aeroplane.

'Competition has changed the whole psychology of the industry,' said Robens: 'it means we've really got to *sell* coal, and provide a service all the way through. For twenty years the nation had been a captive market for coal. What we want is a few large customers, not millions of small ones. Mechanisation is being planned to a degree undreamt of three hundred years ago. The miners, thank God, aren't Luddites: they don't mind machines, provided they get the money.'

In the four years of his chairmanship, Robens has seen a remarkable change in his industry. By 1962 coal made a profit for the first time for sixty years, and maintained it in 1963. Mechanisation doubled in three years, and by 1964 was up to 70 per cent of the total. Great friction continued between the Coal Board and the mineworkers' union, but the new profitability of coal helped to boost the miners' morale. Robens has not been shy about emphasising his rôle: 'When I went to the Coal Board in 1960,' he told sceptical miners at the Scottish TUC in April, 1964, 'pits were being closed, coal was being poured on the ground, and there was no future. It is a very different picture today. I have no apologies to make for the way I have run the National Coal Board. If I had had as much help from everybody in the industry as the time and energy I put into the industry myself, we would have been further along the road today.' But by 1965 coal was facing a new crisis, with the growth of absenteeism, the imports of oil and gas, and the resulting loss of profits.

RAILWAYS

When the 'Big Four' railway companies were nationalised in 1947, the new British Transport Commission became the biggest employers in the country, employing more men than the army, the navy and the air force put together. They took over not only railways, but canals, docks, road haulage, Pullman cars, Cook's travel agents, Pickford's and Carter Paterson's delivery services. They became the biggest hoteliers and caterers in the country, with a chain of Victorian railway palaces. They inherited the most extravagant railway system in the world: no country had such a large amount of railway track (50,000 miles) for its size. You have only to compare a railway map of Britain, with its veins stretching out to remote country areas, with one of Germany or France. And in 1960 it was found that on the average, three out of four seats on British Railways were left unoccupied.[1] Like mines, the railways were built with cheap labour. Armies of navvies covered the country with railway tracks. They built no fewer than 13 main-line terminals in London—New York has two. This complex of stations, viaducts, tunnels, bridges, workshops, marshalling yards, engines and rolling stock is by far the most expensive property in Britain. In 1960 the British Transport Commission estimated that the gross replacement value 'could hardly be less than £5,000 million'.[2] The railways became the most embarrassing of all Britain's Victorian leftovers. In the 150 years

[1] *See Select Committee on Nationalised Industries*, 1960, para. 326.
[2] *Ibid.*, para. 243.

since they came into being, they acquired a picturesque, feudal and delightful way of life of their own, presided over by top-hatted stationmasters in cavernous station halls.

It is difficult to remember that the railways were once as daring as supersonic jets today. The question of profits gradually receded into the background, as mysteriously happens with old industries: the system of railway accounting, riddled with what the select committee called 'financial archaeology', has been the despair of investigators. Ever since the arrival of the internal combustion engine, all railways have been in difficulties. But in Britain, where the railways are the oldest, the problem is thorniest.

BEECHING

Into the midst of this placid railway empire there arrived in October, 1959, the disturbing phenomenon of Ernest Marples, then Minister of Transport. It is dangerous in Whitehall to give credit for changes to the men who claim it, but the personality of Marples was central. He was a self-made tycoon, with a passionate interest in business which distinguished him from the rest of the cabinet. He saw himself less as a politician than a technician, devoted to efficiency. When he became Minister of Transport in 1959, the snarled-up situation exactly suited him—London crawling with traffic jams, British Railways losing millions, roads built without planning or research. He bustled into his new office, read every available book on transport, hired Colin Buchanan, flew round America and Europe inspecting fly-overs and traffic systems, and devised new schemes for London parking, one-way streets, and long-term road-plans. 'I'm a great believer in committing myself,' he told me: 'that's how you get things done, by committing other people too. You get the experts and then you say, "well, now you must do it".'

He did not disguise his contempt for the incompetence of the railways and he was visibly out of sympathy with their then chairman, Sir Brian Robertson. He inspected the modernisation plans, the costing systems, the potato-peelers and the frying pans, the centralised lump of administration, and compared it all to his business experience. He appointed the Stedeford Committee with wide terms of reference, and after their secret report appointed one of its members, Dr. Richard Beeching, a director of ICI, to be the new chairman of the railways. Soon afterwards two other new full-time members of the Transport Commission were appointed—Philip Shirley, an Australian accountant from Unilever at £12,000 a year, and Leslie Williams from Shell at £7,500 a year. The new appointments—one each from the three pillars of private enterprise—underlined the new order in nationalisation.

There are some people who said that Marples' most important achievement was the hiring of Beeching, who approached his vast problem—itself a kind of caricature of all Britain's problems—with the dispassionate expertise of a surgeon. (The fact that he is always known as Doctor reinforced the image.) He is a big, relaxed man with a high dome, a bristle moustache and a slow gravelly voice; he might be mistaken at first for one of those large phlegmatic men who tell long stories over a pint of beer in a country pub. He rose through ICI with apparent effortlessness. The son of a journalist, he took a first in physics at the Imperial College, did research into electrons, and in ICI soon showed a flair for management. He built up a reputation both for efficiency and for fundamental niceness. He takes life easily, arrives at the office at ten, and generates an atmosphere of homely confidence. He gives the impression above all of a striking intellectual honesty, and the political shibboleths about nationalisation seem to dissolve in his presence.

His arrival in British Railways quickly produced a new situation. He succeeded, remarkably quickly, in obtaining the trust of the unions, but he had little sympathy with the traditional attitude of assuming that all railways (like coal mines) were permanent and unchangeable, and that it was their duty to provide any service that was required. He was visibly astonished by the sheer lack of *information* about traffic and costs, through all the years of furious controversy. He described the deficit as an 'open-ended sock' and brought a whole new vocabulary of words like 'fine-scale cross-subsidisation', 'conditions of origin' and 'built-in flywheel'. He shuffled about general managers, introduced accountants, and wobbled the staircase of promotion. Against the anger this produced was the realisation by able men, stuck in a long and inevitable queue, that their talents might now be noticed. 'You can't have a confused set of motives,' he said to me in 1962: 'you can't say one day that you're giving a service and ignoring the profit, and the next day that you're hoping to make it pay . . . It's true that it's not so nerve-racking to be deep in the red as it is to be hovering between the red and the black; but on the other hand being in the red can be very demoralising.'

The full implications of the Beeching revolution burst on to the public on March 27, 1963, when the drastic 'Reshaping Plan' of the British Railways Board (as the railway part of the Transport Commission had become) was published, accompanied by ballyhoo and nation-wide protests. The plan aimed to prune one-third of Britain's railway system, and to close up most of the unprofitable lines, including a large part of the Scottish and Welsh railway system. In a brilliantly-presented film, to launch the Plan, Beeching described with ruthless analysis how uncommercial these country lines had become, and how with ruthless changes the railways could be put on to a business footing.

In the following year the Plan began to take effect, though the closing of lines was always hotly contested and sometimes repealed. In January 1964 the Railways Board could announce that the deficit had been reduced by £17 million. There were also bold schemes for fast trains on main-line routes, and new 'Liner Trains' for express freight. By 1963 there were more than five hundred trains travelling at more than a mile-a-minute, for the first time in the history of the railways; and the electrification of the London to Manchester line—the busiest main line in the world—was expected to produce much smoother and cleaner travel.

The Beeching revolution not only brought a new commercial dynamic into railways; it also became a prototype, or a symbol, of a new kind of ruthlessness in Britain. 'Doing a Beeching' became a phrase for any drastic reassessment—even in the Church; and in the mood of 1963, after Britain's failure to enter the Common Market, the cold logic of Beeching served in some ways to provide some of that harsh reassessment that the Common Marketeers hoped would come from the continent. Beeching is a very different kind of hero from war leaders, colonial governors or flying pioneers; but in the thankless task of wrenching Britain into the nineteen-sixties, his rôle has been crucial and even heroic. There was much talk of Beeching becoming overlord for all transport under the Labour government, but he refused the job, with its difficult conditions, and announced that he would return to ICI in June 1965.

GAS AND ELECTRICITY

The other nationalised industries gradually became more accustomed to competition, and gas found a quite new prospect. The incandescent flame was invented by William Murdoch in

1798; the Gas Light and Coke Company was formed in 1798 and the next year Westminster bridge was lit by gaslight. It was an astonishing innovation, which revolutionised urban society. For most of the next century gas had the field to itself, until in 1881 the first electric light system was installed, in Godalming in Surrey: (Lord Salisbury, the prime minister, was one of the first people to have his house lit by electricity—showing an aristocratic interest in technical innovations not much followed since). Electricity won in lighting, but gas kept its supremacy in cooking. Competition made gas more efficient, and forced it to find ways to cheapen production and use its by-products (which include coal tar, benzine and ammonia).

Gas was built up by a number of local firms—some private, some municipal—which after nationalisation in 1948 kept much of their local character. It is the most decentralised of the nationalised industries: though the Gas Light and Coke Company was renamed North Thames Gas, it remained a proud and separate entity, still setting the pace for others. The Gas Council (the co-ordinating centre) allows the local boards a great deal of autonomy. Only five years ago the gas business seemed to be a rather sad kind of joke. The very word itself (invented in the seventeenth century by a Dutchman) had developed nasty associations with poison and suicide; the smell was horrible; gasholders defaced the countryside; and for everything except cooking, electricity seemed altogether more splendid. The gas people were sadly aware that their fuel was the one that people could do without. But since then many things have happened in the Battle of the Fuels. New processes have been developed which made gas much cheaper, and produced a boom in gas central heating. Natural gas has been discovered abroad in all kinds of odd places, and may soon be discovered under the North Sea. And the gas people will soon be able to liberate themselves from their old dependence on coal—which will make gas not only cheaper but also non-poisonous. (It may also, incidentally, mean the end of coke.)

Encouraged by this new world, the Gas Council have become much more aggressive and cocky. They fought the Coal Board—and all their formidable lobby of miner MPs—with gusto and cunning; they insisted, against all the pressures, on importing gas in liquid form, in special refrigerated ships, from the Sahara; and they launched a big new advertising campaign, which abandoned the old pre-war image of Mr. Therm (the man who made all those jokes in theatre programmes) and substituted the brisk

'High-speed Gas, heat that *obeys* you', which made electricity seem disgracefully sluggish and self-willed. Another cheeky advertisement, aimed at electricity pylons, showed a beautiful cornfield with the caption 'a year ago the gas underground grid was laid through here'. They even considered changing the name of gas altogether, but settled for HSG.

The gas knights at Murdoch House, the headquarters of the Gas Council, assumed a much more confident and defiant look: Sir Henry Jones, the Chairman, a silver-haired Welshman from an old gas family, and Sir Kenneth Hutchison, his deputy, a big Scottish scientist with technocrat's eyebrows, now appeared not as liquidators of a Victorian empire but as heirs to a glorious new gas age.

And *if* large pockets of natural gas *are* found in the North Sea, the new age will have come. The mysterious, powerful fuel which (when it rose up from the Po Valley) first made the fame of Mattei in Italy, which redeemed the Sahara and is now reviving Holland, could upset all our calculations of energy, and will threaten oil, till now the most powerful fuel of all. It could make the Middle East seem much less important; and it could give Britain her first big new discovery of natural wealth since coal was unearthed. (In all the current diagnoses of Britain's malaise, it is easy to forget how much of our balance of payments difficulties would disappear if we were to find rich raw materials on our doorstep.)

Whether or not gas is found in the North Sea, the gas revival and developments in other fuels have already knocked all the post-war predictions sideways: the alarm about the 'Energy gap', the obsessions about the world shortage of oil, and the determination to dig coal at any cost have all now been completely outdated. Is there a moral in this, for economists and planners? None at all, except that You Never Can Tell.

ELECTRICITY

Between a coal mine and a power station there is all the difference of two centuries. One new power station of two million kilowatts (of the kind now being built) will produce enough electricity to run two Birminghams. Labour accounts for 60 per cent of the cost of coal, but only 18 per cent of the cost of electricity. In spite of tremendous capital costs, electricity has consistently made a profit. The capital cost of building power stations has gone down from around £64 per kilowatt ten years ago to £38 per kilowatt today. While the output of electricity has *more than doubled* in ten years, the number of employees has gone up by only one-fifth. This is due more to world-wide trends and improvements than to the efforts of the staff: ('Anyone would think,' said one member of the board, 'from the way some electricity people talk, that *they* were responsible for doubling consumption'). But the expansion and profitability has given it a special dynamic, and it has the advantage of a very short past.

Electricity has a confusing organisation, devised by a new Act in 1957. There is a Central Electricity Generating Board in charge of producing electricity, twelve area boards in charge of distributing it, and an Electricity Council which in theory is the central, decisive body. The Council, as its chairman explained it to me, is 'a cross between a holding company and a federation, with some of the characteristics of both'.

The Chairman of the Electricity Council, Sir Ronald Edwards, is one of the most surprising of all the top people in government pay. He is a mixture of don, accountant, businessman and politician, and this ability to cross frontiers, and to represent one field to another has, as with many other high-fliers, given him obvious strength. He runs the Council with quiet confidence and obvious enjoyment, from luxurious offices at the bottom of the Vickers skyscraper on the Thames: the Council has a huge conference room with a table shaped like a squashed circle, and Sir Ronald—an unobtrusive but very articulate man with thick spectacles—inhabits a resplendent office with walls of Japanese silk paper. He believes that one of the first essentials for a nationalised chairman is that he should be able to get another job at any time, and thus be able to speak his mind; and for this he is clearly qualified.

Sir Ronald's career does not fit into any fixed pattern of the past, but it may seem less surprising in the future. His father was a gas engineer, and he started work at the age of fifteen in the office where his father worked. He saw an advertisement for a correspondence college, and decided to become an accountant by correspondence, which enabled him to become a taxation expert. He then took an economics degree, again by correspondence, and through Sir Arnold Plant, who saw his papers, he was offered a job at the London School of Economics. The war—during which he worked as a civil servant in Aircraft Production—gave to him, as to so many others, a quite new set of experiences and contacts ('It meant that now there are about 300 people in all kinds of different fields who I can ring up on Christian name terms'); and after the war, with the advantage of this mixed background, he began regular seminars on Tuesday evenings at the LSE, where academic economists and businessmen met to discuss their joint problems. (Some of the evidence and findings of the seminars were later embodied in Edwards' book *Business Organisation in Great Britain.*) On this nearly-empty frontier between business and donnery, Edwards was clearly well-placed as an administrator, and through his friendship with Hugh Gaitskell, at the Ministry of Fuel and Power, he found himself first involved in electricity in 1947. He continued his connection with the LSE, where he became Professor of Economics, but he became increasingly involved in Whitehall. He was called in to join the Herbert Committee on Electricity and then (like Beeching) he turned from outsider to insider and in 1961 became head of the industry he had criticised. But he remains an informal, outspoken don in many of his attitudes, and like Lord Robens, Sir Ronald has brought a new confidence and flamboyance to his industry.

But while the Council is the centre of the electricity industry, it is its sister-organisation, the Generating Board, which actually owns, commissions and places the power stations which provide the stuff. 'CEGB'S dilemma,' wrote *The Economist* in July 1963, 'is that it is investing huge sums on which it at least seeks a commercial return at the same time as it is assisting with orders, at the bidding of the government, private firms floundering in a new technology.'[1] The chairmanship of the board is thus a highly controversial position; until 1964 it was firmly held by Lord Hinton, a tall and formidable technocrat who had supervised the building of the first nuclear power station at Calder Hall: Hinton often aroused great resentments: he was accused in the House of Lords by Lord Colyton, who was chairman of one of the consortia building power stations, as 'exerting an economic dictatorship on a pretty wide scale'; but he also gave drive and enthusiasm to the industry, and stimulated much wider research. In 1964 he was succeeded by Stanley Brown, a professional electrical engineer with a keen interest in economics. Brown's career has been much less flamboyant and localised than Hinton's: he went to school and to university in his home town, Birmingham, and started work in the electricity supply department for Birmingham Corporation. By 1957 he was a member of the board of the CEGB, and two years later became its deputy-chairman.

[1] 'The Profligate Atom'. *The Economist*, July 13, 1963.

The most controversial achievements of the Generating Board are the nuclear power stations, which Lord Hinton had begun. They cost as much to build as a small town: the biggest of them at Sizewell will have cost £60 million to build, employing a peak labour force of 2,000 workers: it is rising from a cliff on the Suffolk coast, a silent and solitary factory, sucking in 27 million gallons of seawater an hour, and spewing it out again, through tunnels ten feet high. It will produce 580,000 kilowatts of electricity —enough to supply a city of three-quarters of a million people— but after twenty years it will be unusable, a colossal monument to the earlier nuclear age. The largest nuclear power station yet planned will be at Wylfa Head in North Wales. It is due to start up in 1968, and will have double the output of Sizewell: it is the most powerful nuclear station so far projected in the world.

Will the nuclear power stations prove white elephants? So far, they have been very extravagant—partly because electricity-from-coal has become cheaper: in 1962 nuclear power stations were costing about £100 a kilowatt to build, compared to £40 a kilowatt for 'conventional' stations. But Hinton has insisted that by about 1970 nuclear power should be cheaper.

AIRWAYS

'We're the most competitive industry in the world,' said Lord Douglas of Kirtleside, the former chairman of British European Airways: 'and that makes us different from the other nationalised industries.' The two national airlines are far smaller than the other corporations: they have less than 10 per cent of the staff of British Railways. But their business expands by roughly 15 per cent a year, and they are involved, unlike the others, in a world-wide battle. The competition between national airlines becomes each year more hectic, but it is a very circumscribed competition, controlled by the most formidable cartel in the world, the International Air Transport Association (IATA), which settles everything from fares and legroom to the size of luggage and sandwiches —leaving the airlines to compete with planes, hostesses, courtesy and advertising. The more similar the services become, as with detergents, the more intense the advertising.

Airlines have a separate, international atmosphere of their own, and their staff has a classless, placeless character, freed from the past, as different from railways as coffee-bars from pubs. But in their short lives the airways have already accumulated entrenched bureaucracies and a self-contained 'Kremlin'—as the BOAC headquarters is called: 'There are too many people flying typewriters in this place and not enough flying aircraft,' as one pilot put it.

Britain, being compact and crowded, is one of the least air-minded countries: London Airport, although it is the world's biggest *international* airport, with 450 planes a day from 51 airlines, is smaller than a dozen airports in America.

For British European Airways the competition is fairly unhampered by obligations—apart from a few routes like the Scottish 'Highlands and Islands' service, which loses around £350,000 a year. For fifteen years their chairman was Lord Douglas of Kirtleside, a huge square man with a chin like a spade, who presided over the office as an indestructible father-figure. In 1964 he was succeeded by Anthony Milward, who had been his chief executive for eight years, and his right-hand man in building up the corporation. Milward is a less exotic man: he came into flying during the war, as a Fleet Air Arm pilot, and then joined BEA. He is a Conservative, unlike Douglas, and BEA people sometimes complain about his 'housemaster' attitude: but he is accessible, sensitive, considerate about crews and staff, respected by the unions, and unwaveringly devoted to his corporation.

The history of BOAC, the second biggest airline in the world, has been much less happy: few phenomena are odder or sadder than the way in which this brand-new industry, without any of the historical clutter and Victoriana of railways or mines, has in twenty years become despondent and bogged down in past commitments. BOAC have had many difficulties which BEA have not. They have had to maintain costly routes for the sake of prestige, to serve as a link between the Commonwealth countries, and to subsidise awkward associates, including Nigerian, West Indian and Middle Eastern airlines. They have suffered bad luck in the buying of jet planes, beginning with the three original Comet disasters in 1954, which set back their jet programme by four years. And their troubles have been increased by the growth of the commercial 'independent' airlines, led by the merger of British United Airways and British Aviation Services, who have 80 per cent of the independent business. Their board represents a large slice of city interests, including Sir Andrew Crichton of P and O, and Anthony Cayzer of British and Commonwealth Shipping. Both nationalised airlines are bitter about the Conservative government allowing private competitors to use profitable routes, without paying for unprofitable ones.

But the major difficulty of BOAC, providing its most pressing current problems, is its relationship with the British aircraft industry, which depends so heavily on it for survival. Between BOAC's obligation to make a profit, and its obligation to provide work for aircraft factories, there have been a succession of cross-purposes and bungles. In the words of Roy Jenkins (who three months afterwards became Minister of Aviation): 'It has been buffeted in the past few years between the uncertain peaks of commercial solvency and support for the British aircraft industry, and doubtfully encouraged on its way by the fitful and increasingly irritable appearances on the flight-deck of successive Ministers of Aviation.'[1] Since 1945 there have been no fewer than nine different chairmen of BOAC, including Sir Miles Thomas, Lord Knollys, Gerard d'Erlanger (a part-time banker) and Rear-Admiral Sir Matthew Slattery. Each of them has come up against these two incompatible obligations: 'I think the financial structure of the corporation and the way it is expected to operate is bloody crazy,' said Sir Matthew in 1962. *The Economist* has suggested that the initials might appropriately stand for 'Before Ordering, Act Carefully', and part of their present crisis has stemmed from the ordering by Sir Gerard d'Erlanger in 1958, under pressure from the Government, of 35 VC 10's—British jet planes with a doubtful advantage over the new American ones. The Select Committee on the Nationalised Industries—which has done much to induce realistic thinking into this territory—published in June 1964 a report which blamed this decision for much of BOAC's subsequent frantic and expensive expansion.

The newest chairman to face this stark problem is Sir Giles Connop McEacharn Guthrie, whose appointment was announced in November 1963, to the astonishment of parliament. For Sir Giles, like Sir Gerard before him, came from the sheltered and privileged world of merchant banking. He was a wealthy Old Etonian Baronet of forty-seven; his father Sir Connop had left half a million pounds; and Guthrie had moved from Eton to Cambridge to the staid merchant bank of Morgan Grenfell, and then to Brown, Shipley (where he met Edward Heath, who was doing a short stint as a trainee at the bank). Guthrie had also had a life-long interest in flying; he won the Portsmouth-Johannesburg air race in 1936, and like Milward spent the war as a Fleet

[1] 'The Great BOAC Bungle': *The Observer*, July 12, 1964.

Air Arm pilot. He maintained his interest in aviation, and in 1959 joined the board of BEA. It was there that in 1963 he attracted the attention of the Minister of Aviation, Julian Amery (who had been at Eton at the same time, though he did not then know him). Amery met Guthrie at a lunch in August 1963 to discuss BEA's affairs, and was so impressed by him that he decided, soon afterwards, to ask Guthrie to take over BOAC. Soon after his appointment was announced Guthrie described, with engaging openness, the advantages of his City position:

> It's not how well-known you are that counts, but who you know, and who knows you. The public doesn't know me, but—for instance—how many of the public know the name of the Governor of the Bank of England? As it happens I know him by his Christian name and that's the point. Things work differently in the City.
>
> Knowing Edward Heath didn't enable me to get the BOAC job, but when my name came up it helped prevent me from being blackballed.
>
> One meets an enormous amount of people through, for instance, a thing like the Society of Merchants, which is a dining club of merchant bankers or, if you prefer something more pompous, of eminent city men. In the City this isn't at all mysterious. You know someone and he discovers he knows someone else. Like David Ormsby-Gore and the Kennedys.[1]

It was not long before Guthrie was in the thick of a row. Determined that BOAC should at all costs be profitable, he insisted on cancelling the British VC 10's that his predecessor had ordered, at a cost of £60 million pounds penalty to the aircraft company, and concentrating instead on American Boeings. This bold stand brought to a head once again the old argument about obligations; but there are signs that the chairman of BOAC, like those of Coal, Railways and Electricity, is achieving a more powerful and independent position, where he can present his case direct to parliament and the public, and be allowed to emerge as a tycoon in his own right.

THE NEW TECHNOCRATS

It is a favourite trick of Whitehall to make the greatest changes with the least possible noise, as in the transformation of the nationalised industries. Three years ago few people knew the names, or the policies, of their chairmen: they were much better

[1] *Sunday Times*, December 8, 1963.

known in their previous jobs—Sir James Bowman as a trade unionist, Sir Brian Robertson and Sir Ian Jacob as wartime generals. To the public, and even perhaps to themselves, they seemed part of the entangled undergrowth of government, enmeshed with ministries and embarrassed by parliament. Showmanship was deplored and anonymity was encouraged, almost as if the industries were part of Whitehall itself. If there was any talking, the Minister could do it in Parliament.

But today these chairmen are household names, better known than most cabinet ministers. Beeching was the most spectacular: no one thought of him as part of Whitehall. He became, in his own right, a major political figure, but a party-less one, seeming to inhabit a classless world of his own, bound round with his own expertise. Lord Robens sells coal, attacks oil, and flies about in his own plane, almost as if he were a private tycoon: while hardly anyone can remember who is the man who is technically his boss, the Minister of Power. Sir Ronald and Sir Giles are quite prepared to appeal direct to the public helped by the new power of television, and even in the BBC (as we shall see in chapter 36) the arrival of Sir Hugh Greene has brought about radical changes.

Nor are these simply changes in the public image. For the most important thing about Beeching and Greene is not so much that they are public figures as that they are professionals, with a strong commercial sense. They have mastered their job, and they have surrounded themselves with men of their kind, who are much more interested in efficiency than in politics. Beeching has brought in allies from Shell and Unilever; Greene has promoted his team of young executives who are experts, above all, in mass television. The new breed of chairmen, in fact, show signs of being the first of the British technocrats. They base their authority and support not on party following or public service so much as on technical mastery and commercial success—a very un-British idea. They are beginning to show some of the tough independence of French technocrats, such as Louis Armand in the railways or Dreyfus in Renault. They can appeal direct to the public, and a government—particularly a government which has dedicated itself to efficiency—defies them at its peril.

Moreover, most nationalised industries now make such long-term plans, for five or ten years ahead, that it becomes harder and harder for Parliament—which is still geared to an annual inspection—to keep track of them. Beeching's wisdom or folly will become really clear only in five years' time, just as it was only in the cold winter of 1962–3 that the public discovered the Electricity Council's mistakes of five years' earlier.

Did parliament realise that these giant industries, which in theory they owned were to be rapidly liberated, and handed over to technocrats? The seeds of the new system were sown in the Treasury White Paper of April 1961, largely written by an influential Treasury Under-Secretary, Mark Stevenson. The Select Committee on Nationalised Industries had for years been urging more independence for them, and their report on the railways foreshadowed many of Beeching's recommendations: the Select Committee is, in Sir Ronald Edwards' words, 'Bit by bit helping to hammer out a general philosophy for running nationalised industries.'[1] Clearly the cabinet had decided, in appointing strong men such as Beeching and Robens, that greater autonomy was the only solution. But parliament were quite unaware of the extent to which their industries had disappeared from their ken. And it is doubtful whether even the cabinet realised quite the magnitude of the genie that they were letting out of the bottle.

The running of the nationalised industries still presents an unsolved problem to both political parties. They have not reached the comfortable confidence of private industry—self-perpetuating, self-financing, self-admiring. The relations between Whitehall and the state industries—the largest of all parental problems—is still unhappy. As private enterprise bosses move to public industries, civil servants switch to private industry, and industrial managers acquire a stronger professional sense, the old contrast between public service and private ambition will become blurred, and the question of ownership less relevant. 'The Labour party recognises that, under professional managements, large firms are as a whole serving the nation well. Moreover we recognise that no organisation can operate effectively if it is subjected to persistent and detailed intervention from above.'[2] 'The basic fact,' wrote Anthony Crosland in 1956, 'is the large corporation, facing fundamentally similar problems, and acting in fundamentally the same way whether publicly or privately owned.'[3]

At the centre of the political battle is the most powerful and profitable industry of all, the steel industry—nationalised in 1950, de-nationalised in 1951, expecting re-nationalisation in 1965.

[1] 'Objectives & Control in Nationalised Industry': Electricity Council, 1963.
[2] *See Industry and Society*. Labour Party, 1952.
[3] *See* C. A. R. Crosland: *The Future of Socialism*, 1956, p. 480.

The arguments have raged ever since 1934, when the Labour party first called for public ownership of steel, and since then they have flared up at each post-war election. Many of the big steel companies continued to be controlled by wealthy Conservative families, with interlocking directorships, and the left-wing of the Labour party still insists that nationalisation could transform the industry. But in the midst of all the debate, the steel companies have become more managerial, more vulnerable, and more easily influenced by government pressure, particularly by the government's watchdog, the Iron and Steel Board; and in 1963 politicians were surprised to observe a state-owned steel company (Richard Thomas and Baldwin) competing with a privately-owned one (Stewarts and Lloyds) to take over a third one, (Whitehead's). To many workers and managers, the difference between nationalised and de-nationalised is hardly perceptible.

How public services can be dynamic, competitive and animated with profit, while still remaining 'high custodians' and servants of democracy, remains a recurring problem for many Western countries. As Britain becomes more exposed to competitive winds so the essential services may, as in America, become regarded as the tail-end-charlies, the forgotten drudges under the pavements and pit-heads. This should be a field where Britain, with her old democratic conscience, should make a major contribution: and now that the furious party controversies are subsiding, and the muddles and elephantiasis of the public corporations are being dispassionately analysed, there could still arise new organisms, having vigour without selfishness and service without somnolence.

33

TRADE UNIONS

You have heard, I doubt not, of the Trades' Unions; a fearful engine of mischief, ready to riot or assassinate; and I see no countervailing power.

Dr. Arnold.

We left Trafalgar Square a long time ago.

George Woodcock, 1963.

SINCE the war in the whole of industry, nationalised and otherwise, there has been one force with which all managers and directors have had to come to terms—the force of organised labour. Trade unions have been hailed, praised and cursed as the 'fifth estate', and no one can ignore them. Their position has enormously changed since the pre-war years. As they have become closer to government, less militant, less sure of their real destination, so their power has become harder to analyse. 'The trade unions', one observer has written, 'have never been more powerful—and seldom used their power less. They have never attracted so many members—and have never had members so apathetic. There is an intense deep-seated loyalty—and there are frequent revolts against the chosen leadership. They hold the future in their hands—and cling to the present.'[1]

But they have remained insistently separate from the other estates, their smoother metropolitan world, their façades, and pomposities. In the trade union world things usually *are* what they seem, and their leaders have kept an inherent suspicion of 'them' and the corridors of power—most notable in their attitude to the nationalised industries for which they had been so long pressing. 'They weren't always willing to cross over, nor were their men always willing for them to go in,' said Lord Attlee: 'A curious contradiction, because they talked of labour running the show and yet when you put a trade unionist in they tended to regard him as a bosses' man.'[2]

The separateness of trade unions is evident at the TUC's annual

[1] Eric Wigham: *Trade Unions*, Home University Library, p. 6.
[2] Francis Williams: *A Prime Minister Remembers*, 1961, p. 92.

conference—so different from the sort of meetings of peers, commoners, churchmen or directors which mark the other estates. In a concert hall or opera house the delegates sit on tip-up seats, in rows according to their trade—garment workers in open-necked shirts, civil service clerks in dark suits; it is like the Labour Party conference, which takes place a month later, but with the intellectuals and the constituency radicals noticeably absent. In the gallery are academic observers, personnel officers from the corporations, foreign labour attachés. The numbers of outsiders in the unions' caravan increase every year.

On the platform, sitting behind green cloth, are the thirty-four members of the General Council. The chairman—appointed annually—sits in the middle behind a large silver-plated bell; to his left is George Woodcock, the general secretary, behind leather-bound volumes in the front row are ex-chairmen, three of them knights—the 'Trade Union Establishment', or 'Old Pals Club'. There is Sir Tom O'Brien, the small, dapper ex-cinema worker, who began as an errand-boy at twelve, and has toured the world as a trade unionist. There is Sir William Carron, the ex-turner from Hull who is now a Director of the Bank of England. And most prominent of all is the great shape of Ted Hill, General Secretary of the Boilermakers—the embodiment of the tough, immovable union spirit of the thirties: an enormous Cockney, shaped like a hippo, with a deep voice growling 'nuffink', 'where is 'e?' or 'get on wiv it'. Since as a boy he mended boilers, for P and O at the London Docks, he has never swerved from his distrust of all bosses, who he still often refers to as 'rascals', and he retains a simple, vivid approach to national problems. 'Our economy's like Tower Bridge,' he said in 1960, 'always up and down.' 'I don't trust the Tories,' he said in 1963; 'I would not trust them further than I can throw them—and I'm an old man.'

Proceedings are homely but brisk: in ninety-seven years the congress has evolved its own language and ritual, combining emotional appeal to men with strict authority. The atmosphere is mainly North Country and Scottish: only three of the thirty-four councillors are Londoners. Tough bargaining will be interrupted by waves of sentimentality. At the end retiring members are given gold medals and make nostalgic speeches about colleagues and wives, which may end in tears. A vote of thanks is proposed to the Press (who have a close though touchy relationship) and Auld Lang Syne is sung by the whole hall holding hands.

Rows of bald heads shine under the arc-lights, for most delegates are over fifty. They have taken part in the General Strike of 1926, seen the dole queues of the thirties. 'The Movement' has a magnificent history of struggle and 'the giants'—Bevin, Deakin and Lawther—who forged it. Much has changed since the days of the giants, but what still distinguishes the TUC from other power-groups is the sense of being on the receiving-end of all the legislation and management decisions which emanate from Whitehall or the West End boardrooms. Here you feel the human outcome of the committees, the management studies, the rationalisations and maximisations. It is not the geopolitical resolutions—so often forgotten or reversed by the following year—that matter most to the rank and file, but the scores of tiny resolutions about occupational deafness, home confinement grants or protection against fire. Yet the passionate views on defence, foreign policy and nationalisation, however little material result they may have, are still a very important part of the movement, distinguishing it from most other trade union movements. For they reveal the residual ideological strains—Catholicism, Methodism, Marxism—which lie behind the ideology of 'trade unionism' and give it dignity and passion.

GENERAL SECRETARIES

Ten years ago you could talk about the TUC as a solid political force: three big leaders—Arthur Deakin, Sir Thomas Williamson and Sir Will Lawther—commanded a majority of votes, and together urged wage restraint, supported Gaitskell against Bevan, defended the H-bomb and the Atlantic Alliance. But since Lawther retired and Deakin died—to be succeeded a year later by Frank Cousins—the balance has been upset. The individual leaders have large and personal powers, fortified by tough constitutions and publicity, and massively increased by TV. In most cases, only one man stands out in each union. 'When Bevin was there, who'd heard of Deakin?' said one general secretary: 'When Deakin was there, who'd heard of Cousins?'

When you see the thirty-four people on the dais you can easily imagine them as a miniature cabinet; but their power in fact is only the total of the powers of the individual unions, frequently at loggerheads: 'Baronies in a kingless kingdom,' as one general secretary said. The general secretaries of the biggest unions, who are all members of the Council, are the sinews of the movement; they have grown out of the rank and file, and spent their lifetime working—with small salaries and hard lives. They are an isolated group, cut off from others in this book. Several live in the north-west suburbs of London, commuting to their London offices and periodically touring the branches. At home they live quiet domestic lives, and are nearly all keen on gardening. At work, they are immersed in their own unions, usually seeing their opposite numbers only at TUC meetings, at deputations in Whitehall, on trade union delegations abroad, or at social occasions, such as embassy parties. One moment they will be facing rows of spectacles and pens in the Treasury, the next pleading in a branch office with inarticulate strikers. They cut across all classifications. Their background (as Anthony Crosland has said) is working-class, their way of life middle-class, their power upper-class. They have the influence of eighteenth-century dukes, the background of factories. They do not, like politicians, create dynasties, and their sons often go into white-collar jobs (like Woodcock's son in ICI or Cousins' son in AEA) where the movement is weak.

Most of the leaders have gained power late in life. Some have been caught up in a high-living round of conferences, parties and continental tours; but their wives usually act as a sheet-anchor, and most trade unionists remain solidly unpretentious and very accessible: to talk to them you do not need to make long-term appointments, you need only buttonhole them in the passage at a conference. Many of them enjoy protocol and legalistic jargon, like Peter Sellers in the film 'I'm All Right, Jack'; but this is more common in the middle ranks of the movement. Few leaders stayed at school after sixteen. They are the only group who show no signs of being invaded by graduates: of the thirty-five members only one, Woodcock, has a degree. They are the only group of leaders who could never be mistaken for any other group—judges, civil servants, accountants or managers. Will the impact of the 'meritocracy', catching all clever boys at the age of eleven, drain the movement of future giants, leaving 'no more Bevins'?

THE BIG SIX

Of about 9,000,000 trade unionists in Britain, 8,056,493 are affiliated to the TUC. Their range is exotic, and the conference mixes ancient and limited crafts with new technicians and mass-producers. The smallest unions include, in 1964:

32 London Jewish Bakers
30 Wool Shear Workers
90 Spring Trapmakers
72 Coal Trimmers
148 Military and Orchestral Musical Instrument Makers
110 Sailmakers
252 Shuttlemakers

and delegates come from such surprising trades as

11,468 Actors
5,711 Doctors
32,471 Musicians
2,160 Footballers
2,646 Variety Artistes
17,306 Journalists

But the weight is with the giants, and in 1964 six big unions held half the membership as the list overleaf shows.

Two of the biggest are 'general unions', which straddle scores of industries. Others, like the railwaymen, miners, or seamen, are 'Industrial Unions', within a single industry. Many smaller ones are 'craft unions' linked to the apprentice system, but most have been diluted with unskilled labour.

The cost of the untidiness, 175 unions, is heavy; they argue about 'demarcation' and one union by striking may put members of other unions in the same factory out of work. Britain has paid the price for pioneering trade unions, as for the industrial revolution which begot them. Each union has a proud, jealous history; the desperate pressures of the twenties and thirties persuaded small ones to combine. Now, with less pressure, there is less chance of effective merging, and their constitutions are as diverse as South American governments, 'While we are all diffused in our structure,' said George Lowthian, President of the TUC in 1964, 'this new unionism of the twentieth century will be unobtainable.'

TRANSPORT AND GENERAL

The biggest union in the Western World is the Transport and General Workers', whose leadership has become one of the most influential posts in Britain. Its 1,373,560 members—ranging from London bus-drivers to North Wales quarrymen, with the militant dock workers at the heart—command a sixth of the votes at the TUC. In forty years its membership has quintupled, and has risen by 150,000 in the last five years. It traces its origin back to the dock strike of 1889, and celebrated its jubilee in 1964. But the present amalgamation was formed by Ernest Bevin from fourteen separate unions in 1922, when wage cuts and unemployment had produced a critical need for workers' unity. After *ten years* of discussions, Bevin persuaded them to yield their autonomy: 'nothing in his career more clearly bore the stamp of his own creation'.[1] To impose unity Bevin framed a constitution to give huge powers to one man, the general secretary—the job he himself filled from 1922 till 1940, when he became Churchill's Minister of Labour. The general secretary is the only full-time official who is elected by a ballot of all the members and on the union's council he is much the most powerful: for the rest are all part-time members. The general secretary of the 'T and G' enjoys the same kind of power as the president of the United States:[2] he is the only member of his cabinet who has been directly chosen by the majority of his people. But, unlike the President, the general secretary is appointed until retiring age.

This one-man rule is sometimes resented—particularly the fact that full-time officers are all appointed. A persuasive general secretary can make sure that officials are sympathetic to him, and his election by the very unsophisticated rank and file encourages demagogy. All the general secretaries of the T and G, from Bevin to Cousins, have been powerful speakers. But the organisation gives a lot of freedom to the five thousand branches and the sixteen 'trade groups': and more than any other, the T and G suffers from the threat of breakaways—which compels the leaders to take notice.

The headquarters of the T and G, 'Transport House', is a plain brick building in Smith Square, Westminster, part of which is used by the Labour party. Bevin saw it opened in May 1928: 'To him it was nothing short of marvellous that a working men's organisation, with a subscription of sixpence a week, could rise from renting a house in a back street, to building, at a cost of well over £50,000, an eight-storey office building of its own within a stone's throw of the House of Lords.'[3]

Since its foundation the T and G has had only four secretaries —Ernest Bevin, Arthur Deakin, Jock Tiffin (who died a few months after taking office) and Frank Cousins, elected in May

[1] Alan Bullock: *Life and Times of Ernest Bevin*, p. 185.
[2] V. L. Allen: *Power in the Trade Unions*, p. 207.
[3] Alan Bullock, *Life and Times of Ernest Bevin*, p. 406.

Union	*Union Head*	*Members (Sept. 1964)*	*MPs (1964)*	*Affiliation Fees*
Transport and General Workers (TGWU)	Frank Cousins	1,373,560	21	£85,847
Amalgamated Engineering (AEU)	Bill Carron	980,639	18	61,289
General & Municipal Workers (NUGMW)	Jack Cooper	781,940	9	48,871
National Union of Mineworkers (NUM)	Will Paynter	501,643	29	31,352
Shop, Distributive & Allied Workers (USDAW)	Alf Allen	354,701	10	22,168
National Union of Railwaymen (NUR)	Sid Greene	282,801	6	17,675

1956. We have already seen[1] the large impact of 'Big Frank' Cousins on the Labour Party—the most startling example of the individual power of union leaders. In the setting of his union he appears a less isolated figure and his relentless suspicion of bosses reflects the resentments of dock workers and lorry-drivers. Like Hill he has stuck to his pre-war attitudes: 'Every time that we ease—every time we slacken off a little—then capitalism shows its teeth against us, and shows that it has not removed its thinking very far from where we were twenty years ago.' At one time in 1960 his militancy seemed close to bringing a crisis between the unions and the party, but since then his support—though still formidable—has waned. He is convinced that the trade unions and the Labour party are inseparable, but he dislikes the middle-class leadership: 'I would prefer to see a trade unionist in leadership of the party.' In 1964 he joined Harold Wilson's cabinet as Minister for Technology, seconded from his union, and his place was temporarily taken by Harry Nicholas, a much less vocal trade unionist, who has been a union official since 1936, and assistant secretary for the past eight years.

AMALGAMATED ENGINEERING UNION

The Amalgamated Engineering Union, the second biggest, has a more confiding character; its vast and unwieldly Rule Book is constantly under criticism. The present union was formed in 1920, out of ten craft unions, which have since become diluted with unskilled workers, and even with women (all craft unions are suspicious of women). An elaborately democratic constitution was drawn up, headed with the words 'United we stand—divided we

[1] *See* Chapter 7.

fall', and influenced by the Soviet trade unions (before their powers were circumscribed by Stalin). In theory, the AEU is ideally democratic. Every full-time official in the union is elected for three or five years: the factory workers elect the district committees, who elect the divisional committees, who elect the National Committee of 52 members, while the Executive Council of seven is elected by the whole membership in each of seven regional divisions. But in practice less than one in twelve members usually vote, and the AEU leadership is quite unrepresentative. 'It is,' as one of them described it to me, 'even more self-perpetuating than the board of ICI.' In 1960, according to the president, Bill Carron, 12 of the committee of 52 were Communists, and 6 fellow-travellers: the 'ten per cent democracy' of the AEU has become a by-word.

With this awkward constitution the president, who is the most powerful official, is never in a strong position: but the current president, Sir William Carron, has nevertheless had a massive impact on the movement. He is a short, bald man with a jutting chin, large shrewd eyes, small turned-up eyebrows and the impassive expression of a mandarin. He is unpompous, fond of photography and television, not attracted by banquets, and completely dedicated. A Roman Catholic, he first stood as a union candidate when he was a young turner in Hull in 1931 to keep Communists out, and ever since he has been unremittingly anti-Communist. As the right-wing head of a left-wing union, he has had awkward situations, but he is tough, persistent, with superb stamina: he can go on arguing till late at night, unswerving and good-humoured. He is one of the most loved and respected men in the movement. He has two knighthoods (one from the Queen, one from the Pope), an Oxford M.A.; but he remains very close to his union colleagues.

Like others', Carron's attitudes were forged by the general strike and the depression, but he accepts that the unions' outlook must change. He told me how when he talks to his daughter, he realises the different assessments of the young. 'I can't help remembering the time when my wife was in hospital having a baby, and I asked my foreman if I could take a few hours off to see her: he said, "Why must you people always be bothering about your families: you're here to *work*".' 'That's one of the moments,' said Carron, 'which gave me my outlook on politics: but you can't expect young people, who haven't experienced that kind of thing, to think the same.'

GENERAL AND MUNICIPAL WORKERS

The General and Municipal Workers have a similar wide range of unskilled workers to the T and G, and similar strong powers for the general secretary: until Cousins, the two were traditional allies—the core of organised manual labour. 'Thorne House', the headquarters of the 'NUGMW' in Bloomsbury (which, like Clapham, is a favourite trade union quarter of London), has big metal doors with engravings of all the jobs, from road-menders to gasworkers, which made the union. There have been only four general secretaries of the G and M—Will Thorne, who founded the oldest part of the union (the Gas Workers and General Labourers' in 1889); Charles Dukes, later Lord Dukeston; Sir Thomas Williamson, who ruled for sixteen years; and Jack Cooper, who took over from Williamson in 1962. He is the son-in-law of Lord Dukeston—a rare example of the beginnings of a union dynasty. He went to a council school, made soap for Levers, worked his way up through the G and M and Manchester City Council, and for a year was a Labour MP. In politics he is a moderate, more independent than his predecessor Williamson, but equally at loggerheads with Frank Cousins.

Cooper is a vigorous propagandist for better industrial relations, and is particularly interested in the Swedish trade unions; he is one of the delegation of British trade unionists who toured Sweden in 1962, and later wrote a pamphlet about it, drawing some conclusions. 'The first, most important, and most difficult task confronting us in Britain,' he wrote, 'is the development of a new, positive attitude towards industrial relations on the part of both trade unionists and employers, an attitude based on the proposition that the purpose of industrial relations is to promote industrial peace and harmony. The late R. H. Tawney defined industry as the conquest of nature for the service of man. It ought to be one of the functions of industrial relations to help rather than hinder the attainment of that purpose.'[1]

MINERS

The most distinctive and close-knit is the National Union of Mineworkers. No miner can work without a union card. There is no 'ten per cent democracy' about them: their self-contained communities have an intense union tradition, and every pit-head

[1] Jack Cooper: *Industrial Relations: Sweden shows the way*. Fabian Society, 1963.

has its local office. They have the most sponsored MPs of any union, and parliament is full of their Welsh or Yorkshire accents (though like other unions they tend to regard parliament as a secondary service—a resting-place, not a front line). At conferences, the miners sit and cheer together, stay in their own hotels, sing their own songs.

Because of their local loyalties, they are the most decentralised union; only in 1945 did their forty-one organisations combine in a single body. They have a modern black office in the Euston Road, with a sculpture of an underground miner in the entrance, but most of their staff are scattered through branches. Their general secretary, Will Paynter, is perhaps best known as the leading Communist at the TUC—though he was voted off the General Council in September 1961. His influence with miners is partly counterbalanced by a very anti-Communist president, Sid Ford. But Paynter is a forceful leader—short, wiry, and eloquent in a soft Rhondda accent. He went down the South Wales pits at fourteen, and joined the Communist party at twenty-nine. He has never lost touch with his fellow-miners. He sits in a polished office in London with red leather chairs and white telephones, but is constantly away touring the pit-heads, and though he lives at Edgware two of his seven sons are miners.

Paynter is convinced that the TUC have lost contact with *their* rank and file, and he mocks their 'statesmen': 'There's a tremendous ferment at the lower levels: it's got to be harnessed somewhere,' he told me. 'And when the recession comes, the young people will be much more rebellious than *we* were. They don't have the restraint and inhibitions that we had. The difference between the workers' share and the employers' is as great as it ever was.' He insists that his Communist and trade union activities are kept quite separate, and laughs at suggestions that he is in secret contact with other Communist leaders.

RAILWAYMEN

The railwaymen—the other big nationalised labour force—are less close-knit. The National Union of Railwaymen (NUR) is far the biggest railway union, but they have two proud rival unions, the Associated Society of Locomotive Engineers and Firemen (ASLEF) and the white-collared Transport Salaried Staff Association (TSSA)—who both look down on the ordinary railwaymen. The NUR (telegraphic address 'Beware') has always been a forceful union but seldom militant. They have had only one one-day strike in almost forty years.

The general secretary, Sidney Greene, began his career as a Paddington porter and now seems the quintessence of the modern moderate—clerical grey, quiet voice, garden in Middlesex. He was voted one of the ten best-dressed men for 1963.

Greene's railwaymen are among the lowest paid of all workers and their bargaining power is weakened by the heavy loss made by the railways. But the NUR are inclined to see the British Railways Board as an ally against the meanness of the Treasury, not as the government's agents. In a rapidly retracting industry Greene's hardest tasks are to safeguard his members' interests and make them aware of their rôle: 'You've got to make the rank and file feel that they've got a niche in the industry.' Railwaymen more than any others can bring British industry to a halt but, said Greene, 'I'm a bit afraid of the extent of our economic strength, I hope we never have to use it: it can so easily turn public opinion against us.'

USDAW

A more expanding and very different group are the Union of Shop, Distributive and Allied Workers (USDAW); for their members are involved with 'service industries'[1]—shop assistants, clerks, packers—between the open-necks and the white-collars. They are on the wage-earning end of the boom in service industries since the war, and they represent an important part of the union movement of the future. USDAW has difficulty in organising, because 47 per cent are women, who usually move or marry: the manual unions are inclined to regard them as a 'cosseted union'. Much of their original membership was in the Co-operative movement, which encouraged trade unionists. But USDAW has shot ahead since the war, creeping into the big chain stores (Marks and Spencer, Great Universal Stores, Woolworths, etc.) which are the bane of their organisers. Their secretary, Alf Allen, who took over in 1962, is a Bristol man who began in the Co-op, and worked his way up through the union.

The youngest of the General Secretaries is Clive Jenkins, aged thirty-eight, who belongs to one of the most rapidly-growing

[1] *See* p. 555.

unions, a body of 35,000 white-collar workers, prominent in air-airlines and the 'aerospace industry' called ASSET—the Association of Supervisory Staffs, Executives and Technicians. Jenkins is a smooth and left-wing Welshman, who has written two books about the conspiracies of power and a polemic against trade union leadership. He brings to his union an ingenious energy. ASSET has started its own insurance company, advertises for members on television, and has bought small holdings in all the large companies in which it has membership—so that Jenkins can complain at shareholders' meetings. Jenkins belongs to a tiny circle of intellectual trade unionists, writes a weekly column in *Tribune*, and even founded a highbrow trade union journal.

UNIONS AND BUSINESS

All the big unions face similar problems—most notably the fact that with full employment factory workers can bargain directly with the bosses, and the union leaders thus have difficulty in keeping and controlling their members. Most unions since the war have been challenged by 'wildcat strikes' and rebellious shop-stewards. It is the shop-stewards who collect union dues at the factories, recruit new members, and enforce the factory agreements: the T and G has 25,000 of them, and altogether there are said to be 200,000[1]—more shop-stewards than soldiers. Ever since a menacing 'Shop-Stewards' Movement' grew up during the first world war, the unions have tried to keep stewards in check. But with full employment, power drifts towards them, for they can often make better bargains than at the national level—producing a 'two-tiered' system—with the union headquarters negotiating one agreement in London and shop-stewards negotiating a better agreement at the factory.[2]

Another problem for unions: how far should they take on the pattern of 'business unionism', as in America and Germany, where the big unions are capitalist businesses in their own right? How far should union leaders have the salaries and surroundings of top businessmen? Do they need trained economists and financiers to assess their wage claims and to look after the unions' investments? There has been a long tradition in the British movement that union leaders should be self-sacrificing men, living close to their people. Cars, chauffeurs and big salaries are suspect, as signs that the

[1] Henry Wilton: *The Trade Unions, the Employers and the State*, 1959, p. 116.
[2] *See* B. C. Roberts: *Trade Union Government and Administration.* Bell, 1956.

leaders may have joined the bosses. And the members hate to increase their subscriptions; in 1958 the men paid an average of ·75 per cent of their basic wages to the unions, compared to 1·5 per cent in 1939. The dues for the AEU were 4 per cent of wages in 1912, but only 1 per cent in 1959. In 1964 subscriptions varied from 1/3d. a week (9*d.* for women) in the 'T and G', to from 8/- to 11/1*d.* in the National Graphical Association.

Many unions still dislike being mixed up with 'tar'—the goings-on of capitalists. The nominal capital of trade unions in 1962 was over £100 million, an average of £11/16/5*d.*[1] per member, but very little of this is invested in industry (which would have multiplied its value over twenty years). The American mineworkers think nothing of buying up large shares in coalfields, but British unions are only now beginning to make tentative investments, usually in unit trusts, which avoids the embarrassment of having holdings in a particular industry. Several unions still have rules forbidding investment in equities.

The background of trade unionism as a class struggle has left a strong prejudice against importing specialists, graduates and middle-class men from outside the movement, but gradually a more professional attitude is emerging. An example is Harry Douglass, a big benign Yorkshireman, Secretary of the Iron and Steel Trades Confederation. He comes from one of the richest unions, the steelworkers, who earn up to and over £40 a week: they are the aristocrats of trade unionists and in their booming towns—Middlesbrough, Scunthorpe, Corby—acres of cars wait outside the steelworks. In their co-operation with bosses and lack of class feeling they are closer to American unions. Harry Douglass, with his well-cut suit, his salary of £4,000 and his chauffeur-driven car, could easily be mistaken for a steelmaster, and he is the most business-minded of the leaders. 'The trade union movement today is a very powerful machine,' he said at the 1960 Congress, 'and it can only be driven by experts . . . Are we going to be like the sons of rich men, having inherited a wonderful machine, to allow it to be destroyed by our envy, and our selfishness?'

Another equally pressing problem is the growth of the white collared and white-coated workers—the growing middle class of bank and insurance clerks, civil servants, local government officers, teachers. About a million and a half 'white-collared

[1] Report of the Chief Registrar of Friendly Societies for the year 1962. Part 4.

workers *are* represented at the TUC—including for instance the 145,000 members of the Civil Service Clerical Association, or the 42,500 members of the Inland Revenue Staff Federation. The Post Office Workers, under Ron Smith, have emerged as one of the most militant groups, and Smith himself has become a significant member of 'Neddy'. Others, like the National Union of Teachers and the National and Local Government Officers (NALGO)—a very fast-growing union, which jumped from 146,000 to 326,500 between 1946 and 1963—are outside the TUC. But insurance office workers, bank clerks, or white-coated workers in laboratories fight shy of unions.[1]

The proportion of white-collared to manual workers is steadily rising, and the total figure of trade union membership has been slowly falling—accelerated by the big drop in mining, textiles and railways. About 25,000,000 people are engaged in *some* kind of work in Britain, including cabinet ministers, bookmakers, bishops, stockbrokers and others reluctant to join trade unions, and hundreds of thousands of farm labourers, builders' men, dock workers and odd-job men who are too apathetic, temporary or far-flung to be reached by the unions. But they include, too, the lower-middle-class who see themselves as growing socially superior to trade unions. The table opposite shows how much the numbers have shifted from one industry to another in four years.

The unions still dominate the vital industries—mining, railways, power stations, lorries—which could bring the country to a halt. But as they move away from militant strikes towards a closer relationship with the government. so these 'key industries' become a less viable weapon, and white-collared workers—who bring strength in negotiations and a larger stake in the future—become more important. Trade unionists know from their own sons and daughters that the future Britain will be a white-collar country. Recently, with the pay-pause and the resulting militancy, there have been signs of a new solidarity, and both NALGO and the teachers seem likely to join the TUC. But the conjunction is difficult; for while the white-collar people, conditioned to large bureaucracies and committee-work, bring a negotiating skill, they are often less articulate and persuasive than the manual workers, who have been used to fighting from the beginning. The TUC needs both talents equally—to be able to stir up its people at mass-meetings, and then bargain skilfully in committee-rooms—

[1] *See* p. 425.

TOTAL WORKING POPULATION OF GREAT BRITAIN: AUGUST 1963[1]

Industry or Service	*End-June 1959*	*Mid-August 1963*	*Change 1959–1963*
Agriculture and fishing	999,000	908,000	− 91,000
Mining and quarrying	826,000	680,000	− 146,000
Food, drink, tobacco	818,000	851,000	+ 33,000
Chemicals, etc.	520,000	510,000	− 10,000
Metal manufacture	576,000	583,000	+ 7,000
Engineering and electrical goods	1,938,000	2,139,000	+ 201,000
Shipbuilding and marine engineering	264,000	210,000	− 54,000
Vehicles	869,000	868,000	− 1,000
Metal goods	519,000	556,000	+ 37,000
Textiles	851,000	792,000	− 59,000
Clothing and footwear	565,000	561,000	− 4,000
Other manufactures	1,557,000	1,658,000	+ 101,000
Total in manufacturing industries	8,477,000	8,728,000	+ 251,000
Construction	1,523,000	1,662,000	+ 139,000
Gas, electricity, water	374,000	398,000	+ 24,000
Transport and communication	1,672,000	1,662,000	− 10,000
Distributive trades	3,209,000	3,381,000	+ 172,000
Services—professional, financial, scientific, etc.	4,874,000	5,292,000	+ 418,000
National government service	505,000	532,000	+ 27,000
Local government service	738,000	780,000	+ 42,000
Total in civil employment	23,197,000	24,023,000	+ 826,000
Males	15,308,000	15,669,000	+ 361,000
Females	7,889,000	8,354,000	+ 465,000
Wholly unemployed	379,000	492,000	+ 113,000
Males	275,000	362,000	+ 87,000
Females	104,000	130,000	+ 26,000
HM Forces and Women's Services	565,000	424,000	− 141,000
Males	550,000	407,000	− 143,000
Females	15,000	17,000	+ 2,000
Total working population	24,145,000	24,939,000	+ 794,000
Males	16,137,000	16,438,000	+ 301,000
Females	8,008,000	8,501,000	+ 493,000

[1] In nearest thousands. *Ministry of Labour Gazette*, October 1963.

but they fit uncomfortably, and white-collar people remain alarmed by the political connections of the TUC.

TUC

From Easter until August the individual unions hold their seaside conferences, where delegates come together to pass resolutions on anything from peptic ulcers to missile bases. If the resolution is passed, by however small a majority, it then stands as the corporate opinion of the whole union, and the delegates are sent on to the Trades Union Congress meeting armed with the 'block vote' of the total membership. The block vote is often spoken of as a kind of modern pocket borough, as if the union bosses could do what they like with it. But though a persuasive leader may be able to swing his conference behind him, a current feature of many unions is the opposite: general secretaries, including Carron and Greene, have found their unions' block vote adamant against them.

In September the unions come together for their conference, and for one week in the year the TUC suddenly blazes into the headlines, its leaders fill the TV screens, its dramas and conflicts become exposed and analysed. The TUC itself is relatively tiny. The actual Council of thirty-four is made up of busy general secretaries (including those of all the six biggest, except Will Paynter), who normally meet only once a month round the horseshoe desk in the new Congress House in Bloomsbury (with a statue outside of one worker pulling up another). Few central union organisations are as weak as Britain's. The TUC cannot order a union to strike or not strike: it can only advise, cajole or bring careful pressure. In 1961 the unions paid only 1/3d. per year per member to it, producing a total of about half a million pounds a year, which had to pay for staff, scholarships, publicity, international affiliation fees, and organising the conference.

The actual staff of the TUC consists of only 96 people, including maintenance staff. The senior people are engaged in researching, reporting and recommending: each subject has a special subcommittee, headed by a member of the General Council. Probably the most influential is the Economic Committee, whose chairman is Sir Harry Douglass; and this committee has become more important since the formation of 'Neddy' and the new pressure towards planning, of which Douglass is an eloquent advocate. 'Trade unions have for too long been kept on the defensive,' he said at the 1963 Congress; 'We must seize the initiative wherever we can. We have a right and a duty to help shape planning and we must recognise that the nature and methods of trade unions will be shaped by it. . . . We are not interested in employers or governments, or for that matter NEDC councils, who give lip-service to planning. Nor dare we be guilty of it ourselves. If we are afraid of planning, afraid that it will challenge our own forms of conservatism, then let us say so here and now and have done with it. But if we do accept it and are confident in our ability to use it, not to prop up an outmoded economic system, but to open a way to a better future for the working people of Britain and of other countries—then we must be prepared to justify our attitudes, our practices, and indeed the structure of our organisations.'

GEORGE WOODCOCK

The most important figure at headquarters, and probably in the whole movement, is the general secretary, George Woodcock. He is the only full-time member of the Council, and he runs the permanent staff, with a salary of about £2,500 a year. He is a kind of secretary to the cabinet, but his cabinet is less cohesive and more fitful than the government's, and he has none of the limitations of a civil servant: he can, and does, speak boldly at meetings and emerges as a tough political figure in his own right. He is unmistakable, with a shock of grey hair above enormous black bushy eyebrows; he has a soft Lancashire voice, precise and measured, which conceals surprising passion and impatience. Like a wise ghost, he is nearly always to be seen at TUC gatherings, looking, listening, watching, nodding, occasionally speaking out. Alone in the movement, he combines a working-class upbringing with a (literally) first-class education. He was the son of a Catholic millworker, and at twelve he was working half-time on the loom near Preston, to help his family's wages: at twenty-five, he had won a scholarship to Ruskin College, Oxford, then to New College where he took a first-class degree. (His Economic Adviser at the TUC, Len Murray, is also a New College man.) Woodcock fought shy of political trade unionism, and dislikes soap-boxes. He worked for a time with the civil service, which bored him, and then for ten years was senior economist at the TUC. Walter Citrine—one of the moulders of the movement—impressed Woodcock with professionalism and careful decisiveness. He was also strongly influenced by Bevin, who taught him how to run committees. For fourteen more years Woodcock was assistant to the next general secretary, Sir Vincent Tewson, when he could watch the Council at work, but had no power; and in 1960, after his long and awkward vigil, he became general secretary himself.

He is one of the most articulate men about his job that I encountered, and he is wide awake to the new problems of the TUC. The crucial change, for him, was during the war, when the government accepted responsibility for wages and employment: he remembers Neville Chamberlain telling the TUC delegation in 1938: 'We have only a little more control over labour than we do over the weather.' But since 1944, when the government accepted responsibility for the economic weather, the trade unions' job (Woodcock thinks) is bound to be different. 'We created the Labour party to get what we wanted. Now we've got it, we don't need it in the same way. The Labour party's job is to get votes. Our job is to get wages.'

He sees his own rôle as very limited. 'The TUC doesn't *do* anything: it can't tell the unions what to do. All I can do is to try and see the way things are going, and help them along. I have to try to get the feeling of the council, and then help them to reach a decision.' He admits the shortage of young trade unionists, and the old-fashionedness of many attitudes. 'But it will change as the men at the bottom change. Trade unions are not like family firms, or a religion: the movement is made by the people who come into it at the bottom, and they're pulled into it not by personal ambition but by their own self-respect. We'll have to buy economists and experts in the market-place, and pay well for them: but the men who run the movement will always come up from the rank and file.'

THE ETU AFFAIR

The TUC has always been tolerant, and slow to criticise. Only occasionally is it compelled to take action against one of its unions, but such a moment came with the Communist-controlled Electrical Trades Union. The ETU is the seventh biggest union, with a quarter of a million members. Its Communism is not entirely due to its leadership: it was noted by Marx, among others, that the most radical workers are not the lowest paid—such as railwaymen or dustmen—but prosperous, semi-skilled men, such as lorry-drivers, engine-drivers or electricians. The electricians—who began as a small group of telephone men in Manchester in 1889—

know their power and potential, in everything from television to aircraft. 'We are in everybody's business.'

But after the war, the ETU was captured by the Communists—partly through the apathy of others, partly by simply rigging the ballot. Their offices in a suburb in Kent were shrouded in evasion and secrecy. For years they remained an open scandal, exposed by the press and television, on the initiative of Woodrow Wyatt, but still tolerated by the TUC. Then in 1961, the unsuccessful candidate for secretary, John Byrne, brought a court case against the executive, including the Communist secretary Frank Haxell. Mr. Justice Winn found Haxell and others guilty of 'fraudulent and unlawful devices': 'Not only was the Union managed and controlled by the Communist Party,' he said, 'but so run as to suit the ideals of the party.' Haxell was ordered to resign, and John Byrne took his place.

After long, worried meetings, the TUC decided that it could not tolerate the ETU in its midst. At their meeting at Portsmouth in September 1961, George Woodcock sadly and soberly recounted the sins of the union—not the sins of Communism but the sins of fraud. At last the president, Ted Hill—an old friend of Foulkes—slowly announced: 'It is with profound regret that I have to ask the ETU delegation to withdraw from Congress and surrender their credentials.' Frank Foulkes sadly walked out of the hall, saying 'au revoir, Ted'. 'It was like some very unfortunate family severance'—as one observer put it[1]—'in which all the instincts of flesh and blood give way, in the last analysis, to the good of the greater number.' Four months later the ETU was thankfully readmitted.

The Communist president Frank Foulkes (who had been found guilty by association) did not resign immediately, but in July 1962, he, too, was expelled from the union. Leslie Cannon, the new president, elected in 1963, is fiercely anti-Communist, and despite the party's repeated attempts throughout 1963 to regain control of the union, they are in a 3–8 minority on the executive, elected in December 1963 to serve for two years. At the TUC Congress in Blackpool in 1964, ETU members voted 3 to 1 in favour of banning Communists from holding office.

THE POWER OF THE UNIONS

The strength of the unions is now much harder to define than in

[1] Peter Jenkins: *Time and Tide*, September 7, 1961.

the pre-war head-on clashes. It is not a mailed, but a kid-gloved fist, showing itself little in actual strikes. In 1963, according to the Ministry of Labour, the time lost by strikes amounted to only 0·4 per cent of the total working time, 60 per cent of the time lost by strikes was in four industries, which account for only 7 per cent of the working population—motor-cars, docks, ship-building and coal mines, all known for their bad labour relations and old-fashioned management. Britain is not, contrary to frequent impressions, a country very prone to strikes. These were the total number of days lost per 1,000 workers in mining, manufacturing, construction and transport in the Western industrial countries in 1963:

Italy	1,150
France	770
US	620
Norway	360
Canada	330
Australia	300
UK	140
Finland	140
Belgium	140
W. Germany	130
Denmark	40
Switzerland	50
Netherlands	20
Sweden	10

Two big factors restrict strikes. One is the unions' small funds, which amount only to an average week's wages to each man. The other is public opinion, which looms like a genie: the TUC knows well that strikes by public services, as by the London busmen in 1958, can make the genie scowl.

Much of the unions' power treads softly and invisibly, through the corridors of Whitehall, through boardrooms of nationalised industries (where trade unions have their nominees), and through a hundred joint committees—the British Productivity Council, the National Production Advisory Council on Industry, the Minister of Labour's National Joint Advisory Council, and now the most important, the National Economic Development Council. At the factories there is always suspicion that at those pow-wows the leaders are being bought off by the glamour of government. Many militant demagogues have become fascinated by London power and society. *From Workman's Cottage to*

Windsor Castle was John Hodge's autobiography, and J. H. Thomas, the railway leader, was mocked for his love of aristocracy. The dubbing of trade union knights—'the knights and belted earls of the TUC',[1] as the ETU has called them—has added to suspicion.

The unions' power in this kid-glove era hangs on a tricky balance. The TUC must be close enough to government and boards to influence them, yet separate enough to bargain ruthlessly, keeping their members behind them, clenching the fist inside the glove. With their militant street-corner past, the unions are still unequipped for this balance: lobbying, persuasion and public relations have become complex arts, and the TUC lacks sophisticated negotiators, with economics and tactics at their fingertips. Chairmen and politicians concur: 'We all want a strong trade union movement,' said one minister: 'The trouble is, how can we help them to achieve it? If they think we're interfering, they'll do the opposite.' The reintroduction of planning—with the invitation to the TUC to take part in NEDC—has brought trade unions further into Whitehall, with greater conflicts between their two loyalties. To many of the old street-corner school, this secret committee-world is inherently sinister, and many are very sceptical of the Treasury's good intentions. But to the more modern unionists, planning is a new and exciting responsibility.

The real test of the unions' interest in planning is the acceptance of some kind of 'incomes policy', which was tried by the Conservatives but renewed, with more success, by George Brown in the 1964 Labour government. An incomes policy can, and does, mean quite different things to trade unions and employers; but its object is to regulate wages, to prevent inflation or 'stop-go' policies, in return for restrictions of prices on the side of the bosses. The first hurdle was passed in December 1964, when George Brown persuaded the employers' organisations to join with the government and the TUC, in signing the 'statement of intent' on productivity, prices and incomes. The statement was hailed by George Brown, with some justification, as 'a victory for the nation as a whole', and *The Times* commented: 'Mr. George Brown has achieved in sixty days what eluded Mr. Maudling for months'. But the TUC were careful to add their own qualifications, and Lord Collison, the chairman of the TUC, made it clear that the

[1] In 1961 there were 5 knights on the Council, but no earls: the union peers are Lord Citrine, Lord Geddes, Lord Crook, Lord Williamson and Lord Collison.

planning of incomes was only part of a plan for economic expansion and social equity. The difficulties of obtaining any real agreement between men who earned £20 a week and those who earned £200 a week remained huge. As one union secretary said to me: if the FBI and the TUC agree, there must be something wrong.'

34
LEISURE

All the time we keep avoiding leisure we keep talking about it.
Sloan Wilson.

WHILE trade unionists fight successfully for shorter hours, scientists perfect new substitutes for labour, and computers, TV and supermarkets take over the drudgery of industry, the problem of leisure looms larger. No institutions can be kept in perspective without reference to this large outside, which is changing everyone's character. The old nonconformist ethos, the sense of work being itself virtuous and self-improving, is being undermined by the new prosperity. The success story of today is less likely to be about a man who got up earlier and worked later, like Ernest Marples: even the 'hard day's toil' of the civil service is not necessarily desirable. The modern tycoon often gives the impression of work being not an improving drudgery, but a glorious romp: and the dress-designers, restaurateurs or decorators who are today's young heroes would have appalled Samuel Smiles. The notion that a worker or clerk can reach the top by working harder has become less convincing, and further undermined by gambling. Who would have imagined, even thirty years ago, that a British government would be putting out advertisements like this:

There was a clerk with a worried frown
Who got his fellow workers down
Until one happy day he found
He'd won a prize—£1,000

Behind the daunting façades of British institutions, the drab architecture, economists, and the Board of Trade, Britain has been in a state of galloping consumption. At one extreme leisure is organised and commercialised with juke boxes or glossy magazines, at the other it revolves round philosophical paperbacks and evening classes (in 1963 357,000 people went to evening classes in the LCC area alone). But either way there is more of it, and more money to spend on it. The average working week dropped from about 50 hours in 1939 to 44 hours in 1961, the teenagers alone spend £850 million a year on themselves.

The traditional pursuits of rich Englishmen have taken on a new lease of life: of the three classic sports only shootin' is still largely the preserve of the gentry and the rich. A lot of estates where the owner cannot afford to run a shoot by himself are now shot over by syndicates. But syndicates do not make shooting less private, and anyone answering the rare 'gun wanted' advertisement will be carefully screened to make sure that he's 'safe'. Hunting, on the other hand, which does not need a big private estate, has been taken up by far more people. The number of packs of foxhounds has stayed at about 200 since 1905, but while before the war the hunts had difficulty in finding enough subscribers, today they are booming, and famous hunts like the Belvoir and the Quorn can usually muster over 200 mounted followers. The Horse as a focal point of country life has made a comeback with prosperity in the same way as the London clubs. But the Pony has had an even more startling success. The countryside is fuller of shaggy little horses than ever—membership of the Pony Club has risen from 17,000 in 1947 to 77,000 in 1963[1]—reaching their climax in the summer gymkhanas:

> Oh wasn't it naughty of Smudges?
> Oh, Mummy, I'm sick with disgust.
> She threw me in front of the judges,
> And my silly old collarbone's bust.[2]

Side by side with these ancient country activities, a jazzier social world has grown up round the 'cocktail belt' outside big towns—a world of stockbrokers' Tudor houses in large gardens where people drink Pimms in the summer. Social life centres round the golf and country clubs, and the club dance is the annual equivalent of the hunt ball. Weekends are in American style, with tennis, barbecues, martinis and swimming-pools—hectic in comparison with the country walks and quiet dinners of the deep county. Some of the clubs can be as exclusive as their American counterparts, and it may take a long probation to get into one. The world of the cocktail belt (typified by Sunningdale) still follows the English ideal of country life and the great outdoors, but it is based on money, not land, and peopled by successful businessmen and managers.

[1] *Britain: An Official Handbook*. COI, 1964.
[2] John Betjeman: *Collected Poems*, John Murray, 1958.

The pastimes of the old, and even the new, aristocrats are gradually becoming less relevant. The leisure of the British fifty years ago could be analysed in class terms, from caviare to fish and chips, from the Riviera to Blackpool: the tastes of upper and lower only met in a few national obsessions like cricket, gardening or the races. But since the war there has been more money to spend and mass media have multiplied. There has been a spectacular change. Traditional leisure is losing ground. Cricket and football, though still enormously popular (Charlie Chaplin and Professor Ayer are devoted followers of Fulham and Spurs), have dwindling devotees. (It is impossible to imagine a campaign for 'brighter cricket' before the war.) The cinema has lost its hold—except among unmarried teenagers, two-thirds of whom go at least once a week, perhaps to snog in the doubles—and audiences have dropped from 1,365 million in 1951 to 415 million in 1962, producing a fall in expenditure from £108 million to £60 million. Television is largely to blame, but these are some of the other things people are finding to do instead:

Motor racing is booming, from the big national meetings to odd local events like hill climbs organised by the 500 driving clubs. Between the leisurely atmosphere of Ascot, with its careful status distinctions between Royal Enclosure, Silver Ring and Heath, and the noise, fumes and thousands of classless young men in sweaters and girls in tight trousers at Brands Hatch, there is the gulf of a social revolution.

Bowling. Some cinemas have turned themselves into bowling alleys, an American import; it's a brilliant answer to the demand for gregarious, exhausting, 'fun for all the family' evenings—with licensed clubs for drinks and snack bars.

Bingo. Since the Betting Act of 1961 made them possible, Bingo halls have taken over from cinema shows. Four out of five British adults gamble in some way, and Bingo has provided a safe new excitement for housewives, with the tense dedication of a casino and without the disasters. The washing is abandoned at 3 p.m. as wives rush out to get a good place at the Bingo tables. It costs 2/6 or 5/- to get in, and as much again to play—but it's almost impossible to lose more than a pound a session.

Sailing. There has been a 1,000 per cent increase in owners of boats over the past ten years: in 1961 the Royal Yachting Association's small boat class was 14,770, and this is probably only a third of the small boats in the country. It has been estimated that there are well over a quarter of a million people 'messing around with boats'. The only likely future snag is a shortage of parking space: already friends are arranging their weekend's sailing on a 'you can have our mooring and we'll take yours' basis.

Another old playground of the rich, Abroad, has been invaded. In 1962 four million Britons went abroad for their holidays—the numbers have more than doubled since 1950 and trebled since 1937. Most families still prefer an August week by the sea, but many young people who used to flood holiday camps have discovered that the £15 a week can be better spent in Spain. The repercussions of travel can be seen in the changing face of Britain's town life: Britain has come out of dowdy isolation and responded to gay foreign influences—Italian shoes, French fashions, Gaggia coffee machines, juke boxes, delicatessens—and people are bringing back new tastes like garlic eating or wine drinking.

Dancing. The British have become increasingly a nation of dancers—five million people go dancing at least once a week in the 4,000 dance halls, and 4,000 dancing schools teach them. Five million people watch ballroom dancing competitions on television. Ballroom dancing is one of the few world championships which Britain holds.

Eating. Tastes in food are more adventurous, and foreign restaurants—Chinese, Italian, Indian, even vegetarian—have proliferated over big towns, notably in the north. Spaghetti bolognese has become a staple lunch-time food for thousands of secretaries. Tax dodges have encouraged big lunches, smoked salmon and champagne on expenses. (We are the world's biggest importers of champagne, drinking 26 million glasses a year.) If Britain's past greatness depended on being able to talk politics after dinner, her future may depend more on talking business soberly after a four-course lunch. But even outside the expense-account round, eating-out in the evenings has become much more of a habit as in France, and new restaurants quickly produce new clientèles.

Pubs and Clubs. Although there are 30,000 fewer pubs than before the war, they are fuller—largely because, like other male bastions, women have invaded them. On the whole Britain is a sober country—Frenchmen drink three times as much alcohol, New Zealanders drink more beer—and consumption of alcohol has gone up very little in ten years. But real night life depends almost entirely on clubs, thanks to the amazing and tortuous laws. To buy a drink after 11, play roulette, or see an uncensored film, you must join a club, and nearly all clubs are booming: almost anyone can get a licence to start one with twenty signatures and five shillings. There are jazz clubs for teenagers, strip clubs for middle-aged businessmen, night clubs for debs, dining clubs for gourmets, and, since 1961, gambling clubs for millionaires.

Clothes. A new gayness, style and kinkiness has emerged in British fashion. Marks and Spencer started a revolution with mass-produced copies of foreign designs, and others followed. Here too there is no longer one style for the rich and one for the poor; Britain, once only recognised, rather drearily, for the 'quality' of her tweeds and twinsets, is now famous for the speed and cheapness with which Paris copies are imported. Men are becoming more dandified, lured by the trade into fads like buttoned collars and square-ended ties, and men's boutiques are radiating from Carnaby Street. Long hair is no longer a prerogative of the Fabians, and since the advent of the Beatles and the Rolling Stones it is often difficult to distinguish men from girls. Mockery of Italian men for their vanity and toiletry is now less often heard.

The increase in spending power of the young people, together with the unexpected surge in the post-war birth-rate, has produced a much bigger and more noticeable gulf between the young and old. As Dr. Mark Abrams has put it, in an important survey of changing habits:[1]

> It is hardly surprising that the sense of alienation between the generations should seem more than normal in contemporary Britain. On the one hand we have over 12½ million people who were all born well before the First World War and who, for the most part, acquired their schooling, their working skills, their cultural and entertainment tastes and their political loyalties at a time when radio broadcasting was a barely credible novelty, when Liberal politicians were prime ministers, when the literary lions were Chesterton and Belloc, Shaw and Wells, and when Mary Pickford and Charlie Chaplin were winning film awards. Between this generation which today contains almost all those who exercise political, financial and administrative power and the 16 million young people born and brought up after the defeat of Hitler the contrast in formative experience must often seem an unbridgeable chasm.

[1] Dr. Mark Abrams: *The Newspaper Reading Public of Tomorrow*, Odhams Press, 1964. p. 14.

Important geographical changes have occurred in the past decade which have changed leisure habits. To quote Dr. Abrams again: 'By 1961 the total of inhabitants living in the six great English conurbations had actually fallen slightly. Population in the large towns outside the conurbations (100,000 or more residents) had moved up very slightly; but population had jumped by over two million in towns with less than 50,000 population and in the rural districts; many of the former are, in fact, suburbs, and most of the latter, at least in the south, are little more than commuter dormitories. Over 40 per cent of the English people now live in these small towns and rural districts.'[1]

Within one decade, the pattern of spending has been transformed, above all by the increase in motor-cars; between 1952 and 1963 the number of private cars went up from 2½ million to nearly 7½ million. But household equipment, too, has very suddenly come to the majority of the population: this has been the percentage of adults in Britain living in homes with various equipment:[2]

	1952	*1963*
Television	11%	85%
Washing Machine	10%	52%
Refrigerator	6%	37%
Vacuum Cleaner	40%	80%
Lawn Mower	34%	51%

In his survey, Dr. Abrams does not find a spectacular change in leisure habits: 'By and large people at home are now doing more comfortably and spaciously what they have always done. Even in the middle of winter very little time is allocated by the average person to pursuits likely to exercise and satisfy any sense of craftsmanship or specialised intellectual curiosity. The one major addition to the traditional pattern is the large amount of time spent on watching television and this is mainly a replacement of the time previously spent listening to radio.'[3] But he does find encouragement in the broader horizons and interests of the younger generation: 'The steady increase in the reading of middle-brow and even high-brow books, the expanded sales of records and classical music, the almost doubling of the number of musical societies in the past ten years, the new interest in drama and painting have all sprung largely from the younger generation.'[4]

[1] *Ibid.*, p. 16.
[2] *Ibid.*, p. 33.
[3] *Ibid.*, p. 48.
[4] *Ibid.*, p. 74.

The social philosophy of the industrial revolution—the doctrines of self-help, hard work and profit concealing the undergrowth of poverty and drunkenness—still lingers to promote austere notions of leisure: material prosperity and full employment have undermined their basis, but little has come up to replace the old puritanism, shown for instance in the State's attitude to the arts. 'The purchase of instruments of amusement for the rich with money raised by taxes on rich and poor alike is depredation,' said Bentham, giving as examples: 'Edifices, although for the use of the public, in so far as rendered costly by ornament . . . Pictures, statues and other products of the imitative arts.' The *total* annual government grant to the arts in 1963 was £11 million —one 200th of the defence budget—which included £5½ million for the upkeep of art galleries and £1½ million for preserving stately homes. Private patronage, with its huge potential influence, is largely in the hands of commercial middlemen who sponsor the safest mediocrity—the cinema distributors, property developers,[1] building societies, television tycoons. They blame mass tastes, but some of the nicest tastes, like olives, have to be acquired by familiarity.

But the increase in time, money and education *has* helped to spread culture, with egghead paperbacks and classical LPs in the forefront. The British are buying and borrowing more books: 17,000 separate titles were published in 1930, 25,000 in 1962—twice as many as in America—of which 19,000 were new titles. Audiences at concerts are growing; before the war the Proms ran for 30 nights in a hall holding 2,000, now they run 48 nights in the Albert Hall, which holds 7,000. The total number of concerts has risen from 400 before the war to 2,000 today. The greatest single musical influence, the BBC, under its new musical director William Glock, has been weaning the public from endless Tchaikowsky and Tannhauser to modern and little known works. Do-it-yourself music still goes strong: in 1949 there were 617 'official' music clubs and societies belonging to the National Federation of Music Societies: now there are 820 with 80,000 members. The growing interest in music and theatre makes the dearth of patronage all the sadder. While in Germany the state supports a symphony orchestra in every town, and the Berlin Philharmonic alone gets £150,000 a year, the Arts Council have to finance orchestras and theatres, amateur societies, exhibitions, opera and ballet on its £3 million a year.

[1] *See* p. 468.

The visual arts too are booming, from the stately homes business to the Tate Gallery's Picasso exhibition of 1960, which drew a record crowd of 460,000. But the art market is one preserve of the rich which has not been invaded. Dealers and auction rooms are prospering, but the growing attitude to pictures as investments has made them, like diamonds, a rich man's game.

But against these cultural advances has to be set the more spectacular advances in the oldest and most characteristic of British leisure activities—gambling. Since R. A. Butler's Betting and Gaming Act of 1960, which legalised betting shops and gaming in clubs, the growth has been phenomenal. When Henry Paley, an American official from the New York State Assembly, visited Britain in August 1963 to look into British betting laws, he was astonished; he found that many punters in Brixton were regularly betting two or three pounds a week from weekly earnings of twelve to fifteen pounds. 'There has been a wholesale increase in betting and gambling,' he said; 'A considerable part and a larger part, of the British economy is being devoted to this enterprise. Turnover appears to be about 65 per cent of what is spent on defence.[1]

The Churches' Council on Gambling, a watchdog which produces an annual report and lament on the state of the vice, complained again in 1964 that the government were permitting the commercial stimulation of gamblers: 'Most gambling today springs not from an absolute inward impulse but from a response to a commercially offered impulse . . . how many had previously known that what they wanted was more and better bingo?'

This was how the Council reckoned the turnover on gambling in 1963 and 1961:

	1961 *£ million*	*1963* *£ million*
Horse racing	540	560
Greyhound racing	115	110
Football pools	85	68
Fixed odds football betting	60	65
Bingo in commercial clubs	30	35
Premium Bonds	15	18
Other forms (funfairs, etc.)	8	10
	£853m.	£866m.

[1] *The Times,* August 23, 1963.

It revealed that 44 per cent of the people questioned had bet on a horse or a dog in the previous year; that 36 per cent gambled at least once a week; that 8 per cent played bingo once a week or more often; and that 20 per cent filled in football pool coupons every week.[1]

The pattern of gambling has changed. Greyhound racing, which after the war—when there was not much else to do—enjoyed a fantastic boom, has steadily declined: in 1946 the tote turnover was £200 million, in 1962 it was only £52 million. The pools, too, have declined. 'The pools offer something which works much like a lottery,' said the Churches' Council in 1963, 'and bingo offers an alternative lottery, in the form of a game where the prizes are won straight away the same evening. There is also some companionship and corporate excitement.' Bingo has emerged as the new national sport—of a kind that requires no intelligence, exertion or choice: in 1963 there were over fourteen million members of Bingo clubs.

But with all the new activities, tastes and expanding interests, there remains a strong antisocial element in the national character. George Orwell wrote of the 'English characteristic which is so much a part of us that we barely notice it, and that is an addiction to hobbies and spare-time occupations, the *privateness* of English life. We are a nation of flower-growers . . . of stamp collectors, pigeon fanciers, amateur carpenters, coupon snippers, darts players, crossword puzzle fans'.[2] Fishing, the most defiantly private sport, is booming, and the National Federation of Anglers has 390,000 members. There are nineteen million spare-time gardeners, from banking magnates to trade unionists. Pets abound —there are four million dogs in Britain, six million cats and about nine million pet birds, mostly budgerigars.

Will the privacy and mild eccentricity of English leisure be gradually worn down by the bombardments of motor cars, Wimpy bars, bowling alleys and, above all, mass advertising and TV— producing a gregarious Americanised society, with the same status-races? If 'growth' (the catchword of industry) is taken to mean only steel-production, consumer durables and industrial productivity, then the ultimate achievement will be a country clogged with honking cars and criss-crossed with motorways. But if growth also means social services, education, books, art and

[1] *Daily Telegraph*, April 1, 1963.
[2] *The Lion and the Unicorn*, 1941.

gardens, then Britain—whose aristocratic and landed tradition has produced more subtle (and often more sensible) status symbols —may not only find her own solution to the problems of twentieth-century leisure, but even export it.

35

ADVERTISING

I'm the most superficial man on earth, and yet I am the dean of my profession. So there must be something wrong with my profession.

Albert Lasker (the 'founder of modern advertising').

The trade of advertising is now so near perfection that it is not easy to propose any improvement.

Dr. Johnson, 1759.

To put it mildly, advertising people feel that they are not respectable.

Jeremy Tunstall, 1964.

THE British have always regarded themselves as more resistant to advertising than Americans. But during and since the war (which made great use of it) the admen's prestige has steadily grown. In America, Madison Avenue has suffered a partial setback: bogus television quizzes, payola, faked-up commercials, and the cut-throat competition between agencies revealed an ugly and pathetic mendacity and damaged the admen's social position. In Britain, advertising has been steadily on the up, and the agencies have attracted some of the ablest university graduates. As so often Britain is accepting what America is rejecting: here once more the two ships seem to be crossing in mid-Atlantic. As Britain becomes saturated with increasingly similar goods, so her advertising comes closer to the American pattern. The more identical the soaps or detergents, the more the adman is in his paradise, using all his skill to devise the 'unique selling proposition', to unearth irrational motives to dress soap with romance, sex, security or self-advancement.

There have been some signs of revulsion. Commercial TV has made advertising much more aggressive, and more dislikeable; the growth of political advertising (the Conservatives spent half a million pounds before the last election) has aroused suspicions and the Consumers' Association and their magazine *Which?*, with a circulation of 429,000[1] in 1964—far bigger than *The Times*

[1] It has been estimated that *Which?* has between 3 and 4 readers per copy, giving it a total readership of around 1½ million.

—has begun to make some readers more sceptical. Admen, even more than stockbrokers, are aware of an unfavourable image. But the energy, ingenuity and vast resources of advertising have not yet come up against any effectively organised resistance.

The total amount spent on advertising in 1962 was £479 million pounds; but out of this colossal figure—more than was spent on schools—less than half was devoted to the 'consumer display advertising'—in the press, posters and television—with which advertising agencies are basically concerned; and admen are insistent that the proper figure for *their* expenditure was £225 million, or at most £290 million. This is how the total amount is made up:[1]

ADVERTISING EXPENDITURE 1962

'Consumer Display Advertising'	£225 m.	
Sales Promotion Activities (Catalogues, leaflets, window and shop display, exhibitions, free samples and gift schemes)		£122 m.
Classified Advertising (Personal, Jobs, Houses, Goods, Services)		35 m.
Trade and Technical Advertising		32 m.
Retail and Financial Announcements		65 m.
	£254 m.	
Total Advertising	£479 m.	

After a rapid increase in the post-war years—to make up for the wartime lull—the expenditure on advertising appears now to have settled down to about 2·1 per cent of the net national income—about the same as it was in 1938. This was the percentage of net national income spent on all forms of advertising in various countries over ten years:[2]

	1953	*1956*	*1959*	*1962*
USA	2·6	2·8	2·8	2·7
UK	1·6	1·8	2·1	2·1
W. Germany	1·6	1·6	1·7	1·8
France	0·6	0·7	0·7	0·8
Italy	0·3	0·5	0·6	0·8
Japan	0·8	1·0	1·5	1·6
Canada	2·0	2·0	2·1	2·1

[1] *Advertising Expenditure in 1962: a re-appraisal,* by Dr. John Treasure.

[2] Main source: International Advertising Associations. The international comparisons are bedevilled by differences in the definition and estimation of advertising.

Advertising has no direction, no centre, no obvious tycoon. It exists as a hectic go-between, between the two great wheels of industry and the public, taking a succession of quick and temporary decisions, existing from hand to mouth, and constantly surprised by its own existence and wealth. This dependence of advertising men is part of their self-justification. As one of their pundits, John Hobson, has put it: 'Advertising is not (as some people seem to imagine) something in its own right, some separate estate of the realm, like civil administration, or the services, or law. Advertising is an integral part of industry.'[1] You will look in vain (despite what some churchmen think) for a roomful of advertising chairmen plotting how best to corrupt the public mind and extend their power. Only occasionally do they get together to defend their trade or—very rarely—to chuck out a member. In the one great recent advertising revolution—the creation of commercial television—a few agencies took an important rôle, but most were more alarmed than exhilarated by the prospects, as appears in the next chapter.

The influence of advertising on the press is not as bludgeoning and restrictive as many people, including Northcliffe, feared. Advertisers like newspapers to be credible; the more absurd an advertisement is, the more they like it to be alongside convincing news. But advertising has, in less direct ways, immensely influenced the character of the press—more obviously in the 'quality' papers which are more dependent on advertising.[2] Subjects which are supported by advertisers—notably fashion, travel and consumer goods—have all received mounting editorial attention compared to serious news, and women's magazines and supplements, linked to advertising, have boomed while general news magazines have slumped. No major paper or commercial television channel will dare put forward strong criticism of advertising or advertisers. The influence of advertising on newspapers has not been so much the direct corruption of the editorial puff or boost, as the general muffling of criticism, the magnification of the adman's interests, and the tendency for advertisers to press newspapers into the same mass markets as themselves. Advertisers have also encouraged a debased new travesty of journalism, the 'advertising supplement', with vapid articles of praise printed alongside advertisements. The only medium which is effectively independent

[1] John Hobson (Chairman of Hobson, Bates and Partners) in the *Journal of the Royal Society of Arts*, July 1964, p. 566.

[2] *See* p. 151.

of advertising is the BBC, which has begun to exploit its advantage in a televised consumer report called 'Choice'; when in 1964 they had a panel of a doctor, a dentist and a dermatologist to criticise patent medicines, the advertisers made a howl of protest, and Lord Robens, ironically the current chairman of the Advertising Association, visited his nationalised colleague, Sir Hugh Greene of the BBC, to protest.

Modern advertising was an American invention. There were British pioneers, like Lever and Lipton, but the pace was set by New York. High-pressure advertising began with a young Texan-Jewish salesman called Albert Lasker, who in 1904 first developed the principle of 'salesmanship in print'. He transformed advertising from a series of sedate announcements into a cunning art of appealing to secret desires, and in the next forty years he made forty-five million dollars out of it.[1] But as the business became more complicated, so advertising became less of an art, more of a science. On to the original wagon of salesmanship was loaded an extraordinary baggage of statistics, pollsters, committees and analysts: the technique of probing and goading the human mind became more specialised. 'Advertising', complained Lasker, who had a gift for epigram, 'has been lost in the advertising business.'

But advertising, in spite of its impedimenta, still has the histrionic atmosphere of a second-hand Hollywood. Advertising agencies are a compound of ballyhoo, calculations and creative energy: in their curious caravan are included accountants, film producers, salesmen, poets, artists, showmen and straightforward businessmen. But it is an industry which still manufactures only one fragile commodity—ideas; nothing is actually *made* in an agency building except words and pictures, and when all the committees are finished, the advertisement still depends on someone to write it. The copywriters who compose the advertisements and the artists who design them make up the frail heart of the advertising business: as the flood of advertising has swelled, so these 'creative men' have moved from agency to agency at ever higher salaries. Advertising and television between them have created a sudden and insatiable market for the more malleable kinds of creative talent: and a talented copy-writer in his early thirties can earn £5,000 a year. Here is one of the most spectacular changes in thirty years; with the growth of TV, advertising and 'posh' journalism, any creative talent is in furious demand, and

[1] *See* John Gunther: *Taken at the Flood*, 1960.

anyone prepared to bend his talent to commerce is more likely to collapse from overeating at the White Tower than from starving in an attic.

The trade of the admen depends on harnessing abstract ideas to the machinery of selling, and the resulting conflict shows itself in their characters. They are like lawyers—as they often point out—in their one-sided advocacy, but without the law's object of the whole truth. The earlier, pre-war generation of admen were often reluctant recruits, writing sonnets or painting abstract pictures between slogans. But since the war, advertising has become much more a self-contained career, with its own circles and revolting obscurantist jargon ('Environmentally and market-wise', an accomplished adman will tell his client, 'I think we've minored this too much. We need to make a *major*: we've got to plus it up a bit.') The modern advertising man likes to think of himself as less of a salesman than a 'consumption engineer' who turns the wheels between the manufacturer and the consumer. 'The advertising man,' wrote Jeremy Tunstall of the London School of Economics, 'seems to me to be the clearest example of the consumption engineers who are likely to take over from the manufacturers as the predominant group of business managers within the next generation.'[1]

The smoothest of the admen are the account executives, who look after clients; they are the salesmen for salesmanship. They are masters of ploy and one-upmanship—knowing just where to live, who to know, what to say, where to take their clients to lunch. They inhabit the Connaught, the Savoy or the Stafford, welcomed by waiters and signing vast bills with casual bravura. The art directors can be seen at the Arts Club in Dover Street, full of large men gripping each other by the shoulder, exchanging bonhomie. Two different elements can be noted in the British adman—the Madison Avenue type, with lightweight suits and Italian ties, constantly searching for lusher and more expensive restaurants, and the Guards officer type, frequenting mahogany regions: the Guards Club itself is now a favourite advertising haunt.

Most senior admen come from Oxford or Cambridge.[2] Advertising is a favourite destination for the public school boy, and men who thirty years ago might have gone out to rule India or pace the quarterdeck may now be selling detergent campaigns at

[1] *The Listener*, March 12, 1964.

[2] At the LPE, for instance, three-quarters are from Oxbridge.

the Connaught. 'Advertising seems to need face-to-face communicators,' said Dr. Mark Abrams, the detached and tireless market researcher at the London Press Exchange, 'which is the special skill which Oxbridge provides: people who know when to be flippant and when to be serious, who can say the right things about Wimbledon and Glyndebourne.' Advertising is a very professional affair, with a large front of professional amateurism. 'Never have I met,' someone said, 'such a high ratio of ignorance to intelligence.'

There are about five hundred advertising agencies in Britain, but about half do 90 per cent of the business. These were the twelve biggest agencies in 1963, together with their 'billings'—the total cost of the advertising they placed—in 1963 and 1960:

(All figures in £ million)	*1960* *Total*	*1963* *Total*
A—J. Walter Thompson	15·2	17·0
London Press Exchange	14·6	17·0
S. H. Benson	10·9	15·0
Mather & Crowther	9·0	11·3
Masius & Fergusson	7·3	9·1
A—Erwin Wasey, Ruthrauff & Ryan	8·2	8·9
Colman, Prentis & Varley	9·6	7·9
A—Young & Rubicam	6·8	7·3
Lonsdale-Hands Organisation	5·8	7·1
A—McCann-Erickson	5·0	6·8
A—Hobson, Bates & Partners	—	6·4
Brunning Advertising & Marketing Ltd.	—	6·0

Five of them (marked A) are American-owned. In the last few years several big American agencies have bought London firms, or set up their own branches—bringing a new surge of ballyhoo, statistics, and higher salaries. Some admen have complained that this American invasion is destroying the authentic British way of life: and that American sledgehammer tactics are quite un-British. But others are doubtful whether there is any longer such a thing as a British approach, in such a very American business. Or rather the British approach seems to have become American while the American has become less so.

J. WALTER THOMPSON

The dominating agency in Britain—and in Australia, Argentina or India—is the giant American firm of J. Walter Thompson, which celebrated its centenary in December 1964. 'The great days of advertising are over,' said Commodore James Walter Thompson, a bearded pioneer, when he sold his agency in New York in 1916: since then the turnover has increased by 120,000 per cent, and the firm has spawned over the world. J. Walter Thompson is not a typical agency (there is no such thing) but, both in America and Britain, it has set the pace for others. It was the first agency to develop exhaustive research about markets—ever since 1912 when it produced a small dry book called *Population and its Distribution.* JWT men in New York like to regard themselves as a 'University of Advertising', and to think of themselves as part of a serious profession: they are opposed to nepotism, and there is hardly a son-in-law in the business. Their entrance tests rival those of the Foreign Service. They are anti-romantic and thorough, and have imposed bureaucracy and science on the young wild trade of advertising: the poets and artists, like scientists, bishops or trade unionists, have found themselves sucked into committees.

Thompson's have pioneered 'Reason why' advertising, which unearths motivations for buying products and then projects them to the public. They love testimonials from famous people (Pond's Cream, Lux Soap, etc.) and have a special testimonial department. Gilbert Harding earned £5,000 a year advertising indigestion cures, but most subjects are much cheaper, and film stars are usually free. Thompson's also go in for scientific evidence ('laboratory tests show that . . .'), and they have a whole team of highly-paid consultants from universities to help them with special ingredients and secret formulae. Thompson people are taught to ask themselves five questions—known as the 'Thompson T Square':

What are we selling?
To whom are we selling?
Where are we selling?
When are we selling?
How are we selling?

The London office of J. Walter Thompson, though ultimately controlled from New York, sees itself as thoroughly British. The chairman, vice-chairman and directors are all British, and

New York (which holds 65 per cent of the shares) only rarely interferes. When you walk through Thompson's offices—nine floors in Berkeley Square—you feel immediately the heightened atmosphere of the 'Agency Game'. Activities which might seem merely fatuous outside the building, like collecting testimonials for face cream, immediately acquire an urgent significance. In advertising, ends are forgotten in the excitement of means and techniques, and the one question which cannot be asked is '*why* are we selling?' Young men in bow ties and suede shoes stride through the corridors, pretty, confident secretaries sit talking in clusters (pretty girls are very important for impressing the clients), senior executives sit with their doors open, occasionally shouting a Christian name into the passage. Words like 'creative', 'emote', 'subconscious' are bandied about like merchandise. Even the notice boards have an extravagantly theatrical atmosphere: 'Dear Art Department, just to thank you for my lovely, lovely rug.'

Along the corridors are long display boards, covered with sexy photographs, seductive advertisements and slogans such as 'The best creative people are definitely unreasonable'. Inside the offices are framed advertisements and glass cases containing packets of Kelloggs, Persil or Horlicks—like a museum. These names are the gods of Thompson's business, referred to with a mixture of familiarity and reverence. Into their promotion goes the care that went, in medieval times, into church building. JWT use five hundred artists and 67 writers—writing, unwriting, rewriting their lines of praise. In the Thompson pub, the 'Coach and Horses' behind Berkeley Square, you can hear stories of past campaigns ending with 'and the sales went up like this'—and the speaker tilts his hand to suggest a steep graph.

Some of the Thompson campaigns are legendary. There were those heavenly Black Magic chocolates in the thirties, with a page from a romantic letter, implying that chocolates were the prelude to love. There was the invention of 'night-starvation', with endless strip-cartoons showing haggard and unloved girls being transformed into successful beauties by Horlicks. There was the procession of film stars washing themselves with Lux, starting in 1928, which began the long association between Unilever and J. Walter Thompson. 'Both Unilever and JWT,' said Unilever's glossy magazine, *Progress*, 'are modestly proud of having so successfully analysed the woman/soap/complexion/glamour relation.' And there was the 'what is a Mum' campaign on television from Persil, which is Thompson's most enduring success.

'An agency is like an army consisting entirely of officers,' said Thompson's managing director, 'and that makes it difficult to run.' Out of Thompson's staff of 1,100 about 260 are 'creative', and no fewer than 41 are 'associate directors': it helps to impress the clients. Television has swelled this creative army: it has brought the admen into the heart of show business, and the film-makers are becoming the aristocracy of advertising. Above all, TV has made the big advertising agencies much richer.

Thompson, like all advertising agencies, is a young man's world—and a young woman's (advertising is one of the few fields where women enjoy near-equality with men). The right enthusiasm, ideas and salesmanship are all more likely to be found in the young than in the old. The managing director, Tom Sutton, who looks after the day-to-day administration, is the quintessence of the modern adman. He is only forty, and he joined Thompson's from Oxford, in 1949—one of the first of the post-war rush of Oxford men into advertising. As a young man he was sent to start up a new Thompson office in Frankfurt, and built it up to a staff of three hundred; when he left to become managing director, he was presented by his staff with a juke-box, with a supply of records about himself. Sutton is boyish, extrovert, full of enthusiasm for every product and campaign. He delights in the professionalism of the job, and has tried to bring a new group of young 'technocrats' to the top of the agency. He enjoys practical jokes. He gives no hint of the guilt pangs sometimes ascribed by social commentators to admen.

AGENCY WARFARE

The five hundred agencies exist in a state of jungle competition, not only for clients but for staff: successful writers or account executives move from camp to camp, sometimes taking clients with them. But the larger agencies are beginning to settle down to a more placid existence. The oldest agency, the London Press Exchange, was founded in 1893 as a news agency supplying a London Letter to the provinces—hence the odd name (their chairman, R. C. Sykes, is the son of the founder). Soon they discovered—as others have found since—that advertising is more profitable than journalism, and with the help of such a lucrative client as Cadbury's chocolate they have grown into one of the biggest agencies in Europe.

The agencies are perpetually wooing, with lunches, diagrams, drinks and statistics, the large industrial companies—particularly the tiny group of giants like Unilever, Imperial Tobacco or Shell—on which their fortunes depend. They subsist on the fifteen per cent commission from the placing of advertising, and the transfer of one million-pound product brings £150,000 a year to an agency, which produces around £15,000 net profit. The meetings with the clients or prospective clients mark the tense climax of an agency's salesmanship. Magnificent lunches are spread out in private rooms. Tape-recorders, films, sheafs of drawings and dossiers of figures are marshalled. Sometimes a whole book is produced for the agency's 'presentation'.

ADVERTISING AND INDUSTRY

The collision of the youthful world of advertising with the reticent world of business is bizarre. In Britain, as opposed to America, businessmen have inherited a distrust of advertising and a feeling that, if what they make is good enough, there will be no need to boast about it. They have regarded advertising as a useful luxury, not an essential tool. An elderly director of a family firm and a young advertising executive from Mayfair talk different languages. But gradually the admen and salesmen have come closer to industry: 'Thirty years ago people were shocked at the idea of a marketing man on the board,' said Dr. Mark Abrams: 'accountants and engineers were all right, but not people who *sold* things. In those days an advertising man was likely to have a chat with a manager at Lyons Corner House: now he'll be talking to a member of the board in the directors' dining-room.'

But many industries in Britain have been built on advertising and never forget it. Margarine, patent medicine, cigarettes or cosmetics were born into an age of posters, and the firms which make them, like Unilevers or Beechams, are dominated by 'marketing men'. It is the older industries, which existed before posters or newspapers—like food, beer or coal—which resist advertising most strongly. This was how the cost of advertising on press and television compared to the total consumer expenditure, for some products in 1962:

All alcoholic drink	0·9 per cent
Beer	0·6
All tobacco	0·9
All food	1·0
Bread	0·5

Butter	0·8
Margarine	5·9
Soups	11·5
Ready-to-eat cereals and porridge oats	8·6
Fresh fruit	0·3
Frozen foods	2·4
Canned fruit	1·0
Proprietary food drinks	17·2
Household soaps and detergents	10·2
Indigestion remedies	29·0
Cough and cold remedies	4·3
Hair preparations	13·6
Clothing	0·7
Footwear	0·6
Motors and motor-cycles	0·7
Motor oil	4·5
Durable goods and household equipment	2·9
Coal	0·4

In advertising circles, a special magic surrounds products which spend more than a million pounds a year. These were the ten products which spent most on advertising in 1963, and the firms that made them:

Rolls Washing Machine (John Bloom)	£1,724,187
National Milk Publicity Council	1,401,524
Persil (Unilever)	1,178,940
Daz (Procter & Gamble)	1,150,760
Omo (Unilever)	1,078,104
C & A Modes	977,880
Ford Cars	951,271
Stork Margarine (Unilever)	943,979
Oxo	935,490
National Coal Board	815,809

To see how fickle this business can be, one has only to note that the biggest client, Rolls Washing Machines, went into liquidation in the following year; and to compare this list with that for 1960:

Persil (Unilever)	£1,160,000
Tide (Procter & Gamble)	1,124,000
Omo (Unilever)	1,030,000
Daz (Procter & Gamble)	945,000
Stork (Unilever)	800,000
Guinness	891,000
Nescafé (Nestlé's)	862,000
Surf (Unilever)	855,000
Maxwell House (Alfred Bird)	669,000
Ford Cars	642,000

Some indication of our cockeyed economy is provided by the fact that Daz, Tide and Omo between them spend more on advertising than the Arts Council spends altogether in a year.

Where the ratio of advertising to cost is small, the effectiveness of advertisements is hard to judge: no one, for instance, *knows* whether 'Drinka Pinta Milka Day' makes more people drink milk. ('Half my advertising is wasted,' said the first Lord Leverhulme, 'but I do not know which half.') But with cold cures, detergents or hair oil, the sales ebb and flow with advertising, and the adman enters the heart of business. Often the adman not only provides the posters, television commercials and newspaper displays: he moves in to redesign the packaging, to analyse the market, to recommend on the strategy of selling and even—in some cases—to suggest new kinds of products. Like bankers or management consultants, advertising men can act as mercenaries to feeble régimes.

PRESTIGE ADVERTISING

Since the war there has been an uprush of big-business advertisements not obviously concerned with selling, displaying high-minded sentiments about life in general, and ironically most prominent in the left-wing *New Statesman*. This is 'prestige advertising', 'company advertising', 'reputation advertising', 'institutional advertising', 'good-will advertising'—the multiplicity of names, as for lavatories, suggests embarrassment. Sometimes the object is clear: South Africa justifies apartheid, gas attacks electricity, television is mindful of Pilkington. But often the advertising has a broader objective —a fostering of good-will, a 'projecting of a corporate image'—to use a favourite advertising expression. 'Company advertisements,' says a significant pamphlet issued by the Institute of Practitioners in Advertising, 'can influence the public to regard the company in a certain way: as forward-looking people with a vigorous policy of scientific research; as friendly, helpful people with enough humanity to laugh at themselves; or as craftsmen in the English tradition to whom "automation" and "assembly line" are naughty words.'

The growth of institutional advertising since the war has been spectacular: one advertising chairman estimated that it now constituted ten per cent of the total. It marks an important trend, for it shows advertising trying to act as interpreter for the business corporations, and beginning, in some fields, to usurp the rôle of journalism. There are several ways of describing its rôle. According to Colonel Varley of CPV, it is a question of 'producing a fusion between the consumers' and the producers' attitude. You have to find out where technological developments are taking you, and try to equate those with consumers' attitudes.'

Many Leviathans avoid institutional advertising. Unilever, for instance, prefer to remain a shadowy presence (when, recently, they conducted a poll among the intelligentsia, to discover attitudes to detergent advertising, they found that many were shocked by Omo advertising, but had no idea who was responsible). Few people connect Pepsodent with Unilever, Lucozade with Beechams, Dettol with Reckitt and Colman. But other firms love to proclaim themselves to the public. The eccentricity of Accles and Pollock, the whimsicality of Albright and Wilson, the heroism of English Electric, the enterprise of Bowaters, the sensitivity of the Electricity Generating Board, the broadmindedness of De La Rue—all these have entered into bogus folklore. Frequently, the advertising has very little relation to the real personality of the company: as the IPA pamphlet points out, it may like to suggest that an assembly-line is really a group of craftsmen. The jolly, eccentric directors in the advertisements, singing ditties and exchanging merry quips, can hardly be more different from the actual boards.

PUBLIC RELATIONS

Organised lying.
Malcolm Muggeridge.

A most degrading profession.
Harold Wilson.

The deliberate, planned and sustained effort to establish and maintain mutual understanding between an organisation and its public.
Definition by the Institute of Public Relations.

The trade of public relations had an appropriately disreputable beginning. The first public relations officer was Ivy Lee, a persuasive American who was employed by the first Rockefeller in 1914 to explain away the massacre of strikers in Colorado: in 1934, when he was had up in court, he turned out to be acting as PR man to the Nazi government. Since Lee's day public relations in America has galloped ahead: in 1961 there were reckoned to be

100,000 American PR men, spending two billion dollars a year.

Britain has advanced more cautiously, and (as so often) about thirty years behind America. The first PRO in Britain was Sir John Elliot, who began on the *Daily Express* (which his father edited), became the first PRO for Southern Railways, later chairman of the London Transport Executive, now chairman of Thomas Cook's. Before the war public relations—except in fashion or show business—was regarded with suspicion. The war made it, like advertising, respectable and Whitehall found PROs very convenient for explaining unpopular actions. Since the war the trade has raced ahead. In 1948 the Institute of Public Relations was founded with 248 members: in 1965 it had 2,194 members. One public relations man—Eric Williams of McCann-Erickson—has estimated that by 1970 there will be 10,000 of them: 'Everyone will want to get into the PR act.' Already the Church of England, Paul Getty, Hambro's bank, debutantes, the Army, the Aga Khan, all have their PROs: even the Queen has her PRO, Commander Colville (though he is as much concerned with keeping his client *out* of the papers).

British public relations have roughly followed the American pattern, but there are important differences. In America PR is a trade very separate from advertising, with its own large firms: in Britain, most advertising agencies have their own PR departments, and this combined front makes the machine more formidable. Another difference is that Britain has stronger traditional social networks and communications—the networks of schools, universities, clubs, families, or parliament—which public relations persuaders come up against. But this does not necessarily make PR less effective: by operating *through* clubs, school ties and old boys nets it can and does take over traditional networks, and public relations is a lucrative field for the old boy net and the public school proletariat.[1]

The general shabbiness of the trade was well reflected in the results of a survey which the Institute of Public Relations rather rashly published in 1964.[2] A thousand of their members answered a questionnaire, and the replies revealed that

32 per cent of members went to university
19 per cent graduated
32 per cent went to public or private schools

[1] *See* p. 397.
[2] *The Times*, February 1, 1964.

41 per cent went first into journalism
14 per cent went first into advertising or selling
15 per cent are women.

The survey deduced that 'men tend to get their professional training elsewhere and go into public relations after thirty'. It reckoned that the typical PRO was aged 41 and earned more than £2,300, and that their members handled about £23 million of spending a year, of which £13½ million was devoted to public relations. The survey claimed that the picture which emerged was 'of a relatively young, well-paid profession whose members appear to exercise a very notable degree of power and influence'.

Hundreds of public relations men are steadily employed by large corporations, keeping newspapers and television informed of their employers' achievements, suffused in a rosy light. Many others are employed by advertising agencies to supplement their other services. But there are also more subtle, independent practitioners, often called 'consultants', who work in a more personal way and are the aristocrats of the profession; their average annual income in 1964 (according to the Institute's survey) was £3,000, as opposed to only £2,000 for those in commerce. They have firms of their own, with plush offices in the West End. They work among chandeliers and marble mantelpieces, telephoning, entertaining, introducing, arranging, conciliating, explaining — lubricating the groaning wheels between corporations and the public. Sometimes they make use of institutional advertising, but their real art consists of *unseen* promotion—inspiring headlines, television programmes, questions in parliament, letters to *The Times*. They cultivate an old-fashioned, long-established atmosphere: they wear stiff collars and dark suits and sit in Regency offices.

They are the new fixers of British society: they have the suavity, the social poise, the adaptability and flexibility of diplomats, and a sprinkling of titles and double-barrelled names. There is the Earl of Kimberley, whose clients include Gilbey's gin and Gina Lollobrigida: Lady Joubert de la Ferté, who looks after the London Fashion Designers: Alan Campbell-Johnson, once Lord Mountbatten's press attaché, now explaining Esso, Procter and Gamble, and Imperial Tobacco.

One of the most celebrated is Toby O'Brien, a languid, soft-voiced Irishman (he has a brother known as 'Post Office Toby', who is PRO to the GPO). O'Brien wears a black coat, striped trousers and a monocle: he sits in an office in Old Burlington

Street with a soft carpet, a grandfather clock and a huge oil painting of William O'Brien, a seventeenth-century ancestor on horseback, and he is descended from Lord Inchiquin, Monarch of All Ireland.

O'Brien was once part of 'Peterborough', the gossip-column of the *Daily Telegraph*: later he became Public Relations Officer to the Conservative party, and helped to reconstruct their propaganda machine after 1945. He works in a personal and intimate way, giving small parties for selected opinion-moulders in Old Burlington Street, arranging little wine-tastings, press conferences, statements and expeditions. 'I've always been brought up to believe that public relations people should be seen and not heard,' he said: 'it's your job to boost your clients, not yourself.' His clients include Cunard, the Channel Tunnel, Gonzalez Byass sherry, the Royal Tournament, the Saudi Arabian Government, Cartier and the Portuguese African Colonies. 'The point is I never take anything on that I can't believe in a hundred per cent,' he told the *Daily Mail* in 1961 . . . 'They are still cannibals you know, literally.'

Public relations is penetrating further into the world of politics—both national and international. Several of the PR consultants are employed by foreign governments (a relationship forbidden in America), and are taking over part of the rôle of ambassadors: they have an informality and a technique with the press which conventional diplomats lack. Among these quasi-ambassadors are Michael Rice, a young Conservative who has publicised Ghana; Patrick Dolan and Associates, who have handled the publicity for Western Nigeria; and Frank Owen, a former Fleet Street editor who has represented, among other people, the King of Siam.

The most celebrated political advisers are Colman, Prentis and Varley who (with their subsidiary public relations firm, called Voice and Vision) have advised the Conservative party, the army and Sir Roy Welensky's government in Rhodesia. The success of their free plane trips, tours and advertising in influencing members of parliament pointed dramatically to the power of public relations, as the organisers were quick to demonstrate. 'The public relations gimmick of bringing out parties of British MPs on fact-finding tours of the Federation has paid off handsomely,' the Federal Director of Press and Public Relations is reported to have said in Lusaka on November 14, 1961: 'Public relations men "went to town" on various media to get Sir Roy Welensky terrific coverage for his recent speech at the Institute of Directors.'[1] The fact that MPs are dependent on 'gimmicks' for their excursions abroad has caused worry among some cabinet ministers,[2] but MPs who want to travel find it hard to resist invitations.

Writing a newspaper column one soon uncovers the mechanism of public relations, bombarding the office with handouts and gimmicks to attract attention. In the course of a year I received an invitation written on a plate, another written on silk, several invitations by telegram, a pile of visiting cards with my name printed in Greek (to advertise *The Guns of Navarone*). There was an invitation to a tea party at the Imperial Turkish Baths (to meet 'Miss Slenderleaf' of Tetley's teas); there was a jumping party in a gymnasium to advertise a book; a champagne party to look at a £250,000 man's suit; an invitation to meet a Haitian Voodoo priestess; and an invitation from Derry and Toms which began:

His Royal Highness the Duke of Edinburgh
having graciously consented to a
Display of the Personal Gifts . . .

The PROs outbid one another to find spectacular and exclusive venues for their parties; lately they have taken to invading clubland and parliament—of which increasing numbers of PR men are members. The *Financial Times* estimated that there were twenty Conservative MPs working in some capacity for PR or advertising agencies: 'the question "whom do you represent" ' they commented, 'may become quite ambiguous.'

The public relations officers have become part of the daily machine for manufacturing news: behind every issue of a newspaper lie their contraptions—the handouts, outings, free trips, press conferences or fashion shows. Journalists oscillate between the undoubted agreeableness of the PR men's blandishments—the plane trips to Athens, the lunches at the Connaught, the ready-made photographs and printable little stories—and an uneasy sense of dependence and obligation. Women journalists in particular are uncomfortably aware that, but for the PR machine, the whole calendar of fashion news would collapse.

As Britain becomes more fragmented, more professionalised, so the persuaders enter their kingdom. The old methods of com-

[1] Letter to *The Times* from Gerald Percy: December 1, 1961.
[2] *See* Chapter 3.

munication—the club, the coterie, the country house, even the newspapers—are weak in the face of this well-oiled machine. Some people have suggested that the attempt to influence MPs is no *more* sinister than the pressure of dinner-parties and country houses before the war. But public relations is much more directed and purposeful than any private hostess, and their 'social engineering'—a favourite PR phrase—is far more resourceful.

The picture that Britons have of themselves is already warmly coloured by public relations and advertising. In front of every corporation and institution, like the court praiser dancing and singing in front of a shaky Zulu king, is the PR man—explaining, interpreting, scattering handouts, telling stories of fabulous achievements.

The public relations men are comfortably aware that, after their years of tribulation, the future is theirs. 'If all these forecasts are realised,' Eric Williams has written, after adumbrating the glorious future, 'how splendid it will be for PR wives. At last, without uncertainty, evasion or embarrassment, they will be able to reply quite simply (even without a slight soupçon of status?) to the neighbourly query about their spouses' occupation: he is in public relations.

'And there will be a smile of instant mutual understanding . . .'

It is easy to adopt, as I have done here, an intolerant approach to the whole business of advertising, and much harder to work out what its relationship should be to contemporary Britain. Advertising is an inescapable part of the capitalist system, the visible part of the iceberg, which has to be faced. But the British, because of the traditional reticence and intimate character of the old institutions, have often tried to forget it and to wish that (like science) it wasn't there. Partly as a result, advertising and public relations have been associated with the newer, more ruthless, and often mendacious causes.

In fact, of course, the need for some kind of 'social engineering' is implicit in the complexity of modern society; but the more idealistic and entrenched institutions, including Whitehall departments, the United Nations, the BBC and the Labour party, maintain their suspicion of all kinds of advertising. As advertising trespasses further into journalism, so the resulting imbalance becomes more serious. The public faces a barrage from tobacco makers, industrial corporations, political pressure groups, the fashion industry, but hears scarcely a word from the social services or Whitehall. The older institutions are apt to suspect all new forms of communication, both external and internal, and continue to behave in a club-like, secretive way long after they have grown themselves into mass organisations: and the dangers of this withdrawn tradition were very abruptly discovered by the BBC.

36

TELEVISION

Television has affected nearly every other estate in the country. Commercial TV was not something, like schools, universities or the press, which 'just growed'. It was an innovation more sudden and dramatic than the nationalised industries, and like them full of doctrinal implications: while *they* stood as a monument to socialist doctrine, commercial TV is a monument to the free-enterprise lobby of the Conservative party. In five years it grew from an idea in the minds of a few tough enthusiasts into colossal companies, the most powerful patrons in the country, with profits larger than newspaper groups. Commercial TV, with the combined assault of technology and big-business, has undermined many old attitudes, and turned the managerial revolution on its head; while the new medium itself is still having repercussions on parliament, the monarchy, the Church, the press and particularly the position of the prime minister.

BBC

I believe that the success of a business depends on one man.

Lord Reith[1]

It is already difficult to recall the days of an unchallenged British Broadcasting Corporation, for as with other competitors—life peers v. hereditary ones, Shell v. Esso, Lloyd's v. Insurance companies—the rivals are becoming more alike. But basic differences remain, and much of the BBC's character is the product of its short but spectacular history. Its thirty-year monopoly, from the royal charter of 1927, seemed for most of that time as inevitable as that of the air force and it acquired its own massive character. It has some claim to be the first public corporation, for largely through the personality of J. C. W. Reith it succeeded in wresting itself away from the control of the Post Office, its nominal master, to become a separate organism, responsible to parliament only, who renewed its charter every five years. (The rivalry between the BBC and the GPO continued, and helped to let in the commercial

[1] Interview with John Freeman: *The Listener*, November 10, 1960.

lobby.) But the BBC had none of the anonymity and apparent headlessness of later nationalised industries, for its whole personality revolved round Reith. As one of his staff, Mary Adams, later recalled it, 'He was Queen Victoria, Genghis Khan, Leonardo, rolled into one. He was Headmaster, Field-marshal, Permanent Secretary, Commoner, Captain of the Ship, Father wielding a cane, a baton, a pen, a telephone, a secretary with an effortless ease. . . . Around him we were all dwarfs.' Partly from Reith, partly from its closeness to government, the BBC acquired that reverent attitude to British institutions—particularly the monarchy —which made it the most visible and disliked symbol of the Establishment. The image of the BBC has been transformed in the past ten years, but some of its reverential tone persists, most aptly expressed in the hushed tones of Richard Dimbleby. Its authority reached its peak in the war, with the nine o'clock news and Churchill's speeches. A competitor to the BBC would in those days have been unimaginable.

With its quick expansion and wartime accretions, the BBC became an unparalleled 'cultural bureaucracy', far larger than newspapers or advertising agencies. Like the AEA or ICI it had to combine disciplined hierarchy with a wild strain of creative energy. It had—and has—a substructure of civil service rules with an eccentric over-layer. Most BBC offices have the same passive squalor as Whitehall departments, and directors are likely to receive the CBE. But in the midst of the workaday bureaucracy are subversive poets, mutinous scriptwriters and unreliable actors.

Television took the BBC farther away from the austere discipline of Lord Reith, and showmanship quickly impinged on the informational, civil-service habits: 'You couldn't just stare into the camera looking anonymous,' one of the news announcers said to me: 'you *had* to start smiling and putting across a personality.' Showmen and cantankerous panellists, like Gilbert Harding, became national figures, and the size and resources of the cultural bureaucracy multiplied: by 1948 the BBC was able to put no fewer than a thousand people to cover the Olympic Games at Wembley: and today it employs over 20,000 people. Television bent its old character, but did not break it: the hierarchy were still 'sound men'. The governors still came from the sheltered worlds of universities and public service.

At the top the BBC has a stately organogram, leading down from governors to controllers to producers, with this at the summit in 1964:

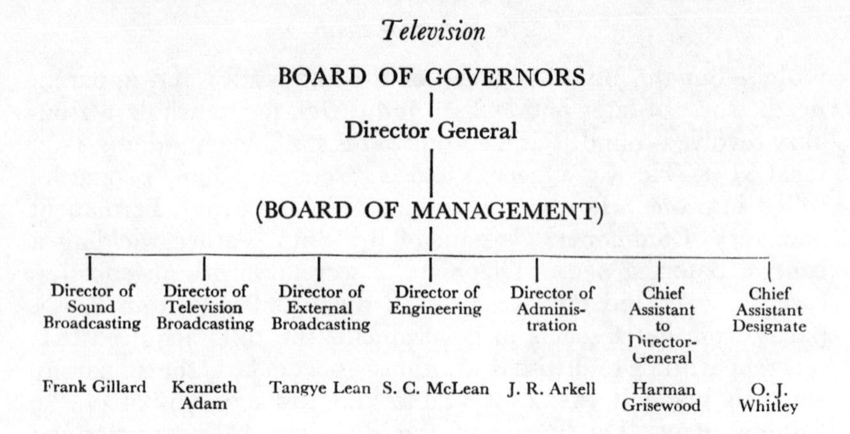

The governors are chosen from the usual pool of house-trained committee-people on the amateur principle, and they are not required to have an interest in, or knowledge of, broadcasting. These were the governors in 1964:

Lord Normanbrook (Chairman) .. Ex-Head of the Civil Service[1]
Sir James Duff (Vice-Chairman) .. Ex-Vice-Chancellor of Durham
Sir David Milne (Scotland) .. .. Ex-Permanent Under Secretary, Scottish Office
Mrs. Rachel Jones (Wales) .. .. Sociologist
Sir Richard Pim (Northern Ireland) Ex-Inspector-General, Ulster Constabulary
Gerald Coke .. .. Chairman, Rio Tinto Company
Robert Lusty .. .. Chairman and Managing Director, Hutchinsons
Sir Ashley Clarke .. .. .. Ex-Ambassador in Rome
Dame Anne Godwin .. .. .. Trade Unionist

Before Lord Normanbrook was appointed in 1963, it was widely rumoured that the new chairman would be armed with larger powers, in order to curb the independence of the director-general. But no change was evident. Lord Normanbrook, a lifelong administrator with a passion for secrecy and a hatred for publicity, took over his new office with infinite discretion, and appeared to be on excellent terms with the director-general. He and the other governors are not much more apparent than the governors of a school with a strong headmaster, and their main task is the choosing of a D-G, who is the executive head. These are the seven director-generals since 1927, with their previous occupations:

[1] *See* p. 281.

Lord Reith (1927–1938) Gen. Manager, Wm. Beardmore & Co.
Sir Frederick Ogilvie (1938–1942) Vice-Chancellor, Queen's University, Belfast
{ Sir Cecil Graves (1942–1943) BBC
R. W. Foot (1942–1944) Gen. Manager, Gas Light & Coke Co.
Sir William Haley (1944–1952) *Manchester Guardian*
Sir Ian Jacob (1952–1960) Chief Staff Officer, Ministry of Defence
Sir Hugh Greene (1960) BBC

Sir Hugh Greene[1] is the first D-G to have made his career in the corporation, and his appointment suggests that the BBC hierarchy has now become self-perpetuating. In his background Greene has some elements which suggest the typical BBC executive. He is a tall, pale man, with a quiet smile and intimidating reserve, like a cultivated permanent secretary, but quite without pomposity. He is one of the four sons of the headmaster of a public school, Berkhamsted, which educated them all: one, Graham, became a novelist; another, Raymond, is an eminent physician who climbed Everest; a fourth, Herbert, has been an ardent defender of the nine o'clock news and opponent of his brother Hugh's policies. After Oxford Hugh became Berlin correspondent for the *Telegraph*, and joined the BBC in wartime, specialising in propaganda to Germany. He had tact, drive and administrative skill, and he rose quickly through the hierarchy, becoming Director-General in January 1960, at the age of only fifty-one.

From his office in Broadcasting House—with a bronze bust of Lord Reith outside—Hugh Greene supervises his jumbled empire, from cowboy films to electronic music. He does not have grand ideas about the power of broadcasting. 'Can one point to any single occasion on which in its short life broadcasting has changed the course of history . . . ?', he said in Germany in April 1959. He believes that the BBC is the best possible system and that the alternatives of purely commercial broadcasting (as in America) or state-controlled broadcasting (as in France) are far more dangerous: 'Radio and television are too powerful in their eventual long-term effects for their control to be entrusted to politicians—or businessmen.' He does not have the grand Hegelian ideas of Lord Reith; but while accepting that the BBC must be impartial between Right and Left, he insists that it cannot be neutral between Right and Wrong. 'I should not for a moment admit that a man who wanted to speak in favour of racial intol-

[1] Formerly Hugh Carleton Greene. He incorporated 'Carleton' into his surname while at Oxford, and dropped it when he was knighted. 'I've been wanting to get rid of it for ages,' he told me.

erance has the same rights as a man who wanted to condemn it.' He maintains that the BBC is quite independent of government pressure, and he has not disguised his contempt for 'the commercial monster' and the men who control it. 'Commercially controlled television tends in the long run to undermine the intelligence, at any rate of its constant listeners and viewers.'

When Greene first took over his directorship, it was widely assumed that, coming from inside the bureaucracy, he would be still more cautious than his predecessors. But he was determined to break out of the reverent surroundings of his job. 'The director-general is partly a sort of glorified PRO,' he said in 1962, 'so I set out to destroy the old Auntie BBC image by meeting and talking to as many people as I could. In my first year I accepted every invitation I got. It meant a hell of a lot of dining, but I think it did a little to destroy the idea of the BBC as a distant, monolithic organisation no one could approach.'[1] Moreover, he had firm views about the rôle of the BBC. 'It's always been my belief,' he told me in 1964, 'that the BBC should not be part of the Establishment—or Establishments—but that it should be looking at the various powers-that-be with an enquiring, a critical, and sometimes a satirical eye. That can make us a more valuable institution.'

His special concern as director-general was with News and Current Affairs; and here he took the bold step of promoting two young producers, Donald Baverstock and Michael Peacock. Both of them had been protegés of a formidable BBC egghead, Grace Wyndham-Goldie, who was in charge of television talks, and who had helped to establish the BBC's pre-eminence in news-magazine programmes. Baverstock, a tireless irascible Welshman, had produced 'Tonight', the daily miscellany; and Peacock, a confident innovator with a flare for publicity, had produced Panorama, the most prestigious and influential of all BBC programmes. The most visible result of these promotions, and of Greene's quiet nerve, appeared in November 1962, when the satirical programme 'That Was The Week That Was' first broke on to a bewildered public. The project had been brewing for some time, with a good deal of opposition from inside the BBC. It was supervised by Baverstock, and produced by Ned Sherrin, a tall suave young impresario with a strong hold on his actors and writers, who devised a quite new kind of programme, blending music-hall, cabaret and the new-found satire of 'Private Eye' with TV techniques. Greene, having approved the venture, left

[1] Interview with John Pearson in the *Sunday Times*, June 17, 1962.

the producers to themselves, and watched the first night, with trepidation, not knowing what was to come. The result was spectacular. 'TW3', as it came to be called, brought irreverence and sharp political satire into the heart of the BBC. It made fun of politics, the government, and the churches, and came near to mocking the monarchy. Nothing could seem further than the awed commentaries of Dimbleby. TW3 destroyed, almost at one stroke, the concept of the BBC as a monolith, or part of the Establishment. The number of viewers went up, at its peak, to twelve million.

The programme, which seemed briefly to have become part of the British way of life, had a short lease; by the end of 1962 its brilliance had faded, some of its stars had become over-familiar, and it faced (it thought) an impending election. Greene decided to stop it, and in 1964 a rather feeble derivative appeared. 'The power of laughter,' he said to me in 1964, 'is an enormous power. We could not responsibly make use of that power with politics in the state they were in at the beginning of that year.' The BBC were accused of cowardice and retreat; but the new independent position which had been captured by TW3 still remained. The BBC, like other nationalised industries[1] but with wider implications, had proclaimed its autonomy and its right to speak out for itself. It was now on its own, more vulnerable but also more powerful. As Greene commented wryly afterwards: 'It was in my capacity of "subversive anarchist" that I yielded to the enormous pressure of my colleagues who were also subversive anarchists to put on "That Was The Week That Was". It was as a pillar of the establishment that I yielded to the Fascist hyena-like howls to take it off again. As you see, some of these criticisms tend to cancel each other out.'[2]

THE COMMERCIAL LOBBY

We have our typically British way of resolving problems of taste, just like any other problem.

Sir David Maxwell Fyfe (later *Lord Kilmuir*), *June 11, 1952*

The launching of Commercial TV was an operation which throws light on several people and institutions in this book, and provides a unique glimpse of the mechanism of power. It was due, not to any strong popular movement, but to the misgivings about

[1] *See* p. 592.
[2] Speech to the Foreign Press Association, December 3, 1963.

monopoly of two leading Conservative politicians, a vague sense of dissatisfaction with the BBC and the old-time attitudes of the cabinet among younger Tory backbenchers, and the active political pressure of a handful of lobbyists with a strong financial interest. The influence and tactics of this lobby have now become apparent from the important study by Professor Wilson of Princeton University, to which I am indebted for part of this material.[1] The lobbying was certainly made easier by the small majority (only 17) of the Conservative party, which enabled a few backbenchers to become a tail wagging a dog.[2] But the success of the lobby, against a united Labour party, an apathetic public and a divided Conservative party, remains an extraordinary and still partly unexplained phenomenon.

The first strong criticism of the BBC came from one dissenting member of the Beveridge Committee in 1951, Selwyn Lloyd, who criticised the BBC for its size (it had expanded from 2,500 to 12,000 between 1935 and 1951), for its monopoly and for its excessive power: he quoted critically Lord Reith's statement that 'it was the brute force of monopoly that enabled the BBC to have become what it did; and to do what it did; that made it possible for a policy of moral responsibility to be followed,' and he complained that 'it is just as though a British Press Corporation were to be set up with a monopoly of publishing newspapers.'

After the report a committee of ten Conservative backbenchers was set up, including John Rodgers, then a director of J. Walter Thompson, Charles Orr-Ewing, and John Profumo, who reported that the broadcasting monopoly should be broken. But in debates in the Commons and the Lords there was little apparent discontent with the BBC, with the important exception of Lord Woolton, an ex-salesman and shopkeeper who was excited by the idea of mass-marketing. When the Conservatives took office in October 1951 there was no enthusiasm in the cabinet. But a strong lobby of advertising and other MPs had formed itself, including Lady Tweedsmuir, Ian Harvey of Crawford's advertising, and Anthony Fell of Pye Radio. In March 1952 Lord Woolton became minister in charge of broadcasting, while as chairman of the Conservative party organisation he saw the potential of the new medium and under him the Central Office helped to promote it. In May 1952 a white paper was published, saying that 'in the

[1] Professor H. H. Wilson: *Pressure Group*, 1961. Some important material is also in 'The Men and the Money in ITV': *Sunday Times*, May 14–28, 1961.

[2] *See* Chapter 3.

expanding field of television, provision should be made to promote some element of competition'.

Lord Reith in the House of Lords bitterly attacked the white paper: 'Somebody introduced Christianity into England and somebody introduced smallpox, bubonic plague and the Black Death. Somebody is minded now to introduce sponsored broadcasting. . . . Need we be ashamed of moral values, or of intellectual and ethical objectives? It is these that are here and now at stake'. He was supported by Lords Halifax, Waverley, Hailsham and Brand. In the Commons, there was less Conservative opposition, and John Profumo effectively attacked the 'guardians of the BBC', who were 'almost powerful enough to be able to intimidate the government', and insisted 'we are not a nation of intellectuals'. But there was not much enthusiasm either, and as John Rodgers later said, most of the credit was due to 'five or six Conservative backbenchers who worked day and night on the project'. 'It is still not clear,' wrote Professor Wilson, 'how so small a group was able to make its influence decisive.'

Working behind parliament was the 'unique and powerful triumvirate' (as Wilson calls them)—Norman Collins, Sir Robert Renwick and C. O. Stanley—who between them brought together three quite different strands of influence, and who are all still major influences on the TV scene. Norman Collins, the novelist, journalist and publisher, had been controller of BBC Television from 1947 until, in 1950, he was passed over for the newly made post of TV Director, and promptly resigned. Rarely can a passing-over have had such momentous consequences. Collins immediately devoted all his energies to destroying the BBC monopoly, disgusted by 'an organisation which hadn't even got a TV set in the board-room'. He set about the attack with what he later called 'sheer bloody-mindedness'.[1] He brought invaluable energy and respectability to the campaign, for he knew the inside workings of the BBC, could convincingly attack its monopolism, and persuaded bishops and dons that a commercial rival would not mean Americanisation or excesses.

With him was Sir Robert Renwick, an adventurous stockbroker in Old Etonian braces, who held fourteen directorships in the electrical industry. He had wide contacts; he was on the council of the Institute of Directors, he had been wartime controller of communications at the Air Ministry, and he had close Tory connections, including a friendship with Orr-Ewing, one of the early

[1] *Sunday Times*, May 14, 1961.

supporters. 'Some participants in this controversy,' wrote Wilson, 'believed that Renwick's influence in party circles and with Lord Woolton may have been enhanced by what they assumed to have been his substantial assistance to raising the Conservative Fighting Fund.'[1] Renwick had been chairman of one of the biggest electricity companies, and was a believer in untrammelled enterprise: 'After the war very few Tories really believed in free enterprise,' he told me: 'my industry was nationalised, so I wanted to try and get my own back.' Both Renwick and Collins thus derived their main stimulus from getting their own back. In 1964 Renwick was made a baron 'for political and public services'.

The third, Charles Orr Stanley, is a chubby Irishman who had built up Pye Radio from small beginnings into an international company. Stanley is one of those implacable non-Englishmen who never succumb to the charms of monopoly or rings: he saw the commercial prospects of commercial TV at an early stage and set about pressing for it remorselessly through allies in parliament and elsewhere. The triumvirate worked closely together, and met at the Reform Club to work out their tactics and extend their allies.

The oddest feature of the ensuing campaign was the indifference or even hostility of most groups which were to benefit from commercial TV. The cinema industry, including Sidney Bernstein's Granada Theatres and Sir Philip Warter's ABC group, were originally opposed to it, as were the West End Theatre managers, including Prince Littler. The majority of radio manufacturers were apathetic. 'I am amazed that in a young and virile industry such as yours there should be such hesitation and timidity in putting the competitive television knob on the set,' complained Sir Robert Renwick. Nor were most of the advertising agencies at all enthusiastic: 'They were making too much money too happily to be interested in TV,' Collins told me in 1961: 'but in fact they've done better out of it than anyone—15 per cent of £50 million.' Many agencies resented American infiltration, and were afraid of the capital expansion and know-how required ('we'll have to get an American in to run it'); only a few of the biggest—notably Thompson's, Erwin Wasey (American) and the London Press Exchange—were enthusiastic. The City of London, which might have been expected to be alive to the commercial prospects, remained bored and sceptical, with the notable exceptions of Harley Drayton, Siegmund Warburg and Renwick.

[1] *Pressure Group*, p. 147.

Newspapers were equally sceptical, or afraid. When Renwick organised a lunch of newspaper proprietors, only Cecil King of the *Daily Mirror* (who later became a shareholder in Associated Television) showed any interest. 'In a hundred years there may not be newspapers,' he said later, 'but there will certainly be television. We want to learn about it and we are in it for keeps.' The *Daily Express* were furiously opposed, until they bought shares in ATV in 1964.

Not only was there this commercial apathy, but by June 1953 an impressive counter-lobby, the National Television Council, organised by Christopher Mayhew, had been set up to dissuade the government, with supporters including Lords Halifax, Brand and Waverley, Lady Violet Bonham Carter, ABC cinemas and the chairman of the TUC, Sir Tom O'Brien. The new council, with its strong Establishment flavour, alarmed the cabinet, and its warnings of vulgarisation were helped by the recent American televising of the Coronation, which had been heralded by commercials featuring J. Fred Muggs, the TV chimpanzee.

But Collins, Renwick and Stanley were undeterred by the counter-attack, and with the support of Lord Woolton they prepared a more impressive front. In July the Earl of Bessborough—a merchant banker and ally of Renwick's—met with the Earl of Derby and Norman Collins at the Turf Club, to invite Derby to become president of a new 'Popular Television Association', with support from Pye and others, and with the collaboration of the Conservative Central Office and unofficial blessing of Woolton. The new association succeeded in presenting a non-party front, attracting Socialists including A. J. P. Taylor, and had as its main object 'to awaken the national conscience to the dangers, social, political and artistic, of monopoly in this rapidly expanding field of television'. It had less impressive names than the anti-commercial council, but it had large funds, masterly techniques, and three tireless men. While the government gave the impression that changes would be distant and vague, the lobbyists, pressed for a quick Bill, and devised ingenious ways of satisfying Conservative qualms. All the usual public relations devices were employed, and 'Aims of Industry', the anti-socialist PR firm (which had invented 'Mr. Cube', the champion of private-enterprise sugar) worked closely with the association. Massive letters-to-the-editor campaigns were organised, public figures, including Lord Derby, Alec Bedser and Gillie Potter made suitable speeches, and a service of news items were provided for newspapers: an impression was conveyed of a nation demanding TV advertising. The campaign, together with back-bench and cabinet pressures (whose details are still obscure), had its effect, and by the end of 1953 the cabinet had decided to press through with commercial TV. 'This study would seem to establish the fact,' concluded Professor Wilson, 'that a small number of MPs, well organised with good connections among both party officials and outside interests, and pushing a definite, limited programme, may exert considerable influence and even overwhelm an organised majority in their own party.'[1]

By March 1954 the Television Bill came up for its second reading: the debate was bitter and split the two wings of Conservative thinking—those who believed in the paternal, aristocratic rôle of government, and those who believed in commercial free enterprise at all costs. It was partly a division between the Salisbury-type and Macleod-type Tories, but many liberal Conservatives were torn between the dislike of monopoly and the dislike of unrestricted salesmanship. In the end no Conservative MPs voted against; the Bill was passed by 296 votes to 269, and fourteen months later the first television advertisement—for toothpaste—appeared.

ITA

> 'Television, this titan of communication between man and man, this surging, sweeping power, rationed and controlled for us before, is in our hands.'
>
> *Sir Robert Fraser, September 24, 1955.*

To supervise this sudden innovation a new public body, the Independent Television Authority, was constructed, to erect the transmitters and give licences to 'contracting companies'—a system partly copied from Chicago. The ITA was empowered by the Act to provide 'television broadcasting services, additional to those of the BBC and of high quality both as to transmission and as to the matter transmitted' and that 'nothing is included in the programmes which offends against good taste or decency or is likely to encourage or incite to crime . . .' A Chairman and 'Members of the Authority' were appointed by the government, not unlike BBC governors, and not necessarily interested in television: their first chairman was Sir Kenneth Clark, the art historian, and the second Sir Ivone Kirkpatrick, former head of the Foreign Office. As with the BBC, the executive head was the director-general, a job first advertised in *The Times* in 1953. Sir Robert Fraser, sunbathing in Spain, saw the advertisement and

[1] *Pressure Group*, p. 208.

applied for the job, in some of the same spirit of adventurousness as Reith twenty-seven years before. Fraser had worked with Sir Kenneth in the war, he had the right background and experience, and he was chosen.

But Fraser had none of Reith's austerity or Calvinism. For their offices the ITA now have a brand new building next to Harrods, with hand-picked furniture, pent-house flats and tinkling lifts, outdoing the TV companies themselves in its comfort. Fraser himself was an unusual paradox—Australian, once an intellectual Socialist, close friend of Laski, Dalton and Durbin, wrote leaders for the *Daily Herald* and stood as Labour candidate. Worked in information during the war, and later ran the Central Office of Information. He was confident, very convincing, well attuned to modern publicity, and loved talking about his job. His new post surprised many of his old left-wing friends, but he justified it at length. He regarded himself as a 'liberal with a small l', and saw himself as a Benthamite, believing in democratic choice, in contrast to the Platonic ideals of the BBC. He liked to think of Commercial TV as 'people's television'. 'If you decide to have a system of people's television,' he said in Manchester in 1960, 'then people's television you must expect it to be, and it will reflect their likes and dislikes, their tastes and aversions, what they can comprehend and what is beyond them.'

The most important job of the ITA was to choose the contracting companies. The selection was made by all members of the authority, but Fraser's influence was often decisive. At first the pessimism about the new medium was such that competition was not very intense. Only when profits were apparent did the value of the ITA's patronage become obvious: 'There's been nothing like it since Charles II doled out patents for making soap,' said one TV lawyer. But in the first year the potential losses were so large that only the richest groups were prepared to contemplate investment, and the eventual result was to make big groups bigger, and rich men richer. The allocation of TV stations resulted in many situations which parliament had most hoped to avoid: the extension of the power of a few already powerful showmen, the exclusion of newspapers (largely through their own fault) from all but one of the biggest stations, and an effective tie-up between the 'big four' producing an effective monopoly of commercial TV, making apparent nonsense of the stipulation of the Act that they should be 'independent of each other both as to finance and as to control'. These were the fourteen commercial TV stations in 1965:

	Staff numbers	Area	Chairman (with main other interest)	Main Shareholders
Associated Television	1,322	London weekends Midlands weekdays	Lord Renwick (stockbroking)	Moss Empires Daily Mirror Daily Express Pye Norman Collins, Val Parnell, etc.
Rediffusion	1,253	London weekdays	J. Spencer Wills (buses)	British Electric Traction (50%) Rediffusion (37½%) J. S. Wills, H. C. Drayton, etc.
Granada	980	Lancashire and Yorkshire weekdays	Sidney Bernstein (cinemas)	Granada Group (85% Bernstein family)
ABC	982	Lancashire and Yorkshire weekends Midlands weekends	Sir Philip Warter (cinemas)	Associated British Pictures (large holding by Warner Brothers)
Scottish	406	Scotland	Lord Thomson (newspapers)	Thomson interests (80%) Howerd & Wyndham (10%)
Southern	356	Southern England	John Davis (cinemas)	Rank Organisation (37½%) Associated Newspapers (37½%) D. C. Thomson (25%)
Television Wales and the West (TWW)	500	S. Wales and West of England	Earl of Derby (land)	Lord Derby (25%) News of the World (20½%) Liverpool Daily Post (14½%) Jack Hylton
Tyne-Tees	440	Newcastle area	E. G. Fairburn	George and Alfred Black (21%) Daily News (21%) Northern Mercantile and Investment (17%)
Westward	181	South West England	Peter Cadbury (ticket agency)	Keith Prowse Emile Littler
Anglia	340	East Anglia	Marquess Townshend (land)	Guardian (20%) Romulus & Remus films (20%) Local interests, industry Norwich Union (55%)
Ulster	163	N. Ireland	Earl of Antrim (land)	Belfast Newsletter, Lord Antrim, etc.
Border	126	The Border	John Burgess (cinemas)	Cumberland Newspapers George Outram and Co. Sir Michael Balcon
Grampian	142	East Coast of Scotland	Sir Alexander King (cinemas)	700 shareholders, mostly local
Channel	65	Channel Islands	W. H. Krichefshi	Unrevealed

THE TV COMPANIES

The first company to be formed, Associated Television, had as its nucleus the original triumvirate of lobbyists who all still have shares in it: Collins' original investment of £2,250 was worth £501,750 by November 1958. But the triumvirate did not originally have enough money to satisfy the ITA; and in the meantime two prominent showmen, Lew Grade and Val Parnell, on the initiative of a publicity agent, Miss Suzanne Warner, had combined to form their own TV company, financed with the help of Warburg's bank,[1] who were quick to see the potential. But they were refused a station—partly because Parnell's theatre company, Moss Empires, was already thought powerful enough, and they therefore eventually merged with Collins' group, which already had a contract. Since the showmen had most of the money, they gained control, and Prince Littler, chairman of Moss Empires, became chairman: later, after ATV suffered heavy losses, Cecil King (again through Warburg's) brought in the *Daily Mirror* with a 19 per cent share.

These different strains formed—and still do—a bizarre partnership. But the showmen's influence made ATV a kind of 'Palladium of the Air', with its climax in Val Parnell's 'Sunday Night Spectacular'. Lew Grade is now managing director, with huge unused scope for patronage. He is a legendary figure often depicted as a modern Sam Goldwyn, credited with the same kind of stories. He came, called Louis Gradowsky, to England from Odessa as a child-refugee with his two brothers, and from being a Charleston champion climbed up to running (with his brother Leslie) the biggest variety agency (credited with saying 'the trouble with this business is that the stars keep ninety per cent of my money'). He is a jovial, uninhibited man with loud ties and fat cigars, a long nose jutting from a bald head, and a combination of shrewdness and salesmanship.

The original prime mover, Norman Collins, now occupies a less central position: he sits in a huge leather club chair, in which he is usually photographed, in a panelled office with Sheraton furniture and a TV set behind a Chinese cabinet. He is vice-chairman, supervises the more cultural programmes, and as the company becomes more dignity-conscious his position has become more important. But the business pace—fast and relentless—is set by Grade. In 1963 Prince Littler resigned as chairman, and was

[1] *See* p. 439.

succeeded by the omnipresent Lord Renwick, who comes in from the city in the afternoons. In 1964 ATV extended its links with the entertainment industry: it took over Stoll Theatres, including the Victoria Palace, the London Hippodrome and Drury Lane; and the *Daily Express* bought a share of ATV.

More than any company, ATV has an international, half-American feel, and its offices themselves—foliage in the waiting-room, Muzak in the hall, open-plan corridors—have the de-nationalised character of airports or UN agencies; ATV has produced a race of compères with mid-Atlantic accents, in contrast to the public school tones of the BBC. They have close relations with America, both buying and selling programmes, and therefore producing their own programmes with a not-too-British flavour for export.

The other London company, Rediffusion, had a quite different genesis, and here we are back again into the territory of Harley Drayton, who had such confidence in the new medium that he not only put up a large share but, when the losses were biggest, bought out his co-owner, Lord Rothermere.[1] Now 50 per cent of the shares are owned by Drayton's British Electric Traction, and another 37½ per cent by Rediffusion, the piped-radio company in which BET has a large interest: part of the remaining 12½ per cent, too, is personally owned by Drayton. But Drayton himself is almost as aloof from the company as he is from the Antofagasta Railway; he normally never goes there, and the company was established by people with no previous experience of show business, films or newspapers. The chairman, John Spencer Wills, is an accountant who worked his way up through the bus business of the Drayton group. The managing director is a former radio engineer, Paul Adorian, who came from Hungary as a young man and helped to build up piped radio. Until 1964 the general manager, in charge of the day-to-day workings, was a retired naval officer, Captain Brownrigg, who ran the business with the brisk, insensitive authority of the quarter-deck. But since Brownrigg's retirement, Rediffusion has showed some signs of undergoing a kind of managerial revolution, with the producers taking over more of the planning of programmes. In 1964 John Macmillan, an Australian who had earlier come from the BBC, took over as

[1] For a fascinating account of this transaction—which had very serious consequences for the future of the *Daily Mail* and the character of Fleet Street—*see* John Spencer Wills' account in 'fusion/18', April 1961.

general manager, and later in the year Stuart Hood, the greatly respected former Controller of TV at the BBC, joined Rediffusion as their controller of programmes. These two, with the help of younger executives such as Cyril Bennett and Lord Windlesham, may succeed in giving Rediffusion a positive televisual character, more divorced from simply commercial incentives.

ABC Television, unlike any others, is wholly owned by one company, the Associated British Picture Corporation, which runs 400 cinemas in Britain, and in which the American Warner Brothers has a large stake. The chairman, Sir Philip Warter, is one of the most respected men in the medium: he is a quiet, civilised businessman, who married the daughter of the man who built up the cinema chain; he has also been vice-chairman of the British Transport Commission, and keenly interested in railways. But ABC are as bound by profit-motive as other companies, and rigorous in their pursuit of mass viewing.

Granada, based on Manchester, is the only major company dominated by a single personality—its chairman, Sidney Bernstein, who with his family owns 85 per cent of the shares: Paul Adorian has said, 'only one man has *real* power in this business—Bernstein.'[1] He belongs to the small group of left-wing millionaires (including Jack Hylton, Lord Walston, Lord Sainsbury, Lewis Cohen, etc.) and is the only major tycoon who proclaims strong political views, with strong links with the Left. He talks passionately about the social and cultural rôle of television and describes himself as a 'Reithian'. He is the most autocratic of the chairmen, supervising details of presentation, typography, publicity and taste. His wide range of interests include the publishing firm McGibbon & Kee. He also collects pictures and cattle, has many Labour friends and loves showmanship: he is a lifelong admirer of Barnum, and a friend of Alfred Hitchcock. Probably alone of the contractors, he would like to have the same kind of power as a newspaper-owner, commanding editorials and crusades, and presenting a consistent political view. He is the nearest that television has to a Northcliffe or a Beaverbrook: but he is deprived of editorials, columnists or comment, and to Bernstein the neutralising requirements of ITA present a constant frustration. But in other respects Bernstein's career has been less frustrating, for he has the biggest personal holding of anyone in commercial TV. His programmes

[1] Quoted by Clive Jenkins. *Power Behind the Screen* 1961. p. 93.

are culturally superior to others and his patronage more enterprising, but he is not markedly less interested in ratings and advertising revenue.

The smaller TV stations which followed have a less heavy influence from showmen; as TV became more obviously profitable, respectability was considered more important for candidates. More traditional directors have emerged, and TV has provided a large bonanza for the local aristocracy. Rival contenders for Sir Robert Fraser's favours have tried to outdo each other with lord lieutenants and mayors, and a marquess, three earls, three viscounts and coveys of local gentry have appeared on the boards, alongside entertainers and popular newspapers. The most blue-blooded is the Earl of Derby, now chairman of Television Wales and the West, with a 25 per cent holding, next to the *News of the World* (20½ per cent), followed by the chairman of Ulster Television, the Earl of Antrim. Probably the most mixed group is Anglia Television, whose chairman is the Marquess Townshend, descendant of the turnip pioneer, whose managing director is Aubrey Buxton, a landowner, bird-watcher and bird-shooter, and whose board includes representatives from Cambridge University, the *Guardian* and Norwich Union Insurance. Anglia was welcomed with high hopes that it would be unusually cultural and enterprising, but it has ended up as dominated by commerce as the others. The most spectacular of the secondary TV tycoons is Lord Thomson,[1] with the major interest in Scottish Television. The ITA originally expected that newspaper groups would extend their influence into commercial television, but Thomson turned the process on its head. By acquiring Scottish TV—a 'licence to print money'—he made enough to buy the *Sunday Times* and its surrounding provincial newspapers, and thus brought the restless salesman's world of TV into the heart of Fleet Street.

The small stations give the appearance of local autonomy with their boards and programmes, and provide (in theory) a fixed proportion of the programmes from their own studios; but they are heavily dependent on the Big Four for their syndicated programmes arranged by the 'Network', which effectively prevents competition between stations, and gives the country the same mass-produced pabulum.

[1] *See* p. 146.

POWER OF THE TYCOONS

What does the power of these new tycoons amount to? Their political scope is severely limited by the ITA. Labour views must be balanced by Tories, and contentious programmes are submitted beforehand. But in the social and cultural character of their programmes, the tycoons can still have enormous scope. Their sudden emergence has defied the managerial revolution: they are a throwback to the days of early press barons. The personal influence of the owners stands out in all companies: they control the key business of 'programming'—arranging for the worst programmes to go on at the peak viewing times, and the best late at night; and they can, if they wish, allow experiment. But few of the TV contractors are much interested in television, art, plays, or news; like insurance companies, popular newspapers or advertising agencies, they have preferred to abdicate their power of patronage in favour of plain profitability.

The influence of advertisers, as with newspapers, has been more general than specific. The TV Act was framed to prevent any kind of link-up between advertisers and programmes, but the pressure of big advertisers is such that it forces programmes into the same mass-mindedness as soap and detergents, squeezing minorities into the late evening.

Looking back on the original TV debates, it seems absurd how much the two sides were considered in black and white—a rigid monopoly on one side, a huckster's free-for-all on the other, a choice between the governess state and the Omo state. Many supported commercial TV mainly out of exasperation with BBC complacency, and the sluggishness of the BBC provoked the vulgarity of commercial TV. Here again we find the deep British gulf between the old collegiate tradition on the one side and the brash outsiders on the other, between Gentlemen and Players. The lack of awareness in the BBC of the forces that were assembling against it was one of its most astonishing characteristics. The BBC was an outstanding example of an institution which could not apparently move except under applied forces.

PILKINGTON AND AFTER

As usual, a synthesis between the two opposites is gradually emerging. An important reassessment of commercial TV came in June 1962, when the report of the Pilkington Committee was published, headed by an austere and independent-minded glassmaker, Sir Harry Pilkington, and including a radical don, Richard Hoggart, author of *The Uses of Literacy*. Inspired by Hoggart's indignation, the committee were shrilly critical of the triviality and debasement of commercial television, and full of praise for the BBC's uprightness. They firmly criticised the weakness of the ITA: 'The Authority's power to control the companies, once they are appointed programme contractors, is illusory and negligible. . . . We recall that the Authority stated that it was satisfied with independent television's service. We do not consider that its grounds for satisfaction are well-founded.' They concluded—among their many spectacular findings—that the planning of programmes and selling of advertising time should henceforth be taken over by the ITA.

The publication of Pilkington was followed by anxious speculation, and many of the programme companies (which for some time previously had been on their best behaviour) expected much tougher legislation. But the consequences were anti-climactic. Macmillan's government put through the Television Act of 1963 with no very fundamental new limitations. A levy on TV advertising was imposed—which gave companies the excuse for further economies—and a new chairman of the ITA, Lord Hill of Luton, was appointed to keep a closer eye on the companies. Lord Hill's appointment seemed a convincing one. As a former cabinet minister—axed by Macmillan in 1962—he knew the inward workings of power, and he had understood the arts of communication ever since his time as The Radio Doctor, talking about bowels and indigestion in his deep earthy voice. Lord Hill made it clear that he would be watchful and firm, but the results have not been spectacular. He insisted that the companies' programme schedules would be drawn up in consultation with the ITA; he strengthened the 'advertising advisory committee' and appointed Sir Harold Evans, the former publicity adviser to Harold Macmillan, to the new post of head of information and research. But when the companies' contracts expired in 1964, all fourteen were renewed, and the same tycoons continued in charge. There has been no obvious improvement in the meanness and philistinism of the companies, and the power of the Network has scarcely lessened.

But the character of the companies has been gradually changing. Sidney Bernstein likes to quote an old Hollywood saying: 'There was a time when you couldn't afford to be honest: but later you couldn't afford to be dishonest.' The fat years of TV profits are probably already over; the huge profits are steadily being nibbled away by the unions, the actors and the usual Parkinsonian tendencies; the tycoons are beginning to diversify their interests, and have sold out part of their holdings. Out of its wild origins, from show business, bus business, box offices and stately homes, commercial TV will gradually throw up a new race of professional television managers: in twenty years' time the first fat years will seem as legendary as the old days of Hollywood. But the origins, no doubt, will still stamp the corporate characters, as Mond and McGowan stamped ICI, or Reith the BBC.

A further consequence of Pilkington was the establishment in 1964, after unprecedented ballyhoo, of a second channel for the BBC. This decision indicated a victory for the Corporation; but in fact none of the existing commercial stations wanted a second advertising channel (because it would diminish their own revenue) with the important exception of Associated Television, which continued to lobby energetically both for more commercial TV, and for commercial radio. The indefatigable C. O. Stanley, with his interest in making TV and radio sets as well as in the programmes, was determined to extend the territory of private enterprise, and in 1964 became a partner in Radio Manx, an advertising programme from the Isle of Man.

BBC 2 brought to the fore the new thrusting character of young BBC executives; nowhere is the distinction between two generations—the withdrawn public servants and the new self-aware—more marked than in broadcasting. As *The Economist* described these 'apparatchiks': 'Just as the Russians would talk in party meetings in Marxist terms and then go out and copy the best that Detroit or Dusseldorf have in technical matters, so these young men have a double persona: Reithian in their sense of public service, in their actual management they resemble the commercial opposition.' BBC 2 was lobbied for, advertised and launched with all the brashness and zest of a big-business operation; the symbols of the new channel, appropriately enough, were two kangaroos called Hullaballoo and Custard. The head of the channel, Michael Peacock, constantly proclaimed in person the coming marvels. But BBC 2 turned out a heavy anticlimax. The programmes appeared much the same, if not worse, than the other channels; few people bothered to have their sets converted for the new fine screen; and after a few months the programmes were drastically altered, and a batch of old Hollywood films were purchased in order to lure more viewers to the unwatched channel.

Yet in spite of all the conflicts, commercialism and corruption in British television, it has to be said that its programmes on average can make some claim to be the best in the world. In comparison with the frenzied hucksterism of American TV, or the bleak state control of French TV, or the dull second-rateness of Italian TV, it succeeds in combining the vigour of commercialism with some of the standards of public service. However crude was the commercial explosion of 1955, it has become increasingly hard to maintain that television without it would have been better.

TELEVISION CIRCUS

Whoever runs it, the impact of television will continue. Britain is the second biggest TV market in the world, but while in America commercial TV rose out of an established jungle of commercial radio, salesmen's attitudes, publicity machines and a vast film business, in Britain it burst into a more tribal and placid territory with the suddenness of an invasion. This mobile column has barged through the middle of many old British institutions: it threatens to by-pass parliament by bringing major discussions straight to the viewer, so that politicians bother more about the screen than about the back-benchers.[1] It provides new scope for the Church to project discussions both serious and ridiculous. It has changed the whole pace of consumer buying, bringing salesmen into the drawing-room and regulating the movements of packets in supermarkets. It gives new scope for the love of pageantry, and the quasi-religious attitude to monarchy. It provides a huge new weapon of education and information. And it projects a classless, Americanised, competitive world, full of mid-Atlantic accents and sleek cars, into the remotest villages where TV aerials stick up with the regularity of chimney-pots.

No doubt its influence is often exaggerated; TV has a fairytale quality, and a knack of draining subjects of their meaning, leaving the faces remembered, but not what they said. But its indirect, insidious power of projecting images, ways-of-life and associations of ideas is such that no institution can afford to ignore it. The keys to this new magical kingdom are essential for anyone concerned with salesmanship, politics or simply fame. TV already has its 'New Boy Net' of men who have mastered this publicity machine:

[1] *See* Chapter 3.

as the Old Boy Net has its magic of antiquity, with the Palace in the background, so the New Boys have a new synthetic magic, which can turn nonentities into national heroes.

At the big studios outside London the ephemeral dream-world of television is carefully concocted by technicians and producers, in their factories of images and fame. Under the cameras dangling like bats from the roof, the disparate subjects assemble—an archbishop talking to a pop singer, a trade unionist talking to a Tory MP: they troop on and off in endless cavalcade, all mixed together—professors, jugglers, cabinet ministers, ventriloquists, dukes, chairmen, compères and diplomats—all punctuated by quick glimpses of detergents and toothpaste. On the magic screen people who have never met each other before chat away with Christian names, as if they jostled together every day in some inner world of fantasy power.

37

BRITAIN'S CHANGING ANATOMY

The hall of fame has many rooms,
And most of them are full.
And some doors are marked push,
And some are labelled pull.

Anon.

If we want things to stay as they are, things will have to change.

Tancredi, in The Leopard.

Have you ever witnessed the fidget and distraction of the great? It is the most painful sight. It leaves one wondering whether it is after all necessary to be struggling, day in and day out, to be anything but a bum.

Coz Idapo, in DRUM magazine (Nigeria).

REWRITING this book after three years and retracing my steps, the changes seem quite spectacular. In politics, in the boardrooms, the senior common rooms, the Inns of Court and even in the BBC, the familiar chorus of 'Old Freddies'—of peers, soldiers or courtiers—has begun to troop off-stage. Harold Macmillan's family party has almost disappeared. The splendours and follies of the Empire, and of the last world war, have faded and the angry debates about Suez, Cyprus or Central Africa seem to belong to a quite separate era.

Reverence and stuffiness are out of fashion, and nearly everyone, from the head of the BBC to the Lord Chancellor, likes to think of himself as being 'anti-Establishment'. After 1963, year of frenzied satire, even the excitement of impudence has lessened. The old Aunt Sallies like the palace, the House of Lords or the Foreign Office, have become drabber and less important; and as the Freddies retreat, so the professional anti-Freddies, like Malcolm Muggeridge, are left high and dry, to refight old battles, and man their rusty barricades, while the rest of Britain gets down to the harder problem of Britain's commercial survival.

TWO GENERATIONS

All my life I have watched the gyrations of the British Establishment. They move like a flight of starlings. One turns, all turn!

Richard Crossman, 1964.

Pragmatism is less often talked about, and the phrase 'it's odd but it works' is less often heard. The decimal system and Continental road signs are on their way. Reorganisation and rationalisation have become national slogans, and after Dr. Beeching's surgery on the railways, nearly every institution has wanted, or pretended to want, its Beeching. Parliament, the Law, the Church, Oxford, the Foreign Office, have all been investigated. The fighting services have been marshalled into a single vast organogram and the First Lord of the Admiralty has ceased to exist. Lord Plowden and Lord Franks, the two omnipresent inquisitors, have tiptoed round from committee to committee, tactfully suggesting that all is not quite what it might be. Management consultants, led by McKinsey's, have invaded the big corporations, to redraw the lines of responsibility, and strengthen the profit motive. Even Buckingham Palace has called in efficiency experts. The Bank of England no longer insists on being protected by a troop of guardsmen in full dress, marching through the traffic, but allows them to arrive in battle dress, in a truck, like Shakespearean actors in modern dress.

Introspection has become a national hobby, and everywhere the sociologists and Prodnose people, armed with statistics and surveys, have entered their unfriendly kingdom. No profession is now complete without its figures to show how few of them went to university, and how many want to emigrate.

The ancient debate between amateurs and professionals, or gentlemen and players, has lost much of its point, for only a few top people, like Sir Alec Douglas-Home, would now dare admit to amateur attitudes. Long lunches and long weekends may be as unhurried as ever, but they are more discreet; and the importance of political house-parties, kept high by Harold Macmillan, has been undermined by the awareness of the austere confidence of senior civil servants, or Harold Wilson. The two networks co-exist awkwardly, with a mutual suspicion and cross-purposes which wastes a good deal of their energies. The *salon* world of drawing-room politics is still cultivated by Lord Snow or George Weidenfeld; but it has much less relevance in the face of the unsocial telephone methods of Harold Wilson or Herbert Bowden.

In Whitehall, in industry or even in the city, a new post-war generation of men has emerged near the top, with a much more thrusting and self-aware attitude than their pre-war elders; and this split between generations, accentuated by the post-war birth-rate,[1] can be seen running through every British institution. (My own age-group—I was thirteen when the war broke out—is perhaps specially aware of the difference, for we lie uneasily between two more defined generations. At Oxford after the war, where colonel undergraduates mixed with teenager undergraduates, I felt the cross-currents between the opposed values of two eras, and the confusion of the post-war world, without heroes, villains or causes.)

On the one hand are the outstanding men in their fifties, who started their careers in the slump years of the thirties, and who are now permanent secretaries, directors or ambassadors. They joined their government department or corporation often with a mixture of a genuine sense of service, and thankfulness for a safe job in bad times. They were loyal to their institution as they were loyal to their college, and however unsettled the world and the rest of Britain might be, the colleges, clubs or departments remained—looking with hindsight—extraordinarily *there*. The Indian army, the hierarchies of the Indian and colonial services and the huge protocol of the pre-war navy, gave a military backbone to the middle-classes. However impoverished, they could and did lead whole lives with no thought of commercial competitiveness, either for themselves or for their country. Of course many of this generation did make fortunes, and remain to this day acquisitive and crafty. But even in the city, if you set out to make a fortune, it was helpful to do so behind a military moustache, and with a handle to your name.

The last war, when so many men proved themselves, encouraged the feeling that companies should be run like armies: and after the war, however much the English liked to think of themselves as a civilian nation, the colonels and generals moved confidently and briskly into the city, industry, British Railways or the BBC, inspired by thoughts of patriotism and loyalty, rather than commercial or technical efficiency. Looking back now on the Britain of the fifties, where generals and brigadiers ran everything, it is hard to remember how little analytical thought, or commercial drive, went into British institutions.

But now a generation of administrators has come up who were at school during or after the war, who have been brought up alongside a crumbling Empire, a dwindling army, and recurring balance of payments crises. They do not have the same loyalty (as their elders sadly assured me) to their institutions. At university,

[1] *See* Mark Abrams, p. 621.

the ablest realised that they would be much in demand, and if they felt they were not properly valued by one employer, they could move elsewhere. 'Officer-like qualities' were far less required, and a drunken poet who could write silly ditties for commercials might earn twice as much as a long service manager. And, as an extra training ground for the ambitious, America loomed closer: ten times as many people crossed the Atlantic in 1960 as did in 1930: and many of them brought back new techniques of salesmanship, efficiency and commercial vigour.

And the new generation were much more aware of themselves—their value, their reputation and their power: 'they've read their Theodore White and their C. P. Snow,' as one permanent secretary said. Talking to civil servants or industrial managers in both age-groups, you cannot fail to notice the difference. The younger men are reluctant to accept the old tradition of reticence and anonymity, or to feel calmly detached from their work as if it were an extension of Greek verse or mediaeval history. They feel themselves in the midst of a shifting scene, and part of the scenery, with cold winds blowing, and arc lights glaring. The public service is no longer so cut off from private industry; permanent secretaries troop out to profitable jobs in industry, and some industrialists, even, stride into the Treasury building.

Any British outfit, given half a chance, will settle down into behaving like an Oxford college, or a country estate. But in the last few years that illusion has been harder to maintain. In industry, the competition from America and Europe, and the end of the fat years of a seller's market, has at last produced a new competitiveness, in which the word 'profits' is mentioned without shame. In ICI, Unilever, Bowaters, AEI, English Electric or General Electric, new chairmen have generated a new ruthlessness, and (as John Tyzack put it) 'We are at last coming back to accepting that the job of management is to manage. We are trying to jump over a generation, and to put into senior management young men who have been conditioned since the war to the new world.' The word entrepreneur, which for so long had a stigma, has come back into fashion; and for thousands of young managers John Bloom, until his crash, was a kind of hero.

And playing all round this changing, competitive scene, with glitter and fantasies, is the glaring light of publicity. It opens up secret places, makes heroes overnight, and quickens the pace of envy and self-awareness. It is hard to recall what Britain was like eight years ago, before that first television toothpaste advertisement, and the whole noisy invasion of jingles and ephemeral fame which followed it. Television broke through the high walls which separate British institutions from each other, and dragged almost everyone into its studios; but most of all it knocked down its own wall, between private and public enterprise, and turned the BBC, the most influential of the nationalised industries, inside out. The young 'apparatchiks' there became the central figures in the New Boy Net, who hold the keys to promotion, salesmanship and fame. They demolished much of the stateliness of the existing Old Boy Networkers, and have built up their own jolly show-biz parade, with teenagers and David Frost as their pacemakers—a parade which any strong, silent man joins at his peril. They have unleashed 'the power of laughter' (in Sir Hugh Greene's phrase), which makes stuffiness and squareness the deadliest sins.

OUTSIDERS INSIDE

> Power is rather like how Oscar Wilde described society. Being in it is a bore. Being out of it is a tragedy.
>
> *A Labour Minister, 1965.*

All these changes of attitude have been accompanied by a change of government. The wand has been waved over Whitehall, and magically 107 outsiders have become insiders. The government Humbers wait outside front doors which, only a few months ago, seemed insignificant, and theorists suddenly become men of power. Change, overnight, becomes politically respectable, even essential, and the projects and plans accumulated over thirteen years take shape in a few hectic weeks. The Treasury is cut in half, new ministries are invented, intellectuals surge into Whitehall, and the whole civil service (in Arthur Schlesinger's phrase) 'crackles with spirit'. The transformation has underlined both the necessity, and the weakness, of the two-party system. On the one hand, a party out from the wilderness easily confuses the talkers and the doers; and the first few months of power lead, almost inevitably, to blunders, retreats, 'I told you so', and cabinet changes. On the other hand, only a new party, fresh from the wilderness, and uncluttered with commitments, can bring real stimulus to the passive engines of Whitehall.

At the head of the new government is a man of determined isolation and professionalism, different from any previous inhabitant of Downing Street. Harold Wilson has not been diverted or delighted by the historical splendours of his office, and he talks with puzzled amusement about the social foibles of his predecessors. He is quite prepared to use honours, or invitations, or social flattery, for political ends, but he has no wish or ability to create a personal mythology. Like Lyndon Johnson succeeding Kennedy, Wilson has blown away the courtly trappings of his office: he invites visitors or journalists, to inspect the mystery, and (like an anti-conjurer) shows them that there is nothing inside, but a tough, clever man pulling levers. He operates, like LBJ, a kind of 'government by boredom', in which pretensions and passions dissolve in the dry atmosphere of technical discussion.

I went to see him in January 1965, sitting in the cabinet room with his feet on the table, leaning right back in his chair. No one could have been more different from Harold Macmillan, whom I had seen in the same chair, and who had seemed part of the stately furniture.

Macmillan talked slowly and theatrically, relishing the history and accoutrements of his job. Wilson talked quickly and drily, constantly returning to technicalities. I asked Wilson how he found the job of being prime minister:

> Taking a decision here is basically no harder than any other decision. The red boxes are full every night—sometimes with sixty different papers on sixty different subjects—but everything has been carefully sifted out and briefed, so that you know exactly the arguments on either side.
>
> I don't get tired when I'm working; the only time I feel tired is when I'm bored, and I'm not bored when I'm with professionals. I'm not bothered by loneliness—there are plenty of people around in this building to talk to. I'm always stimulated by talking to people who know their jobs.
>
> I want this place to be a power-house, not a monastery.

Do you find your surroundings have an effect on you?

> I haven't had time to see much of my surroundings: I haven't looked at the pictures, except that one of Walpole above me. If you're interested in who you're talking to, you don't notice the pictures.

Do you find the job cuts you off from other people?

> No, not at all: I spend a lot of the time at the House: I go into the tea room quite often, and I have lunch with members who happen to be around. But I'm convinced that you could

never run the British government and run a social life of your own—I wouldn't want to anyway.

How far had his government been able to produce real changes?

After all the talk about the difficulty of changing the civil service, I think we produced, in forty-eight hours, the biggest revolution in Whitehall since Lloyd George. I decided from the start that we should take decisions as if we had a majority of 400, not 4—and they like getting decisions.

As far as pressing buttons is concerned, the buttons in Whitehall have never failed to register—sometimes they even register before I'm quite ready for it. But I can't press a button and get those lorries moving into the docks, or suddenly improve exports—this is the price we pay for years of inertia.

It'll be a long job getting things properly moving. You've got to appeal to the Dunkirk spirit, but you can only do that if you weren't responsible in the first place for getting them into the mess. We've got that advantage, as Churchill had in 1940.

A lot of people realise in January 1965 that something has got to be done, and are looking for people to lead them—which wasn't so in January 1964. The complacency's gone.

The motto of this government is that there are no sacred cows, unless they've been examined and found to deserve that status. Like Kennedy, we've re-examined all the old assumptions. We've tried to lay down the ground rules of sacred cowmanship.

Have you felt much reaction from the old social 'Establishment'? Are they still totally hostile?

The Establishment can make noises, drinking gins and tonics at their New Year's Eve parties, but that doesn't have much effect on politics. Politics is a question of power, and power has been transferred. Whatever people say at an election, the members of the old Establishment only have one vote each at the end of the day. So has each engineer and miner in my constituency.

As for that part of the Establishment which makes up the civil service machine—if you call it an Establishment—I know most of the permanent secretaries quite well from my time in the war, or my period as the chairman of the Public Accounts Committee. They're real professionals, and I've never seen an operation to compare with those first forty-eight hours.

How far can you change the conservative atmosphere at Number Ten?

Well, I've decided to use Number Ten for a definite type of functional entertaining: I'm going to use it as a centre for professional groups—vice-chancellors, heads of CATs, technologists and so on. I'll have them to a meal upstairs, and sit round the table with them, and discuss their problems. I'm going to have monthly meetings with a group of technologists.

So far I've only had two major receptions—one for the Olympic Team—three hundred of them—and one for the Olympic Paraplegics. I spend my own time on this floor and the second floor—I usually don't bother about the first floor, where the state rooms are.

This place is like a tremendous organ—anything you play comes out the other end.

TWO WORLDS

While long-established English institutions tend to be illogical and wasteful, the values which they promote, however limited in their scope, are morally and aesthetically far superior to anything which the new world of admass tastes and applied science can show.

Simon Raven

In this new climate, both social and political, there are not many politicians—except a few of the generation of Captain Waterhouse—who dare suggest that Britain can survive without major change. Change is being urged everywhere, and every day new changes are announced.

And yet, inspecting British institutions, one cannot fail to notice the huge discrepancy between what is urged and commanded, and what actually happens. Up on the bridge, the captain rings through, full speed ahead and hard a port; the bells ring, the signals run up the mast, the officers all come up on deck. But nothing actually seems to happen; the ship shudders a bit, and then goes on, on the same course, heading steadily for the sandbanks.

No country can be analysed and redesigned like a machine, and least of all Britain, with its social obscurities, its web of unwritten understandings, its gentlemen's agreements, and its institutions which live in a 'curious half-light'[1] between competition and monopoly. The planners draw up their charts and organograms, and make neat divisions of responsibility between the Treasury and the Department of Economic Affairs. They even abolish the First Lord of the Admiralty, and merge the War Office and the Air Ministry. But somehow the mysterious personalities of institutions, and their gentlemanly muddle, always seem to take over. A supposedly powerful new body becomes subtly demoralised, and old offices again reassert their ancient status. When the three separate service ministries were merged (as the Estimates Committee found to their alarm), the total staff actually went up by 300. These institutions are like clouds; from outside they look clear and definite enough, but inside one, they seem shapeless, damp and very foggy.

I have tried to dwell on the social characters of institutions in this book rather than on their strictly constitutional rôle; believing that this is the most useful rôle of a reporter, and that the social differences, for instance, between the Treasury and the Bank of England, or between ministers and permanent secretaries, are an essential part of the anatomy. But how can these powerful social characters be changed, or created?

How can technologists or vice-chancellors be given the same dignity and weight as viceroys or field-marshals? How can the mysterious aura that hangs over St. James's Street or the House of Lords be moved towards the Institution of Civil Engineers? How can the stage army of Establishment heroes, who shuffle through the newspapers and television screens be extended to include men who can really change the face and fortunes of the country? Harold Wilson has done something to try to redress the balance. He has shorn his own office of its snobbish surroundings. He has put technocrats and engineers into the House of Lords. He invites heads of CATs to Downing Street. His 'functional entertaining', though not exactly exciting, stresses the importance of new men and shop talk as opposed to amusing conversations, and contrasts with the amateur get-togethers at the palace.

But British society, and the influence that goes with it, still moves with its own momentum, like a heavy flywheel. *The Times* court page, with its Establishment birthdays, its country notes,

[1] *See* p. 428.

and its weddings in order of precedence, projects a Britain that is complacent and silly, but still influential. The columns of all newspapers still prefer to record the scandals of a duke to the achievements of a Nobel scientist. Very few people, who could rattle off twenty British historians or fifty actors, could mumble the names of five living engineers. It is not only the press, the palace and the pageantry which encourages this love of antiquity; it is the whole dead weight of inherited wealth, both individual and corporate, which enriches and romanticises ancient pursuits, so that young undergraduates still prefer the rich and cosy irrelevance of All Souls to the modern purpose of Nuffield. The wealth of colleges and schools is self-perpetuating, for their old boys will rarely refuse to fork out for appeals for lavish rebuilding.

The old Britain, whether rich or poor, has enveloping charms. There are many men in their thirties, caught between pre-war muddle and post-war efficiency, who find it difficult to embrace the technological age. They feel like Bill Maitland, the hero of John Osborne's play *Inadmissible Evidence*, who shakily affirms his belief in 'the technological revolution, the pressing, growing, pressing, urgent need for more and more scientists, and more scientists, for more and more schools and universities and schools . . .' The complacent arrogance of the old orders breeds an aggressive philistinism in the new. The two extremes, the country-house amateurs and the suburban technocrats, thrive on the contrast. Lord Bowden, the computer-technologist, loves to appear more philistine than he is, and terrifies the House of Lords with his rat tat-tat of technological terms. Faced with this line of harsh alternative, many prefer in the end to be wrong with Macmillan than to be right with Wilson.

'If I care,' Simon Raven wrote,[1] 'to spend my day writing Latin verses or watching cricket, as opposed to selling some beastly machine or rubbishy gimmick over a fat expense account luncheon, who is to say I am not the better man for it? Certainly not Mr. Sampson. (Westminster and the House.)'

But the choice between commerce and culture is, and always has been, a fake one. The leisure and cultivation of most of the current prosperous middle class, their cricket lawns and libraries, were built on the profits of Victorian technology, a more sudden and ruthless phenomenon than anything today. Growing leisure and culture depends on improved technology, and the apparent

[1] *The Listener*, July 12, 1962.

conflict has only happened because inherited wealth has become cut off from the skills which once produced it.

OUT OF EUROPE

It is a shower we enter, not a Turkish bath.
Harold Macmillan, 1962.

However much Britain analyses and discusses herself, the only quick cure for her lethargic conditions can be a stimulus from outside. The country is like Oblomov—a tired, impoverished aristocrat, lying in bed, speculating and worrying about his condition, but never actually getting out of bed. The only sure remedy is to be tipped out. No appeal to the Dunkirk Spirit can be effective unless there is a visible Dunkirk.

It is painful to remember how far, three years ago, the hopes of politicians and industrialists were geared to the prospect of joining the Common Market. It seemed to me then, writing this book, that nearly every institution was girding itself for the challenge. Harold Macmillan and Edward Heath staked their careers on the prospect, and the Tories prepared for a Disraelian crusade. 'If we don't get into Europe,' one cabinet minister said to me at the time, 'we'll just become like Portugal, that's all.' When de Gaulle's veto came, it came as a shock so abrupt and humiliating that, like a childhood trauma, it had to be forgotten. To a journalist, it was eerie to see the subject of Europe dropped, almost overnight, out of the public mind.

Britain can never flourish in isolation. Its settled quasi-aristocratic society has difficulty nowadays in generating dynamic movement. Much of its current energy comes not from the English, but from the immigrants—Welsh, Scottish, Canadian, Jewish or West Indian. Examining the top people in Britain one is quickly struck by the dominance of immigrants, particularly in the fastest growing industries—in electronics, in television, in hire-purchase or in advertising. The English may deplore the success of Lord Thomson, or gloat over the failure of John Bloom, but it is hard to imagine how dull and inactive a country England would be without such men as Sir Leon Bagrit, Sir Billy Butlin, Sir Eric Roll, Sir Jules Thorn or Sir Solly Zuckerman. The financial and intellectual drive of immigrants (as Dr. Barna has pointed out) is visible in many countries, but England is more monolithic and settled than most, and it has been the special knack of the English aristocracy that they have provided a stable and adaptable society, which can attract and absorb new blood and new money. But there is not now the same wave of talent as came in before and after the war, and even the supply of ambitious Scots from the Highlands is dwindling. In the past, the governing of the Empire and the shake-up of two world wars provided colossal challenges: among the most dynamic top people, it is striking how many had their first break either in the war, or in challenging jobs in distant places, such as George Cole of Unilever has described.[1] Africa and Asia still provide escape and scope, particularly for idealistic young men. But the independent Commonwealth cannot generate the same economic opportunities as were provided by the lonely responsibilities of the Empire. The sons of the men who ruled India or fought through the desert are now more likely to be settled in London offices, sitting on co-ordinating committees or mounting advertising presentations. It was the prospect of a new shake-up, the 'cold shower' that encouraged so many politicians and industrialists to enter the Common Market. De Gaulle's veto *was* a kind of Dunkirk—and there have been rumblings of change; but to visit the capitals of the Common Market is to see how much the new sense of mobility and opportunity, and the awareness of competitive neighbours, can help to bring new vigour to old countries. It is hard to see how Britain can quickly break out of her supine contentment, without this kind of immediate challenge.

ETON AND THE REST

> The way to the top is being rebuilt. But the process is confused and muddling; and no one seems to know whether we are making a narrow ladder or a broad highway.
>
> *Anthony Crosland, 1961.*

The long-term prospects of Britain lie not with an immediate shake-up, or with tinkering with institutions, but with the drastic reform of the educational system which has helped to fix so many of our antique attitudes. The biggest and most hopeful change in the country is the intense public awareness of the importance of schools, and the rush of new universities; and I have tried to reflect this in the structure of this book. Education is rightly beginning to take the key rôle in politics and controversy that was

[1] *See* p. 494.

occupied by the Empire, and it is to the headmasters and vice-chancellors that we must turn for our revival. To look back on the complacency of Oxford in the fifties, and the doctrine of 'more means worse' is to survey a quite different era. Thinking about education, if not actual education, has undergone a revolution.

The Labour government has done something to introduce new blood from new places into the centre of power; but the influence of a relatively tiny group of people from a few public schools, and particularly from Eton and Winchester, remains one of the most astonishing features of contemporary Britain. The Foreign Office, BOAC, the Conservative party, the Bank of England, Associated Television, and a large part of the city, are run by Old Etonians, and within the Tory party the influence of Eton is only slowly waning. There is something inherently absurd and dispiriting in the idea of a large part of this industrial country being run by this stage army of men, awarding each other GCMGs, and dressing up for ceremonies in fancy dress as if they were still in the school play.

It is silly to suggest that wealth and nepotism are the only reasons for this situation; and some of the prominent Old Etonians are men of exceptional ability. But their most valuable asset is confidence—confidence both from themselves, and from others. In any uncertain situation, in a boardroom or in the Tory party, the voting is likely to favour the calm assurance of the man who is quietly convinced of his superiority. In a military society, this automatic leadership is valuable, for confidence is a large part of success. But in a commercial or technical situation, this unquestioning self-assurance can be disastrous, and (as in the Tory party) it can easily demoralise more able men. This monopoly must be broken if Britain is to make proper use of her brains and her energy. The ablest boys must be able to acquire not only a first-class education, but social confidence in themselves.

The stultifying effect of our present educational system—as shown in the graph on page 196—is visible in the make-up of management, all through this book.

The public schools and the richer colleges not only perpetuate the class system (as is now much more widely admitted), and project a view of Britain which is out-of-date and often irrelevant. They also insulate their alumni from taking a serious interest in education as a whole. A public school politician may show a wide-ranging and disinterested concern in foreign affairs, penal reform or even economics; but when he thinks about education, his mind inevitably turns towards his own and his children's school. There is nothing an Old Etonian, however old, enjoys more than talking about Eton. He may encourage the comprehensive and praise technical universities, but when he receives an appeal for expensive new buildings in Eton or Christ Church, he will willingly pay. What the state system needs is not only the ablest children, but the most demanding and critical parents, who will insist on better teaching and conditions. It is one of the strongest arguments for integrating public schools into the state system that only thus can the right kind of interest be attracted.

It is in education, more than anywhere else, that the old British faith in pragmatism, and institutions which 'just grow' is being broken. The comprehensives or the new technological universities have sprung up from nowhere, creating new traditions, and new kinds of people. It is their heads who can, like the old empire-builders, forge a new kind of Britain, which will emerge in the next decade. But so long as these state innovations grow up in a cut-off compartment, quite separate from the old tradition of the public schools and Oxbridge, so long will the rift, which runs right through this book, remain. The public school men, with their confidence, culture, and ignorance, will look with dread and defensiveness at the new technocrats; and the technocrats, with their expertise and drive, will produce an efficient but bleak new Britain.

Any prosperous arts graduate from Oxbridge who rails against incompetence, the lethargy and the lack of technology in contemporary Britain finds himself, in the end, in an awkward posture. He demands change, competition and stimulus; but he has to admit that all these are uncomfortable, particularly for others, and that England remains for him a country of freedom and ease, where the countryside continues to defy the competitive pressures of the towns. And behind all the ugly conservatism—maintaining privilege, poverty, and injustice, there is the justifiable conservatism of a country which can offer peace, humanity, freedom and leisure, in a way for which one looks in vain elsewhere.

INDEX

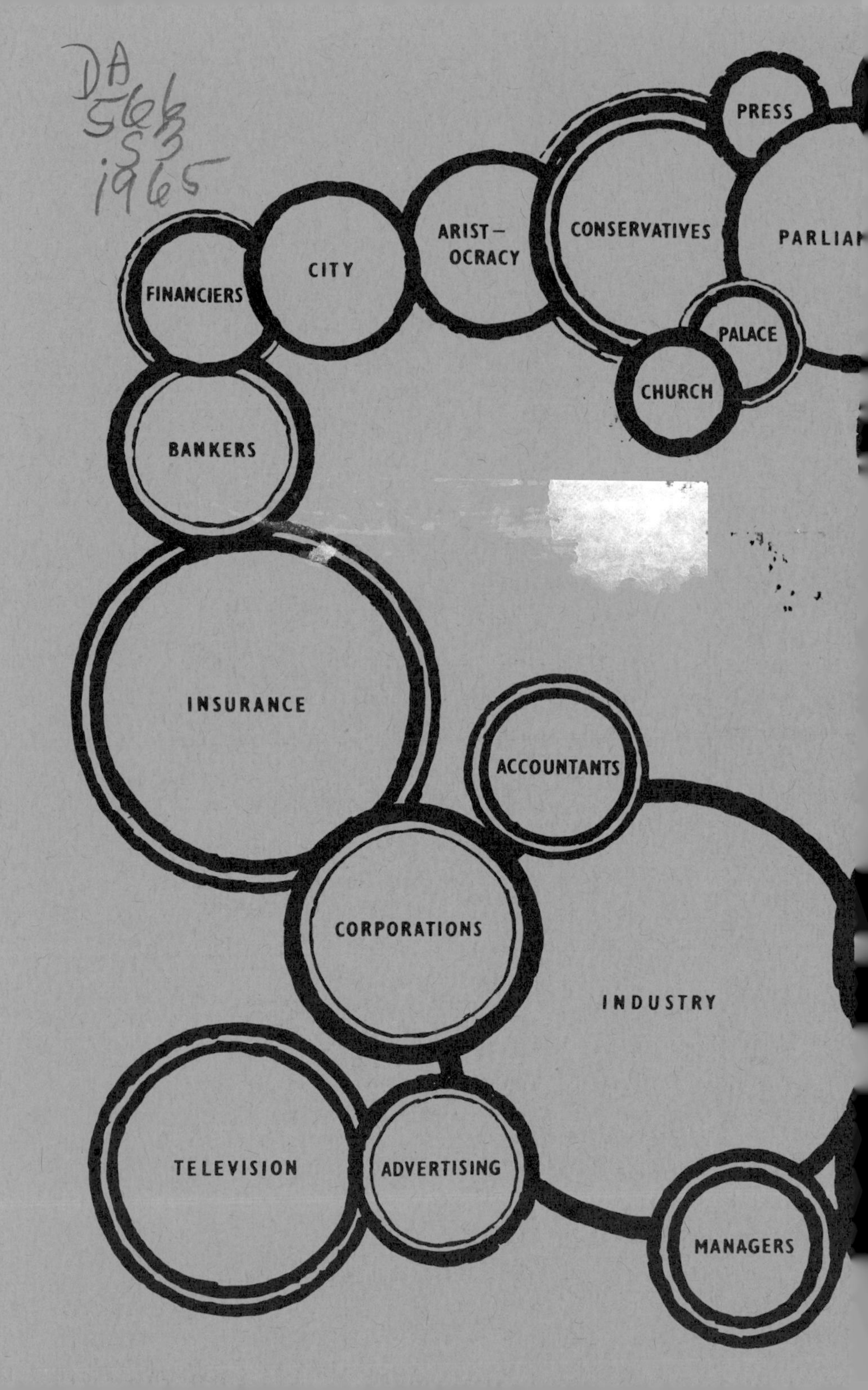
PRESS
FINANCIERS
CITY
ARIST-
OCRACY
CONSERVATIVES
PALACE
CHURCH
BANKERS
INSURANCE
ACCOUNTANTS
CORPORATIONS
INDUSTRY
TELEVISION
ADVERTISING
MANAGERS